Economic Psychology

BPS Textbooks in Psychology

BPS Wiley presents a comprehensive and authoritative series covering everything a student needs in order to complete an undergraduate degree in psychology. Refreshingly written to consider more than North American research, this series is the first to give a truly international perspective. Written by the very best names in the field, the series offers an extensive range of titles from introductory level through to final year optional modules, and every text fully complies with the BPS syllabus in the topic. No other series bears the BPS seal of approval! Many of the books are supported by a companion website, featuring additional resource materials for both instructors and students, designed to encourage critical thinking, and providing for all your course lecturing and testing needs. For other titles in this series, please go to http://psychsource.bps.org.uk.

Economic Psychology

EDITED BY

ROB RANYARD
CENTRE FOR DECISION RESEARCH,
UNIVERSITY OF LEEDS, UK

The British
Psychological Society

WILEY

Registered Offices
John Wiley & Sons, Inc., 111 River Street, Hoboken, NJ 07030, USA
John Wiley & Sons Ltd, The Atrium, Southern Gate, Chichester, West Sussex, PO19 8SQ, UK

Editorial Office
The Atrium, Southern Gate, Chichester, West Sussex, PO19 8SQ, UK

For details of our global editorial offices, customer services, and more information about Wiley products visit us at www.wiley.com.

Wiley also publishes its books in a variety of electronic formats and by print-on-demand. Some content that appears in standard print versions of this book may not be available in other formats.

Library of Congress Cataloging-in-Publication Data

Names: Ranyard, Rob, editor.
Title: Economic psychology / edited by Rob Ranyard.
Description: Hoboken : Wiley-Blackwell, 2017. | Series: BPS textbooks in psychology ; 2380 | Includes bibliographical references and index. | Identifiers: LCCN 2017014502 (print) | LCCN 2017016417 (ebook) | ISBN 9781118926475 (pdf) | ISBN 9781118926390 (epub) | ISBN 9781118926482 (hardback) | ISBN 9781118926345 (paper)
Subjects: LCSH: Economics—Psychological aspects. | BISAC: BUSINESS & ECONOMICS / Consumer Behavior.
Classification: LCC HB74.P8 (ebook) | LCC HB74.P8 .E3196 2017 (print) | DDC 330.01/9—dc23
LC record available at https://lccn.loc.gov/2017014502

Cover Design: Wiley
Cover Image: © from2015/Gettyimages

Set in 11/12.5 pt Dante MT Std by Aptara Inc., New Delhi, India

10 9 8 7 6 5 4 3 2 1

The British Psychological Society's free Research Digest email service rounds up the latest research and relates it to your syllabus in a user-friendly way. To subscribe go to http://www.researchdigest.org.uk or send a blank e-mail to subscribe-rd@lists.bps.org.uk.

Contents

Preface

The 28 chapters of this book present an overview of contemporary economic psychology in a manner suitable for the core text of a course at the intermediate or final-year level of a UK honours degree in psychology, or equivalent. The 50 chapter authors are internationally recognized experts in their fields of research. Our focus is on individual and household economic decision-making, ranging widely across financial matters such as borrowing and saving, and economic behaviour such as trading and entrepreneurial activity. Part 1 presents an introduction to the field and to important theoretical developments in economic decision theory. Next, in Part 2, material to equip the student to understand a range of contemporary research methods and to undertake an empirical study in economic psychology is presented. Following this, Parts 3–5 deal with central aspects of economic psychology in everyday life. In addition to reviewing current knowledge on each topic, they also consider its practical and policy implications for supporting economic decision-making. Finally, we consider two broader perspectives. Part 6 presents a life-span developmental approach, from childhood to old age; and Part 7 deals with important societal issues such as charitable giving and pro-environmental behaviour. There is growing interest in both economic psychology and behavioural economics; graduate students and researchers in both areas will find the book useful and insightful.

A course in economic psychology was first introduced in a European university by Karl-Erik Wärneryd at Stockholm University in 1957, assisted by Folke Ölander who subsequently moved to Denmark to teach the subject at Aarhus University. Later, in 1972, Gery van Veldhoven and Fred van Raaij developed economic psychology courses at Tilburg in The Netherlands, and the field began to slowly spread across the continent.

At the same time, researchers were investigating economic behaviour, though with little communication with each other. For example, Reynaud and Paul Albou in Strasbourg, France, and Hermann Brandstäetter in Augsburg, Austria, were developing research centres. This somewhat scattered scenario was to change in 1976, when a group of twelve economic psychologists gathered in Tilburg to discuss their findings and experience in the area, in an informal setting (a pizza parlour), that would, nevertheless, have important consequences: this would be the first colloquium of a long series of annual conferences that began to gather researchers not only from Europe, but other parts of the world as well. This organization is today known as the *International Association for Research in Economic Psychology* (IAREP), created in 1982. Just before that, in 1981, the *Journal of Economic Psychology* was founded; 2016 saw the 53rd volume, with six parts a year, and growing visibility and impact.

A round-table on the history of economic psychology took place at the IAREP Conference in Prague, the Czech Republic, in 2005, when experienced pioneer researchers in the area (Karl-Erik Wärneryd, Folke Ölander, Fred van Raaij and

Stephen Lea) discussed the recent history of the discipline, which allowed data about this period to be gathered (Ferreira, 2007). In 2016, the 41st IAREP-SABE Conference took take place, in Wageningen, The Netherlands (SABE is the Society for the Advancement of Behavioral Economics, also created in 1982).

Finally, we should mention two important textbooks that contributed to the establishment of contemporary economic psychology (1) *The Individual in the Economy: A Survey of Economic Psychology* (1987) by Stephen Lea, Roger Tarpy and Paul Webley; and (2) the *Handbook of Economic Psychology* (1988) edited by Fred van Raaij, Gery van Veldhoven and Karl-Erik Wärneryd. The present volume aims to document developments in the field over the following decades and to introduce a new generation of readers to this fascinating area of psychology.

REFERENCES

Ferreira, V. R. M. (2007). Psicologia Econômica: origens, modelos, propostas [Economic psychology: origins, models, proposals]. Doctoral thesis, Social Psychology Graduate: Studies Program, PUC-SP, São Paulo.

Lea, S., Tarpy, R., & Webley, P. (1987). *The individual in the economy: A survey of economic psychology.* Cambridge: Cambridge University Press.

van Raaij, F., van Veldhoven. G., & Wärneryd, K.-E. (Eds.). (1988) *Handbook of economic psychology.* New York: Springer.

Notes on Contributors

Gerrit Antonides is a Professor Emeritus of Economics of Consumers and Households at Wageningen University, The Netherlands. He obtained his PhD at Erasmus University, Rotterdam, in 1988 and has published in the areas of behavioural economics, economic psychology, and consumer behaviour. He has been an editor of the *Journal of Economic Psychology*, has (co-)authored several textbooks in consumer behaviour and economic psychology and is past President of the Society for the Advancement of Behavioural Economics (SABE). The behavioural aspects of consumer decision-making concerning issues of finance, household, environment and health, are an important part of his current research activities.

John K. Ashton is a Professor of Banking at Bangor University, UK, Editor of the *Journal of Financial Regulation and Compliance* and Academic Director of the Chartered Banker MBA at Bangor Business School. John has previously worked at the University of Leeds, the University of East Anglia and Bournemouth University, publishing numerous academic articles on pricing, regulation, monetary policy transmission and competition within retail banking markets. These academic outputs have been informed by a career teaching banking through universities and with appropriate professional bodies.

Jan Willem Bolderdijk received his PhD in Environmental Psychology in 2011 from the University of Groningen The Netherlands. He is fascinated by people's tendency to make 'irrational' decisions, and frequently employs field experiments to explore new research ideas in realistic consumer settings. He currently works as an Assistant Professor at the Department of Marketing, University of Groningen, where he studies ways to promote sustainable consumer behaviour. He was awarded a 'Veni' career grant by the Dutch National Research Council (NWO) in 2014.

Nicolao Bonini is full Professor of Psychology of Consumer Choice in the Department of Economics and Management, at the University of Trento, Italy. His research training was at the University of Padua, from where he graduated in 1987. Then he was awarded a PhD on experimental psychology at the University of Trieste. Subsequently, he has held various research and lecturing posts in psychology, including Professor of Psychology at the University of Trento from 1999 to the present. He has undertaken psychological research using a range of methods, and has published widely on economic psychology and decision research. He has served the European Association of Decision Making as President, President-Elect, and a member of the steering board.

Christopher J. Boyce is currently a Research Fellow at Stirling Management School, the University of Stirling, UK. He graduated from the University of Surrey with a BSc in Economics in 2005 and then moved to the University of

Warwick to complete an MSc in Economics. At Warwick, he completed a PhD in Psychology in 2009 on the topic of subjective well-being. After his PhD he held positions as a Research Fellow at the Paris School of Economics, the University of Manchester, and at the Institute of Advanced Studies. His current research crosses the boundaries of economics and psychology, and he tries to unite ideas from both disciplines. Specifically he is concerned with understanding how an individual's health and happiness are influenced by the world around them.

Wändi Bruine de Bruin holds a University Leadership Chair in Behavioural Decision Making at the Leeds University Business School, UK, where she co-directs the Centre for Decision Research. She is also affiliated with Carnegie Mellon University, the University of Southern California, and the RAND Corporation. She holds a PhD in behavioural decision-making and psychology and an MSc in behavioural decision theory from Carnegie Mellon University, as well as an MSc in cognitive psychology and a BSc in psychology from the Free University Amsterdam. Her research focuses on judgement and decision-making, risk perception and communication, as well individual differences in decision-making competence across the life-span.

W. Ray Crozier is Honorary Professor in the School of Social Sciences, Cardiff University, UK. Previously, he has held chairs in psychology in Cardiff University and the University of East Anglia. He received research training at the University of Keele, where his PhD was on risky decision-making. He has published widely on topics in social and educational psychology including the emotions, shyness in childhood and adulthood, and artistic creativity. He is a Fellow of the British Psychological Society.

Michael Daly is a Reader affiliated to the Behavioural Science Centre of the Stirling Management School, the University of Stirling, UK. Previously, he has been a Fulbright Scholar visiting Florida State University, a lecturer in the University of Manchester School of Psychology, and a CARA Fellow at the University of Aberdeen Institute of Applied Health Sciences, funded by the Marie Curie Programme. His research focuses on how ideas shaped at the interface of psychology and economics can be investigated and applied to policy. Michael has published a broad set of papers on human health and well-being, how they are interrelated, and how they are determined by psychological traits (e.g., self-control) and economic circumstances (e.g., unemployment).

Liam Delaney is SIRE Professor of Economics and Co-director of the Behavioural Science Centre in the Stirling Management School, the University of Stirling, UK,. He is also PhD Director of the Scottish Graduate Programme in Economics, and Director of Research and Deputy Head of the Stirling Management School. He is a Marie Curie Career Integration Fellow and an investigator with the ESRC-funded Scottish Centre on Constitutional Change. In 2009, he received the Statistical and Social Inquiry Society of Ireland's Barrington Medal. He was a 2011 Fulbright Fellow at Princeton University. His main research interests involve using novel measures of well-being and time preferences to shed light on long-running questions about the determinants of health and well-being.

Fabio Del Missier is senior research scientist and tenured Assistant Professor in the Department of Life Sciences at the University of Trieste, Italy, and an affiliated

research scientist at Stockholm University, in the Department of Psychology. After graduating with a PhD in Psychology from the University of Trieste, he was a postdoc researcher at the University of Trento. His research focuses on memory and cognitive underpinnings of decision-making, basic memory and control processes, and decision-making competence across the adult life-span. His work has been published in the main cognitive psychology, neuropsychology, and decision-making journals.

Artur Domurat is an Assistant Professor in the Faculty of Psychology, at the University of Warsaw, Poland, where he graduated in 2004 with a PhD on psychological methods. His background lies both in economics (Warsaw School of Economics, M.Sc., 1998) and psychology (University of Warsaw, M.A., 2000). He has also been collaborating with the Centre for Economic Psychology and Decision Sciences at Kozminski University since 2001. His interdisciplinary research interests encompass studies in judgement and decision-making (risk-taking, heuristics and Bayesian reasoning) and economic psychology (psychology of entrepreneurship and investing).

Mark Egan is a PhD student at the Behavioural Science Centre, the Stirling Management School, the University of Stirling, UK. His research draws on large, longitudinal data-sets to examine how individual psychological differences in childhood and adolescence predict future economic and health outcomes. Prior to his PhD, he graduated from the MSc Human Decision Science programme at Maastricht University.

Antony Elliott is Chief Executive of the Fairbanking Foundation. He has a degree in Banking and International Finance from City University, London, and a Master's degree in Operational Research from Imperial College, London. In 2014, he was awarded an OBE for services to bank customers. Antony has been actively involved in researching the field of financial well-being since 2004 and has published a large number of reports in the field. He was lead author for the Money Advice Service report, *Transforming Financial Behaviour* (2010), examining the role of behavioural economics in improving financial capability. He founded the Fairbanking Foundation in 2008, which conducts research, provides advice and is the certification body for the Fairbanking Mark.

Vera Rita de Mello Ferreira has a PhD in social psychology, and is a member of NEC, the Behavioural Studies Center at CVM (the Brazilian Securities Exchange Commission). She is an economic psychology lecturer at B3 Educacional, in São Paulo, and at other institutions in both São Paulo and other states, an independent consultant for organizations and policy-making (VERTICE PSI), in Brazil and abroad, and author of the first Brazilian books on economic psychology. She is the representative in Brazil of IAREP, and a former member of the Executive Committee of the International Confederation for the Advancement of Behavioral Economics and Economic Psychology (ICABEEP). Vera has been directly involved in the development of economic psychology in Brazil since 1994.

Bruno S. Frey is Professor of Economics at the University of Zurich, Switzerland, and Research Director of CREMA – Center for Research in Economics, Management and the Arts, Zurich, Switzerland. He was Distinguished Professor of Behavioural Science at the Warwick Business School at the University of Warwick, UK, from 2010 to 2013, Professor of Public Finance at the University of Constance, Germany, from 1970 to 1977 and Professor of Economics at the University of Zurich, Switzerland, from 1977 to 2010. He seeks to extend economics beyond standard neo-classics by including insights from other disciplines, including political science, psychology and sociology. According to the Institute for Scientific Information, he belongs to the group of 'the most highly cited Researchers'.

Jana Gallus is an Assistant Professor at UCLA's Anderson School of Management, USA. She holds a PhD in Economics from the University of Zurich. Switzerland. As a scholarship holder of the German National Merit Foundation, she previously studied at the Institut d'études politiques de Paris (IEP Paris/Sciences Po) in France, the University of California at Santa Barbara (UCSB) in the United States, and the University of St Gallen (HSG) in Switzerland.

Amelie Gamble is an Associate Professor in the Department of Psychology, and is affiliated with the Centre for Finance, School of Business, Economics, and Law at the University of Gothenburg, Sweden. She graduated in 2005 in psychology from the University of Gothenburg. Her research interests are economic decision-making and well-being.

Tommy Gärling is Emeritus Professor of Psychology affiliated with the Department of Psychology and Centre for Finance at the School of Business, Economics, and Law at the University of Gothenburg, Sweden. He graduated with a PhD from Stockholm University in 1972 and held university positions at the Royal Institute of Technology in Stockholm and the University of Umeå before being appointed Professor of Psychology at the University of Gothenburg. He is a Fellow of the International Association of Applied Psychology and has conducted research and published extensively in environmental psychology, economic psychology and transportation psychology.

Agata Gasiorowska is an Associate Professor affiliated to the Centre for Research in Economic Behaviour, SWPS University of Social Sciences and Humanities, Poland. She received her PhD in management from Wroclaw University of Technology in 2003 and her PhD in psychology from the University of Wroclaw in 2009. She has undertaken research on the psychology of money and consumer behaviour, and is currently the Polish representative for the International Association for Research in Economic Psychology, and the President of Polish Academic Association for Economic Psychology.

Anouk Griffioen received her MSc degree in Social Psychology at the VU University, Amsterdam. She is now a Climate-KIC PhD student at Wageningen University, The Netherlands. Her project, 'Saving energy when others pay the bill: A field experimental approach to behavioural aspects of energy conservation' aims to improve knowledge about stimulating pro-environmental behaviour when financial incentives are absent. An additional goal is to translate these findings into functioning interventions in practice. To accomplish this, she has collaborated closely with the Student Hotel, a hotel chain which provides a 'living lab' by allowing experimental test interventions for energy conservation.

Michel Handgraaf received his PhD in social psychology from Leiden University. Since 2011, he has been an Associate Professor at Wageningen University, The Netherlands. Most of his research using (field) experimental methods and surveys can be described as 'behavioural economics'. It mainly deals with differences between what rational economic theories would predict and the psychology behind deviations from such predictions. Besides research on fairness and ethics, his current research focuses on decisions in the environmental domain. These decisions typically feature uncertainty, temporal trade-offs and social trade-offs.

Nigel Harvey is a Professor of Judgement and Decision Research, University College London, UK, and Visiting Fellow in the Department of Statistics at the London School of Economics and Political Science. He is a past President of the European Association for Decision Making and is co-editor of the *Blackwell Handbook of Judgment and Decision Making*. He works on judgement in forecasting, advice-taking, and the calibration of subjective probabilities.

Bill Hebenton teaches and researches at the Centre for Criminology and Criminal Justice in the School of Law and is a Research Associate of the Manchester Centre for Chinese Studies, Manchester University, UK. He has published widely on comparative criminology and criminal justice, and has a particular research interest in China and Greater China. He is chief editor of the Palgrave Macmillan book series 'Palgrave Advances in Criminology and Criminal Justice in Asia'. His other research interests can be categorized broadly around three themes: demystifying the 'smoke and mirrors' of contemporary crime and criminal justice, including sexual crime, sentencing and 'enforcement' of judicial penalties; applications of crime science; and situational versus dispositional explanation and implications for criminology.

Martin Hedesström is an Associate Professor of Psychology, University of Gothenburg, Sweden, and is affiliated with the Centre for Finance at the same university. His research is mainly experimental and often related to savings and investments in the stock market. Current research interests also include behavioural spillover from moral decisions and choice architecture.

Erik Hoelzl is Professor of Economic and Social Psychology at the University of Cologne, Germany. He obtained his PhD in 2000, and his Habilitation in 2005, from the University of Vienna, Austria. He moved to the University of Cologne in 2010. His major research interests are decisions about the use of money, ranging from consumer spending over credit to taxation. He has published in international, peer-reviewed journals on economic and applied psychology. He was Editor-in-Chief of the *Journal of Economic Psychology* (jointly with Erich Kirchler). His interests also include the development of the scientific method, and meta-research. He is member of several scientific societies and on the editorial board of several scientific journals.

Erich Kirchler is Professor of Economic Psychology at the University of Vienna, Austria. He obtained his PhD in 1973, from the University of Vienna and his Habilitation in 1989, from the University of Linz, Austria. His first academic position was at the University of Linz. He moved to the University of Vienna in 1992. His major research interests are household financial decision-making and tax behaviour. He is an advisor at the Austrian Science Fund (FWF), was President of the International Association for Research in Economic Psychology (IAREP) and the Austrian Psychological Society (ÖGPs). He was Editor-in-Chief of the *Journal of Economic Psychology* and past-president of Division 9 (Economic Psychology) of the IAAP (International Association of Applied Psychology).

Tehila Kogut is an Associate Professor at the Department of Education and the Center for Decision Making and Economic Psychology at Ben-Gurion University in Israel. She received her PhD from the Hebrew University. Her research is in the field of social psychology and decision making, focusing on pro-social decisions among children and adults.

Zeev Krill is a senior researcher in the Chief Economist Department, Ministry of Finance, in Israel. His interests include macroeconomics and fiscal policy, lay understanding of economics and nudge economics. Before joining the ministry, he worked as a consultant and as a lecturer in Economics at Ben-Gurion University, from where he also received a BA in Economics and Psychology and an MA in Economics.

Anton Kühberger is Professor of Psychology working at the Department of Psychology, and is also a member of the Centre for Cognitive Neuroscience at the University of Salzburg, Austria. He has carried out extensive research into judgement and decision-making, especially in the context of risk.

David Leiser is Full Professor of Economic and Social Psychology in the Department of Psychology, Ben-Gurion University, Israel. He was educated in Mathematics (Hebrew University of Jerusalem BSc, 1972), Adult Education (University of Illinois at Urbana Champaign, MSc, 1973), and Psychology (Université de Genève, Switzerland, PhD, 1978). He was the founder and director (2003–2013) of the Center for Decision Making and Economic Psychology, and Co-Founder of the Center for Research on Pension, Insurance and Financial Literacy (2014–), both at Ben-Gurion University. He served as President (2010–2014) of IAREP and currently is President (2014–) of the Economic Psychology Division of the International Association for Applied Psychology. His current work centres on the analysis of lay understanding, in particular in the economic domain.

Cäzilia Loibl, Ph.D., CFP®, is an Associate Professor in the Department of Human Sciences, Ohio State University Columbus, Ohio, USA, and held an appointment as Marie Curie Fellow at the Centre for Decision Research at Leeds University Business School, UK (2014–2016). Her research focuses on consumer financial decision-making.

Sandie McHugh is an Associate Researcher in Psychology, at the University of Bolton, UK. She originally studied social and economic history at the University of Manchester and became interested in applied psychology during a career in the civil service and as a member of the GB Women's Target Sports National Squad. She has been involved in a series of research projects in the Household Financial Decision Making group of the Psychology Department and is the co-author of published papers. She is a representative on the University of Bolton's Centre for Worktown Studies and has published on happiness research conducted in the town of Bolton.

Simon McNair is currently a Leverhulme Early Career Research Fellow in the Centre for Decision Research, Leeds University Business School, UK. He was awarded his PhD in 2013 by Queen's University, Belfast, for research on the cognitive psychology of Bayesian reasoning. Simon's interest in economic psychology developed as a post-doc, when he conducted research for Grant Thornton UK LLP, a leading consumer financial insolvency firm. More recently, Simon has conducted research in the area of financial capability (with partners Suitable Strategies), and from 2016 will begin a three-year project in partnership with the Citizens Advice Bureau to develop more effective financial support provision.

Ellen K. Nyhus is Professor of Marketing in the Department of Management, School of Business and Law, the University of Agder, Norway. She is also a senior researcher at the Department of Innovation at Agderforskning AS. She has held former positions at the Norwegian School of Economics and Business Administration, Bergen, Norway, and at the Centre for Economic Research in Tilburg, The Netherlands. Ellen is past President of IAREP and an editorial board member of the *Journal of Economic Psychology*. She is conducting research in the field of consumer behaviour, behavioural economics, labour market behaviour, socialization processes and travel and tourism.

Annette Otto is a researcher in the field of economic and developmental psychology and is currently teaching at the Johannes Gutenberg University, Mainz, Germany. She earned her PhD from the University of Exeter in 2009 on the economic psychology of adolescent saving. Her research focuses on the development of saving behaviour within the social context of the family and adolescent learning within the family and school context. She is a member of the academic research group of 'Child and Youth Finance International'. Her work has been published in the *Journal of Economic Psychology*, the *Economics of Education Review*, and the *Journal of Consumer Affairs*.

Davide Pietroni is a senior research scientist, a tenured Assistant Professor in the Department of Business Studies at the University d'Annunzio of Chieti-Pescara, Italy, and a trainer in the area of personal and organizational development. After attaining his PhD in cognitive science at the University of Padua, he consolidated a research partnership with the Social Psychology Department at the University of Amsterdam. His research focuses on conflict management and negotiation with an emphasis on the interpersonal effects of emotions in bias mitigation and coordination; most recently his research is centred on the use of nudging to promote wealth and well-being. His work has been published in the leading social psychology journals and he has authored four books on negotiation.

Rob Ranyard is a freelance researcher and Visiting Professor affiliated to the Centre for Decision Research, University of Leeds, UK. His research training was at the University of Stirling, from where he graduated in 1972 with a PhD on the psychology of decision-making. Subsequently he has held various research and lecturing posts in psychology, including Professor of Psychology at the University of Bolton from 2001 to 2014. He has undertaken psychological research using a range of methods, has published widely on economic psychology and decision research, and is currently the UK representative for the International Association for Research in Economic Psychology. He is an Associate Fellow of the British Psychological Society.

Daniel Read is Professor of Behavioural Science at Warwick Business School University of Warwick, UK. He has previously held positions at the University of Leeds, the London School of Economics and Durham Business School, and has held lengthy visiting positions at Carnegie Mellon University, Pittsburgh, USA, the University of Rotterdam, and the Yale School of Management. He has published widely in prestigious journals including *Management Science, Organizational Behavior and Human Decision Process, Psychological Review*, and the *Journal of Experimental Psychology*. Most of Daniel's research has been in the area of intertemporal choice, including many papers with Marc Scholten. He is also interested in Bayesian inference, choice heuristics, strategic thinking, and applications of behavioural science to social problems.

Ilana Ritov is a Professor of Psychology at the School of Education in the Hebrew University of Jerusalem, Israel. She is the Director of the Center for Empirical Studies of Decision Making and the Law at the Hebrew University. Her research area is the psychology of judgement and decision-making, with a special focus on choice in social contexts. The issues she studies include, among others, determinants of altruistic behaviour, the role of social comparison, and the distinction between abstract choices and those involving identified individuals.

Marc Scholten has been, since 2013, Associate Professor with Habilitation at the Universidade Europeia Lisbon, Portugal. In 1993, he took his PhD in Economic Psychology at Tilburg University. Since 2002, his research has expanded on the simple, but not innocuous, premise that people make direct comparisons between available options in reaching a decision. This was the premise underlying his journal articles on a model of decisional conflict (*Journal of Experimental Psychology: General*, 2006) and on a later model of intertemporal choice (*Psychological Review*, 2010). Most of his subsequent publications have been an orchestrated effort to cement this perspective on decision-making, both theoretically and methodologically. Recently, his research has shifted attention from choices between options with single consequences to choices between options with multiple consequences.

Michael Schulte-Mecklenbeck is a lecturer in Consumer Behaviour, at the University of Bern, Switzerland, and an Adjunct Researcher at the Max Planck Institute for Human Development, Berlin. He received his PhD from the University of Fribourg, Switzerland, in 2005, and worked in industrial consumer research at a large food company and in different academic institutions in Europe and the United States. His research focuses on the cognitive processes in decision-making, consumer behaviour and food choice. Furthermore, he is interested in research methods to capture and understand human data acquisition.

Joyce Serido is an Associate Professor in Family Social Science at the University of Minnesota-Twin Cities, USA. She holds an MBA in finance from Seton Hall University and an MS and PhD in family studies and human development from the University of Arizona. Her research focuses on financial behaviour, specifically, the intersection of family processes and personal well-being of youth and young adults. As principal investigator for the *Arizona Pathways to Life Success for University Students (APLUS)* research initiative, she leads a multi-university team in the first longitudinal, multidisciplinary study of young adults' financial behaviours. Dr Serido currently serves on the editorial boards for the *Journal of Consumer Affairs* and *Journal of Financial Counseling and Planning*.

Stefanie J. Sonnenberg is a Senior Lecturer in Psychology at the University of Portsmouth, UK. She completed an MSc in Economic Psychology at the University of Exeter in 1998 and a PhD in Social Psychology at the University of St Andrews in 2004. Stefanie's research interests span a range of topics within social and economic psychology, including the social psychology of money and household money management. Her specific interests in these broad domains concern the ways in which we conceptualize the 'self' and the role identity plays in understanding socio-economic processes.

John Thøgersen is Professor of Economic Psychology in the School of Business and Social Sciences at Aarhus University, Denmark, where he heads the Marketing and Sustainability research group. He received his MSc and PhD from Aalborg University, Denmark, in 1980 and 1985, and his advanced doctoral degree, Dr. Merc., from Aarhus School of Business in 1999. His research focus is on sustainable consumption in a broad sense, including sustainable lifestyles and 'spillover', social norms, values, intergenerational transfer, eco-labelling, energy consumption, travel mode choice, and organic food. He is editor of the *Journal of Consumer Policy*.

Tadeusz Tyszka is Head of the Centre for Economic Psychology and Decision Sciences, Kozminski University, Warsaw, Poland. He has been involved in research on human judgement and decision-making for many years, including: decision-making in situations of conflicts of interests; decision-making among multi-attribute alternatives; and risk perception. Results of these studies have been published in international journals. His group also edits its own multi-disciplinary journal in Polish/English – *Decyzje/Decisions*. He has been President of IAREP (1992–1994) and President of the Economic Psychology Division in the International Association of Applied Psychology (2006–2010).

Ivo Vlaev is Professor of Behavioural Science at Warwick Business School, University of Warwick, UK, and received a DPhil (PhD) in Experimental Psychology from the University of Oxford. His research is to advance understanding of human decision-making (behavioural economics) and behaviour change. It is a convergence of psychology, neuroscience and economics, which achieves results that none of the disciplines can achieve alone. Ivo is also a co-author of the UK Cabinet Office MINDSPACE report, advising policy-makers on how to effectively use behavioural insights.

Kathleen Vohs is Land O'Lakes Chair in Marketing at the Carlson School of Management, Minneapolis, USA, and has an extensive background in psychology. She applies her understanding of psychological science to business issues in order to advance new areas of marketing research. Her research specialties include self-regulation; self-esteem; the psychology of money; meaningfulness in life, and heterosexual sexual relations as predicted by economic principles. She has authored more than 160 scholarly publications and served as the editor of eight books. She has written invited articles for *Scientific American*, the *New York Times*, and *Science*.

Alex M. Wood is Professor and Director of the Behavioural Science Centre, the Stirling Management School, the University of Stirling, UK. He was possibly the youngest full professor in UK history, gaining his first Chair in 2012 when aged 29. After his PhD in Psychology at the University of Warwick in 2008, he was Lecturer then Senior Lecturer at the University of Manchester, which also awarded him an honorary Chair in 2013. His 100 papers related to well-being have been published in leading journals across psychology, medicine, and economics. He is an expert on psychometrics as he believes that evaluating the quality of the measurement of well-being is integral to the validity of the subsequent scientific literature. He balances work with travel, philosophy, reading, wild swimming, and hanging out with his Scottish musician friends.

Juemin Xu is currently a PhD student in the Department of Experimental Psychology at University College London, UK. Her research interests include gambling and financial decision-making. She has studied online gambling and risk taking in daily economic activities.

Tomasz Zaleskiewicz is Professor of Psychology at the SWPS University of Social Sciences and Humanities in Wroclaw, Poland, and graduated in 1998 with a PhD in psychology. His research focuses on different aspects of economic psychology (mainly psychology of money, saving, behavioural finance) and decision-making under risk. His work has been published in international journals and handbooks on economic psychology, decision sciences and social psychology. He is currently Honorary Secretary of IAREP, President Elect of the Division of Economic Psychology, International Association of Applied Psychology, and Associate Editor of the *Journal of Economic Psychology*.

Acknowledgements

Support from the following colleagues is much appreciated for their careful and insightful reviews of, in some cases, several chapters: Gerrit Antonides, Wändi Bruine de Bruin, W. Ray Crozier, Michael Daly, Fabio Del Missier, Mark Egan, Tommy Gärling, Nigel Harvey, Erik Hoelzl, Bernadette Kamleitner, Erich Kirchler, Anton Kühberger, Cäzilia Loibl, Simon McNair, Ellen K. Nyhus, Barbara Summers, Karl-Erik Wärneryd, Mathew White and Tomasz Zaleskiewicz.

PART 1
Fundamentals

PART 1

Fundamentals

1 Introduction to Economic Psychology: The Science of Economic Mental Life and Behaviour

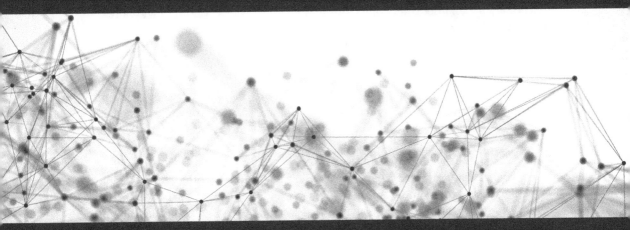

ROB RANYARD AND VERA RITA DE MELLO FERREIRA

CHAPTER OUTLINE

LEARNING OUTCOMES

BY THE END OF THIS CHAPTER YOU SHOULD BE ABLE TO:

1. Understand and describe the nature, origins and scope of economic psychology.
2. Discuss the relationship between economic psychology and behavioural economics, and their perceived similarities and differences.
3. Give examples of a range of studies and findings from recent economic psychology research.

1.1 INTRODUCTION

Economic psychology has important contributions to make in a changing economic world in which individuals and households are expected to take more responsibility for their own economic well-being. Consider first that the international financial crisis of 2007–2008, and the subsequent Great Recession, were not predicted by mainstream economics. One reason, argued Paul Krugman, was that most economists had 'turned a blind eye to the limits of human rationality' (2009, p. 1). Economic psychology has an important contribution, then, to provide economics with a realistic and insightful understanding of human rationality in the economic domain. This extends to other psychological factors that may play a role in financial crises; our emotional tendencies, such as fears in the face of financial risk, and our social nature, including our tendency to compare ourselves with and to follow others (Gärling, Kirchler, Lewis, & Van Raaij, 2009). Consider, second, that both household and personal economic decision-making are becoming increasingly complex and have significant consequences for our quality of life and psychological well-being. Decisions about saving for a rainy day or for retirement, borrowing to improve today's lifestyle, how to manage tax affairs or financial risks, how to make sense of advertisements for loans, savings and insurance, are all issues that economic psychology can contribute towards understanding and improving. Consider finally, that people's thoughts and feelings about material possessions, money, prices, the economy and inflation are at the core of economic mental life, and that the psychology of such things is fascinating and worthy of study for its own sake.

Our description of economic psychology as the *science of economic mental life and behaviour* reflects a contemporary approach to psychology, conferring equal status on the twin endeavours of understanding mental life and understanding behaviour. As is well known, the history of psychology has been characterized as a series of paradigm shifts, or fundamental changes in perspective. For example, the early twentieth century saw a shift from introspectionism's reliance on self-reports of mental activity to behaviourism, which eschewed such methods and concepts to focus on observable behaviour. This held sway until what became known as the cognitive revolution from the mid-1950s. Once again, evidence from self-reports of mental experience was deemed admissible and mental elements were accepted as the nuts and bolts of cognitive theory. One of the leading players in this development was George Miller (1962a) through his work, for example, on our capacity to process information. He wrote an inspiring introductory text which signalled psychology's cognitive shift. He called it *Psychology: The Science of Mental Life* (Miller, 1962b), from which our description of economic psychology is derived. It should be noted that although our definition also encompasses behaviour, it signals a distinctive orientation from the burgeoning, related field of behavioural economics which primarily focuses on behavioural prediction.

Box 1.1 summarizes further defining characteristics of economic psychology. First, it is a *branch of applied psychology*, recognized as such by the International Association of Applied Psychology, in which both theory and application are central. This means that economic psychologists take seriously the responsibility of providing the basis for research-informed policies to support people's economic well-being and the health of the economy. Second, it identifies an important characteristic of economic

1.5 FINANCIAL BEHAVIOUR AND ECONOMIC ACTIVITY

The quality of decisions to spend, save or borrow is central to the financial well-being of individuals and households. In Chapter 12, Vlaev and Elliott describe a psychological framework that defines what it means to be a financially capable citizen who makes informed decisions on such matters. They argue for a deeper notion of capability that includes, in addition to appropriate knowledge and cognitive skills, people's reflective and automatic motivations and the social and physical opportunities that their environment provides for capable action. The authors describe a range of interventions that have successfully supported people's ability and motivation, and consequent financial decision-making, particularly in the domain of saving behaviour. They show how their psychological framework facilitates our understanding of when interventions will have successful outcomes.

Understanding individual and household saving and borrowing is important to economists, since on the aggregate level such behaviour affects the macro-economy; as Lea et al. (1987) wrote, we need to understand how individuals affect the economy as well as vice versa. In Chapter 13, Nyhus explains some of the influential ways that economists have theorized about saving behaviour, such as Keynes' (1936) *absolute income hypothesis* and Modigliani and Brumberg's (1954) *life-cycle hypothesis*. She points out that there is agreement that income is a major driver of saving and that most economic analyses hold that the effects of individual psychological factors cancel out at the aggregate saving level. On the other hand, psychologists such as Katona (1975) have argued that, as has been observed, individual expectations of future income do predict aggregate saving and borrowing. In Chapter 13, Nyhus reviews research on important psychological determinants of saving, including time orientation, attitudes towards, and motives for saving. Not surprisingly, Ranyard, McHugh and McNair show in Chapter 14 that some of the same psychological factors, for example, time orientation, are also associated with borrowing. Other psychological characteristics associated with borrowing include materialistic values and less active money management. Ranyard et al. also review research on the information borrowers need to make good credit and repayment choices, and the causes and consequences of over-indebtedness. They conclude with some suggestions for improving credit information disclosure, the role and content of financial education, and support for over-indebted borrowers.

Ordinary citizens as well as professionals are increasingly engaged in financial markets. For example, recent policy changes in many countries have resulted in many more people managing their own pension investment portfolios. In Chapter 15, Hedesström reviews research on the cognitive, emotional and social influences on investment behaviour. He concludes that the research shows that investors tend to trade too often, which may be associated with overconfidence or thrill-seeking, and they sell rising shares too soon and falling shares too late. Hedesström argues that such short-termism may be counteracted if, as Gärling et al. (2009) suggest, bonuses to portfolio managers are linked to long-term performance.

Taxpaying is another aspect of economic behaviour that has broader implications, since if people evade or avoid their taxes, this has a serious negative impact on the economy and society. Kirchler and Hoelzl's illuminating review in Chapter 16

1.4   ECONOMIC MENTAL REPRESENTATIONS

In the fourth century BC, the invention of money changed the nature of human social and commercial exchanges. According to the credit definition, money is a scale of economic value used across society to monitor and record balances of credit and debt that are transferable to third parties (for a nontechnical account, see Martin, 2013). This definition focuses on the role of money as a tool to facilitate the practicalities of trade, and in economic theory it is seen as an interchangeable tool usable in any economic transaction. However, one of the earliest contributions of psychology to behavioural economics was research showing that psychologically money is not completely interchangeable, since the way people use money depends on how they mentally categorize it (Shefrin & Thaler, 1988; Tversky & Kahneman, 1981). In Chapter 8, Antonides and Ranyard review research demonstrating the rich diversity of such mental accounting phenomena. Before that, in Chapter 7, Zaleskiewicz, Gasiorowska, and Vohs consider core aspects of what money means to people. They describe an extensive series of ingenious experiments showing that reminding people about money affects economic behaviour in surprising ways. These money priming studies reveal that the psychological meaning of money runs much deeper than that of a mere tool. They show, for example, that money is associated with feelings of agency and independence, and with both negative values of selfishness and positive values of fairness and reciprocity.

Other aspects of money, the processes of evaluating specific prices, and perceptions and expectations of price inflation, are reviewed in Chapter 10 by Ranyard, Del Missier, Bonini, and Pietrioni. They argue that it is important to understand the former since judging whether a given price is cheap or expensive is a fundamental process underlying consumer behaviour. Also, it is important to understand the latter especially because (1) inflation expectations affect individual and household economic behaviour, and (2) surveys of inflation expectations are used to inform monetary policy.

Other key aspects of economic mental representations are explored in Chapters 9 and 11. In Chapter 9, Leiser and Krill present a novel analysis of lay understanding of the macro-economy. They point out that modern economies are complex with multiple direct, indirect and feedback effects of, for example, the rate of unemployment on economic growth. As Simon (1955) argued, the human capacity to deal with such complexity is bounded. The authors present fascinating evidence of how lay people use metaphors and heuristics to understand the economy. They are doubtful that any resulting misunderstandings can be corrected by financial education, but whether their doubts are justified is an open question for future research. Finally, in Chapter 11, Crozier reviews extensive research revealing the psychological meanings of material possessions, and shows that it demonstrates a strong link between a sense of ownership and self-identity. He also considers materialism, the importance people attach to material possessions, as an individual difference. Research has consistently shown it to be negatively correlated with subjective well-being, defined as both a reflective judgement on satisfaction with one's life and the balance of positive and negative emotions one experiences. His analysis of the causes, consequences and implications of this relationship contains many valuable insights.

approach, with economic psychology being prepared to employ a more eclectic range of research methods (see Section 1.3 and Part 2), including the study of behaviour in realistic, hypothetical scenarios and a range of methods to elicit self-reports (Ranyard & Svenson, 2011). In contrast, behavioural economics deems a narrower range of methods to be scientific, and requires data to be either from the real economic world or to be motivated by meaningful incentives. Third, Fetchenhauer et al. further explain that another significant contrast between the two disciplines relates to research ethics. Specifically, whereas economic psychologists allow the deception of research participants, as long as an appropriate ethical code is adhered to, such as that of the British Psychological Society (BPS, 2014), this is not acceptable, according to behavioural economics research ethics. Finally, it should be noted that behavioural economics adopts a distinctive political position concerning the role of interventions to effect behavioural change, *libertarian paternalism*. Applying this philosophy, those in power use behavioural economic research findings to change the decision environment so that people are more likely to make the decisions that those in power deem to be in the people's best interests. Some in the wider economic psychology community accept this 'nudge' approach to policy, while for others it is more controversial.

In conclusion, nowadays the distinctions between behavioural economics and economic psychology are becoming blurred. For example, behavioural economics is today more influenced by broader psychological theories, while economic psychology has been influenced by developments in behavioural economics. Kahneman recently expressed a similar view of the relationship between the related disciplines as follows: 'We need a common label for our shared activities … a descriptively correct label is "applied behavioral science" … I would be proud to call myself an applied behavioral scientist' (Kahneman, 2013, p. ix).

1.3   RESEARCH METHODS

Quantitative research methods have dominated economic psychology, although qualitative methods have made important contributions, often within multi-method research strategies, for example, case studies of specific economic events or phenomena, or in-depth interviews about core economic experience. Antonides presents a comprehensive overview of research methods in Chapter 4. He details an extensive range of studies to illustrate how each method has made a substantive contribution to the field. In quantitative economic psychology research, the measurement of psychological variables, or psychometrics, has been of central importance. Consequently, the two other chapters in Part 2 (Research Methods) are devoted to this. In Chapter 5, McNair and Crozier describe published measures of psychological dispositions and states relevant to economic behaviour. The scales they evaluate can be recommended for use in new research projects since they possess the sound psychometric properties of sensitivity, reliability and validity. In Chapter 6, Wood and Boyce explain how new subjective scales of personality, preferences and well-being can be developed for research purposes and when this might be appropriate. They provide a detailed guide to the process suitable for researchers new to psychometrics and a checklist of good practice for those more familiar with it.

Kahneman. He derived explanations from their influential work on judgemental heuristics and biases (Tversky & Kahneman, 1974) and prospect theory (Kahneman & Tversky, 1979), discussed in Chapter 2.

One of the first interdisciplinary collaborations in behavioural economics was research showing that economic behaviour can violate *homo economicus*'s (expected) utility maximization principle because people's evaluation of the same good can vary, depending on whether they own it or not (Kahneman, Knetsch, & Thaler, 1990; Thaler, 1980; see Chapter 11). They explained this *endowment effect* in terms of prospect theory's value function, which assumes that: (1) economic outcomes are evaluated as gains or losses relative to a reference point, and (2) people are loss-averse. The other key element of their explanation is that owners 'frame' the evaluation of the good from a different reference point to non-owners. In Kahneman's view, 'The concept of loss aversion is certainly the most significant contribution of psychology to behavioral economics' (2011, p. 300). Other framing effects, where the same decision alternatives are viewed from different reference points, likewise leading to preference reversals that violate utility theory (Tversky & Kahneman, 1981), have also made significant contributions. Perhaps the outstanding achievement of behavioural economics since the early 1980s has been its impact on public policy. For example, the recognition that framing the decision to donate organs after death as the default, with opting out being the alternative, increases rates of organ donation compared to the opposite frame (Johnson & Goldstein, 2004). Kahneman notes that the book *Nudge* (Thaler & Sunstein, 2008) can be considered to be the bible of behavioural economics, and that its international impact includes the establishment in the United Kingdom of the *Behavioural Insights Team* to advise the government on measures to support policy objectives, such as increasing the take-up of occupational pensions. Recently, more nuanced views of the impact of behavioural economics have been aired (Harford, 2014).

The similarities between behavioural economics and economic psychology are perhaps more important than their differences. First, both acknowledge many of the same historical roots described earlier, with both, for example, identifying Herbert Simon as a founding parent. This is not surprising since he was a polymath, making outstanding contributions to psychology, economics, artificial intelligence, and the philosophy of science. Indeed, a case can be made that he was the first psychologist to be awarded the Nobel Prize for Economics – in 1978, for his pioneering research into the decision-making process in economic organizations. Second, both disciplines are essentially empirical sciences, placing a premium on the validity of theories tested against behavioural evidence. Finally, both are applied sciences motivated to develop effective support for individuals and society in the economic domain.

Although both disciplines draw on psychology and economics, their main differences concern their ontological and epistemological assumptions and the research ethics of their parent disciplines. First, economic psychology draws broadly on contemporary psychology, which, as argued earlier, includes the primary goal of modelling mental life. On the other hand, the psychological component of behavioural economics is dominated by the approach to the psychology of judgement and decision-making developed by Tversky and Kahneman and their colleagues. In that sense, then, perhaps behavioural economics can be seen as a school within a broader interdisciplinary endeavour, in much the same way that the Chicago School is viewed in economics. Second, Fetchenhauer et al. (2012) note differences in epistemological they would be satisfied that their business would be more than viable. That is, they were motivated to reach an aspiration level. He later coined the term 'satisficing' to refer to simple decision rules, or heuristics, in which aspiration levels, rather than the goal of maximization, play a major role (Simon, 1955). His work on bounded rationality, an alternative view to 'rational economic man', was both a seminal and enduring contribution to psychology's cognitive revolution (Simon, 1959, 2000) that laid the ground for subsequent psychological theories of decision-making, such as prospect theory (Kahneman & Tversky, 1979). In Chapter 2, Kühberger and Schulte-Mecklenbeck review these developments, based on what they describe as the bedrock concepts of risk and value. They consider how judgement and decision heuristics have been viewed as both adaptive mechanisms for dealing with a complex environment and maladaptive failures of rationality. They conclude that our understanding of the psychology of economic decision-making has advanced by exploring the process of making decisions and by investigating the joint roles of emotional and affective influences and cognitive mechanisms.

Another major development in economic decision theory concerns choices between alternative courses of action whose outcomes are distributed over time, for example, either spending now or saving for a pension; or at the societal level, continuing to burn fossil fuels or developing energy sources less harmful to the planet in the long term. These are known as intertemporal choices. Koopmans (1960) developed a discounted utility model based on the rational principle that, other things being equal, one should have a time preference for a positive event sooner rather than later. As Read and Scholten explain in Chapter 3, much influential theory developing the concept of time preference has been tested in the laboratory with variants of the simplest intertemporal choice, 'smaller sooner or larger later?', for example: 'would you prefer £10 today or £12 in two months?' As well as time preference, other psychological dimensions of time perspective, such as planning horizons, concern for future consequences, expectations and uncertainty about the future, have been found to predict everyday economic decisions, for example, saving and borrowing (see Chapter 13 and Chapter 14 in this volume). Further research is needed to clarify the relative importance of these different aspects of time perspective in economic decision-making.

1.2.3   Behavioural Economics and Economic Psychology

Behavioural economics, more usually known by its American spelling (behavioral), is the branch of economics that uses psychological concepts and theories to better understand economic behaviour. This seems rather similar to aspects of our definition of economic psychology, summarized in Box 1.1, so what are the differences between the two disciplines? As Fetchenhauer et al. (2012) asked in the title of their article, are they 'monozygotic twins or unrelated stepchildren?' Before addressing this question, we first present some background on behavioural economics.

According to recent autobiographical accounts (Kahneman, 2011; Thaler, 2015), the discipline was born of a fruitful interaction between psychologists Daniel Kahneman and Amos Tversky, and the economist Richard Thaler in the 1970s. After Thaler had identified some patterns of economic behaviour inconsistent with rational economic theory, he explored how to explain these anomalies with Tversky and which disciplines such as psychology, biology, political science and history should play a major role. For many years, he strove to convince economics to absorb these per-spectives, but did not really succeed. Economists argued against this interdisciplinary approach on the grounds that economic theories – including those making assump-tions about human nature and the psychological mechanisms of economic agents – would suffice for their studies (Ferreira, 2007, 2008; van Raaij, 1999).

Wärneryd (2005a) and Kirchler and Hoelzl (2003) identified other advances in economic psychology in the United States in the early 1900s, with Wärneryd noting that they tended to be classified as consumer psychology. An *Association of Economic Psychology* was created in 1916, led by psychologists and businessmen interested in using psychology for practical purposes, such as recruitment and selection, publicity and sales, although information about the association is sparse, possibly because of the turmoil during and following the First World War (Wärneryd, 2005a).

To some authors, modern economic psychology starts in the mid-twentieth century, with George Katona (Ferreira, 2007, 2008; Webley & Walker, 1999). Indeed, the pioneering work of Katona, a Hungarian psychologist who emigrated to the United States and worked for the Department of Agriculture and the University of Michigan, is considered to be a landmark in the history of economic psychology. He was responsible for some of the first large surveys of attitudes, beliefs and expec-tations regarding economic behaviour.

In the early 1940s, economists were predicting from theoretical models that a major recession would follow the end of the Second World War because the popu-lation would be motivated to save their money after the traumatic events of the war. However, from his large-scale surveys of the American population, Katona predicted that the opposite was more likely, with people eager to buy goods, spend money and enjoy life after the war – and he was right. An economic boom took place after the war in the United States, and the economic community and other researchers were surprised that a psychologist could get it right, while economists went so astray in their forecasting (Ferreira, 2007, 2008).

In 1952, Katona created the 'Index of Consumer Sentiment' (ICS) that assesses people's economic expectations (see Chapter 13). The ICS was subsequently adopted by many countries and is still very much in use. In 1975, he published his major work, *Psychological Economics*, which integrated the findings from his many regular surveys. The reason he would prefer this for the title of his book to the inverse – *economic psychology* – remains unclear. Apparently, he used both, as well as the term *behavioural economics*, making no obvious distinction between them (Cruz, 2001).

1.2.2   Economic Decision-Making

Working at the same time as Katona, Herbert Simon began to develop an equally influential contribution to economic psychology. Like Katona, Simon's research was grounded in empirical investigation. His fundamental criticism of the behavioural assumptions of mainstream economic theory, based on *homo economicus*, was that they were just that – assumptions; neither based on, nor tested against, empirical data. In his classic study of how firms actually work, *Administrative Behaviour*, Simon (1947) found that business people did not seek to maximize their profits, as would be expected from standard economic theory. Rather, they set target levels above which

Besides Adam Smith, other economists of the eighteenth and nineteenth centuries wrote about psychological aspects of economic phenomena. Jeremy Bentham (1748–1832) developed Smith's concept of self-love and characterized utility as the permanent hedonistic pursuit of pleasure and avoidance of pain, along with calculations to maximize utility (MacFadyen & MacFadyen, 1986; Wärneryd, 2005a). John Stuart Mill (1806–1873) conceived the still respected (among mainstream economists) model of the *homo economicus*, a rational individual who makes rational decisions that maximize utility, is self-interested, capable of learning from experience, and with stable, consistent preferences (Lea et al., 1987; Wärneryd, 2008a). Mill believed that economics should be based on 'an obvious psychological law' (the universal preference for a greater gain as opposed to a smaller one). W. Stanley Jevons (1871) derived marginal utility theory from Mill's model, while adding deductive mathematics to establish some basic assumptions, later tested empirically. Finally, in the 1870s, Karl Menger and his collaborators, Böhm-Bawerk, von Wieser, Sax and others, formed what became known as the *Austrian Psychological School*, or the *Marginalist School*, that emphasized the importance of subjective elements in the economy. They claimed that a psychological analysis ought to provide the foundation for economics, arguing that introspection was the only method necessary to examine needs and attributions of value (Descouvières, 1998; Reynaud, 1967). In addition, thinkers throughout the centuries have routinely observed and discussed human relations involving choices, exchanges, ownership, loans, payments, investments, planning and other matters involving the allocation of scarce resources (Lea et al., 1987; Wärneryd, 2005a).

Economic psychology as a discipline can be traced to the late nineteenth century (Ferreira, 2008; Wärneryd, 2005b). The earliest record of the term can be found in an 1881 article in the journal *Philosophical* by the French jurist and social thinker, Gabriel Tarde, about the relationship between psychology and economics (Barracho, 2001; van Raaij, 1999; Wärneryd, 2008b). This was around the same time as psychology itself was being established as a science, in 1879, with Wilhelm Wundt's pioneering Introspectionist School in Leipzig (Schultz & Schultz, 2004). These developments allowed psychologists and some economists to start questioning the nature of the psychological assumptions used in economic theory, aiming at a more complex theory of rationality, or its rejection altogether (Wärneryd, 2005a).

Tarde, also considered to be one of the pioneers of social psychology, claimed that economic phenomena demanded a minute analysis of the psychology involved in them. In his earlier work, he discussed how imitation, repetition, and innovation could be used to analyse social and economic behaviour (van Raaij, 1999). However, it was in 1902 that he published *La psychologie économique*, believed by several authors to mark the birth of the discipline (Barracho, 2001; Descouvières, 1998; Ferreira, 2007, 2008; Kirchler & Hoelzl, 2003; Lea et al., 1987; Reynaud, 1967; van Raaij, 1999; Wärneryd, 2008b). This two-volume book was never translated into other languages, and Tarde passed away shortly after publishing it, in 1904. After that, the progress of economic psychology in Europe was to stall for several decades.

Around the same time, Thorstein Veblen, an American social thinker, published in 1899 *The Theory of the Leisure Class* in which he criticized the excessive life-style of American millionaires (Kirchler & Hoelzl, 2003; van Raaij, 1999). He argued that the basic human drive was towards social and economic status, and the means to achieve these could vary according to time and social and economic conditions (Lea et al., 1987). Veblen defended a broader approach to analysing economic phenomena, in

Box 1.1 Defining characteristics of economic psychology

- The science of economic mental life and behaviour
- A branch of applied psychology
- The study of 'how individuals affect the economy and how the economy affects individuals' (Lea, Tarpy, & Webley, 1987, p. 2)
- An interdisciplinary field of study

psychology famously broadcast in the influential textbook, *The Individual in the Economy: A Survey of Economic Psychology*, by Lea, Tarpy, and Webley (1987). It is the study of 'how individuals affect the economy and how the economy affects individuals' (p. 2). Consequently, it is an interdisciplinary endeavour, with increasingly fruitful collaborations with mainstream and behavioural economics and other biological and social sciences.

In Section 1.2, we describe the emergence of economic psychology as a discipline, including key developments in theories of economic decision-making, and we consider the relationship between behavioural economics and economic psychology. Following this, our introduction to the field reflects on the topics discussed in each part of the book, beginning with an outline of the main research methods that have been used (Part 2 of the book). We next discuss the various aspects of economic mental representations considered in Part 3. We then move on to aspects of personal and household financial decision-making and economic activity (covered in Parts 4 and 5). Finally, we introduce some of the economic-psychological issues related to life-span development and to society that are covered in Parts 6 and 7.[1]

1.2 THE EMERGENCE OF THE DISCIPLINE

1.2.1 *From Adam Smith to George Katona*

The origins of economic psychology can be traced to Greek philosophers and, more recently, to seventeenth-century economists who reflected on psychological matters, notably Adam Smith. Twenty years before writing *An Inquiry into the Nature and Causes of the Wealth of Nations* in 1776, Smith had published *The Theory of Moral Sentiments*, considered by some to be the starting point for economic psychology (e.g., Descouvières, 1998). He explored the concept of self-love and the importance of being able to take others' roles, as in the social interactions necessary for trading. In addition, he claimed that happiness and well-being were derived from the happiness and well-being of others, and explored several psychological concepts, including sympathy, emotions, and virtues in general (Barracho, 2001; Kirchler & Hoelzl, 2003; Wärneryd, 2005a).

describes how audits and fines, attitudes towards taxes and non-payment, social norms and notions of fairness influence an individual's tax behaviour. They argue that effective policies to minimize avoidance and evasion require that tax authorities use their powers wisely and foster a climate of trust with taxpayers. They conclude by suggesting several specific measures that could contribute to an approach to regulation based on cooperation and trust.

As well as financial matters, the scope of economic psychology encompasses important aspects of work and leisure, three of which are explored in Part 4 of the book. Since people have both intrinsic and extrinsic motivations to work, the role of money as an incentive for employees and volunteers is not straightforward. For example, research has shown that pay for volunteers crowds out their intrinsic motivation to contribute something positive to society (Frey, 1997). In Chapter 17, Frey and Gallus argue that both volunteer and for-profit organizations face similar problems of incentivizing workers. They focus on the role of public recognition by awards, outlining how they differ from monetary incentives. They conclude with some potentially useful suggestions for how organizations could effectively use awards to support the motivation of their volunteers.

Although voluntary work is important to the economy, entrepreneurial activity has a crucial role since it creates and expands economic activity, especially by identifying and exploiting new products. In Chapter 18, Domurat and Tyszka explore the economic and cultural conditions, and the personal motivations that stimulate entrepreneurial activity. Following a critical evaluation of research on the psychological characteristics associated with entrepreneurial status, they conclude that some statistically significant, though rather weak, associations have been found. They also find that entrepreneurs may be susceptible to cognitive biases in different ways from non-entrepreneurs. Finally, they detail some of the positive outcomes of training programmes for those embarking on entrepreneurial activity.

As well as the world of work, the world of leisure is a fascinating domain for economic psychology. Here we consider gambling behaviour, the one example in which risk, monetary value and affect are central. The study of gambling is interesting because, on the one hand, it is a major branch of the leisure industry and a source of pleasure for millions of people, yet on the other, *problem* gambling is a source of significant psychological and financial distress. In Chapter 19, Xu and Harvey discuss different forms of gambling, from simple jackpot lottery games of pure chance to more complex forms, arguably involving some skill, such as sports betting and card games. The authors document research that has advanced our understanding of the cognitive, affective and neurological determinants of gambling behaviour. They show that at least for those whose problem gambling is not due to some prior underlying psychopathology, cost-effective interventions based on education or counselling techniques can provide effective support.

1.6 LIFE-SPAN PERSPECTIVES

In 2001, Webley, Burgoyne, Lea and Young published the first thorough treatment of economic psychology that took a life-span developmental perspective. In Part 6 we offer four chapters that selectively enrich such an approach. In Chapter 20, Otto and

Serido begin by showing how one such developmental framework, that of Bronfen-brenner (2005), can offer insights on economic behaviour. They then review research on the role of parents in economic socialization which, it can be argued, is at least as important as school-based financial and economic education. Finally, they present an illuminating overview of how the economic understanding and behaviour of children, adolescents and young adults progress towards the goal of adult financial autonomy. A complementary perspective on the childhood psychological predictors of lifelong economic outcomes is presented by Egan, Daly and Delaney in Chapter 21. Their theoretical perspective emphasizes the notion of critical periods of develop-ment particularly before the age of 3 years old, while their review of the literature focuses on longitudinal surveys of development from child to adult, and on well-controlled studies of the impact of early interventions. In a thoughtful consideration of policy implications, they recommend that priority be given to early interventions supporting infants and pre-school children, and their parents.

Chapters 22 and 23 turn to developments across the adult years. In the former, Sonnenberg considers the economic psychology of couples' joint financial decision-making and of money management in households. She explains that research on the former shows how joint purchase decisions depend on a couple's relationship quality, their previous decision histories and on each partner's use of social influence strat-egies. She then shows how intra-household money management systems affect each partner's access to monetary resources, with women tending to be disadvantaged. Sonnenberg further argues that social norms such as fairness, and stereotypic expec-tations such as entitlements to earned income, are important psychological determi-nants of household financial behaviour. She concludes that further research could explore such factors more fully with new methods to reveal the dynamics of joint decision processes.

In Chapter 23, Bruine de Bruin examines the role of cognitive functioning, knowl-edge, emotions and motivation in personal economic decision making. She focuses on how age-related changes across adulthood impact on the quality of decision pro-cesses. The research she reviews shows how declines in fluid cognitive abilities, such as information processing speed, result in older adults having greater difficulties as the complexity of decisions increase. In other respects, both positive and negative effects of age-related changes have been observed. On the positive side, for example, older adults seem to dwell less on past negative events, which can be useful. Bruine de Bruin argues that support for economic decision-making across adulthood can be improved if such life-span psychological developments are taken into account. She contributes a valuable analysis of how decision aids, lifelong education and financial advice could benefit from such an approach.

1.7 ECONOMIC PSYCHOLOGY AND SOCIETY

The aspects of economic life and behaviour considered in Part 7 all have rather impor-tant implications for society. In Chapter 24, Kogut and Ritov present an in-depth anal-ysis of research on the psychology of charitable giving. As they point out, Adam Smith (1756) believed that helping others is a fundamental human motivation, and recent research has elaborated this. For example, Andreoni and Payne (2003) found that the act of giving a sum to a charitable cause gave people more pleasure than merely knowing that the same amount of the tax they paid went to that cause. Kogut and Ritov show how various characteristics of charitable causes influence donation behaviour, including the extent to which those in need elicit empathy. In addition, they analyse certain cognitive biases in charitable giving such as the *singularity effect*; the finding that donations are greater when the target of help is an identifiable individual rather than a group. Clearly, a rich understanding of charitable giving can be of great value to organizations for public benefit that rely on donations.

Earlier we mentioned Crozier's reflections on the negative association between material values and subjective well-being. In Chapter 25, Gärling and Gamble explore the measurement, causes and consequences of the latter in greater detail. Subjective well-being, they argue, is an important goal at both the societal and individual levels. Their review identifies a range of determinants of subjective well-being, including engagement in goal-directed activities, material wealth and supporting others. They also discuss important consequences such as good health and a longer life. Gärling and Gamble conclude that further research is needed to better understand the complex interrelationships between such factors and the directions of causality between them.

Poverty, generally defined as gap between the material resources people need to live and those they actually have, clearly has a negative impact on subjective well-being. In Chapter 26, Loibl reviews recent research on the negative effects of poverty on the financial behaviour of vulnerable groups. A series of recent studies have shown how preoccupation with the problems of everyday life in poverty can impair economic decision processes (Mullainathan & Shafir, 2013). Loibl begins by considering the various ways that poverty is defined and then reviews the effects on the economic behaviour of people living in poverty of the financial environment, financial literacy, limited margins for decision error and pressure on mental resources. She presents a thoughtful discussion of three particularly vulnerable groups that, she argues, are doubly disadvantaged: older adults, children and single mothers.

Chapter 27, by Handgraaf, Griffioen, Bolderdijk and Thøgersen, takes an economic psychological perspective on pro-environmental behaviour. Among other things, the authors show how psychological dispositions such as pro-environmental attitudes and concern for future consequences are associated with pro-environmental behaviour, and that certain cognitive biases, such as a preference for the status quo, and misunderstandings of effectiveness, can be barriers to pro-environmental actions. They conceptualize environmental problems as large-scale social dilemmas in which social norms may be used to overcome some of the problems of financial incentives for behaviour change in the interest of saving the planet – the ultimate societal challenge of our times.

In the final chapter, Ranyard, Ashton and Hebenton consider individual and societal issues surrounding personal and household insurance. Their overarching concerns relate to different facets of the moral hazards inherent in insurance: the insured may take unwarranted risks or make fraudulent claims, while insurers can mis-sell their products or turn a blind eye to false claims. In the first part of the chapter the authors present a bounded rationality perspective of insurance decisions as a means of protection against financial loss. In the second part, they discuss the causes of mis-selling and related consumer protection matters and in the final part they explore the prevalence of insurance fraud and approaches to prevention.

1.8 SUMMARY

Economic psychology, the science of economic mental life and behaviour, is increasingly relevant as people are expected to take more responsibility for their household and personal economic decisions. This chapter serves as a brief introduction to the field as well as to the following chapters of the book, which are organized into seven parts. We first traced the emergence of the discipline, from Adam Smith to George Katona and Herbert Simon, and discussed its relationship with behavioural economics. We also introduced important theories of economic decision-making based on risk, value and affect, and theories of intertemporal choice (Part 1). Then, after a brief look at methodology (Part 2), we examined the nature and behavioural consequences of economic mental representations about such things as material possessions, money and the economy (Part 3). We next turned to central aspects of economic psychology in everyday life – financial behaviour such as saving and tax-paying, and matters, such as entrepreneurial activity (Parts 4 and 5). In these and other chapters we noted some of the important implications of the research for supporting individuals and the economy. Finally, we considered two broader perspectives on economic psychology: life-span psychological development from childhood to old age (Part 6); and societal issues such as charitable giving and pro-environmental behaviour (Part 7). We hope that our selective review of the fascinating field of economic psychology is sufficient to whet the appetite of our readers.

NOTE

1. Readers should note that neuropsychological perspectives on economic behaviour are outside the scope of our coverage.

REVIEW QUESTIONS

1. What role has the notion 'homo economicus' had in the development of economic psychology?
2. Why are mental representations important in understanding economic behaviour?
3. Consider how a person's time perspective might be both a cause and a consequence of personal financial decisions.
4. Discuss the insights into economic behaviour arising from a life-span developmental perspective.

REFERENCES

Andreoni, J., & Payne, A. (2003). Do government grants to private charities crowd out giving or fund-raising? *American Economic Review, 93*, 792–812.

Barracho, C. (2001). *Lições de psicologia econômica* [Lessons on economic psychology]. Lisbon: Instituto Piaget.

BPS (2014). *Code of human research ethics.* Leicester: British Psychological Society.

Bronfenbrenner, U. (2005). *Making human beings human: Bioecological perspectives on human development.* Thousand Oaks, CA: Sage.

Cruz, J. E. (2001). Psicología económica [economic psychology]. *Suma Psicológica, 8*(2), 213–236.

Descouvières, C. (1998). *Psicología económica: temas escogidos* [Economic psychology: selected issues]. Santiago de Chile: Editorial Universitária.

Fetchenhauer, D., Azar, O. H., Antonides, G., et al. (2012). Monozygotic twins or unrelated step-children? On the relationship between economic psychology and behavioral economics. *Journal of Economic Psychology, 33*(3), 695–699.

Ferreira, V. R. M. (2007). Psicologia Econômica: origens, modelos, propostas [Economic psychology: origins, models, proposals]. Doctoral thesis, Social Psychology Graduate:Studies Program, PUC-SP, São Paulo.

Ferreira, V. R. M. (2008). *Psicologia econômica: estudo do comportamento econômico e da tomada de decisão* [Economic psychology: the study of economic behaviour and decision-making]. Rio de Janeiro: Campus/Elsevier.

Frey, B. S. (1997). *Not just for the money: An economic theory of personal motivation.* Cheltenham: Edward Elgar Publishing.

Gärling, T., Kirchler, E., Lewis, A., & Van Raaij, F. (2009). Psychology, financial decision making, and financial crises. *Psychological Science in the Public Interest, 10*(1), 1–47.

Harford, T. (2014, March 21). Behavioural economics and public policy. *Financial Times.* Retrieved from: http://www.ft.com/cms/s/2/9d7d31a4-aea8-11e3-aaa6-00144feab7de.html

Jevons, W. S. (1871). *The theory of political economy.* London: Macmillan.

Johnson, E. J., & Goldstein, D. G. (2004). Defaults and donation decisions. *Transplantation, 78,* 1713–1716.

Kahneman, D. (2011). *Thinking, fast and slow.* New York: Farrar, Straus and Giroux.

Kahneman, D. (2013). Foreword. In E. Shafir (Ed.), *The behavioral foundations of public policy.* Princeton, NJ: Princeton University Press.

Kahneman, D., Knetsch, J. L., & Thaler, R. H. (1990). Experimental tests of the endowment effect and the Coase theorem. *Journal of Political Economy,* 1325–1348.

Kahneman, D., & Tversky, A. (1979). Prospect theory: An analysis of decision under risk. *Econometrica, 47,* 263–292.

Katona, G. (1975) *Psychological economics.* New York: Elsevier.

Keynes, J. M. (1936). *The general theory of employment, interest, and money.* London: Macmillan.

Kirchler, E., & Hoelzl, E. (2003). Economic psychology. *International Review of Industrial and Organizational Psychology, 18,* 29–81.

Koopmans, T. C. (1960). Stationary ordinal utility and impatience. *Econometrica: Journal of the Econometric Society,* 287–309.

Krugman, P. (2009, September 2). How did economists get it so wrong? *New York Times.*

Lea, S. E. G., Tarpy, R. M., & Webley, P. (1987). *The individual in the economy: A survey of economic psychology.* Cambridge: Cambridge University Press.

Lewis, A., Webley, P., & Furnham, A. (1995). *The new economic mind: The social psychology of economic behaviour.* London: Harvester/Wheatsheaf.

MacFadyen, A. J., & MacFayden, H. W. (Eds.). (1986). *Economic psychology: Intersections in theory and application.* Amsterdam, The Netherlands: Elsevier Science Publishing.

Martin, F. (2013). *Money: The unauthorised biography.* London: Random House.

Miller, G. A. (1962a). The magical number seven, plus or minus two: Some limits on our capacity for processing information. *Psychological Review, 63,* 81–97.

Miller, G. A. (1962b). *Psychology: The science of mental life.* Oxford: Harper & Row.

Modigliani, F., & Brumberg, R. H. (1954). Utility analysis and the consumption function: An interpretation of cross-section data. In K. K. Kurihara (Ed.), *Post-Keynesian economics* (pp. 388–436). New Brunswick, NJ: Rutgers University Press.

Mullainathan, S., & Shafir, E. (2013). *Scarcity: Why having too little means so much.* New York: Times Books.

Ranyard, R., & Svenson, O. (2011). Verbal data and decision process analysis. In M. Schulte-Mecklenbeck, A. Kühberger, & R. Ranyard (Eds.), *A handbook of process tracing methods for decision research: A critical review and user's guide* (pp. 115–137). New York: Psychology Press.

Reynaud, P.-L. (1967). *A Psicologia econômica (La psychologie économique, in the original)*. São Paulo: Difusão Européia do Livro.

Schultz, D. P., & Schultz, S. E. (2004). *A history of modern psychology*. Belmont, CA: Thomson Higher Education.

Shefrin, H., & Thaler, R.H. (1988). The behavioral life-cycle hypothesis. *Economic Inquiry, 26*, 609–643.

Simon, H. A. (1947). *Administrative behavior: A study of the decision-making process in administrative organization*. New York: Macmillan.

Simon, H. A. (1955). A behavioral model of rational choice. *The Quarterly Journal of Economics, 69*, 99–118.

Simon, H. A. (1959). Theories of decision-making in economics and behavioral science. *The American Economic Review, 49*(3), 253–283.

Simon, H. A. (2000). Bounded rationality in social science: Today and tomorrow. *Mind & Society, 1*(1), 25–39.

Smith, A. (2010 [1756]). *The theory of moral sentiments*. London: Penguin.

Smith, A. (1982 [1776]). *The wealth of nations: Books I–III*. London: Penguin.

Thaler, R. H. (1980). Toward a positive theory of consumer choice. *Journal of Economic Behavior & Organization, 1*(1), 39–60.

Thaler, R. H. (2015). *Misbehaving: The making of behavioral economics*. New York: W W Norton & Company.

Thaler, R. H., & Sunstein, C. R. (2008). *Nudge: Improving decisions about health, wealth, and happiness*. New Haven, CT: Yale University Press.

Tversky, A., & Kahneman, D. (1974). Judgment under uncertainty: Heuristics and biases. *Science, 185*, 1124–1131.

Tversky, A., & Kahneman, D. (1981). The framing of decisions and the psychology of choice. *Science, 211*, 453–458.

Van Raaij, W. F. (1999). History of economic psychology. In P. Earl, & S. Kemp (Eds.), *The Elgar companion to consumer research and economic psychology*. Aldershot: Edward Elgar.

Veblen, T. (1899). *The theory of the leisure class*. New York: Macmillan.

Wärneryd, K. E. (2005a). Consumer image over the centuries. Glimpses from the history of economic psychology. In K. Grunert, & J. Thögersen (Eds.), *Consumers, policy and the environment: A tribute to Folke Ölander*. New York: Springer Verlag.

Wärneryd, K. E. (2005b). Psychology and economics. In T. Tyszka (Ed.), *Psychologiaekonomiczma*, Gdansk, Poland: Gdanskie Wydawnictwo Psychologiczne (author's original manuscript in English).

Wärneryd, K. E. (2008a). Economics and psychology: Economic psychology according to James Mill and James Stuart Mill. *Journal of Economic Psychology, 29*, 777–791.

Wärneryd, K. E. (2008b). The psychological underpinnings of economics: Economic psychology according to Gabriel Tarde. *The Journal of Socio-Economics, 37*(5), 1685–1702.

Webley, P., Burgoyne, C., Lea, S. E. G., & Young, B. (2001). *The economic psychology of everyday life*. Hove, East Sussex: Psychology Press.

Webley, P. & Walker, C. M. (Eds.). (1999). *Handbook for the teaching of economic and consumer psychology*. Exeter: Washington Singer Press.

FURTHER READING

Gärling, T., Kirchler, E., Lewis, A., & Van Raaij, F. (2009). Psychology, financial decision making, and financial crises. *Psychological Science in the Public Interest, 10*(1), 1–47.

Webley, P., Burgoyne, C., Lea, S. E. G., & Young, B. (2001). *The economic psychology of everyday life*. Hove, East Sussex: Psychology Press.

2 Theories of Economic Decision-Making: Value, Risk and Affect

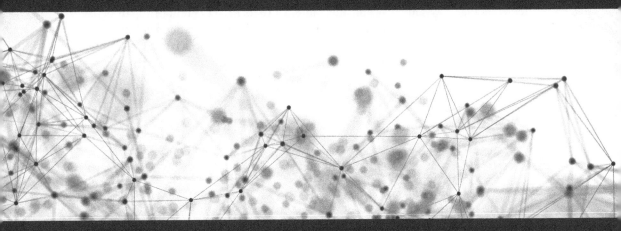

ANTON KÜHBERGER AND MICHAEL SCHULTE-MECKLENBECK

CHAPTER OUTLINE

LEARNING OUTCOMES

BY THE END OF THIS CHAPTER YOU SHOULD BE ABLE TO:

1. Identify and explain the major models of combining value and uncertainty.
2. Calculate the utility of a prospect according to SEU, and according to prospect theory.
3. Explain how affect and emotion can interact with cognitions in risky decision situations.

2.1 INTRODUCTION

Economic decision-making deals with various aspects of people's economic choices. In this process, the value of options is evaluated; but often options are not available for certain, and in such situations, risk becomes important. People may feel happy or sad about a situation or the outcomes of a choice, thus affect plays an important role. Understanding how value, risk and affect interact to form a coherent group of behaviours called risky decision-making is the main aim of this chapter. In what follows, we will give an overview of relevant concepts, such as value and utility, risk and ambiguity, affect and emotion, review the empirical research that informs the development of theory, and discuss relevant developments and interactions.

2.2 VALUE AND UTILITY

Theories of decision-making have their roots in economics (see Caplin & Glimcher, 2014), when researchers began to ask how the prices of traded goods come about. A striking first idea was that the price of a good produced by human effort depends on the number of labour hours it takes to produce it (the labour theory of value). It soon became clear that value accrues not only from labour. The so-called *marginal revolution* solved this problem. The new idea was to construe price as the marginal value of a good instead of its average value. Crucially, the marginal value of some good decreases as its total amount increases. Thus, for instance, stones are cheaper than diamonds because they are plentiful in most circumstances. If they were to become rare, their price would increase. An immediate question followed: why would someone be willing to pay so much more for exactly the same good if it was rare rather than plentiful? A person derives more happiness from the first item of a good compared to the, say, fifth item in her possession. Pricing thus follows from the decision-makers' goal to maximize happiness and/or satisfaction. Using the magical word: people are *utility*-maximizers.

The concept of utility became one of the backbones of the theory of economic decision-making. The historical record identifies a central paper on utility written by Nicolaus Bernoulli and published by his brother Daniel in the *St. Petersburg Academy Proceedings*. Bernoulli (1954 [1738]) proposed a solution for the so-called St. Petersburg Paradox (Box 2.1).

To solve the paradox, Bernoulli suggested distinguishing the utility – the desirability or satisfaction – of an outcome from its monetary amount (i.e., its value), and assuming a *principle of decreasing marginal utility*. This principle states that marginal utility (i.e., the utility obtained from an increment of some good) decreases as the quantity consumed increases. In other words, each additional amount of a good consumed is less satisfying than the previous one. Bernoulli additionally suggested a reasonable functional form for utility: the logarithm of the amount. By doing this the sum of expected utilities reaches a limit and the St. Petersburg game is worth the equivalent of about £4.00. The rational gambler, then, would pay any sum less than £4.00 to play. Thus, Bernoulli presented an ingenious solution of the paradox, and decreasing marginal utility became a new yardstick for reason and rationality.

Box 2.1 The St Petersburg Paradox

Consider the following gamble: you flip a fair coin until it comes up tails. The total number of flips, n, determines the prize you get, which equals £2^n. Thus, if the coin comes up tails the first time, the prize is £2^1 = £2, and the game ends. If the coin comes up heads, you flip it again. If it comes up tails the second time, the prize is £2^2 = £4, and the game ends. If it again comes up heads, it is flipped again. And so on. What is the value of this gamble? It is the sum of the payoffs of all the possible outcomes. In the first toss, the probability of tails is ½, and the payoff is £2. There are further possible outcomes, however: heads first, then tails. The probability of this sequence is ¼, and the payoff is £4. On we go, as long as further possibilities exist: heads, heads, tails. The probability of this sequence is ⅛, and the payoff is £8. We see that the probability of longer sequences of heads decreases, but never reaches zero. Calculation of the to-be-expected value (EV) shows:

$$EV = ½ \times 2 + ¼ \times 4 + ⅛ \times 8 + \ldots$$
$$= 1 + 1 + 1 + 1 + \ldots \text{ ad infinitum}$$

EV is an infinite large sum. Thus, a rational gambler should be willing to bet his or her entire fortune to play this gamble. Alas, paradoxically, 'few of us would pay even $25 to enter such a game' (Hacking, 1983, p. 563).

Researchers began to treat utility as something real, and tried to measure it. Consider this example, however. Imagine Tom prefers apples over oranges, oranges over bananas, and apples over bananas (i.e., apples > oranges > bananas). To explain Tom's preferences, we assign a 'fruit' utility to him of 3 for apples, 2 for oranges, and 1 for bananas. Unfortunately, we could also double, or halve the utilities, to predict the same preferences. The assigned utilities are useful for ordering things, but they fail on one simple test of rationality. This test has become famous as the *money pump* (Davidson, McKinsey, & Suppes, 1955). Box 2.2 gives an example of the logic behind it.

Box 2.2 The money pump

Imagine you prefer apples over oranges or you are indifferent; you prefer oranges over bananas or you are indifferent; you prefer bananas over apples or you are indifferent. Formally:

apples ≳ oranges; oranges ≳ bananas; bananas ≳ apples

You have a banana. Now you are offered an orange for your banana plus 1¢. You accept – recall that you like oranges more than bananas. Then you are offered an apple for the orange plus 1¢. Again, you accept (apples are better than oranges). Finally, you are offered to sell back your original banana for the apple plus 1¢. Again, you accept (as you prefer bananas over apples). Based on your preferences you consider each trade a good one, however, looking at the final state, you own your original banana and you have lost 3¢. Obviously, this is not a good deal: because of your inconsistent preferences, it turns you into a money pump in repeated choices.

2.3   RISK AND UNCERTAINTY

We face uncertainties in many situations throughout our lives. Tannert, Elvers, and Jandrig (2007) proposed a taxonomy of uncertainty that pits the mismatch between the knowledge required and the knowledge available for rational decision-making. Their basic distinction is between *objective* and *subjective uncertainty*. Kahneman and Tversky (1982) proposed a similar distinction between *externally* attributed uncertainty and *internally* attributed uncertainty. External uncertainty is based on frequencies or on propensities; internal uncertainty can be based on arguments or on knowledge. Kahneman and Tversky showed that people use different ways to resolve these different forms of uncertainty.

In addition, it is useful to distinguish two further variants of uncertainty based on frequencies: whether the distribution of possible outcomes is known, or is not known (Knight, 1921). In decisions under risk, the outcomes and the associated uncertainties are known. Most experimental work on human choice has focused on decisions under risk (Weber, Shafir, & Blais, 2004). However, many real-world decisions come with uncertainty, rather than risk, because the distribution of outcomes is unknown. For example, accepting one job over another entails many uncertainties about the possible states of the world if one had decided differently.

2.3.1   *From Expected Value to (Subjective) Expected Utility*

How can we combine uncertainty and value? Early considerations resolved around a quite mundane problem: how to bet wisely in a lottery. Blaise Pascal recognized that choosing wisely involves picking the option that provides the best combination of value (*v*) and probability (*p*). He proposed calculating $v \times p$, i.e., the *expected value* (*EV*), and to evaluate lotteries according to this property. Mathematical expectation, and its maximization (i.e., choosing the option with the highest EV), became the central doctrine of how to choose in a rational manner.

Yet, there are problems with this approach. First, lotteries are a simplified model of the uncertainties faced in the world. It is questionable whether they provide an adequate description of real-life decisions (see Box 2.1, the St Petersburg Paradox), Indeed, people often fail to maximize EV, making EV a poor predictor of choice.

Second, how can the doctrine of EV be applied to uncertain (i.e., ambiguous) situations? The best-known solution is to turn uncertainty into risk by replacing objective probabilities by subjective ones (Savage, 1954). Objective probabilities are determined by physical facts, whereas subjective probability (or perceived risk) is the personal or social construction of belief that can be independent of physical facts. This conception of risk led to a new model – the *subjective expected utility* model (SEU).

Imagine a choice between two insurance policies. One covers your damage with 90% probability, and the other does the same with 45% probability. Is the first policy exactly twice as good as the second?

To answer such questions, von Neumann and Morgenstern (1944) formulated a set of axioms that need to be fulfilled when measuring subjective expected utility (see Box 2.3). They stated the transitivity axiom as a basis for ordering lotteries. They then took care that there were no abrupt jumps in preference following from small

---

Box 2.3 Important axioms of SEU, technically stated, and examples

Axiom of completeness: Either a $\succsim$ b, or b $\succsim$ a, or a $\sim$ b.

Example (colour preference): Either you prefer azure over blue, or blue over azure, or you are indifferent between azure and blue.

Axiom of transitivity: If a $\succsim$ b and b $\succsim$ c, then a $\succsim$ c.

Example: If you prefer azure over blue, and blue over cyan, you also prefer azure over cyan.

Axiom of continuity: b $\sim$ pa + (1-p)c.

Example: If it is true that azure $\succsim$ blue $\succsim$ cyan, then you are indifferent between blue and (azure with probability p and cyan with probability 1-p).

Axiom of independence: If a $\succsim$ b, then xa + (1-x)c $\succsim$ xb + (1-x)c.

Example: If you prefer azure over blue, and blue over cyan, you also prefer (50% azure and 50% blue) to (50% azure and 50% cyan).

---

differences in value or probability, by introducing the continuity axiom. Finally, they introduced the independence axiom, which ensures that adding or subtracting a common prize to a pair of lotteries does not change preference.

Armed with these axioms, it is possible to measure utility by having people decide between lotteries. However, researchers discovered that many decisions do not conform to this set of axioms. Investigating the scope of violations of the axioms has been one of the major issues of behavioural decision theory in the last 50 years. Among the classic demonstrations of failure of some axioms are: the *Allais paradox* (Allais, 1953; also called the *certainty effect*, Kahneman & Tversky, 1979); risk aversion for losses (*loss aversion;* Kahneman & Tversky, 1979); *ambiguity aversion* as demonstrated in the *Ellsberg effect* (Ellsberg, 1961); failure of descriptive invariance of identical situations (the *framing effect;* Tversky & Kahneman, 1981). To account for these violations, SEU was adapted and extended.

2.4 DEVELOPMENTS BASED ON SUBJECTIVELY EXPECTED UTILITY (SEU)

Imagine playing the popular television game show *Deal or No Deal*. As the show approaches the end, two possible prizes are left: the largest prize (£100,000) and the smallest one (£1). One of those prizes is in a box next to you. The gameshow host offers you £20,000 for that box: you thus have to choose between £20,000 for sure (EV: 20,000 × 1 = 20,000), or a 50% chance of £100,000 and a 50% chance of £1 (EV: 100,000 × .50 + 1 × .50 = 50,000.5). What do you choose? Wouldn't it be tempting to take the £20,000, even though that has a much lower expected value?

This example shows a clash between the clever thing and the rational thing to do. Many of those clashes are addressed by another, if not the, prominent theory of risk and uncertainty, which we will discuss next.

2.4.1 Prospect Theory

The most successful development of SEU was prospect theory (PT), proposed by Kahneman and Tversky (1979); this was further developed as cumulative prospect theory by Tversky and Kahneman (1992). PT entails separate functions for the evaluation of probabilities, and for the translation of objective value into subjective utility.

The theory distinguishes two phases of decision-making: the editing phase, in which outcomes are assigned a subjective value by coding them in relation to some reference point, and probabilities are translated into decision weights. In the subsequent evaluation phase, the prospect with the highest evaluation is chosen. One of PT's essential new ideas relates to the editing phase and its value function. This function is defined over gains and losses relative to some reference point, shows diminishing sensitivity in both gains and losses, and is steeper for losses than for gains.

These properties of valuation have important consequences. Diminishing sensitivity is a general feature of evaluative processes, reflecting the basic psychophysical principle that the difference between £1 and £2 seems bigger than the difference between £101 and £102. Above the reference point, the value function is concave, below the reference point, it is convex. The shape of the value function is also steeper when losses are involved. This reflects loss aversion: for identical amounts, the reaction to losses is stronger than the reaction to gains.

PT's weighting function applies diminishing sensitivity to probabilities: There are two salient reference points for the evaluation of probabilities, namely, certainty ($p = 1$), and impossibility ($p = 0$). As people move away from these reference points, they become less sensitive to changes. They thus show a stylized pattern: they overweigh very small and underweigh very large probabilities. This gives rise to a weighting function that is concave near impossibility and convex near certainty (see Figure 2.1).

PT is formulated as:

$$V(x, p; y, q) = \pi(p)v(x) + \pi(q)v(y).$$

V denotes the value function for an option with two possible outcomes, x with probability p, and y with probability q; $v(0) = 0$, and π denoting the weighting function

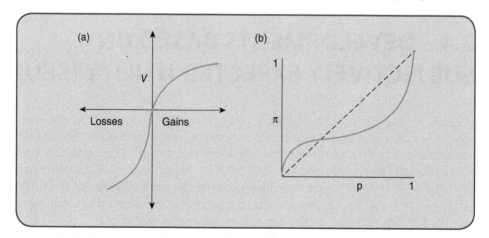

FIGURE 2.1 *Schematic form of (a) value-function and (b) weighting-function in prospect theory.*

Source: Adapted from Dreher 2007 with permission of Elsevier.

with $\pi(O) = 0$, and $\pi(1) = 1$ (Kahneman & Tversky, 1979, p. 276). PT descriptively explains a large number of so-called biases in risky decisions, such as loss aversion (Kahneman, Knetsch, & Thaler, 1991), the framing effect (Tversky & Kahneman, 1981), the endowment effect (Knetsch & Sinden, 1984; but see Kogler, Kühberger, & Gilhofer, 2013), the status quo bias (Samuelson & Zeckhauser, 1988), or the fourfold pattern of risk attitude (cumulative prospect theory: Tversky & Kahneman, 1992). This work was honoured in 2002 by the award of the Nobel Prize in Economics to Daniel Kahneman.

2.5   BEYOND UTILITY-BASED THEORIES

2.5.1   *Process Models of Risky Choice*

Until now we have only looked at the final choice as the central dependent measure. This allows for the construction of input-output models of risky choice. However, many researchers asked for tools and analyses also covering the information acquisition process, before a choice takes place (for an overview, see Schulte-Mecklenbeck, Kühberger, & Ranyard, 2011). Many of the more recent process-tracing tools are freely available, such as MouselabWeb (http://www.mouselabweb.org/) or MouseTracker (http://www.mousetracker.org/). Box 2.4 gives an example of a process-tracing approach.

Box 2.4 Inspection patterns of the priority heuristic

The priority heuristic (Brandstätter, Gigerenzer, & Hertwig, 2006) assumes that, rather than calculating SEU, decision-makers follow three rules when making risky choices. The rules (for gains) are:

1. *Priority rule.* Consider the components of a gamble in the following order: minimum gain, probability of minimum gain, maximum gain.
2. *Stopping rule.* Stop examination if the minimum gains differ by 1/10 (or more) of the maximum gain (aspiration level); otherwise, stop examination if probabilities differ by 1/10 (or more) of the probability scale.
3. *Decision rule.* Choose the gamble with the more attractive gain (probability).

Following these rules implies clear-cut and testable process predictions, which have been investigated with reaction time analysis in the original paper, and with attention and search sequence measures by Johnson, Schulte-Mecklenbeck and Willemsen (2008). For instance, the priority rule predicts that information should be acquired in the following order: minimum gain, probability of minimum gain, maximum gain. In conjunction with the stopping rule, it follows that the minimum outcomes will be inspected more often and longer than the maximum outcomes. Johnson et al. (2008) found that attention was actually equally distributed over minimum and maximum outcomes, thus providing no support for the priority and stopping rules. Note, however, that the predictive validity of the priority heuristic for choices is high (Brandstätter et al., 2006).

2.5.2 Heuristics

Ironically, organisms simpler in cognitive architecture may be able to follow the principles of rational choice better (Stanovich, 2013), because the axioms all end up saying, in one way or another, that choices should be unaffected by context, given that complete, well-ordered, and stable preferences exist. Surely, however, your preference for aspirin depends on whether or not you have a headache. That is, aspirin increases happiness only in case of a headache; its value thus is relative. It is a general finding of decision research that most preferences fail to be stable and rather are constructed on the fly (Lichtenstein & Slovic, 2006).

The heuristics-and-biases programme (Gilovich, Griffin, & Kahneman, 2002) deploys the intuition that people do not integrate all available information but use simple rules to navigate the vast amount of information available in the world. The programme developed in Berlin by the ABC Research Group (Gigerenzer, Todd, & the ABC Research Group, 1999), fast and frugal heuristics, argues that heuristics are essential tools to navigate large amounts of information successfully, in their appropriate ecology. In this tradition, heuristics are defined in a stringent and testable manner consisting of three rules: (1) a search rule (defining how search unfolds); (2) a stopping rule (defining when the search stops); and (3) a decision rule (defining how a final decision is made). The fast-and-frugal view takes an idea of Herbert Simon (1955; 1990) seriously, namely that the rationality of a choice not only depends on internal criteria (e.g., following the axioms) but also on the structure of the environment. Rationality is like a pair of scissors – one blade representing the structure of the environment, the other the computational capacities of the person – a proper conceptualization of rationality is only possible by understanding both the person and the environment they act in.

Unlike the SEU model, the heuristic approach does not assume that the organism needs to calculate value. Rather, valuation can be a consequence of simple comparisons, as in the priority heuristic. Decision-by-sampling theory (Stewart, Chater, & Brown, 2006) is exemplary of this approach, modelling decision-making as simple binary, ordinal comparisons. Decision-making works like a pan balance, indicating which of two items is heavier by tipping to one side, while providing no read-out of weight. Direct comparison, rather than value, is fundamental to choice. Reason-based choice is another comparative model, seeing choice as the balance of reasons for and against various alternatives (Shafir & Tversky, 1992). This account of decision-making is typical in the politics of business discourse. Reason-based analyses can explain non-experimental historic, legal and political decisions. In contrast, value-based approaches have dominated experimental research in standard economic analyses. Note that the idea of reason-based choice is very close to the way we normally think and talk about choices, thus providing a natural way to understand the conflict that often characterizes decision-making (i.e., that there are good reasons for and against each option, or conflicting reasons for competing options).

2.5.3 Decisions from Experience

The developments of psychological decision theory, as briefly summed up above, show that people frequently do not follow SEU theory. In contrast, SEU theory neatly predicts the behaviour of animals (e.g., Real, 1996). Where does this difference come from?

First, animal behaviour is tested in real life or at least in elaborate simulations of real life, while humans, by contrast, are tested using abstract analytical models of real life (e.g., lotteries). One such abstraction is to describe probabilities and payoffs to human participants in terms of summary measures (e.g., the probability of an event in the long run: decisions by description) rather than having them find out about the different outcomes of choice alternatives by repeatedly sampling them (decisions by experience). These two modes of decision-making could not be more different: In decisions from description, people get a written or graphical description of a situation, upon which they base their choices. Within this description, value and risk are numerically available and nicely summed up. In decisions from experience, people either need to consult their memory, or to actively sample information from the environment. You might recall from above, that prospect theory predicts, for a description situation, that low probability events are overweighted and high probability events are underweighted. In decisions from experience, the reverse pattern has been found (Hertwig et al., 2004): people behave as if rare events had much less impact than they would objectively deserve. This reverse pattern – the description-experience gap (Hertwig & Erev, 2009) – instigated a research programme of exploring a broad array of questions ranging from decisions in the medical world to the economic domain (for a comprehensive overview, see Wulff et al., 2016). Indeed, only humans have the ability to process abstract, symbolic representations of risky prospects, and animals' decisions are by necessity experience-based. It seems that there are striking similarities between the choices of humans and animals when humans make decisions from experience (Weber, Shafir, & Blais, 2004). This experience side of the *homo economicus* is widely underdeveloped and still neglected in research on risky decision-making.

2.6   HOT DECISIONS

Recently attention in decision research has turned to how emotions and feelings influence judgements and decisions: 'hot' processes became a hot topic. The relationship between affect and decision-making is bilateral, as there is evidence for an impact of affect on decisions (e.g., physiological and psychological arousal changes decisions; Ariely & Loewenstein, 2006), as well as for decisions on affect (e.g., Lerner & Tiedens, 2006) or regret (Connolly & Butler, 2006).

Lerner et al. (2015) identify various themes of affective influences on decision-making. Theme 1 is the integral effect of emotions on decision-making, that is, the effect of emotions that arise directly from the choice at hand. For instance, feeling anxious about a risky outcome may induce the choice of a safer, yet less lucrative, option. Compelling evidence for this type of influence comes from the work of Damasio (e.g., 2006), showing that injuries to the ventromedial prefrontal cortex reduce both patients' ability to feel emotions, and the optimality of their decisions. Many of those patients are risk-prone to the point of bankruptcy. Damasio's somatic marker hypothesis assumes that this is due to patients' inability to experience emotional signals – the somatic markers – that lead healthy people to feel, for example, fear in the presence of high risks. Theme 2 is the influence of incidental emotions. These are emotions unrelated to the decision, having a carry-over effect on choices. For instance, economists have reported a positive correlation between the amount of sunshine and stock market performance (Hirshleifer & Shumway, 2003). Other important themes are emotional influences on the content of thought (e.g., when fear induction leads to increased risk perception; Lerner et al., 2003), and emotional influences on the depth of thought (e.g., when negative mood leads to systematic processing while positive mood leads to heuristic processing; Schwarz, 1996). The interested reader may consult Lerner et al. (2015) for additional themes; here we will concentrate on some focal findings concerning risky decisions.

2.6.1 Predicted Emotions

Quite obviously, the positive or negative outcome of a decision can profoundly affect the decision-maker's feelings after a decision. Research on the consequences of acting unwisely (i.e., regretting a decision) or attaining an unwanted state of affairs (i.e., being disappointed by an outcome) gives testimony of two distinct emotions that may result from experiencing negative outcomes.

People may also experience positive emotions (e.g., joy, pride) following decision-making, though these emotions are only rarely investigated in decision research. The reason for this seems to be that positive emotions have, in contrast to negative emotions, only vague and unspecific action tendencies. According to Fredrickson's (2001) broaden-and-build theory, negative emotions tend to call for specific action tendencies (e.g., flight, or fight) and thus narrow an individual's momentary action repertoire. In contrast, positive emotions broaden an individual's action repertory (e.g., play, explore, savour), since no specific action is called for from experiencing a positive emotion: from feeling good, no specific action follows.

An implicit assumption of research that compares positive to negative emotions is that all positive, or all negative, emotions, are essentially equivalent for decision-making. There is reason to doubt this, since there is evidence that even affective states of the same valence can have distinct influences on decision-making. This is because different positive affective states (e.g., pride vs. cheerfulness), or different negative affective states (e.g., anger vs. sadness), may activate different implicit goals (see also Theme 3 in Lerner et al., 2015).

2.6.2 Risk-as-Feelings and the Affect Heuristic

Schwarz (2000) distinguishes two principled ways in which affect (i.e., weak emotion that is experienced as a quality of 'goodness' or 'badness'), and emotion can influence decision-making: as anticipated emotions (i.e., predictions about the emotional consequences of a decision), or as immediate emotions which are experienced at the time of decision-making. In the risk-as-feeling hypothesis (Loewenstein, Weber, Hsee, & Welch, 2001), risk has a specific affective feature: it is the instinctive and intuitive reaction to danger. Thus, risk is not calculated, but felt – as an immediate visceral reaction (e.g., fear, anxiety, dread). Feelings such as worry, fear, dread, or anxiety can result when people evaluate risky alternatives at a cognitive level. These feeling states can respond to factors that do not enter into cognitive evaluations (e.g., the immediacy of a risk; the vividness with which consequences can be imagined; personal exposure to or experience with the risk), leading to emotional reactions to risks that can diverge from cognitive evaluations of the same risks.

Slovic et al. (2002) have used the term 'affect heuristic' to characterize reliance on such feelings. The idea that current affect has an important role in decision-making, independent of cognitively mediated consequential deliberations, is also central to the affect heuristic. The affect heuristic proposes that the representations of choice situations in people's minds are tagged to varying degrees with affect. In the process of making a judgement or decision, people consult or refer to an 'affect pool' containing all the positive and negative tags consciously or unconsciously associated with the representations. Just as imaginability, memorability, and similarity serve as cues for probability judgements (e.g., the availability and representativeness heuristics), affect may serve as a cue for many important judgements (Slovic et al., 2007).

Thus, this heuristic is a cognitive short-cut that allows quick decisions based on current, negative, but also positive, affect. It is the equivalent to 'going with your gut' – note the similarity to Damasio's somatic marker hypothesis.

Research on risk perception offers a nice example of the affect heuristic. In general, it is true for hazardous activities that risk and benefit are positively correlated (i.e., high-risk activities have greater benefits than low-risk activities). This is not necessarily true for how people understand this correspondence: risk and benefit are often perceived as being negatively correlated. This inverse relationship between perceived risk and perceived benefit is mediated by affect: if I feel uneasy with, say, nuclear power, I tend to consider it a technology of high risk, and at the same time, a technology offering little benefit (Finucane et al., 2000). Thus, affect has informational value. The affect-as-information model (Schwarz & Clore, 1996) is another well-known example of this principle. However, in high levels of emotion, the direct effect is detrimental as it overrides cognition: individuals are 'out of control' (Loewenstein, 1996), acting against their own self-interest. These direct effects also vary depending on the qualitative character of the emotion, that is, the different action-tendencies evoked by different emotions.

Especially interesting are the indirect effects of current emotions on changing expectation and valuation. For instance, people become optimistic when in a good mood (e.g., Bower, 1991). Recent research has shed some light on specific effects of being emotional on the way that people deal with numbers, and on how they evaluate magnitudes. Two such effects, scope insensitivity, and hot-cold empathy gaps, will be discussed next.

2.6.3 Scope Insensitivity

Valuation depends on whether people are in a 'feeling', or a 'calculative' thought mode. Valuation by calculation is a process that relies on some sort of algorithm (e.g., the typical price of a piece of music) that takes into account the nature of the stimulus (e.g., that the piece is performed by the Vienna Philharmonic Orchestra), and its scope (e.g., that an offer contains two symphonies with 15 pieces each). In contrast, valuation by feeling relies on a gut feeling about the stimulus (e.g., that one likes music played by the Vienna Philharmonic Orchestra), but ignores its size (e.g., makes no difference between offers including one symphony or two). The general idea is that when people rely on valuation by feeling, they are sensitive to only basic differences in scope (i.e., the presence or absence of a stimulus) but are largely insensitive to further variations of scope (e.g., three, five or eight items all become 'some'). In contrast, when people rely on calculation, they show sensitivity to scope (Hsee & Rottenstreich, 2004).

Size insensitivity due to affective valuation, that is, the assessment of preference based on the sign and intensity of the emotional response can also exist when evaluating probability. For instance, Rottenstreich and Hsee (2001) asked participants for their willingness-to-pay for either a 1% or 99% chance of winning a $500 coupon, which could be used either for tuition payments (affect-poor) or towards expenses associated with a vacation (affect-rich). At 1%, people were willing to pay more for the vacation coupon than for the tuition coupon, but at 99% the picture reversed. People thus were more sensitive to the variation in probability between 1% and 99% when the prize was affect-poor than when it was affect-rich. In terms of prospect theory, the distinction between valuation by calculation and valuation by feeling translates into different forms of the value and the probability weighting functions. Both functions show more curvature under valuation by feeling.

Thinking in the calculative mode can have important consequences in real life: it can make people less receptive to other people's suffering. Slovic (2007) has described such a process – psychic numbing – in which thinking about large numbers of suffering humans leads to insensitivity towards the number of people involved, and thus mitigates emotional reactions to the suffering others. Indeed, as the number of suffering individuals becomes excessively high – as in genocide, mass famine, or other large-scale crisis – emotions can dissipate to a degree that people become less emotionally responsive to a large-scale as compared to a small-scale suffering.

2.6.4   Empathy Gaps

Predicting future feelings following from a decision can be especially difficult if these feelings are different from the current feelings. Such situations are called empathy gaps (e.g., Loewenstein, 2004) and come in two variants: (1) intrapersonal empathy gaps (predicting how one would feel in a different situation); (2) and interpersonal empathy gaps (predicting how others would feel). With respect to emotion, empathy gaps have two generic forms: hot-to-cold empathy gaps, and cold-to-hot empathy gaps. In hot-to-cold empathy gaps, people who are in emotional (i.e., hot) states tend to underestimate the extent to which their predicted preferences are under the influence of their present emotional state. They tend to underappreciate the influence of transient affect and thus overestimate the stability of their own current preferences. In cold-to-hot empathy gaps, people are not currently affectively aroused, but have to predict their behaviour in arousing situations. People then tend to underestimate the motivational forces of their own future hot states, and thus often fail to self-control. The classic example of a cold-to-hot empathy gap is substance abuse. The failure to empathize with future affective states due to alcohol abuse, or smoking, for instance, will cause decision-makers to underweigh the future consequences of those behaviors. Empathy gaps can specifically influence situations that involve intense emotions like fear, anxiety, or pain, thus, many medical decisions pertain to this category.

2.7   SUMMARY

Theories of economic decision-making have two bedrock concepts: value and risk. Theoretical work focused on ideas how to combine these two to arrive at sound decisions. This work culminated in the formulation of axioms that enable the measurement of utility, and the description of the ideal: the *homo economicus*, who seeks to maximize subjective expected utility. Subsequent empirical work revealed numerous instances where people fall short of this ideal: frequently they neither act in accordance to the axioms, nor maximize utility. Much of this research comes under the heading of 'heuristics'. However, interpretations differ, emphasizing either the negative (i.e., biased and irrational), or the positive (i.e., ecologically rational) consequences of relying on heuristics. In addition, directly investigating the process of decision-making, rather than merely its result, led to a wealth of interesting new findings that informed the development of new models, not following the expectancy-value structure. Finally, it became obvious that decision-making is not a purely cognitive process. Rather, emotional and affective influences are integral features, mediating and moderating the whole process of economic decision-making. These developments inform a new understanding of rational decision-making as a blend of cognitive and emotional processes that result in adaptive choices, dependent on the characteristics of the chooser, the context, and the relationship between chooser and context.

REVIEW QUESTIONS

1. What is the idea of expected utility theory? Explain in words and formula.
2. Explain the idea of the risk-as-feeling model.
3. Decisions-by-description versus decisions-by-experience: Discuss relevant similarities and differences in experimental operationalization and empirical findings.
4. How do emotion and affect interact with cognition? Explain the interaction for the case of magnitudes.

REFERENCES

Allais, M. (1953). Le comportement de l'homme rationnel devant le risque: Critique des postulats et axiomes de l'école américaine. *Econometrica: Journal of the Econometric Society*, 503–546.

Altman, M. (2004). The Nobel Prize in behavioral and experimental economics: A contextual and critical appraisal of the contributions of Daniel Kahneman and Vernon Smith. *Review of Political Economy*, 16, 3–41.

Ariely, D., & Loewenstein, G. (2006). The heat of the moment: The effect of sexual arousal on sexual decision making. *Journal of Behavioral Decision Making*, 19, 87–98.

Bernoulli, D. ([1738] 1954). Exposition of a new theory on the measurement of risk. (Ed. & Trans.) *Econometrica*, 22(1), 23–36. DOI:10.2307/1909829.

Bower, G. H. (1991). Mood congruity of social judgment. In J. Forgas (Ed.), *Emotion and social judgment* (pp. 31–54). Oxford: Pergamon Press.

Brandstätter, E., Gigerenzer, G., & Hertwig, R. (2006). The priority heuristic: Making choices without trade-offs. *Psychological Review, 113*, 409–432.

Caplin, A., & Glimcher, P. W. (2014). Basic methods from neoclassical economics. In P. W. Glimcher, & E. Fehr (Eds.), *Neuroeconomics* (2nd ed.; pp. 3–17). New York: Elsevier.

Connolly, T., & Butler, D. (2006). Regret in economic psychological theories of choices. *Journal of Behavioral Decision Making, 19*, 139–154.

Damasio, A. R. (2006). *Descartes' error* (2nd ed.). New York: Random House.

Davidson, D., McKinsey, J. C. C., & Suppes, P. (1955). Outlines of a formal theory of value, I. *Philosophy of Science*, 140–160.

Dreher, J-C. (2007). Sensitivity of the brain to loss aversion during risky gambles. *Trends in Cognitive Sciences, 11*, 270–272.

Finucane, M. L., Alhakami, A., Slovic, P., & Johnson, S. M. (2000). The affect heuristic in judgments of risks and benefits. *Journal of Behavioral Decision Making, 13*, 1–17.

Fredrickson, B. F. (2001). The role of positive emotions in positive psychology. *American Psychologist, 56*, 218–226.

Gigerenzer, G., Todd, P. M., & the ABC Research Group (1999). *Simple heuristics that make us smart*. New York: Oxford University Press.

Gilovich, T., Griffin, D., & Kahneman, D. (Eds.). (2002). *Heuristics and biases*. New York: Cambridge University Press.

Hacking. I. (1983). *Representing and intervening: Introductory topics in the philosophy of natural science.* New York: Cambridge University Press.

Hertwig, R., Barron, G., Weber, E. U., & Erev, I. (2004). Decisions from experience and the effect of rare events in risky choice. *Psychological Science, 15*, 534–539.

Hertwig, R., & Erev, I. (2009). The description–experience gap in risky choice. *Trends in Cognitive Sciences, 13*, 517–523.

Hirshleifer, D., & Shumway, T. (2003). Good day sunshine: Stock returns and the weather. *The Journal of Finance, 58*, 1009–1032.

Hsee, C. K., & Rottenstreich, Y. (2004). Music, pandas, and muggers: On the affective psychology of value. *Journal of Experimental Psychology: General, 133*, 23–30.

Johnson, E. J., Schulte-Mecklenbeck, M., & Willemsen, M. C. (2008). Process models deserve process data: Comment on Brandstätter, Gigerenzer, and Hertwig (2006). *Psychological Review, 115*, 263–272.

Kahneman, D., Knetsch, J. L., & Thaler, R. H. (1991). Anomalies: The endowment effect, loss aversion, and status quo bias. *The Journal of Economic Perspectives, 5*, 193–206.

Kahneman, D., Slovic, P., & Tversky, A. (Eds.). (1982). *Judgment under uncertainty: Heuristics and biases*. New York: Cambridge University Press.

Kahneman, D., & Tversky, A. (1979). Prospect theory: An analysis of decision under risk. *Econometrica, 47*, 263–292.

Kahneman, D., & Tversky, A. (1982). Variants of uncertainty. *Cognition, 11*, 143–157.

Knetsch, J. L., & Sinden, J. A. (1984). *Willingness to pay and compensation demanded: Experimental evidence of an unexpected disparity in measures of value. The Quarterly Journal of Economics, 99*, 507–521.

Knight, F. H. (1921). *Risk, uncertainty, and profit*. New York: Hart, Schaffner & Marx.

Kogler, C., Kühberger, A., & Gilhofer, R. (2013). Real and hypothetical endowment effects when exchanging lottery tickets: Is regret a better explanation than loss aversion? *Journal of Economic Psychology, 37*, 42–53.

Lerner, J. S., Gonzalez, R. M., Small, D. A., & Fischhoff, B. (2003). Effects of fear and anger on perceived risks of terrorism: A national field experiment. *Psychological Science, 14*, 144–150.

Lerner, J. S., Li, Y., Valdesolo, P., & Kassam, K. S. (2015). Emotion and decision making. *Annual Review of Psychology, 66*, 799–823.

Lerner, J. S., & Tiedens, L. Z. (2006). Portrait of the angry decision maker: How appraisal tendencies shape anger's influence on cognition. *Journal of Behavioral Decision Making, 19*, 115–137.

Lichtenstein, S., & Slovic, P. (Eds.). (2006). *The construction of preference.* New York: Cambridge University Press.

Loewenstein, G. F. (1996). Out of control: Visceral influences on behavior. *Organizational Behavior and Human Decision Processes, 65,* 272–292.

Loewenstein, G. F. (2004). Hot-cold empathy gaps and medical decision making. *Health Psychology, 24,* 49–56.

Loewenstein, G. F., Weber, E. U., Hsee, C. K., & Welch, N. (2001). Risk as feelings. *Psychological Bulletin, 127,* 267–286.

Payne, J. W., Bettman, J. R., & Johnson, E. J. (1993). *The adaptive decision maker.* Cambridge: Cambridge University Press.

Real, L. A. (1996). Paradox, performance, and the architecture of decision-making in animals. *American Zoologist, 36,* 518–529.

Rottenstreich, Y., & Hsee, C. K. (2001). Money, kisses, and electric shocks: On the affective psychology of risk. *Psychological Science, 12,* 185–190.

Samuelson, W., & Zeckhauser, R. (1988). Status quo bias in decision making. *Journal of Risk and Uncertainty, 1,* 7–59.

Savage, L. J. (1954). *The foundations of statistics.* New York: Wiley.

Schulte-Mecklenbeck, M., Kühberger, A., & Ranyard, R. (Eds.). (2011). *A handbook of process tracing methods for decision research: A critical review and user's guide.* London: Psychology Press.

Schwarz, N. (2000). Emotion, cognition, and decision making. *Cognition and Emotion, 14,* 433–440.

Schwarz, N., & Clore, G.L. (1996). Feelings and phenomenal experiences. In E. T. Higgins & A. Kruglanski (Eds.), *Social psychology: Handbook of basic principles* (pp. 433–465). New York: Guilford.

Shafir, E., & Tversky, A. (1992). Thinking through uncertainty: Nonconsequential reasoning and choice. *Cognitive Psychology, 24,* 449–474.

Simon, H. A. (1955). A behavioral model of rational choice. *Quarterly Journal of Economics, 69,* 99–118.

Simon, H. A. (1990). Invariants of human behavior. *Annual Review of Psychology, 41,* 1–19.

Slovic, P. (2007). 'If I look at the mass I will never act': Psychic numbing and genocide. *Judgment and Decision Making, 2,* 79–95.

Slovic, P., Finucane, M. L., Peters, E., & MacGregor, D. G. (2002). The affect heuristic. In T. Gilovich, D. Griffin, & D. Kahneman (Eds.), *Heuristics and biases: The psychology of intuitive judgment* (pp. 397–420). New York: Cambridge University Press.

Slovic, P., Finucane, M. L., Peters, E., & MacGregor, D. G. (2007). The affect heuristic. *European Journal of Operational Research, 177,* 1333–1352.

Smith, D. V., & Huettel, S. A. (2010). Decision neuroscience: Neuroeconomics. *Wiley Interdisciplinary Reviews: Cognitive Science, 1,* 854–871.

Stanovich, K. E. (2013). Why humans are (sometimes) less rational than other animals: Cognitive complexity and the axioms of rational choice. *Thinking & Reasoning, 19,* 1–26.

Stewart, N., Chater, N., & Brown, G. D. (2006). Decision by sampling. *Cognitive Psychology, 53,* 1–26.

Tannert, C., Elvers, H-D., & Jandrig, B. (2007). The ethics of uncertainty. *EMBO Reports, 8,* 892–896.

Tversky, A., & Kahneman, D. (1981). The framing of decisions and the psychology of choice. *Science, 211,* 453–458.

Tversky, A., & Kahneman, D. (1992). Advances in prospect theory: Cumulative representation of uncertainty. *Journal of Risk and Uncertainty, 5,* 297–323.

von Neumann, J. V., & Morgenstern, O. (1944). *Theory of games and economic behavior.* Princeton, NJ: Princeton University Press.

Weber, E. U., Shafir, S., & Blais, A-R. (2004). Predicting risk sensitivity in humans and lower animals: Risk as variance or coefficient of variation. *Psychological Review, 111,* 430–445.

Wulff, D. U., Mergenthaler, M., & Hertwig R. (2016). A meta-analytic review of two modes of learning and the description–experience gap. (Manuscript under review).

FURTHER READING

Caplin, A., & Glimcher, P. W. (2014). Basic methods from neoclassical economics. In P. W. Glimcher, & E. Fehr (Eds.), *Neuroeconomics* (2nd ed.; pp. 3–17). New York: Elsevier.

Johnson, J. G., & Busemeyer, J. R. (2010). Decision making under risk and uncertainty. *Cognitive Science*, 1(5), 736–749.

Lerner, J. S., Li, Y., Valdesolo, P., & Kassam, K. S. (2015). Emotion and decision making. *Annual Review of Psychology*, 66, 799–823.

3 Future-Oriented Decisions: Intertemporal Choice

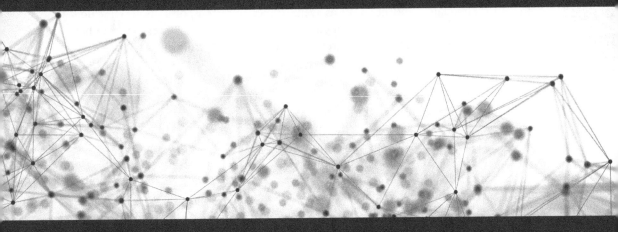

DANIEL READ AND MARC SCHOLTEN

CHAPTER OUTLINE

LEARNING OUTCOMES

BY THE END OF THIS CHAPTER YOU SHOULD BE ABLE TO:

1. Describe the basic results of the economic model of intertemporal choice.
2. Describe anomalies to the basic model, and explain why they are considered anomalies (and why they might not necessarily be).
3. Critically evaluate the question of what we measure when we measure discounting, and whether there are better alternatives.

3.1 INTRODUCTION

This chapter is about the economics and the psychology of *intertemporal choice*. Intertemporal choices involve trade-offs among outcomes that differ in their timing, and often in their quality and quantity as well. Typical intertemporal choices include whether to start work early or get an education before getting a better job; whether to smoke or to enjoy better health later; whether to save for a new car or get the car now by taking out a loan; whether the right time to have children is during your studies or after your career is well established; and whether you should publish now or wait for definitive results. It can, indeed, be argued that all choices are intertemporal in a broad sense. To illustrate this, consider what appears to be a non-intertemporal choice. You must decide whether to stay at home and read or go to a movie. Both actions span the same evening. However, the opportunity cost of the book is the enjoyment of the movie, whereas the opportunity cost of the movie is not only the enjoyment of the book, but also the enjoyment of the goods attainable with the money spent on the movie. This turns the decision into an intertemporal choice. The choice is between, on the hand, the movie tonight and, on the other hand, the book tonight and the other goods further on in the future. Similarly, a choice between having a rich, fattening dessert or an apple is intertemporal, because the consequences of what you eat can extend well into the future, which is why people diet.

A complete account of the field of intertemporal choice would sacrifice too much depth for breadth. Our goal is to cover a decent amount of terrain and to give enough detail to allow you to understand the current literature and perhaps to contribute to it, and to provide some understanding of how the literature on intertemporal choice relates to everyday behaviour. There are other excellent recent reviews out there which take different perspectives and emphasize different issues and we have not attempted to duplicate these (e.g., Kalenscher & Pennartz, 2008; Story, Moutoussis, & Dolan, 2016; Urminsky & Zauberman, 2014). We have also mostly avoided technical work on choice modelling (e.g., Arfer & Luhmann, 2015; Dai & Busemeyer, 2014; Doyle, 2013; Ericson White, Laibson, & Cohen, 2015; Scholten, Read, & Sanborn, 2014) although given that we ourselves conduct research in this area, it is not surprising that we make occasional references to it. The chapter is divided into three main sections. The first provides a brief account of the economic model of intertemporal choice, as it applies to individual decision-makers. We next consider some key behavioural departures from this model and, in particular, how to interpret these departures. Finally, we consider what people are *actually* doing when they make choices in the laboratory between money now and money later.

3.2 RATIONAL INTERTEMPORAL CHOICE

Although intertemporal choices are diverse, most research focuses on a restricted domain of choices we collectively refer to as 'standard tasks' in which people trade off early money against later money. This will also be the focus of this chapter. In a typical experiment, respondents choose between Smaller Sooner (*SS*) and Larger Later (*LL*) options (*choice*), or else must specify an option which is equivalent in value to a provided option (*matching*). It is useful to have some notation to enable us to speak in general terms. If we define $SS = (x_S, t_S)$ and $LL = (x_L, t_L)$, where x is an amount to be received (or paid), t is the time before the payment or receipt occurs, and the subscripts $_S$ and $_L$ index whether the later or earlier option is being discussed. For instance, imagine you have a choice between $100 now and $110 in one year. Then $SS = (x_S = \$100, t_S = 0)$, and $LL = (x_L = \$110, t_L = 1)$. In cases of matching, the respondent might specify what amount in one year would be equivalent to receiving $100 now (or what amount received now is equivalent to $110 in one year).

An intertemporal decision or choice can be conceptualized as follows: the later amount x_L is the outcome from investing x_S at an *experimental interest rate*, i_E, over the interval separating the outcomes. That is, because you can get x_L by not receiving x_S now, it is just like depositing x_S in the bank and waiting a year for it to grow into x_L. The banker is the experimenter. In our example, i_E is 10% (0.1) as can be worked out as follows:

$$x_L = x_S(1 + i_E)^{t_L - t_S} \text{ or } \$110 = \$100(1 + .1)^{1-0}$$

Most theories in economics and psychology hold that the decision-maker evaluates choices between delayed outcomes by comparing the experimental interest rate with a personal 'interest rate' (often called a 'discount rate') which we will denote i_ψ. Theoretically, people will choose LL over SS only if the experimenter offers a return greater than i_ψ.[1] In our example with an annual experimental interest rate (i_E) of 10%, a decision-maker with $i_\psi > 10\%$ would take SS, one with $i_\psi < 10\%$ would take LL, and one with i_ψ equal to exactly 10% would be indifferent.

Economic theory assumes a rational agent who minimizes *opportunity cost*, which is the value of what you have to give up to get something. When it comes to money over time, the opportunity cost is dictated by the credit market (Coller & Williams, 1999; Fisher, 1930; Price, 1993) – how much you can earn by investing money, and how much you would pay to borrow it. Consequently, for each individual, i_ψ *will be equal to the highest rate of interest at which that individual can save or invest money, or the lowest rate of interest at which they can borrow*.

To see how this works, consider two examples. If Mary is currently saving at 3% per year, then 3% is her opportunity cost. If the experimenter offers Mary a 10% return (i_E), Mary will choose LL, since 10% is higher than 3%. Suppose, on the other hand, John carries credit card debt charging 28% on the unpaid balance and has no savings (which he will not have, if he is rational, since he will already have used his savings to draw down his debts).[2] If offered an option earning 10%, he should take SS because, for John, money received now will 'earn' 28% if he used it to reduce his debt.

This rational theory of intertemporal preferences has important implications. One is that an individual's personal degree of impatience will not influence the intertemporal decisions they make for money, at least not for relatively small amounts. We cannot describe this implication more concisely than Richard Thaler (1981):

> In the case of perfect capital markets, everyone behaves the same way *at the margin* since firms and individuals borrow or lend until their marginal rate of substitution between consumption today and consumption tomorrow is equal to the interest rate. (p. 201, italics added)

To see this, imagine two people who are identical in terms of their circumstances, except one is more patient than another. Call the patient one Anna (the 'ant' from Aesop's fable of the ant and the grasshopper) and the impatient one Gretchen (the 'grasshopper'). Both earn $5,000 a month which they can save at 3%. The feckless Anna spends $4,000 and saves $1,000, whereas the frugal Gretchen spends $1,000 and saves $4,000. They are both saving *something* but Anna is clearly much more impatient than Gretchen as reflected in her spending. Suppose Anna and Gretchen are offered an extra $1 which they can choose to save or spend. Because they are both saving money, it means that they are already spending as much as they want out of $5,000, so they have no pressing need to spend that extra (or 'marginal') dollar and will be indifferent between spending and saving it. Another way of putting this is that both will be indifferent between receiving $1 today, or receiving $1.03 in one year. Clearly, Anna is much more impatient than Gretchen, but theoretically this should not be reflected in their i_ψ measured in terms of decisions over the marginal dollar. As it turns out, however, people in apparently identical circumstances do display very different preferences in whether they want to save or spend the marginal dollar, even when the interest rates on offer are very different from the market rate. It is this fact that drives empirical research into intertemporal choice.

3.3 ANOMALIES IN INTERTEMPORAL CHOICE

The most studied findings in intertemporal choice are called 'anomalies' because they contradict the baseline model just described, or a close relative of that model similarly designed to reflect economic rationality (see Loewenstein & Thaler, 1989; Roelofsma, 1996; Thaler, 1981). One widely cited close relative is the *exponential discounting* model which holds that if you discount some experiences at a certain rate over some period, you should discount all experiences at the same rate over all periods. Exponential discounting is not quite the standard economic model (although it is sometimes described as such): it specifies that i_ψ be constant over time, whereas the standard model only specifies that i_ψ correspond to the prevailing rate of interest which can differ over time and over places; and, moreover, most discussions of the exponential discounting model do not specify that i_ψ corresponds to that prevailing rate of interest.

Most anomalies concern how differences in options influence preference in ways that deviate from exponential discounting. There are two classes of such anomaly: In the first class, differences in the objective properties of options influence preferences over those options; in the second class, economically irrelevant variations in choice circumstances or option description produce variations in preference. We start with the first class.

3.3.1 The Common Difference Effect

The *common difference* effect is that adding an additional delay to both options in a choice pair will increase choices of *LL* (Loewenstein & Prelec, 1992). Using our example, someone who chooses $100 today over $110 in one year might nonetheless choose $110 in two years over $100 in one year: the one-year delay matters more if it starts now than if it starts in one year. The common difference effect, sometimes under different names, is widely discussed because it seems to reflect an important and fundamental human characteristic: the tendency to make far-sighted plans that are undermined when it comes time to enact them. For instance, a dieter might plan to have a low-calorie salad for tomorrow's dinner (reflecting his long-term plans, or *LL* in our terminology), but when the one-day delay is removed and dinner is about to be served, he might well change his mind and opt for the high-calorie Beef Wellington (*SS* in our terminology). There is much evidence of such realistic versions of the common difference effect, with people in the lab, as well as in the real world, falling prey to temptations available now but not to temptations available next week (e.g., Kirby & Herrnstein, 1995; Read, Loewenstein, & Kalyanaraman, 1999; Read & Van Leeuwen, 1998). But with respect to choices involving money, evidence for the common difference effect is much more fragmentary. Some researchers have obtained evidence for it (e.g., Ainslie & Haendel, 1983; Green, Fristoe, & Myerson, 1994; Halevy, 2015; Scholten & Read, 2006). Others have not (Andreoni & Sprenger, 2012; Baron, 2000; Glimcher, Kable, & Louie, 2007; Luhrmann, 2013; Read, 2001). The effect appears highly dependent on specific features of the choice context (Dai & Fishbach, 2013; Read, Frederick, & Airoldi, 2012; Read, Frederick, Orsel, & Rahman, 2005). To give examples, Read et al. (2005) find an effect when time is described in terms of dates, but not in terms of delays; Dai and Fishbach (2013) find that when the decision-maker actually has to wait over the interval prior to *SS* being made available, they become more patient and so more likely to choose *LL* when both options are available immediately than when they are delayed. There are even cases where the effect reverses (e.g., Read, Olivola, & Hardisty, 2016; Sayman & Öncüler, 2009).

3.3.2   *Subadditive Discounting*

The common difference effect, to the degree that it does occur, appears to reflect *present bias*, or *hyperbolic discounting*. That is, rather than i_ψ having a constant value, its value decreases with delay from the present (McAlvanah, 2010; Read, 2001). In the example we gave, the value of i_ψ would be higher (more discounting) for the first year than for the second. Another way discount rates vary as a function of time is what we will call the *subadditive effect* (an effect which, unfortunately, is also often called hyperbolic discounting). We can illustrate the subadditive effect by comparing preferences for three choices having $i_E = 10\%$, compounded annually:

$(0 \rightarrow 1)$: $100 today OR $110 in one year

$(0 \rightarrow 3)$: $100 today OR $133 in three years

$(2 \rightarrow 3)$: $100 in two years OR $110 in three years.

The numbers in parentheses give the discounting interval $(t_S \rightarrow t_L)$. More people will choose *LL* given a $(0{\rightarrow}3)$ choice than either a $(0{\rightarrow}1)$ choice[3] or a $(2{\rightarrow}3)$ choice. What this shows is that people discount at a higher rate over a shorter interval and, quite important from a theoretical perspective, this is primarily due to the length of the interval and not whether the interval itself starts sooner or later. Read (2001) called this *subadditive* discounting because it means the discount rate i_ψ will be greater over an interval when that interval is divided into segments; dividing the interval

$0 \rightarrow 3$ into three one-period segments and measuring discounting over each segment will produce more discounting than measuring discounting over the undivided interval. For example, while Scholten and Read (2010) find moderate evidence of a common difference effect (e.g., $(2 \rightarrow 3) > (0 \rightarrow 1)$), they find much stronger effects of subadditivity. Interval effects such as these are in strong contradiction with the economic models of intertemporal choice that assume choice is driven by a single value of i_ψ, or by a value of i_ψ defined in terms of the financial opportunity cost.

3.3.3   The Sign Effect

The *sign effect* is that the inferred value of i_ψ is higher when choosing among delayed losses than gains (Thaler, 1981). For instance, if we compare choices between receiving $100 today or $110 in one year, or *paying* $100 today or $110 in one year, we would find a much higher proportion would pay today than receive in one year. This contradicts the standard model since anyone with $i_\psi < 10\%$ would take the later money and pay today, while anyone with $i_\psi > 10\%$ would take the earlier money and pay later. The sign effect is even more extreme than this, since many people will prefer to pay *more* now than to pay later, even if there is no financial advantage in waiting and indeed often even if the amount to be paid is greater now than later (e.g., Hardisty, Appelt, & Weber, 2013; Yates, 1975). As we discuss shortly, this has implications for the magnitude effect.

3.3.4   The Magnitude Effect

This is perhaps the most robust anomaly in intertemporal choice (see Scholten & Read, 2010). People are more patient (inferred i_ψ is lower) when deciding over larger amounts than smaller ones, if we hold i_E and the discounting interval constant. Someone currently indifferent between receiving gains of $x today or $y > $x in one year and who is offered a choice between $cx today and $cy in one year (where $c > 1$) will take LL in the second case. This violates the constant rate model just described, and also is likely to violate any version of the standard model, because in the outside world the opportunity cost of money does not typically depend greatly on the amounts of money being considered.

The magnitude effect is an anomaly in another economic or decision theoretic sense: someone who displaces the magnitude effect can be turned into a 'money pump', or someone whose inconsistent preferences can lead an arbitrager to extract money from them, while they receive no benefit from the transaction (see Echenique, Lee, & Shum, 2011). To illustrate how the magnitude effect can create a money pump, imagine John prefers $100 today over $111 in one year; and prefers $1,100 in one year over $1,000 today. John's preferences are consistent with a very small magnitude effect. You can money pump John as follows. First offer John $1,100 in one year in exchange for $1,000 today. John will agree and give you $1,000. Next, take the $1,000 and break it into ten $100 chunks, and then make a series of separate offers to switch each of these $100 chunks for $111 in one year. John will agree to each exchange, and at the end of the set of transactions you will owe John $1,100 in one year, and he will owe you $1,110 in one year. You now start again by offering John $1,100 in one year in exchange for $1,000 today, and the process continues. In theory, with these preferences, John can be induced to part with his entire fortune.

In reality, John is unlikely to be pumped since he will quickly recognize he is being conned and stop dealing with you. But money pump arguments suggest how people might make themselves worse off when making individual intertemporal (and other) choices, even when those choices are independent. For instance, someone might make many small purchases on credit cards at high interest rates and carry over that debt, even when they have money in the bank earning much less than that credit card debt. This implies the money pump pattern just described: a willingness to save large amounts for a relatively modest future return, while accelerating small amounts of consumption in exchange for proportionately much higher payments later. (For more on what might be called 'distributed' money pumps, see Rabin & Thaler, 2001.)

3.4 EXPLAINING ANOMALIES

One approach to anomalies is to demonstrate they are not anomalies at all – that they are the result of rational processes missing from the economic analysis. The other way is to identify psychological processes that will produce the anomaly. Here we will consider both approaches as they apply to the magnitude effect.

To give a flavour of how to rationalize the magnitude effect, consider that the costs of waiting might be (proportionally) larger for small payoffs than large ones. There may be, for instance, a psychological or financial burden associated with separate transactions, such as a cost of making sure future payments actually take place, or to remember to cash a cheque. A magnitude effect can arise because the cost of a transaction makes it worthwhile to wait for a large gain, but not for a small one. To illustrate, suppose the cost to John of remembering to collect any individual payment in one year is a fixed $5. Then $1,100 in one year is reduced to $1,095 and $110 in one year is reduced to $105. But if there are ten separate payments of $110, their total value is reduced to $1050, and it is consistent to prefer to $1,095 in one year to $1,000 now, while preferring $1,000 now to $1050 in one year.

Another possibility is that small amounts can yield greater returns than larger ones. For instance, suppose you could invest $100 at 15% but could only get 5% for $1,000. Then you would rationally take $100 now over $110 in a year, but $1,100 in a year over $1,000 now. An example like this is described by Banerjee and Duflo (2012), when discussing how microfinance might benefit the very poor. They observe the total benefits from a small loan can often be (proportionally) much greater than those from a large loan. The intuition is based on diminishing marginal returns to additional investments – a car dealer might get a huge proportional return on investment by stocking one additional car, but find that with two additional cars the average sale price drops, and with three cars, one is left unsold. Although Banerjee and Duflo do not make the connection to the magnitude effect, this would entail that people should be willing to forego a larger interest rate on very small amounts, but accept it for larger amounts.

Rationalizations like these likely do not apply over the full range of circumstances in which the magnitude effect has been observed. For instance, the effect occurs if payments are described as direct deposits or withdrawals from one's bank. This requires us to draw on non-economic explanations. The most likely explanation is surprisingly simple. Most models of intertemporal choice assume that the preference is determined by ratios between payment values. We propose that, in addition, people are sensitive to *differences* between amounts (see also Killeen, 2009; Leland, 2002; Leland & Schneider, 2016; Rubinstein, 2003). We model this by proposing an attribute-based model to intertemporal choice, first summarized in (Scholten & Read, 2010).[4] In our model, options are directly compared along their attributes, and the option with the largest advantage is chosen. Thus, '$100 today' has a time advantage over '$110 in one year', but the latter has an outcome advantage. These advantages are transformed mathematically, and the option whose advantage is the greatest is chosen. So instead of the comparison between i_E and i_ψ determining choice (as in the economic model, and most psychological variants), it is a comparison between a function of time differences and a function of outcome differences (or more specifically, between a function of differences between functions of time, and a function of differences between functions of amounts).

To produce a magnitude effect, the outcome advantage has to exhibit what we call *augmenting proportional sensitivity*. Increasing a pair of amounts by a constant increases the size of the outcome advantage: for example, if $100 and $110 are tripled to $300 and $330, the outcome advantage is increased. Many functions display this effect, including a *linear advantage function* where $f(x_1, x_2) = \beta(x_2 - x_1)$.[5] This feature of the trade-off model explains another curious result – the magnitude effect can *reverse* in losses (Hardisty, Appelt, & Weber, 2013; Scholten , Read, Walters, Erner, & Fox, 2017). To see this, assume a linear difference function, and assume as well there is a sign effect and magnitude effect. Someone indifferent between *receiving* $100 today and $120 in one year (positive time preference), would also be indifferent between $1,000 today and $1,020 in one year, displaying a huge magnitude effect. Now imagine someone who displays negative discounting for losses, so that they are indifferent between, say, paying $100 today and paying $110 in one year (i.e., β is negative for losses). With the linear difference function, this person would also be indifferent between paying $1,000 today, and paying $1,010 in one year: the same difference between outcomes, but a higher, because less negative, discount rate. Consistent with this view, Scholten et al. (2017) show that people differ in their time preference for losses (positive for some, negative for others), and that, *in the aggregate*, implied discount rates increase, from negative to positive, as the magnitude of losses increases.

3.5 FRAMING EFFECTS

The preceding discussion has addressed anomalies to the economic model due to *objective* changes in the options, such as changes in outcome sign, delay or magnitude. There is also much evidence that preferences can vary among identical options due to changes in option description. We will call these *framing effects*. Framing effects violate the fundamental idea that preferences should be determined entirely by the options on offer, and when they will be experienced. For instance, imagine a choice between $100 now and $110 in one year, and another between $100 now and $110 in 52 weeks. It would be hard to rationalize having different preferences for these two choice pairs, although in fact far fewer people will choose the $110 when it is only one year away than when it is as many as 52 weeks (Read, Frederick, Orsel, & Rahman, 2005). Similarly, Robles and Vargas (2007; Robles, Vargas, & Bejarano, 2009) observed much more impatience when identical lists of intertemporal choice items were presented in the order of low interest rate (i_E) to high interest rate, than when presented in the opposite order. It is not the options that determine preference but (in this case) also the method used to elicit that preference. Other framing effects include the delay/speed-up asymmetry (Loewenstein & Prelec, 1992), the date/delay effect (Read et al., 2005), the rate/amount asymmetry (Read, Frederick, & Scholten, 2013), and the (asymmetric) hidden zero effect (Magen, Dweck, & Gross, 2008; Read & Scholten, 2012; Read, Olivola, & Hardisty, 2016; Scholten, Read, & Sanborn, 2016; Wu & He, 2012).

The earliest and best-known framing effect in intertemporal choice is the delay/speed-up asymmetry (Loewenstein, 1988; Malkoc & Zauberman, 2006). For positive outcomes (e.g., the receipt of a new bicycle), time matters more when the outcome will be delayed, than when it will be speeded up (i.e., expedited). For negative outcomes, the reverse is true. To illustrate this, imagine Mary is expecting her new bicycle to arrive in one month, but learns it is possible to receive it tomorrow instead. How much extra will Mary pay to speed up delivery? Call that speed-up fee $S. Now imagine Nira is expecting her new bicycle tomorrow, but could delay delivery by one month for a discount. What discount will be enough? Call that discount $D. It turns out that $D likely to be greater than $S, suggesting the benefit to Mary of getting her bicycle early is greater than the inconvenience to Nira of getting it late. The delay/speed-up asymmetry is a classic framing effect, in that it seems to reflect loss aversion, just like the endowment effect (although it does not depend on the Willingness to pay/Willingness to accept discrepancy – see Loewenstein, 1998; Scholten & Read, 2013).[6] Loewenstein and Prelec (1992) explained it this way: delaying an option entails an early loss of an option, compensated by a later gain of an identical option. Because of loss aversion, the earlier loss does not sufficiently compensate for the later gain, even if there was no change in timing. The compensation demanded therefore reflects compensation for losing the earlier option, as well as compensation for delay. Scholten and Read (2013) suggested that, in fact, the loss in the problem was a loss of time – delaying a positive outcome was seen as a loss of time.

When applied to consumer goods, it is possible to rationalize this framing effect. For instance, suppose Nira has made plans to go on a cycling trip with her friends on the day she receives her bike. Receiving the bike later will throw these plans in disarray. Mary will not, however, have made plans to go cycling *before* she anticipates receiving the bike, so this upset does not apply to her. A delay can easily be disruptive, but the failure to achieve an unplanned speed up cannot be. The delay/speed-up asymmetry, however, also applies to decisions involving *money* – delaying and speeding up receipts or payments – results which require the kinds of rationalization discussed in the preceding section.

Other framing effects are more difficult to rationalize with plausible arguments. One example is the hidden zero effect, which can be illustrated by comparing a choice between '$100 now OR $110 in one year' and '$100 now and $0 in one year OR $0 now and $110 in one year.' Magen, Dweck, and Gross (2008) found that the second choice pair yielded much more patience (choices of *LL*) than the first. This finding has been replicated many times (Loewenstein & Prelec, 1991, 1993 – who predated its rediscovery; Radu et al., 2011; Read & Scholten, 2013; Wu & He, 2012). The effect is entirely due to the 'zero' attached to the *SS* option – learning that you will get $0 in one year if you choose *SS* makes you more inclined to choose the *LL* option (Read, Olivola & Hardisty, 2016).

How to explain this? Read et al. (in press) propose attention plays a key role. Framing draws attention to some option features, and reduces attention to others. The amount of attention focused on a feature determines its decision weight. Introducing the 'zeroes' focuses attention on the opportunity costs of each option. This effect is asymmetric, which is why adding a zero to the *SS* option makes people more patient, while adding a zero to the *LL* option has no effect. People readily understand that choosing the *LL* option entails giving up something now, but are normally much less aware that choosing the *SS* option entails giving up something later.

There are numerous other framing effects. Read, Frederick, and Scholten (2013) proposed the DRIFT model to capture some of these, drawing on the same idea of attentional salience just described. The DRIFT model is a multi-attribute model, in which the role played by any given attribute is determined by salience. Outcomes have numerous features including the four factors denoted DRIF (the 'T' stands for time): the difference (D) between them (e.g., $110 - $100, as discussed earlier in relation to the magnitude effect), their ratio (R: $110/$100), the experimental interest rate (r_E), and whether they are framed in financial terms (F). Read et al. (2013) found that describing options in terms of these factors strongly influenced preference. Specifically, if D(ifferences) between options were emphasized, the standard anomalies of intertemporal choice were very strong, especially the magnitude effect, subadditivity,[7] and excessive discounting (i.e., a discount rate much higher than the market rate). In short, emphasizing only differences yielded the typical results from intertemporal choice studies. If R(atio) information was emphasized, however, the magnitude effect was *greatly* diminished although not eliminated, as was the average level of discounting, although the subadditive effect remained strong. When I(nterest) rate information was emphasized, the effect was to again reduce the magnitude effect and the overall level of discounting, but also to *reverse* the subadditive effect. Now, people showed a higher discount rate (or, were more likely to choose *LL*) when the interval was longer than when it was shorter. Finally, if F(inance) considerations were emphasized, people discounted considerably less in general. These effects on patience all make sense if we treat framing effects as the result of attentional focus, with greater attention being put on those attribute dimensions explicitly mentioned in the outcome frame. In this way, framing effects are the experimental equivalent of marketing.

3.6 WHAT DO WE CARE ABOUT WHEN WE MEASURE INTERTEMPORAL CHOICE?

The ultimate goal of studying time preferences for money is not to find out how people make monetary trade-offs (although we do care about this) but to find out how they value their future selves.[8] Here is one way of thinking of this. Imagine our life can be described in utilitarian terms, as a stream of 'instantaneous utility', or happiness and misery, pleasure and pain. The choices we make will often involve trading off pleasures and pains at different times. Smoking a cigarette, for instance, might be seen as a trading off the early pleasure from smoking against delayed negative health consequences. The discount rate we often want to measure, therefore, is the rate at which we substitute delayed for early happiness. To give a simple example, a person might want to take 10 units of happiness today in exchange for 11 units in one year.

Choices for money payments, while they are not necessarily the same as choices for non-monetary goods, nonetheless do tell us something about the psychological discount rate. Many studies show a correlation between time preference measured using money, and real-world outcomes associated with consumption decisions, such as obesity, smoking and drug addiction (e.g., Chabris, Laibson, Morris, Schuldt, & Taubinsky, 2008; Estle, Green, Myerson, & Holt, 2007; Kirby, Petry, & Bickel, 1999; Robles, 2010; Smith, Bogin, & Bishai, 2005). In addition, monetary time preference is correlated with age in ways that make sense if money was treated as equivalent to consumption, with older people typically discounting less than younger ones (Reimers, Maylor, Stewart, & Chater, 2009). Time preference is also related to intelligence and other measures of cognitive ability (Shamosh & Gray, 2008). It appears we can use choices between *SS* and *LL* options as a rough index of impatience, and to the degree that impatience is a trait that rough index can often predict other behaviours associated with that trait. But many years of intertemporal choice research leave us with unanswered questions about the relationship between discounting in the laboratory, and how much people value themselves in the future. While in this chapter we have largely restricted our attention to intertemporal choices for money, there is a larger research project yet to come in which we delve into the question of whether people truly value their future self less than their current self and, if so, how we can characterize this future valuation.

3.7 SUMMARY

Intertemporal choices are choices between outcomes that differ in time, usually between smaller sooner (*SS*) and larger later (*LL*) options. The economic model of intertemporal choice makes clear predictions, that, on the margin, people will choose between options that offer a rate of return equal to the market rate of interest. In reality, people show many anomalies to this prediction. They discount large amounts at a lower rate than small ones, losses at a lower rate than gains, and at a rate that increases as the interval between outcomes gets smaller. The anomalies are economically irrational in that they can in principle turn people into money pumps. But it is possible to rationalize some (perhaps even all) standard anomalies, if the opportunity cost of one class of option is different from that of another. Framing effects, in which identical options are discounted at different rates depending on how they are described, are more challenging to rationalize. Although we often study delay discounting for money, in reality, we are interested in how people value their future selves.

NOTES

1. This section makes some simplifying assumptions that do not substantively change the conclusions. See Cubitt and Read (2007), and Hirshleifer (1965) for more thorough accounts.

2. We know, however, that many people simultaneously roll over credit card debt and keep savings earning much less than that debt (Banks, Smith, & Wakefield, 2002; Gross & Souleles, 2002).

3. This effect is the basis for many measures of the hyperbolic discounting parameter k, although the term hyperbolic discounting should be applied to the common difference effect (Read, 2001; Scholten & Read, 2010). To see this, consider that hyperbolic discounting predicts people will be more likely to choose LL given the $(2\rightarrow3)$ choice than the $(0\rightarrow3)$ choice, yet in fact choices will go (very strongly) in the opposite direction.

4. It is possible for a standard attribute-based model to mimic attention to attribute differences with an *increasingly elastic* value function. Such a function is found in the hyperbolic discounting model proposed by Loewenstein and Prelec (1992). This approach cannot model interval effects, such as the subadditive/hyperbolic effect described earlier.

5. Diminishing proportional sensitivity requires is only that the output of the advantage function increases in proportional increases in both outcomes, or that $f(cx_1, cx_2) > f(x_1, x_2)$, where $c > 1$. Several formal models incorporate this basic idea, such as the DRIFT model (Read, Frederick, & Scholten, 2013) and the ITCH model (Ericson et al., 2015).

6. Choice studies in which no payments are made rule out the WTA/WTP discrepancy. For instance, Scholten and Read (2013) presented one group with delay questions like the following: 'You are entitled to receive $100 today. Choose between: (A) Receive $100 today, as planned; (B) Delay the receipt and receive $200 in 1 year instead', and another group with similar speed-up questions: 'You are entitled to receive $200 in 1 year. Choose between: (A) Speed up the receipt and receive $100 today instead; (B) Receive $200 in 1 year, as planned.' The result was that most people chose A in the delay frame, and B in the speed-up frame.

7. Subadditivity as measured by comparing two intervals that begin now, as in the $0\rightarrow1$ and $0\rightarrow3$ comparisons made earlier. This is also called hyperbolic discounting, but here we avoid the term because of its ambiguity.

8. An important current line of research investigates the relationship between how people identify with their future selves, and how they discount future outcomes (Bartels & Rips, 2010; Bartels & Urminsky, 2011; Frederick, 2002). This work is inspired by the philosopher Derek Parfit (1984).

REVIEW QUESTIONS

1. What will happen to an individual's choices between SS and LL amounts of money if (a) the interest rate increases?; (b) they are uncertain about their job prospects?

2. The money pump is one of the main theoretical devices in decision theory. Can you devise a money pump for someone who displays a sign effect? As a further exercise, investigate money pumps in other aspects of decision-making.

3. How do frames work? One effect of framing is to influence choice behaviour, with some frames producing more choices of the LL option than others. In your opinion, are frames that increase LL choices actually increasing patience, or something else? How would you test your hypothesis?

4. How would you investigate time preference for non-monetary goods? Try to come up with an alternative to choices between SS and LL quantities of those goods.

REFERENCES

Ainslie, G., & Haendel, V. (1983). The motives of the will. In E. Gottheil, K. A. Druley, T. E. Skoloda, & H. M. Waxman (Eds.), *Etiologic aspects of alcohol and drug abuse* (pp. 119–140). Springfield, IL: Charles C. Thomas.

Allais, M. (1953). Le comportement de l'homme rationnel devant le risque: critique des postulats et axiomes de l'école américaine. *Econometrica, 21,* 503–546.

Andreoni, J., & Sprenger, C. (2012). Estimating time preferences from convex budgets. *American Economic Review, 102,* 3333–3356.

Arfer, K. B., & Luhmann, C. C. (2015). The predictive accuracy of intertemporal-choice models. *British Journal of Mathematical and Statistical Psychology, 68,* 326–341.

Banerjee, A., & Duflo, E. (2012). *Poor economics: A radical rethinking of the way to fight global poverty.* New York: Public Affairs.

Banks, J., Smith, Z., & Wakefield, M. (2002). The distribution of financial wealth in the UK: evidence from 2000 BHPS data. IFS Working Paper W02/21. Available at: http://www.ifs.org.uk/workingpapers/wp0221.pdf

Baron, J. (2000). Can we use human judgments to determine the discount rate? *Risk Analysis, 20,* 861–868.

Bartels, D. M., & Rips, L. J. (2010). Psychological connectedness and intertemporal choice. *Journal of Experimental Psychology: General, 139,* 49–69.

Bartels, D. M., & Urminsky, O. (2011) On intertemporal selfishness: The perceived instability of identity underlies impatient consumption. *Journal of Consumer Research, 38,* 182–198.

Chabris, C. F., Laibson, D., Morris, C. L., Schuldt, J. P., & Taubinsky, D. (2008). Individual laboratory-measured discount rates predict field behavior. *Journal of Risk and Uncertainty, 37,* 237–269.

Chabris, C. F., Laibson, D., & Schuldt, J. P. (2006). Intertemporal choice. In S. Durlauf, & L. Blume (Eds.), *The new Palgrave dictionary of economics* (2nd edn.). London: Palgrave Macmillan.

Coller, M., & Williams, M. B. (1999). Eliciting individual discount rates. *Experimental Economics, 2,* 107–127.

Cubitt, R. P., & Read, D. (2007). Can intertemporal choice experiments elicit time preferences for consumption? *Experimental Economics, 10,* 369–389.

Dai, J., & Busemeyer, J. R. (2014). A probabilistic, dynamic, and attribute-wise model of intertemporal choice. *Journal of Experimental Psychology: General, 143,* 1489–1514.

Dai, X., & Fishbach, A. (2013). When waiting to choose increases patience. *Organizational Behavior and Human Decision Processes, 121,* 256–266.

Doyle, J. R. (2013). Survey of time preference, delay discounting models. *Judgment and Decision Making, 8*(2), 116–135.

Echenique, F., Lee, S., & Shum, M. (2011). The money pump as a measure of revealed preference violations. *Journal of Political Economy, 119,* 1201–1223.

Ericson, K. M. M., White, J. M., Laibson, D., & Cohen, J. D. (2015). Money earlier or later? Simple heuristics explain intertemporal choices better than delay discounting does. *Psychological Science, 26,* 826–833.

Estle, S. J., Green, L., Myerson, J., & Holt, D. D. (2007). Discounting of monetary and directly consumable rewards. *Psychological Science, 18,* 58–63.

Fisher, I. (1930). *The theory of interest.* New York: Macmillan.

Frederick, S. (2003). Time preference and personal identity. In G. Loewenstein, D. Read, & R. Baumeister (Eds.), *Time and decision* (pp. 89–113). London: Russell Sage Foundation.

Frederick, S., Loewenstein, G., & O'Donoghue, T. (2002). Time discounting and time preference: A critical review. *Journal of Economic Literature, 40,* 351–401.

Glimcher, P. W., Kable, J. W., & Louie, K. (2007). Neuroeconomic studies of impulsivity: Now or just as soon as possible? *American Economic Review, 97,* 142–147.

Green, L., Fristoe, N. & Myerson, J. (1994). Temporal discounting and preference reversals in choice between delayed outcomes. *Psychonomic Bulletin and Review, 1,* 383–389.

Gross, D. B., & Souleles, N. S. (2002). Do liquidity constraints and interest rates matter for consumer behavior? Evidence from credit card data. *Quarterly Journal of Economics, 117,* 149–185.

Halevy, Y. (2015). Time consistency: Stationarity and time invariance. *Econometrica, 83*(1), 335–352.

Hardisty, D. J., Appelt, K. C., & Weber, E. U. (2013). Good or bad, we want it now: Fixed-cost present for gains and losses explains magnitude asymmetries in intertemporal choice. *Journal of Behavioral Decision Making, 26,* 348–361.

Hirshleifer, J. (1965). Investment decision under uncertainty: Choice-theoretic approaches. *The Quarterly Journal of Economics,* 510–536.

Kalenscher, T., & Pennartz, C. M. (2008). Is a bird in the hand worth two in the future? The neuro-economics of intertemporal decision-making. *Progress in Neurobiology, 84*(3), 284–315.

Killeen, P. R. (2009). An additive-utility model of delay discounting. *Psychological Review, 116,* 602–619.

Kirby, K. N., & Herrnstein, R. J. (1995). Preference reversals due to myopic discounting of delayed reward. *Psychological Science, 6*(2), 83–89.

Kirby, K. N., Petry, N. M., & Bickel, W. K. (1999). Heroin addicts have higher discount rates for delayed rewards than non-drug-using controls. *Journal of Experimental Psychology: General, 128,* 78–87.

Leland, J. W. (2002). Similarity judgments and anomalies in intertemporal choice. *Economic Inquiry, 40,* 574–581.

Leland, J. W., & Schneider, M. (2016). Salience, Framing, and decisions under risk, uncertainty, and time. ESI Working Paper 16-08. Retrieved from http://digitalcommons.chapman.edu/esi_working_papers/186/

Loewenstein, G. (1987). Anticipation and the valuation of delayed consumption. *Economic Journal, 97,* 666–684.

Loewenstein, G. (1988). Frames of mind in intertemporal choice. *Management Science, 34,* 200–214.

Loewenstein, G., & Prelec, D. (1991). Negative time preference. *American Economic Review, 81,* 347–352.

Loewenstein, G., & Prelec, D. (1992). Anomalies in intertemporal choice: Evidence and an interpretation. *Quarterly Journal of Economics, 107,* 573–597.

Loewenstein, G., & Prelec, D. (1993). Preferences for sequences of outcomes. *Psychological Review, 100,* 91–108.

Loewenstein, G., & Thaler, R. H. (1989). Anomalies: Intertemporal choice. *The Journal of Economic Perspectives, 3*(4), 181–193.

Luhmann, C. C. (2013). Discounting of delayed rewards is not hyperbolic. *Journal of Experimental Psychology: Learning, Memory, and Cognition, 39*(4), 1274.

Magen, E., Dweck, C. S., & Gross, J. J. (2008). The hidden-zero effect. Representing a single choice as an extended sequence reduces impulsive choice. *Psychological Science, 19,* 648–649.

Malkoc, S. A., & Zauberman, G. (2006). Deferring versus expediting consumption: The effect of outcome concreteness on sensitivity to time horizon. *Journal of Marketing Research, 43,* 618–627.

McAlvanah, P. (2010). Subadditivity, patience, and utility: The effects of dividing time intervals. *Journal of Economic Behavior & Organization, 76*(2), 325–337.

Myerson, J., Baumann, A. A., & Green, L. (2014). Discounting of delayed rewards: (A)theoretical interpretation of the Kirby questionnaire. *Behavioural Processes, 107,* 99–105.

Parfit, D. (1984). *Reasons and persons.* Oxford: Oxford University Press.

Price, C. (1993). *Time, discounting and value.* Oxford: Blackwell.

Rabin, M., & Thaler, R. H. (2001). Anomalies: risk aversion. *The Journal of Economic Perspectives, 15*(1), 219–232.

Radu, P. T., Yi, R., Bickel, W. K., Gross, J. J., & McClure, S. M. (2011). A mechanism for reducing delay discounting by altering temporal attention. *Journal of the Experimental Analysis of Behavior, 96*(3), 363–385.

Read, D. (2001). Is time-discounting hyperbolic or subadditive? *Journal of Risk and Uncertainty, 23*, 5–32.

Read, D. (2004). Intertemporal choice. In D. J. Koehler, & N. Harvey (Eds.), *Blackwell handbook of judgment and decision making* (pp. 424–443). Malden, MA: Blackwell Publishing.

Read, D. (2007). Experienced utility: Utility theory from Jeremy Bentham to Daniel Kahneman. *Thinking & Reasoning, 13*(1), 45–61.

Read, D., Frederick, S., & Airoldi, M. (2012). Four days in Cincinnati: Longitudinal tests of hyperbolic discounting. *Acta Psychologica, 140,* 177–185.

Read, D., Frederick, S., Orsel, B. & Rahman, J. (2005). Four-score and seven years from now: The date/delay effect in intertemporal choice. *Management Science, 51,* 1326–1335.

Read, D., Frederick, S., & Scholten, M. (2013). DRIFT: An analysis of outcome framing in intertemporal choice. *Journal of Experimental Psychology: Learning, Memory, and Cognition, 39,* 573–588.

Read, D., Loewenstein, G., & Kalyanaraman, S. (1999). Mixing virtue and vice: Combining the immediacy effect and the diversification heuristic. *Journal of Behavioral Decision Making, 12*(4), 257.

Read, D., Olivola, C. Y., & Hardisty, D. (2016). The value of nothing: Asymmetric attention to opportunity costs drives intertemporal decision making. *Management Science,* published online October.

Read, D., & Powell, M. (2002). Reasons for sequence preferences. *Journal of Behavioral Decision Making, 15,* 433–460.

Read, D., & Scholten, M. (2012). Tradeoffs between sequences: Weighing accumulated outcomes against outcome-adjusted delays. *Journal of Experimental Psychology: Learning, Memory, and Cognition, 38,* 1675–1689.

Read, D., & Van Leeuwen, B. (1998). Predicting hunger: The effects of appetite and delay on choice. *Organizational Behavior and Human Decision Processes, 76*(2), 189–205.

Reimers, S., Maylor, E.A., Stewart, N. & Chater, N. (2009). Associations between a one-shot delay discounting measure and age, income, education and real-world impulsive behavior. *Personality and Individual Differences, 47,* 973–978.

Reuben, E., Sapienza, P., & Zingales, L. (2010). Time discounting for primary and monetary rewards. *Economics Letters, 106,* 125–127.

Robles, E. (2010) Delay and loss of subjective value. *Journal of Behavior, Health, and Social Issues, 5,* 105–118.

Robles, E., & Vargas, P. A. (2007). Functional parameters of delay discounting assessment tasks: Order of presentation. *Behavioural Processes, 75*(2), 237–241.

Robles, E., Vargas, P. A., & Bejarano, R. (2009). Within-subject differences in degree of delay discounting as a function of order of presentation of hypothetical cash rewards. *Behavioural Processes, 81*(2), 260–263.

Roelofsma, P. H. (1996). Modelling intertemporal choices: An anomaly approach. *Acta Psychologica, 93,* 5–22.

Rubinstein, A. (2003). 'Economics and psychology?' The case of hyperbolic discounting. *International Economic Review, 44,* 1207–1216.

Sayman, S., & Öncüler, A. (2009). An investigation of time inconsistency. *Management Science, 55,* 470–482.

Scholten, M., & Read, D. (2006). Discounting by intervals: A generalized model of intertemporal choice. *Management Science, 52,* 1426–1438.

Scholten, M., & Read, D. (2010). The psychology of intertemporal tradeoffs. *Psychological Review, 117,* 925–944.

Scholten, M., & Read, D. (2013). Time and outcome framing in intertemporal tradeoffs. *Journal of Experimental Psychology: Learning, Memory, and Cognition, 39,* 1192–1212.

Scholten, M., Read, D., & Sanborn, A. (2014). Weighing outcomes *by* time or *against* time? Evaluation rules in intertemporal choice. *Cognitive Science, 38,* 399–438.

Scholten, M., Read, D., & Sanborn, A. (2016). Cumulative weighing of time in intertemporal tradeoffs. *Journal of Experimental Psychology: General, 145,* 1177–1205.

Scholten, M., Read, D., Walters, D. J., Erner, C., & Fox, C. R. (2017). A diagnosis of tolerance and aversion to debt. Working Paper.

Shamosh, N., & Gray, J. (2008). Delay discounting and intelligence: A meta-analysis. *Intelligence, 36,* 289–305.

Shapiro, J. M. (2005). Is there a daily discount rate? Evidence from the food stamp nutrition cycle. *Journal of Public Economics, 89,* 303–325.

Smith, P. K., Bogin, B., Bishai, D. (2005). Are time preference and body mass index associated? Evidence from the National Longitudinal Survey of the Young. *Economics and Human Biology, 3,* 259–270.

Story, G. W., Moutoussis, M. & Dolan, R. J. (2016). A computational analysis of aberrant delay discounting in psychiatric disorders. *Frontiers in Psychology, 6,* 1–18.

Strotz, R. H. (1955–1956). Myopia and inconsistency in dynamic utility maximization. *Review of Economic Studies, 23,* 165–180.

Thaler, R. H. (1981). Some empirical evidence on dynamic inconsistency. *Economics Letters, 8,* 201–207.

Urminsky, O., & Zauberman, G. (2014). The psychology of intertemporal preferences. In G. Keren & G. Wu (Eds.), *The Wiley-Blackwell handbook of judgment and decision making.* Chichester: John Wiley and Sons, Ltd.

Wu, C.-Y., & He, G.-B. (2012). The effects of time perspective and salience of possible monetary losses on intertemporal choice. *Social Behavior and Personality, 40,* 1645–1654.

Yates, J. F., & Watts, R. A. (1975). Preferences for deferred losses. *Organizational Behavior and Human Performance, 13*(2), 294–306.

Zauberman, G., Kim, B. K., Malkoc, S. A., & Bettman, J. R. (2009). Discounting time and time discounting: Subjective time perception and intertemporal preferences. *Journal of Marketing Research, 46,* 543–556.

FURTHER READING

Read, D., Frederick, S., & Airoldi, M. (2012). Four days in Cincinnati: Longitudinal tests of hyperbolic discounting. *Acta Psychologica, 140,* 177–185.

Thaler, R. H. (1981). Some empirical evidence on dynamic inconsistency. *Economics Letters, 8,* 201–207.

Urminsky, O., & Zauberman, G. (2014). The psychology of intertemporal preferences. in G. Keren & G. Wu (Eds.), *The Wiley-Blackwell handbook of judgment and decision making.* Chichester: John Wiley and Sons.

PART 2
Research
Methods

4 Research Methods for Economic Psychology

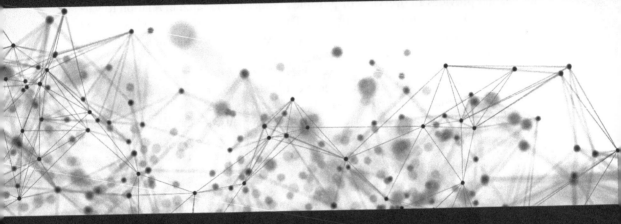

GERRIT ANTONIDES

CHAPTER OUTLINE

LEARNING OUTCOMES

BY THE END OF THIS CHAPTER YOU SHOULD BE ABLE TO:

1. Understand and explain the differences between theoretical and empirical, and between descriptive and explanatory types of research.

2. Decide at what stage of theory development to apply qualitative or quantitative research, and choose an appropriate qualitative or quantitative method.

3. Detect and avoid the most common biases that can occur in different types of experiments.

4.1 INTRODUCTION

Economic psychology uses a variety of research techniques and resources to acquire knowledge of the determinants, processes and effects of economic decision-making. This chapter provides an overview of possible avenues for research in relation to various key economic-psychological problems. The chapter is more practically oriented than philosophical or technical. For example, the long-term development of theories or methods of analysis fall outside the scope of this chapter.

Economic psychology includes the word 'psychology', implying that this type of research includes individual, subjective elements in the economy that distinguish the field from, for example, pure economic market modelling. Since psychology comprises many different areas, notably social, cognitive, personality, developmental, clinical, and neuropsychology, economic psychology borrows from knowledge gathered in all these fields. This is evident from research topics including group decision-making and social dilemmas, individual decision-making, preferences, learning, abnormal economic behaviours, and the tracing of cognitive and emotional processes in the brain. The different fields each have their own methodologies which are applied in economic psychology. Two basic distinctions in type of research are between theoretical and empirical, and between descriptive and explanatory research, to be explained next.

Theoretical research mainly comprises (mathematical) modelling of economic psychological processes. The starting point for theoretical research often is literature search and observation of behaviour. For example, Bernoulli (1954 [1738]) laid the foundations for expected utility theory after observing people's gambling behaviour, which deviated from the expected value model. Other examples of this type of research are the modelling of emotions in economic decision-making. Mui (1995) has modelled the role of envy in retaliation, and how punishment by the government may reduce it. Kim (2006) modelled the development of will power over time as a function of past resistance to temptation. Gómez-Miñambres (2012) studied a principal–agent model in which production goal-setting, not payment, stimulates the agent's intrinsic motivation to perform. Theoretical research usually is deductive, that is, predictions of economic behaviour are derived from several assumptions, and tested in subsequent empirical research.

Empirical research is based on data gathering and can be either deductive – testing hypotheses based on theory – or inductive – theory is constructed after data analysis, without testing *a priori* hypotheses. Empirical methods may differ across different stages of theory development. Exploratory – usually inductive – research typically is conducted in the early stages of theory development, in order to identify important concepts and variables of interest. For example, Wundt (1973 [1911]) used introspection to study perceptual processes, explaining how physical stimuli are transformed into mental representation via sensations. Introspection may lead to hindsight bias (Roese & Vohs, 2012), that is, past events are deemed more predictable after than before their occurrence. Another reporting failure may occur because by focusing on a particular topic, respondents may overweight specific information (Kahneman, 2011; Schkade & Kahneman, 1998). Such reporting biases constitute a weakness of several research techniques relying on self-reports.

Descriptive research aims at describing a particular state of affairs or trends in society of economic psychological interest. This includes, for example, statistical measures of savings, or opinion research about consumer confidence or inflationary expectations as measured in the Business and Consumer Surveys of the European Commission. The difference to exploratory research is that the concept and variables of interest are defined *a priori*.

Explanatory – usually inductive – research aims to test relationships between defined key concepts and variables related to economic behaviour and its determinants and effects. Examples of such relationships are the effects of decreased mood after the end of popular TV series on stock investments (Lepori, 2015), or the effects of watching TV on life satisfaction (Frey, Benesch, & Stutzer, 2007). An extension of explanatory research is predictive research, where the results of explanatory research are forecast in a fresh sample. For example, Uhl (2014) predicts the Dow Jones Industrial Average index from positive and negative sentiments in Reuters news articles.

All four types of research offer not only specific strengths and weaknesses, but also specific ethical challenges. In order to ensure researchers' ethical conduct, ethical guidelines have been written (e.g., American Psychological Association, Centre for Economic Research of the University of York), and ethical committees have been set up in many universities judging the ethical issues in research proposals. In addition, a number of scientific journals require approval of research proposals by ethical committees.

4.2   QUALITATIVE METHODS

A common distinction in empirical research methods is between qualitative and quantitative methods. Qualitative methods are usually applied to understand and interpret human behaviour by extracting subjective information from (economic) actors or observers. Qualitative methods are most useful in the beginning stages of the research process and can help in developing concepts, becoming aware of relationships between concepts and behaviour, and making sense of an often overwhelming amount of data (as in Big Data available in marketing, business, and telecommunications).

There are a number of qualitative methods. Here we provide an overview of the most frequently applied methods in economic psychology by describing typical examples of research applications, that is, in-depth interviews, focus groups, and content analysis.

4.2.1   In-Depth Interviews

In order to acquire a deeper understanding of people's motives and reasons for economic behaviours, the in-depth interview is a feasible instrument. Typically, in-depth interview questions are unstructured or semi-structured, which is different from a survey in which questions usually are highly structured. Dittmar and Drury (2000) conducted in-depth interviews on normal and excessive shoppers in order to find differences in impulse buying, regret experiences and relations with the self. Although their sample of 59 men and women was not representative, different age ranges, education, occupations and family types were included. Excessive shoppers were recruited from a shopping addiction self-help organization, whereas normal shoppers were recruited from a mail survey sample. The interview questions were semi-structured, so that the same topics were raised in each interview, but with no fixed order. The respondents' answers were read, interpreted and categorized – a process which the authors themselves characterize as involving interpretation and judgement. In reporting the results, the responses were summarized by aspects of the behaviour under study and illustrated by quotes. Then, a summary of the behaviour was given, for example 'impulse buying is characterised by little deliberation, and by psychological motivations – desire, wanting, treat, thrill – overtaking financial considerations' (2000, p. 125). As limitations to their study, the authors note that women tended to respond in a more personal and psychological way than men, thus leading to different views on excessive buying behaviour. Also, the responses of a few women might have been biased because they were already dealing with their excessive buying behaviour in the self-help organization. No attempt at quantifying the responses was made, although the interview study was triangulated with an experimental study and a diary study among similar types of respondents, reported separately.

Other examples of in-depth interviews in economic psychology are Burgoyne et al. (2007) dealing with household money management systems, and Olivero and Lunt (2004) dealing with online data collection for marketing purposes. The latter study employed in-depth interviews by e-mail in a 'snowball sample' of experienced internet and e-mail users, that is, people who found new respondents themselves rather than the researchers.

4.2.2   Focus Groups

A quite efficient instrument to elicit a wide range of views concerning a particular topic is the focus group. Focus groups typically consist of 5–10 people who are familiar with the topic under study. The focus group moderator structures the discussion about the topic using a discussion guide. Because of the social nature of the discussion, all kinds of detail concerning the topic may be triggered by the various statements of the participants. Kleijnen, Lee, and Wetzels (2009) conducted focus group discussions about resistance to new product innovations, studying 8 different groups for a total of 58 active male and female consumers below 30 years of age. All participants were selected on the basis of a screening question to ensure they had made a conscious decision not to adopt a new product or service in the recent past. Three of the groups discussed rejection of an innovation, 3 dealt with opposition, and 2 with postponement. The moderator welcomed the participants and explained the topic to be discussed, followed by a brainstorming exercise to generate examples of innovations that had been resisted in the recent past. This task also helped to 'break the ice' in order to let the participants discuss their opinions and experiences freely. The moderator took care of encouraging views of different types. Another member of the research team acted as an observer of the process, taking additional notes. Discussions lasted between 1.5 and 2 hours and were audio-taped. Next, three trained individuals coded the focus groups' transcripts in detail, using single statements about a subject as the unit of analysis (e.g., risk, usage pattern, perceived image, traditions or norms). In total, 1925 such units were coded, with a coding agreement of 95%. The authors mention conformity with prevailing opinions in the group, as well as the non-representative sample as a threat to the external validity of the study, limiting the generalization of the findings.

Fox et al. (2009) conducted focus groups with food-allergic patients to discuss issues of economic costs, welfare and well-being associated with having a food allergy. The discussions were used to guide the development of a questionnaire to measure the economic impact of having a food allergy. Examples of other studies using focus groups are West, Bailey and Winter (2010), dealing with renewable energy; and Guerrero and Rodríguez-Oreggia (2008), supplementing their quantitative study of corruption with focus group discussions.

4.2.3   *Content Analysis*

The use of content analysis is aimed at finding systematic trends, differences or patterns in verbal or symbolic material. Therefore, after analysing content, often statistical analysis is applied to find relationships among categories of the material, or between categories and other types of data. Categorization may take place at different levels, for example, words, themes, concepts, paragraphs, persons (names), or entire communications (e.g., books, letters, etc.) (Berg & Lune, 2012).

Rudmin (1994) asked 253 respondents to list things they did not own and for which they felt little sense of ownership, and things they did not own but felt some sense of ownership, then asked them to describe what their sense of ownership consisted of. The listed items were categorized post-hoc into 52 categories, with as little interpretation as possible. A second researcher independently classified the answers into the categories with a resulting reliability of 0.85. The frequencies of categories used by male and female respondents were then compared, and differences between genders were interpreted. For example, men were found to focus on property as unrestrained rights, autonomy and exclusivity, whereas women focused on responsibility, self-connection and pride.

Gould and Kramer (2009) studied people's value construction process in joint versus separate evaluation of dictionaries – resulting in a preference reversal – by asking open questions concerning how they made their willingness-to-pay decisions and why. The answers were analysed for content, partly using interpretive analysis, looking for personally salient experiences of the participants, explaining their answers. Here, the qualitative analysis was used to provide interpretation for the quantitative result of the preference reversal effect.

Other examples of content analysis in economic psychology are Zullow (1991), who analysed pessimistic rumination in popular songs and news magazines to predict negative growth in gross national product in the United States a year later; Garz (2013), who used pre-analysed media content from a news reporting agency to predict unemployment expectations in Germany; or Ranyard and Craig (1995), who content-analysed interview material on instalment credit to find consumers' mental accounts of their financial budgets.

4.2.4 Other Qualitative Methods

Several other, less practised, qualitative methods have been distinguished, including diary methods, ethnographic studies and case studies:

- *Diary studies* aim at obtaining detailed reports of people's activities. Kirchler (1988) used retrospective diaries of couples' purchasing decisions to study the partners' influence in the process. Kahneman, Krueger, Schkade, Schwarz, and Stone (2004) asked participants to break the previous day up into episodes of activities (e.g., 'having dinner') and report on their feelings to construct a measure of experienced happiness.

- *Ethnographic studies* aim at studying people in their natural environments. Voordouw et al. (2009) studied food-allergic consumers in their natural shopping environment while shopping for safe food. During the shopping event, they were questioned about the choice of food in order to learn about the use of information labels.

- *Process-tracing studies* aim at revealing the process of decision-making. Ranyard, Hinkley, Williamson, and McHugh (2006) presented participants with minimal information about several instalment credit options. The participants could then ask for more information and subsequently make a choice. By studying the type and amount of information requested, the process of decision-making was traced. Milch, Weber, Appelt, Handgraaf, and Krantz (2009) applied query theory to both individual and group decisions about risk-taking in gain versus loss frames, and intertemporal choice in advance versus delay frames. For individual decisions, participants were asked to write down their reasons for making a decision; for group decisions, this step was supplemented by transcripts of the group discussions leading to the group decision. It appeared that both the reasons and discussion content mediated the effect of framing on decision-making, thus indicating that the framing effect was driven by the prevailing thoughts evoked by the frames.

- *Case studies* aim at acquiring all kinds of information about a phenomenon or business from various sources. The case is usually limited to a certain part of the world or part of business. Choi and Fielding (2013) conducted a case study on the willingness to pay (WTP) for protection of endangered species in the Demilitarized Zone between North and South Korea. They conducted focus groups, expert consultations and a nationwide survey to elicit WTP measures from their sample, together confirming earlier research findings in this area.

4.3 QUANTITATIVE METHODS

When constructs have been defined in the beginning stages of research, quantitative data analysis becomes feasible. Quantitative analysis may be focused on construct measurement, database construction, or structural relationships between constructs.

Other methods for studying structural relationships are using (statistical) observations, either or not in time series analyses, for example, between actual and perceived inflation (Antonides, 2008), or between happiness, consumption and saving (Guven,

2012). Other examples are physiological and brain studies in which structural relationships between biological functions and behaviour are sought. For example, electrical stimulation of the right lateral prefrontal cortex (known to be involved in norm compliance) resulted in strong effects on donations in a dictator game where the recipient could punish the allocator (Ruff, Ugazio, & Fehr, 2013). Next, several quantitative methods will be considered in more detail.

4.3.1   Test Construction

Much economic psychological research has dealt with test construction. An example is the Consideration of Future Consequences scale (McKay, Morgan, van Exel, & Worrell, 2015; Petrocelli, 2003; Strathman, Gleicher, Boninger, & Edwards, 1994), measuring people's orientation towards the present or the future. This construct is important because it is related to time preference and to a number of economic behaviours, including saving (Joireman, Sprott, & Spangenberg, 2005; Webley & Nyhus, 2006), ego depletion and self-control (Joireman, Balliet, Sprott, Spangenberg, & Schultz, 2008), eating and exercising (Van Beek, Antonides, & Handgraaf, 2013). Other examples of economic-psychological test construction are social preferences (Murphy, Ackermann, & Handgraaf, 2011), and tax compliance measures (Kirchler & Wahl, 2010). A relatively new development is the measurement of economic preferences by experimental tasks, for example, lotteries for measuring risk preference, trust games for measuring trust, and time trade-off measures for time preference (Almlund, Duckworth, Heckman, & Kautz, 2011).

4.3.2   Surveys

Surveys are self-report questionnaires, either cross-sectional, at one or more time periods; or longitudinal, where questionnaires are administered to the same sample of participants at two or more points in time. As argued above, surveys are intended to quantify and test theoretical relationships between constructs. In any case, a population to be studied has to be defined, variables have to be selected from theory, then operationalized by questionnaire measures, the questionnaire has to be assembled, a sample of the population has to be drawn, data is collected, analysed and reported.

A number of economic-psychological variables have been included in large longitudinal databases for use in secondary data analysis. Examples of such databases, all including extensive economic household information, are the German Socioeconomic Panel (GSOEP, since 1984), including the Big Five personality traits and several economic preferences (Almlund et al., 2011; Proto & Rustichini, 2015); the British Household Panel Survey (BHPS, since 1991), including some subjective measures of subjective well-being and attitudes (cf. Brown & Taylor, 2014); and the DNB Household Survey (DHS, since 1993), including saving motives and preferences, consideration of future consequences, locus of control, and happiness (Kapteyn & Teppa, 2011; Nyhus & Pons, 2012; Van Rooij, Lusardi, & Alessie, 2011). Economic psychologists have made extensive use of these panels in two ways: (1) as existing sources of data on which new, original analyses have been conducted to address specific economic psychological research questions; and (2) by adding new specific questions to one or more waves of a survey, thereby collecting new data.

Economic-psychological data has been used to study structural relationships between economic behaviour and specific concepts of interest, using a variety of methods and statistical techniques. Surveys have been employed to study associations between (reported) economic behaviours, choices and intentions, on the one hand, and socio-demographic variables, attitudes, emotions, situations, and personality variables, on the other. Examples, in addition to those based on longitudinal data mentioned above, are Onwezen, Bartels, and Antonides (2013), who studied relationships between pro-environmental behaviour, attitudes and emotions; Gathergood (2012), who studied relationships between over-indebtedness, financial literacy and self-control; and Antonides, De Groot, and Van Raaij (2011), who studied relationships between mental budgeting and household financial management.

Wenzel (2005) used longitudinal data from the same taxpayers in the years 2000 and 2001 to study the effects of background variables in 2000 on tax compliance and tax ethics in 2001, thus suggesting causal effects. Gangl et al. (2013) used a one-shot survey among taxpayers to study the effect of background variables and perceived service orientation of tax authorities on tax compliance intentions.

4.3.3 Observations of Economic Activity

Statistical offices (e.g., Eurostat, the statistical office of the European Union; Euromonitor, a private company that collects consumer and business data) collect a number of observational data on aggregate economic activities on a regular basis. Examples are time-series of consumer price indexes; credit and savings; consumption expenditures; unemployment; and population statistics. Such observational data is useful in studying economic trends, and finding relationships between economic variables and subjective information from repeated cross-section and longitudinal surveys.

Madsen and McAleer (2001) use a number of country data from OECD, national accounts and national banks to study consumers' sensitivity to income changes affecting the amount of consumption. According to the life-cycle permanent income hypothesis (Modigliani, 1986), income changes should be unrelated to current consumption. They study three hypotheses explaining deviations from the life-cycle model by econometric analysis: liquidity constraints, uncertainty, and temptation to spend current income. The latter two appear to outperform the first hypothesis. Both Ramalho, Caleiro, and Dionfsio (2011) and Vuchelen (2004) studied the relationship between consumer sentiment and a number of economic variables, all measures taken from Eurostat and the European Commission.

4.3.4 Experiments

Although survey analysis often suggests causal relationships, the very nature of the data does not guarantee causality because the endogeneity of explanatory variables, omitted variables, and reverse causality problems may be present (Angrist & Krueger, 2001). For this reason, experimental methods have been used extensively. The experimental method is applied in both economic psychology and in experimental economics to study perceptions, intentions or behaviour. By manipulating the absence or presence of variables causing an effect in different conditions, and random assignment of individuals to the conditions, the effect should be considered to be causal. Since manipulation requires strict control over the experiment, most experiments are run in laboratories.

Different types of experiments are carried out in both disciplines, including laboratory, field, and survey-based experiments. Experiments can be conducted between subjects (different subjects allocated randomly to different conditions) or within subjects (same subjects allocated to more than one condition). Within-subject experiments need less subjects than between-subjects experiments and have more statistical power in finding results because individual sources of error variance (e.g. different age, gender, etc.) are removed. However, within-subject experiments may suffer from several disadvantages (cf. Charness, Gneezy, & Kuhn, 2012). Since in within-subjects experiments participants provide similar responses to different manipulations, all kinds of practice, sensitization and carry-over effects may occur. Also, subjects may guess the purpose of an experiment in a within-subjects design because they are exposed to several conditions. They may then act according to this purpose, which is known as the *demand effect*. Furthermore, in within-subjects experiments, participants may become aware of a range of manipulations, hence provide more variation in their responses than participants in a between-subjects experiment (*range effect*). From research on evaluability (Hsee, 1996), it is known that items evaluated in isolation may be judged on easy-to-evaluate attributes, whereas items evaluated in combination may be judged on difficult-to-evaluate attributes. *Evaluability effects* may contribute to different findings from between-subjects and within-subjects experiments.

Laboratory experiments range from very simple decision tasks, such as choosing between lottery A or B, to quite complex, realistic simulations of everyday economic tasks, such as budgeting or tax compliance. Control of conditions is usually very high, thus maximizing the chances of finding significant results. Field experiments range from pure experiments, with random allocation of participants to conditions, to quasi-experiments for which randomization is either not appropriate or not possible, such as gender and income. Control is often less but external validity is relatively high. Survey-based experiments comprise different versions of questionnaires, randomly allocated to participants, to investigate differences in attitudes, intentions or reported behaviours. Survey responses often deal with hypothetical choices or comprise reported behaviour.

An example of a laboratory experiment is Savadori and Mittone (2015), who let people choose between a high-probability low-outcome bet (p-bet) and a low-probability high-outcome bet ($-bet) of equal expected value, under two different conditions. In one condition, the bet was paid out immediately after the experiment (near), in another condition the bet was paid out in the future (distant). Participants were randomly assigned to one of the conditions. In the near-condition, the p-bet was chosen more often than in the distant-condition. It was concluded that the risk delay caused people's lower risk aversion.

The control exerted in a laboratory experiment often limits the realism of the experimental task performed by the participants. Hence, the result may not be generalizable to situations outside the laboratory, that is, the external validity of the results may be questioned. For this reason, field experiments may be conducted, taking place in natural situations. An example is Madrian and Shea (2001), who studied the effect on contribution rates in retirement savings of a change in default. In the control condition, the default was no contribution, unless individuals opted in to contribute.

The change in the default implied a contribution at a 3% rate, unless individuals opted out of the program. One year after changing the default, the participation rate had changed from 49% in the control group to 86% in the treatment group. The change in default situation thus brought about significantly more retirement savings.

An example of a survey-based experiment is Pfeffer and DeVoe (2009), studying willingness to volunteer. In their control condition, participants in a survey calculated the average wage per hour in the United States from average annual earnings, number of hours typically worked per week, and number of weeks worked in a year. In the experimental condition, participants calculated their own wage per hour from their own reported earnings, working hours and working weeks. Next, participants completed a questionnaire concerning volunteer work. Since participants in the experimental condition were being reminded of how much they earned and how long they worked for it, they were less willing to volunteer than those in the control condition. Also, experience with hourly payment was negatively related to willingness to volunteer.

Survey-based experiments may suffer from hypothetical bias (List & Gallet, 2001), meaning that participants in hypothetical choices may overstate their preferences. Another methodological issue in experimental studies is the use of student participants. Although some differences have been found between the behaviour of students and other people (Levitt & List, 2007), Alm et al. (2015) found no differences in experimental tax games. Other issues are the level of the stakes (Andersen, Ertaç, Gneezy, Hoffman, & List, 2011), and learning (Levitt & List, 2008), both of which tend to make people behave more rationally.

Hertwig and Ortmann (2001) note that psychologists generally use a flat show-up fee as a reward for participating, whereas economists use incentives depending on the behaviour of participants. Also, economists more often use repeated trials of experimental tasks in contrast to psychologists. Another difference is the deception of participants in psychological experiments, which is totally avoided in economic experiments. Many experimental economists refrain from asking questions of their participants. We believe that using additional self-reports, if only as a manipulation check, may lead to faster progress in theory development than endless manipulations without asking any questions.

4.3.5   *Physiological and Brain Methods*

A number of physiological and brain methods have been applied to study human decision-making. Although economic theory assumes rational decision-making, many decisions are taken on the basis of affective or subconscious processes, which are less easily studied by observing behaviour. Camerer, Loewenstein, and Prelec (2005) state that tracing brain activity during decision-making not only reveals which parts of the brain are involved, but also how these parts interact and react to different decision tasks. Several neuroscience methods are available, including an electro-encephalogram (EEG) to measure electrical activity, positron emission topography (PET) to measure blood flow in the brain by tracing a nuclear substance injected into the blood, and functional magnetic resonance imaging (fMRI), to measure the blood flow by changes in magnetic properties due to blood oxygenation. For example, Sanfey, Rilling, Aronson, Nystrom, and Cohen (2003), using fMRI, found that the anterior insula in the brain is involved in responding to unfair offers in an ultimatum game, indicating that emotions are involved in responders' decisions. Van 't Wout, Kahn, Sanfey, and Aleman (2006) used additional galvanic skin responses to investigate the involvement of emotions in the ultimatum game, resulting in similar findings as with the fMRI method. Other physiological methods include heart rate, blood pressure and pupil dilation.

Especially strong experimental evidence for brain activity causing decisions is obtained when brain functions are manipulated, such as in Ruff, Ugazio, and Fehr (2013). Another example is De Dreu et al. (2010), who used the neuropeptide oxytocin, affecting the amygdala, hippocampus, brain stem and spinal cord – involved in trust and cooperation – and other neural circuitries involved in empathy. Participants who were given oxytocin through a nasal spray behaved more cooperatively to in-group members (due to empathy and cooperation) in a prisoner's dilemma-type of game than those given a placebo, whereas no effect was observed towards out-group members (where less empathy was involved).

4.4 CONCLUSION

Economic psychology is characterized by a number of different research methods which can be applied in different stages of theory development. In our view, there is a need for triangulation of methods both within economic psychology, and between economics and psychology. Triangulation is the combined use of different research methods, or different data sources, to investigate the same phenomenon (Rothbauer, 2008). Through triangulation, results of one study can be validated by another study, using different methods or data sources.

- *Multiple methods* were used by Masson, Delarue, Bouillot, Sieffermann, and Blumenthal (2015) to elicit consumer perceptions of eight coffee cups. A *sorting task* comprised grouping the eight cups in at least two and maximally seven categories, then describing the categories. A *repertory grid method* comprised of indicating the two most similar coffee cups from a set of three and asking why these cups differed from the third and repeating this task for eight different triads. A *word association task* asked for the first words coming to mind when presenting the product, combined with a *sentence completion task* asking participants to continue a sentence with a statement. An *image association task* asked the participants which pictures of kitchens, coffee types and coffee makers were to be associated with each cup, then asking for an explanation of the picture choices. A kind of *laddering task* asked participants to rank order the cups according to preference, then asked for reasons for liking the cups (in order of most to least preferred), and reasons for disliking the cups (in order of least to most preferred). Finally, a *focus group discussion* was conducted about the cups. The methods were compared on the number of attributes (associations directly related to the product) and evocations (associations unrelated to the product) elicited. It appeared that the word association and sentence completion task elicited the most associations out of the six methods. There were no great differences in understanding, easiness or appreciation of the methods by the participants.

- Vidal, Ares, and Giménez (2013) used online questionnaires, including a word association task, a dialogue completion task, and two shopping lists from which the personality of the buyer had to be indicated, to elicit consumer perceptions of ready-to-eat salads. Wood and Essien-Wood (2012) employed semi-structured interviews, non-participant observation, a focus group, and an unstructured *concept mapping task* in which participants had to depict factors affecting their success in college by diagrams, narratives, poems, drawings and listings.

4.5 SUMMARY

Economic psychology deals with individual, subjective elements in the economy. For this reason, a wide range of methods is used to acquire knowledge about these elements. Economic psychology is mostly an empirical discipline in which inductive or deductive research is used in different stages of theory development, that is, exploratory, descriptive and explanatory research.

A broad classification of qualitative and quantitative methods can be made. Qualitative methods are used relatively often in the beginning stages of the research process, including in-depth interviews, focus groups and content analysis. Quantitative methods are used mainly in the later stages, including test construction, surveys, observations, experiments, and physiological and brain methods. A need for triangulation of methods, in which research findings are validated using different methods in different contexts, is apparent.

REVIEW QUESTIONS

1. What do you think physiological and brain studies can contribute to the theory of economic behaviour over and above qualitative and other quantitative methods?
2. Evaluate potential problems of focusing, hindsight and hypothetical bias in each of the qualitative research methods.
3. Explain how experimental findings can be confirmed or problematized by triangulation with each of two qualitative methods of your choice.

REFERENCES

Alm, J., Bloomquist, K. M., & McKee, M. (2015). On the external validity of laboratory tax compliance experiments. *Economic Inquiry, 53*, 1170–1186. http://dx.doi.org/10.1111/ecin.12196

Almlund, M., Duckworth, A. L., Heckman, J., & Kautz, T. (2011). Personality psychology and economics. In E. A. Hanushek, S. Machin, & L. Woessmann (Eds.), *Handbook of the economics of education* (vol. 4, pp. 1–181). Amsterdam: Elsevier. http://dx.doi.org/10.3386/w16822

American Psychological Association (n.d.). *Ethical principles of psychologists and code of conduct.* Retrieved from http://www.apa.org/ethics/code/ (retrieved March 16, 2015).

Andersen, S., Ertaç, S., Gneezy, U., Hoffman, M., & List, J. A. (2011). Stakes matter in ultimatum games. *American Economic Review, 101*, 3427–3439. http://dx.doi.org/10.1257/aer.101.7.3427

Angrist, J. D., & Krueger, A. B. (2001). Instrumental variables and the search for identification: From supply and demand to natural experiments. *Journal of Economic Perspectives, 15*(4), 69–85. http://dx.doi.org/10.1257/jep.15.4.69

Antonides, G. (2008). How is perceived inflation related to actual price changes in the European Union? *Journal of Economic Psychology, 29*, 417–432. http://dx.doi.org/10.1016/j.joep.2008.04.002

Antonides, G., De Groot, I. M., & Van Raaij, W. F. (2011). Mental budgeting and the management of household finance. *Journal of Economic Psychology, 32*(4), 545–555. http://dx.doi.org/10.1016/j.joep.2011.04.001

Berg, B. L., & Lune, H. (2012). *Qualitative research methods for the social sciences.* Boston: Pearson.

Bernoulli, D. (1954 [1738]). Specimen theoriae novea de mensura sortis. *Commentarii Academiae Scientiarium Imperialis Petropolitanae, 6*, 175–192. Translated by Sommer, L. (1954). Exposition of a new theory on the measurement of risk. *Econometrica, 22*, 23–36. http://dx.doi.org/10.2307/1909829

Brown, S., & Taylor, K. (2014). Household finances and the 'Big Five' personality traits. *Journal of Economic Psychology, 45*, 197–212. http://dx.doi.org/10.1016/j.joep.2014.10.006

Burgoyne, C. B., Reibstein, J., Edmunds, A., & Dolman, V. (2007). Money management systems in early marriage: Factors influencing change and stability. *Journal of Economic Psychology, 28*, 214–228. http://dx.doi.org/10.1016/j.joep.2006.02.003

Camerer, C., Loewenstein, G., & Prelec, D. (2005). Neuroeconomics: How neuroscience can inform economics. *Journal of Economic Literature, 43*, 9–64. http://dx.doi.org/10.1257/0022051053737843

Centre for Experimental Economics (n.d.) *Ethical statement.* Retrieved from http://www.york.ac.uk/media/economics/images/exec/Ethical%20Statement.pdf. (retrieved March 16, 2015).

Charness, G., Gneezy, U., & Kuhn, M. A. (2012). Experimental methods: Between-subject and within-subject design. *Journal of Economic Behavior & Organization, 81*, 1–8. http://dx.doi.org/10.1016/j.jebo.2011.08.009

Choi, A. S., & Fielding, K. S. (2013). Environmental attitudes as WTP predictors: A case study involving endangered species. *Ecological Economics, 89*, 24–32. http://dx.doi.org/10.1016/j.ecolecon.2013.01.027

De Dreu, C. K. W., Greer, L. L., Handgraaf, M. J. J., Shalvi, S., Van Kleef, G. A., Baas, M., Ten Velden, F. S., ... Feith, S. W. W. (2010). The neuropeptide oxytocin regulates parochial altruism in intergroup conflict among humans. *Science, 328*, 1408–1411. http://dx.doi.org/10.1126/science.1189047

Dittmar, H., & Drury, J. (2000). Self-image – is it in the bag? A qualitative comparison between 'ordinary' and 'excessive' consumers. *Journal of Economic Psychology, 21*, 109–142. http://dx.doi.org/10.1016/S0167-4870(99)00039-2

Fox, F., Voordouw, J., Mugford, M., Cornelisse, J., Antonides, G., & Frewer, L. (2009). Social and economic costs of food allergies in Europe: Development of a questionnaire to measure costs and health utility. *Health Services Research, 44*(5), 1662–1678. http://dx.doi.org/10.1111/j.1475-6773.2009.00993.x

Frey, B. S., Benesch, C., & Stutzer, A. (2007). Does watching TV make us happy? *Journal of Economic Psychology, 28*, 283–313. http://dx.doi.org/10.1016/j.joep.2007.02.001

Gangl, K., Muehlbacher, S., De Groot, I. M., Goslinga, S., Hofmann, E., Kogler, C., ... Kirchler, E. (2013). 'How can I help you?' Perceived service orientation of tax authorities and tax compliance. *Public Finance Analysis, 69*(4), 487–510. http://dx.doi.org/10.1628/001522113X675683

Garz, M. (2013). Unemployment expectations, excessive pessimism, and news coverage. *Journal of Economic Psychology, 34*, 156–168. http://dx.doi.org/10.1016/j.joep.2012.09.007

Gathergood, J. (2012). Self-control, financial literacy and consumer over-indebtedness. *Journal of Economic Psychology, 33*, 590–602. http://dx.doi.org/10.1016/j.joep.2011.11.006

Gómez-Miñambres, J. (2012). Motivation through goal setting. *Journal of Economic Psychology, 33*, 1223–1239. http://dx.doi.org/10.1016/j.joep.2012.08.010

Gould, S. J., & Kramer, T. (2009). 'What's it worth to me?' Three interpretive studies of the relative roles of task-oriented and reflexive processes in separate versus joint value construction. *Journal of Economic Psychology, 30*, 840–858. http://dx.doi.org/10.1016/j.joep.2009.08.003

Guerrero, M. A., & Rodríguez-Oreggia, E. (2008). On the individual decisions to commit corruption: A methodological complement. *Journal of Economic Behavior & Organization, 65*, 357–372. http://dx.doi.org/10.1016/j.jebo.2005.09.006

Guven, C. (2012). Reversing the question: Does happiness affect consumption and savings behavior? *Journal of Economic Psychology, 33*, 701–717. http://dx.doi.org/10.1016/j.joep.2012.01.002

Hertwig, R., & Ortmann, A. (2001). Experimental practices in economics: A methodological challenge for psychologists? *Behavioral and Brain Sciences, 24*, 383–451.

Hsee, C. (1996). The evaluability hypothesis: An explanation for preference reversals between joint and separate evaluations of alternatives. *Organizational Behavior and Human Decision Processes, 67*, 247–257. http://dx.doi.org/10.1006/obhd.1996.0077

Joireman, J., Balliet, D., Sprott, D., Spangenberg, E., & Schultz, J. (2008). Consideration of future consequences, ego-depletion, and self-control: Support for distinguishing between CFC-immediate and CFC-future sub-scales. *Personality and Individual Differences, 48*, 15–21. http://dx.doi.org/10.1016/j.paid.2008.02.011

Joireman, J., Sprott, D., & Spangenberg, E. (2005). Fiscal responsibility and the consideration of future consequences. *Personality and Individual Differences, 39*, 1159–1168. http://dx.doi.org/10.1016/j.paid.2005.05.002

Kahneman, D. (2011). *Thinking fast and slow*. New York: Farrar, Straus and Giroux.

Kahneman, D., Krueger, A. B., Schkade, D. A., Schwarz, N., & Stone, A. A. (2004). A survey method for characterizing daily life experience: The day reconstruction method. *Science, 306*, 1776–1780. http://dx.doi.org/10.1126/science.1103572

Kapteyn, A., & Teppa, F. (2011). Subjective measures of risk aversion, fixed costs, and portfolio choice. *Journal of Economic Psychology, 32*(4), 564–580. http://dx.doi.org/10.1016/j.joep.2011.04.002

Kim, J.-Y. (2006). Hyperbolic discounting and the repeated self-control problem. *Journal of Economic Psychology, 27*, 344–359. http://dx.doi.org/10.1016/j.joep.2005.06.018

Kirchler, E. (1988). Diary reports on daily economic decisions of happy versus unhappy couples. *Journal of Economic Psychology, 9*, 327–357. http://dx.doi.org/10.1016/0167-4870(88)90039-6

Kirchler, E., & Wahl, I. (2010). Tax compliance inventory TAX-I: Designing an inventory for surveys of tax compliance. *Journal of Economic Psychology, 31*, 331–346. http://dx.doi.org/10.1016/j.joep.2010.01.002

Kleijnen, M., Lee, N., & Wetzels, M. (2009). An exploration of consumer resistance to innovation and its antecedents. *Journal of Economic Psychology, 30*, 344–357. http://dx.doi.org/10.1016/j.joep.2009.02.004

Lepori, G. M. (2015). Investor mood and demand for stocks: Evidence from popular TV series finales. *Journal of Economic Psychology, 48*, 33–47. http://dx.doi.org/10.1016/j.joep.2015.02.003

Levitt, S. D., & List, J. A. (2007). What do laboratory experiments measuring social preferences reveal about the real world? *Journal of Economic Perspectives, 21*(2), 153–174. http://dx.doi.org/10.1257/jep.21.2.153

Levitt, S. D., & List, J. A. (2008). *Homo economicus* evolves. *Science, 319*, 909–910. http://dx.doi.org/10.1126/science.1153640

List, J. A., & Gallet, C. S. (2001). What experimental protocols influence disparities between actual and hypothetical stated values? *Environmental and Resource Economics, 20*, 241–254. http://dx.doi.org/10.1023/A:1012791822804

Madrian, B. C., & Shea, D. F. (2001). The power of suggestion: Inertia in 401(k) participation and savings behavior. *Quarterly Journal of Economics, 116*(4), 1149–1187. http://dx.doi.org/10.1162/003355301753265543

Madsen, J. B., & McAleer, M. (2001). Consumption, liquidity constraints, uncertainty and temptation: An international comparison. *Journal of Economic Psychology, 22*, 61–89. http://dx.doi.org/10.1016/S0167-4870(00)00037-4

Masson, M., Delarue, J., Bouillot, S., Sieffermann, J.-M., & Blumenthal, D. (2015). Beyond sensory characteristics, how can we identify subjective dimensions? A comparison of six qualitative methods relative to a case study on coffee cups. *Food Quality and Preference*. Advance online publication. http://dx.doi.org/10.1016/j.foodqual.2015.01.003

McKay, M. T., Morgan, G. B., Van Exel, N. J., & Worrell, F. C. (2015). Back to 'the future': Evidence of a bifactor solution for scores on the consideration of future consequences scale. *Journal of Personality Assessment, 15*, 287–298. http://dx.doi.org/10.1080/00223891.2014.999338

Milch, K. F., Weber, E. U., Appelt, K. C., Handgraaf, M. J. J., & Krantz, D. H. (2009). From individual preference construction to group decisions: Framing effects and group processes. *Organizational Behavior and Human Decision Processes, 108*(2), 242–255. http://dx.doi.org/10.1016/j.obhdp.2008.11.003

Modigliani, F. (1986). Life cycle, individual thrift, and the wealth of nations. *American Economic Review, 76*(3), 297–313. http://dx.doi.org/10.1126/science.234.4777.704

Mui, V.-L. (1995). The economics of envy. *Journal of Economic Behavior and Organization, 26*, 311–336. http://dx.doi.org/10.1016/0167-2681(94)00079-T

Murphy, R. O., Ackermann, K. A., & Handgraaf, M. J. J. (2011). Measuring social value orientation. *Judgment and Decision Making, 6*, 771–781. http://dx.doi.org/10.2139/ssrn.1804189

Nyhus, E., & Pons, E. (2012). Personality and the gender wage gap. *Applied Economics, 44*(1), 105–118. http://dx.doi.org/10.1080/00036846.2010.500272

Olivero, N., & Lunt, P. (2004). Privacy versus willingness to disclose in e-commerce exchanges: The effect of risk awareness on the relative role of trust and control. *Journal of Economic Psychology, 25*, 243–262. http://dx.doi.org/10.1016/S0167-4870(02)00172-1

Onwezen, M., Bartels, J., & Antonides, G. (2013). The Norm Activation Model: An exploration of the functions of anticipated pride and guilt in pro-environmental behaviour. *Journal of Economic Psychology, 39*, 141–153. http://dx.doi.org/10.1016/j.joep.2013.07.005

Petrocelli, J. V. (2003). Factor validation of the consideration of future consequences scale. *Journal of Social Psychology, 143*, 404–413. http://dx.doi.org/10.1080/00224540309598453

Pfeffer, J., & DeVoe, S. E. (2009). Economic evaluation: The effect of money and economics on attitudes about volunteering. *Journal of Economic Psychology, 30*, 500–508. http://dx.doi.org/10.1016/j.joep.2008.08.006

Proto, E., & Rustichini, A. (2015). Life satisfaction, income and personality. *Journal of Economic Psychology, 48*, 17–32. http://dx.doi.org/10.1016/j.joep.2015.02.001

Ramalho, E. S., Caleiro, A., & Dionfsio, A. (2011). Explaining consumer confidence in Portugal. *Journal of Economic Psychology, 32*, 25–32. http://dx.doi.org/10.1016/j.joep.2010.10.004

Ranyard, R., & Craig, G. (1995). Evaluating and budgeting with instalment credit: An interview study. *Journal of Economic Psychology, 16*, 449–467. http://dx.doi.org/10.1016/0167-4870(95)00020-O

Ranyard, R., Hinkley, L., Williamson, J., & McHugh, S. (2006). The role of mental accounting in consumer credit decision processes. *Journal of Economic Psychology, 27*, 571–588. http://dx.doi.org/10.1016/j.joep.2005.11.001

Roese, N. J., & Vohs, K. D. (2012). Hindsight bias. *Perspectives on Psychological Science, 7*, 411–426. http://dx.doi.org/10.1177/1745691612454303

Rothbauer, P. (2008). Triangulation. In L. M. Given (Ed.), *The Sage encyclopedia of qualitative research methods* (pp. 892–894). London: Sage. http://dx.doi.org/10.4135/9781412963909.n468

Rudmin, F. W. (1994). Gender differences in the semantics of ownership: A quantitative phenomenological survey study. *Journal of Economic Psychology, 15*, 487–510. http://dx.doi.org/10.1016/0167-4870(94)90026-4

Ruff, C. C., Ugazio, G., & Fehr, E. (2013). Changing social norm compliance with noninvasive brain stimulation. *Science, 342*, 482–484. http://dx.doi.org/10.1126/science.1241399

Sanfey, A. G., Rilling, J. K., Aronson, J. A., Nystrom, L. E., & Cohen, J. D. (2003). The neural basis of economic decision-making in the ultimatum game. *Science, 300*, 1755–1758. http://dx.doi.org/10.1126/science.1082976

Savadori, L., & Mittone, L. (2015). Temporal distance reduces the attractiveness of p-bets compared to $-bets. *Journal of Economic Psychology, 46*, 26–38. http://dx.doi.org/10.1016/j.joep.2014.11.004

Schkade, D. A., & Kahneman, D. (1998). Does living in California make people happy? A focusing illusion in judgments of life satisfaction. *Psychological Science, 9*, 340–346. http://dx.doi.org/10.1111/1467-9280.00066 S

Strathman, A., Gleicher, F., Boninger, D. S., & Edwards, C. S. (1994). The consideration of future consequences: Weighing immediate and distant outcomes of behavior. *Journal of Personality and Social Psychology, 66*, 742–752. http://dx.doi.org/10.1037/0022-3514.66.4.742

Uhl, M. W. (2014). Reuters sentiment and stock returns. *Journal of Behavioral Finance, 15*, 287–298. http://dx.doi.org/10.1080/15427560.2014.967852

Van Beek, J., Antonides, G., & Handgraaf, M. J. J. (2013). Eat now, exercise later: The relation between consideration of immediate and future consequences and healthy behaviour. *Personality and Individual Differences, 54*(6), 785–791. http://dx.doi.org/10.1016/j.paid.2012.12.015

Van Rooij, M. C. J., Lusardi, A., & Alessie, R. J. M. (2011). Financial literacy and retirement planning in the Netherlands. *Journal of Economic Psychology, 32*(4), 593–608. http://dx.doi.org/10.1016/j.joep.2011.02.004

Van 't Wout, M., Kahn, R. S., Sanfey, A. G., & Aleman, A. (2006). Affective state and decision-making in the Ultimatum Game. *Experimental Brain Research, 169*, 564–568. http://dx.doi.org/10.1007/s00221-006-0346-5

Vidal, L., Ares, G., & Giménez, A. (2013). Projective techniques to uncover consumer perception: Application of three methodologies to ready-to-eat salads. *Food Quality and Preference, 28*, 1–7. http://dx.doi.org/10.1016/j.foodqual.2012.08.005

Voordouw, J., Cornelisse-Vermaat, J. R., Yiakoumaki, V., Theodoridis, G., Chryssochoidis, G., & Frewer, L. J. (2009). Food allergic consumers' preferences for labelling practices: A qualitative study in a real shopping environment. *International Journal of Consumer Studies, 33*, 94–102. http://dx.doi.org/10.1111/j.1470-6431.2008.00735.x

Vuchelen, J. (2004). Consumer sentiment and macroeconomic forecasts. *Journal of Economic Psychology, 25*, 493–506. http://dx.doi.org/10.1016/S0167-4870(03)00031-X

Webley, P., & Nyhus, E. (2006). Parents' influence on children's future orientation and saving. *Journal of Economic Psychology, 27*, 140–164. http://dx.doi.org/10.1016/j.joep.2005.06.016

Wenzel, M. (2005). Motivation or rationalisation? Causal relations between ethics, norms and tax compliance. *Journal of Economic Psychology, 26*, 491–508. http://dx.doi.org/10.1016/j.joep.2004.03.003

West, J., Bailey, I., & Winter, M. (2010). Renewable energy policy and public perceptions of renewable energy: A cultural theory approach. *Energy Policy, 38*, 5739–5748. http://dx.doi.org/10.1016/j.enpol.2010.05.024

Wood, J. L., & Essien-Wood, I. (2012). Capital identity projection: Understanding the psychosocial effects of capitalism on Black male community college students. *Journal of Economic Psychology, 33*, 984–995. http://dx.doi.org/10.1016/j.joep.2012.06.001

Wundt, W. M. (1911). *Einführung in die Psychologie*. Leipzig: R. Voigtländer. English translation, 1973. *An introduction to psychology*. New York: Arno Press.

Zullow, H. M. (1991). Pessimistic rumination in popular songs and news magazines predict economic recession via decreased consumer optimism and spending. *Journal of Economic Psychology, 12*, 501–526. http://dx.doi.org/10.1016/0167-4870(91)90029-S

FURTHER READING

Berg, B. L., & Lune, H. (2012). *Qualitative research methods for the social sciences*. Boston: Pearson.

Brocas, I., & Carrillo, J. D. (2008). The brain as a hierarchical organization. *American Economic Review, 98*, 1312–1346.

Fréchette, G. R., & Schotter, A. (2015). *Handbook of experimental economic methodology*. Oxford: Oxford University Press.

Glimcher, P. W. (2011). *Foundations of neuroeconomic analysis*. Oxford: Oxford University Press.

Silverman, D. (2004). *Qualitative research*. London: Sage.

Spector, P. E. (2013). Survey design and measure development. In T. D. Little (Ed.), *The Oxford handbook of quantitative methods* (vol. 1, pp. 170–188). Oxford: Oxford University Press.

5 Assessing Psychological Dispositions and States that Can Influence Economic Behaviour

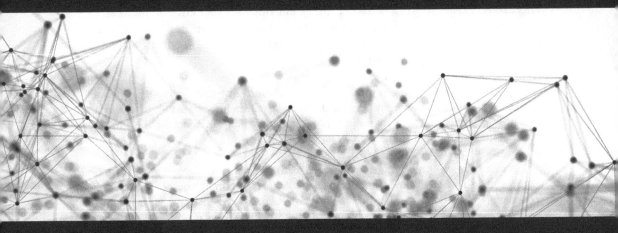

SIMON MCNAIR AND W. RAY CROZIER

CHAPTER OUTLINE

LEARNING OUTCOMES

BY THE END OF THIS CHAPTER YOU SHOULD BE ABLE TO:

1. Distinguish between economic 'dispositions' and 'states', and list some key examples of each.
2. Identify instruments/scales that could be used to assess prominent economic dispositions and states.
3. Recognize specific methodological issues to be conscious of when reading or conducting economic psychology research.

5.1 INTRODUCTION

People's mental experiences comprise a constantly shifting mix of transient factors and more predictable, stable characteristics; psychologists attempt to infer how such factors translate into thoughts, feelings, and actions. For instance, while it is well established that debt is associated with increased stress (Brown, Taylor, & Wheatley Price, 2005; Taylor, Jenkins, & Sacker, 2011), individuals' experience of and reactions to stress will differ (Folkman & Lazarus, 1985), which in turn has implications for how different people may respond to financial difficulty (Caplan & Schooler, 2007). Consider the following two people:

> Kate is always thinking about what she needs to do next. At work, she keeps her desk free from clutter, and methodically organized. On Friday afternoons she is sure to take time to schedule her next week. Kate resolves not to carry a credit card, because she knows she sometimes finds it difficult to resist a sale.

> Jeff takes things as they come. He prefers to focus on the here-and-now rather than think too much about the future. Although he's not rich, he is content, and he feels that things generally work themselves out. Sometimes, though, towards the end of the month he becomes worried about whether his income will stretch to pay day.

Kate may be a saver, for example, and have a well-thought-out retirement plan, while Jeff may not conflate happiness with wealth as others might. Distinguishing the psychological differences that might underlie people's financial behaviours can help economic psychologists to understand how financial advice, guidance, and education might be most effective.

This chapter introduces some key psychological constructs – both dispositional and situational – studied in economic psychology, and some of the specific instruments that psychologists use to gauge these factors. Typically, these tools take the form of questionnaires or inventories, where respondents read short statements or adjectives and indicate the extent to which they endorse them, or feel they are reflective of their own behaviours, attitudes, or opinions. Respondents use a numbered scale known as a Likert scale to rate their level of agreement for each individual statement, often having five to seven options ranging from 'Strongly Disagree' to 'Strongly Agree'. An overall composite score is generally calculated, based on the respondent's cumulative ratings to each statement/adjective, giving a quantified sense of their 'level' of that factor. Often, instruments will comprise sub-scales, scored in the same fashion, giving researchers insight into how people vary on particular aspects of a factor.

Section 5.2 covers the assessment of some of the key psychological dispositions that are associated with differences in financial behaviour. Section 5.3 details the assessment of more transitory psychological states, covering both objective and subjective indicators of financial well-being; current financial mental health; and how people perceive their own future economic states. In Section 5.4, we consider some methodological issues associated with how these factors are typically measured in research (e.g., validity), and with the types of instruments used (e.g., scale length), that readers should be mindful of when conducting their own research.

5.2 PSYCHOLOGICAL DISPOSITIONS AND ECONOMIC BEHAVIOUR

Here we consider three broad classes of dispositional factors: (1) financial attitudes; (2) time orientations; and (3) pragmatic characteristics, and describe some of the key tools used to investigate such factors. We refer readers to the accompanying tables for further details on each instrument.

5.2.1 Financial Attitudes

Table 5.1 lists some attitude scales widely used in economic psychology research. Attitudes reflect one's particular way of thinking, and are considered a central influence in shaping behavioural intentions (e.g. Jaccard & Becker, 1985). Measuring attitudes elucidates the kinds of reasoning that informs behaviour, which may aid a debt advisor, for instance, to identify problematic thinking that could undermine behavioural change.

Table 5.1 *Attitudes and associated measurement instruments*

Scale	Dimensions measured	Items	Source
Money attitudes			
Money Beliefs & Behaviours Scale	Power, Security, Obsession, Retention, Inadequacy, Effort	60	Furnham (1984)
Money Ethics Scale; Brief Money Ethics Scale	Good, Evil, Respect, Achievement, Budget, Freedom	30 (12 in Brief)	Tang (1992, 1995)
Money Attitudes Scale	Power, Generosity, Security, Autonomy	16	Furnham, Wilson, & Telford (2012)
Borrowing attitudes			
Attitudes to Credit Scale	Affective, Cognitive, Behavioural	20	Hayhoe, Leach, & Turner (1999)
Attitudes to Debt Scale	Pro- vs. Anti-debt	14	Davies & Lea (1995)
Materialistic attitudes			
Material Values Scale; Brief Material Values Scale	Success, Centrality, Happiness	18, 9, 6, & 3 items	Richins & Dawson (1992) Richins (2004)
Compulsive Buying Scale	Habitual urges to spend	7	Faber & O'Guinn (1992)
Cognitive/Affective Impulsive Buying Scales	Deliberation/emotional involvement in purchases	10	Verplanken & Herabadi (2001)

Psychologists understand attitudes to comprise an affective, cognitive and behavioural component. To illustrate, Hayhoe, Leach, and Turner's (1999) Attitudes to Credit Scale asks respondents to rate statements such as 'Because I use credit my debt rises every day' (cognitive); 'Credit makes me feel happy' (affective); and 'I always apply for more credit' (behavioural). Both Hayhoe et al. (1999) and Xiao, Noring, and Anderson (1995) find that people holding more credit cards in particular rate affective statements more positively. While financial attitude scales do not typically explicitly distinguish between the different attitudinal components in this way, the different statements they pose are nonetheless usually delineated into several specific attitude domains. Scales developed by Furnham (1984; Furnham, Wilson, & Telford, 2012) measure attitudes such as using money as a source of power ('I sometimes "buy" friendship with money'), or as a tool for generosity ('I demonstrate my generosity by buying people things'). Tang's (1992, 1995) Money Ethics Scales take a similar approach, assessing the extent to which people see money as a source of good or evil, or as a symbol of achievement and respect. Other scales focus purely on sentiment (reflecting a combination of cognitive and affective factors): Davies and Lea's (1995) Attitudes to Debt Scale, for example, poses eight 'pro-debt' (e.g. 'It is better to have something now and pay for it later'), and eight 'anti-debt' statements (e.g. 'Owing money is basically wrong'), with their findings indicating that those in debt tend to show more positive debt attitudes, and an increase in positive attitudes with age.

Materialism is one of the most widely studied consumer attitudes in economic psychology, and concerns beliefs, values, and traits that elevate the acquisition of material goods as an indicator of affluence and as a projection of status (see Chapter 11 in this volume). The most widely used measure of materialism – the Material Values Scale (Richins & Dawson, 1992) – assesses three tenets of materialistic attitudes: (1) possessions as success ('I admire people who own expensive goods'); (2) centrality of possessions ('I usually only buy the things I need'); and (3) possessions as a source of happiness ('I'd be happier if I could afford to buy more things'). Scales also exist that allow for the investigation of materialism in terms of specific behavioural, cognitive, and affective components. At the behavioural level, Faber and O'Guinn's (1992) Compulsive Buying Scale asks about respondents' tendencies to buy things knowing they cannot afford them, or insistence on spending any remaining income at the month's end. Materialism is also characterized by more *impulsive* spending behaviours (Dittmar & Bond, 2010), and Verplanken and Herabadi (2001) offer both a cognitive (e.g., 'I am used to buying things on the spot'), and affective impulsive buying scale (e.g., 'I buy things because I want them, not because I need them').

5.2.2   *Temporal Dispositions*

Economic decisions often entail a trade-off between an immediate or a more delayed result; those trading in stocks, for example, must decide whether to sell now when the price is high or wait longer and see if the price possibly rises further. There are three key temporal dispositions of note in this example: (1) time perspective; (2) planning behaviour; and (3) delay of gratification. Table 5.2 lists instruments used to study each of these facets of temporal disposition.

Time perspective concerns whether one is psychologically oriented more towards the past, present, or future. Zhang, Howell, and Bowerman's (2013) Brief Time

Table 5.2 *Temporal dispositions and associated measurement instruments*

Scale	Dimensions measured	Items	Source
Temporal orientation			
Brief Time Perspective Scale	Past (Positive, Negative) Present (Fatalism, Hedonism) Future	15	Zhang, Howell, & Bowerman (2013)
Future Orientation Scale	Anticipation Planning	15	Steinberg et al., (2009)
Consideration of Future Consequences Scale	Focus on present/ future outcomes	12	Strathman, Gleicher, Boninger, & Edwards (1994)
Planning			
Propensity to Plan Scale	Money (Short/Long-term) Time (Short/ Long-term)	24	Lynch, Netemeyer, Spiller, & Zammi (2010)
Delaying gratification			
Delaying Gratification Inventory	Physical, Money, Food, Social, Achievement	35	Hoerger, Quirk, & Weed (2012)
Monetary Choice Questionnaire	Preference for immediate/delayed rewards	35	Kirby, Petry, & Bickel (1999)
Three-Option Adaptive Discount Rate (ToAD)	As above	10	Yoon & Chapman (2015)

Perspective Scale offers past- and present-oriented statements framed both negatively (e.g., 'Painful past experiences keep playing in my mind'), and positively (e.g., 'It is important to lead an exciting life'), yielding four subscales. Steinberg et al.'s. (2009) Time Perspective Scale comprises a present/future orientation measure, while additionally adding subscales for *anticipation* of future consequences (e.g., 'Some people just act – they don't waste time thinking about consequences'), and planning behaviour. Steinberg et al.'s (1999) scale takes a different measurement approach, presenting pairs of opposing statements; respondents indicate which statement is relatively truer of them, then further indicate if the chosen statement is 'Really true' or 'Sort of true of me'. A more standard Likert approach is adopted in Strathman, Gleicher, Boninger, and Edwards' (1994) Consideration of Future Consequences Scale, which presents items that focus exclusively on prospective outcomes (e.g., 'I am willing to sacrifice immediate happiness to achieve future outcomes'). Evaluating planning behaviour is also the exclusive focus of Lynch, Netemeyer, Spiller, and Zammit's (2010) Propensity to Plan Scale, which incorporates subscales distinguishing how people plan both their time and money. The scale assesses both short-term (e.g., 'I decide in advance how my money will be spent in the coming days') and long-term planning behaviour (e.g., 'I consult my diary to see how much time I have left in the coming 1–2 months') in each domain, yielding four separate scores.

The third disposition of interest in the stock trader example concerns delaying gratification, or one's willingness to forego a more immediate positive outcome in favour of a distant but more positive outcome. Hoerger, Quirk, and Weed's (2012) Delaying Gratification Inventory represents the most current instrument, and includes a subscale specific to financial behaviour (e.g., 'I enjoy spending money the moment I get it'), as well as social, physical, and eating behaviours. The authors offer an in-depth 35-item version, or a shorter 10-item version. Perhaps the more traditional approach to measuring delayed gratification, as discussed in Chapter 2, involves mathematically deriving a quantification of how much someone 'discounts' the future; this measure, known as one's 'discount rate', represents the factor by which a delayed reward must be increased to reach the same level of subjective value as a more immediate reward. It follows that those with higher discount rates are less likely to delay gratification. This method involves presenting people with a series of choice pairs in which smaller, more immediate rewards are offered against larger, more delayed rewards (e.g., 'Would you prefer $50 now, or $100 in two weeks?'). Using the values of the rewards, length of the delays, and how the respondent chooses, one can compute the individual's discount rate using a standard formula. Kirby, Petry, and Bickel's (1999) Monetary Choice Questionnaire (MCQ)[1] is the most widely cited discount rate measure using such an approach. More recently, Yoon and Chapman's (2015) new online ToAD measure (Three-option Adaptive Discount)[2] takes the same mathematical approach, automatically calculating discount rates in as little as a minute, using 10 choice-pair items.

5.2.3   Pragmatic Dispositions

People's disposition may also manifest in terms of their general financial management skills or behaviours, financial knowledge, and perceived agency with respect to having control over their outcomes. Table 5.3 contains details of pertinent scales in these areas.

Measures of financial management skills typically ask people to indicate the frequency with which they engage in particular behaviours, using the standard Likert scale procedure. Garðarsdóttir and Dittmar's (2012) Money Management Skills scale quickly assesses basic behaviours, such as preparing a budget, checking bank statements, and 'keeping an eye on cash flow', for instance. Dew and Xiao's (2011) Financial Management Behaviours scale asks how often respondents have behaved in certain ways over the past six months, with behaviours subdivided into categories of consumption (e.g., actively comparing a range of prices when shopping), credit management (e.g., maximizing credit cards), cash management (e.g., keeping records), and investment (e.g., saving accounts, buying stocks).

Financial knowledge scales generally assess people's awareness and understanding of financial products and markets (and concepts therein), and researchers have assessed both subjective and objective knowledge. This is an important distinction, as many people *overestimate* their level of knowledge, with direct implications for behaviour. Subjective knowledge scales typically ask individuals to rate how well they feel they understand how products work or how to engage in good financial practices. Grable, Park, and Joo's (2009) Subjective Financial Knowledge Scale, for example,

Table 5.3 *Pragmatic dispositions and associated measurement instruments*

Scale	Dimensions measured	Items	Source
Financial management			
Money Management Scale	Basic financial management tendencies	9	Garðarsdóttir & Dittmar (2012)
Financial Management Behaviors Scale	Consumption, Credit, Cash, Saving, Investment	15	Dew & Jiao (2011)
Financial Management Behaviors Scale	As above plus Risk, Capital, Retirement	20	Porter & Garman (1993)
Financial knowledge/ literacy			
Subjective Financial Knowledge Scale	Subjective comprehension of basic financial matters	5	Grable, Park, & Joo (2009)
Objective Financial Knowledge Scale	Factual and computational understanding of basic financial matters	20	Knoll & Houts (2012)
Basic & Sophisticated Financial Literacy Items	As above	3 basic 8 sophisticated	Lusardi & Mitchell (2009)
Locus of control			
Internal-External LoC Scale	Internal, External	29	Rotter (1966)
Levenson IPC Scale	Internal, External, Powerful Others	24	Levenson (1981)

simply asks people to rate how much they know in relation to overarching topics such as credit management and investing money, but does not target specific behaviours or concepts. Objective knowledge scales, such as Knoll and Houts' (2012) Financial Knowledge scale, pose questions in a variety of domains (e.g., risk, inflation, debt management, interest) to assess the breadth and factual accuracy of people's understanding. The scale also includes several items testing people's calculation abilities in areas such as compound interest. Several of these items are taken from the Basic, and Sophisticated Financial Literacy scales of Lusardi and Mitchell (2009), which assess people's numeracy in the financial domain. Research using such knowledge scales indicates that people with greater financial knowledge exercise better financial management practices (Antonides, Manon de Groot, & Fred van Raaij, 2011; Grable et al., 2009).

A further dispositional characteristic concerns the extent to which people believe that their behaviour makes a meaningful difference to their circumstances. One influential characterization of these beliefs is in terms of having an internal or external *locus of control*. Rotter's (1966) locus of control scale takes a similar forced-choice approach to Steinberg et al. (2009) noted earlier, with respondents reading pairs of contrasting statements and selecting appropriately, for example: 'When I make plans I am almost certain to make them work' (Internal) vs. 'It is not wise to plan ahead as many things happen due to luck' (External). Alternatively, Levenson's (1981) I-P-C scale takes a more standard six-point Likert scale approach, with the instrument's three subscales giving rise to the scale's name. As well as an Internal locus of control score, the scale discriminates between two External scores: one concerning the degree of influence one feels that 'powerful others' have ('Getting what I want involves pleasing those above me'), and the other concerning the influence of chance ('I find that what is going to happen will happen').

5.3 PSYCHOLOGICAL STATES AND ECONOMIC BEHAVIOUR

Economic psychologists also have the task of understanding how an individual's current, acute situational circumstances may influence their financial behaviours. In this section we outline state-based indicators that help researchers to ascertain an individual's current financial state – both actual and perceived – as well as associated impacts on people's current mental state. Unless otherwise stated, the questionnaires discussed below follow the same inventory and Likert scale format as previously described.

5.3.1 Financial Well-Being

Shim, Xiao, Barber, and Lyons (2009) argue that 'financial well-being' is founded on financial knowledge and attitudes, and observe it to be directly predictive of life satisfaction, as well as physical and mental health (see also Porter & Garman, 1993). While a more economics-based approach might focus on objectively quantifying financial well-being in terms of levels of relative income, or debt-to-income ratios, in economic psychology it is becoming clear that increases in income produce differential improvements in *subjective* well-being contingent upon personality factors such as neuroticism (Proto & Rustichini, 2015), and locus of control (Keese, 2012). Indeed, Aldana and Liljenquist (1998) report that financial well-being is more likely to be influenced by people's perceived ability to meet their financial responsibilities than by overall income (see also Keese, 2012), while Fox and Chancey (1998) found that subjective perceptions of financial status were more closely associated with individual and family well-being than were objective measures. Economic psychologists, then, typically tend to solicit both objective and subjective assessments when studying financial well-being. Details about the discussed objective and subjective scales can be found in Table 5.4.

Table 5.4 *Measurement instruments associated with financial well-being*

Scale	Dimensions measured	Items	Source
Objective			
Material Deprivation Scale	Living standards/poverty	15	McKay (2010)
Economic Hardship Scale	Cutbacks in everyday living expenses, current financial status	12	Lempers, Clark-Lempers, & Simons (1989)
Financial Strain Scale	Difficulties affording basic living expenses	5	Caplan & Schooler (2007)
Financial Stressor Events Scale	Frequency of financial shocks	23	Kim, Garman, & Sorhaindo (2003)
Subjective			
Subjective Financial Well-being Scale	Self-perceived financial security/health	8	Norvilitis, Szablicki, & Wilson (2003)
Perceived Financial Well-being Scale	Positive/negative sentiment about financial status	4	Kim, Garman, & Sorhaindo (2003)
Perceived Financial Well-being Scale	Overall evaluation of current financial status	1	Porter & Garman (1993)
Financial Threat Scale	Concern about current financial status	5	Marjanovic, Greenglass, Fiksenbaum, & Bell (2013)

5.3.2   Objective Indicators

While research suggests that income level positively correlates with overall life satisfaction, the relationship is weak (e.g., Blanchflower & Oswald, 2004), and appears to reach a plateau at income levels of around $75,000 per annum (Kahneman & Deaton, 2010). One issue, however, is that participants may confuse concepts such as household and personal income, or gross and net income (Collins & White, 1996); or may simply not know their income (Schräpler, 2006). Given these and many other difficulties regarding income measurement (see Moore, Stinson, & Welniak, 2000), we focus instead on questionnaire-based measures that quantify the extent or frequency with which people face specific instances of economic difficulty in their daily lives.

Such an approach has recently been adopted by the UK government, which introduced the Material Deprivation Index in 2011 to assess national economic well-being alongside income. This 15-item instrument asks whether respondents have access to certain items (e.g. a warm coat), experiences (e.g. socializing), and services (e.g. phone line), with overall scores determined by a relative weighting system that ascribes more or less impact to each item conditional on their prevalence within the sample being studied (see McKay, 2010, for a detailed overview). The UK government uses the Index in their yearly Family Resources Survey, data from which inform reports on UK poverty levels. This approach of asking people about specific, basic living requirements and areas of everyday living expenditure is a feature of two further, widely used financial state instruments. First, Lempers, Clark-Lempers, and Simons' (1989) Economic Hardship Scale (EHQ) asks how frequently someone has had to 'make cutbacks' such as reducing heating or electricity use, changing eating or food shopping habits, and foregoing medical care to save money. Two broader questions ask more directly about (1) overall financial status (No problems – Minor Problems – Major Problems – Extreme Problems), and (2) changes to income in the previous six months (Increased a Lot – Increased Somewhat – Stayed the Same – Decreased Somewhat – Decreased a Lot). Second, Caplan and Schooler's (2007) Financial Strain Scale asks about basic living expenses such as food and clothing, and household costs such as rent/mortgage and utilities; respondents indicate how often they cannot afford to sufficiently meet such expenses. Finally, Kim, Garman, and Sorhaindo (2003) devised an instrument enquiring about a range of 23 'financial shock events' including receiving overdue notices or phone calls from creditors; being late on credit repayments; and more serious concerns such as having wages appropriated, or items repossessed. Respondents indicate whether events have occurred Never, Once, or More than Once. While broader in scope and severity of events, this scale does not inquire about financial difficulty regarding food and eating, often taken as a critical indicator of objective financial well-being.

Those interested in pursuing income-based indicators should consult Hansen and Kneale (2013), who compare the effectiveness of different approaches. The scale-based measures considered above offer several further merits, including a higher fidelity of insight into people's specific experiences. Furthermore, as these measures include a temporal element, they afford at least some degree of assurance about the individual's typical financial state that an otherwise 'snapshot' income-based measure might lack.

5.3.3   Subjective Indicators

Two individuals with similar debt-to-income ratios may not necessarily perceive a similar degree of *subjective* financial burden. Porter and Garman (1993) suggest that the essence of subjective financial well-being (SFWB) appears to be manifest most clearly as a sense of how adequate one feels one's income is for one's needs. However, as Keese (2012) notes, perceptions of SFWB are not exclusively tied to objective financial state. We might also expect behavioural differences between those who perhaps over- or underestimate the severity of their objective financial status: those who do not feel so constrained typically assume more debt, for example (Brown et al., 2005). At the psychological level, SFWB is also directly associated with psychological stress (e.g. Brown et al., 2005); depression (Taylor et al., 2011); and in extreme cases, suicidal ideation (Meltzer et al., 2011).

The construct of SFWB is thus more complex than it may first appear. First, 'well-being' is multifaceted, and can refer to acute sentiments in the more immediate present, or broader evaluations of one's overall long-standing contentment. Furthermore, different scales may either ask about how 'pleased' or 'unhappy' someone is with their financial situation. This is not a trivial issue, as the presence of negative feelings does not necessarily mean the absence of positive feelings (and vice versa) (Diener, Emmons, Larsen, & Griffin, 1985). Perhaps the most neutrally framed SFWB measure comes from Porter and Garman (1993), who use a single 'ladder' item that asks respondents to imagine the top and bottom 'rungs' as their best and worst possible financial circumstances. Once self-anchored in this way, respondents are asked to indicate where they feel they currently stand on this ladder. Kim et al.'s (2003) subjective scale does distinguish between positive and negative affect, posing items referring to satisfaction and stress, as well as one's more general state of 'perceived financial wellness', for example.

In contrast, some SFWB scales focus more exclusively on negative emotional experiences. Norvilitis, Szablicki, and Wilson's (2003) Financial Well-being scale evaluates how preoccupied respondents are with their debt burden (e.g., 'I think a lot about the debt I am in'), as well as their future expectations about difficulty in repaying (e.g., 'One year from now I will not be in debt'). Similarly, Marjanovic, Greenglass, Fiksenbaum, and Bell's (2013) five-item Financial Threat Scale (FTS) taps into the 'mixture of fear, uncertainty, and cognitive preoccupation' associated with financial difficulty, with items inquiring specifically about how uncertain, at risk, threatened, and worried respondents are about their current financial situation. Findings indicated that although financial threat was related to objective income indicators, the FTS still predicted health outcomes separately from these, further underlining the importance of distinguishing objective and subjective statuses.

5.3.4 *Financial Mental Health*

We conceive of 'financial mental health' as representing people's psychological appraisal of their capacity to engage with their financial matters; to confidently and adaptively make financial decisions; and to have belief in one's ability to achieve financial goals. Difficulties with such factors may present psychological barriers that undermine people's attempts to apply otherwise practical knowledge and skills. Table 5.5 details information about scales in the area of financial mental health.

5.3.5 *Financial Coping Style*

Where one person might thoughtfully lay out a plan of action to ameliorate stress, another may, in contrast, avoid their problems, or deny they exist. At the most fundamental level psychologists distinguish between 'emotion-focused' and 'problem-focused' stress

Table 5.5 *Measurement instruments associated with financial mental health*

Scale	Dimensions measured	Items	Source
Financial Coping Style	Emotion-, and Problem-Focused coping	9	Caplan & Schooler (2007)
Financial Self-Confidence Scale	Perceived ability to make good financial decisions	10	Norvilitis & Mao (2013)
Financial Self-Efficacy Scale	Perceived ability to succeed and achieve goals	6	Lown (2011)

coping styles (Folkman & Lazarus, 1985). Emotion-focused coping entails attempts to regulate how people *feel* about their situation, while problem-focused coping is centred on identifying specific behaviours people might engage (or disengage) to overcome the stressor. Caplan and Schooler (2007) constructed a short instrument assessing emotional and problem-focused coping with financial stress specifically, in which emotion-focused financial coping is characterized in statements such as 'I tell myself "money is not worth getting upset about"', in contrast to problem-focused strategies such as 'I try to cut expenses'. Their findings indicated that lower socio-economic status was associated with increased emotional coping, with problem-focused coping contingent upon individuals feeling confident they can effect a change through their behaviour. Only problem-focused coping led to reduced financial distress, but its dependency on agency suggests that those who lack material resources may find it especially difficult to form active behavioural strategies to combat financial stress.

5.3.6   *Financial Self-Confidence and Self-Efficacy*

People's economic behaviours are also in part determined by their sense of self-assuredness and their sense of engagement in competently achieving goals. For financial advisors or debt counsellors, for example, understanding how clients perceive their own capabilities may help identify where a client may need particular supplemental encouragement or guidance. Here, we distinguish between self-confidence and self-efficacy which, while related (confidence typically increases with efficacy), are differently poised.

Self-confidence entails an assertion of trust in one's own ability, and evidence attests that people are generally overconfident, which can lead to problems. Overconfident male traders trade more frequently, for example, and tend to suffer lower overall returns (Barber & Odean, 2001. See Skala, 2008, for more on overconfidence in financial contexts.) Norvilitis and Mao (2013) have developed a specific financial self-confidence scale where items pertain to confidence in money management ('I am confident I know how to handle my money'), financial products ('I am confident in my abilities to handle credit cards'), and where to seek financial advice ('If I had questions about money, I know where to ask for advice'). Higher financial self-confidence scores predicted higher subjective financial well-being, a finding of interest as this relationship was independent of income level.

Self-efficacy embodies the more applied competency with which people feel they can complete specific tasks, or accomplish specific goals. Given the degree to which people are often overconfident in their practical ability, it is useful to separately assess how assured one feels one could, for instance, adapt to a financial setback or stick to a specified financial plan. While research on financial self-efficacy remains very limited, Lown (2011) recently adapted items from a generalized measure of self-efficacy to produce a six-item scale pertaining specifically to financial matters (e.g., 'When unexpected expenses occur, I usually have to use credit'). Lown observed that higher financial self-efficacy was linked to having more sophisticated retirement plans in place. Elsewhere, lower self-efficacy has been associated with greater credit card debt (Tokunaga, 1993), and is thought to be more prevalent in impoverished households (Boardman & Robert, 2000).

5.4 METHODOLOGICAL ISSUES IN ASSESSING DISPOSITIONS AND STATES

Although a fuller deconstruction of the merits of surveys and scales is beyond the scope of this chapter (see Chapter 6 in this volume), we briefly orient the reader towards several key issues to be mindful of when conducting research using scales.

5.4.1 Repetition of Items and Length of Scales

While longer scales are generally regarded as more statistically reliable due to aggregated random errors cancelling out, they often entail a degree of item repetition and redundancy. Longer scales lead to decreased response rates particularly in volunteers sampled from the general population, compared to samples comprising university students completing studies for course credit (McCarty, House, Harman, & Richards, 2006). Shorter scales place less burden on the respondent, and mitigate issues of boredom and fatigue (Robins, Hendin, & Trzesniewski, 2001). Single item measures of constructs, including life satisfaction (Campbell, Converse, & Rodgers, 1976), subjective well-being (Diener, 1984), self-esteem (Robins et al., 2001), and affect (Russel, Weiss, & Mendelsohn, 1989) have shown comparable merit with equivalent longer scales.

5.4.2 Correlational Data and Large Sample Sizes

Questionnaire and survey-based data are typically analysed in correlational terms meaning that, by definition, the research cannot infer causation between statistically related measurements. Without the scientific control afforded by an experiment, one must always assume that statistical relationships *might* be explained by other constructs not expressly measured by the survey. Furthermore, many of the scales described in this chapter are often used as part of very large, nationally representative longitudinal questionnaires, such as the American Life Panel Survey in the United States (5000+ respondents), and the Dutch LISS Panel (Longitudinal Internet Studies for the Social Sciences) (8000+ respondents). It should be noted that p values become highly sensitive to even minor fluctuations in measurements such that very small correlations of $r = .01$ will appear statistically significant at sample sizes of 1000. Lin, Lucas, and Shmueli (2013, p. 106) comment that larger samples become 'too big to fail'. As such, if administering scales to larger groups, researchers should augment any significant correlations by also referring to confidence intervals (an estimated range of scores for which the observed score likely falls), and/or effect size (e.g., R^2 for correlations, representing the extent of the variance accounted for by the scale).

5.4.3 Systematic Measurement Error

Systematic measurement error occurs when scale scores deviate from their *true* value by a fixed amount. To illustrate, a respondent may inadvertently and consistently overestimate how frequently they engage in money management behaviours such that their overall score is somewhat elevated, presenting them as more of a money manager than they actually may be. This 'social desirability' bias, whereby respondents answer items as they feel they *should* be answered in order to paint themselves in a favourable light, can produce spurious relationships or mask true relationships (Ganster, Hennessey, & Luthans, 1983). This is further compounded by people's tendency to strive for consistency in their responses across items (Podsakoff & Organ, 1986). Further artificial relationships may occur due to acquiescence, whereby respondents have a general tendency to agree with positive statements and disagree with negative statements when in doubt; scales using a range of positively and negatively framed items are thus preferable.

5.4.4   *Predictive Validity*

The so-called 'person-situation' debate in psychology concerns whether dispositional variables are truly sufficiently stable to provide predictive validity for behaviour (e.g., Funder, 2009; Mischel, 2009). Behavioural economists argue instead that behaviour is ultimately driven by situational considerations (typically changes in utility), which invites the possibility that characteristics may show domain-specificity. Several studies show, for instance, that people's propensity for risky behaviours varies depending on whether the risks pertain to areas such as finance, health, or social decisions (e.g., Blais & Weber, 2006; Slovic, 1962; Weber, Blais, & Betz, 2002). Further evidence indicates the changing nature of personality over the lifespan (see Roberts, Walton, & Viechtbauer, 2006), which is to say that the continuing development of our social, cultural, and economic circumstances is associated with shifts in our perspectives. In even more reductive terms, the mood that you are experiencing on any day may affect how you respond to a survey.

The more contemporary argument is conciliatory, and recommends that researchers be mindful of both stable characteristics and situational considerations (Fleeson, 2001). Our point is not to discourage the use of instruments such as those described in this chapter but rather to argue that such tools in and of themselves will only paint part of the picture. Where possible, longitudinal designs that allow for assessment of within-subject variability, and designs that expressly attempt to relate dispositions to actual observed actions offer stronger theoretical bases upon which to infer the psychological basis of economic behaviour.

5.5   SUMMARY

This chapter has introduced measures of several dispositional and state-based psychological factors that can be useful in distinguishing individual-level variations in people's economic thoughts, feelings and actions.

We considered three classes of dispositional factors: (1) financial attitudes; (2) time orientations; and (3) pragmatic characteristics. Attitudes can be analysed at affective, cognitive, and behavioural levels and scales in the financial domain cover attitudes at these levels to credit and debt, to the role of money, and to materialism. Measures of temporal dispositions include time perspective, propensity to plan ahead, and preferences for immediate or delayed gratification. Measures of pragmatic characteristics include financial management skills and practices, financial awareness and understanding, and people's feelings of direct control over their circumstances.

This chapter also considered the importance of more state-based assessments that give an indication of people's current, or recent, situational circumstances. We distinguished between *objective* and *subjective* financial well-being. The former is typified by assessments of income, or the financial security to access basic products/ services, while examples of subjective financial status are instruments that inquire about people's perceptions of the level of debt burden or feelings of fear and uncertainty about their current financial situation. A further category of state-based measure we discussed was that of financial mental health, assessing how people cope with financial pressure and how effectively and confidently they feel they can make financial decisions.

We concluded the chapter by considering some methodological limitations relevant to research that uses these kinds of instruments, including problems associated with lengthy or repetitive questionnaires; instrument validity, and the limitations of correlational research for making causal inferences. While paying due attention to these issues, the study of individual variation in psychological dispositions and states makes an important contribution to economic psychology.

NOTES

1. See http://kuscholarworks.ku.edu/handle/1808/15424, for a useful Excel template that calculates discount rates for the MCQ.
2. See http://decisiontimes.org/toad-demo, for more information.

REVIEW QUESTIONS

1. How might a psychologist categorize different types of economic attitudes? What benefits might this confer on a financial advisor, for example?
2. What are some key differences between objective and subjective indicators of financial well-being? Why might it be important to distinguish between these?
3. What are some key methodological caveats to be mindful of when assessing psychological dispositions and states?

REFERENCES

Aldana, S. G., & Liljenquist, W. (1998). Validity and reliability of a financial strain survey. *Financial Counselling and Planning*, 9(2), 11–19.

Antonides, G., Manon de Groot, I., & Fred van Raaij, W. (2011). Mental budgeting and the management of household finance. *Journal of Economic Psychology*, 32(4), 546–555. http://doi.org/10.1016/j.joep.2011.04.001

Barber, B. M., & Odean, T. (2001). Boys will be boys: Gender, overconfidence, and common stock investment. *The Quarterly Journal of Economics*, 116(1), 261–292. http://doi.org/10.1016/S0169-2070(03)00031-1

Blais, A., & Weber, E. U. (2006). A Domain-Specific Risk-Taking (DOSPERT) scale for adult populations. *Judgement and Decision Making*, 1(1), 33–47.

Blanchflower, D. G., & Oswald, A. J. (2004). Well-being over time in Britain and the USA. *Journal of Public Economics*, 88(7–8), 1359–1386. http://doi.org/Doi 10.1016/S0047-2727(02)00168-8

Boardman, J.D. & Robert, S.D. (2000). Neighborhood socioeconomic status and perceptions of self-efficacy. *Sociological Perspectives*, 43 (1), 117–136

Brown, S., Taylor, K., & Wheatley Price, S. (2005). Debt and distress: Evaluating the psychological cost of credit. *Journal of Economic Psychology*, 26(5), 642–663. http://doi.org/10.1016/j.joep.2005.01.002

Campbell, A., Converse, P. E., & Rodgers, W. L. (1976). *The quality of American life: Perceptions, evaluations, and satisfactions*. New York: Russell Sage Foundation

Caplan, L. J., & Schooler, C. (2007). Socioeconomic status and financial coping strategies : The mediating role of perceived control of socioeconomic status and financial coping strategies. *Social Psychology Quarterly*, 70(1), 43–58. http://doi.org/10.1177/019027250707000106

Collins, D., & White, A. (1996). In search of an income question for the 2001 census. *Survey Methodology Bulletin*, 39(7), 2–10.

Davies, E., & Lea, S. (1995). Student attitudes to student debt. *Journal of Economic Psychology*, 16, 663–679. http://www.sciencedirect.com/science/article/pii/0167487096800146

Dew, J., & Xiao, J. J. (2011). The Financial Management Behavior Scale: Development and validation. *Journal of Financial Counseling and Planning*, 22(1), 43–59.

Diener, E. (1984). Subjective well-being. *Psychological Bulletin*, 95(3). 542–575. http://doi.org/10.1037/0033-2909.95.3.542

Diener, E., Emmons, R., Larsen, J., & Griffin, S. (1985). The satisfaction with life scale. *Journal of Personality Assessmemt*, 49(1), 71–75. http://doi.org/10.1207/s15327752jpa4901_13

Dittmar, H., & Bond, R. (2010). I want it and I want it now: Using a temporal discounting paradigm to examine predictors of consumer impulsivity. *British Journal of Psychology*, 101, 751–776. http://doi.org/10.1348/000712609X484658

Faber, R. J., & O'Guinn, T. C. (1992). A clinical screener for compulsive buying. *Journal of Consumer Research*, 19(3), 459. http://doi.org/10.1086/209315

Fleeson, W. (2001). Toward a structure-and process-integrated view of personality: Traits as density distributions of states. *Journal of Personality and Social Psychology*, 80(6), 1011–1027.

Folkman, S., & Lazarus, R. S. (1985). If it changes, it must be a process: Study of emotion and coping during three stages of a college examination. *Journal of Personality and Social Psychology*, 48(1), 150–170. http://doi.org/10.1037/0022-3514.48.1.150

Fox, G. L., & Chancey, D. (1998). Sources of economic distress: Individual and family outcomes. *Journal of Family Issues*, 19(6), 725–749. http://doi.org/10.1177/019251398019006004

Funder, D. C. (2009). Persons, behaviors and situations: An agenda for personality psychology in the postwar era. *Journal of Research in Personality*, 43(2), 120–126. http://doi.org/10.1016/j.jrp.2008.12.041

Furnham, A. (1984). Many sides of the coin: The psychology of money usage. *Personality and Individual Differences*. http://doi.org/10.1016/0191-8869(84)90025-4

Furnham, A., Wilson, E., & Telford, K. (2012). The meaning of money: The validation of a short money-types measure. *Personality and Individual Differences*, 52(6). http://dx.doi.org/10.1016/j.paid.2011.12.020

Ganster, D. C., Hennessey, H. W., & Luthans, F. (1983). Social desirability response effects: Three alternative models. *Academy of Management Journal*, 26(2), 321–331.

Garðarsdóttir, R. B., & Dittmar, H. (2012). The relationship of materialism to debt and financial well-being: The case of Iceland's perceived prosperity. *Journal of Economic Psychology*, 33(3), 471–481. http://doi.org/10.1016/j.joep.2011.12.008

Grable, J. E., Park, J. Y., & Joo, S. H. (2009). Explaining financial management behavior for Koreans living in the United States. *Journal of Consumer Affairs*, 43(1), 80–107. http://doi.org/10.1111/j.1745-6606.2008.01128.x

Hansen, K., & Kneale, D. (2013). Does how you measure income make a difference to measuring poverty? Evidence from the UK. *Social Indicators Research*, 110(3), 1119–1140. http://doi.org/10.1007/s11205-011-9976-5

Hayhoe, C. R., Leach, L., & Turner, P. R. (1999). Discriminating the number of credit cards held by college students using credit and money attitudes. *Journal of Economic Psychology*. http://doi.org/10.1016/S0167-4870(99)00028-8

Hoerger, M., Quirk, S. W., & Weed, N. C. (2012). Development and validation of the Delaying Gratification Inventory. *Psychological Assessment*, 23(3), 725–738. http://doi.org/10.1037/a0023286

Jaccard, J., & Becker, M. A. (1985). Attitudes and behavior: An information integration perspective. *Journal of Experimental Social Psychology*, 21(5), 440–465. http://doi.org/10.1016/0022-1031(85)90029-0

Kahneman, D., & Deaton, A. (2010). High income improves evaluation of life but not emotional well-being. *Proceedings of the National Academy of Sciences*, 107(38), 16489–16493. http://doi.org/10.1073/pnas.1011492107

Keese, M. (2012). Who feels constrained by high debt burdens? Subjective vs. objective measures of household debt. *Journal of Economic Psychology*, 33(1), 125–141. http://doi.org/10.1016/j.joep.2011.08.002

Kim, J., Garman, E. T., & Sorhaindo, B. (2003). Relationships among credit counseling clients' financial well-being, financial behaviors, financial stressor events, and health. *Journal of Financial Counseling and Planning*, 14(2), 75–88.

Kirby, K. N., Petry, N. M., & Bickel, W. K. (1999). Heroin addicts have higher discount rates for delayed rewards than non-drug-using controls. *Journal of Experimental Psychology. General*, 128(1), 78–87. http://doi.org/10.1037/0096-3445.128.1.78

Knoll, M.A.Z., & Houts, C.R. (2012) The financial knowledge scale: An application of item response theory to the assessment of financial literacy. *Journal of Consumer Affairs*, 46(3), 381–410. http://dx.doi.org/10.1111/j.1745-6606.2012.01241.x

Lempers, J. D., Clark-Lempers, D., & Simons, R. L. (1989). Economic hardship, parenting, and distress in adolescence. *Child Development*, 60(1), 25–39. http://doi.org/10.2307/1131068

Levenson, H. (1981). Differentiating among internality, powerful others, and chance. In H. M. Lefcourt (Ed.), *Research with the locus of control construct* (vol. 1, pp. 15–63). New York: Academic Press.

Lin, M., Lucas, H. C., & Shmueli, G. (2013). Too big to fail: Large samples and the p-value problem. *Information Systems Research*, 24(4), 906–917. http://doi.org/http://dx.doi.org/10.1287/isre.2013.0480

Lown, J. M. (2011). Development and validation of a financial self-efficacy scale. *Journal of Financial Counseling and Planning*, 22(2), 54–63.

Lusardi, A., & Mitchell, O. S. (2009). How ordinary consumers make complex economic decisions: Financial literacy and retirement readiness (NBER Working Paper # 15350). Retrieved from http://www.nber.org/papers/w15350

Lynch, J. G. Jr., Netemeyer, R. G., Spiller, S. A., & Zammit, A. (2010). A generalizable scale of propensity to plan: The long and the short of planning for time and for money. *Journal of Consumer Research*, 37(1), 108–128. http://doi.org/10.1086/649907

Marjanovic, Z., Greenglass, E. R., Fiksenbaum, L., & Bell, C. M. (2013). Psychometric evaluation of the Financial Threat Scale (FTS) in the context of the Great Recession. *Journal of Economic Psychology*, 36, 1–10. http://doi.org/10.1016/j.joep.2013.02.005

McCarty, C., House, M., Harman, Je., & Richards, S. (2006). Effort in phone survey response rates: The effects of vendor and client-controlled factors. *Field Methods*, 18(2), 172–188. http://doi.org/10.1177/1525822X05282259

McKay, S. (2010). Using the new Family Resources Survey question block to measure material deprivation among pensioners (DWP Working Paper # 89). Retrieved from www.gov.uk/government/uploads/system/uploads/attachment_data/file/214387/WP89.pdf

Meltzer, H., Bebbington, P., Brugha, T., Jenkins, R., McManus, S., & Dennis, M. S. (2011). Personal debt and suicidal ideation. *Psychological Medicine*, 41(4), 771–778. http://doi.org/10.1017/S0033291710001261

Mischel, W. (2009). From Personality and Assessment (1968) to Personality Science (2009). *Journal of Research in Personality*, 43(2), 282–290. http://doi.org/10.1016/j.jrp.2008.12.037

Moore, J. C., Stinson, L. L., & Welniak, E. J. J. (2000). Income measurement error in surveys: A review. *Journal of Official Statistics*, 16(4), 331–361. Retrieved from http://www.jos.nu/Articles/abstract.asp?article=164331

Norvilitis, J. M., & Mao, Y. (2013). Attitudes towards credit and finances among college students in China and the United States. *International Journal of Psychology*, 48(3), 389–398. http://doi.org/10.1080/00207594.2011.645486

Norvilitis, J. M., Szablicki, P. B., & Wilson, S. D. (2003). Factors influencing levels of credit-card debt in college students. *Journal of Applied Social Psychology*, 33, 935–947. http://doi.org/10.1111/j.1559-1816.2003.tb01932.x

Podsakoff, P. M., & Organ, D. W. (1986). Self-reports in organizational research: Problems and prospects. *Journal of Management*, 12(4), 531–544.

Porter, N. M., & Garman, E. T. (1993). Testing a conceptual model of financial well-being. *Financial Counseling and Planning*, 4(803), 135–164.

Proto, E., & Rustichini, A. (2015). Life satisfaction, income and personality. *Journal of Economic Psychology*, 48, 17–32. http://doi.org/10.1016/j.joep.2015.02.001

Richins, M. L. (2004). The Material Values Scale: Measurement properties and development of a short form. *Journal of Consumer Research*, 31(1), 209–219.

Richins, M. L., & Dawson, S. (1992). A consumer values orientation for materialism and its measurement: Scale development and validation. *Journal of Consumer Research*, 19(December), 303–316.

Roberts, B. W., Walton, K. E., & Viechtbauer, W. (2006). Patterns of mean-level change in personality traits across the life course: A meta-analysis of longitudinal studies. *Psychological Bulletin*, 132, 1–25. doi: 10.1037/0033-2909.132.1.1

Robins, R. W., Hendin, H. M., & Trzesniewski, K. H. (2001). Measuring global self-esteem: Construct validation of a single-item measure and the Rosenberg Self-Esteem Scale. *Personality and Social Psychology Bulletin*, 27(2), 151–161. http://doi.org/10.1177/0146167201272002

Rotter, J. B. (1966). Generalized expectancies for internal versus external control of reinforcement. *Psychological Monographs: General and Applied*, 80(1), 1–28. http://doi.org/10.1037/h0092976

Russel, J. A., Weiss, A., & Mendelsohn, G. A. (1989). Affect grid: A single-item scale of pleasure and arousal. *Journal of Personality and Social Psychology*, 57(3), 493–502.

Schräpler, J. P. (2006). Explaining income nonresponse: A case study by means of the British Household Panel Study (BHPS). *Quality & Quantity*, 40(6), 1013–1036. http://doi.org/10.1007/s11135-005-5429-z

Shim, S., Xiao, J. J., Barber, B. L., & Lyons, A. C. (2009). Pathways to life success: A conceptual model of financial well-being for young adults. *Journal of Applied Developmental Psychology*, 30(6), 708–723. http://doi.org/10.1016/j.appdev.2009.02.003

Skala, D. (2008). Overconfidence in psychology and finance: An interdisciplinary literature review, MPRA Working Paper #26386. Retrieved from https://mpra.ub.uni-muenchen.de/26386/

Slovic, P. (1962). Convergent validation of risk taking measures. *The Journal of Abnormal and Social Psychology*, 65(1), 68.

Steinberg, L., Graham, S., O'Brien, L., Woolard, J., Cauffman, E., & Banich, M. (2009). Age differences in future orientation and delay discounting. *Child Development*, 80(1), 28–44. http://doi.org/10.1111/j.1467-8624.2008.01244.x

Strathman, A., Gleicher, F., Boninger, D. S., & Edwards, C. S. (1994). The consideration of future consequences: Weighing immediate and distant outcomes of behavior. *Journal of Personality and Social Psychology*, 66(4), 742–752. http://doi.org/10.1037/0022-3514.66.4.742

Tang, T. L. (1992). The meaning of money revisited. *Journal of Organizational Behavior*, 13(2), 197–202. http://doi.org/10.1177/0002764206289140

Tang, T. L. (1995). The development of a short money ethic scale: Attitudes toward money and pay satisfaction revisited. *Personality and Individual Differences*, 19(6), 17–22. http://dx.doi.org/10.1016/s0191-8869(95)00133-6

Taylor, M. P., Jenkins, S. P., & Sacker, A. (2011). Financial capability and psychological health. *Journal of Economic Psychology*, 32(5), 710–723. http://doi.org/10.1016/j.joep.2011.05.006

Tokunaga, H. (1993). The use and abuse of consumer credit: Application of psychological theory and research. *Journal of Economic Psychology*, 14(2), 285–316. http://doi.org/10.1016/0167-4870(93)90004-5

Verplanken, B., & Herabadi, A. (2001). Individual differences in impulse buying tendency: Feeling and no thinking. *European Journal of Personality*, 15(S1), S71–S83. http://doi.org/10.1002/per.423

Weber, E. U., Blais, A., & Betz, E. N. (2002). A domain-specific risk-attitude scale measuring risk perceptions and risk behaviors. *Journal of Behavioral Decision Making*, 15(August), 263–290. http://doi.org/10.1002/bdm.414

Xiao, J. J., Noring, F. E., & Anderson, J. G. (1995). College students' attitudes towards credit cards. *Journal of Consumer Studies & Home Economics*, 19(2), 155–174. http://doi.org/10.1111/j.1470-6431.1995.tb00540.x

Yoon, H., & Chapman, G. (2015). A closer look at the yardstick: A new discount rate measure with precision and range. *Journal of Behavioral Decision Making*. http://doi.org/10.1002/bdm

Zhang, J. W., Howell, R. T., & Bowerman, T. (2013). Validating a brief measure of the Zimbardo Time Perspective Inventory. *Time & Society*, 22(3), 391–409. http://doi.org/10.1177/0961463X12441174

FURTHER READING

Almlund, M., Duckworth, A. L. Heckman, J. J., & Kautz, T. D. (2011). Personality psychology and economics. NBER Working Paper No. 16822. Retrieved from http://www.nber.org/papers/w16822

6

Developing, Evaluating, and Using Subjective Scales of Personality, Preferences, and Well-Being: A Guide to Psychometrics for Psychologists and Economists

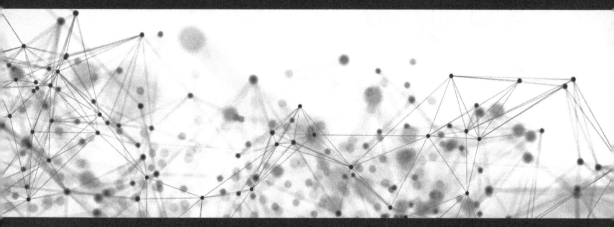

ALEX M. WOOD AND CHRISTOPHER J. BOYCE

CHAPTER OUTLINE

LEARNING OUTCOMES

BY THE END OF THIS CHAPTER YOU SHOULD BE ABLE TO:

1. Understand the importance of psychometrics for economic psychology research.
2. Understand the necessary steps involved in developing a psychometrically valid and reliable scale.
3. Be able to critically evaluate research that uses subjective scales but also to use appropriate measures in your own research.

6.1   INTRODUCTION

Subjective measures of well-being, attitudes, psychological states, and personality are increasingly being used in economic research (see Chapter 5 in this volume; Borghans, Duckworth, Heckman, & Weel, 2008; Dolan, Peasgood, & White, 2008). They have not only played an important role in overturning traditional economic models (Kahneman, Wakker, & Sarin, 1997) but they have also helped our understanding of how individuals react to changing socio-demographic circumstances (Boyce & Wood, 2011; Clark, Diener, Georgellis, & Lucas, 2008). This burgeoning economic research has introduced many advanced statistical econometric techniques to psychological research and this has helped establish important causal relationships and yield potentially important policy conclusions (O'Donnell, Deaton, Durand, Halpern, & Layard, 2014). However, the credibility of these results depends on how accurately and with what precision variables are measured (reliability) and whether the variable being measured is that which is claimed to be being measured (validity). Analogically, there would be little value to an astronomer in having a poorly calibrated telescope pointed at the right galaxy (low reliability, high validity) or a well-calibrated telescope pointed at the incorrect galaxy (high reliability, low validity).

Psychometrics, an area of psychology that has developed to specifically ensure psychological constructs are measured with optimum reliability and validity, is virtually unheard of in economics. Psychometrics is also a specialization within psychology, and there is a need for greater dissemination among psychology students who use but do not design scales. In this chapter, we therefore offer a guide to the necessary steps in developing subjective measures[1] and in doing so we hope to introduce researchers to psychometrics, enabling them to evaluate measures used by others and use appropriate measures in their own research.

6.2   THE IMPORTANCE OF PSYCHOMETRICS FOR ECONOMIC PSYCHOLOGY RESEARCH

Psychometrics as a field essentially reduces to a set of techniques designed to construct a subjectively reported instrument with optimum reliability and validity (and to test the performance of existing instruments on these two dimensions). Fifty years ago, in psychology, it would be common to use instruments in studies which had not been developed or tested according to the then poorly understood psychometric principles. However, over the last few decades it has become almost unthinkable to publish in a reputable journal a paper reporting instruments which have *not* undergone such testing. As the study of subjective constructs within economics is far newer, and there has not been dissemination of psychometric practice within economics, understandably, practice is as it was historically in psychology. A consequence of this is that there are often inappropriate or unvalidated scales contained within large panel datasets, which likely do not measure what they purport to measure, or at the very least do not do so as well as they might have done had they been developed according to psychometric principles. Further, if the importance of scale development is not fully understood, then researchers may make the mistake of confusing one measurement with another just because it 'appears' to be the same.

One informative example is that of subjective measures of well-being (see Chapter 25 in this volume). For example, life satisfaction and positive affect are often interchangeably referred to as 'happiness', and this has caused great confusion in the literature. However, life satisfaction, representing an individual's evaluation of their life overall, is very different from how an individual feels in a given moment (affect). It has been shown, for example, that life satisfaction and positive affect have different relationships with both income (Kahneman & Deaton, 2010) and unemployment (Knabe, Rätzel, Schöb, & Weimann, 2010). In developing a scale, it is therefore essential to have the right meaning of the construct represented in the items or any conclusions based on its use risk being invalid. Given the suggestion to evaluate the progress of society based on national indicators of subjective well-being alongside more traditional economic indicators, such as GDP growth (O'Donnell et al., 2014; Stiglitz, Sen, & Fitoussi, 2009), it is important to ensure we understand exactly what is being measured. While it would be unthinkable for the national policies of OECD countries to be based on economic data that could not be verified, some subjective measures being collected do not meet the most rudimentary psychometric standards.

The use of subjective measures within economics, while fast growing, is nevertheless still a fringe activity and we routinely encounter scepticism as to the appropriateness of using such measures (e.g., Johns & Ormerod, 2012). To the extent that these refer to measures that have not been psychometrically validated then we would share this scepticism. But to the extent that these criticisms refer to the practical possibility of measuring subjective constructs, they simply represent a lack of knowledge of psychometrics and the huge amount of validation that has overwhelmingly supported the reliability and validity of the most validated scales. Thus, knowledge of psychometrics allows an evidence-based response to criticism of the use of subjective measures within economics, and the widespread knowledge of psychometrics in the field would allow such criticism to be more appropriately targeted at specific uses rather than generalizations about the endeavour.

We stress that we do not mean to be overly critical of existing work within economics that use such scales (which includes our own), as at the moment there is a trade-off between collecting one's own data (as commonly used by psychologists) with optimally psychometrically defined variables, and using existing very large ($N > 5,000$) representative longitudinal datasets (as commonly used by economists). The trade-off is often currently in favour of using these large datasets with non-optimal variables. However, even within these constraints, psychometrics can be used to test the performance of the measures in these datasets (either with the information contained within, or as small supplementary validation studies) and can also help individual researchers to more accurately assess the limitations of their research. In the longer term, we hope that wider knowledge of psychometrics in economics will encourage better scales to be included in new and revised surveys.

This chapter is the first, to our knowledge, to introduce psychometrics to an economics audience. Many excellent textbooks on psychometrics do exist (e.g., Coaley, 2010) as do highly cited guides introducing psychometrics to sub-fields within psychology (e.g., Worthington & Whittaker, 2006), and excellent overviews of specific psychometric techniques (e.g., Clark & Watson, 1995; Hunsley & Meyer, 2003; Smith & McCarthy, 1995). We would recommend these references are read alongside this chapter. However, the textbooks require substantial time investment for the typical user and this chapter therefore offers a clear overview of psychometrics that will not only help economists interpret research using subjective measures but will be useful for advanced psychology students interested in economic psychology.

We organize the remainder of this chapter around designing a new scale. A common question from colleagues within economics working with subjective measures is: 'Is this a good scale?' and the best way to evaluate a scale is to ask how many of the standard steps of psychometric development have been applied to the scale and how convincing the demonstration of each step is.

6.3   STEPS IN DEVELOPING A SCALE

Table 6.1 gives examples of commonly used and well-validated psychometric measures from psychology that may be of interest to people at the interface of economics and psychology (see also Chapter 5). As should be apparent, they represent very different psychological constructs. The steps used in the development and evaluation of any such scales are, however, the same as they would be for other self-report scales, such as ones for use in marketing, business, or consumer psychology research. The basic underlying steps are outlined below and represent a toolkit that can be applied to any new problem at hand. Much of the information in this section is quite complex, and readers would not be expected to fully understand every last process described, but it is hoped that the basic message will be conveyed and the information here will act as a useful overarching guide.

Table 6.1 *Commonly used and well-validated psychometric measures assessing well-being, mental health, physical health, personality, and related constructs*

Scale	Authors and date	Number of items	What it measures
Subjective well-being			
Satisfaction with Life Scale (SWLS)	Diener, Emmons, Larsen, & Griffin (1985)	5	An individual's global overview of their life. A one-item version of this scale is typically contained in large nationally representative datasets used by economists.
Positive and Negative Affect Schedule (PANAS)	Watson, Clark, & Tellegen (1988)	20	Reflects an individual's positive and negative moods at a specific time (e.g., 'right now', 'last month'). Together with life satisfaction, this can be used to operationalize 'Subjective Well-being' (SWB) or the 'pleasantness' of an individual's life.
Psychological Well-Being (PWB)	Ryff & Keyes (1995)	Variable	Perceptions of positive relationships, personal growth, autonomy, environmental mastery, purpose in life and self-acceptance

(continued)

Table 6.1 (*Continued*)

Scale	Authors and date	Number of items	What it measures
Happiness Scale	Lyubomirsky & Lepper (1999)		Sidesteps the issue of defining happiness by simply asking participants in various ways whether they are happy, without providing a definition
Mental health			Health economists are often interested in specific mental health conditions
General Health Questionnaire (GHQ)	Goldberg & Williams (1991)	Variable	Initially designed as a general screening measure to identify participants in large datasets with probable mental health problems. Often included in large nationally representative datasets used by economists.
Centre for Epidemiologic Studies Depression (CES-D) Scale	Radloff (1977)	20	One of the most commonly used measures of depression
Patient Health Questionnaire-9 (PHQ-9)	Spitzer, Kroenke, & Williams (1999)	9	This is the best of the very short depression scales
Depression, Anxiety, and Stress Scale (DASS-21)	Ng et al. (2007)	21	Measures three common mental health concerns
Perceived Stress Scale (PSS)	Cohen (1988)	10	Assesses stress based on a conception of environmental demands exceeding coping ability
Generalised Anxiety Disorder-7 (GAD-7)	Spitzer, Kroenke, Williams, & Löwe (2006)	7	Focuses on general feelings of anxiety
Physical health			Physical health is often better rated objectively, although there are times when subjective reports of health are needed, and these are more common in large datasets
SF-36	Ware & Sherbourne (1992)	36	The most common measure of subjective health, it provides a total score and sub-scores on sub-domains of health

Scale	Authors and date	Number of items	What it measures
Physical Health Questionnaire	Schat, Kelloway, & Desmarais (2005)	14	Less commonly used, but useful in measuring the milder psychosomatic complaints (sleep disturbance, headaches, gastrointestinal problems, and respiratory infections) so may pick up non-clinical sub-optimal health
Pittsburgh Sleep Inventory	Buysse, Reynolds III, Monk, Berman, & Kupfer (1989)	19	Measures various aspects of impaired sleep
Personality			Personality is normally assessed via the Big Five
Big Five Inventory	John & Srivastava (1999)	44	One of the most respected measures of the Big Five
Mini-International Personality Item Pool (Mini-IPIP)	Donnellan, Oswald, Baird, & Lucas (2006)	20	A good measure of the Big Five that has the practical minimum of items per factor
Ten Item Personality Inventory	Gosling, Rentfrow, & Swann Jr. (2003)	10	The shortest Big Five inventory for use only where the mini-IPIP is not possible
NEO PI-R	Costa & McCrae (2008)	120–360	Comprehensively measures the Big Five and the six facets of each for a total of 30 traits
Other measures			
Perceived Social Support (PSS)	Cohen, Mermelstein, Kamarck, & Hoberman (1985)		Assesses people's perception of how much practical, emotional, and guidance support they have
Brief Cope	Carver (1997)		Assesses the habitual adaptive and maladaptive coping strategies people use to deal with stressful situations
Social Desirability Scale-17 (SDS-17)	Stöber (2001)	17	Provides a set of plausible socially desirable statements with which everyone would like to agree, but no one can. High scores indicate the person is not answering a questionnaire accurately.
Gratitude Questionnaire-6	McCullough, Emmons, & Tsang (2002)	6	Gratitude is one of the strongest predictors of well-being and an emotion that Adam Smith believed to be essential to most successful transactions (see Wood, Froh, & Geraghty, 2010)

6.3.1 Step 1: Identify the Need for the Scale

This step may appear obvious, but it is actually the step that is most likely to be omitted from subjective scale development exercises. More than 50 years of work within psychology have resulted in subjective scales for pretty much whatever one would want to measure. Indeed, in the 1980s and 1990s a relatively easy way to get a publication was to develop a new scale; hence this was taken advantage of, and scale development was often suggested to PhD students as a way to contribute to knowledge, given the resources that they typically have. The benefit of this is that there are now a huge number of useful subjective scales available. However, the cost has been that multiple scales have emerged that measure similar but not quite identical constructs, often using slightly different terms for the construct and framing in terms of different prior literature. Such a multiplicity of scales has the advantage of being able to operationalize latent constructs with multiple scales, but has the disadvantage of making it more difficult for literature reviews to make substantive conclusions – are, for example, differences between studies due to substantive factors, such as the populations studied, or are they simply due to the use of different scales? As a result of these concerns, publishing scale development papers has gone from one of the easiest 'wins' to being among the most difficult category of papers to get published. Nevertheless, this is also the category of papers that generally gets the most citations – if a scale is genuinely needed and accepted as reliable and valid, then it is likely to be highly used. It is notable that of the 100 most cited research papers of all time, the only entries from psychology are explicit scale development papers (Van Noorden, Maher, & Nuzzo, 2014). Occasionally there is a genuinely unstudied fundamental construct. Sometimes there is a need for a shorter version of a lengthy scale. In applied research, new developments in services sometimes need new scales designed to assess progress. For example, advances in genetics have created new genetic testing services, which provide such information as the likelihood of any children having the same disorder as the parent. To support individuals going through this process, new genetic counselling services emerged, and in order to inform health care management, a scale was developed to assess whether patients' needs were being met (McAllister, Wood, Dunn, Shiloh, & Todd, 2011). Even more commonly, there is a need to validate older scales that perhaps were developed before optimal practice became the norm; or, as is sadly the case for many scales in management consultancy, developed with commercial rather than scientific interests in mind. Thus, although psychometrics is still a thriving discipline, it is essential that a scale development exercise begins with a full systematic literature review to ensure that the scale does not already exist, and to locate theoretically related scales (the latter will also be needed in later steps). A proper systematic review and strong rationale in the introduction will help ensure the contribution of the scale is apparent, and adherence to the remaining steps will ensure the scale is suitably reliable and valid. See Hinshaw (2009) for a starting point of how to conduct such a review.

6.3.2 Step 2: Define the Construct and Develop Items

To begin with, a large pool of items that covers the full terrain of the construct is developed. There will commonly be around 100 items, both to ensure that as many factors as are genuinely in the data have enough items out of which to emerge, and to allow the deletion of worse performing items in the next step. A key challenge at this stage is how to map out the full terrain of the construct, and there are several ways in which this may be achieved, of varying levels of acceptability.

- *Qualitative work.* This is an example of where the mixed methods approach – almost unheard of in economics – is the most appropriate. Often it makes sense for the end user community to define the construct. Key decisions for the researcher would be the choice of community and the form of qualitative analysis. In the genetic counselling example, we asked people with the condition to describe what they wanted from their treatment. Other approaches could have been used, such as drawing the construct definition from the service, researchers, or an existing theoretical model, but this would go against the intention to have a 'patient reported outcome measure (PROM)' and it was the patients' experiences that were meant to be the point of the scale. Here it is clear that the researcher's conception is inappropriate as they are not part of that community, and the choice of participants and qualitative method (interviews) was relatively mandated. However, even in cases where the researcher is part of the community, there is benefit in using qualitative research to define the construct – not least as other approaches (such as one's intuition or previous work in the field) may not be fully inclusive of the construct. In a second example, a scale was designed to measure 'pre-sleep cognitions', the thoughts that people have while falling asleep (it was subsequently shown that positive thoughts improved sleep whereas negative thoughts impaired it, Wood, Joseph, Lloyd, & Atkins, 2009). In this step, the developers gave participants a voice-activated Dictaphone and asked them to speak aloud whatever they were thinking. Excluding the most common theme (that they could not sleep due to speaking aloud into the Dictaphone), a quite exhaustive database of thoughts was collected that formed the basis of the item pool.

- *Pre-existing complete lists.* A reason to omit the qualitative stage is if there happen to be a full list of items already developed. This is rare, but was seen in the development of the dominant 'Five Factor Model' of personality, where personality at the highest level of abstraction is represented by agreeableness, conscientiousness, extraversion, neuroticism and openness (John & Srivastava, 1999). These (and their attendant scale items) were developed through having participants rate every single adjective in the English language dictionary that described a person (excluding those that referred to skills or non-psychological differences). Hence, assuming that all words considered to describe a culturally important characteristic of a person become represented in language, this may be seen as a complete list.

- *Existing theoretical model.* This is where practice can become non-optimal. Quite commonly, researchers design items around an existing conception (that, e.g., specifies that a trait or form of well-being has three factors). This can be acceptable, as long as it is made very clear in the paper and all subsequent research that the scale is not designed to measure the construct, but rather a particular conception of it. This can be acceptable if the aim was simply to test predictions of the particular conception (e.g., we developed a measure of authenticity, to assess a conception of it arising from a particular counselling approach, to test the theories associated with that approach, Wood, Linley, Maltby, Baliousis, & Joseph, 2008). However, if the approach is correct in predicting a certain number of factors that underlie the data, then there is no real reason not to develop items that cover the whole domain; if the theory is correct, these should naturally emerge anyway. This approach to item development can be problematic as, once the scale is published, quite likely people will use it as a measure of the whole construct despite cautions not to do this in the development paper.

- *Using items from existing scales.* This is occasionally appropriate, as, for example, when shortening an existing scale or merging two existing scales (a good example of which is found in Griffiths et al., 2015). The key danger is the validity of the resultant measure is totally reliant on the (possibly poorly derived) items in the existing scales.

- *Researchers using their own conceptions.* This is totally unacceptable, as this is based solely on the opinion of a small number of researchers (statistically from very specific backgrounds). Such subjectivity should not have a part in scientific scale development.

- *Finishing the step.* At the outcome of the development phase the researchers would have developed a clear conception and a large pool of items that fully covers it. Quite how the items themselves have been written partially depends on the decisions above. Often it would have been appropriate for the item generation to be an integrative process between researchers and qualitative participants.

6.3.3   Step 3: Identify the Scale's Structure and Select Items Based on Factor Analysis

After the full item pool has been developed, the researchers should give out the item pool to a large sample of participants from the final population who will be using the scale. Once the data is collected, it will be subjected to exploratory factor analysis (EFA). EFA ideally has 450 participants, at which number the factor structures are so stable there is little point in having more. At a minimum, 150 participants are needed, although this is almost certainly too small and only justifiable if it is an exceptionally difficult-to-access population. Several excellent guides should be consulted (Fabrigar, Wegener, MacCallum, & Strahan, 1999; Floyd & Widaman, 1995). This step involves seeing how many factors naturally underlie the data. EFA as a technique essentially looks at how correlations between items naturally group together, asks how many groups there are, and which items are most representative of that group. Determining the correct number of factors is critical and is not a subjective decision; rather, techniques such as parallel analysis test whether each potential factor explains more variance than would be expected had it arisen by chance, using normal standards of significance. This (or the similar Minimal Average Partial technique) should always be used rather than older more subjective criteria (O'Connor, 2000; Velicer, Eaton, & Fava, 2000). Once it has been determined how many factors underlie the data, then the researcher is in a position to choose whether or not to have sub-scales. Again the decision in this step is not subjective; in this case the researcher would be obliged to form sub-scales to represent each substantive factor found in the data. The EFA should also be used to reduce the number of items from the large initial pool to the number required for the final scale. After deciding on how many items are needed, the final items are chosen based on the 'highest-loading' items on the EFA for each factor, corresponding to each sub-scale, that is, the items which are most representative of each. Again, this decision is not subjective; it is not up to the researcher to decide which the 'best' items are, but rather the best items are those that are statistically shown to be the most representative of the construct. Part of the rationale for having so many items originally is to allow the ones that looked sensible but did not perform well to be eliminated. Typically, four items per sub-scale are considered an optimum number. Shorter scales are more likely to be used in the field as they reduce participant burden, although there will undoubtedly be a trade-off with establishing internal consistency (see below), which is normally higher with larger scales. If the improvement in internal consistency from moving from a four-item scale to a five-item scale is trivial, this will provide justification to use the lower number. The outcome of this step is that it produces the final scale, consisting of a low number of items either as a single scale, or as series of subscales. For example, if a measure of personality were being developed, then giving out enough items to initially cover all differences between people, and conducting an EFA (which would have told you there were five factors), and then selecting the four most representative items in each factor would give a final 20-item scale with five sub-scales. The remaining steps here involve showing that this is reliable and valid, but this current step is one of the most important to get right, as in the future steps only the reduced number of items will need to be given out. Once the factor structure and items are determined, there is no going back.

6.3.4   Step 4: Confirm the Factor Structure

The next step involves giving out the scale to several new groups of participants which comprise the most likely user groups of the final scale (the same considerations on numbers apply as in the previous step). On these groups a confirmatory factor analysis (CFA) should be performed. CFA is a technique which differs from EFA in that it does not explore what factor structure is naturally in the data, but rather tests a prior conception (which here arises from your EFA). Ideally a 'multi-group CFA', a technique which shows that the factor structure is stable across your groups, will be carried out and once this is complete, other groups (such as gender and other demographics) can be assessed by combining the samples and splitting by gender. CFA will also ideally be used to test between the *a priori* factor solution and other number of factors that theory may have suggested. Once the factor structure is confirmed, the remaining steps test reliability and validity. Commonly these will use the same samples as used for the CFA (as other measures would be typically collected alongside).

6.3.5   Step 5: Test Internal Consistency (Reliability)

This step involves showing, through Cronbach's alpha, that the items within each subscale correlate as expected. This alpha is the adjusted average inter-correlation between the items, and ranges from zero to one with broadly the same interpretation as a correlation coefficient. In general, values above .80 are excellent, as they indicate equivalence, but below .70 are generally deemed unacceptable as they indicate that the items are measuring too disparate concepts. We offer some caution with interpreting Cronbach's alphas since some scales with a low number of items (three or less), which may be used to limit participant burden, can have low content overlap and therefore typically produce low Cronbach's alphas (Sijtsma, 2009).

6.3.6   Step 6: Test Temporal Stability (Reliability)

In this step the stability of the scale over time is assessed. The scale is given to participants at two time points and it needs to be shown (with the interclass coefficient) that neither the rank order nor the mean level of responses changes substantially over time (values above .80 are again excellent, as they show equivalence). The time period chosen can be tricky. They should be far enough apart to ensure that participants do not simply remember and report what they first stated, but not so far away that meaningful change may have occurred. For many variables, two or four weeks would be appropriate; often one might, with different samples, assess both time periods (as consistent results would remove both concerns above). Ideally, one might show that the scale is sensitive to change when it would be expected to (e.g., that mean levels on a new depression group reduce during psychotherapy relative to a control group who remain on the waiting list).

6.3.7   Step 7: Show Face Validity

This step simply shows that people believe that the items make sense. This should be already justified if Step 1 has been carried out correctly, but this step can be formalized by taking the final items to focus groups of end users (perhaps the same as used in Step 1) or experts. This will avoid the complaint that the items do not make sense to experts or end users later on.

6.3.8   Step 8: Show Convergent Validity

Here, it should be shown that the items correlate with other constructs that they are expected to. If there are any existing measures of the same construct, then these should be used. However, if not, previous theory should be used to determine what the appropriate constructs are. For example, when a gratitude questionnaire was developed, the authors expected it to theoretically relate to well-being and social relationships, so this formed their convergent validity. It has to be argued convincingly in the introduction which constructs were chosen and why. It is also important at this stage to argue what is the magnitude of the correlations you expected to see and show that they are within this range in the results ($r >$ .30 may be sufficient for very different constructs, $r >$ .70 may be appropriate for identical constructs).

6.3.9   Step 9: Show Discriminate Validity

The converse of the last step; this involves showing that the scale does not corre-late with what it is not meant to (this is a near zero correlation, rather than a neg-ative correlation which would be evidence of convergent validity). For example, the social desirability scales (see Table 6.1) should not correlate with the new scale. Finding other measures with which the scale should not correlate is tricky and again depends on theory, which may in some cases be present (e.g., in the development of the PANAS, see Table 6.1, there was the theoretical expectation that high activation positive and negative affect would not strongly correlate based on prior neurolog-ical findings, and their test of discriminate validity showed that this was the case). Sometimes an experiment can be conducted to show that your scale does not differ across groups (e.g., react to a mood induction, if it is not meant to capture moods); Bayesian statistical approaches can get around problems with trying to 'prove the null hypothesis' in this fashion. Again, the argument needs to be made for whatever has been chosen, and since no correlation is ever zero, how small it would have to be to have discriminant validity ($r < .10$ would be a reasonable default). Of course, how convincing the argument is makes the difference; one cannot simply call all small correlations 'divergent validity' and all large ones 'convergent validity' as this would just capitalize on chance characteristics in the dataset.

6.3.10   Step 10: Test Predictive Validity

This step is an extension of Step 8, except here you are showing that the scale can predict some future outcome. This may be changes in an outcome over time within a longitudinal design, or it could be an objective behaviour. Theoretically, Step 9 could also be extended in this way, to show that the measure does not lead to what is not meant to (although this is not seen in the literature). The next step may also be demonstrated longitudinally.

6.3.11   Step 11: Test Incremental Validity

In the first step it is argued that the measure was needed. This is directly tested in what is perhaps the most critical step. Here it is necessary to show that the scale can predict certain expected outcomes beyond existing scales. For example, if it is claimed that the new improved scale of child behaviour has been developed, then it is necessary to show (e.g., through multiple regression) that it can predict some outcome (perhaps objective behaviour) above and beyond the existing childhood behaviour scales. If it does, then this provides direct evidence that it is needed; if it does not, the evidence suggests against the need for the scale. You will have to pick your outcome with care and justify it (as any scale would not be expected to incrementally predict all out-comes) and equally the choice of what to predict needs to justify that a 'tough' test was set by controlling for the theoretically or literally competing scales and constructs. A scale would convince no one if shown to predict outcomes beyond known, but poor predictors, of that outcome (e.g., gender or income). If, however, there is success in this step, then there is empirical demonstration that the scale is a novel contribution.

6.4   OTHER STEPS AND CONCLUSION

The steps above are the practical minimum of what one needs to show for psychometric development. Depending on the scale, other steps may be appropriate. For example, where there are predictions that mean levels of the scale will differ between groups (as in between clinical and non-clinical participants on a well-being measure), this should be shown directly. An 'ROC Curve' analysis may be performed to find the optimum score on the scale to distinguish between groups. Convergence between a person rating themselves on the measure and others rating them may be appropriate. As can be seen, scale development is a complex and very detailed process. One can readily understand psychologists' dismissive attitude of scales that have not been through this. However, if a scale development has met all of these steps, one can have considerable confidence that it is accurately measuring what it claims. Greater dissemination of this knowledge within economics combined with ensuring that only scales are used which have met these steps will help resolve the controversy of using subjective measures within economics. End users of the research will have higher confidence that the research based on the use of these scales is as valid as those using traditional economic indicators.

6.5   SUMMARY

Subjective measures of well-being, attitudes, psychological states, and personality are increasingly being used in economic research. However, the credibility of the results from research relying on subjective measures depends on how accurately and with what precision variables are measured (reliability) and whether the variable being measured is that which is claimed to be being measured (validity). Psychometrics, an area of psychology that has developed to specifically ensure psychological constructs are measured with optimum reliability and validity, is virtually unheard of in economics. Here we highlight the importance of psychometrics for economic psychology research and then overview the essential components of developing psychometrically valid scales. We then provide a step-by-step account of developing a scale, thus enabling researchers not only to evaluate research that uses subjective scales but also to use appropriate measures in their own research.

NOTE

1. A note on terminology. Following conventions within psychology, subjective reports refer to a person answering questions about themselves (self-report) or others (peer-report) on some psychological characteristics (e.g., well-being, attitudes, traits, states etc.). One or (usually) more questions purporting to measure the same construct are referred to as a scale, measure, or instrument; if sub-scores are formed within a scale, these are referred to as sub-scales.

REVIEW QUESTIONS

Imagine that you were designing a scale to measure employee well-being:
1. How would you define the construct and develop the item pool?
2. How would you show reliability (considering each of the relevant steps)?
3. How would you show validity (considering each of the relevant steps)?
4. Who would you use as participants for your answers to each of the questions above?

REFERENCES

Borghans, L., Duckworth, A. L., Heckman, J. J., & ter Weel, B. (2008). The economics and psychology of personality traits. *Journal of Human Resources, 43*, 972–1059. http://doi.org/10.3368/jhr.43.4.972

Boyce, C. J., & Wood, A. M. (2011). Personality prior to disability determines adaptation: agreeable individuals recover lost life satisfaction faster and more completely. *Psychological Science, 22*, 1397–1402. http://doi.org/10.1177/0956797611421790

Buysse, D. J., Reynolds III, C. F., Monk, T. H., Berman, S. R., & Kupfer, D. J. (1989). The Pittsburgh sleep quality index: A new instrument for psychiatric practice and research. *Psychiatry Research, 28*, 193–213. http://doi.org/10.1016/0165-1781(89)90047-4

Carver, C. S. (1997). You want to measure coping but your protocol's too long: Consider the brief cope. *International Journal of Behavioral Medicine, 4*, 92–100. http://doi.org/10.1207/s15327558ijbm0401_6

Clark, A. E., Diener, E., Georgellis, Y., & Lucas, R. E. (2008). Lags and leads in life satisfaction: A test of the baseline hypothesis. *The Economic Journal, 118*, F222–F243. http://doi.org/10.1111/j.1468-0297.2008.02150.x

Clark, L. A., & Watson, D. (1995). Constructing validity: Basic issues in objective scale development. *Psychological Assessment, 7*, 309–319. http://doi.org/10.1037/1040-3590.7.3.309

Coaley, K. (2010). *An introduction to psychological assessment and psychometrics.* Los Angeles, CA: SAGE.

Cohen, S. (1988). Perceived stress in a probability sample of the United States. In S. Spacapan, & S. Oskamp (Eds.), *The social psychology of health* (pp. 31–67). Los Angeles, CA: SAGE.

Cohen, S., Mermelstein, R., Kamarck, T., & Hoberman, H. M. (1985). Measuring the functional components of social support. In I. G. Sarason, & B. R. Sarason (Eds.), *Social support: Theory, research and applications* (pp. 73–94). The Hague, The Netherlands: Springer Netherlands. Retrieved from http://link.springer.com/chapter/10.1007/978-94-009-5115-0_5

Costa, P. T. J., & McCrae, R. R. (2008). The Revised NEO Personality Inventory (NEO-PI-R). In G. J. Boyle, G. Matthews, & D. H. Saklofske (Eds.), *The SAGE handbook of personality theory and assessment: Personality measurement and testing.* Los Angeles, CA: SAGE.

Diener, E., Emmons, R. A., Larsen, R. J., & Griffin, S. (1985). The satisfaction with life scale. *Journal of Personality Assessment, 49*, 71–75. http://doi.org/10.1207/s15327752jpa4901_13

Dolan, P., Peasgood, T., & White, M. (2008). Do we really know what makes us happy? A review of the economic literature on the factors associated with subjective well-being. *Journal of Economic Psychology, 29*, 94–122. http://doi.org/10.1016/j.joep.2007.09.001

Donnellan, M. B., Oswald, F. L., Baird, B. M., & Lucas, R. E. (2006). The mini-IPIP scales: tiny-yet-effective measures of the Big Five factors of personality. *Psychological Assessment, 18*, 192–203. http://doi.org/10.1037/1040-3590.18.2.192

Fabrigar, L. R., Wegener, D. T., MacCallum, R. C., & Strahan, E. J. (1999). Evaluating the use of exploratory factor analysis in psychological research. *Psychological Methods, 4*, 272–299. http://doi.org/10.1037/1082-989X.4.3.272

Floyd, F. J., & Widaman, K. F. (1995). Factor analysis in the development and refinement of clinical assessment instruments. *Psychological Assessment*, 7, 286–299. http://doi.org/10.1037/1040-3590.7.3.286

Goldberg, D. P., & Williams, P. (1991). *A user's guide to the general health questionnaire*. Windsor, Berkshire: NFER-Nelson.

Gosling, S. D., Rentfrow, P. J., & Swann, W. B. Jr. (2003). A very brief measure of the Big-Five personality domains. *Journal of Research in Personality*, 37, 504–528. http://doi.org/10.1016/S0092-6566(03)00046-1

Griffiths, A. W., Wood, A. M., Maltby, J., Taylor, P. J., Panagioti, M., & Tai, S. (2015). The development of the Short Defeat and Entrapment Scale (SDES). *Psychological Assessment*, 27, 1182–1194. http://doi.org/10.1037/pas0000110

Hinshaw, S. P. (2009). For over a century, *Psychological Bulletin* has been the leading source of systematic review articles for the entire discipline of psychology: Editorial. *Psychological Bulletin*, 135, 511–515. http://doi.org/10.1037/a0014869

Hunsley, J., & Meyer, G. J. (2003). The incremental validity of psychological testing and assessment: Conceptual, methodological, and statistical issues. *Psychological Assessment*, 15, 446–455. http://doi.org/10.1037/1040-3590.15.4.446

John, O. P. (1990). The 'Big Five' factor taxonomy: Dimensions of personality in the natural language and questionnaires. In L. A. Pervin (Ed.), *Handbook of personality: Theory and research* (pp. 66–100). New York: Guilford Press.

John, O. P., & Srivastava, S. (1999). The Big Five trait taxonomy: History, measurement, and theoretical perspectives. In L. A. Pervin, & O. P. John (Eds.), *Handbook of personality: Theory and research* (2nd ed., pp. 102–138). New York: Guilford Press.

Johns, H., & Ormerod, P. (2012). *Happiness, economics and public policy*. London: Institute of Economic Affairs.

Kahneman, D., & Deaton, A. (2010). High income improves evaluation of life but not emotional well-being. *Proceedings of the National Academy of Sciences*, 107, 16489–16493. http://doi.org/10.1073/pnas.1011492107

Kahneman, D., Wakker, P. P., & Sarin, R. (1997). Back to Bentham? Explorations of experienced utility. *The Quarterly Journal of Economics*, 112, 375–406. http://doi.org/10.1162/003355397555235

Knabe, A., Rätzel, S., Schöb, R., & Weimann, J. (2010). Dissatisfied with life but having a good day: Time-use and well-being of the unemployed. *The Economic Journal*, 120, 867–889. http://doi.org/10.1111/j.1468-0297.2009.02347.x

Lyubomirsky, S., & Lepper, H. S. (1999). A measure of subjective happiness: Preliminary reliability and construct validation. *Social Indicators Research*, 46, 137–155. http://doi.org/10.1023/A:1006824100041

McAllister, M., Wood, A. M., Dunn, G., Shiloh, S., & Todd, C. (2011). The Genetic Counseling Outcome Scale: A new patient-reported outcome measure for clinical genetics services. *Clinical Genetics*, 79, 413–424. http://doi.org/10.1111/j.1399-0004.2011.01636.x

McCullough, M. E., Emmons, R. A., & Tsang, J.-A. (2002). The grateful disposition: A conceptual and empirical topography. *Journal of Personality and Social Psychology*, 82, 112–127. http://doi.org/10.1037/0022-3514.82.1.112

Ng, F., Trauer, T., Dodd, S., Callaly, T., Campbell, S., & Berk, M. (2007). The validity of the 21-item version of the Depression Anxiety Stress Scales as a routine clinical outcome measure. *Acta Neuropsychiatrica*, 19, 304–310. http://doi.org/10.1111/j.1601-5215.2007.00217.x

O'Connor, B. P. (2000). SPSS and SAS programs for determining the number of components using parallel analysis and Velicer's MAP test. *Behavior Research Methods, Instruments, & Computers*, 32, 396–402. http://doi.org/10.3758/BF03200807

O'Donnell, G., Deaton, A., Durand, M., Halpern, D., & Layard, R. (2014). *Wellbeing and policy*. London: Legatum Institute.

Radloff, L. S. (1977). The CES-D scale a self-report depression scale for research in the general population. *Applied Psychological Measurement*, 1, 385–401. http://doi.org/10.1177/014662167700100306

Ryff, C. D., & Keyes, C. L. M. (1995). The structure of psychological well-being revisited. *Journal of Personality and Social Psychology*, 69, 719–727. http://doi.org/10.1037/0022-3514.69.4.719

Schat, A. C., Kelloway, K. E., & Desmarais, S. (2005). The Physical Health Questionnaire (PHQ): Construct validation of a self-report scale of somatic symptoms. *Journal of Occupational Health Psychology, 10,* 363–381. http://doi.org/10.1037/1076-8998.10.4.363

Sijtsma, K. (2009). On the use, the misuse, and the very limited usefulness of Cronbach's alpha. *Psychometrika, 74,* 107–120. http://doi.org/10.1007/s11336-008-9101-0

Smith, G. T., & McCarthy, D. M. (1995). Methodological considerations in the refinement of clinical assessment instruments. *Psychological Assessment, 7,* 300–308. http://doi.org/10.1037/1040-3590.7.3.300

Spitzer, R. L., Kroenke, K., & Williams, J. B. (1999). Validation and utility of a self-report version of PRIME-MD: The PHQ primary care study. Primary Care Evaluation of Mental Disorders. Patient Health Questionnaire. *JAMA, 282,* 1737–1744.

Spitzer, R. L., Kroenke, K., Williams, J. B., & Löwe, B. (2006). A brief measure for assessing generalized anxiety disorder: The GAD-7. *Archives of Internal Medicine, 166,* 1092–1097. http://doi.org/10.1001/archinte.166.10.1092

Stiglitz, J., Sen, A., & Fitoussi, J.-P. (2009). The measurement of economic performance and social progress revisited. Documents de Travail de l'OFCE No. 2009–33. Paris, France: Observatoire Français des Conjonctures Economiques (OFCE). Retrieved from http://econpapers.repec.org/paper/fcedoctra/0933.htm

Stöber, J. (2001). The Social Desirability Scale-17 (SDS-17): Convergent validity, discriminant validity, and relationship with age. *European Journal of Psychological Assessment, 17,* 222–232. http://doi.org/10.1027//1015-5759.17.3.222

Van Noorden, R., Maher, B., & Nuzzo, R. (2014). The top 100 papers. *Nature, 514,* 550–553. http://doi.org/10.1038/514550a

Velicer, W. F., Eaton, C. A., & Fava, J. L. (2000). Construct explication through factor or component analysis: A review and evaluation of alternative procedures for determining the number of factors or components. In R. D. Goffin, & E. Helmes (Eds.), *Problems and solutions in human assessment* (pp. 41–71). New York: Springer US. Retrieved from http://link.springer.com/chapter/10.1007/978-1-4615-4397-8_3

Ware, J. E., Jr., & Sherbourne, C. D. (1992). The MOS 36-item short-form health survey (SF-36): I. Conceptual framework and item selection. *Medical Care, 30,* 473–483.

Watson, D., Clark, L. A., & Tellegen, A. (1988). Development and validation of brief measures of positive and negative affect: The PANAS scales. *Journal of Personality and Social Psychology, 54,* 1063–1070. http://doi.org/10.1037/0022-3514.54.6.1063

Wood, A. M., Froh, J. J., & Geraghty, A. W. A. (2010). Gratitude and well-being: A review and theoretical integration. *Clinical Psychology Review, 30,* 890–905. http://doi.org/10.1016/j.cpr.2010.03.005

Wood, A. M., Joseph, S., Lloyd, J., & Atkins, S. (2009). Gratitude influences sleep through the mechanism of pre-sleep cognitions. *Journal of Psychosomatic Research, 66,* 43–48. http://doi.org/10.1016/j.jpsychores.2008.09.002

Wood, A. M., Linley, A. P., Maltby, J., Baliousis, M., & Joseph, S. (2008). The authentic personality: A theoretical and empirical conceptualization and the development of the Authenticity Scale. *Journal of Counseling Psychology, 55,* 385–399. http://doi.org/10.1037/0022-0167.55.3.385

Worthington, R. L., & Whittaker, T. A. (2006). Scale development research. A content analysis and recommendations for best practices. *The Counseling Psychologist, 34,* 806–838. http://doi.org/10.1177/0011000006288127

FURTHER READING

Coaley, K. (2010). *An introduction to psychological assessment and psychometrics.* Los Angeles, CA: SAGE.

Worthington, R. L., & Whittaker, T. A. (2006). Scale development research. A content analysis and recommendations for best practices. *The Counseling Psychologist, 34,* 806–838. http://doi.org/10.1177/0011000006288127

PART 3

Economic Mental Representations

7 The Psychological Meaning of Money

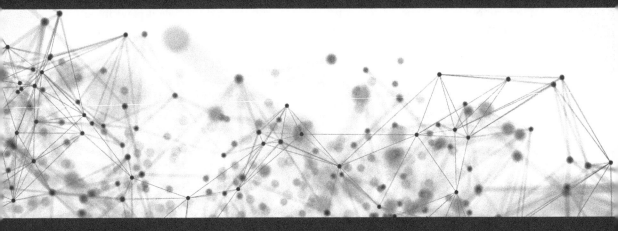

TOMASZ ZALESKIEWICZ, AGATA GASIOROWSKA
AND KATHLEEN D. VOHS

CHAPTER OUTLINE

LEARNING OUTCOMES

BY THE END OF THIS CHAPTER YOU SHOULD BE ABLE TO:

1. Understand and describe the differences between economic and psychological perspectives on money.
2. Discuss the psychological consequences of money for self-regulation and social relations.
3. Give examples of studies that used the money-priming method to investigate the psychological consequences of money.

7.1   INTRODUCTION

The aim of this chapter is to demonstrate the psychological consequences of money. The chapter begins by explaining how the disciplines of economics and psychology differ in how they define the main functions of money and the role it plays in people's lives. We argue that the invention of money several thousand years ago changed the system of trade (by replacing barter), as well as affected processes related to social interactions. Following this line of reasoning are three predictions: (1) money increases people's focus on self and their own goals; (2) money impairs warm, caring social behaviour; and (3) money alters morals and values. We explain how the technique of money priming has been used to test these hypotheses. Finally, we review empirical research conducted to test the above predictions.

7.2   MONEY: ECONOMIC AND PSYCHOLOGICAL PERSPECTIVES

Money is a concept that many people spontaneously associate with economics or finance. From an economic point of view, money is a universal, instrumental, and market-driven force defined by the functions it provides. Money serves as a medium of exchange, a way to store wealth and value, a means of evaluation, and a method of figuring out the value of goods and services (Begg, Fischer, & Dornbusch, 2005). In this sense, the main economic functions of money are purely instrumental; money expresses the value of products (material and immaterial) and is inextricably involved in trade. In other words, from an economic point of view, money cannot become the end in itself. The question arises, though, whether this approach to money sufficiently explains the role it plays in people's lives. Several theories from both psychology (Lea & Webley, 2006) and sociology (Belk & Wallendorf, 1990; Zelizer, 1994) suggest that money, in addition to its economic functions, also has emotional and social meanings. For example, money can evoke positive and negative feelings (Furnham, 2014; Tang, 1992), activate innate proclivities and motivations (Lea & Webley, 2006), compensate for self-esteem (Zhang, 2009), and change the norms within interpersonal relations (Vohs, Mead, & Goode, 2008; Zaleskiewicz & Gasiorowska, 2017). In the present chapter, we show how psychological research complements an economic approach to money, and review research on the consequences of money for both intra- and interpersonal regulation.

In the contemporary world, people have become used to the presence of money. Most of us probably cannot even imagine a world without credit cards or cash. However, from an historical perspective, money is quite a recent instrument; it was invented only about 3000 years ago (Martin, 2014; Weatherford, 1998). Barter – the system of trade, in which goods or services are directly exchanged for other goods or services – preceded the invention of money. It should be noted that differences between barter and money-based trade are not only formal but also psychological. The former system requires both parties to agree on what is fair and to calculate the value of one product in terms of the quantity of the other (Morgan, 1969). To make the process of trade effective and possible, people must recognize each other's needs first, and agree that what the other party offers is exactly what they desire. Before the innovation of money, this requirement (called a 'double coincidence of wants'; Ostroy & Starr, 1990) was likely frustrating and time-consuming. The invention of money solved many drawbacks and limitations of barter.

Possessing money allows people to get goods and services they need – for example, food, clothing and accommodation – from complete strangers without the need to engage in close social interactions. Money ushered in a new social dimension of mutually beneficial relationships with strangers. Consequently, those who have money may focus on their own desires, needs, and goals instead of deliberating on what others would find attractive or useful, as was the case in the barter-based trading system.

7.3 PREDICTIONS

Based on the above argument, we propose three predictions concerning the psychological consequences of money: (1) money promotes a focus on the self; (2) money impairs communal relationships; and (3) money alters personal values. In Sections 7.3.1–7.3.3., we elaborate on the origins of these predictions and then present experimental evidence on the three psychological consequences of money.

7.3.1 Prediction 1: Money Activates Focus on the Self, One's Own Goals and Agency

Baumeister and Vohs (2015) propose 'the idea of money is to activate thoughts along the lines of *getting what I want*' (p. 3). Based on experimental research that used the technique of money priming (see Section 7.4), Vohs, Mead and Goode (2006, 2008) introduced the self-sufficiency hypothesis. 'Self-sufficiency is defined as an emphasis on behaviours of one's own choosing accomplished without active involvement from others. Being in a self-sufficient state would mean being hesitant to allow others to involve the self in their activities' (Vohs et al., 2008, p. 209). A self-sufficient state of mind resulting from being reminded of money is associated with agentic goal pursuit and reduced focus on interpersonal liking or empathetic reactions (see also Ma-Kellams & Blascovich, 2013). If money makes people more individualistically oriented, it should have a negative impact on the quality of their social relations, consistent with the self-sufficiency hypothesis. This leads to the second prediction.

7.3.2 Prediction 2: Money Impairs Communal Relations

Broadly speaking, people can fulfil their needs in two different ways: either by establishing communal relationships or by trading with outgroup members (Clark & Mills, 1993; Fiske, 1992; Zaleskiewicz & Gasiorowska, 2017). Non-contingent helping is arguably the *sine qua non* of communal relationships. People in a communal mode find it natural to be helpful, altruistic, and generous, with friendships and family relations exemplifying such relationships (Clark & Mills, 1993). Conversely, when people engage in exchange relationships, they care about how much they get out of their investment and whether the repayment is of a comparable value. Exchange relationships often involve money because it is an easy means of calculating and expressing value. Research has shown that introducing monetary payments to communal relationships changes them into market-like exchanges or at least impairs attitudes and behaviours that are characteristic of relationships based on communal norms (Ariely, Bracha, & Meier, 2009; Gneezy & Rustichini, 2000; Heyman & Ariely, 2004). For example, Ma-Kellams and Blascovich (2013) found that participants paid with money demonstrated worse performance in detecting other people's emotions than participants in a neutral condition (without monetary payment). In Section 7.3.3, we will show that it is not necessary to implement financial payments to observe how money impairs communal relations. Changing the state of mind by activating the concept of money is enough to move people to dispense with empathetic connection to others and to be less socially oriented.

The two predictions introduced so far suggest that money highlights the self and downplays empathetic relations with others. The combination of these assumptions implies that money affects social norms and values, which is the final prediction.

7.3.3   Prediction 3: Money Alters Values, Ethics and Morals

Money aids both individuals and societies. However, if money stimulates a focus on individual demands, it might motivate people to pursue self-interest and usurp more than is fair. This point of view is consistent with the common correlation of money with greed and selfishness and, more generally, with weakened moral sentiments. When people think about money, they can be driven to engage in immoral behaviour, such as cheating, to get more resources. Ethics is rooted in social relations and to the extent that money weakens communal bonds, the presence of money could decrease the importance of morality (Kouchaki, Smith-Crowe, Brief, & Sousa, 2013).

In contrast to the idea that money impairs ethicality is the notion that the socio-economic system only works if people override unethical desires and follow moral rules. In short, humans benefit from engaging in fair and reciprocal trade (with money). Mutually beneficial, cooperative transactions with people from outside of one's in-group were the catalyst to humanity's success (Fukuyama, 2011). Hence money might also evoke notions of honesty and fairness.

These two lines of reasoning suggest that on a psychological level, money can produce a tension between taking more than is fair and upholding codes of fairness, honesty, and trust (Baumeister & Vohs, 2015). Experiments indicate that, depending on the context, the idea of money can stimulate ethical or unethical behaviour (Yang et al., 2013).

Later in this chapter, we will review studies that were carried out to test the above predictions. However, before we turn to reviewing empirical evidence, we will introduce and explain the money-priming technique that has been widely used by researchers from many countries and cultures to study psychological consequences of money in both adults and children.

7.4 THE METHOD OF MONEY PRIMING: AKIN TO GETTING A TASTE OF BIG MONEY

Most of the research on psychological consequences of money has used an experimental technique called money priming. Priming is defined as the unconscious activation of social knowledge structures or mental representations related to specific ideas, objects, or concepts used as primes (Bargh, 2006). In experiments using money priming, participants are visually or verbally reminded of either money or other objects — but they do not have to deal with gains or losses, and sometimes do not have contact with real, physical money. It is typical of these studies not to directly refer to money in the instructions presented to participants, and participants often are not paid or rewarded based on their performance. Using such a procedure allows the inference that people did not change their behaviour or preferences because they wanted to receive a desired monetary reward, but instead because certain mental representations or knowledge structures related to money had been made salient. As in other experiments based on priming procedures, participants should not be aware that the first task (involving money or control concepts) is linked to the next task (devoted to measuring dependent variable), nor should they realize that the first task had any effect on their subsequent decisions, behaviours, or preferences.

How can the concept of money be primed? Usually participants are instructed to solve word tasks related to money or to perform irrelevant tasks while in close proximity to banknotes, pictures, or animations of coins and notes (Caruso, Vohs, Baxter, & Waytz, 2013; Mogilner, 2010; Vohs et al., 2006). Sometimes, participants imagine that they possess a large amount of money (Briers, Pandelaere, Dewitte, & Warlop, 2006; Vohs et al., 2006) or touch, sort, or count piles of notes or coins (Zaleskiewicz, Gasiorowska, Kesebir, Luszczynska, & Pyszczynski, 2013; Zhou, Vohs, & Baumeister, 2009).

Carefully designed and conducted experimentation using money priming requires choosing an adequate method of priming and, ideally, a manipulation check to ensure that the priming was effective. The most common method used to assess whether the money prime activated the concept of money (relative to the control prime) is a word-stem completion task, a standard implicit measure of cognitive activation (Roediger, Weldon, Stadler, & Riegler, 1992). In such a task, participants receive a set of word-stem items, some of which could be completed as both money-related and non-money-related words (e.g., CO_ _ could be coin, cord or coal). The money-priming procedure is considered effective if the participants exposed to money use a significantly higher number of money-related words to complete the task than those exposed to control concepts (Boucher & Kofos, 2012; Vohs et al., 2006).

To summarize, even subtle money primes can change people's behaviour, decisions and preferences. The effects of money priming have been replicated in independent laboratories in many countries around the world, including Europe, Asia and North America (see Vohs, 2015, for a review). The consistency across countries and continents suggests that these effects are robust in a cross-cultural sense. Moreover, these effects have been observed not only in adults, but also in adolescents (Roberts & Roberts, 2012) and very young children (Gasiorowska, Zaleskiewicz, & Wygrab, 2012; Gasiorowska, Chaplin, Zaleskiewicz, Wygrab, & Vohs, 2016).

7.5   RESULTS

This section reviews results of experiments that were conducted to test predictions presented in Section 7.3. First, we show how money enhances agency. Second, we review studies demonstrating the impact of money on social relationships. Finally, studies revealing how money alters values, ethics and morals are presented.

7.5.1   Result 1: Money Enhances Agency

Recent studies using the money-priming paradigm have shown that money is related to agency, goals and autonomy. First, money enhances agency, making people believe that they can achieve their goals and enhancing their persistence in reaching those goals. For example, money-primed participants, compared to those from a neutral control group, reported greater feelings of self-efficacy (Mukherjee, Manjaly, & Nargundkar, 2013), declared that they felt personally stronger (Gasiorowska, 2014; Zhou et al., 2009), and more agentic (Gasiorowska, 2014). These findings suggest that the concept of money is closely related to the idea of expertise, and indeed priming the concept of money can boost perceptions of agency and competence ascribed to the self and others (Aaker, Vohs, & Mogilner, 2010; Gasiorowska, 2014). Second, money not only makes people feel strong and agentic, but makes them more concentrated on hard work. In a study conducted by Mogilner (2010), diners at a cafe spent more time working at their laptops if they had been primed with money than if they had not. In one of the first experiments using the money-priming paradigm, people reminded of money chose to take on more work themselves even when they had an opportunity to work with others, and worked longer on a challenging and unsolvable task even when they could ask for help (Vohs et al., 2006). Third, as persistence in unsolvable tasks is frequently used as a measure of self-regulation, it is not surprising that money priming increases self-control, which is an important feature of the agentic self. In two studies combining money primes with ego depletion, Boucher and Kofos (2012) have shown that participants who exerted self-control and were then primed with money performed better on the following tasks requiring self-control than those not primed with money after ego depletion. Moreover, using a mediation analysis they demonstrated that money-primed participants were no more motivated during the second self-control task, but did think that the task was less difficult and required less effort (Boucher & Kofos, 2012). Sarial-Abi and Vohs (2012, 2013) demonstrated that reminders of money stimulate motivation, but only when goal pursuit cues are present. These authors showed that it did not matter whether the goal was related to hard work and effort, as in the case of financial, health, or performance issues, or was related to enjoyment.

Our studies (Gasiorowska et al., 2016) demonstrated that effects concerning money and agency can be observed in young children between the ages of 4 and 6, who at this age have a limited understanding of the economic functions of money. In one experiment, children who had been instructed to handle coins as opposed to paper discs persisted longer on an extremely difficult jigsaw puzzle before they gave up. In another study, children who had been exposed to money worked harder on a difficult labyrinth task than other children, and achieved better outcomes, showing a higher level of agency than participants not primed with money (Gasiorowska et al., 2016).

Another stream of research on the psychological consequences of money revealed that money is strongly related to self-focus, feelings of autonomy, and freedom. In one of our studies, participants were asked to perform a task either related or unrelated to money, and then watch one of two versions of an advertisement presenting a sophisticated hi-fi product, one that used self-related arguments ('Only you and the sound that surrounds you' or 'This is the time for you and the music') and the other that used other-related arguments ('You and your friends enjoy the music and dance', 'This is the time for being together'). It was found that people who were primed with money perceived the advertisement that used arguments related to the independent self as more effective and would pay a higher price for the product than for the condition in which the ad's arguments related to the interdependent self. For people not primed with money the reverse pattern of results was observed (Gasiorowska, 2014). Similar results were found by Reutner and Wänke (2013), who discovered that money-primed people, compared to neutral controls, were more likely to follow recommendations framed in terms of costs and benefits to the self that were used in social campaigns for reducing meat eating or arguing against smoking cigarettes. People primed with money were also less prone to follow recommendations framed in terms of costs and benefits to others.

When the concept of money is salient, self-related arguments are convincing likely because money causes people to be focused on personal advancement and their own needs and benefits rather than on the needs or benefits of others. In other words, money causes people to construe themselves in a more independent rather than interdependent manner. Indeed, in another study, we directly demonstrated that money can change self-construal; participants in a money prime condition saw themselves in a more independent manner and slightly less interdependent manner than those in the neutral control condition (Gasiorowska, 2014). Moreover, a study conducted by Mogilner and Aaker (2009) showed that people primed with money used more first-person pronouns, thus referring to their individual selves more, than those exposed to neutral primes.

The focus on self that is triggered by money might be so strong that it impairs the propensity to take the perspective of others. For example, Caruso et al. (2009) asked their participants to draw a $ symbol (money-related) or an S symbol (a similar symbol not related to money) on a card placed on their forehead while the experimenter stood across from them. This task is a commonly used assessment of egocentrism, as it measures whether people draw the orientation of the symbol so that the experimenter observer can read it clearly or whether they draw it so that they could see it clearly if they were standing behind themselves. Caruso et al. found that a greater proportion of people who had first been primed with money drew the $ symbol egocentrically, as though they would read it themselves. These authors suggested that money led to ignoring the perspective of others, because people reminded of money were less willing to correct their egocentric viewpoint and hence adopt the visual perspective of others. In other words, money seems to increase egocentrism – the fundamental tendency to interpret the world in terms of the self and to neglect other dimensions of social life.

Summing up, we argue that money is a cue to agency, hard work, goal attainment, self-focus, and egocentrism. These findings might mean that money restrains behaviours typical for or required in communal relations, such as a focus on others or the adoption of other-oriented goals. Next, we review research showing the other side of psychological consequences of money; money has the power to hinder communal relations.

7.5.2   Result 2: Money Impairs Communal Behaviours

Money allows people to acquire what they need and want while minimizing the need to get along with others (Zhou et al., 2009). From a psychological point of view, money is associated with independence and autonomy to such a strong extent that it might impair communal behaviours, for example being generous towards or taking the perspective of others. Indeed, this is what we might find in studies conducted in the money-priming paradigm. For example, participants exposed to money (in comparison to those exposed to other concepts) were less likely to volunteer their time to others in need (Chatterjee, Rose, & Sinha 2013; Pfeffer & DeVoe, 2009) and to help either the experimenter or the other participant, both in a laboratory setting (Vohs et al., 2006, 2008) and in field studies (Guéguen & Jacob, 2013). The reduced willingness to help caused by exposure to money appears strong; it has been observed not only when participants were supposed to help a stranger, but also when the person who needed help was their partner in a romantic relationship (Mead, Vohs, Savini, Stillman, & Baumeister, 2010). Moreover, our recent research has shown that even young children, aged 3–6, whom we had instructed to handle money, were less helpful to the experimenter and their peers than children who had performed similar tasks with non-monetary objects (Gasiorowska et al., 2012; Gasiorowska et al., 2016).

Reminding people of money also affects generosity, operationalized as the willingness to share resources with non-kin. For example, money primes decreased proneness to donate to charities (Chatterjee et al., 2013; Roberts & Roberts, 2012; Vohs et al., 2006), generosity in a dictator game (Gasiorowska & Helka, 2012), and the willingness to spend money on gifts for relatives or friends (Gasiorowska, 2013). Moreover, we found diminished generosity after exposure to money among very young children: pre-schoolers reminded of money kept more stickers for themselves instead of sharing them with another child more so than pre-schoolers not reminded of money (Gasiorowska et al., 2012, Gasiorowska et al., 2016).

Further research also showed subtle effects of money priming on communal-related behaviours. For example, reminders of money led to committing more errors when recalling information about another person, and to the conviction that the beliefs of other people are much more similar to participants' own opinions (Caruso et al., 2009). Participants reminded of money (compared to neutral controls) were less prone to use communal self-presentation strategies when meeting a new acquaintance – behaviour that is essential for a potential long-term relationship. They behaved in a less likeable and less friendly fashion when interacting with conversation partners, and thus were less effective at making a good impression (Mead & Baumeister, 2009). In other studies, adults and children reminded of money preferred to keep their (physical) distance from others, and spend time alone rather than with others (Park, Gasiorowska, & Vohs, 2015; Vohs et al., 2006).

As already mentioned in Section 7.1, reminders of money might alter feelings of compassion and warmth towards others. Research supports this notion. Counting money instead of paper significantly reduced the suffering induced by social rejection (Zhou et al., 2009). Other studies showed that money cues cause individuals to view themselves in a less relational manner, impairing their compassion and empathy. Activating the concept of money reduced people's compassion and lowered the feelings of empathy for others in need, such as a homeless person and an alleged terrorist who was being starved (Caruso et al., 2013) and customers who lost money due to advice from one's own employer (van Laer, de Ruyter, & Cox, 2013). In a different study, the effect of money primes on reduced compassion was mediated by lowered feelings of empathy and heightened perceptions that it is unprofessional to express emotions (Molinsky, Grant, & Margolis, 2012). These results showed that money might lead to indifference to other people, mostly because the self-focus and autonomy that arise after money priming contradict caring about others. As suggested by Reutner, Hansen and Greifeneder (2015), money causes cold-hearted behaviour.

Why are people who are reminded of money relatively less social? One idea is that money directly impairs interpersonal harmony and hinders communal relationships. Another idea is that the psychological effect of money is the salience of a market mode way of behaving (Gasiorowska et al., 2016; Vohs et al., 2008; Zaleskiewicz & Gasiorowska, 2017), and that diminished helpfulness, generosity, and empathy are by-products of that mentality. For example, because money primes increase perceived agency and competence assigned to self and to others (Aaker et al., 2010; Gasiorowska, 2014), they reduce helpfulness not due to antisocial tendencies, but because others are seen as being able to cope by themselves. Put simply, people reminded of money might perceive both themselves and others as being self-focused and self-sufficient.

So far, we have demonstrated that money cues enhance feelings of agency and impair communal relationships. One might expect that the combination of these two effects would cause people to focus on their own goals to such a degree that they could feel justified to violate ethical norms to fulfil their desires. Empirical evidence will be reviewed in the next paragraph that will partly confirm this assumption. However, it will also suggest that exposure to money might strengthen the motivation to respect the rules of fairness and reciprocity.

7.5.3   Result 3: Money Alters Values, Ethics and Morals

People often associate money with greed, distrust, selfishness, suspiciousness, or evil (Baumeister & Vohs, 2015; Furnham, 2014; Tang, 1992; Yang et al., 2013; Wernimont & Fitzpatrick, 1972). Proverbs show the dark side of money, for example, 'Too much prosperity makes most men fools' or 'When money speaks, the truth keeps silent.' In other words, people seem to draw a clear line between the world of the profane, which is related to money and the world of the sacred, which is not related to money ('You cannot serve God and Mammon' (Matthew 6:24)). One of the most cited verses of the Bible proclaims, 'The love of money is a root of all kinds of evil ...' (1 Timothy 6:10).

Yet, it ought to be clear that people use money on a daily basis and experience its brighter side. Hence money is likely also associated with positive values.

Money facilitates trade and improves the quality of life. In this sense, it propels self-sufficiency and effectiveness and supports sentiments such as fairness or reciprocity (Baumeister & Vohs, 2015). It seems, therefore, that money might activate different sorts of values, both negative and positive. Empirical evidence from studies using the money-priming technique seems to confirm this claim. Later in this section, we review results that indicate that exposure to money can alter values and ethics.

Several authors directly tested the idea that money primes (or wealth primes) promote unethical activities. Kouchaki et al. (2013) compared people exposed to money to those in a neutral control condition and found that the former expressed stronger intention to behave in an unethical way as well as engaged in more immoral behaviour. First, participants were presented with several dilemmas (e.g., whether to steal copy paper from a university office) and indicated the likelihood of them performing the unethical behaviour. People primed with money (compared to controls) declared that they were more likely to behave in an unethical way. Second, participants played a game, in which they could earn more money if they decided to lie to another person than if they did not lie. The authors found that activating the concept of money caused twice as much lying as the control condition. Finally, participants imagined that they worked as managers and could hire a candidate who offered to provide confidential information (i.e., made an unethical proposal). Results showed that participants in the money condition reported that they would be more likely to hire a dishonest job candidate than controls. Altogether, Kouchaki et al. showed that exposure to money is associated with unethical outcomes, which suggests that money might trigger the dark side of human nature.

Other researchers have found similar results. Piff, Stancato, Côte, Mendoza-Denton, and Keltner (2012) have suggested that wealth might be associated with people's engagement in acts that are questionable from an ethical point of view. They showed, using both laboratory and naturalistic methods, that higher social class predicts increased unethical behaviour. Two independent field studies revealed that upper-class individuals (compared to lower-class individuals) were more likely to break the law while driving. For example, people driving higher-status vehicles through a busy four-way intersection with stop signs on all sides more often cut off other vehicles and were more likely to drive through the crosswalk without yielding to the waiting pedestrian. Results from the laboratory confirmed field observations; social class positively predicted unethical decision-making, unethical behaviour at work, cheating to increase one's chances of winning a prize, and lying in negotiations (Piff et al., 2012). Other studies examining the role of socio-economic status in social relationships showed that women possessing personal income more often reported thoughts about divorce while higher-status individuals were less likely to spend time with their children (for a review, see Mead & Stuppy, 2014).

Experiments using a wealth-priming technique revealed quite similar results. In a series of studies conducted by Gino and Pierce (2009), participants were first presented with stimuli related to either wealth (large amounts of money placed in front of them) or small amount of money (only the cash necessary to pay participants placed in front of them), and then engaged in different tasks to gain a financial reward. As a result, participants primed with wealth displayed more frequent cheating compared to controls. For example, they overstated their performance in an anagram task to earn more money. In the wealth condition, not only did more people cheat (higher percentage of cheaters) but people cheated more (higher number of overstatements).

So far, we have reviewed studies revealing that money and wealth have a negative impact on people's intentions and behaviours. Merely activating the concept of money (or the concept of wealth) increases the probability of unethical choices and engagement in immoral acts. Yet, as mentioned at the beginning of this section, money reminders might also trigger values related to positive reciprocity, trust, and fairness. Two contradictory psychological consequences of exposure to money have been shown by Yang and colleagues (2013) in their experiments on clean versus dirty money. These authors considered:

> Clean money presumably comes straight from the government treasury or bank, and these institutions embody laws and fair economic behaviour. This could activate the associated inclinations to act fairly. In contrast, dirty money may have a chequered past, such as being handled recently by shady characters whose hands were dirty because of dirty deeds. Such thoughts could activate a dirty self and inclinations to pursue selfish goals while disregarding moral scruples.
>
> (Yang et al., 2013, p. 474)

On the basis of this argumentation, they hypothesized that clean money (freshly printed bank notes) would activate associations with fair, reciprocating economic behaviour and the need to obey ethical norms. In contrast, dirty money (circulated money that had been buried in a bag of mud for several days) would activate associations of greed, exploitation, and the tendency to treat others unfairly or with the violation of moral rules. These expectations were confirmed in a series of both field studies and laboratory experiments (various behavioural economics games).

Results of games played in a laboratory revealed that people reminded of clean money (compared to those reminded of dirty money) cooperated more in a prisoner's dilemma game and divided money more fairly in a game that involved allocating money between oneself and an anonymous person. Participants were also more likely to reject unfair offers in an ultimatum game in which participants have to decide whether to accept an offer from another player or to reject it (in which case, nobody gets anything). In contrast, people whose first task involved handling or thinking about dirty money demonstrated more greed and selfishness in their choices (Yang et al., 2013).

Field study conducted by the same group of researchers (Yang et al., 2013) confirmed outcomes found in a laboratory environment. It appeared that vendors who had handled dirty money as opposed to freshly printed money were more likely to cheat customers on a subsequent transaction by giving customers less than the quantity for which they paid.

Results collected in this section have shown that being exposed to money might have two distinct effects on people's ethical considerations. On one hand, and in line with common belief, money and wealth trigger greed, selfishness and the preparedness to violate moral norms. On the other hand, money stimulates thinking about social reality in terms of fairness and positive reciprocity. Such ambiguity opens a new, intriguing stream of future research into how money alters the values and ethics that are important in the contemporary free-market society.

7.6   SUMMARY

Economics and consumer sciences typically consider money as a universal force that allows people to buy and possess goods. However, evidence from psychology and sociology suggests that the meaning of money goes far beyond its economic and instrumental functions. The aim of this chapter was to show that money might influence people's intentions and behaviour even if their actions have no monetary consequences.

The invention of money changed the system of trade but also had an impact on social relations. It allowed people to interact with out-group members and to form exchange relationships with strangers. In this sense, the appearance of money in the history of human kind has had important psychological consequences. Those who have money may focus on their own desires, needs, and goals instead of considering what others would find attractive or useful, as was the case in the barter-based trading system. For that reason, we predicted that money is strongly connected to self-focus and thus changes intrapersonal and interpersonal processes; it triggers agency, hampers sociability, and alters values, ethics, and morals, in both negative and positive ways.

Recent studies on the psychological consequences of money have often used the money-priming technique explained in this chapter. We showed three different streams of research with the goal of empirically testing the above-mentioned predictions. First, we demonstrated that reminding people of money activates agency as well as focus on self and own goals. Second, we presented experiments showing that money impairs communal relations, leading to lower generosity, less empathy and socializing, and weaker willingness to help. Finally, we described ambiguous effects of money on ethics and morals. Some results show that money triggers cheating and unethical behaviour aimed at gaining higher profit. Other results suggest that money might promote fairness in economic transactions.

ACKNOWLEDGEMENTS

This work was supported by the SWPS University of Social Sciences and Humanities (Project BST/WROC/2015/04) and the Polish National Science Centre (Grant DEC-2013/11/B/HS6/01316).

REVIEW QUESTIONS

1. How does psychology differ from economics in defining the role of money and its main functions?
2. Explain the money-priming technique.
3. Review empirical evidence showing how activating the concept of money increases people's focus on self.

4. What does it mean that money impairs communal relationships? Give examples of experiments that tested the effects of money priming on social relations.
5. Explain the effects of money priming on children's social behaviour and their persistence in work.

REFERENCES

Aaker, J. L., Vohs, K. D., Mogilner, C. (2010). Non-profits are seen as warm and for-profits as competent: Firm stereotypes matter. *Journal of Consumer Research, 37*(2), 224–237.

Ariely, D., Bracha, A., & Meier, S. (2009). Doing good or doing well? Image motivation and monetary incentives in behaving prosocially. *American Economic Review, 99,* 544–555.

Bargh, J. A. (2006). What have we been priming all these years? On the development, mechanisms, and ecology of nonconscious social behavior. *European Journal of Social Psychology, 36,* 147–168.

Baumeister, R., & Vohs, K. D. (2015). The meanings of money: Behavioral, interpersonal, cognitive, motivational, and affective consequences of money-related thoughts. Manuscript submitted for publication. Florida State University.

Begg, D., Fischer, S., & Dornbusch, R. (2005). *Economics.* Maidenhead: McGraw-Hill Higher Education.

Belk, R. W., & Wallendorf, M. (1990). The sacred meaning of money. *Journal of Economic Psychology, 11,* 35–67.

Boucher, H. C., & Kofos, M. N. (2012). The idea of money counteracts ego depletion effects. *Journal of Experimental Social Psychology, 48*(4), 804–810.

Briers, B., Pandelaere, M., Dewitte, S., & Warlop, L. (2006). Hungry for money: On the exchangeability of financial and caloric resources. *Psychological Science, 17,* 939–943.

Caruso, E. M., Mead, N., & Vohs, K. D. (2009). There's no 'you' in money: Thinking of money increases egocentrism. *Advances in Consumer Research, 36,* 208–209.

Caruso, E. M., Vohs, K. D., Baxter, B., & Waytz, A. (2013). Mere exposure to money increases endorsement of free market systems and social inequality. *Journal of Experimental Psychology: General, 142*(2), 301–306.

Chatterjee, P., Rose, R. L., & Sinha, J. (2013). Why money meanings matter in decisions to donate time and money. *Marketing Letters, 24,* 109–118.

Clark, M. S., & Mills, J. R. (1993). The difference between communal and exchange relationships: What it is and is not. *Personality and Social Psychology Bulletin, 19,* 684691.

Fiske, A. P. (1992). The four elementary forms of sociality: Framework for a unified theory of social relations. *Psychological Review, 99,* 689–723.

Fukuyama, F. (2011). *The origins of political order: From prehuman times to the French Revolution.* New York: Farrar, Straus and Giroux.

Furnham, A. (2014). *The new psychology of money.* London: Routledge.

Gasiorowska, A. (2013). Psychologiczne skutki aktywacji idei pieniędzy a dawanie prezentów [The psychological consequences of mere exposure to money and gift-giving]. *Psychologia Społeczna, 8,* 156–168.

Gasiorowska, A. (2014). *Psychologiczne znaczenie pieniędzy. Dlaczego pieniądze wywołują koncentrację na sobie.* [The psychological meaning of money. Why money induces self-focus]. Warsaw: Wydawnictwo Naukowe PWN.

Gasiorowska, A., Chaplin, L. N., Zaleskiewicz, T., Wygrab, S., & Vohs, K. D. (2016). Money cues increase agency and decrease prosociality among children: Early signs of market mode behaviors. *Psychological Science, 27,* 331–344.

Gasiorowska, A., & Hełka, A. (2012). Psychological consequences of money and money attitudes in dictator game. *Polish Psychological Bulletin, 3*(1), 20–26.

Gasiorowska, A., Zaleskiewicz, T., & Wygrab, S. (2012). Would you do something for me? The effects of money activation on social preferences and social behavior in young children. *Journal of Economic Psychology, 33*, 603–608.

Gino, F., & Pierce, L. (2009). The abundance effect: Unethical behavior in the presence of wealth. *Organizational Behavior and Human Decision Processes, 109*(2), 142–155.

Gneezy, U., & Rustichini, A. (2000). Pay enough or don't pay at all. *Quarterly Journal of Economics, August*, 791–810.

Guéguen N., & Jacob, C. (2013). Behavioral consequences of money: When the automated teller machine reduces helping behavior. *The Journal of Socio-Economics, 47*, 103–104.

Heyman, J., & Ariely, D. (2004). Effort for payment. *Psychological Science, 15*, 787–793.

Kouchaki, M., Smith-Crowe, K., Brief, A.P., & Sousa, C. (2013). Seeing green: Mere exposure to money triggers a business decision frame and unethical outcomes. *Organizational Behavior and Human Decision Processes, 121*(1), 53–61.

Lea, S. E. G., & Webley, P. (2006). Money as tool, money as drug: The biological psychology of a strong incentive. *Behavioral and Brain Sciences, 29*, 161–209.

Ma-Kellams, C., & Blascovich, J. (2013). The ironic effect of financial incentives on empathic accuracy. *Journal of Experimental Social Psychology, 49*, 65–71.

Martin, F. (2014). *Money: The unauthorised biography*. London: Vintage Books.

Mead, N., & Baumeister, R. (2009). Money reduces self-presentation and interpersonal likability in novel social situations. *Advances in Consumer Research, 36*, 208.

Mead, N. L., & Stuppy, A. (2014). Money can promote or hinder interpersonal harmony. In E. H. Biljleveld, & H. Aarts (Eds.), *The psychological science of money* (pp. 243–262). New York, NY: Springer.

Mead, N., Vohs, K. D., Savini, K., Stillman, T., & Baumeister, R. (2010). Reminders of money weaken sociomoral responses. *Advances in Consumer Research, 37*, 36.

Mogilner, C. (2010). The pursuit of happiness: Time, money, and social connection. *Psychological Science, 21*(9), 1348–1354.

Mogilner, C., & Aaker, J. (2009). The time vs. money effect: Shifting product attitudes and decisions through personal connection. *Journal of Consumer Research, 36*, 277–291.

Molinsky, A. L., Grant, A. M., & Margolis, J. D. (2012). The bedside manner of *homo economicus*: How and why priming an economic schema reduces compassion. *Organizational Behavior and Human Decision Processes, 119*, 27–37.

Morgan, E. (1969). *A history of money*. Harmondsworth: Penguin.

Mukherjee, S., Manjaly, J. A., & Nargundkar, M. (2013). Money makes you reveal more: Consequences of monetary cues on preferential disclosure of personal information. *Frontiers in Psychology, 4*, 839. DOI: 10. 3389/fpsyg. 2013. 00839.

Ostroy, J. M., & Starr, R. M. (1990). The transactions role of money. In B. M. Friedman, & F. H. Hahn (Eds.), *Handbook of monetary economics* (vol. I; pp. 3–62). Amsterdam: Elsevier Science B.V.

Park, J. K., Gasiorowska, A., & Vohs, K. D. (2015). Self-affirmation has the power to offset the harmful effects of money reminders. Unpublished manuscript. University of Delaware.

Pfeffer, J., & DeVoe, S. E. (2009). Economic evaluation: The effect of money and economics on attitudes about volunteering. *Journal of Economic Psychology, 30*, 500–508.

Piff, P.K., Stancato, D.M., Côte, S., Mendoza-Denton, R., & Keltner, D. (2012). Higher social class predicts increased unethical behavior. *Proceedings of the National Academy of Sciences of the USA, 109*(11), 4086–4091.

Reutner, L., Hansen, J., & Greifeneder, R. (2015). The cold heart: Reminders of money cause feelings of physical coldness. *Social Psychological and Personality Science, 6*(5), 490–495.

Reutner, L., & Wänke, M. (2013). For my own benefit or for the benefit of others: Reminders of money moderate the effects of self-related versus other-related persuasive arguments. *Social Psychological and Personality Science, 4*(2), 220–223.

Roberts, J. A., & Roberts, C. R. (2012). Money matters: Does the symbolic presence of money affect charitable giving and attitudes among adolescents? *Young Consumers: Insight and Ideas for Responsible Marketers, 13*(4), 329–336.

Roediger, H. L., III, Weldon, M. S., Stadler, M. S., & Riegler, G.H. (1992). Direct comparison of word stems and word fragments in implicit and explicit retention tests. *Journal of Experimental Psychology: Learning, Memory, & Cognition, 18*, 1251–1264.

Sarial-Abi, G., & Vohs, K. D. (2012). The mere presence of money motivates goal achievement. *Advances in Consumer Research, 40*, 795.

Sarial-Abi, G., & Vohs, K. D. (2013). Mere exposure to money motivates goal attainment. *Advances in Consumer Research, 41*, 108–109.

Tang, T.L.P. (1992). The meaning of money revisited. *Journal of Organizational Behavior, 13*, 197–202.

van Laer, T., de Ruyter, K., & Cox, D. (2013). A walk in customers' shoes: How attentional bias modification affects ownership of integrity-violating social media posts. *Journal of Interactive Marketing, 27*, 14–27.

Vohs, K. D. (2015). Money priming can change people's thoughts, feelings, motivations, and behaviors: An update on 10 years of experiments. *Journal of Experimental Psychology: General, 144*, e86–e93.

Vohs, K. D., Mead, N. L., & Goode, M. R. (2006). The psychological consequences of money. *Science, 314*, 1154–1156.

Vohs, K. D., Mead, N. L., & Goode, M. R. (2008). Merely activating the concept of money changes personal and interpersonal behavior. *Current Directions in Psychological Science, 17*, 208–212.

Weatherford, J. (1998). *The history of money*. New York: Three Rivers.

Wernimont, P., & Fitzpatrick, S. (1972). The meaning of money. *Journal of Applied Psychology, 56*, 218–226.

Yang, Q., Wu, X., Zhou, X., Mead, N. L., Vohs, K. D., & Baumeister, R. F. (2013). Diverging effects of clean versus dirty money on attitudes, values, and interpersonal behavior. *Journal of Personality and Social Psychology, 104*(3), 473–489.

Zaleskiewicz, T., & Gasiorowska, A. (2017). The psychological consequences of money for economic and social relationships. In C. Jansson-Boyd, & M. Zawisza (Eds.), *The international handbook of consumer psychology* (pp. 590–619). London: Routledge.

Zaleskiewicz, T., Gasiorowska, A., Kesebir, P., Luszczynska, A., & Pyszczynski, T. (2013). Money and the fear of death: The symbolic power of money as an existential anxiety buffer. *Journal of Economic Psychology, 36*, 55–67.

Zelizer, V. A. (1994). *The social meaning of money*. New York: Basic Books.

Zhang, L. (2009). An exchange theory of money and self-esteem in decision making. *Review of General Psychology, 13*(1), 66–76.

Zhou, X., Vohs, K. D., & Baumeister, R. F. (2009). The symbolic power of money: Reminders of money alter social distress and physical pain. *Psychological Science, 20*(6), 700–706.

FURTHER READING

Bijleveld, E., & Aarts, H. (Eds.) (2014). *The psychological science of money*. New York: Springer.

Dunn, E., & Norton, M. (2013). *Happy money: The science of happier spending*. London: Oneworld Publications.

Furnham, A. (2014). *The new psychology of money*. London: Routledge.

Gasiorowska, A., Chaplin, L. N., Zaleskiewicz, T., Wygrab, S., & Vohs, K. D. (2016). Money cues increase agency and decrease prosociality among children: Early signs of market mode behaviors. *Psychological Science, 27*, 331–344.

Lea, S. E. G., & Webley, P. (2006). Money as tool, money as drug: The biological psychology of a strong incentive. *Behavioral and Brain Sciences, 29*, 161–209.

Vohs, K. D. (2015). Money priming can change people's thoughts, feelings, motivations, and behaviors: An update on 10 years of experiments. *Journal of Experimental Psychology: General, 144*, e86–e93.

8 Mental Accounting and Economic Behaviour

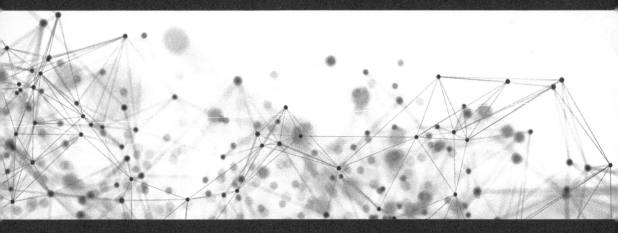

GERRIT ANTONIDES AND ROB RANYARD

CHAPTER OUTLINE

LEARNING OUTCOMES

BY THE END OF THIS CHAPTER YOU SHOULD BE ABLE TO:

1. Understand different conceptualizations of a mental account and how mental accounting can lead to departures from the economic principle that all money is interchangeable.

2. Give examples of studies that demonstrate consequences of mental accounting for economic behaviour and transactions.

3. Evaluate different hypotheses regarding the determinants and functions of mental accounts.

8.1   INTRODUCTION

Imagine your grandmother gives you some money to buy something for yourself, and after a while she asks what you have spent it on. For an economist, this is a silly question, since your granny's money goes into your money pool and may be spent on anything. However, in everyday life, people care about how they would spend it. They would buy something special, say, an ornament, or something to wear, and make a point of showing granny what they had bought. This example shows that people may dedicate part of their money for specific categories of expenditure, thus violating a central assumption of economics that money is fungible; that is, money from all sources is interchangeable. Actually, it is an instance of mental accounting: the psychological separation of events, objects or transactions, based on categorization, with consequent effects on choices or behaviour (Antonides, 2015). Another example of mental accounting is the US gasoline tax, money that has been used exclusively for transportation purposes since 1997 (ITEP, 2013).

The concept of mental accounting was first introduced by Kahneman and Tversky (1984) and developed by Thaler and his colleagues (Shefrin & Thaler, 1988; Thaler, 1985, 1999) to describe mental representations and cognitive processes related in particular to transactions involving money. Whereas financial and managerial accounting records financial transactions in books, and analyses and reports the results, mental accounting describes the ways ordinary people carry out such activities. In this chapter we present an overview, summarized in Table 8.1, of research into mental accounting and its effects on economic behaviour. First, we consider mental accounts posited to broadly categorize financial resources across the life-cycle, and, second, those constructed for specific transactions. Next, we review research showing how economic behaviour can be influenced by the categorization of money by type of income, spending category, the medium of payment, and saving or borrowing purposes. Following this, we discuss the psychological functions and determinants of mental accounting, and, finally, its broader implications and some unresolved issues.

8.2   BROAD MENTAL ACCOUNTS

Shefrin and Thaler's (1988) behavioural life-cycle model assumes that people construct simplified mental representations of their economic resources using three broad mental accounts: (1) *current income*; (2) *current assets*; and (3) *future income*. The current income account, often related to an actual bank current account, is generally associated with the highest marginal propensity to consume, which is the tendency to increase or decrease consumption as the available means increases or decreases. In contrast, the future income account, which represents anticipated future income and pension annuities, is associated with the lowest marginal propensity to consume. That of the current assets account, often linked to a bank savings account for discretionary savings, is in between these two. This psychological model contrasts with the economic life-cycle model which assumes that utility across the life-cycle is maximized and that the marginal propensity to consume of all available money is equal (Friedman, 1957; Modigliani & Brumberg, 1954).

Table 8.1 *Overview of mental accounting and its effects*

Type/process	Examples	Effects	Source
Broad mental accounts	Current income (CI) Current assets (CA) Future income (FI)	Varying budget constraints: CI low, CA medium, FI high	Behavioural life-cycle model; Shefrin & Thaler (1988)
Specific mental accounts	Comprehensive, topical and minimal accounts	Decision outcomes often evaluated at the topical level	Kahneman & Tversky (1984)
Categorization of money	Income framing	Bonuses and rebates spent differently	Epley & Gneezy (2007)
	Spending category	Voucher labels direct spending Mental budgeting	Abeler & Marklein (2008) Heath & Soll (1996)
	Medium of payment	*Denomination effect:* Lower-value notes spent more readily *Plastic effect:* Debit card spending less constrained than cash	Raghubir & Srivastava (2009) Runnemark, Hedman, & Xiao (2015)
	Saving category	Money allocated to saving goals	Soman & Cheema (2011)
	Saving versus credit (the debt puzzle)	Borrowing at a higher interest rate than available savings	Katona (1975)
Mental accounting processes	Integration and segregation	Hedonic editing	Thaler & Johnson (1990)
		Buffering the pain of paying	Prelec & Loewenstein (1998)

One implication of the behavioural life-cycle model is that acquired income will be spent more easily or more reluctantly depending on its categorization or labelling. Large sums may be categorized as belonging to the current asset account and tend to be saved, while smaller sums may be categorized as current income and spent more easily. Shefrin and Thaler (1988) presented evidence from a survey of part-time MBA students who were asked how much they would expect their consumption to increase after receiving a windfall of $2,400. They were given three scenarios differing in whether they would receive it in 12 monthly instalments, as an immediate lump sum, or as a lump sum in five years plus interest. The median reported increase in consumption was $1200, $785 and $0 a year, respectively. The model would predict this pattern of consumption if the smaller instalments were coded as current income, the immediate lump sum as current assets, and the delayed lump sum as future income.

Several studies have failed to replicate the original findings by Shefrin and Thaler, partly because the instalment plan refers to income in the future, thus leading to lower consumption (Selart, Karlsson, & Gärling, 1997; Winnett & Lewis, 1995). Nevertheless, other evidence is more supportive of predictions of the behavioural life-cycle model. Shefrin and Thaler (1988) reviewed some studies, including Landsberger's (1970) survey of spending from real irregular payments that varied in amount across recipients. As they predicted, Landsberger found that the marginal propensity to consume increased as the size of the windfall decreased. Second, Chambers and Spencer (2008) conducted an experiment in which participants were asked how much they would spend of a tax refund paid in different ways. When it was to be paid as a lump sum, the average response was to spend about one-third of the windfall, whereas when it was to be paid in instalments the average response was to spend about four-fifths. Third, Levin (1998) analysed the spending patterns of interviewees between 57 and 62 years from waves of the Longitudinal Retirement History Survey in the 1970s and found that spending was much more sensitive to changes in income compared to changes in assets. Finally, Karlsson, Gärling and Selart (1999) reported similar findings in two experiments investigating students' willingness to buy in scenarios involving different changes in current asset and current income, with total wealth held constant across the scenarios. If participants had to use their current assets to make a purchase, they were less willing to do so than if they had sufficient current income.

In conclusion, Shefrin and Thaler themselves described the behavioural life-cycle hypothesis as a 'simple and stylized version of a mental accounting system' (1988, p. 614). Not surprisingly then, not all predictions of the model have been reliably replicated, and it has been suggested that the mental accounts people develop are complex and varied. Nevertheless, there is strong evidence supporting several predictions, and the model has been very influential in the development of a body of research demonstrating some of the important ways that money is not fungible.

8.3 MENTAL ACCOUNTS FOR SPECIFIC FINANCIAL DECISIONS

In contrast to the broader representation of the behavioural life-cycle model, Kahneman and Tversky (1984) defined a mental account as an outcome frame set up for a specific consumer choice or transaction. A key element of such an outcome frame is the reference point from which outcomes are evaluated. They postulated three levels of account based on the contextual information included in it: minimal, topical, and comprehensive mental accounts. These can be illustrated with reference to one of their scenarios, the Jacket and Calculator decision problem (Tversky & Kahneman, 1981). One group of participants were asked to imagine that they were about to purchase a jacket for $125 and a calculator for $15, and were informed that the calculator was on sale for $10 at another branch of the store, a 20-minute drive away. In the original study, when asked if they would drive to the other store, 68% of participants responded that they would do so. However, when the problem was re-phrased for a second group, with the prices of jacket and calculator reversed (the calculator being $125 in one store and $120 in the other and the jacket $15), only 29% were prepared to drive to the other store. In principle, the price discount could be framed in terms of any of the three levels of a specific mental account: as an absolute saving of $5 relative to the zero reference point (minimal account); or as a saving from the wider context of the whole shopping trip (a comprehensive account), reference point $140; or as a saving from the price of the calculator (a topical account), reference point either $15 or $125. Since the price difference and the cost of the whole shopping trip are the same in both forms of the problem, participants representing the discount in terms of either a minimal or comprehensive mental account would not change their preference across the two versions. Rather, the significant difference in the percentage driving to the other store suggests that the mental account primed for the transaction was the topical account. That is, the reference point from which the price discount was evaluated was derived from the 'topic' of the decision; in this case, the price of the calculator. From the choice patterns to the above and other scenarios, Kahneman and Tversky concluded that people have a tendency to construct topical accounts that incorporate the most relevant, but not all, aspects of the transaction.

The above choice pattern with the Jacket and Calculator scenario has been shown to be robust in several replications (for a review, see Moon, Keasey, & Duxbury, 1999), which also identified some of its boundary conditions. For example, Ranyard and Abdel-Nabi (1993) showed that independently varying the price of the jacket also had a significant effect on choice, whereas Moon et al. found that the effect of the relative price of the calculator disappeared when the absolute value of the discount was above a certain threshold. The former suggests an influence of the comprehensive account and the latter the influence of the minimal account. This suggests that people may view financial transactions from alternative or multiple mental account perspectives.

8.4   OTHER CATEGORIZATIONS OF MONEY

8.4.1   *Income Framing*

Several other mental accounting phenomena concerning the labelling of income have been observed in addition to those related to broad mental accounts. For example, Epley, Mak and Idson (2006) found that income framed as a bonus had a higher marginal propensity to consume than money framed as a rebate. They concluded that this is likely to be due to the fact that a bonus feels like extra money to spend, whereas a rebate just turns a prior loss into a neutral situation (Epley & Gneezy, 2007). Related to this, President Bush signed a law in 2001 entitling tax payers to a tax rebate varying from $300 (for single individuals) to $600 (for married couples). Contrary to standard economic expectations, only 21.8% of the people in a national survey indicated that this money would mostly lead to spending; the remaining people indicated that it would mostly lead to savings or debt pay-offs (Shapiro & Slemrod, 2003). Finally, Kahneman (2011) provides an example in which spending is more likely from stocks sold at a gain than from stocks sold at a loss, thus further pointing to the effect of income categorization on spending.

8.4.2 Coding Money to Specific Spending Categories

In addition to spending per se, categorization of income and assets can affect spending more specifically. For example, in seventeenth-century England, income for a wife's personal use was considered 'pin money', to indicate its marginal significance, perhaps to be spent on trivia. Similarly, at the beginning of the twentieth century, extra income earned by women was considered to be used (in fact labelled) either for extra family expenses or 'discretionary "fun" money' (Zelizer, 1994, p. 62). The labelling or earmarking of income for specific expenditures continues to be rather common. For example, for two-parent households in the Netherlands, the marginal propensity to consume for child clothing from child allowances was about 10% higher than from other income sources, whereas for adult clothing it was not statistically related to child allowances (Kooreman, 2000). These results were even stronger for single-parent households.

Recent research has shown how money received as vouchers or coupons may be allocated to different spending categories. Abeler and Marklein (2008) found that when consumers in a restaurant were given a free €8 voucher labelled 'beverages', they spent more on beverages than when given a voucher labelled 'gourmet'. In another study, when students were given either $5 in cash or as a gift voucher, in the first case, they spent more on everyday items, such as toothpaste, ballpoint pens, paper towels, regular notebooks, bottled water, and tissue boxes, whereas in the second case they spent more on luxury items, such as memorabilia, recycled notebooks, multi-coloured pens, cookies, chips, and candy (Helion & Gilovich, 2014). Finally, it has been found that online grocery customers redeeming a $10 coupon spent more on goods they normally did not buy, for example, frozen seafood and fruit (Milkman & Beshears, 2009).

8.4.3 The Medium of Payment: Cash, Debit and Credit Cards

For obvious practical reasons, cash is available in a range of values, for instance, from €50 to €5 notes, and from €2 to 1 cent coins. A perhaps surprising mental accounting phenomenon is that spending has been shown to vary with the value of the available bank notes. Raghubir and Srivastava (2009) carried out a series of experiments involving real purchases with cash. One of their main observations was that when money was available, for example, as a single €20 note, it was less likely to be spent than when the same amount was available as several smaller value notes. Important aspects of the purchasing environment were controlled in order to rule out explanations based on pragmatic considerations; thus, it could be concluded that the results were due to mental accounting. Raghubir and Srivastava termed this and related behaviour the *denomination effect*. Interestingly, participants with a disposition to control their spending were more susceptible to it.

Comparisons of spending by cash, debit and credit card have also been investigated. Harding (2013), writing in *The Independent*, suggests that young adults in Britain today are children of the plastic generation 'that only knows consumption through the medium of plastic, where the relationship between purchase and funds is disjointed'. As he reflects, the first credit cards appeared in the UK 50 years ago, the first debit cards 25 years ago, and today, 'Money has lost its physical relevance, it has become abstract.' In the UK, there were 47 million debit card holders in 2013, while in Denmark over 80%

of the population possess a debit card (Runnemark, Hedman, & Xiao, 2015). In that country it is the most common method of payment nowadays. Differences in spending between debit cards and cash are particularly interesting because unlike other forms of card payment, that by debit card is, like cash, immediate and widely accepted by traders. Runnemark et al. conducted one of the few controlled experiments to compare actual spending by cash and by debit card. In their study, student participants received 100 DKK which they used to bid for cards redeemable for drinks (beer and coffee) of value 170, 100 or 40 DKK. They were randomly assigned to one of three groups differing only in the method of payment. In the comparison between cash and debit card payment conditions, the mean bid for the drinks was significantly higher with debit card payments, demonstrating a clear 'plastic effect'. Likewise, Prelec and Simester (2001) found 76–113% higher bids for tickets to a basketball game when payments had to be made by credit card than with cash, thus indicating a 'credit card premium'.

Soman (2003) reported a related experiment in which spending on photocopying was higher when payment was via a photocopy card rather than cash. He attributed the plastic effect to the card's lack of payment transparency compared to cash. As in studies of the denomination effect, these experiments were designed to rule out alternatives to a mental accounting explanation.

8.4.4   *Saving and Borrowing*

As well as allocating income to different spending categories, people also earmark money for savings. This was found to be quite effective among low-income households who received their weekly wages in cash (Soman & Cheema, 2011). For this group, when part of the wage was put in a sealed envelope, meant to be saved, savings increased by over 300% over a period of 14 weeks. Furthermore, if the same amount was spread over two different envelopes the saved amount was even doubled.

A further example of mental accounting is simultaneous borrowing and saving, which is often practised to ensure that savings will be used to reach particular goals. Since borrowing and saving usually take place at different interest rates, this behaviour is considered irrational and is known as the *debt puzzle* (Gross & Souleles, 2002; Katona, 1975; Laibson, Repetto, & Tobacman, 2003). In this case, current assets are clearly separated from future income, such that both accounts should be closed in a positive way. If these two accounts were not kept separate, the benefits of the saving goals may not be reached.

8.5   FUNCTIONS OF MENTAL ACCOUNTS

Mental accounting has several important psychological functions, although it is not considered rational in standard economic theory. One function is to simplify decision-making, and related to this, to apply self-control in order to spread positive outcomes across the life-cycle. These combine to contribute to successful money management and budgeting. Additionally, the mental accounting processes of integration and segregation may have hedonic functions, such as buffering the pain of payment or distributing positive experiences in an enjoyable way.

8.5.1 Simplification

The categorization of money and decision outcomes into mental accounts serves the important cognitive function of simplifying aspects of the complex economic world. As such, it is one of the devices people use to achieve bounded rationality (Simon, 1957). The topical account, for example, enables a potentially complex purchasing decision to be mentally represented in a way that allows the consumer to focus on the key information for a good decision. In fact, all the examples of mental accounting described so far simplify some aspect of the economic environment; it is much easier to deal with a limited number of expenditures within a smaller budget than with a myriad of expenditures within a huge budget. In former days, people used all kinds of physical means to keep budgets for different expenses, for example, envelopes, boxes and tin cans (Zelizer, 1994), hence the name 'tin can accounting'.

8.5.2 Self-Control and Money Management

A second function of mental accounting is self-control imposed by the budget constraints associated with different mental accounts. Setting a budget has the effect of an imposed ceiling on expenditures within the account, thus facilitating keeping control over expenses. A budget also serves as an anchor against which expenses are tracked (Heath & Soll, 1996). Furthermore, purchases from almost depleted budgets tend to yield lower customer satisfaction with the product – a phenomenon called the *bottom dollar effect* (Soster, Gershoff, & Bearden, 2014).

The application of mental accounting in managing financial affairs has been referred to as mental budgeting. The mental budgeting process consists of several stages. The first stage is setting budgets for different types of expenses, which are considered binding (Heath & Soll, 1996). Setting budgets is an imperfect process since most expenses cannot be predicted exactly. Hence, budgeting may both lead to overconsumption (if budgets are set too high) and underconsumption (if budgets are set too low). Second, expenses are tracked against the set budgets by noticing ('booking') and assigning expenses ('posting') to a particular budget (Heath, 1995). Posting expenses is facilitated by the ease of categorization, which is higher for typical expenses (e.g., petrol expenses in the transportation budget) than for atypical expenses (e.g., cost of a cup of coffee consumed on the road). Third, compensation for past expenses may take place by postponing, reducing or cancelling future expenses within a particular budget, even if there is money left in another budget category.

Mental budgeting tends to improve one's overview of expenses and to keep expenses within one's means to make ends meet (Antonides, De Groot, & Van Raaij, 2011). For marketers, it should be useful to know in which budgets consumers post expenses on their products. For example, will expenses for a new bicycle be posted in the recreation budget or in the work-related budget? And with which other expenses is the bicycle purchase competing?

A special instance of mental accounting may happen with sequential choices, that is, choices made consecutively over time. Sequential choices can be made in broad brackets, for example, in the case of keeping one's weight down by not consuming more than 14,000 calories per week. Alternatively, narrow bracketing may be applied, for example, by not consuming more than 2,000 calories per day (Read, Loewenstein, & Rabin, 1999). In the latter case, self-control would be accomplished more easily than in the former case, presumably because there are more decision points to which one has to pay attention (Cheema & Soman, 2008).

8.5.3 Hedonic Editing

A third function of mental accounting is hedonic editing (Thaler & Johnson, 1990), based on psychological evaluations of choice outcomes. In particular, it has been found that positive events are preferred more when the outcomes are mentally segregated, or separated, rather than integrated. This finding is explained by the concave value function for gains of prospect theory (Kahneman & Tversky, 1979; see Chapter 2), which means that the sum of the separate evaluations of gains is higher than the evaluation of the integrated gain (see Box 8.1). That is, adding up separate values, for example, enjoying several shorter holidays at different times of the year, induces more pleasure than valuing integrated outcomes, for example, enjoying one long holiday. Likewise, negative events are more preferred when the outcomes are mentally integrated than segregated, such as all expenses pooled on one's credit card bill, because of the convex shape of the value function for losses (Thaler, 1985). For mixed outcomes, it appears that small gains are preferred when segregated from large losses ('silver lining'), whereas small losses are preferred when integrated with larger gains ('cancellation').

The hedonic editing rules do not apply under all circumstances. When people are given the opportunity to segregate losses at different points in time, they prefer to do so. It appears that people experience coping problems if too many losses come at the same time, and they prefer to spread them out over time (Thaler & Johnson, 1990). So, for example, having to pay the repair bill for one's broken washing machine and municipality taxes at the same time is very unpleasant, whereas paying the second bill in the next month would be considered less unpleasant. Hedonic editing rules are relevant to marketing; for example, an extra charge for service will be preferred when integrated with the total service price.

8.5.4 Buffering the Pain of Payment

An important question regarding the use of credit cards and other types of borrowing is whether the gains and losses of a transaction are integrated or segregated, for example, whether the pleasure of acquiring and using a new car is segregated from, or integrated with, the pain of paying for it. Prelec and Loewenstein's (1998) double-entry mental accounting theory argues that gains (the black = income, consumption) and losses (the red = paying) are mentally represented in separate accounts that interact in different ways, particularly depending on how such outcomes are distributed over time. If they are coupled, then the pain of payment, as they describe it, can be buffered by the pleasure associated with the purchase. Conversely, the pleasure of consumption can be diminished by association with painful thoughts about the cost. In one of their survey items with hypothetical scenarios, Prelec and Loewenstein found that the majority of participants expressed

Box 8.1 Hedonic editing

The mental accounting of a combination of events is based on hedonic editing, using the value function, V, in prospect theory (see Figure 8.1), sometimes called mental arithmetic. The value function is concave for gains (right of the 0 reference point), and convex and relatively steep for losses (left of the reference point). Consequently, it appears from the shape of the value function that the segregated evaluation of two gains, x and y, amounts to V(x)+V(y), which is preferred to the integrated evaluation of these gains, V(x+y), since this value lies higher on the value function. The latter expression first integrates the events, then evaluates, whereas the former keeps the values of events separate.

Likewise, Figure 8.1 shows that the integration of two losses, v and w, amounts to V(v+w), which is preferred to the segregated evaluation of these losses, V(v)+V(w). A similar calculation can be made for mixed events, combining a gain and a loss. It can be shown easily that segregating a small gain, x, and large loss, v, is preferred to integrating these events ('silver lining'). Likewise, integrating a small loss, w, and a large gain, y, is preferred to segregating these events ('cancellation'). We leave these calculations as an exercise for the reader.

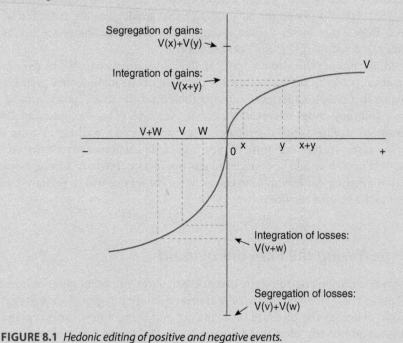

FIGURE 8.1 *Hedonic editing of positive and negative events.*

a preference for prepayment for a holiday experience. They interpreted this as support for the idea that such payment schedules buffer the negative experience of payment with the prospect of a positive consumption experience, and leave the consumer free to enjoy their purchase without having to think about its cost. They argue also that people are generally averse to post-payment, and borrowing for consumption in general, partly because thoughts of payments to come tend to spoil the pleasure of the item purchased. On the other hand, they found a preference to postpone payment for a washer-dryer machine. In this case the utilitarian nature of the purchase does not interfere with the pain of paying. Credit card debt, they argue, is particularly disagreeable because repayments are not easily linked to specific consumption experiences that could buffer the pain of payment. One of their survey findings supports this idea by showing that an unexpected tax rebate used to repay a credit card debt was more agreeable when it would be used to pay for some other specific items.

In general, however, clear evidence of the mental coupling and decoupling of consumption and payment is somewhat limited, and some research has found substantial individual variability (as did the original surveys mentioned above). For example, Kamleitner and Kirchler (2006) carried out interviews with a sample of people who were about to, or had already, made a purchase with a personal bank loan. They found that participants often reported associating, or coupling, the loan repayments with the goods purchased, thereby buffering the impact of the cost. On the other hand, they seldom reported associating the goods with the loan repayments, thereby decoupling, which protected their enjoyment. However, these effects varied with context (e.g., were stronger for furniture than vehicle purchases) and diminished towards the end of the loan period. This again suggests a pattern of substantial individual and contextual differences as well as a lack of stability of effects over time.

8.6   DETERMINANTS OF MENTAL ACCOUNTING

As discussed earlier, mental accounting is considered irrational according to standard economic theory (Thaler, 1985). In fact, it has been found that cognitive abilities (Frederick, 2005) as well as education (Abeler & Marklein, 2008; Benjamin, Brown, & Shapiro, 2006) decrease the use of heuristics and biases. However, other factors seem to be related to mental accounting. Since it has been considered to be a self-control device (Cheema & Soman, 2006; Wertenbroch, 2003), it may be used less by impatient people with low self-control resulting in impulsiveness. Karlsson, Gärling, and Selart (1997) found that the willingness to use savings for unforeseen events was higher for replacing products that were accidentally broken than to buy a desired item, suggesting that saving goals may be related to mental accounting. Also, the availability of money may decrease the need for mental accounting, whereas lack of money may increase it.

Antonides, De Groot, and Van Raaij (2011) found evidence for the above-mentioned effects by using a four-item mental budgeting scale, applied to household financial management, in a survey. The four items dealt with making reservations for different expenses, not spending more than a fixed amount on a particular type of expense, spending less after having spent more, and spending less in the next month after having spent more in the current month. They found that a higher score on the mental budgeting scale was positively associated with long-term time orientation, having debts, having saving goals, and knowledge of financial products and investments. Mental budgeting was negatively associated with household income, home equity, savings, higher education, and being male.

8.7   CONCLUSION

The range of decision phenomena that have been elucidated by mental accounting theory since the 1980s is extensive. Important insights have been gained into consumers' responses to discounts and surcharges (Kimes & Wirtz, 2002), their reactions to unexpected price changes, consumer credit decisions, and evaluations of the bundling or separation of product features (Johnson, Herrmann, & Bauer, 1999). Also, our understanding of important aspects of personal finance, such as saving and tax-related behaviour, has been advanced. In addition, boundary conditions and other limitations have been identified.

Several attempts have been made to apply mental accounting theory to non-monetary resources, for example, chocolate consumption and gambling behaviour (Cheema & Soman, 2008). Apparently, wrapped pieces of chocolate in a box suggest a partitioning of consumption experiences, as opposed to unwrapped chocolates, resulting in decreased chocolate consumption. Furthermore, the effect of earmarking has been related to recreational versus work time. Rajagopal and Rha (2009) found that people were more upset about a flight delay on a business trip than a delay on a vacation trip, showing that the evaluation of time is work-related. Also, they found that when people who wanted to consult a bookstore for recreation purposes discovered that it was closed for the next hour, they tended to spend the extra time on non-work-related activities, such as having coffee with friends. In contrast, people who wanted to visit the bookstore for work-related purposes tended to spend the extra time more on work-related activities, such as working on a laptop. So, it seems that people matched their time budget (either work or recreation related) to the type of activity they choose, which is similar to the income framing effect.

Mental accounts have even been related to emotions and feelings. For example, Levav and McGraw (2009) found that a money gift from an uncle who was just diagnosed with an illness was less likely to be spent on hedonic items, such as ice-cream sundae, designer sunglasses, or stereo equipment, than on a plain gift. This result was explained by the experience of negative feelings associated with the uncle's illness, which did not match with the hedonic expense. One way to overcome the negative feelings was 'money laundering', in which the money could be spent on utilitarian items, such as educational expenses, which seemed to match better with the sad feelings associated with the uncle's illness.

Although mental accounting is considered irrational in the standard economic model, it fulfils some useful functions in everyday life. It makes financial management easier and serves as a self-control device, thus facilitating the accomplishment of people's own objectives. A negative aspect of mental accounting is the felt need to close every account in a positive way, thus neglecting the overall view of one's financial situation. In policy-making and marketing, mental accounting might be used to support financial measures and the positioning of products and services in particular spending categories.

One criticism of mental accounting theory has been that mental accounts are in practice rather malleable, with money mentally transferred from one to the other rather easily (Cheema & Soman, 2006). Also, the over-extensive use of the term mental accounting to refer to basic coding and editing processes has been criticized as adding little to what is understood via prospect theory and cognitive process models of decision-making. Nevertheless, the fundamental insight of mental accounting theory, that financial resources are not fungible, has been consistently validated and shown to be important across many areas of economic life.

8.8 SUMMARY

In standard economic theory, money from all sources is fungible, or interchangeable. In contrast, economic psychological research has proposed that money from different sources may be integrated into one mental account or segregated into several different ones. In this chapter, we discuss models based on broad mental accounts across the life-cycle, specific ones constructed for a single transaction and other categorizations of money based on, for example, income source, spending and saving categories, and medium of payment. We review research showing that such categorizations can lead to anomalies of economic behaviour not predicted by economic theory; for example, higher spending by debit card compared to cash. We argue that although empirical studies support the general notion, mental accounts are probably more complex and varied than current models allow. We also review the evidence, which is contested, for several psychological functions of mental accounts including simplification, self-control and buffering the pain of payment. Finally, we present research on the determinants of mental accounting, such as wealth, cognitive capacity and present/future orientation. We conclude that despite criticisms of mental accounting research, the important finding that financial resources are not fungible has been consistently validated and shown to be important across many areas of economic life.

REVIEW QUESTIONS

1. Mention three broad consumer financial accounts in which the Marginal Propensity to Consume (MPC) is different. Which account has the highest MPC, which has the lowest MPC? In addition to the three financial accounts, bonuses, rebates, and windfalls also influence the MPC. How?
2. Provide your best definition of mental budgeting. Why is mental budgeting considered irrational in standard economic theory? What types of people apply mental budgeting most?
3. How could mental budgeting help improve people's financial outcomes?
4. Show the silver lining, and cancellation effects for mixed positive and negative outcomes, by using Figure 8.1.

REFERENCES

Abeler, J., & Marklein, F. (2008). Fungibility, labels, and consumption. *Discussion Paper* 3500. Bonn: IZA.

Antonides, G. (2015). Mental accounting. In M. Altman (Ed.), *Real world decision making: An encyclopedia of behavioral economics* (pp. 260–262). Santa Barbara, CA: Praeger.

Antonides, G., De Groot, I. M. & Van Raaij, W. F. (2011). Mental budgeting and the management of household finance. *Journal of Economic Psychology, 32*, 546–555.

Benjamin, D. J., Brown, S. A., & Shapiro, J. M. (2006). Who is 'behavioral'? Cognitive ability and anomalous preferences. *Journal of the European Economic Association, 11*(6), 1231–1255.

Chambers, V., & Spencer, M. (2008). Does changing the timing of a yearly individual tax refund change the amount spent vs. saved? *Journal of Economic Psychology, 29*, 856–862.

Cheema, A., & Soman, D. (2006). Malleable mental accounting: The effect of flexibility on the justification of attractive spending and consumption decisions. *Journal of Consumer Psychology, 16*(1), 33–44.

Cheema, A., & Soman, D. (2008). The effect of partitions on controlling consumption. *Journal of Marketing Research, 55*, 665-675.

Epley, N., & Gneezy, A. (2007). The framing of financial windfalls and implications for public policy. *Journal of Socio-Economics, 36*, 36–47.

Epley, N., Mak, D., & Idson, L. C. (2006). Bonus or rebate? The impact of income framing on spending and saving. *Journal of Behavioral Decision Making, 19*, 213–227.

Frederick, S. (2005). Cognitive reflection and decision making. *Journal of Economic Perspectives, 19*(4), 25–42.

Friedman, M. (1957). *A theory of the consumption function.* Princeton, NJ: Princeton University Press.

Gross, D. B., & Souleles, N. S. (2002). Do liquidity constraints and interest rates matter for consumer behavior? Evidence from credit card data. *Quarterly Journal of Economics, 117*(1), 149–185.

Harding, N. (2013). Plastic people: How credit cards changed our relationship with money. *The Independent*, 10 August.

Heath, C. (1995). Escalation and de-escalation of commitment in response to sunk costs: The role of budgeting in mental accounting. *Organizational Behavior and Human Decision Processes, 62*(1), 38–54.

Heath, C., & Soll, J. B. (1996). Mental budgeting and consumer decisions. *Journal of Consumer Research, 23*, 40–52.

Helion, C., & Gilovich, T. (2014). Gift cards and mental accounting: Green-lighting hedonic spending. *Journal of Behavioral Decision Making, 27*, 386–393.

ITEP (2013). *A federal gas tax for the future.* Washington, DC: Institute of Taxation and Economic Policy.

Johnson, M. D., Herrmann, A., & Bauer, H. H. (1999). The effects of price bundling on consumer evaluations of product offerings. *International Journal of Research in Marketing, 16*(2), 129–142.

Kahneman, D. (2011). *Thinking fast and slow.* New York: Farrar, Straus and Giroux.

Kahneman, D., & Tversky, A. (1979). Prospect theory: An analysis of decision making under risk. *Econometrica, 47*, 263–291.

Kahneman, D., & Tversky, A. (1984). Choices, values, and frames. *American Psychologist, 39*(4), 341–350.

Kamleitner, B., & Kirchler, E. (2006). Personal loan users' mental integration of payment and consumption. *Marketing Letters, 17*(4), 281–294.

Karlsson, N., Gärling, T., & Selart, M. (1997). Effects of mental accounting on intertemporal choice. *Göteborg Psychological Reports, 27*(5), 1.

Karlsson, N., Gärling, T., & Selart, M. (1999). Explanations of effects of prior income changes on buying decisions. *Journal of Economic Psychology, 20*, 449–463.

Katona, G. (1975). *Psychological economics.* Oxford: Elsevier.

Kimes, S. E., & Wirtz, J. (2002). Perceived fairness of demand-based pricing for restaurants. *Cornell Hotel and Restaurant Administration Quarterly, 43*, 31–37.

Kooreman, P. (2000). The labeling effect of a child benefit system. *American Economic Review, 90*, 571–583.

Laibson, D. L., Repetto, A., & Tobacman, J. (2003). A debt puzzle. In P. Aghion, R. Frydman, J. Stiglitz, & M. Woodford (Eds.), *Knowledge, information, and expectations in modern macroeconomics: In honor of Edmund S. Phelps* (pp. 228–266). Princeton, NJ: Princeton University Press.

Landsberger, M. (1970). The life-cycle hypothesis: A reinterpretation and empirical test. *American Economic Review, 60*(1), 175–183.

Levav, J., & McGraw, P. (2009). Emotional accounting: How feelings about money influence consumer choice. *Journal of Marketing Research, 46*, 66–80.

Levin, L. (1998). Are assets fungible?: Testing the behavioral theory of life-cycle savings, *Journal of Economic Behavior & Organization, 36*, 59–83.

Milkman, K., & Beshears, J. (2009). Mental accounting and small windfalls: Evidence from an online grocer. *Journal of Economic Behavior and Organization, 71*(2), 384–394.

Modigliani, F., & Brumberg, R. H. (1954) Utility analysis and the consumption function: An interpretation of cross-section data. In K. K.Kurihara (Ed.), *Post-Keynesian economics* (pp. 388–436). New Brunswick, NJ. Rutgers University Press.

Moon, P., Keasey, K., & Duxbury, D. (1999). Mental accounting and decision making: The relationship between relative and absolute savings. *Journal of Economic Behavior & Organization, 38*(2), 145–153.

Prelec, D., & Loewenstein, G. (1998). The red and the black: Mental accounting of savings and debt. *Marketing Science, 17*(1), 4–28.

Prelec, D., & Simester, D. (2001). Always leave home without it: A further investigation of the credit-card effect on willingness to pay. *Marketing Letters, 12*(1), 5–12.

Raghubir, P., & Srivastava, J. (2009). The denomination effect. *Journal of Consumer Research, 36*, 701–713.

Rajagopal, P., & Rha, J.-Y. (2009). The mental accounting of time. *Journal of Economic Psychology, 30*, 772–781.

Ranyard, R., & Abdel-Nabi, D. (1993). Mental accounting and the process of multiattribute choice. *Acta Psychologica, 84*(2), 161–177.

Read, D., Loewenstein, G., & Rabin, M. (1999). Choice bracketing. *Journal of Risk and Uncertainty, 19*, 171–197.

Runnemark, E., Hedman, J., & Xiao, X. (2015). Do consumers pay more using debit cards than cash? *Electronic Commerce Research and Applications*. Available online 20 March 2015. doi.org/10.1016/j.elerap.2015.03.002.

Selart, M., Karlsson, N., & Gärling, T. (1997). Self-control and loss aversion in intertemporal choice. *Journal of Socio-Economics, 26*, 513–524.

Shapiro, M., & Slemrod, J. (2003). Consumer response to tax rebates. *American Economic Review, 93*, 381–396.

Shefrin, H. M., & Thaler, R. H. (1988). The behavioral life-cycle hypothesis. *Economic Inquiry, 26*, 609–643.

Simon, H. A. (1957). *Models of man: Social and rational.* New York: John Wiley & Sons, Inc.

Soman, D. (2003). The effect of payment transparency on consumption: Quasi-experiments from the field. *Marketing Letters, 14*, 173–183.

Soman, D., & Cheema, A. (2011). Earmarking and partitioning: Increasing saving by low-income households. *Journal of Marketing Research, 48*, S14–S22.

Soster, R. L., Gershoff, A. D., & Bearden, W. O. (2014). The bottom dollar effect: The influence of spending to zero on pain of payment and satisfaction. *Journal of Consumer Research, 41*(3), 656–677.

Soster, R. L., Monga, A., & Bearden, W. O. (2010). Tracking costs of time and money: How accounting periods affect mental accounting. *Journal of Consumer Research, 37*, 712–721.

Thaler, R. H. (1985). Mental accounting and consumer choice. *Marketing Science, 4*(3), 199–214.

Thaler, R. H. (1999). Mental accounting matters. *Journal of Behavioral Decision Making, 12,* 183–206.

Thaler, R. H., & Johnson, E. J. (1990). Gambling with the house money and trying to break even: The effects of prior outcomes on risky choice. *Management Science, 36*(6), 643–660.

Tversky, A., & Kahneman, D. (1981). The framing of decisions and the psychology of choice. *Science, 211,* 453–458.

Wertenbroch, K. (2003). Self-rationing: Self-control in consumer choice. In G. Loewenstein, D. Read, & R.Baumeister (Eds.), *Time and decision: Economic and psychological perspectives on intertemporal choice* (pp. 491–516). New York: Russell Sage Foundation.

Winnett, A., & Lewis, A. (1995). Household accounts, mental accounts, and savings behaviour: Some old economics rediscovered? *Journal of Economic Psychology, 16,* 431–448.

Zelizer, V. A. (1994). *The social meaning of money.* New York: Basic Books.

FURTHER READING

Cheema, A., & Soman, D. (2006). Malleable mental accounting: The effect of flexibility on the justification of attractive spending and consumption decisions. *Journal of Consumer Psychology, 16*(1), 33–44.

Kamleitner, B., & Kirchler, E. (2006). Personal loan users' mental integration of payment and consumption. *Marketing Letters, 17*(4), 281–294.

Thaler, R. H. (1999). Mental accounting matters. *Journal of Behavioral Decision Making, 12,* 183–206.

9 How Laypeople Understand the Economy

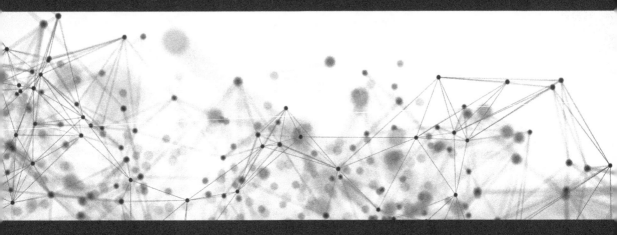

DAVID LEISER AND ZEEV KRILL

CHAPTER OUTLINE

LEARNING OUTCOMES

BY THE END OF THIS CHAPTER YOU SHOULD BE ABLE TO:

1. Describe the main cognitive challenges presented by economic theory.
2. Discuss the Good-Begets-Good heuristic and how it enables non-economists to interpret the economy.
3. Describe the contribution of metaphors and the dangers of using them to understand economic issues.

9.1 INTRODUCTION: UNDERSTANDING ECONOMICS IS HARD YET EXPECTED

Economics is notoriously hard to understand. The domain is inherently difficult (Arthur, 2000) and, in contrast to some other domains, the human mind is not particularly equipped to think about macroeconomics (Pinker, 2002; Rubin, 2003), as it constitutes a domain that was irrelevant to humankind's evolutionary past. As a consequence, lay people's understanding of the economy frequently contradicts accepted professional knowledge.

Recent years have seen a significant increase in the number of studies investigating how lay people understand economic phenomena (Caplan, 2011; Gangl, Kastlunger, Kirchler, & Voracek, 2012; Leiser & Drori, 2005; Loix & Pepermans, 2009; Ranyard, Missier, Bonini, Duxbury, & Summers, 2008; van Bavel & Gaskell, 2004; Williamson & Wearing, 1996). This chapter will sketch what is known about lay understanding of economics by first discussing several features of lay understanding in general, and then suggesting how they account for lay economic understanding.

Beyond the inherent interest of the topic, it is of major practical significance for two distinct reasons. First, citizen understanding is essential for democracy (Caplan, 2011; Davies, 2015) and it affects public policy through the political process (Fornero, 2015). Policy-makers may hesitate to pursue what they consider the best policy if they know that the public will not understand its rationale or its necessity and oppose it. Indeed, the public tends to judge unpopular policies as more necessary if they have a better understanding of them (Huston, 2010, 2012). Moreover, economic beliefs affect economic behaviour (Roos, 2007, 2008), and constitute an important component of economic modelling (Darriet & Bourgeois-Gironde, 2015).

9.1.1 *The Complexities of Macroeconomics*

Why is economics so difficult to understand? Several factors contributing to this impenetrability may be distinguished. One is that economic theory functions as a complex causal system, whereas people are remarkably poor at combining causal links into a system (Grotzer, 2012; Perkins & Grotzer, 2005). Even when aware of a given link (A causes B), people tend not to think of the feedback effects (B affects A in return) or of further, indirect effects (A affects B and B affects C, so A affects C too). This means that the *scope* of explanations tends to be overly narrow, and to involve too few aspects. Another reason is that many of the basic factors in economic theory, and especially in macroeconomics, are aggregate variables, such as money supply, inflation rates, and Gross Domestic Product. Consider, for instance, a definition of money supply: it is *the sum total of currency and other liquid instruments in a country's economy as of a particular time*. The kind of causality that links such variables is the cumulative outcome of countless individual transactions that are not individually known. People do have the cognitive wherewithal to understand other people (Shahaeian, Peterson, Slaughter, & Wellman, 2011; Wellman, Fang, & Peterson. 2011), and can grasp their needs, knowledge, motivations and actions, but they are ill-equipped to cope with the aggregate effects of the individual decisions of many. Related to this, the type of causality invoked by economic theory is not intuitive. It routinely

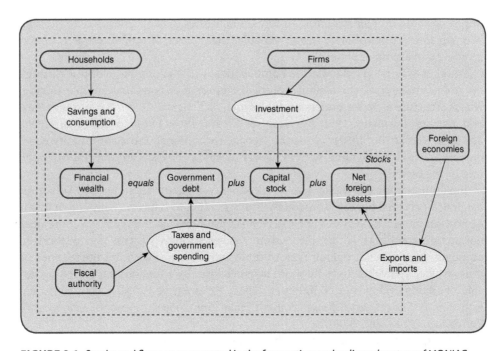

FIGURE 9.1 *Stocks and flows as represented in the forecasting and policy subsystem of MONIAC.*

Source: Reserve Bank of New Zealand Bulletin 2007. Reproduced with permission of Reserve Bank of New Zealand.

explains outcomes by the 'equilibrium seeking' of a complex dynamic system. A striking implementation of this way of thinking was the MONIAC hydraulic economic model of 1949 (see Figure 9.1): a physical model of the economy in which flows of consumption, saving, investment and other economic forces were represented by liquid moving through tubes and pipes as monetary and fiscal variables varied, and the whole system could be observed as it came to an equilibrium (Ng & Wright, 2007). This equilibrium seeking is not the kind of causation people are comfortable with.

And yet, despite the difficulty in understanding economics without proper formal training in the discipline, discourse addressed to the public on matters economic conveys that it is expected to understand it, and such discussions are exceedingly common. Newscasts and the written press will discuss such things as whether the present time is a good time to buy a house and why, the economic circumstances of the latest decisions by the central bank governor and its likely consequences, or the probable macro-economic significance of 'Brexit' (the UK withdrawal from the European Union). This state of affairs is very different from that observed in other domains. News programmes, for example, rarely invite civil engineers to talk to the public about the precise technical mishap that caused a bridge to collapse, doubtless on the reasonable ground that people would not be capable of following the explanation.

9.1.2   How to Understand What You Cannot

Faced with the implicit expectation that they can and ought to understand those issues, lay people tend to feel guilty at their ignorance, and try to make sense them. To do so without proper training, they must assimilate this discourse in some way, by imposing some simpler structure, or rely on heuristics or other means. The rich and complex interactions of large sets of variables that economic models strive to master is reduced to a simpler pattern.

Another way people handle the complexities of the economic world is through the use of metaphors, the assimilation of the intractable issue to a familiar domain whose structure is better understood (Holyoak & Thagard, 1989). For instance, several authors (Furnham, 1988; Furnham & Cleare, 1988; Leiser & Zaltsman, 1990; Sevón & Weckström, 1989) discuss the view of the national or the community economy as akin to a family unit, with the government or the local administration in the role of the parent.

Finally, intentional and teleological accounts come naturally to people. Whatever happened occurred because someone wilfully made it to happen. Thinking in terms of how an interlocking system of causal links produces an emergent outcome does not come naturally to lay people. Recent studies strongly suggest that goal-driven accounts constitute the default way to understand causes, with the other types of causality being invoked only by more advanced thinkers functioning under favourable conditions (Donovan & Kelemen, 2011; Kelemen & Rosset, 2009; Kelemen, Rottman, & Seston, 2013; Leiser & Beth Halachmi, 2006; Lombrozo, Kelemen, & Zaitchik, 2007; Rosset, 2008).

This explanatory mode leads to the personalization of economic matters, looking for people responsible for a state of affairs, to animism and personification, even to the ascription of wants and volition to entities such as the stock market (Morris, Sheldon, Ames, & Young, 2007). We will discuss the conspiratorial style in economics, the tendency to see occult and conspiratorial causes behind economic events, which constitutes a prime expression of the intentionality bias.

If the public crudely oversimplifies the interactions of large sets of variables that economic models strive to master, yet feels it does understand the situation tolerably well, this has consequences, political and economic. A simple illustration: retirement funding in many countries is actuarially untenable, due to a combination of increased life expectancy, lowered return on investments, and demographic changes in ageing countries. In responsibly run countries, this concern requires certain policy changes. The consequence is often that people who do not understand how pension funds function and in particular its mutual responsibility dimension, feel that they are being cheated of their hard-earned pension rights. It is not just that they object to policies that lower their income: they consider them morally wrong, a breach of contract. It is natural for people to feel unhappy if their pension rights are curtailed, but their indignation is partly caused by their failure to grasp the way pension funds are meant to function, in a way that is fair inter-generationally. Conversely, financial literacy would facilitate the introduction of better economic policies through democratic processes and lay the foundations for the political sustainability and effectiveness of reforms (Fornero, 2015). Political leaders, who are usually not trained in economics, may sometimes unwittingly rely on their uneducated intuitions to pursue wrongheaded policies, or pander to the unsophisticated members of the public by advocating populist ones (Thomadakis, 2015). As Caplan (2002a, 2002b) points out, the issue is not just that the public randomly support policies in a way that the support might cancel out. Rather – to use the phrase made famous by Ariely and Jones (2008) – their mode of understanding is *predictably irrational*. The many misconceptions, simplifications and distortions that plague non-expert understanding are systematic. The challenge for researchers is to identify these systematic misconceptions, and use this knowledge to facilitate communication with non-specialists (Bruine de Bruin & Bostrom, 2013).

This is of course not to say that non-expert understanding is necessarily misguided, nor to claim that modern liberal economics is the gold standard that represents truth. Economic theory is an historically derived conception, and certainly not the only possible one, as attested by fundamental debates opposing alternate conceptions. Yet it remains the case that, hampered by a severely limited understanding of many fundamental aspects of the economy (as documented below), popular participation in those debates is somewhat ineffective. 'Democratic debate stagnates into discussions between small elite groups over small differences behind the backs of an increasingly disillusioned and unrepresented public. This … is a grave threat to our democracy' (Inman, 2015).

9.2 INTERACTING VARIABLES

In the following section we discuss lay knowledge regarding macroeconomics, centring the discussion around the concept of inflation. The reason for this focus is that the understanding of inflation was studied more than that of other macroeconomics variables, and because psychological inflationary expectations actually affect price dynamics. We will show how it is understood, with a restricted scope; how people perceive the relation between inflation and unemployment; how relations between macroeconomics variables are understood in general, on the basis of the Good-Begets-Good heuristic; and discuss macroeconomic consequences. We do not cover here biases in the *perception* of inflation, an important topic treated in Chapter 10 in this volume. Our focus lies in how people *understand* inflation and its relations to other macroeconomics variables.

9.2.1 Lay Views on Inflation

Leiser and Drori (2005) examined lay beliefs about inflation in different groups of society. There were interesting differences between the groups. Individuals operating as price-setters (e.g., shopkeepers) tend to associate the notion of inflation to increases in their operating costs (mainly to higher interest payments on debt) and to lower demand. In contrast, people receiving a salary (e.g., state-employed teachers) believe that in an inflationary episode, updates of (nominal) wages lag behind increases of the consumer price index. However, the core of non-expert representation of the phenomenon is nearly identical across the groups, and at variance with the concept held by professional economists. To the economically naïve individual, inflation is perceived as something bad that befalls prices and money: money is worth less, prices are higher. Its consequence is a lower value of the local currency and devaluation. Missing from their account are wages, unemployment, the government, the central bank, and indeed, any understanding of economics as a system. This conception could not be more different from Milton Friedman's famous helicopter image. 'When we economists hear the term "inflation"', writes Mankiw, 'we naturally start thinking about helicopters dropping money over the countryside. We imagine a continuing change in the unit of account that alters all nominal magnitudes proportionately' (Mankiw, 1997). The simplified understanding by non-experts is not useless, as it features understanding of some key antecedents of national price inflation and important consequences, such as currency devaluation (Ranyard et al., 2008).

Little wonder, then, that contrary to most economists, non-economists are categorically averse to inflation. To them, zero inflation is best. Robert Shiller (1997) interviewed lay people, and asked them why they so dislike inflation. His conclusion: it is because they believe that inflation makes them poorer. His respondents cite various inconveniences associated with inflation, such as making it harder to judge whether a price is advantageous, and to plan for the future. Another source of concern is the perception that inflation provides the opportunity for some economic agents to take advantage of others, and that inflation makes us feel good but ultimately deceives us, that it will weaken the country's currency, damage its national prestige, and so increase political instability (the causation they see is from inflation to instability). Still, as Shiller stresses, the supposed direct effect of inflation on the standard of living is paramount, while people are comparatively indifferent to the inconveniences it produces (Scheve, 2003; Shiller, 1997). The naïve concept of inflation is significant beyond the prediction of the rate of inflation. For instance, Savadori, Nicotra, Rumiati, and Tamborini (2001), who studied the content and structure of mental representation of economic crises in Italy, showed that inflation is considered a prime symptom of economic crisis, even though persistent inflation has a tendency to become the normal state of affairs in an economy. Again, the introduction of the euro was perceived as being accompanied by inflation – a negative phenomenon to lay people. A common inference was that it was the introduction of the euro that was responsible for the (putative) inflation (Rosa, Jesuino, & Gioiosa, 2003). These examples illustrate how reception of economic policy by the public depends on how it grasps the situation and the causal forces at work.

9.2.2   Inflation and Unemployment

Expectations of inflation are the beliefs held by the public about the likely path of inflation for the future. The 'Phillips curve' states that there is an inverse relationship (a 'trade-off') between the rate of unemployment and the rate of inflation in an economy. More accurately, unemployment varies with unanticipated inflation. But lay people do not believe in the Phillips curve. Dixon, Griffiths, and Lim (2014) analysed a long-running survey (Melbourne, 1995–2011) comprising over 220,000 observations of consumers' views about the expected state of the economy. The questionnaire included many questions, of which we will be concerned with two: on inflation: Thinking about the prices of things you buy, by this time next year, do you think they'll have gone: (1) up, (2) down or (3) stayed the same? (4) Don't Know; the other on unemployment: Now about people being out of work during the coming 12 months, do you think there'll be (1) more unemployment (2) About the same / Some more some less (3) Less unemployment (4) Don't Know. The respondents answered separate questions involving their perceptions of likely (un)favourable changes for unemployment and predicted prices. Looking at the pattern of answers to these questions, Dixon et al. (2014) show that, except for rare special cases such as during the financial crisis, the answers correlate positively. This was confirmed by Dräger,

Lamla, and Pfajfar (2016) who exploited the data accumulated over the years by the University of Michigan Survey of Consumers, which collects consumers' expectations regarding the main macroeconomics variables on a monthly basis.

9.2.3   The Good-Begets-Good Heuristic

The studies just summarized relied on participants' independent assessment of expected movements in the levels of economic activity. We now turn to people's explicit *beliefs* about how such variables are related. In one early study, Rubin (2003) provided participants with index cards carrying the name of dozens of variables and asked them to pick pairs of variables that are causally related, in the sense than an increase in one will cause the other to increase or to drop. When collating all the cards selected by a given participant, we obtain a conceptual map, such as Figure 9.2. that lays out (part of) one participant's answers to individual propositions (of the form, *A raises B*). This, however, is a synoptic map created by the experimenter – but unless they have been professionally trained, participants are quite incapable of grasping how their individual insights combine into a system: they understand its fragments piecemeal, as is known for other domains of knowledge as well (Barbas & Psillos, 1997; Grotzer, 2012; Leiser, 2001; Lundholm & Davies, 2013; Perkins & Grotzer, 2005).

And yet, there is structure to their understanding. Leiser and Aroch (2009) presented some 20 macroeconomic variables to participants. These included measures of aggregate economic activity (like the GNP), the rate of economic growth, corporate profits, wages, private spending, private investments on the stock market, the rate of inflation, the rate of unemployment. For every pair of variables, they were asked to judge explicitly whether they were causally related. For example, *If the unemployment rate increases, how will this affect the inflation rate?* Specifically, they were asked,

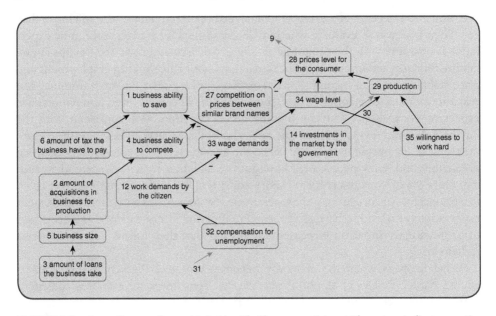

FIGURE 9.2   *Synoptic map of causal links identified by one participant. The – signs indicate negative correlations.*

for every pair of variables A and B: *If variable A increases, how will this affect variable B?* Possible answers were: B will increase / B will decrease / B will not be affected / 'I don't know'. The average rate of 'Don't Know' answers was 27%. An illuminating pattern was found when one plots all the variables on a line, putting them close together the more they are positively associated (A increases B), and far from one another the more they are negatively associated (A decreases B). It turns out that this ranking almost perfectly matches rankings of how good or bad an increase in each variable is judged to be by lay people. Changes in economic variables are considered to be good or bad, and this provides the (dubious) grounds for their answers: if both A and B belong to a same pole (good or bad), an increase in one will raise the other; if they belong to opposite poles, a raise in one will cause the other to drop. This heuristic was called the *Good-Begets-Good (GBG) heuristic*. It is a simple heuristic, that instantiates the general human tendency to bi-polar thinking (Brown, 1991), and explains the pattern of their answers.

The GBG heuristic is not absurd. Also professional economists commonly look at the economy as being in a good or bad state and have even devised economic indices to suggest an overall evaluation of the state of the economy. The latest avatar of the 'misery index', introduced by Merrill Lynch's economists (*The Economist*, 12 January 2006), adds unemployment and inflation rates, interest rates and the budget and current-account balances, then subtracts GDP growth. Its rationale is that high unemployment, inflation, and interest rates are bad, whereas a positive budget and current account balances and a high GDP growth rate are good. Still, GBG is just an approximation based on a general sentiment rather than on the understanding of economic mechanisms, and it is far from being generally valid, as we will presently see.

9.2.4 Macroeconomic Consequences of the GBG Heuristic

We return to Dräger et al. (2014), who analyzed the microdata of the Michigan Survey. Their goal was to evaluate whether US consumers form macroeconomic expectations consistent with the economic concepts we discussed here: the Phillips curve, linking inflation and unemployment rates; the Taylor rule (linking employment and price stability) and the Income Fisher equation, linking inflation with nominal and real interest rates (or income). They report that 50% of the surveyed population have expectations consistent with the Income Fisher equation, 46% consistent with the Taylor Rule and only 34% are in line with the Phillips Curve. These figures overestimate what lay people understand, since the analysis relies on correlations between predictions and many people may have got the direction right without understanding. Only 6% of consumers form theory-consistent expectations with respect to all three concepts. Unsurprisingly, those relatively few consumers with theory-consistent expectations also tend to have lower absolute inflation forecast errors, and are closer to professionals' inflation forecasts, suggesting that they follow economic news rather closely.

What happens when the economy becomes unstable? Predictions become, of course, harder. Dräger et al. (2014) observe that consumers are even less consistent with the Phillips curve and the Taylor rule during recessions and when inflation exceeds 2%. From the perspective of the central bank, stabilizing the economy and leading it to growth becomes more of a challenge. In addition to the economic complexities involved, lay people's model plays a role. GBG implies that rising actual and expected rates of inflation ('negative' developments) are predicted to lead to lower actual and future economic growth, higher unemployment and lower corporate profits. As the expected rate of inflation increases, individuals become more pessimist about the future prospects of the whole economy. In times of crisis, this lessens the chances of recovery. It is well known that the concept of overall sentiment about the economy has a large psychological component (Bovi, 2009; Resende & Zeidan, 2015) and the GBG explains in part how this component functions.

As we saw above, Dixon et al. (2014) showed in their analysis of expectations of economic change that lay predictions of inflation and unemployment conform to the GBG heuristic, and is at variance with the Philips curve. Gaffeo and Canzian (2011) further showed that the GBG heuristic has real-world economic consequences, and in particular that it complicates the task of the central banks. The Taylor rule is a monetary-policy rule that stipulates how much the central bank should change the nominal interest rate in response to changes in inflation, output, or other economic conditions. The GBG heuristic means that the public perceives the economic situation in a simplistic manner, as improving or deteriorating, and this generates waves of optimism or pessimism. A wave of sentiment among the public can trigger a corresponding change in aggregate demand. 'Such waves triggered by inflation dynamics but also governed by the GBG heuristic enhance the effectiveness of monetary policy when the volatility of the public's sentiment is relatively low, but act as a destabilizing device when intense.' The authors conclude that controlling the system by means of monetary policy is a much tougher task than predicted by the received wisdom on the stabilizing properties of the Taylor principle.

9.3   USING METAPHORS

Section 9.2 presented one way by which lay people try to come to grips with the overwhelming complexity of macroeconomics: they use an heuristic to generate (sometimes invalid) answers, accompanied by a (spurious) feeling of competence. In this section, we briefly present another way to attain the same goal, namely, by the use of metaphors or similes. Metaphors offer a bridge from the known to the unknown, from the familiar to the unfamiliar. This is often beneficial, as metaphors provide an organized structure to understand a domain, and thereby make it possible to go beyond the piecemeal grasp described above.

According to Carey (2009; see also Dunst & Levine, 2014), the human capacity for conceptual understanding and efficient reasoning relies on rich developmental primitives that developed in humans faced with cognitive domains, such as the biological, the physical, the psychological-interpersonal domains, and the moral. Some of these developmental primitives are embedded in systems of core cognition, while other structures are acquired in the course of development (Gopnik & Wellman, 2012; Xu, 2011). When having to deal cognitively and emotionally with matters for which humans are not particularly equipped, people may try to assimilate into one of those other domains. This is how they come to describe complex economic processes in physical or biological terms (Cheng & Ho, 2015), or with concepts useful to understand social relations (Lakoff, 2002).

Those domains form the backdrop for the wide-ranging specific metaphors used to understand particular economic areas and phenomena. Oberlechner, Slunecko, and Kronberger (2004) examined metaphorical conceptualizations of the foreign exchange market held by market participants, and concluded that their understanding of financial markets relies on seven metaphors: the market as a bazaar, as a machine, as gambling, as sports, as war, as a living being, and as an ocean (see also Christandl, Oberlechner, & Pitters, 2013). Crucially, each metaphor highlights and hides from view certain aspects of the foreign exchange market. Some of the metaphors imply market predictability, other do not, and indeed, the sports and the machine metaphors were found to be associated with fixed rules and predictability, whereas the bazaar and war metaphors correlated with unpredictability. Morris et al. (2007) showed how, in stock market commentary, agentic metaphors (i.e., that describe price movements as volitional, such as 'jumped' versus 'got caught') cause investors to expect that a trend will continue. As Paul Krugman urges, those misleading metaphors should be blocked:

> America's economy isn't a stalled car, nor is it an invalid who will soon return to health if he gets a bit more rest. Our problems are longer-term than either metaphor implies. And bad metaphors make for bad policy. The idea that the economic engine is going to catch or the patient rise from his sickbed any day now encourages policy makers to settle for sloppy, short-term measures when the economy really needs well-designed, sustained support.
>
> (Krugman, 2010)

Among the different cognitive explanatory stances, one stands out: the personal, intentional one. Intentionality is the default mode of understanding causality. Faced with some phenomenon, people tend to see it as a wilful action, though of course they can also think again, and adopt another perspective. This psychological bias comes out very clearly in studies about the causes of the world-wide economic crisis. Leiser, Bourgeois-Gironde, and Benita (2010) conducted a cross-national study analyzing how people from several countries account for the crisis. Respondents came from the United States, Germany, France, Russia, Israel and Sub-Saharan Africa. The authors found that respondents tend to attribute the responsibility for the crisis to moral, cognitive, and character failures of individuals, rather than to systemic features of the economy. The finding that relatively few respondents blamed the system is striking because the financial crisis would have been a natural opportunity to take stock of capitalism and globalization. These findings were confirmed in Austria by Gangl et al. (2012) who comment: 'Contrary to our expectations that the participants would criticize the economic system in general, especially neoliberalism, as this critique was also part of the public discourse about the crisis ..., we rarely found such information.' Working in Iceland, a country hit hard by the economic crisis, Thórisdóttir and Karólínudóttir (2014) too found that people were most likely to blame human foibles for the crisis (moral failures, stupidity, deliberate negligence, lax regulation and supervision), and were less prone to point to the capitalist system or to the notion that the economy 'spun out of control'. Also in line with these findings, a qualitative analysis of Irish lay explanations of the financial crisis disclosed a wide range of ideas about society, power, morality, public sphere and personhood. The crisis was not a strictly economic event but a political, social and moral one (O'Connor, 2012). Summarizing, the public holds mainly a moral/intentional view about the origin of the crisis, rather than seeing it as a complex impersonal system that malfunctioned or is structurally doomed to fail (Aprea & Sappa, 2014; Leiser, Benita, & Bourgeois-Gironde, 2016).

An extreme case of intentional causality is presented by conspiratorial thinking. Leiser, Wagner-Egger and Duani (2017) presented lay people in Switzerland, Israel and the United States with possible accounts for a range of economic concepts (the business sector, stock markets, globalization, etc.). Four statements corresponded to contrasting types of accounts: (A) the liberal economics textbook explanation; (B) government malfunction – the government is to blame; (C) the conspiracy explanation – small and powerful groups manipulate the markets; and (D) the 'bad' invisible hand – the natural market equilibrium is not socially optimal. Participants rated their agreement with each statement. To illustrate:

> Stock markets ... (A) ... are a necessary tool, a mechanism that allows for sophisticated financial activity, which is an indispensable component of modern economies. (B) ... have evolved uncontrollably in the past decades, and the government is not acting vigorously enough to regulate their activity, (C) ... are easily manipulated by the select few who can influence it via speculation, causing many small players and individuals to lose a great deal of money. (D) ... are an effective way for businesses to develop, but it also allows wealthy individuals more power over the economy and over the development of other businesses.

The authors found that there exists indeed a conspiratorial style in economics; people who endorsed the conspiratorial style (C) tended to do so consistently. Moreover, they were also more likely to give credence to classic conspiracy theories regarding such events as the allegedly fake Apollo moon landing and foul play in the death of Princess Diana.

9.4 FINANCIAL LITERACY

It would be impossible to conclude this chapter without making reference to the topic of financial literacy. Recent pension reforms, in particular, the shift from Defined Benefits to Defined Contributions plans, have placed the onus of financial management on the individual consumer. With it has come increased attention to individuals' capacity to manage their financial affairs, and the extent of their understanding of economic topics. The phrase 'financial literacy' was coined to refer to this ability. Recent research has documented great gaps in the ability of savers to manage their savings, due to lack of basic financial knowledge (Lusardi & Mitchelli, 2007). As a means to increase people's level of financial abilities, leading organizations, such as the OECD and the World Bank, promote educational programmes, as do many governments and financial institutions.

The topic of the this chapter is therefore very timely, but its corollary for teaching economic and financial literacy are not very encouraging. While knowledge is certainly to be encouraged, extensive academic research questions the 'financial literacy' approach to the improvement of financial abilities. That research suggests two conclusions:

1. Changing economic understanding is hard. Many misconceptions persist even after a year of college study (Busom & Lopez-Mayan, 2015). Participating in an economics course did not even improve minimal economic knowledge (Wobker, Kenning, Lehmann-Waffenschmidt, & Gigerenzer, 2014).

2. Attempts to increase financial literacy have a negligible effect on financial behaviour, that moreover decays over time (Fernandes, Lynch Jr, & Netemeyer, 2014). So too, Collins and O'Rourke (2010) find that counselling programmes have only a modest positive effect. Financial decisions are also affected by biases, psychological factors and external factors that may overshadow the gains of financial education (De Meza, Irlenbusch, & Reyniers, 2008; van Overveld, Smidts, Peffer, & Atkinson, forthcoming). Accordingly, financial literacy research is broadening towards 'financial capability' which focuses on actual financial practice and decisions rather than knowledge (Johnson & Sherraden, 2007). By asking people to report common behaviours in four distinct financial categories (managing money, choosing products, staying informed, and planning ahead), researchers are able to diagnose specific financial abilities (Atkinson, McKay, Collard, & Kempson, 2007). A meta-analysis performed by Miller, Reichelstein, Salas, and Zia (2015) that took this approach was able to identify specific areas where financial intervention can make the difference (e.g., increasing savings but not reducing loan defaults).

Economics suffuses modern society but is not understandable without professional training. The disparity between our innate cognitive endowment and what would be required to grasp our social and economic environment is vast. Deriving from this realization ways to enable people to live economically sound lives in a democratic society is a major and increasingly pressing challenge. Two routes need to be combined. In a democracy, economic-financial literacy may be crucial to the success of economic reforms (Fornero, 2015), especially when the political stamina is found wanting, and promoting it is a crucial but daunting challenge. Meeting it will require mapping the main components of a mature grasp of macro-economics, with a view to see whether aspects of it might be made usefully accessible to non-economists. At the level of individual decisions, we recommend that the inherent difficulty of understanding the economy and taking sound financial decisions be realistically acknowledged. For a government intent upon improving the economic life of its citizens, sponsoring financial literacy is no substitute to proper regulation. For major economic decisions, the authorities should use their regulatory powers to provide informed guidance and assistance to citizens to enable them to make the most appropriate decisions.

9.5 SUMMARY

Understanding the economy is a challenge, and people without training are not equal to it. This chapter submits that the difficulty stems from a mismatch between the cognitive proclivities of humans and the mode of functioning of modern economies. The limited scope of mental structures typically developed to come to grip mentally with a domain of knowledge means that indirect and feedback effects are not taken into account, so that policies may be endorsed with a mistaken apprehension of their consequences. The tendency to assume that causality involves intent is at variance with the complex interplay and equilibrium-seeking of aggregated variables. Lay people rely on various makeshift approaches as substitutes to proper understanding.

One of them is the use of metaphors, and in particular the notorious equation of state and household budgets. Another is the reliance on heuristics. One important heuristic we discussed at some length is the 'Good-Begets-Good' (GBG) heuristic: people assume that good (or bad) economic changes are mutually reinforcing. Such assumptions have consequences for the economy and citizen participation.

REVIEW QUESTIONS

1. What are the main psychological traits mentioned in the chapter that explains economic misconceptions; why are these misconceptions important?
2. What is the Good-Begets-Good heuristic, and how does it affect the economy?
3. Why do people rely on metaphors, and what might be their danger?
4. What is the conspiratorial mind set in understanding economics correlated with?

REFERENCES

Aprea, C., & Sappa, V. (2014). Variations of young Germans' informal conceptions of financial and economic crises phenomena. *Journal of Social Science Education, 14*, 57–67.

Ariely, D., & Jones, S. (2008). *Predictably irrational*: New York: HarperCollins.

Arthur, W. B. (2000). Cognition: The black box of economics. In D. Colander (Ed.), *The complexity vision and the teaching of economics*. Northampton, MA: Edward Elgar.

Atkinson, A., McKay, S., Collard, S., & Kempson, E. (2007). Levels of financial capability in the UK. *Public Money and Management, 27*(1), 29–36.

Barbas, A., & Psillos, D. (1997). Causal reasoning as a base for advancing a systemic approach to simple electrical circuits. *Research in Science Education, 27*(3), 445–459.

Bovi, M. (2009). Economic versus psychological forecasting. Evidence from consumer confidence surveys. *Journal of Economic Psychology, 30*(4), 563–574. doi:http://dx.doi.org/10.1016/j.joep.2009.04.001

Brown, D. E. (1991). *Human universals*. New York: McGraw-Hill.

Bruine de Bruin, W., & Bostrom, A. (2013). Assessing what to address in science communication. *Proceedings of the National Academy of Sciences, 110* (Supplement 3), 14062–14068.

Busom, I., & Lopez-Mayan, C. (2015). Student preconceptions and learning economic reasoning. Available at SSRN 2704371.

Caplan, B. (2002a). Straight talk about economic illiteracy. Retrieved from http://www.the-dissident.com/illiteracy.shtml May 2016

Caplan, B. (2002b). Systematically biased beliefs about economics: Robust evidence of judgemental anomalies from the survey of Americans and economists on the economy. *The Economic Journal, 112*(479), 433–458.

Caplan, B. (2011). *The myth of the rational voter: Why democracies choose bad policies* (new ed.). Princeton, NJ: Princeton University Press.

Carey, S. (2009). *The origin of concepts*: Oxford; Oxford University Press.

Cheng, W., & Ho, J. (2015). A corpus study of bank financial analyst reports semantic fields and metaphors. *International Journal of Business Communication*, 1–25.

Christandl, F., Oberlechner, T., & Pitters, J. (2013). Belastung oder Gelegenheit: Eine Metaphornanalyse zur Wahrnehmung der Finanzkrise durch wirtschaftliche Laien [Burden or opportunity: A metaphor analysis on the perception of the financial crisis by economic lay people]. *Wirtschaftspsychologie, 2*, 48–60.

Collins, J. M., & O'Rourke, C. M. (2010). Financial education and counseling: Still holding promise. *Journal of Consumer Affairs, 44*(3), 483–498.

Darriet, E., & Bourgeois-Gironde, S. (2015). Why lay social representations of the economy should count in economics. *Mind & Society*, 1–14. DOI:10.1007/s11299-015-0177-9.

Davies, P. (2015). Towards a framework for financial literacy in the context of democracy. *Journal of Curriculum Studies, 47*(2), 300–316.

De Meza, D., Irlenbusch, B., & Reyniers, D. (2008). *Financial capability: A behavioural economics perspective*: London: Financial Services Authority.

Dixon, R., Griffiths, W., & Lim, G. (2014). Lay people's models of the economy: A study based on surveys of consumer sentiments. *Journal of Economic Psychology, 44*, 13–20.

Donovan, E., & Kelemen, D. (2011). Just rewards: Children and adults equate accidental inequity with intentional unfairness. *Journal of Cognition and Culture, 11*(2), 137–150.

Dräger, L., Lamla, M. J., & Pfajfar, D. (2016). Are consumer expectations theory-consistent? The role of central bank communication and news. *European Economic Review, 85*, 84–111.

Dräger, L., Menz, J.-O., & Fritsche, U. (2014). Perceived inflation under loss aversion. *Applied Economics, 46*(3), 282–293.

Dunst, B., & Levine, A. (2014). Conceptual change: Analogies great and small and the quest for coherence. In *International handbook of research in history, philosophy and science teaching* (pp. 1345–1361). New York: Springer.

Fernandes, D., Lynch Jr, J. G., & Netemeyer, R. G. (2014). Financial literacy, financial education, and downstream financial behaviors. *Management Science, 60*(8), 1861–1883.

Fornero, E. (2015). Economic-financial literacy and (sustainable)pension reforms: Why the former is a key ingredient for the latter. *Bankers, Markets & Investors, 134*, 6–16.

Furnham, A. (1988). *Lay theories: Everyday understanding of problems in the social sciences*. Oxford: Pergamon Press.

Furnham, A., & Cleare, A. (1988). School children's conceptions of economics: Prices, wages, investments and strikes. *Journal of Economic Psychology, 9*, 467–479.

Gaffeo, E., & Canzian, G. (2011). The psychology of inflation, monetary policy and macroeconomic instability. *Journal of Socio-Economics*. DOI:10.1016/j.socec.2011.05.005

Gangl, K., Kastlunger, B., Kirchler, E., & Voracek, M. (2012). Confidence in the economy in times of crisis: Social representations of experts and laypeople. *The Journal of Socio-Economics, 41*(5), 603–614.

Gopnik, A., & Wellman, H. M. (2012). Reconstructing constructivism: Causal models, Bayesian learning mechanisms, and the theory theory. *Psychological Bulletin, 138*(6), 1085–1108. DOi:10.1037/a0028044

Grotzer, T. A. (2012). *Learning causality in a complex world: Understandings of consequence*. Lanham. MD: Rowman & Littlefield Education.

Holyoak, K. J., & Thagard, P. (1989). Analogical mapping by constraint satisfaction. *Cognitive Science, 13*, 295–355.

Huston, S. J. (2010). Measuring financial literacy. *Journal of Consumer Affairs, 44*(2), 296–316.

Huston, S. J. (2012). Assessing financial literacy. *Student Financial Literacy, 56*, 109–124.

Inman, P. (2015). Lack of financial literacy among voters is a 'threat to democracy'. *The Guardian*, 16 March.

Johnson, E., & Sherraden, M. S. (2007). From financial literacy to financial capability among youth. *Journal of Society & Social Welfare, 34*, 119–146.

Kelemen, D., & Rosset, E. (2009). The human function compunction: Teleological explanation in adults. *Cognition, 145*, 1–6.

Kelemen, D., Rottman, J., & Seston, R. (2013). Professional physical scientists display tenacious teleological tendencies: Purpose-based reasoning as a cognitive default. *Journal of Experimental Psychology: General, 142*(4), 1074–1083.

Krugman, P. (2010). Block those metaphors, Op-Ed. *New York Times*. Dec. 12. Retrieved from www.nytimes.com/2010/12/13/opinion/13krugman.html

Lakoff, G. (2002). *Moral politics: How conservatives and liberals think*. Chicago: University of Chicago Press.

Leiser, D. (2001). Scattered naive theories: Why the human mind is isomorphic to the internet web. *New Ideas in Psychology, 19*(3), 175–202.

Leiser, D., & Aroch, R. (2009). Lay understanding of macroeconomic causation: The good-begets-good heuristic. *Applied Psychology, 58*(3), 370–384.

Leiser, D., Benita, R., & Bourgeois-Gironde, S. (2016). Differing conceptions of the causes of the economic crisis: Effects of culture, economic training, and personal impact. *Journal of Economic Psychology, 53*, 154–163. DOI: http://dx.doi.org/10.1016/j.joep.2016.02.002

Leiser, D., & Beth Halachmi, R. (2006). Children's understanding of market forces. *Journal of Economic Psychology, 27*(1), 6–19.

Leiser, D., Bourgeois-Gironde, S., & Benita, R. (2010). Human foibles or systemic failure: Lay perceptions of the 2008–2009 financial crisis. *Journal of Socio-Economics, 39*(2), 132–141. doi:10.1016/j.socec.2010.02.013

Leiser, D., & Drori, S. (2005). Naïve understanding of inflation. *Journal of Socio-Economics, 34*(2), 179–198. DOI:10.1016/j.socec.2004.09.006

Leiser, D., Duani, N., & Wagner-Egger, P. (2017). The conspiratorial style in lay economic thinking. *PLoS ONE, 12*(3), e0171238.

Leiser, D., & Zaltsman, J. (1990). Economic socialization in the kibbutz and the town in Israel. *Journal of Economic Psychology, 11*(4), 557–565.

Loix, E., & Pepermans, R. (2009). A qualitative study on the perceived consequences of poverty: Introducing consequential attributions as a missing link in lay thinking on poverty. *Applied Psychology, 58*(3), 385–402.

Lombrozo, T., Kelemen, D., & Zaitchik, D. (2007). Inferring design. *Psychological Science, 18*(11), 999–1006.

Lundholm, C., & Davies, P. (2013). Conceptual change in the social sciences. In S. Vosniadou (Ed.), *International handbook of research on conceptual change* (pp. 288–304). New York: Routledge.

Lusardi, A., & Mitchelli, O. (2007). Financial literacy and retirement preparedness: Evidence and implications for financial education. *Business Economics, 42*(1), 35–44.

Mankiw, N. G. (1997). Comment on 'Why do people dislike inflation?' In C. Romer, & D. Romer (Eds.), *Reducing inflation: Motivation and strategy*. Chicago: University of Chicago Press.

Miller, M., Reichelstein, J., Salas, C., & Zia, B. (2015). Can you help someone become financially capable? A meta-analysis of the literature. *The World Bank Research Observer, 30*(2), 220–246.

Morris, M. W., Sheldon, O. J., Ames, D. R., & Young, M. J. (2007). Metaphors and the market: Consequences and preconditions of agent and object metaphors in stock market commentary. *Organizational Behavior and Human Decision Processes, 102*(2), 174–192.

Ng, T., & Wright, M. (2007). Introducing the MONIAC: An early and innovative economic model. *Reserve Bank of New Zealand Bulletin, 70*, 46–52.

Oberlechner, T., Slunecko, T., & Kronberger, N. (2004). Surfing the money tides: Understanding the foreign exchange market through metaphors. *British Journal of Social Psychology, 43*(1), 133–156. DOI:10.1348/014466604322916024

O'Connor, C. (2012). Using social representations theory to examine lay explanation of contemporary social crises: The case of Ireland's recession. *Journal of Community & Applied Social Psychology, 22*(6), 459–469. DOI:10.1002/casp.1125

Perkins, D. N., & Grotzer, T. A. (2005). Dimensions of causal understanding: The role of complex causal models in students' understanding of science. *Studies in Science Education, 41*, 117–166.

Pinker, S. (2002). *The blank slate*. New York: Viking.

Ranyard, R., Missier, F. D., Bonini, N., Duxbury, D., & Summers, B. (2008). Perceptions and expectations of price changes and inflation: A review and conceptual framework. *Journal of Economic Psychology, 29*(4), 378–400. DOI:10.1016/j.joep.2008.07.002

Resende, M., & Zeidan, R. (2015). Psychological biases and economic expectations: Evidence on industry experts. *Journal of Neuroscience, Psychology, and Economics, 8*(3), 160–172. DOI:10.1037/npe0000043

Roos, M. W. M. (2007). Nonexpert beliefs about the macroeconomic consequences of economic and noneconomic events. *Public Choice, 132*(3–4), 291–304. DOI:10.1007/s11127-007-9152-2

Roos, M. W. M. (2008). Predicting the macroeconomic effects of abstract and concrete events. *European Journal of Political Economy, 24,* 192–201.

Rosa, A. S. de, Jesuino, J., & Gioiosa, C. (2003). Euro currency system: Familiarisation processes the introduction of the euro. Paper presented at the The Euro: Currency and Symbol, Vienna, Austria.

Rosset, E. (2008). It's no accident: Our bias for intentional explanations. *Cognition, 108*(3), 771–780.

Rubin, P. (2003). Folk economics. *Southern Economic Journal, 70*(1), 157–172.

Savadori, L., Nicotra, E., Rumiati, R., & Tamborini, R. (2001). Mental representation of economic crisis in Italian and Swiss samples. *Swiss Journal of Psychology, 60*(1), 11–14. Doi: 10.1024// 1421-0185.60.1.11

Scheve, K. (2003). Public demand for low inflation. Bank of England Working Paper No. 172, International Economic Analysis Division. Available at SSRN: http://ssrn.com/abstract=392361 or http://dx.doi.org/10.2139/ssrn.392361.

Sevón, G., & Weckström, S. (1989). The development of reasoning about economic events: A study of Finnish children. *Journal of Economic Psychology, 10,* 495–514.

Shahaeian, A., Peterson, C. C., Slaughter, V., & Wellman, H. M. (2011). Culture and the sequence of steps in theory of mind development. *Developmental Psychology, 47*(5), 1239.

Shiller, R. J. (1997). Why do people dislike inflation? In C. D. Romer & D. H. Romer (Eds.), *Reducing inflation: Motivation and strategy* (pp. 13–70). Chicago: University of Chicago Press.

Thomadakis, S. B. (2015). Growth, debt and sovereignty prolegomena to the Greek crisis (GreeSE Paper No. 91.). Retrieved from London School of Economics and Political Science.

Thórisdóttir, H., & Karólínudóttir, K. E. (2014). The boom and the bust: Can theories from social psychology and related disciplines account for one country's economic crisis? *Analyses of Social Issues and Public Policy, 14*(1), 281–310.

van Bavel, R., & Gaskell, G. (2004). Narrative and systemic modes of economic thinking. *Culture and Psychology, 10*(4), 417–439.

van Overveld, M., Smidts, A., Peffer, G., & Atkinson, A. (forthcoming). Financial capability and financial litteracy: Two sides of the same coin? Examining the relationship between financial knowledge, financial skills, personality traits and emotion regulation. *The International Journal of Research in Marketing.*

Wellman, H. M., Fang, F., & Peterson, C. C. (2011). Sequential progressions in a theory-of-mind scale: Longitudinal perspectives. *Child Development, 82*(3), 780–792.

Williamson, M. R., & Wearing, A. J. (1996). Lay people's cognitive models of the economy. *Journal of Economic Psychology, 17*(1), 3–38.

Wobker, I., Kenning, P., Lehmann-Waffenschmidt, M., & Gigerenzer, G. (2014). What do consumers know about the economy? *Journal für Verbraucherschutz und Lebensmittelsicherheit, 9*(3), 231–242.

Xu, F. (2011). Rational constructivism, statistical inference, and core cognition. *Behavioral and Brain Sciences, 34*(03), 151–152.

FURTHER READING

Lewis, A., Webley, P. & Furnham, A.F (1995). *The new economic mind.* Brighton: Harvester Wheatsheaf.

Lundholm, C., & Davies, P. (2013). Conceptual change in the social sciences. In S. Vosniadou (Ed.), *International handbook of research on conceptual change* (pp. 288–304). New York: Routledge.

10 The Citizen's Judgements of Prices and Inflation

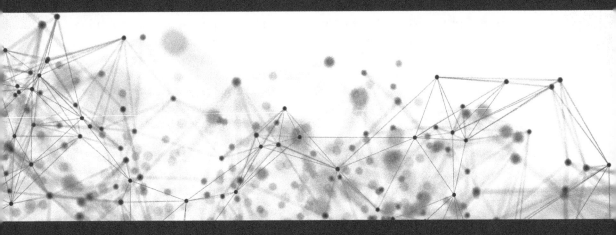

ROB RANYARD, FABIO DEL MISSIER, NICOLAO BONINI AND DAVIDE PIETRONI

CHAPTER OUTLINE

LEARNING OUTCOMES

BY THE END OF THIS CHAPTER YOU SHOULD BE ABLE TO:

1. Understand and describe the principal theoretical accounts of price perception.
2. Identify and describe the main factors affecting price perception.
3. Define perceived inflation and inflation expectations and identify their underlying psychological determinants and consequences.

10.1 INTRODUCTION

This chapter provides an introduction to the economic psychology of price and inflation judgements, focusing on the main findings and the more relevant psychological theories. The first part of the chapter (Section 10.2) is devoted to the process of price evaluation. This is a fundamental process underlying individual economic and consumer behaviour, because purchase decisions usually imply a judgement of the price of a target product or service, and price is a fundamental evaluation dimension. Thus, it is important to understand the processes that lead individuals to deem a given price as cheap or expensive (Putler, 1992). In Section 10.2, we will initially focus on theories centred on the construct of a reference price, defined as a benchmark price used in relative evaluation processes. These theories share the assumption that one or more reference prices, stored in memory or available in the external environment, are used to make sense of the target price via comparative evaluation processes (Monroe, 1990). We then briefly consider how prices are evaluated according to three psychological theories (prospect theory, decision by sampling, and norm theory), which provide further insight into evaluation processes and their effects. Finally, we will take into account the factors affecting retrieval of reference prices and briefly mention other aspects relevant to price evaluation.

Section 10.3 is devoted to perceived inflation and inflation expectations. Inflation refers to changes in the value of money over time. From an individual's point of view, inflation is revealed as changes in the cost of living (price inflation) and changes in income, for example, wage inflation. Past price inflation is officially measured by the annual percentage change in the total cost of a basket of goods and services purchased by the typical consumer. In contrast, official measures of price inflation *expectations* are forecasts of price changes in the basket of goods – the most widely used being based on complex models of the economy. People's perceptions of past and expectations of future inflation have been found to differ from official statistics, often substantially (for a review, see Ranyard, Del Missier, Bonini, Duxbury, & Summers, 2008). It is important to understand how this occurs, since, as we show, perceived inflation influences expected inflation, which in turn affects economic behaviour such as wage negotiations, borrowing, saving and spending. Furthermore, because of such effects on individual and household behaviour, and because public expectations are used to inform monetary policy, perceived and expected inflation indirectly affect the performance of the macro-economy (Armantier et al., 2013). After reviewing evidence of how people's perceptions and expectations are formed, we turn to research demonstrating some of their consequences. The chapter concludes by outlining some of the policy implications of the research reviewed.

10.2 PRICE EVALUATION

10.2.1 Reference Price Theories

Different conceptions of reference price exist and are used in different contexts (cf. Briesch, Krishnamurthi, Mazumdar, & Raj, 2010; Niedrich, Sharma, & Wedell, 2001; Winer, 1988). The more typical assume that consumers evaluate the price of a product by comparing it with other prices in their memory (*internal* reference prices) or available in the environment (*external* reference prices) (Jacobson & Obermiller, 1990). This comparison process is assumed to be psychologically crucial for making sense of a price. Although reference price theories differ in the type of comparison and evaluation postulated, it is usually supposed that the comparison process involves the subjective (perceived) value of prices and not their nominal values (cf. Niedrich et al., 2001). In other words, consumers react to their psychological perception of prices and not to their face value.[1]

Imagine being a habitual espresso coffee drinker with extensive experience of the coffeehouses of your area. The price of a standard espresso cup in your area is usually between €0.80 and €1.30, with a modal value of €1.00. A new coffeehouse opens and you go there to taste their espresso. You are asked for €1.20, without any apparent reason motivating this price (e.g., better quality of the blend, fair trade production, coffeehouse environment). You end up judging this price as expensive. In this case, the price judgement relies on *internal* reference prices stored in your memory. Now imagine you are attending a hotel-based meeting. You are supposed to give a talk within one hour. Suddenly, your belt breaks and you rush to a clothes shop in the hotel. Not being a habitual belt shopper, you have no clear idea about the prices. So you examine a few suitable models within the rather restricted set of options available in the hotel shop and compare their prices and the other features. In this case, the judgement of the price will depend on the *external* prices of the products considered (i.e., the prices displayed on product labels). Generally, external reference prices are used more frequently when the consumer is not able to remember product prices or is not sufficiently motivated to retrieve them (Briesch et al., 2010). There are also hybrid situations, in which the consumer relies both on internal and on external reference prices (Mayhew & Winer, 1992; Rajendran & Tellis, 1994).

Reference price theories differ with respect to the nature of the comparison processes involved. According to adaptation level theory (Helson, 1947, 1964), the evaluation of a price depends on the difference between the price to be evaluated and the *adaptation level*. The adaptation level can be conceived as a weighted mean of the prices in a given reference category, representing a kind of prototypical reference price derived from encountered prices. In our coffeehouse example, the adaptation level could be a dynamically updated mean of the espresso prices that our coffee drinker has encountered in his or her area, in which the more recent prices are weighted more. Thus, the evaluation of the espresso price in the new expensive coffeehouse will reflect the distance between the price and the adaptation level (Figure 10.1).

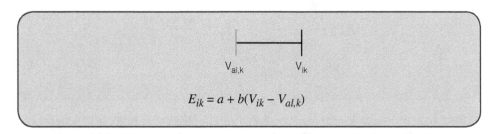

$$E_{ik} = a + b(V_{ik} - V_{al,k})$$

FIGURE 10.1 *Price evaluation according to adaptation level theory (see Niedrich et al., 2001). V_{ik} is the price to be evaluated (in the evaluation context k) and $V_{al,k}$ is the adaptation level. The price judgement (E_{ik}) depends on the distance between the target price and the adaptation level.*

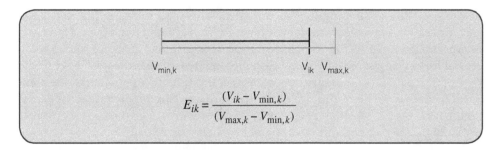

FIGURE 10.2 *Price evaluation in range theory (see Niedrich et al., 2001). V_{ik} is the price to be evaluated (in the evaluation context k), $V_{min,k}$ and $V_{max,k}$ are the minimum and the maximum consumer's reference prices. The price judgement (E_{ik}) depends on the ratio of the difference between the target price and the minimum price, and the range.*

According to range theory (Volkmann, 1951), a target price is instead evaluated by taking into account the minimum and the maximum reference prices, more specifically by taking into account the proportion of the contextual range of reference prices that is lower than the target price (Figure 10.2). Thus, our coffee drinker should evaluate the price in relation to the lowest and highest reference price of espresso coffees in her or his memory (€0.80, €1.30).

Range-frequency theory (Parducci, 1965, 1995) assumes that the whole frequency distribution of reference prices affects the judgement of a target price, beyond the influence of extreme values. The evaluation of the target price can be conceived as a weighted average between a range-based evaluation and a frequency-based evaluation (Figure 10.3). In the frequency-based evaluation, the target price is evaluated considering its rank (relative position) within the distribution of reference prices. Following our coffee example, the frequency-based evaluation will appraise the rank of the price paid (€1.20) within the distribution of coffee prices paid in the area.

The three theories we have just summarized are probably the ones more supported by empirical evidence. There have been some attempts to contrast them experimentally by manipulating critical factors (such as the range of presented

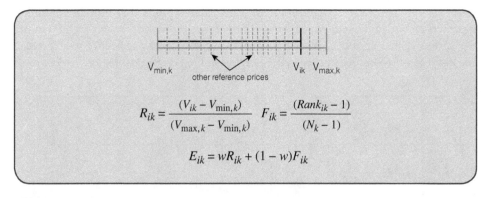

FIGURE 10.3 *Price evaluation in range-frequency theory (see Niedrich et al., 2001). V_{ik} is the price to be evaluated (in the evaluation context k), $V_{min,k}$ and $V_{max,k}$ are the minimum and the maximum consumer's reference prices. The price judgement (E_{ik}) depends on a weighted mean of the range-based evaluation (R_{ik}) and the frequency-based evaluation (F_{ik}), where $Rank_{ik}$ is the rank of the target price and N_k the number of contextual prices.*

prices and their frequency distribution). Janiszewski and Lichtenstein (1999) compared adaptation level theory and range theory by manipulating the range of presented prices while keeping the mean constant, finding that the range of prices affected the judgement of the mean of presented prices. Niedrich et al. (2001) manipulated the range, mean and distribution of presented prices, asking participants to evaluate given prices. Their findings supported range-frequency theory, showing that participants were sensitive not only to the range, but also to the relative rank of a price within the distribution. One study showed that participants were more affected by extreme reference prices (and thus by the range) when the judgement was memory-based versus based on externally available prices, possibly because extreme values are easier to recall and thus they may represent effective anchors in a memory-based judgement.

However, it seems rather implausible from a psychological viewpoint that consumers would recall an entire distribution of prices when evaluating a target price. Alternatively, the evaluation may rely on more intuitive and global judgements reflecting the price distribution or on a sample of retrieved prices (e.g., Dougherty, Gettys, & Ogden, 1999; Kahneman & Miller, 1986; Stewart, Chater, & Brown, 2006).

10.2.2   Price Evaluation in Prospect Theory, Decision by Sampling, and Norm Theory

Other theories relevant to the field of economic psychology have been applied to price evaluation. In this context, some aspects of the evaluation process implied by prospect theory are worth mentioning (Kahneman & Tversky, 1979; Tversky & Kahneman, 1992).[2] First, categorizing the situation as a gain or as a loss in relation to a reference point (usually the status quo or a given reference price) changes the evaluation (Kalyanaram & Winer, 1995; Putler, 1992). Second, owing to diminishing returns or sensitivity, the same differences between lower versus higher nominal values are evaluated differently at different absolute values (e.g., a price increase from €10 to €20 will be judged as more unpleasant than one from €110 to €120). Finally losses have a greater impact than corresponding gains, which means loss aversion (e.g., the pain of losing €10 will be approximately double the pleasure of gaining €10). As a consequence, consumers should react more strongly to perceived losses (e.g., price increases) than to perceived gains (e.g., price decreases) (Brachinger, 2006; Hardie, Johnson, & Fader, 1993). Prospect theory captures important aspects of price perception, as the difference between subjective gains and losses. However, it has been criticized for its reliance on descriptive psychoeconomic functions that do not actually provide an explanation of price evaluation in terms of psychological processes.

The decision by sampling theory (Stewart et al., 2006) overcomes this criticism and explains a series of 'traditional' evaluation findings and phenomena in terms of more plausible psychological mechanisms (sampling and rank-based evaluation). The theory challenges the assumption that there are stable internal scales or functions to evaluate monetary changes, temporal intervals, or probabilities. During the evaluation process, a sample of instances is derived from memory and/or from the external environment in relation to the item to be evaluated (e.g., a set of reference prices for a target price). Given that memory is assumed to reflect occurrences in the environment (Anderson & Schooler, 1991), a stochastic memory sampling process will represent the stimuli typically encountered in people's experience. The judgement of the item to be evaluated is assumed to reflect the rank of the target item in relation to the sampled items (e.g., the relative position of the target price within the retrieved sample of reference prices), which can be determined by a series of binary comparisons (Kornienko, 2004). Therefore, the theory naturally incorporates a frequency-based judgement. Range-related effects can be explained by assuming that sampled elements do not belong only to the immediate context but are retrieved from long-term memory (Stewart et al., 2006).

Another theory sharing the idea of memory recruitment is norm theory (Kahneman & Miller, 1986), according to which evaluation takes place in relation to a set of relevant items (the norm) activated in parallel starting from the target item and its features. Thus, if a price of a product has to be judged, the product will activate similar products and their prices that will be used for evaluation. However, norm theory does not assume that the items composing the norm are sampled into working memory or processed with awareness, which seems to capture what happens in some price evaluation contexts. Starting from the norm items, distributions of values for relevant attributes are obtained and their values are weighted according to their activation. These distributions underlie a judgement potentially sensitive to the effects of range and frequency.

10.2.3   Factors Affecting Price Memory and Evaluation

It should be noted that consumers are not always able to accurately remember the prices of products (Monroe & Lee, 1999) and their knowledge seems to depend both on experience with the product category (Briesch et al., 1997) and on price variability in the market (Aalto-Setälä, & Raijas, 2003). Among the other factors contributing to accurate price memory, are recency and frequency of exposure or purchase (Brachinger, 2006; Dickson & Sawyer, 1986; Krishna, Currim, & Shoemaker, 1991), and item distinctiveness and salience, which may explain why extreme values assume more importance in memory-based judgements (Niedrich et al., 2001). The idea that memory accessibility of reference items (e.g., products or prices) at the time of the judgement affects the evaluation of a target price or dimension has been supported by priming studies showing that pre-activating some products in consumer memory affects subsequent product evaluation (e.g., Herr, 1989) and inflation evaluation (Del Missier, Ranyard, & Bonini, 2016). Moreover, given that products are evaluated in relation to similar products (Kahneman & Miller, 1986; Stewart et al., 2006), prices of the products similar to the one to be evaluated are more likely to be retrieved. It has also been proposed that similarity between the price to be evaluated and reference prices may affect not only retrieval but also price evaluation (Qian & Brown, 2005).

Finally, it should be noted that other factors matter for price evaluation, including consumers' characteristics, price presentation characteristics, and context (for a review, see Raghubir, 2006). For instance, different purchase contexts may lead to the use of different reference prices (Thaler, 1985, 1999). Indeed, consumers' willingness to pay for a cold beer during a hot day on the beach is much higher if the purchase has to take place in a fancy resort hotel vs. a small, run-down grocery store (Thaler, 1985, but see also Ranyard, Charlton, & Williamson, 2001).

10.3 INFLATION

10.3.1 The Formation of Inflation Perceptions

As mentioned earlier, surveys have revealed differences between official inflation measures and the citizen's perception of past price changes, particularly after a currency change (see Ranyard et al., 2008). One reason for such differences is that most people do not routinely purchase the typical basket used to calculate the official measures. For example, a recent analysis by the Office for National Statistics (ONS, 2014) estimated that although in the past decade UK price inflation was 2.6% on average, UK citizens in the lowest decile of expenditure experienced an inflation rate about 1% higher. A second reason relates to how survey questions are worded. A typical wording to elicit judgements of expected inflation, for example, is: *During the next 12 months, do you think that prices in general will go up, or go down ... By about what percent do you expect prices to go [up/down] on the average?*, as used by the Michigan Survey of Consumers in 2015. Bruine de Bruin et al. (2012) compared expectation judgements elicited by this question with an alternative in which the words *prices in general* were replaced by *US inflation*. With the alternative wording, US survey respondents' median estimate of expected inflation, and its dispersion (standard deviation), were significantly lower. The authors suggest that the original wording biases judgements upwards because *prices in general* (or as is sometimes used, *the prices you pay*) cues memories for specific higher price increases respondents had experienced. However, this is only part of the story, as we elaborate below.

As illustrated in Figure 10.4, various sources of information contribute to perceived inflation judgements, including personal experience of price changes, media reports, official statistics and expectations (Ranyard et al., 2008). It has been hypothesized that

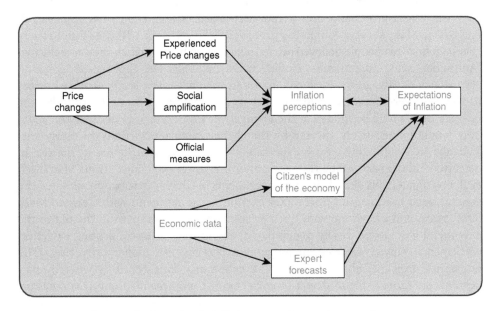

FIGURE 10.4 *Sources of information for inflation perceptions and expectations.*

if inflation judgements are constructed from memory of personal experience of price changes, then those that are more available, or easier to recall, will have a disproportionate influence. Evidence supporting an availability mechanism was described by Jungermann, Brachinger, Belting, Grinberg, & Zacharias (2007), who showed experimentally that perceived inflation was related to product frequency of purchase, with more frequently bought products contributing more to the judgement. This was confirmed by Huber (2011) in three experiments of simulated purchases in which the frequency of products with increased prices was manipulated, while overall expenditure increases, and the relative price increase of individual products, were controlled. Finally, in a more direct test of the availability mechanism, Del Missier et al. (2016) primed products that had either risen or fallen in price in the previous year. In two experiments with different procedures, priming influenced perceived inflation judgements significantly in the direction that was primed.

It has also been suggested that personal experience of price changes can bias perceived inflation because people pay more attention, and give more weight, to larger and/or negative price changes (Bates & Gabor, 1986; Jungermann et al., 2007). In addition, as Wärneryd (1986) observed, people can learn about inflation both directly from exposure to prices and indirectly from social communication, including via the media. A consequence of this is that an individual's asymmetric attention to, and evaluation of, large price increases compared to other changes may be amplified by media reports, which may further bias inflation perceptions. Soroka (2006) found evidence for such an effect in an analysis of 1986–2000 UK economic indicators, media reports of them, and public opinion. This was corroborated with Swedish survey data by Dräger (2011), who concluded that these biasing influences of the media on perceived inflation were stronger under high or volatile inflation.

Finally, turning to the role of expectations, Bates and Gabor (1986) suggested that believing inflation to be high can generate a general expectation that biases perceptions of past price changes. Evidence for the role of expectations was provided by German researchers investigating what they referred to as illusory price increases after the 2002 Euro changeover (Traut-Mattausch, Schulz-Hardt, Greitemeyer, & Frey, 2004). Many surveys comparing perceived inflation to the CPI after the currency change found that people believed prices to have risen by more than they actually had (Antonides, 2008; Aucremanne, Collin, & Dhyne, 2005; Del Giovane & Sabbatini, 2005; Fluch & Stix, 2005). Respondents in an Irish interview study expected prices to rise for several reasons, including that price conversions would be rounded up, or price rises would be hidden at the changeover to the Euro, or because the economy would be negatively affected by the change in currency (Ranyard, Burgoyne, Saldanha, & Routh, 2005). Such expectations could have contributed to the rise in perceived inflation across the Eurozone after the currency change. Traut-Mattausch et al. investigated this directly in four experiments in which participants estimated the general trend in restaurant prices after examining an old menu with German Mark (DM) prices and a new one with Euro prices. The inflation rate from the old to the new menu was systematically manipulated, and in spite of disconfirming evidence, participants showed a consistent judgement bias towards higher price rises. The researchers explained this in terms of an expectancy-consistent bias whereby participants are more likely to detect or correct conversion calculation errors contrary to their expectations. In another study, Greitemeyer, Schulz-Hardt, Traut-Mattausch and Frey (2005) induced price trend expectations experimentally (higher prices versus stable prices). They asked participants to read a fictitious article that had allegedly appeared in a well-respected German magazine and then, using the menu paradigm, they investigated whether the induced expectations biased judgements of inflation. As predicted, the expectation of rising prices led participants to perceive increased prices when they were actually stable, whereas the expectation of stable prices led them to underestimate price increases.

10.3.2   The Formation of Inflation Expectations

The rational expectations hypothesis, that people can learn to use the available economic information to form an unbiased forecast of future inflation, has been a basic assumption of mainstream macro-economic theory. It is therefore important to test it empirically, since if it is not valid, then predictions of macro-economic theory may be flawed. The rational expectations hypothesis has been investigated via three research questions: (1) Are the citizen's inflation expectations homogeneous and unbiased?; (2) Do lay models of the economy differ from expert models in important ways?; and (3) Do people use available economic information efficiently in forming expected inflation judgements?

As indicated earlier, inflation expectations have been measured in surveys for many years. One way their accuracy might be assessed is by comparing, for example, forecasts of inflation one year ahead with the CPI value realized at that point in time. However, Jonung and Laidler (1988) argued that apparent biases in judgements can occur with this approach because people may rationally take into account future events that are probable at the time of forecast but do not actually happen before the forecast's target date. The authors argue that instead, the prediction of the rational expectations hypothesis that inflation *perceptions* are unbiased should be tested, since it is not subject to the above criticism. As we have seen, there is evidence against this prediction. Furthermore, in their analysis of Swedish survey data from 1978 to 1985, when inflation was running at about 15%, Jonung and Laidler found that although average perceptions were relatively unbiased compared to the CPI, Swedish respondents systematically underestimated *changes* in inflation. This produced significant autocorrelation of estimation errors not consistent with the hypothesis.

Another way to assess the accuracy of lay expectations is to compare them to expert forecasts. Armantier et al. (2013) found that average one year ahead inflation expectations from the Michigan Consumer Surveys for the years 2007–2012, i.e., across the Great Recession, followed the same temporal pattern of a survey of professional forecasters. However, they were consistently higher on average and were more variable. Interpretation of the survey question wording, as discussed earlier, is likely to be one factor underlying these differences.

Finally, as shown in Figure 10.4, some of the sources of information people may use to form inflation expectations include mental models of the economy, perceived inflation and expert forecasts. If a person's mental model of the economy is a primary source, and if the rational expectations hypothesis has some validity, then people may be able to use relevant economic data such as the CPI, the central bank interest rate, and recent oil prices and unemployment trends (but see Chapter 9 in this volume). Burke and Manz (2014) investigated the extent to which people use such information efficiently in an online experiment with US students and non-student adults. A US bank's computer model of the US economy was adapted to create a realistic simulation of the time course of a national economy. Participants had access to relevant data as described above, and also to some plausible but inefficient data, such as recent milk price trends. In a series of exercises their task was to forecast inflation one year and five years ahead. Prior to making the inflation forecast, the typical participant most frequently consulted recent CPI information, which is the most efficient variable in the bank's model. They also, however, often considered recent milk price trends, which had little predictive power. The main finding, though, was that forecast accuracy, as measured by deviation from the model's forecast, was significantly related to a measure of participants' economic literacy, which included monetary and financial knowledge and numeracy (see also Bruine de Bruin, van der Klaauw, Downs, Fischhoff, Topa, & Armantier, 2010). The authors concluded that their findings highlight the importance of education to raise citizens' economic literacy.

In large-sample, cross-national online experiments in both a high and a low inflation country (Argentina and the United States), Cavallo, Cruces and Perez-Truglia (2014) manipulated two sources of information: supermarket purchases and their price changes, and the CPI. Participants first estimated past inflation and then received further information (either the official CPI or supermarket price changes, or both, or neither) before forecasting the inflation rate one year ahead. They found that in both countries 'inflation expectations are very reactive to information about inflation statistics ... [however] ... individuals assigned significant weight to their own memories of price changes' (p. 33). The finding that people can appropriately use past inflation statistics was corroborated by Armantier et al. (2014), who found in their online US experiments that participants, when given average 12-month past food price change information, revised their inflation rate expectation in the predicted direction (compared to a control group). The finding that experience of (and memory for) specific price changes can influence inflation expectations was corroborated experimentally by Gärling and Gamble (2008) and by Bruine de Bruin, van der Klaauw and Topa (2011). Finally, few studies have examined whether people use expert forecast information when it is available. Recently, however, in the above-mentioned study, Armantier et al. demonstrated that this was the case.

To date, then, it is clear that ordinary people, especially those with higher monetary and financial literacy, can use expert forecasts and economic data efficiently in forming inflation expectations. However, there is a strong general influence of both perceived inflation and perceptions of specific price changes that can bias expectations substantially. Further research is needed to identify the relative contribution of these different sources of information to inflation expectations and to identify ways to debias expectation judgements.

10.3.3 Consequences of Inflation Perceptions and Expectations

Individual perceptions and expectations of inflation have significant consequences for national economies because of their effects on economic behaviour. This link has been demonstrated in several studies. First, Eppright, Arguea and Huth (1998) showed that the average 12-month inflation expectation, as measured by the University of Michigan Index of Consumer Expectations, was a significant predictor of future aggregate US expenditure, contributing predictive power over and above that of objective economic data. Second, inflation perceptions have been found to be related to wage bargaining behaviour, with consequent impacts on the macro-economy (Du Caju, Gautier, Momferatou, & Ward-Warmedinger, 2008). Third, Sorić (2013) identified effects on aggregate consumption expenditure of both perceptions and expectations of inflation in a cross-national study of survey data from eight post-communist European countries. Using structural vector autoregression (VAR) methodology, he found that, in line with rational models, perceptions of sharp increases in recent inflation were followed by immediate and durable decreases in aggregate consumption, whereas one-year-ahead expectations of sharp increases were followed by a temporary consumption boost. Related to the latter, D'Acunto, Hoang and Weber (2015) found that German consumers increased their spending on consumer durables relative to other goods after an announcement of a future Value Added Tax (VAT) rise, which obviously changed inflation expectations.

Other recent studies have reported effects of inflation expectations on investment and saving behaviour. In two incentivized, web-based investment choice experiments (N = 771, 734), Armantier et al. (2015) found that choice of inflation index-linked investment versus a fixed return in 12 months was significantly related to judgements of expected inflation. With respect to saving behaviour, Arnold, Dräger and Fritsche (2014) found that higher inflation expectations affected planned savings adjustments because higher interest rates were expected.

10.4   POLICY IMPLICATIONS

First let us consider some implications of price evaluation research for consumer policy. Overall, price evaluation appears to be a reference-based and, to some extent, situation-specific process, which can be rather malleable unless the consumer has an accurate knowledge of prices. Thus, to help consumers evaluate prices of less familiar purchases, real-time market-derived reference prices could be provided via information services. Public services for some product categories already exist in some countries in the form of SMS or apps. Ideally this information should be easy to evaluate, allowing the consumer to understand where the price of a given product falls within the price distribution and range. Web-based price comparison tools of products and services may be helpful as well, provided that they offer really unbiased and evaluable information.

We now turn briefly to the implications of research on inflation judgements for financial education. The rate of recent and future inflation can have a significant impact on the outcomes of important economic decisions that individuals and households must make. However, as we have seen, people's perceptions and expectations of the rate of inflation can be significantly biased. Furthermore, understanding of the impact of inflation may vary widely. Although the research has shown that the average citizen can demonstrate useful knowledge, the understanding of those with lower economic literacy may be rather poor (see Chapter 9 in this volume). For example, a recent UK survey of 3,000 adults found that: 'When asked to identify whether inflation at 5% would have eroded the purchasing power of money in an account paying 3% interest, a third of people got this wrong ... this rose to 44% of those aged under 35' (Money Advice Service, 2014). This and the research findings described earlier suggest that there is need for financial education and advice concerning changes in the rate of inflation over time and its effects.

10.5 SUMMARY

Research on two aspects of the citizen's price judgements was reviewed: price evaluation, and judgements of aggregate trends in prices, i.e., perceptions of past, and expectations of future, inflation. The former is a fundamental process underlying consumer behaviour, while the latter influences economic behaviour, such as wage negotiations, spending, saving and borrowing.

Price evaluation is usually considered a comparative process, in which consumers make sense of a price to be judged in relation to reference prices stored in their memories or available in the external environment. However, reference price theories differ with respect to the evaluation process postulated and the prices considered. Other theories provide further insight into price evaluation phenomena (e.g., gain-loss asymmetry) and into the psychological processes underlying price evaluation. However, it is currently not completely clear to what extent price evaluation depends on explicit retrieval of prices, even though price judgements are affected by price and product accessibility and by previous experiences with product prices, together with other relevant aspects (e.g., purchase context, price presentation, and product features).

Inflation perceptions are formed using several sources of information: prior expectations, personal experience of price changes (which are biased by frequency of purchase and salience), media reports (which amplify such biases) and official statistics. The formation of expectations of future inflation involves the same sources, and in addition, lay mental models of the economy, and expert forecasts (when available). Inflation judgements of people with higher financial and economic literacy are more in line with official statistics and expert forecasts. Finally, both survey and experimental evidence have demonstrated that the effects of inflation judgements are consistent with prescriptions of rational models of economic behaviour, especially for those higher in financial literacy. It is concluded that further research is needed to evaluate initiatives to facilitate better judgement and knowledge of prices and inflation.

NOTES

1. To capture the influence of subjective perception, when modelling the evaluation process, subjective values (V) are usually derived from the nominal ones (P) via a logarithmic transformation (i.e., Fechner's law) or power transformation (e.g., $V = P^r$, where r is empirically estimated).

2. According to prospect theory, prices are evaluated by their subjective values, with the translation from the nominal values being usually modelled by a power value function (Kahneman & Tversky, 1979; Tversky & Kahneman, 1992). When the situation is perceived as a gain (e.g., a price reduction or a price that is lower than a reference price), the relation between the nominal and the subjective value can be expressed as $V = X^\alpha$, where X is the

nominal value and the parameter α is estimated (typically .88, which captures diminishing returns). When the situation is perceived as a loss (e.g., a price increase, a price higher than a reference price), the value function is $V = -\lambda\text{-}X^{\alpha}$ (with typical values: $\alpha = .88$ and $\lambda = 2.25$, the latter capturing gain-loss asymmetry).

REVIEW QUESTIONS

1. What are internal and external reference prices? What are the main theories of price evaluation based on reference prices and how do they differ?
2. Prospect theory, norm theory, and decision by sampling can be applied to price evaluation. What psychological insights do they offer into price evaluation phenomena and underlying mechanisms?
3. Do people have an accurate perception of inflation? Are inflation expectations rational? If there are biases in inflation perception and expectations, how they can be explained and what can be their consequences?

REFERENCES

Aalto-Setälä, V., & Raijas, A. (2003). Consumer price knowledge before and after the euro changeover. *International Journal of Consumer Studies, 27*, 210–217.

Anderson, J. R., & Schooler, L. J. (1991). Reflections of the environment in memory. *Psychological Science, 2*, 396–408.

Antonides, G. (2008). How is perceived inflation related to actual price changes in the European Union? *Journal of Economic Psychology, 29*, 417–432.

Armantier, O., Bruine de Bruin, W., Potter, S., Topa, G., van der Klaauw, W., & Zafar, B. (2013). Measuring inflation expectations. *Annual Review of Economics, 5*, 273–301.

Armantier, O., Bruine de Bruin, W., Topa, G., van der Klaauw, W., & Zafar, B. (2015). Inflation expectations and behavior: Do survey respondents act on their beliefs? *International Review of Economics, 56*, 505–536.

Armantier, O., Nelson, S., Topa, G., van der Klaauw, W., & Zafar, B. (2014). The price is right: Updating of inflation expectations in a randomized price information experiment. *Review of Economics and Statistics*, posted Online November 7, 2014. DOI:10.1162/REST_a_00499

Arnold, E., Dräger, L., & Fritsche, U. (2014). Evaluating the link between consumers' savings portfolio decisions, their inflation expectations and economic news. Retrieved from https://www.wiso.uni-hamburg.de/repec/hepdoc/macppr_2_2014.pdf

Aucremanne, L., Collin, M., & Dhyne, E. (2005). Is there a discrepancy between measured and perceived inflation in the euro area since the euro cash changeover? Retrieved from http://www.oecd.org/dataoecd/54/49/35011554.pdf

Bates, J. M., & Gabor, A. (1986). Price perception in creeping inflation: Report on an enquiry. *Journal of Economic Psychology, 7*, 291–314.

Brachinger, H. W. (2006). Euro or 'Teuro'?: The Euro-induced perceived inflation in Germany. Working Paper No. 5. Department of Quantitative Economics Working Paper Series, University of Fribourg, Switzerland.

Briesch, R. A., Krishnamurthi, L., Mazumdar, T., & Raj, S. P. (1997). A comparative analysis of reference price models. *Journal of Consumer Research, 24*, 202–214.

Bruine de Bruin, W., van der Klaauw, W., Downs, J. S., Fischhoff, B., Topa, G., & Armantier, O. (2010). Expectations of inflation: The role of financial literacy and demographic variables. *Journal of Consumer Affairs, 44*, 381–402.

Bruine de Bruin, W., van der Klaauw, W., Downs, J. S., Fischhoff, B., Topa, G., & Armantier, O. (2010). Expectations of inflation: The role of demographic variables, expectation formation, and financial literacy. *Journal of Consumer Affairs, 44*, 381–402.

Bruine de Bruin, W., van der Klaauw, W., Potter, S., Rich, R., & Topa, G. (2010). Improving survey measures of household inflation expectations. *Current Issues in Economics and Finance, 16*, 1–7.

Bruine de Bruin, W, van der Klaauw, W., & Topa, G (2011) Inflation expectations: The biasing effect of thoughts about specific prices. *Journal of Economic Psychology, 32*, 834–845.

Bruine de Bruin, W., van der Klaauw, W., Topa, G., Downs, J.S., Fischhoff, B., & . Armantier, O. (2012). The effect of question wording on consumers' reported inflation expectations. *Journal of Economic Psychology, 4*, 749–757.

Burke, M. A., & Manz, M. (2014). Economic literacy and inflation expectations: Evidence from a laboratory experiment. *Journal of Money, Credit and Banking, 46*(7), 1421–1456.

Cavallo, A., Cruces, G., & Perez-Truglia, R. (2014). *Inflation expectations, learning and supermarket prices: Evidence from field experiments (No. w20576)*. Washington, DC: National Bureau of Economic Research.

D'Acunto, F., Hoang, D., & Weber, M. (2015). Inflation expectations and consumption expenditure. Retrieved from http://faculty.chicagobooth.edu/michael.weber/research/pdf/inflationExpectations.pdf

Del Giovane, P., & Sabbatini, R. (2005). La divergenza tra inflazione rilevata e percepita in Italia. In P. Del Giovane, F. Lippi, & R. Sabbatini (Eds.), *L'euro e l'inflazione* (pp. 17–74). Bologna: Il Mulino. http://www.oecd.org/dataoecd/24/55/34975994.pdf

Del Missier, F., Ranyard, R., & Bonini, N. (2016). Perceived inflation: The role of product accessibility and attitudes towards inflation. *Journal of Economic Psychology, 56*, 97–106.

Dickson, P. R., & Sawyer, A. G. (1986). The price knowledge and search of supermarket shoppers. *Journal of Marketing, 54*, 42–53.

Dougherty, M. R. P., Gettys, C. F., & Ogden, E. E. (1999). MINERVA-DM: A memory processes model for judgments of likelihood. *Psychological Review, 106*, 180–209.

Dräger, L. (2011). Inflation perceptions and expectations in Sweden: Are media reports the missing link? *Oxford Bulletin of Economics and Statistics, 77*, 681–700.

Du Caju, P., Gautier, E., Momferatou, D., & Ward-Warmedinger, M.(2008). *Institutional features of wage bargaining in 23 European countries, the US and Japan*. Paris: Banque de France.

Eppright, D. R., Arguea, N. M. & Huth, W.L. (1998). Aggregate consumer expectation indexes as indicators of future consumer expenditures. *Journal of Economic Psychology, 19*, 215–235.

Fluch, M., & Stix, H. (2005). Perceived inflation in Austria: Extent, explanations, effects. *Monetary Policy and the Economy, 3*, 22–47.

Gärling, T. & Gamble, A. (2008). Perceived inflation and expected future prices in different currencies. *Journal of Economic Psychology, 29*, 401–416.

Greitemeyer, T., Schultz-Hardt, S., Traut-Mattausch, E., & Frey, D. (2005). The influence of price trend expectations on price trend perceptions: Why the Euro seems to make life more expensive. *Journal of Economic Psychology, 26*, 541–548.

Hardie, G. G. S., Johnson, E. J., & Fader, P. S. (1993). Modeling loss aversion and reference dependence effects on brand choice. *Marketing Science, 12*, 378–394.

Helson, H. (1947). Adaptation-level as frame of reference for prediction of psychophysical data. *American Journal of Psychology, 60*, 1–29.

Helson, H. (1964), *Adaptation-level theory*. New York: Harper & Row.

Herr, P. M. (1989). Priming price: Prior knowledge and context effects. *Journal of Consumer Research, 16*, 67–75.

Huber, O. W. (2011). Frequency of price increases and perceived inflation: An experimental investigation. *Journal of Economic Psychology, 32*, 651–661.

Jacobson, R., & Obermiller, C. (1990). The formation of expected future price: A reference price for forward-looking consumers. *Journal of Consumer Research, 16*, 420–432.

Janiszewski, C., & Lichtenstein, D. R. (1999). A range theory account of price perception. *Journal of Consumer Research, 25*, 353–368.

Jonung, L., & Laidler, D. (1988). Are perceptions of inflation rational? Some evidence for Sweden. *The American Economic Review, 78*, 1080–1087.

Jungermann, H., Brachinger, H. W., Belting, J., Grinberg, K., & Zacharias, E. (2007). The euro changeover and the factors influencing perceived inflation. *Journal of Consumer Policy, 30*, 405–419.

Kahneman, D., & Miller, D. T. (1986). Norm theory: Comparing reality to its alternatives. *Psychological Review, 93*, 136–153.

Kahneman, D., & Tversky, A. (1979). Prospect theory: An analysis of decisions under risk. *Econometrica, 47*, 263–291.

Kalyanaram, G., & Winer, R. S. (1995). Empirical generalizations for reference price research. *Marketing Science, 14*, 161–169.

Kornienko, T. (2004). A cognitive basis for cardinal utility. Working Paper. Department of Economics, University of Stirling.

Krishna, A., Currim, I. S., & Shoemaker, R. W. (1991). Consumer perceptions of promotional activity. *Journal of Marketing, 55*, 4–16.

Mayhew, G. E., & Winer, R. S. (1992). An empirical analysis of internal and external reference prices using scanner data. *Journal of Consumer Research, 19*, 62–70.

Money Advice Service (2014). *The Financial Capability of the UK.* https://www.moneyadviceservice.org.uk/en/corporate/the-financial-capability-of-the-uk

Monroe, K. B., & Lee, A. Y. (1999) Remembering versus knowing: Issues in buyers' processing of price information. *Journal of the Academy of Marketing Science, 2*, 207–225.

Monroe, K. P. (1990). *Pricing: Making profitable decisions.* New York: McGraw-Hill.

Niedrich, R. W., Sharma, S., & Wedell, D. H. (2001). Reference price and price perceptions: A comparison of alternative models. *Journal of Consumer Research, 28*, 339–354.

ONS (2014). *Variation in the inflation experience of UK households: 2003–2014.* Newport: Office of National Statistics, UK. Retrieved from http://webarchive.nationalarchives.gov.uk/20160105160709/http://www.ons.gov.uk/ons/rel/elmr/variation-in-the-inflation-experience-of-uk-households/2003-2014/sty-variation-in-the-inflation-experience-of-uk-households.html

Parducci, A. (1965). Category judgment: A range-frequency model. *Psychological Review, 72*, 407–418.

Parducci, A. (1995). *Happiness, pleasure, and judgment: The contextual theory and its applications.* Mahwah, NJ: Erlbaum.

Putler, D. (1992). Incorporating reference price effects into a theory of consumer choice. *Marketing Science, 11*, 287–309.

Qian, J., & Brown, G. D. A. (2005). Similarity-based sampling: Testing a model of price psychophysics. In *Proceedings of the 27th Annual Conference of the Cognitive Science Society* (pp. 1785–1790). Mahwah, NJ: Erlbaum.

Raghubir, P. (2006). An information processing review of the subjective value of money and prices. *Journal of Business Research, 59*, 1053–1062.

Rajendran, K. N., & Tellis, G. J. (1994). Contextual and temporal components of reference price. *Journal of Marketing, 58*, 22–34.

Ranyard, R., Burgoyne, C., Saldanha, G., & Routh, D. (2005). A qualitative study of adaptation to the Euro in the Republic of Ireland: I. Attitudes, the 'Euro Illusion' and the perception of prices. *Journal of Community and Applied Social Psychology, 15*, 95–107.

Ranyard, R., Charlton, J. P., & Williamson, J. (2001). The role of internal reference prices in consumers' willingness to pay judgments: Thaler's Beer Pricing Task revisited. *Acta Psychologica, 106*, 265–283.

Ranyard, R., Del Missier, F., Bonini, N., Duxbury, D., & Summers, B. (2008). Perceptions and expectations of price changes and inflation: A review and conceptual framework. *Journal of Economic Psychology, 29*, 378–400.

Sorić, P. (2013). Assessing the sensitivity of consumption expenditure to inflation sentiment in post-communist economies. *Post-Communist Economies, 25*(4), 529–538.

Soroka, S. N. (2006). Good news and bad news: Asymmetric responses to economic information. *The Journal of Politics, 68*, 372–385.

Stewart, N., Chater, N., & Brown, G. D. A. (2006). Decision by sampling. *Cognitive Psychology, 53*, 1–26.

Thaler, R. H. (1985). Mental accounting and consumer choice. *Marketing Science, 4*, 199–214.

Thaler, R. H. (1999). Mental accounting matters. *Journal of Behavioral Decision Making, 12*, 183–206.

Traut-Mattausch, E., Schulz-Hardt, S., Greitemeyer, T., & Frey, D. (2004). Expectancy confirmation in spite of disconfirming evidence: The case of price increases due to the introduction of the Euro. *European Journal of Social Psychology, 34*, 739–760.

Tversky, A., & Kahneman, D. (1992). Advances in prospect theory: Cumulative representation of uncertainty. *Journal of Risk and Uncertainty, 5*, 297–323.

Volkmann, J. (1951). Scales of judgment and their implications for social psychology. In J. H. Rohrer, & M. Sherif (Eds.), *Social psychology at the crossroads* (pp. 273–294). New York: Harper & Row.

Wärneryd, K.-E. (1986). The psychology of inflation. *Journal of Economic Psychology, 7*, 259–268.

Winer, R. S. (1988). Behavioral perspectives on pricing: Buyer's subjective perceptions of price revisited. In T. Devinney (Ed.), *Issues in pricing: Theory and research*. Lexington, MA: Lexington Books.

FURTHER READING

Niedrich, R. W., Sharma, S., & Wedell, D. H. (2001). Reference price and price perceptions: A comparison of alternative models. *Journal of Consumer Research, 28*, 339–354.

Raghubir, P. (2006). An information processing review of the subjective value of money and prices. *Journal of Business Research, 59*, 1053–1062.

Ranyard, R., Del Missier, F., Bonini, N., Duxbury, D., & Summers, B. (2008). Perceptions and expectations of price changes and inflation: A review and conceptual framework. *Journal of Economic Psychology, 29*, 378–400.

11 Materialism and the Meanings of Possessions

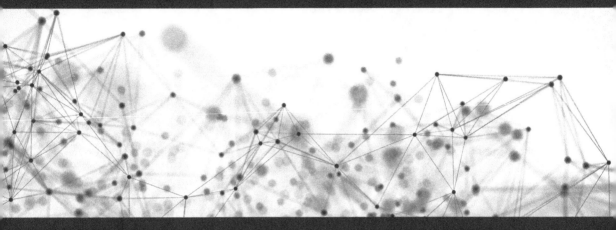

W. RAY CROZIER

CHAPTER OUTLINE

LEARNING OUTCOMES

BY THE END OF THIS CHAPTER YOU SHOULD BE ABLE TO:

1. Understand the distinction between objective and psychological ownership.
2. Compare different interpretations of research findings of an inverse relationship between materialist values and subjective well-being.
3. Appraise the contribution of psychology to explaining variation in relations among materialism, income and happiness.

11.1 INTRODUCTION: THE SOCIO-ECONOMIC CONTEXT OF POSSESSIONS AND MATERIALISM

There are many kinds of material objects and possessions and a variety of motives for owning them. One person might purchase and retain possessions for purely financial reasons, perhaps as an investment, buying a house but never living in it or bidding for an artwork unseen. Someone else might pay much more than an object is apparently worth in order to acquire the final item in a set that he or she has been collecting for years or even to prevent a rival from making the acquisition. One family might occupy the same house for generations, whereas nomads take all their possessions from one place to another, while the homeless can fit everything they own into a few carrier bags. Within the developed world – the 'consumer society' as it is often called – the ownership of material goods has come to occupy a crucial economic role. This is not new. The paintings of domestic interiors by artists such as Vermeer illustrate the range of possessions imported by the recently wealthy Dutch traders in the seventeenth century (Brook, 2009). The objects and clothing depicted as well as the pictures themselves are signs of their owners' social status, showing that they are sufficiently wealthy to own these items; they also constitute evidence of the importance of global trade to the Dutch economy in that era. Since the late-eighteenth century, consumerism has become intertwined with developments in industrialization, urbanization and mass consumption. The well-being of societies is premised on remorseless economic growth which requires increased productivity, fresh markets, and novel products and designs within existing markets. The status quo is not an option if investors are to be attracted, profits made and dividends paid out. This has led to the growth of marketing and advertising practices which range from simple notices of availability of products to sophisticated psychological campaigns, the invention of brands and the creation of brand awareness and loyalty. All these provide impetus towards ownership of material possessions.

The significance of these pressures has been studied extensively and is the province of political science, economics, history and anthropology. The sociologist Thorstein Veblen published the classic *The Theory of the Leisure Class* in 1899, which introduced the term 'conspicuous consumption'. Has psychology a role to play? Have material possessions psychological dimensions over and above their instrumental and functional properties? Does the pursuit of material possessions have undesirable consequences? These questions are the focus of this chapter.

Section 11.2 considers what is meant by ownership of material possessions, whether it is relevant to distinguish psychological ownership from objective or legal ownership and how possessions relate to people's sense of self. Section 11.3 covers definitions of materialism, approaches to its measurement and explanations of the origins of individual differences. Section 11.4 considers whether the pursuit of material goals has psychological consequences. It provides an overview of the substantial body of research that has examined the relationship between materialist values and psychological well-being, both at the individual level, examining relations between inter-individual variation in materialist values and aspirations and measures of psychological health, and at the national level, comparing relations across different economies. It also considers the relationship between income and well-being.

11.2   THE PSYCHOLOGICAL MEANINGS OF POSSESSIONS

11.2.1   *Subjective and Objective Ownership*

The notion of possessions might appear unproblematic. I type this text at a computer in the university library, wearing and surrounded by my possessions. I know that the computer I am working at does not belong to me, although it is mine temporarily and no one else is likely to take it from me unless the library staff exert a greater claim, for maintenance purposes or to close the building. I am conscious that the draft copy of this document that I print out (it is a university printer) will be my sole possession – until I pass it to the publisher. I can take the journal offprint I have just downloaded away with me but there are (copyright) restrictions on what I can do with it. I purchased (with a credit card – potentially the bank's money?) an e-book copy of Tim Kasser's *The High Price of Materialism* but I am uncertain whether or not I do own this – I cannot give it to anyone else, for example. Already I have slipped into equating possessions with ownership: Are these the same? I have also construed ownership/possessions in legal terms, for example, mentioning the question of copyright. Is psychological possession equivalent to legal possession? We can possess and exert control over property without necessarily owning it and we can own something even if not currently in possession of it (these issues become salient in the field of housing, in the matter of leases, mortgages and rents). I own my savings in a bank but this money is not in my possession and that distinction becomes all too obvious when there is a banking crisis; hence the long queues in 2007 outside branches of the Northern Rock building society across Britain when depositors feared that they would lose their funds which were in Northern Rock's possession. During sales frenzies in department stores it is not unknown for customers to fight for possession over the same item even though neither of them yet owns it. Psychologically, we might feel that we own something even though we have no legal entitlement to it or even 'own' another person and become possessive if we believe that someone else is taking undue interest in him or her. Ownership extends beyond material goods to encompass the intangible, for example, the 'personal space' surrounding ourselves or our thoughts, plans and ideas, our intellectual property. (I heard the late Professor Colin Martindale joke in a lecture that when he was a graduate student, he kept his ideas to himself fearful that other students would steal them, but now he found that he couldn't give his ideas away.)

Ownership has psychological consequences. Studies show that items are valued more highly merely because we own them. In the endowment effect (Thaler, 1980), a research participant who owns an item, such as a coffee cup or a chocolate bar – even if it has only just been received from the researcher – demands more money to part with the item than another participant who has been randomly assigned to the role of purchaser is willing to pay for it. This is a robust phenomenon that has been explained in terms of loss aversion; according to prospect theory, losses weigh more heavily in our mind than gains do, therefore we require more money to compensate for the loss of an item than we would pay to acquire it (Kahneman, 2011). An alternative explanation is in terms of ownership rather than loss aversion; Morewedge et al. (2009) reported the endowment effect in cases where there was ownership without loss aversion but an absence of the effect in circumstances where there was loss aversion without ownership. Reb and Connolly (2007) went further, demonstrating the significance of subjective ownership as opposed to actual ownership.

I have suggested that legal and psychological ownership are not the same and we can readily conjure up illustrations of this. But why are they not the same? Why is legal entitlement not necessary and sufficient for the experience of ownership and why do we feel this in circumstances where we lack such entitlement? Pierce, Kostova and Dirks (2003) set out a conceptual framework for the study of psychological ownership that facilitates addressing these questions. They defined psychological ownership as a complex state where there is a sense of possession and the object is perceived as having a close connection with the self. They propose that ownership is based upon three fundamental motives or needs: (1) to have the power to produce desired outcomes; (2) to define self-identity and communicate this identity to others; and (3) to have a place where one belongs. Pierce et al. (2003, pp. 92–93) also suggest three pathways towards a sense of psychological ownership: (1) having control over the target of ownership; (2) coming to know the target, to 'live with it'; and (3) investing the self in the target. The greater the sense of control, the better one knows it and the more the self is invested in it, the stronger the sense of psychological ownership. Rudmin and Berry (1987) found that control over an object, attachment to it and whether or not it has been purchased were regarded by participants as the most important criteria of ownership for specific objects already in their possession, but when evaluating arguments for ownership in general, participants reported that whether an object was purchased, was received as a gift or had been made by themselves proved more convincing arguments than control and attachment.

It is evident that the self plays a key role in this account of the motives for psychological ownership and its formation. The power to exercise control over objects relates to feelings of self-efficacy. Possessing your own space facilitates a sense of personal security, is often accompanied by personalizing the space and using it for self-presentation, and is expressed in the complex cognitive and emotional states that are associated with the notion of 'home' and the German *Heimat* and the Welsh *hiraeth*, both difficult concepts to capture in English. Invasion of one's home is perceived as a threat to, or violation of the self and people whose home has been burgled typically report feeling very differently about their home for long afterwards.

Involvement of the self helps explain circumstances where we have legal ownership without a corresponding sense of psychological ownership. I might purchase cars on a regular basis, changing them for financial reasons, without forming an attachment to any of them; they make no contribution to my identity. On the other hand, I might have a sense of ownership of my rented apartment if I have inhabited it for a long time, have some sense of control over it, have been able to personalize it through decoration, displaying pictures and photographs and so on, and if I have memories of happy and self-fulfilling experiences, such as having a romantic relationship or starting a family there.

11.2.2   The Self–Possessions Link

The notion of the relevance of possessions to the individual's self-concept or sense of identity is long-standing. William James (1890, p. 291) wrote:

> *In its widest possible sense, however, a man's Self is the sum total of all that he* CAN *call his*, not only his body and his psychic powers, but his clothes and his house ... his land and horses,

and yacht and bank account … if they wax and prosper, he feels triumphant; if they dwindle and die away, he feels cast down.

Possessions can be more than 'mine', they become part of 'me'. Empirical studies of people's grief reactions to the loss of possessions, whether through accident or theft, demonstrate the psychological significance of possessions for personal identity and feelings of self-worth and substantiate the thesis that possessions form part of what Belk (1988) in a seminal article has called an 'extended sense of self'. His conceptualization of the extended self has generated a considerable body of evidence on the psychological meanings of possessions. Our possessions reflect our sense of who we are and who we aspire to be but they do more than this. They are instrumental in forming our identity, in affirming it, and in displaying it to the outside world. Our most treasured belongings are not necessarily the most valuable in financial terms.

Links between possessions and the self are formed when feelings of self-worth are attached to objects which reflect values that are important to the self and come to symbolize important aspects of the self. Medals, trophies, a wedding dress, a lock of hair, photographs of our forebears, all are examples of possessions that are frequently described as 'irreplaceable'. These are the kinds of possessions that recur in surveys of the objects that people treasure most (Csikszentmihalyi & Rochberg-Halton, 1981; Dittmar, 1992). Analysis of the reasons why research participants nominate particular belongings finds that the higher-order category 'self' is by far the most frequently identified category (Csikszentmihalyi & Rochberg-Halton, 1981). However, there are individual differences in the tendency to become attached to such objects. Ferraro, Escalas and Bettman (2011) tested the hypothesis that the strength of self–possession links is associated with the degree to which possessions represent domains of the self on which a person bases his or her self-worth. The degree of recalled and imagined distress at participants' loss of possessions was predicted by the strength of the self–possession link and this in turn was predicted by the degree of match between object domain and self-worth domain.

Dommer and Swaminathan (2012) studied the links between the self and ownership in the context of the endowment effect. They proposed that possessions enhance the self and individuals seek to increase the value of their possessions in order to counter threats to the self, particularly threats of social rejection, and that this effect is more pronounced in selling than in buying since the self–possessions link is more salient in the case of selling. Their research demonstrates that the endowment effect can be modified and even disappear when the attractiveness of goods are manipulated by changing their link with the self.

The self is also prominent in attempts to distinguish psychological ownership from legal or objective ownership of possessions. The psychological proximity of possessions to the self is a key factor in psychological ownership and psychological investment in objects facilitates the sense of ownership over them. Some empirical research has explored everyday conceptions of ownership, although it has tended to be abstract in nature, asking participants to apply general concepts to sample possessions or more broadly to the nature of ownership. Studies of the endowment effect offer one possible route for undertaking more subtle research. As mentioned earlier, Reb and Connolly (2007) were able to show that the effect was produced by psychological feelings of ownership rather than by actual ownership. This paradigm might be extended to examine control and psychological proximity as mediators of subjective ownership. Research has identified pathways to ownership but has yet to explain how psychological proximity to the self, control, familiarity, and so on fit together to contribute to making some possessions more valued than others. Future research can also ask whether some pathways are more relevant for some objects rather than others.

We now turn to consider materialism in terms of definitions, its measurement and explanations of the origins of individual differences in materialist values.

11.3 PSYCHOLOGICAL ASPECTS OF MATERIALISM

11.3.1 *Defining and Measuring Materialism*

Belk (1984, p. 291) defined materialism as:

> the importance a consumer attaches to worldly possessions. At the highest levels of materialism, such possessions assume a central place in a person's life and are believed to provide the greatest sources of satisfaction and dissatisfaction in life either directly (as ends) or indirectly (as means to ends).

This definition refers to individual differences and there is disagreement as to whether these differences should be construed as variation in fundamental personality traits, or in values or beliefs.

The trait approach has been promoted by Belk (1984) who conceptualizes materialism in terms of the traits of possessiveness, lack of generosity and envy. He constructed questionnaire scales to measure these traits, scales which inter-correlate significantly albeit modestly. However, most research is guided by the assumption that materialism is a value, a belief about the relations between conduct and goals that organizes behaviour across contexts (Kasser & Ryan, 1993; Richins & Dawson, 1992; Schwartz, 1994). According to Richins and Dawson (1992), this value comprises three dimensions, namely, (1) the centrality of material possessions and wealth in a person's life; (2) the belief that acquisition of material goods and wealth is essential for happiness; and (3) beliefs that possessions enable judgements to be made about the success of the self and others. They constructed the Material Values Scale (MVS), where participants indicate using a Likert scale the degree to which they endorse 18 statements representing these three dimensions (see Chapter 5 in this volume).

Schwartz (1992) insists that, rather than be studied in isolation, materialism should be investigated in the context of other values. He produced a circumplex measure of ten value priorities, where values that are more compatible are located more closely together on the circle of values whereas values that are opposed are located opposite one another on the circle. The circle can be described along two bipolar orthogonal dimensions, interpreted by Schwartz as higher-order values: (1) openness to change versus conservation and conformity; and (2) self-transcendence (acceptance of others and concern for their welfare) versus self-enhancement (pursuit of self-interest, power and dominance). Self-enhancement – the value of acquiring power and standing out from others in terms of the acquisition of money and status – is closest conceptually to materialism as defined above. Measurement of these values is by means of the 56-item Schwartz Value Survey (SVS; Schwartz, 1994) which has been validated in studies conducted in 73 countries (Schwartz, 2006). There is evidence that scores on the SVS self-enhancement scale correlate significantly with the three MVS scales of materialism (Karabati & Cemalcilar, 2010; Kilbourne, Grünhagen, & Foley, 2005).

Kasser and Ryan (1993) produced the Aspiration Index (AI), a 21-item self-report scale where respondents rate the importance to them and the likelihood of their achieving goals in the domains of self-acceptance, affiliation, community feeling (prosocial values) and financial success. A subsequent theoretical development of the association between intrinsic and extrinsic motivation, on the one hand, and values, on the other, has led to the extension of the scale to incorporate additional values and the construction of a circumplex model of the psychological structure of values that bears some resemblance to Schwarz's model (Grouzet et al., 2005). The AI has been extensively applied in research.

In conclusion, materialism has been variously defined as a personal trait, as a prioritizing of materialist possessions and their significance for personal success and happiness, and as the importance people attach to goals for wealth and material possessions. There is reliance on self-report questionnaires, and the MVS, the SVS and the AI have all been extensively used in research. This variation in conceptualization and methodology ought to be taken into account when evaluating research.

11.3.2   Causes of Individual Differences

The emphasis in research into materialist values is on individual differences and we have little evidence on what causes these differences. What leads some individuals to be more materialistic than their peers? Consider the case of two hypothetical medical graduates from similar backgrounds, one of whom joins a pharmaceutical company while the other goes to the Third World to work for Médécins sans frontières. It is likely that these individuals will have different values where materialism is concerned but what leads to these differences? We can imagine that their values influence their occupational choice and that the experiences they have in these occupations and the values of the people they encounter in and through their work will reinforce their values. Can these influences be teased out?

It is conceivable that particular personality traits or combinations of traits predispose individuals to adopt materialist values. Belk (1984) has argued for the traits of possessiveness, lack of generosity, and tendency to envy others, traits which are presumably not restricted to money or material success but apply more broadly. In consumer-oriented societies where material success is highly valued, these traits may make individuals more susceptible to messages in the media and elsewhere that promote these values. The correlations between materialism and psychological well-being suggest that personality characteristics such as low self-esteem may predispose people to materialism rather than (or in addition to) being consequences of materialist values. Veblen (1899) argued that possessions are used to define social status; social comparison processes have been proposed as a key mediator in the association between materialist values and subjective well-being, suggesting that self-dissatisfaction might be both cause and outcome of these values.

11.4   MATERIALISM AND SUBJECTIVE WELL-BEING

11.4.1   At the Individual Level

The predominant theme in research is that materialism is negatively associated with well-being. In other words, the more materialistic you are, the less content you will be: money doesn't buy happiness. A substantial body of evidence from studies undertaken by Kasser and by other researchers is consistent with this hypothesis (Kasser, 2002). On the other hand, there are suggestions that materialist values can be beneficial. Consumption practices can facilitate the enhancement of social identity, for example, through access to membership of a shared subculture (Kilbourne, Grünhagen, & Foley, 2005). Being insufficiently materialistic is surely also a disadvantage for effective social functioning in a materialist society. Researching this issue poses a number of questions. What is meant by well-being and how is it measured? What is the strength of the relationship? Does it vary from one country to another, for example, is it stronger in 'richer' economies in terms of gross domestic product (GDP), or in countries with greater inequality in wealth, in those with an individualist rather than a collectivist ethos or dominated by neoliberal as opposed to social democratic values? The relationship between materialism and well-being is correlational in nature. Implicit is the thesis that materialism is bad for your mental health and well-being but perhaps these conditions encourage the pursuit of materialist values and goals, or there is a bi-directional relationship between them, or both reflect some other factors, whether cultural or individual.

A meta-analysis of studies undertaken by Dittmar, Bond, Hurst and Kasser (2014) addressed methodological issues in detail and throws light on possible explanations. Their investigation has some striking features. First, the 753 effect sizes from 175 studies in 151 separate reports located by the researchers indicate how extensive is the empirical attention paid to materialism and subjective well-being. Second, this research has used a wide range of measures of materialism and well-being. Third, the meta-analysis incorporated a number of potential moderating factors at the individual level (age, gender, education, personal income, involvement in consumer-related occupations), and at the societal level, including economic indices and cultural values.

Overall, there is a modest but consistent negative relation between materialism and well-being which holds across measures of both variables, including diverse measures of well-being, and across moderating factors.[1] Notwithstanding this consistency, there is variability in effect sizes related to moderating factors and we focus here on some of particular relevance. Effect sizes are larger when broader measures of materialist beliefs and values are involved and smaller when measures refer more specifically to the desire for money and financial success; this implies that the mean effect size would be larger if fewer studies relied upon specific measures. Contrary to predictions, effect sizes were smaller, albeit in the same direction, in societies with greater inequality and with higher growth in GDP. On the other hand, effect size was independent of *level* of GDP, whether a society was free-market rather than regulated or had higher mean materialist cultural values. More systematic sampling is necessary to reach firm conclusions about these influences on well-being. For example, analysis of aggregate data as opposed to the study of individual differences reveals corre-lations between economic inequality within societies and mental health outcomes (Wilkinson & Pickett, 2010). Finally, although materialism was negatively associated with the entire range of measures of well-being, three measures with larger than average effect sizes were compulsive buying, engagement in physical risk-taking such as smoking and alcohol consumption, and negative self-appraisal.

11.4.2   At the Societal Level

Do societies differ in their levels of materialist values and is there variation across time within the same society? It is often asserted that Britain became increasingly materialistic in the 1980s under the Thatcher government, with the rapid expansion of the finance sector and easier access to credit fuelling consumer spending, and price inflation in the private housing market giving rise to feelings of prosperity. Similar trends were apparent in the United States and other capitalist economies. The col-lapse of communist administrations in Russia and across Eastern Europe has wid-ened the adoption of free market economies, globalization and consumerism. Are levels of materialism related to socio-economic conditions of the societies and, if so, which conditions are most relevant?

Kasser, Cohn, Kanner and Ryan (2007) argued that the American corporate capitalist culture of competition and maximizing self-interest and its demand for continuous economic growth through mass consumerism undermines values prior-itizing affiliation, autonomy, benevolence and self-worth. Easterlin (2007) countered that economic growth rather than consumerism is the principal factor responsible for the adverse consequences of materialism. Growth raises expectations across generations. Within generations, social comparison processes increase feelings of self-dissatisfaction while encouraging the belief that satisfaction can be achieved through the attainment of material goals. Schwartz (2007) addressed this question by relating a quantitative measure of different forms of capitalism to material value orientations and priorities across 20 capitalist countries. The measure of capitalism is an empirical index of dimensions of capitalism constructed by Hall and Gingerich (2004). Data from international comparison sources such as the Organisation for Economic Co-operation and Development (OECD) were drawn upon to generate scores on the dimensions and these were submitted to factor analysis to produce a single index of scores. Schwartz (2007) reported that the degree of capitalism in a society and aggregate materialist values were significantly correlated.

Kasser et al. (2014) examined materialism (assessed by the MVS) and well-being in Iceland, which suffered severely from the international banking crisis in 2008. In a longitudinal design, data were collected on two occasions six months apart in 2009. There was an increase in materialist values over this period and materialism was neg-atively correlated with well-being at both measurement points.

Levels of materialism vary across countries although there is yet no consensus on what the critical factors are. Comparative studies have focused on the Western devel-oped world and there is a paucity of data from countries with extreme economic dis-advantages or alternative economic systems. The study in Iceland reported by Kasser et al. (2014) suggests that average levels of materialism within a society are sensitive even in the short term to large-scale economic changes. Within societies, materialist values may be correlated with economic position and factors such as family income, education and occupation. Yet there is no evidence that the link between materialism and well-being is determined by these factors (Dittmar et al., 2014).

This research has wider implications. The OECD World Forum in Istanbul in 2007 'affirmed in a declaration their commitment to measuring and fostering the progress of societies in all dimensions, with the ultimate goal of improving policy making, democracy and citizens' wellbeing' (Organisation for Economic Cooperation and Development, 2007). The UK Office of National Statistics collects population measures of well-being, and publishes reports on findings of its surveys, including data related to well-being such as satisfaction with personal relationships, feelings of loneliness, and access to social support (Siegler, 2015). While the collection and dissemination of these data are valuable, the research does not seek to investigate causal relations between subjective well-being and economic factors. For example, government reports remain silent on how dominant values of materialism are consistent with well-being.

11.4.3   Causal Relations

What is the causal relationship between materialism and well-being? Research using multivariate designs such as structural equation modelling (Dittmar et al., 2014) and regression techniques (Kasser et al., 2014) reports that models predicting well-being from materialism fit data better than alternative models do. Nevertheless causality is not directly studied in these designs and can be investigated more rigorously by experimental methods. Unfortunately these have been rarely reported. Bauer, Wilkie, Kim and Bodenhausen (2012) used a cuing technique to induce increases in materialist aspirations and reported that this increased scores on materialist aspirations and reduced scores on measures of affect, satisfaction with self, and preference for social involvement. The effects of manipulating participants' self-esteem have also been studied. Clark et al. (2011) studied the effects on the monetary evaluation of specific objects of inducing changes in self-perception through priming interpersonal security concerns and reported that inducing greater insecurity led to larger monetary evaluations. Park and John (2011) found that a discrepancy between explicit self-esteem and implicit self-esteem predicted materialism better than either of these forms of self-evaluation. Here 'explicit' refers to responses on a standardized questionnaire and 'implicit' to self-evaluation at an unconscious level which is assessed indirectly, for example through measurement of response times to briefly presented words related either to self or other categories and to pleasant or unpleasant categories.

The effect of priming social comparisons upon materialist values was studied by Maio et al. (2009), drawing upon Schwartz's theory of ten values. Their experimental manipulation involved having participants compare their ratings of the relative importance of values with fictitious value rankings selected by the researchers to provide exemplars of more extreme endorsements of the values; participants were also presented with verbal descriptions of the kinds of people who hold those values. The hypotheses were supported: Priming can change values in ways predicted by Schwartz's model. The priming manipulation in this study draws explicitly on a social comparison process and illustrates how this process can induce changes in values.

Priming methodology represents a promising approach to teasing out the relations between values and subjective well-being. More generally, research needs to go beyond correlational designs to examine in greater depth the important issues that are raised in the study of materialism. Materialist values imply that personal success is defined in materialist terms and this has to be understood in the context of what is available to be consumed; as Rudmin (1993, p. 56) reminds us, 'there is no doubt that property practices are culturally bound'. These values also have to be understood in terms of what others consume – that is, with reference to some group with which we compare ourselves – and where we stand with regard to this comparison: how materialism fits into our other values and what its implications are for our sense of self-worth.

11.4.4   *Income, Materialism and Subjective Well-Being*

Economists are interested in a related issue, the relation between wealth, defined in terms of income, and subjective well-being, or 'happiness' as the literature tends to label it. Discussion of this is beyond the scope of this chapter but it is worth highlighting relevant empirical findings (see Easterlin, 2001, and Layard, 2011, for detailed accounts; see also Chapter 25 in this volume). At any point in time, individuals with larger income are, on average, happier than those with smaller incomes. On average, their level of happiness remains constant across the life-cycle even though their income increases during that time. They tend to believe that they will be happier in the future than they currently are and that they were less happy in the past, in apparent contradiction of findings that happiness overall remains constant. These results obtain across all countries that have been surveyed. At the societal level, richer nations are happier than poor ones but above a certain level of national income there is no systematic relationship between wealth and happiness. How can this apparently puzzling pattern of results be explained? Layard (2011) emphasizes social comparison processes; we take material success to be an indicator of worth in the eyes of others and compare our success with what we perceive to be that of our peers. My joy at receiving a research grant of £100,000 might be reduced when I learn of a rival's award of £200,000 for a similar project. Easterlin (2001) proposed that happiness is influenced by both income and material aspirations and that aspirations increase in proportion to income. Thus, higher income leads to the belief that aspirations will be fulfilled; when we reflect on our past happiness we are comparing our income then with our current aspirations rather than with the aspirations we held at the time. Similarly, prospective happiness is influenced by current aspirations and we fail to take into account that our future aspirations will rise in line with our anticipated future income. Easterlin argues that levels of and changes in aspirations must be taken into account when explaining levels of subjective well-being. Carter and McBride (2013) obtained evidence for the hypotheses that social comparison processes and expected outcomes influence the reference point which we use to judge gains and losses in experienced utility: our satisfaction reflects the outcomes that reference groups obtain alongside our own experiences.

How do these findings relate to research into materialism and subjective well-being? The psychological literature concludes that – among individuals – greater aspirations for material success are associated with negative self-appraisals and poorer adjustment, which is compatible with findings that a higher income does not necessarily result in increases in personal satisfaction. Aspirations, which have to be taken into account alongside actual wealth when predicting happiness, are prominent in explanations in both fields of enquiry. Aspirations are inevitably linked with values: It seems improbable that someone with materialist aspirations will not also have materialist values. In both areas of research – materialist values and income – self-comparison with relevant reference groups influences subjective well-being. Income is not an end in itself nor can it be understood purely in terms of the power to acquire possessions. It is an indication of social status, as is the capacity to acquire the kinds of possessions that are likely to be envied. An illustration of this is the size of the bonuses awarded to already wealthy senior staff in large financial corporations. Bonuses provide status to these staff and also to their employers who demonstrate that they belong to the elite corporations that can afford these payments.[2] If it is the case that aspirations increase in proportion to wealth and that material goals can never be fulfilled, we can understand how materialism does not necessarily lead to subjective well-being.

Finally, it is possible to take a critical view of research into 'happiness'. One risk that Davies (2015) notes is that people will be blamed for their unhappiness in the face of society's promotion of this state as an individual's responsibility, in the same way as the mentally ill were once blamed for their failure to conform to acceptable standards of conduct, or the poor, or people 'on benefits' – in current government-speak – are responsible for their predicament without acknowledging, and at the same time diverting attention from, the economic context in which their difficulties are experienced. Unhappiness can result from the stress and sense of helplessness associated with poor housing, homelessness, insecurity about income or retaining employment, low wages, high rents, and so on, not to mention the stigma associated with their position. That these conditions rise and fall with the economy and with political decisions suggests that more than individual responsibility is involved.

11.5   SUMMARY

Research in economic psychology has produced insights into the personal meanings of material possessions and the relations among materialist values, income and subjective well-being. It is argued in this chapter that psychological ownership can be distinguished from legal or objective ownership and that there is a strong connection between a sense of ownership and the self. Material possessions help define personal identity and communicate this identity to others; they indicate status, wealth and taste. The endowment effect – evaluating objects more highly simply because we own them – is influenced by the strength of the link between the self and possessions.

The chapter showed that research has reported that higher levels of materialism are associated with lower psychological well-being. The correlations are modest but reliable and obtain across alternative measures of materialism and well-being; there seem to be no published studies that report contrary findings. The correlational nature of this research does not permit definite conclusions about causality but the thrust of this research has been on well-being as the outcome variable, claiming that adherence to materialist values makes us discontented because our aspirations cannot be met or because their pursuit diverts us from values that would be more likely to bring us fulfilment. A small number of studies have adopted an experimental design to show that cuing or priming materialist values can produce more negative feelings. Nevertheless, other studies have reported that changes in self-esteem do have effects upon materialism. The two explanations are not contradictory and both processes may be operative in linking materialism with lower levels of subjective well-being. Income is also related to well-being in that greater income does not necessarily produce greater happiness. Explanations have emphasized psychological processes: aspirations and social comparison processes.

Research raises issues about values, aspirations and possessions that are worthy of further examination, and contributes to larger debates about the influence of political and economic systems upon the mental health of the population.

NOTES

1. The mean effect size for independent samples, expressed as a correlation, is $r = -.15$, 95% confidence interval from -.18 to -.13 (Dittmar et al., 2014, p. 889).
2. A survey of executives shows the relevance of social comparison processes (Gosling, 1912). Once a certain remuneration level is reached, being paid more than one's peers matters more than the absolute level of remuneration.

REVIEW QUESTIONS

1. What does the endowment effect tell us about psychological ownership?
2. Has research established a causal link between materialist values and psychological well-being?
3. What is meant by the 'extended self'? How useful is this concept for understanding economic behaviour?

REFERENCES

Bauer, M. A., Wilkie, J. E. B., Kim, J. K., & Bodenhausen, G. V. (2012). Cuing consumerism: Situational materialism undermines personal and social well-being. *Psychological Science*, *23*, 517–523. http://doi.org/10.1177/0956797611429579.

Belk, R. W. (1984). Three scales to measure constructs related to materialism: Reliability, validity, and relationships to measures of happiness. *Advances in Consumer Research*, *11*, 291–297.

Belk, R. W. (1988). Possessions and the extended self. *Journal of Consumer Research*, *15*, 139–168.

Brook, T. (2009). *Vermeer's hat: The seventeenth century and the dawn of the global world*. London: Profile Books.

Carter, S., & McBride, M. (2013). Experienced utility versus decision utility: Putting the 'S' in satisfaction. *Journal of Socio-Economics*, *42*, 13–23. http://doi.org/1010.1016/j.socec.2012.11.009.

Clark, M. S., Greenberg, A., Hill, E., Lemay, E. P., Clark-Polner, E., & Roosth, D. (2011). Heightened interpersonal security diminishes the monetary value of possessions. *Journal of Experimental Social Psychology*, *47*, 359–364. http://doi.org/10 10.1016/j.jesp.2010.08.001.

Csikszentmihalyi, M., & Rochberg-Halton, E. (1981). *The meaning of things: Domestic symbols and the self*. Cambridge: Cambridge University Press.

Davies, W. (2015). *The happiness industry. How the government and big business sold us well-being.* London: Verso Books.

Dittmar, H. (1992). *The social psychology of material possessions.* Hemel Hempstead: Harvester Wheatsheaf.

Dittmar, H., Bond, R., Hurst, M., & Kasser, T. (2014). The relationship between materialism and personal well-being: A meta-analysis. *Journal of Personality and Social Psychology, 107,* 879–924. http://doi.org/1010.1037/a0037409.

Dommer, S. L., & Swaminathan, V. (2012). Explaining the endowment effect through ownership: The role of identity, gender, and self-threat. *Journal of Consumer Psychology, 39,* 1034–1050. http://doi.org/10 10.1086/666737.

Easterlin, R. A. (2001). Income and happiness: Towards a unified theory. *Economic Journal, 11,* 465–484. http://doi.org/1010.1111/1468-0297.00646.

Easterlin, R. A. (2007). The escalation of material goals: Fingering the wrong culprit. *Psychological Inquiry, 18,* 31–33. http://doi.org/10.1080/10478400701389094.

Ferraro, R., Escalas, J., & Bettman, J. R. (2011). Our possessions, our selves: Domains of self-worth and the possession-self link. *Journal of Consumer Psychology, 21,* 169–177. http://doi.org/10.1016/j.jcps2010.08.007

Gosling, T. 2012. Money on the mind: The psychology of pay and incentives. *Forbes Insights.* Retrieved from http://www.forbes.com/sites/forbesinsights/2012/11/26/money-on-the-mind-the-psychology-of-pay and-incentives/ (accessed June 28, 2015).

Grouzet, F. M. E., Kasser, T., Ahuvia, A., Fernandez-Dols, J. M., Kim, Y., Lau, S., ... & Sheldon, K. M. (2005). The structure of goal contents across fifteen cultures. *Journal of Personality and Social Psychology, 89,* 800–816. http://doi.org/10.1037/0022-3514.89.5.800

Hall, P. A., & Gingerich, D. W. (2004). *Varieties of capitalism and institutional complementarities in the macroeconomy: An empirical analysis.* MPHG Discussion Paper 04/5. Max Planck Institute for the Study of Societies, Cologne, Germany. Available at www.mpi-fg-koeln.mpg.de (accessed January 18, 2015).

James, W. (1890). *The principles of psychology,* Vol. 1. New York: Henry Holt.

Kahneman, D. (2011). *Thinking, fast and slow.* London: Allen Lane.

Karabati, S., & Cemalcilar, Z. (2010). Values, materialism, and well-being: A study with Turkish university students. *Journal of Economic Psychology, 31,* 624–633. http://doi.org/10.1016/j.oep.2010.04.007

Kasser, T. (2002). *The high price of materialism.* Cambridge, MA: MIT Press.

Kasser, T., Cohn, S., Kanner, A. D., & Ryan, R. M. (2007). Some costs of American corporate capitalism: A psychological exploration of value and goal conflicts. *Psychological Inquiry, 18,* 1–22. http://doi.org/10.1080/10478400701386579.

Kasser, T., Rosenblum, K. L., Sameroff, A. J., Deci, E. L., Niemiec, C. P., ... & Hawks, S. (2014). Changes in materialism, changes in psychological well-being: Evidence from three longitudinal studies and an intervention experiment. *Motivation and Emotion, 38,* 1–22. http://doi.org/10.1007/s11031-013-9371-4.

Kasser, T., & Ryan, R. M. (1993). The dark side of the American dream: Correlates of financial success as a central life aspiration. *Journal of Personality and Social Psychology, 65,* 410–422. http://doi.org/10.1037//0022-3514.65.2.410.

Kilbourne, W., Grünhagen, M., & Foley, J. (2005). A cross-cultural examination of the relationship between materialism and individual values. *Journal of Economic Psychology, 26,* 624–641. http://doi.org/10.1016/joep.2004.009.

Layard, R. (2011). *Happiness: Lessons from a new science* (2nd edn). London: Penguin.

Maio, G. R., Pakizeh, A., Cheung, W.-Y., & Rees, K. J. (2009). Changing, priming, and acting on values: Effects via motivation relations in a circular model. *Journal of Personality and Social Psychology, 97,* 699–715. http://doi.org/10.1037/a0016420

Morewedge, C. K., Dhu, L. L., Gilbert, D. T., & Wilson, T. D. (2009). Bad riddance or good rubbish? Ownership and not loss aversion causes the endowment effect. *Journal of Experimental Social Psychology, 45*, 947–951. http://doi.org/10.1016/j.jesp2009.05.014.

Organization for Economic Co-operation and Development (2007). *Measuring and fostering the progress of societies.* Retrieved from http://www.oecd.org/site/worldforum06/peopleandorganisationswhosignedtheistanbuldeclaration.htm

Park, J. K., & John, D. R. (2011). More than meets the eye: The influence of implicit and explicit self-esteem on materialism. *Journal of Consumer Psychology, 21*, 73–87. http://doi.org/10.1016/j.jcps.2010.09.001

Pierce, J. L., Kostova, T., & Dirks, K. T. (2003). The state of psychological ownership: Integrating and extending a century of research. *Review of General Psychology, 7*, 84–107. http://doi.org/10.1037//1089-2680.7.1.84.

Reb, J., & Connolly, T. (2007). Possession, feelings of ownership and the endowment effect. *Judgment and Decision Making, 2*, 107–114.

Richins, M. L., & Dawson, S. (1992). A consumer values orientation for materialism and its measurement: Scale development and validation. *Journal of Consumer Research, 19*, 303–316. http://doi.org/1086/209304.

Rudmin, F. W. (1993). Property. In W. J. Lonner, & R. Malpas (Eds.), *Psychology and culture* (pp. 55–58). Boston, MA: Allyn & Bacon.

Rudmin, F. W., & Berry, J. W. (1987). Semantics of ownership: A free-recall study of property. *Psychological Record, 37*, 257–268.

Schwartz, S. H. (1992). Universals in the content and structure of values: Theory and empirical tests in 20 countries. In M. Zanna (Ed.), *Advances in experimental social psychology*, Vol. 25, pp. 1–65. New York: Academic Press.

Schwartz, S. H. (1994). Are there universal aspects in the structure and contents of human values? *Journal of Social Issues, 50*, 19–45. http://doi.org/10.1111/j.1540-4560.1994.tb01196.x

Schwartz, S. H. (2006). A theory of cultural value orientations: Explication and applications. *Comparative Sociology, 5*, 137–182. http://doi.org/10.1163/156913306778667357

Schwartz, S. H. (2007). Cultural and individual value correlates of materialism: A comparative analysis. *Psychological Inquiry, 18*, 52–57. http://doi.org/10.1080/10478400701388963

Siegler, V. (2015). *Office of National Statistics. Measuring national well-being – an analysis of social capital in the UK.* Retrieved from http://www.ons.gov.uk/ons/dcp171766_393380.pdf

Thaler, R. H. (1980). Toward a positive theory of consumer choice. *Journal of Economic Behavior and Organization, 1*, 39–60.

Veblen, T. (1899). *The theory of the leisure class.* New York: Macmillan.

Wilkinson, R. G., & Pickett, K. (2010). *The spirit level: Why greater equality is better for everyone.* London: Penguin.

FURTHER READING

Dittmar, H. (1992). *The social psychology of material possessions.* Hemel Hempstead: Harvester Wheatsheaf.

Dittmar, H., Bond, R., Hurst, M., & Kasser, T. (2014). The relationship between materialism and personal well-being: A meta-analysis. *Journal of Personality and Social Psychology, 107*, 879–924. http://doi.org/1010.1037/a0037409.

Kasser, T. (2002). *The high price of materialism.* Cambridge, MA: MIT Press.

PART 4

Financial Behaviour

12 Defining and Influencing Financial Capability

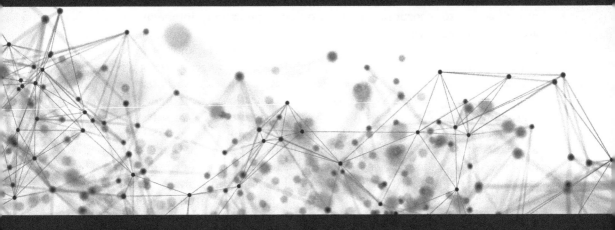

IVO VLAEV AND ANTONY ELLIOTT

CHAPTER OUTLINE

LEARNING OUTCOMES

BY THE END OF THIS CHAPTER YOU SHOULD BE ABLE TO:

1. Understand and describe the nature, origins and scope of behaviour change theory.
2. Discuss the relationship between behaviour change and financial capability, and describe various ways to influence financial capability.
3. Give examples of a range of studies and findings from recent behavioural finance research.

12.1   INTRODUCTION

A person is not 'capable' if they acquire skills and knowledge, but do not put them into practice. This chapter sets out the need for practitioners in the field of money advice to incorporate motivation and opportunity interventions, which are as important as the provision of knowledge and skills. Thus, while the old, traditional definition of financial capability focused on the knowledge and skills to be a financially capable person (such as living within one's means and planning ahead), our expanded definition of financial capability also includes the opportunities and motivations required to be a financially capable person. There is a growing body of behavioural science on which to draw in order to identify specific interventions that are likely to improve financial capability in the population. Section 12.2 gives examples from finance to demonstrate the scope to use the revised definition to drive innovation in the development of initiatives. The components of influencing behaviour can be applied in combinations in order to produce interventions that work for the population group needing advice. Recent evidence of the growing maturity of the discipline of economic psychology (behavioural economics) has already been applied in the financial services industry. Financial institutions are also starting to apply behavioural approaches to produce better outcomes for their customers.

12.2   A NEW CONCEPTUALIZATION OF FINANCIAL CAPABILITY

12.2.1   Re-Defining Financial Capability

In order to help households manage their money better, a necessary first step is to understand and define what it means to be financially capable. The working definition of financial capability, determined by research undertaken in 2006 by the Financial Services Authority in the UK (Financial Services Authority, 2006a, 2006b, 2006c), is based on skills such as making ends meet, keeping track of money, choosing financial products, planning ahead, and staying informed. This rather narrow view of capability is useful, but it is also misleading, because it gives the impression that giving people skills is everything required for them to become financially capable. However, evidence from behavioural sciences has demonstrated that skills and knowledge are not sufficient to change behaviour (Webb & Sheeran, 2006), and other ingredients are needed, such as internal motivations and external opportunities to perform the target behaviour (Michie, van Stralen, & West, 2011; Vlaev & Dolan, 2015). Therefore, we would like to propose a broader, and hopefully more useful, definition of capability in general and financial capability in particular. This will provide us with a more behavioural definition of financial capability, which is ultimately about how understanding how money is used daily, thought about, and felt about in the life of the person.

In essence, 'capability' is defined in the *Oxford Dictionary* as 'as the power or ability to do something'. This official definition reveals that capability relates to every factor (psychological, physiological and environmental) that enables the individual to perform a specific behaviour. Obviously this relates to knowledge and skills to perform an action, but this definition reveals that capability could also include things, such as the forces or resources giving a person or an army the ability to undertake a particular kind of military action; the intuitive ability to bring the best out in people in your team; and the facility on a computer for performing a specified task such as a graphics capability. In summary, *capability*, or what defines a *capable person*, includes all necessary and sufficient conditions that make it possible for an individual to perform a specific behaviour.

Intuitively, and also formally as we shall explain later, this means that in order to act, the person needs enough knowledge and skills, conscious will or unconscious desire, optimal physical conditions and favourable cultural institutions. All these things taken together make the person capable of doing something. For example, imagine a football player who is very skilful and gifted, but lacks the motivation to run around the pitch and pass the ball, and because of his lazy reputation his team mates do not willingly pass him the ball when he is in a position to score. Thus, if he lacks the motivation to play and the opportunity to score, he will hardly ever be seen to play good football, and hence the fans and the media are unlikely to describe him as a capable player. Similarly in the financial domain, a person possessing good financial knowledge and acumen, but lacking the willpower, or emotional resilience, to resist the temptation to buy unnecessary luxuries and live beyond one's means, will hardly ever be seen as, or behave like, a financially capable person.

Therefore, our position here is that how people manage their money, and their financial behaviour in general, are subject to the same wide range of influences, like any other human action. This definition also implies that understanding what makes a financially capable person will also allow us to impact on and improve the capability of that person. This chapter tries to present a broader picture of financial capability, largely based on a behavioural framework, which goes beyond how skills and knowledge affect an individual's approach to their finances. As a result, financial advisory services, such as the Money Advice Service (MAS) in the United Kingdom, who have knowledge of these behavioural influences, should be (ethically and responsively) employing such insights when it comes to providing new services or interventions that have a greater benefit to its users.

Note that the art of influencing people has been practised for millennia, so there is nothing new in this idea. However, there is certainly something new in what we know about how best to do it. Recent research in the behavioural sciences shows that approaches based on education and information alone do not actually work that well (Webb & Sheeran, 2006). Instead, we are each influenced, in remarkably similar ways, by the framing of a decision and by subtle contextual factors (Thaler & Sunstein, 2008). These effects are fast, automatic, and largely unconscious. The aim of this chapter is to review the latest thinking on the various components of behaviour change and to illustrate how to design comprehensive interventions to support household economic decisions. Those intervention strategies can also be used to improve the financial advisory services (Vlaev, Nieboer, Martin, & Dolan, 2015) and customer well-being (Vlaev & Elliott, 2014).

12.2.2 *Understanding and Influencing Behavioural Capability*

Behaviour change is a growing field which includes several disciplines in the social sciences. Using a theoretical approach rooted in sound evidence-based theory to understand behavioural capability and intervention design usually leads to long-term effectiveness and sustainability of the proposed policies (Michie & Prestwich, 2010). Complex interventions to change behaviour and improve behavioural capability should work on several levels – structural or environmental, psychological, and behavioural (Abraham & Michie, 2008; Michie, van Stralen, & West, 2011; Webb & Sheeran, 2006). This approach will enable financial advice services to implement multifactorial interventions, targeting several levels at once (although sometimes simple interventions will be the most cost-effective). This understanding of behavioural capability and intervention design should be informed by recent comprehensive models of behaviour and behaviour change (see Vlaev & Darzi, 2012; Vlaev & Dolan, 2015).

According to recent integrative frameworks for understanding and changing behaviour (Fishbein et al., 2001; Michie et al., 2011), human behaviour is an interacting system in which Abilities,[1] Motivations and Opportunities interact to generate Behaviour, thus producing Behavioural Capability, which in turn influences these components (see Figure 12.1). Thus, three factors are necessary and sufficient conditions for the performance of a specific volitional behaviour: (1) the abilities necessary to perform the behaviour; (2) the motivation (although not necessarily conscious) to perform the behaviour; and (3) environmental opportunities that make it possible to perform the behaviour.

- *Ability* is defined as the individual's psychological and physical capacity to engage in the activity concerned.

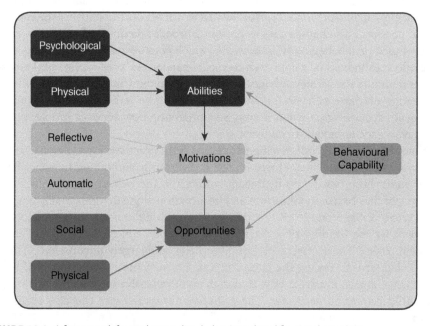

FIGURE 12.1 *A framework for understanding behavioural and financial capability.*

- *Psychological ability* includes having the necessary knowledge and skills and also possessing the capacity to engage in the necessary thought processes such as comprehension, reasoning, and so on. It can be achieved through imparting knowledge or understanding, and by training emotional, cognitive and/or behavioural skills. This is about ability to perform – whether people find it difficult or not (hence why subjective self-efficacy is also important – whether the individuals believe they can do things). For example, in order to help people live within their means (budgeting and not running out of money), interventions could involve using tools to aid budgeting – online or using a spreadsheet/book, or earmarking money for different outgoings – mentally or physically separating them into piles.

- *Physical ability* can be achieved through physical skill development, which is the focus of training. Another key issue here is whether individuals are being limited by their body because they are disabled in some way; and therefore this category also relates to old, sick, or disabled individuals, or those who may have difficulty using the internet or getting to banks in a rural location.

- *Motivations* are defined as all those brain processes that energize and direct behaviour, which includes reflective and automatic mechanisms. The 'dual process' model has often been proposed as a theoretical basis for targeting automatic behaviours with 'nudges' (Marteau et al., 2011). In particular, psychologists and neuroscientists have recently converged on a description of brain functioning that is based on two types of cognitive processes, also interpreted as two distinct systems (or sets of systems): evolutionarily older 'System 1' processes described as automatic, uncontrolled, effortless, associative, fast, unconscious and affective; and more recent, characteristically human 'System 2' processes described as reflective, controlled, effortful, rule-based, slow, conscious and rational (Evans, 2008; Strack & Deutsch, 2004). Neurobiological evidence of separate brain structures for automatic processing of information provides substantial support for this model (Rangel, Camerer, & Montague, 2008). We also employ the dual-process paradigm as a unified framework for population behaviour change, but additionally provide a more nuanced account of how the automatic systems control behaviour.

- *Reflective motivations* involve evaluations (also known as attitudes) weighing up the pros and cons of something; goal setting – thinking about the outcome you want to achieve – including abstract long-term goals and short-term goals; and planning – creating an action plan to achieve an outcome by specifying where, when, and how to execute an action. Reflective motivations are usually targeted in interventions based on cognitive behavioural therapy. Public policies targeting reflective motivation traditionally include information provision and economic incentives. For example, living within one's means would require evaluations about whether or not something is needed, and then making plans so that regular spending habits correlate with this decision. These plans could include setting a financial target in order to achieve a goal (e.g., aim to travel in retirement, take a gap year, buy a house); and then identifying small achievable steps such as making weekly or monthly monitoring and paying into a savings account or making investments.

- *Automatic motivations* are associative in nature and comprise a class of mental phenomena such as habits, impulses, heuristics and biases. Those processes are predominantly influenced by context, in line with the behavioural economics approach embodied in the MINDSPACE framework (Dolan et al., 2012a; 2012b). This mnemonic framework reflects an attempt to establish the most robust effects on behaviour that operate largely through automatic psychological processes. Automatic motivations can also be broken down into more basic motivations that drive human behaviour (see Table 12.1).[2]

- *Opportunities* are defined as all the factors, social and physical, that lie outside the individual that make the behaviour possible or prompt it.

Table 12.1 *The MINDSPACE framework for automatic motivations and behaviour change*

MINDSPACE influences	Automatic motivations and behaviours*
Messenger	We are heavily influenced by who communicates information to us, such as when our decision to listen to or ignore something purely because of who has said it. For example, it matters who told us to keep track of finances, invest or take out pension – it is crucial whether they are friends with an IFA and what we think of them.
Incentives	Our responses to incentives are shaped by predictable mental shortcuts such as strongly avoiding losses, ignoring/discounting future benefits or losses (so we are unable to resist a 'bargain' even if the product is not needed), and creating idiosyncratic mental accounts. For example, individuals may be encouraged to perform mental accounting to keep track of how much money they have.
Norms	We are strongly influenced by what others do – such an automatic conformity with social norms (desire to be like those around us) is a driver of preventative behaviours across many domains. For example, people may budget if their friends or family budget too; and they may plan ahead if their peers have a plan of where they want to be in the future.
Defaults	We 'go with the flow' of pre-set options – defaults are the options that are pre-selected if an individual does not make an active choice. For example, in order to enable consumers to budget and keep track of finances, they could automatically receive information about their bills or bank accounts, and also receive advice how to improve bills and debt repayments.
Salience	Or attention is drawn to what is novel and seems relevant to us – we are more likely to register stimuli that are novel (messages in flashing lights), accessible (items on sale next to checkouts) and simple (a snappy slogan). For example, a simple way to motivate people to keep track of finances is making the bank statements and budget sheets interesting enough to pay attention to.
Priming	Our acts are often influenced by subconscious cues – these could be sounds, sights and smells that draw us in or repel us. For example, credit borrowers may only pay minimal payment on credit card bills as the amount has been suggested or primed, which allows providers to intervene by strategically manipulating this amount.

MINDSPACE influences	Automatic motivations and behaviours*
Affect	Our emotional associations can powerfully shape our actions – we can respond emotionally to words, images and events and our mood can impact our decision-making. Such feelings may motivate people to plan ahead for something they look forward to, such as holidays. Likewise, budgeting may be reinforced by rewarding oneself at the end of the month for keeping within limits.
Commitments	We seek to be consistent with our public promises, and reciprocate acts – if we say we are going to do something, we are more likely to do it. For example, someone may check balances regularly after telling others she will do so; similarly, planning ahead will be encouraged by asking someone to tell others of plans.
Ego	We act in ways that make us feel better about ourselves – we tend to behave in a way that supports the impression of a positive and consistent self-image. For example, individuals could be informed that keeping track of finance projects gives an impression of being on top of things, while living within one's means should be presented as creating a self-image of being frugal.

* Note that the examples in the table are hypothetical and they are provided only to illustrate the application of each principle; while the supporting evidence is provided in the main text.

- *Social opportunity* is afforded by the cultural milieu that dictates the way that people think, including the set of shared values and practices that characterize institutions and groups. This happens when family and friends are encouraging and supportive, such as when they may help us find time and space to study for exams, when they openly discuss and share information about household finances, and when financial awareness is being raised by people we know. For example, in order to improve capability for budgeting and keeping track of finances, others can tell us about the usefulness of online banking or balance text messages, about ways of spending money, about ways of budgeting and tools available. Our planning ahead can similarly be influenced by others telling us about their financial plans, products and investments.

- *Physical opportunity* is about the infrastructure or technology available for people, such as levels of access to financial services or products, so it may not necessarily be about individual behaviour, but this determinant can guarantee sustainability of the target behaviours. For example, enabling individuals to keep track of their finances would require broadband internet access at home, a smartphone with a banking app, and accessing account information at cash points. Similarly, enabling financial planning would require easily being able to contact financial institutions or support services in person or online, availability of choice of products and competition in local area.

In summary, this theoretical framework for understanding financial capability ensures that the most appropriate intervention is implemented once we have better understanding of the role of various determinants in financial behaviour (e.g., see Vlaev, Nieboer, Martin, & Dolan, 2015). For example, some people may be reflectively motivated to budget and keep track of their finances, but lack the physical or social opportunity (i.e., structural and cultural barriers). There are some obvious applications of this framework to changing financial behaviour (the evidence in the academic literature is discussed in Section 12.3). Reflective motivational techniques such as 'providing information on consequences', 'prompting barrier identification', 'prompting specific goal setting', and 'prompting review of behavioural goals' should be encouraged (see Abraham & Michie, 2008). Influencing automatic motivations is another key lever to improve financial capability. For example, information about 'social norms', such as testimonials from people most similar to the target audience, should have powerful, yet automatic influence on motivation (e.g., if the client is a young family with children, the financial adviser could provide information about what other young families are doing with their finances if this is relevant and appropriate to the customer and the provision of best advice). It is also important to inform and reinforce to people that they are not only behaving in ways that are desirable, but continue to be similar to others just like them.

The next sections briefly illustrate how interventions can influence each component of this comprehensive framework.[3]

12.3   WAYS TO INFLUENCE FINANCIAL CAPABILITY

12.3.1   *Influencing Psychological Abilities*

Psychological or cognitive abilities are usually improved through education. Gaurav, Cole and Tobacman (2011) report large-scale randomized field experiments on the uptake of an innovative, but complex, financial product: rainfall insurance for poor farmers in India. The authors invited half the farmers in the sample to a financial education session by a non-governmental organization, in which various financial concepts, including insurance, were explained in an interactive way. This resulted in a beneficial effect of advice (doubled uptake from 8% to 16%) by a source that did not stand to benefit from a sale. The positive effect of the training likely came from the trust the farmers had in an expert and independent source (see Section 12.2 on the characteristics of the adviser). Another example is one of the largest studies on the impacts of financial education – Bernheim and Garrett (2003) found that saving rates increase significantly with the provision of employer-based education. Employees who are offered retirement education are far more likely to participate in 401(k) programmes in the United States, and to make larger contributions to their plans. The effects of education are particularly pronounced among those least inclined to save; however, there is some indication that education stimulates 401(k) contributions among high savers. The authors conclude that the education led to a 1.5% higher saving rate.

Another example of improving psychological capability comes from a recent study addressing the fact that consumers do not accurately compute how incentives accumulate over time. McKenzie and Liersch (2011) show that people drastically underestimate how much wealth they will amass if they save at a certain rate (because they mistakenly expect cumulative savings to grow linearly with contributions rather than exponentially, ignoring the effects of interest on interest). However, visually educating individuals (using graphs and figures) about the higher projected exponential growth makes them more motivated to save than to cut back.

12.3.2 Influencing Reflective Motivation

There are various possible approaches and techniques that can be applied here but probably the most effective strategy should integrate two separate techniques (see Stadler, Oettingen, & Gollwitzer, 2010, for a review of related evidence).

- *Evaluation and goal setting*: This is a motivational technique that helps people to self-regulate their goal commitment by translating expectations of success and value into goal commitment. This technique leads individuals through a specified sequence of three steps: (1) identifying an important wish that is directed towards behaviour change and that a person expects to be able to attain (e.g., 'saving more'); (2) identifying and imagining the most positive outcome of successfully changing the behaviour (e.g., 'greater well-being'); and (3) identifying and imagining the most critical obstacle that stands in the way of wish fulfilment (e.g., 'going out on Friday and Saturday evening').

  There has been a significant growth in the availability of goal-based savings tools from financial institutions in the last three years (see Elliott, 2013). The most advanced tool is provided by RBS / NatWest where the making of a conscious commitment is shown to significantly increase the amount of saving by £190 per month at the end of 2013 compared with non-goal-based savings (the two commitment tools are the setting of a goal and the commitment to a regular payment which is achieved by standing order / direct debit or by making a regular transfer to the account).

- *Planning*: The second technique is known as 'implementation intention' (Gollwitzer & Oettingen, 2015), which involves detailed planning that enables implementing the desired goals, otherwise people forget to act or are distracted when an opportunity to act arises. Implementation intentions are 'if … then …' plans that link critical situational cues to a goal-directed behaviour in the format of 'if (cue), then (response)', which enhances the accessibility of the mental representation of the specified cue and allows people to easily identify the critical situation when they subsequently encounter it. Goal fulfilment is more likely when individuals supplement a goal (e.g., 'I want to save more!') with an implementation plan that details when, where, and how the person wants to act (e.g., 'On every Friday evening before going out, I will transfer £50 into my savings account'). Anticipating critical situations – opportunities and obstacles – is also crucial for implementing behaviour change; and researchers have distinguished such planning techniques directed at action initiation from plans that are directed at dealing with obstacles ('coping planning') to highlight this difference (Stadler, Oettingen, & Gollwitzer, 2010). To implement those two reflective motivation techniques, participants are usually asked to write down each step as described above (and initially rehearse it each day in writing using a diary and also mentally). Those techniques can be applied to short-term goals as well as long-term goals.

12.3.3 Influencing Automatic Motivation

Note that when we design behavioural interventions, our basic assumption is that every effect in the MINDSPACE framework can work as both a driver of behaviour (if properly applied) and also as a barrier to desired behaviours. For example, social norms can encourage people to join in social networking sites if other people are observed to do so, but can also deter young consumers from using consumer education tools if none of their peers are doing so. With this caveat in mind, we briefly outline examples from the literature reporting how nudging automatic motivations has been used to promote adaptive and positive behaviours, using MINDSPACE (**M**essengers, **I**ncentives, **N**orms, **D**efaults, **S**alience, **P**riming, **A**ffect and, **C**ommitments and **E**go).

- *Messengers*: In an experiment on enrolment in the Tax Deferred Account in the United States, a random sample of employees in a subset of departments were encouraged to attend a benefits information fair organized by the university (Duflo & Saez, 2003). Enrolment in the scheme months after the fair was significantly higher in departments where some individuals were treated (i.e., encouraged to attend) than in departments where nobody was treated. The messenger effects are that friends and colleagues in the same department are telling their colleagues about the benefits of enrolment.

- *Incentives*: The incentives principle relates to framing of financial outcomes. This matters because of automatic loss aversion, which can be used to motivate people to take financial action. People are less likely to spend tax cuts delivered as a lump sum or framed as a 'rebate', compared to ones delivered as many small payments or framed as a 'bonus' (Epley et al., 2006). In another study on framing of incentives, respondents were given the choice to take part in a company charity donation scheme, with an amount to be deducted immediately from their salary (Gourville, 1998). The donations were presented as equivalent to either 'per day frame' (e.g., $1 per day for a year) or 'per year frame' (e.g., $350 for the year). Significantly more donations were made in per day frame, but only when amount was typical of per day expenses (e.g., cup of coffee). The per-year frame was favoured for larger amounts. This evidence also shows that both financial value and the timeframe over which financial actions are stated will influence the likelihood that they are ever undertaken.

- *Norms*: The set of shared values and practices that characterize institutions and groups can influence behaviours. In a study of the effect of peer groups, Karlan (2007) tested whether more well-connected groups perform better in terms of loan repayments and savings in Peru, where banks lend to groups rather than individuals. It turns out that stronger social connection within the group led to higher repayment and savings. For example, during the first 4-month loan cycle, moving from the 25th percentile to the 75th percentile in the spatial distance to others in the group implies an increase of 22% of the average savings rate.

Another way to employ social norms is reported by Schultz et al. (2007), who demonstrated that messages describing average energy usage in the neighbourhood produced either desirable energy savings when households were already consuming at a high rate, or undesirable increase in consumption when households were consuming at a low rate. However, a follow-up study adding an 'injunctive' norm conveying social approval or disapproval – by showing smiling or sad faces respectively, eliminated the undesirable increase (households continue consuming at a low rate). A tested practical example of injunctive norms is provided by *thinkmoney*, a supplier of a 'jam jar' bank account (Elliott, 2013). They decided to provide information to customers in the form of a 'smiley' or 'frown' face according to whether based on existing information on forthcoming bills and income they would run out of money in the month ('smiley' or 'frown' face are signals of social approval and disapproval, also known as injunctive norms). The 'frown' face was described as helpful by 94% of the customers that received it and 96% took an action such as contacting a 'Money Manager' at the company. Of course, in addition to communicating a social norm, the faces are also providing salient information that customers would not know otherwise. i.e., running out of money as opposed to projected money in and out (it is forecasting based on information customers provided about regular income and known bills).

- *Defaults*: Defaults are the options that are pre-selected if an individual does not make an active choice. The best examples of defaults have come from financial behaviour. Cronqvist and Thaler (2004) examines the choice of retirement funds in Sweden after the privatization of social security. They found that 43% of new participants chose the default plan, despite the fact that the government encouraged individual choice, and despite the availability of 456 plans. Three years later, after the end of the advertisement campaign encouraging individual choice, the proportion choosing the default plan increased to 92%.

- *Salience*: As a neat example of where attention is automatically directed, Brown et al. (2008) investigated how people think about annuities; consumers asked to think in terms of consumption viewed annuities as valuable insurance, whereas consumers asked to think in terms of investment risk and return viewed annuities as a risky asset because the payoffs depends on an uncertain date of death. The two 'frames' were randomized to a group of individuals 50 years old and over, and the authors found that the vast majority of individuals prefer an annuity over alternative products when the question is framed in terms of consumption, while the majority of individuals prefer non-annuitized products when the questions are presented in terms of risk and return (note that this result is not dependent on the initial purchase price). Salience has caused individuals to focus their attention on either consumption or the risk and return.

A tested practical example of salient information is provided by RBS/ NatWest (see Elliott, 2013). This bank has been introducing messages relating to goal-based savings that are designed to help customers with the pressure to be consistent with the goals they make. Those messages provide salient feedback as to how the customer is progressing towards the goal. Messages have been sent to customers falling behind or stopping saving as a result of over-ambitious goals that are leading to many customers re-setting those goals at more manageable levels. In particular, 23% reset mostly downwards their savings goal and 25% started saving again. Customer responses as to why they found the message helpful included answers such as 'Prompted me to reassess my financial health' and 'I reviewed my savings and made changes to my current plans'.[4]

- *Priming*: Stewart (2009) finds that the minimum-repayment information on hypothetical credit card debt primes (anchors) the size of hypothetical repayments (see also McHugh & Ranyard, 2016). Feinberg (1986) found that being primed with a credit card (i.e., the mere possession or image of a credit card is a prime) makes you more likely to spend more on a good, and spend quicker. Prelec and Simester (2001) report a similar finding that when payment is by credit card, people are willing to pay 60–110% higher than the paying by cash.

- *Affect*: Emotional responses to words, images, and events can be rapid and automatic, which is a powerful force in decision-making. In a consumer credit marketing field experiment in South Africa, Bertrand et al. (2010) find that adding a photo of an attractive smiling female face to a direct mail solicitation increases the likelihood of borrowing by just as much as reducing the interest rate by about 3% (for example, from 10% to 7%), for both men and women alike. In this case, the letter and the loan offer are associated with a positive feeling provoked by the photo.

- *Commitments*: Another type of automatic motivation is activated by commitments. Behavioural research suggests that people feel a strong interpersonal pressure to be consistent with their public commitments and actions. Making a commitment ties a person's sense-of-self to a particular course of action. Studies have shown that asking for a small initial commitment (such as asking someone if they would be willing to call in advance if they have to cancel a restaurant reservation, or verbally repeat back details of a medical appointment), significantly reduces subsequent no-shows (Cialdini, 2007; Martin et al., 2012). Commitments can be strengthened to the extent that they are voluntary, effortful and public. It is advisable, for example, that a financial adviser seeks small voluntary commitments in the early stages of a client engagement and builds on these initial commitments (making those commitments public – perhaps involving a spouse or other family member – may also increase future commitments).

- *Ego*: The Ego principle (that we act in ways that make us feel better about ourselves) has been employed in interventions aiming to change insurance behaviour (see Shu, Mazar, Gino, Ariely, & Bazerman, 2012). Dan Ariely and his colleagues conducted a field experiment with an insurance company in the south-eastern United States asking some of their existing customers to report their odometer reading. When a new insurance policy is issued, each customer has to submit information about the exact current odometer mileage of all cars insured under their policy, along with other information. The researchers sent out automobile policy review forms to policyholders, randomly assigning them to either the original form used by the insurance company or to a slightly redesigned form. The original form asked customers to sign the statement: 'I promise that the information I am providing is true' which appeared at the bottom of the form, usually signed after having completed it; whereas the redesigned form asked customers to sign that same statement but at the top of the form, which should happen usually before filling it out. This was the only difference between the forms. Asking customers to sign at the beginning of the form led to a 10.25% increase in the calculated miles driven over the current practice of asking for a signature at the end. Apparent discrepancies between how people want to view themselves (the ideal self or Ego) and how they actually behave, creates discomfort that drives people to reduce this discrepancy by changing their behaviour to act more in accordance with their ideal self. As this study shows, in the domain of financial deception, this could lead to more honest behaviour.

12.3.4   *Influencing Social Opportunity*

In the realm of 'cultural' determinants, there has been research on who uses web-based advice. People who use the web tend to be younger, better educated and more affluent; and consumers also want web-based advice to be branded, interactive, independent, unbiased and tailored (Joo et al., 2007; Sillence & Briggs, 2007). Therefore, financial interventions can include tailored advice given over the web. In this respect, it is important to consider who would have access to different channels and which demographics would be willing to act on advice from such sources.

12.3.5   *Influencing Physical Opportunity*

Researchers have studied which communication opportunities are seen as the most trusted and useful, which is related to the 'structural' determinants, such as infrastructure and technology. Those studies revealed that the method of service delivery available to the customer will make a difference. Researchers investigated the financial advice available online relative to that given by trainee financial advisers and found mixed results (Ciccotelo & Wood, 2001; Mantel, 2000). The web gave more consistent advice on life insurance and tax benefit issues, but less consistent advice on estate tax and investment. They also found that live advice was less sensitive to complexity in the client's situation, relative to web-based advice. In another study, financial advisers were represented by text-only, video, audio, avatar, or photo and text; and it turned out that audio and video were most popular, but all the media resulted in a similar uptake of advice (Riegelsberger et al., 2005).

12.4   CONCLUSION

Influencing financial behaviours is a key service area that needs to be addressed as more field interventions are needed, while interventions to support household economic decisions will benefit from recent work in laboratory environments. The examples reported here apply to all kinds of financial behaviours and services, because the underlying behavioural principles are the same (e.g., social norms can affect choices in saving, debt repayment, insurance, financial advice, and other financial domains). Therefore, the lessons learned from this chapter, subject to testing, can be applied in many financial contexts; thus revealing the way towards truly innovative policy-making promoting households' financial capability and ultimately their subjective well-being (Vlaev & Elliott, 2014).

We would like also to stress that most of the influences on behaviour operate below conscious awareness and therefore cannot easily be tapped into by the conscious questioning of market research. The recent insights from behavioural sciences reveal that humans are not especially good at knowing what just influenced them, or what will influence them in the future. Crucially, more research is needed on interventions that target automatic motivations, as this is the least understood factor in the behaviour production system presented in Figure 12.1. Conducting such interventions promises to create more effective tools for changing behaviour and improving financial capability across different populations and domains of life.

12.5   SUMMARY

A 'financially capable' person not only acquires skills and knowledge, but also puts them into practice. Thus, while a tradition definition of financial capability focuses on the knowledge and skills to be a financially capable person, our expanded definition of financial capability also includes the opportunities and motivations required to be a financially capable person. Therefore, practitioners in the field of money advice need to appreciate that motivation and opportunity interventions are as important as the provision of knowledge and skills. There is a growing body of behavioural research on which to draw in order to identify specific interventions that are likely to improve financial capability in the population. Further evidence of the growing maturity of the discipline of economic psychology is provided by its use in the financial services industry. Financial institutions are also applying behavioural approaches to produce better outcomes for their customers.

NOTES

1. In the original version of this framework, the authors used the term 'Capability', but we replaced it with 'Ability' in this chapter, so that the term 'capability' used by Fishbein et al. (2001) and Michie et al. (2011) is not confused with our definition of financial capability and general capability to perform a specific behaviour.

2. Note that Messenger, Incentives, Norms and Commitment could be implemented in ways that involved reflective motivation although in most cases they would be focusing on automatic processes.

3. Note that influencing 'physical ability' is less relevant for financial interventions, and has received little attention in the literature, so we do not consider this aspect here.

4. Ipsos MORI survey conducted with 1,188 RBS/NatWest customers who have a Your Savings Goal. Fieldwork was conducted online in October 2013.

REVIEW QUESTIONS

1. Provide your best definition of financial capability. Why is financial capability more than knowledge and skills?

2. Why do we need a general theoretical framework for understanding behaviour?

3. How could behavioural theory help to improve people's financial capability?

4. Explain how automatic motivation works and the ideas summarized in the MINDSPACE framework.

5. Provide examples from academic research and financial services, which illustrate how behavioural science can improve financial capability.

REFERENCES

Abraham, C., & Michie, S. (2008). A taxonomy of behavior change techniques used in interventions. *Health Psychology, 27*, 379–387.

Bernheim, B. D., & Garrett, D. M. (2003). The effects of financial education in the workplace: Evidence from a survey of households. *Journal of Public Economics, 87*, 1487–1519.

Bertrand, M., Karlan, D., Mullainathan, S., Shafir, E., & Zinman, J. (2010). What's advertising content worth? Evidence from a consumer credit marketing field experiment. *Quarterly Journal of Economics, 125*, 263–306.

Brown, J. B., Kling, J. R., Mullainathan, S., & Wrobel, M. V. (2008). Why don't people insure late-life consumption? A framing explanation of the under-annuitization puzzle. *American Economic Review, 98*, 304–309.

Cialdini, R. (2007). *Influence: The psychology of persuasion.* New York: Harper Business.

Ciccotelo, C. S., & Wood, R. E. (2001). An investigation of the consistency of financial advice offered by web-based sources. *Financial Services Review, 10*, 5–18.

Cronqvist, H., & Thaler, R. H. (2004). Design choices in privatized social-security systems: learning from the Swedish experience. *American Economic Review, 94*, 424–428.

Dolan, P., Elliott, A., Metcalfe, R., & Vlaev, I. (2012a). Influencing financial behavior: From changing minds to changing contexts. *Journal of Behavioral Finance, 13*, 127–143.

Dolan, P., Hallsworth, M., Halpern, D., King, D., Metcalfe, R., & Vlaev, I. (2012b). Influencing behaviour: The MINDSPACE way. *Journal of Economic Psychology, 33*, 264–277.

Duflo, E., & Saez, E. (2003). The role of information and social interactions in retirement plan decisions: Evidence from a randomized experiment. *Quarterly Journal of Economics, 118*, 815–842.

Elliott, A. (2013). *Fairbanking ratings: Reaching for the stars.* The Fairbanking Foundation. http://fairbanking.org.uk/research-3/fairbanking-reports/

Epley, N., Mak, D., & Idson, L. C. (2006). Bonus or rebate? The impact of income framing on spending and saving. *Journal of Behavioral Decision Making, 19*, 213–227.

Evans, J. (2008). Dual-processing accounts of reasoning, judgement, and social cognition. *Annual Review of Psychology, 59*, 255–278.

Feinberg, R. (1986). Credit cards as spending facilitating stimuli. *Journal of Consumer Research*, *13*, 348–356.

Financial Services Authority (2006a). *Levels of financial capability in the UK: Results of a baseline survey*. London: FSA.

Financial Services Authority (2006b). *Financial capability in the UK: Establishing a baseline*. London: FSA.

Financial Services Authority (2006c). *Financial capability in the UK: Delivering change*. London: FSA.

Fishbein, M., Triandis, H., Kanfer, F., Becker, M., Middlestadt, S., & Eichler, A. (2001). Factors influencing behaviour and behaviour change. In A. Baum, T. Revenson, & J. I. Singer (Eds.), *Handbook of health psychology* (pp. 3–17). Mahwah. NJ: Lawrence Erlbaum Associates.

Gaurav, S., Cole, S., & Tobacman, J. (2011). Marketing complex financial products in emerging markets: Evidence from rainfall insurance in India. *Journal of Marketing Research*, *48*, S150–S162.

Gollwitzer, P. M., & Oettingen, G. (2015). From studying the determinants of action to analyzing its regulation. *Health Psychology Review*, *9*, 146–150.

Gourville, J. T. (1998). Pennies-a-day: The effect of temporal reframing on transaction evaluation. *Journal of Consumer Research*, *24*, 395–408.

Joo, S. H., Grable, J. E., & Choe, H. (2007). Who is and who is not willing to use on-line employer-provided investment advice. *Journal of Employment Counseling*, *44*, 73–86.

Karlan, D. (2007). Social connections and group banking. *Economic Journal*, *117*, F52–F84.

Mantel, B. (2000). Why don't consumers use electronic banking products? Towards a theory of obstacles, incentives, and opportunities. Emerging Payments Occasional Paper Series, Chicago: Federal Reserve Bank of Chicago.

Marteau, T. M., Ogilvie, D., Roland, M., Suhrcke, M., & Kelly, M. P. (2011). Judging nudging: Can nudging improve population health? *British Medical Journal*, *342*, d228.

Martin, S. J., Bassi, S., & Dunbar-Ress, R. (2012). Commitments, norms and custard creams: A social influence approach to reducing no-shows. *Journal of the Royal Society of Medicine*, *105*, 101–104.

McHugh, S., & Ranyard, R. (2016). Consumers' credit card repayment decisions: The role of higher anchors and future repayment concern. *Journal of Economic Psychology*, *52*, 102–114.

McKenzie, C. R. M., & Liersch, M. J. (2011). Misunderstanding savings growth: implications for retirement savings behavior. *Journal of Marketing Research*, *48*, S1–S13.

Michie, S., & Prestwich, A. (2010). Are interventions theory-based? Development of a theory coding scheme. *Health Psychology*, *29*, 1–8.

Michie, S., van Stralen, M. M., & West, R. (2011). The behaviour change wheel: A new method for characterising and designing behaviour change interventions. *Implementation Science*, *6*, 42.

Prelec, D., & Simester. D. (2001). Credit-card effect on willingness to pay. *Marketing Letters*, *12*, 5–12.

Rangel, A., Camerer, C., & Montague, M. (2008). A framework for studying the neurobiology of value-based decision-making. *Nature Reviews Neuroscience*, *9*, 545–556.

Riegelsberger, J., Sasse, A., & McCarthy, J. D. (2005). Rich media, poor judgment? A study of media effects on users' trust in expertise. *Proceedings of the HCI-05 Conference on People and Computers*, *19*, 267–284.

Schultz, P. W., Nolan, J. M., Cialdini, R. B., Goldstein, N. J., & Griskevicius, V. (2007). The constructive, destructive, and reconstructive power of social norms. *Psychological Science*, *18*, 429–434.

Shu, L. L., Mazar, N., Gino, F., Ariely, D., & Bazerman, M. H. (2012). Signing at the beginning makes ethics salient and decreases dishonest self-reports in comparison to signing at the end. *Proceedings of the National Academy of Sciences*, *109*, 15197–15200.

Sillence, E., & Briggs, P. (2007). Please advise: Using the Internet for health and financial advice. *Computers in Human Behavior*, *23*, 727–748.

Stadler, G., Oettingen, G., & Gollwitzer, P. M. (2010). Intervention effects of information and self-regulation on eating fruits and vegetables over two years. *Health Psychology*, *29*, 274–283.

Stewart, N. (2009). The cost of anchoring on credit card minimum repayments. *Psychological Science*, *20*, 39–41.

Strack, F., & Deutsch, R. (2004). Reflective and impulsive determinants of social behavior. *Personality and Social Psychology Review*, 8, 220–247.

Thaler, R., & Sunstein, C. (2008). *Nudge: Improving decisions about health, wealth and happiness.* New Haven, CT: Yale University Press.

Vlaev, I., & Darzi, A. (2012). Preferences and their implication for policy, health and wellbeing. In T. Sharot, & R. Dolan (Eds.), *Neuroscience of preference and choice* (pp. 305–336). Oxford: Elsevier.

Vlaev, I., & Dolan, P. (2015). Action change theory: A reinforcement learning perspective on behaviour change. *Review of General Psychology*, 19, 69–95.

Vlaev, I., & Elliott, A. (2014). Financial well-being components. *Social Indicators Research*, 118, 1103–1123.

Vlaev, I., Nieboer, J., Martin, S., & Dolan, P. (2015). How behavioural science can improve financial advice services. *Journal of Financial Services Marketing*, 20, 74–88.

Webb, T., & Sheeran, P. (2006). Does changing behavioral intentions engender behavior change? A meta-analysis of the experimental evidence. *Psychological Bulletin*, 132, 249–268.

FURTHER READING

Dolan, P., Elliott, A., Metcalfe, R., & Vlaev, I. (2012a). Influencing financial behavior: From changing minds to changing contexts. *Journal of Behavioral Finance*, 13, 127–143.

Dolan, P., Hallsworth, M., Halpern, D., King, D., Metcalfe, R., & Vlaev, I. (2012b). Influencing behaviour: The MINDSPACE way. *Journal of Economic Psychology*, 33, 264–277.

Michie, S., van Stralen, M. M., & West, R. (2011). The behaviour change wheel: A new method for characterising and designing behaviour change interventions. *Implementation Science*, 6, 42.

13 Saving Behaviour: Economic and Psychological Approaches

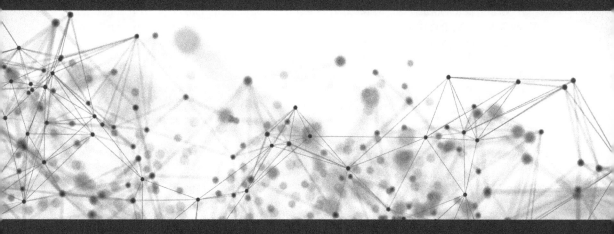

ELLEN K. NYHUS

CHAPTER OUTLINE

LEARNING OUTCOMES

BY THE END OF THIS CHAPTER YOU SHOULD BE ABLE TO:

1. Discuss the implications of both individual and aggregate saving behaviour for individual welfare.
2. Describe the economic and psychological factors that may influence individual saving behaviour.
3. Apply both economic and psychological models in analyses of observed saving behaviour.

13.1   INTRODUCTION

Since the Second World War, the interest in understanding household saving has been steadily increasing, mainly because of the impact that saving has on economic growth. Saving used to be the privilege of a small and rich upper class, but the positive economic development of the post-war period has created a situation where most people have the opportunity to postpone expenditures and save. The sum of these individual saving decisions influences aggregate demand in a nation, which in turn may affect the nation's long-term economic growth. If the majority of households decide to postpone expenditures, then an economic recession may be the result. If the majority decides to spend most of its income and even borrow to increase spending, then the result will be an economic boom. Hence, to explain and predict business cycles, we must have a good understanding of individual saving and consumption decisions (Deaton, 1992), especially if we wish to influence saving behaviour.

Saving behaviour also has important implications for individual welfare. For example, failure to save for retirement may have a severe negative impact on someone's quality of life in old age. Failing to engage in precautionary saving ('saving for a rainy day') may have a negative impact on welfare if such a failure forces someone into expensive credit arrangements. There is a trend in many developed countries in which many welfare-enhancing services that used to be provided by the state are being replaced by systems that are based on the individual accumulation of assets. For example, social housing has been replaced by home ownership made possible through the credit market (Lowe & Meers, 2015). These changes increase not only individuals' freedom but also their responsibility for their own welfare. To identify the most effective policy measures that will help consumers make good decisions, we must understand how consumers think.

In this chapter, the reader will find an overview of the factors believed to be of importance for individual saving behaviour. Identifying them is not an easy task because a person's saving is a result of a wide range of decisions of various levels of significance of whether to spend or not to spend, and each of these decisions may be influenced by different situational factors. For example, in Chapter 8, it is possible to observe how decisions to spend or to save may depend on how one acquired the money or what one planned to spend it on in the first place. Therefore, it is important to identify the factors that will have predictive and explanatory power across the majority of a person's saving and spending decisions. In this chapter, the reader will be introduced to economic models of saving, particularly their underlying psychological foundation. In addition, research on the associations between various psychological concepts, such as motives, attitudes and personality, and saving is described. First, however, we must discuss what we mean by saving behaviour.

13.1.1   *Definitions and Measures*

As shown below, when reading about different saving studies, there is a large variation in the definitions of saving behaviour. For this reason, it is important to pay attention to which aspect of saving behaviour has been analysed when comparing results across studies. Formally, saving is defined as the difference between net worth at the beginning and at the end of a period of time (Wärneryd, 1999). This difference may sound easy to measure, but there are many methods of operational-izing the various components. For example, 'net worth' can be defined in different ways depending on which assets are included in the measure. The 'period' is often a year, but some studies use shorter or longer time intervals.

It is also important to distinguish between saving and savings. *Saving* is a flow variable and refers to the accumulation of assets and debts over a specific period of time. *Savings* is a stock variable and refers to the net worth of a person's assets at a particular moment in time. The *saving ratio* expresses the part of income that is saved during a period and gives us a relative measure of saving. It tells us more about one's tendency to save because it says how large a part of one's income that a person is setting aside.

Katona (1975) defines three types of saving. Putting money in a bank account involves a decision to save made in the current period. Katona labels this *discretionary saving*, which is the type of saving that is often of interest when studying psycholog-ical explanations of saving behaviour. *Contractual saving* is often a result of previous decisions, such as buying goods and services on credit. A down payment on loans is a form of saving performed in the present period but regulated through contracts. Membership in a mandatory pension scheme is another example of forced contrac-tual saving. Finally, *residual saving* is income that is simply not spent during a period and therefore is not a result of a decision. It is accidental saving.

Psychologists also tend to consider additional dimensions of saving behaviour beyond the financial dimensions, and they have studied planned saving (e.g., Rabi-novich & Webley, 2007), saving habits (Furnham, 1985, 1999), and saving intentions (e.g., Wärneryd, 1996). These measures may all be useful and provide insights into various dimensions of saving behaviour.

13.1.2   *Economic Versus Psychological Approaches*

Most research on saving behaviour has been conducted by economists. Their aim is often to make predictions about behaviour that are as good as possible, rather than identifying the real underlying causes for why people act as they do. The develop-ment of theories is achieved by constructing a model of the behaviour under investi-gation, often based on a number of simplifying assumptions, for example, that agents act rationally and that there are no liquidity constraints. Although the realism of the assumptions can be debatable, the assumptions have proven useful for economic analyses (Wärneryd, 1999). Frequently, the goal is to be able to predict behaviour at the macro level, and therefore, the focus is on similarities in behaviour. The goal is to predict the behaviour of the 'average' person.

The (economic) psychological approach to studying saving behaviour has a dif-ferent starting point. Psychologists often focus on the active decisions to save or on saving intentions. They are more interested in studying individual differences than the behaviour of the average person. Hence, psychologists use explanatory variables and methods in their analyses of saving behaviour that are different from those that economists use. For example, economists would typically test the importance of the retirement saving motive by testing the implications of including such a motive in a structural saving model. Psychologists would approach the same research question by simply asking people whether they have a retirement saving motive and whether they consider it important.

In recent decades, saving has also been studied by behavioural economists (e.g., Shefrin & Thaler, 1988). In this research, we can observe how insight from psychology has enriched economic models so that they are more realistic and may therefore provide better predictions of actual saving behaviour. The use of psychological insight has also helped in developing programmes that have increased workers' retirement saving (Thaler, 2015). These behavioural models show how economics and psychology may complement and enrich each other, despite their different approaches.

13.2 ECONOMIC PERSPECTIVES

13.2.1 *Time Preference*

Some of the first models of saving behaviour focused on the intertemporal choice between consuming now or later, in addition to the factors that influence this choice (see Chapter 3). Although several economists in the nineteenth century discussed similar ideas, Böhm-Bawerk (1959 [1889]) and Fisher (1930) are considered the creators of the theory of time preference, a concept that they used to explain the formation of interest rates. The core of their theories is the trade-off between spending and investing or between immediate enjoyment and possible greater deferred enjoyments. A person's time preference expresses his or her impatience to increase consumption in the present period. A person with a high time preference is expected to have a strong preference for present consumption and is therefore unwilling to save and may even borrow to increase consumption.

Fisher (1930) suggested that a person's time preference is established early in life through processes of socialization. He expected people with longer time horizons, longer life expectancy, high self-control and habits of saving to have a low time preference. In addition, he proposed that a person's economic circumstances would influence his or her time preference. Fischer expected that an impatient person, with a higher rate of time preference than the market interest rate, would be willing to borrow to consume more. Similarly, a person with a lower time preference rate than the market interest rate would be willing to postpone consumption and save.

Several researchers have attempted to measure the rate of time preference (see Frederick, Loewenstein, & O'Donoghue, 2002). Antonides (1988) found differences in the discount factors between savers and non-savers. The average monthly discount factor of the savers in his study is 1.4%, whereas it is 2.6% for the non-savers. Ritzema (1992) found that time preference is significantly related to the likelihood of financial problems and total debt. Donkers and van Soest (1999) found a negative relationship between time preference and the probability of owning a house but find a positive relationship with the probability of holding risky assets. Conversely, Chabris et al. (2008) found no significant association between a person's time preference and his or her saving ratio.

One reason for the ambiguous results may be that it is too optimistic to assume that all factors that determine someone's preference for immediate consumption can be expressed in one single parameter. The implication would be that, for example, we are as impatient for furniture as we are for food – that our sofa time preference is the same as our banana time preference. For most people, this is not the case.

13.2.2 Income and the Life-Cycle

Many studies of saving show that household saving is strongly related to household income. It is a natural relationship because the income determines a household's ability to save. Different researchers have used different income measures in their models: past, present, future, or relative income. These are macro-economic models, but they are based on psychological ideas about individual behaviour.

Keynes (1936) proposed that saving is a linear function of present income, which is called *the absolute income hypothesis*. Keynes thought that the distribution and effect of psychological factors would have little impact at the macro level. His hypothesis is based on the idea that psychological traits and saving motives vary between individuals; however, when examining an entire, population, these factors will change very slowly. Keynes' model was criticized and was not supported by long-term data (Kuznets, 1946).

One of the first attempts to define alternative models was based on the notions of habit formation and social comparison (Duesenberry, 1949; Modigliani, 1949). In these models, the role of past income and relative income, rather than the present income, was highlighted. These models challenged the assumption that people's preferences are independent – that they are not influenced by other people's preferences. Duesenberry formulated *the relative income hypothesis*, which states that the propensity to save is related to the relative position of the consumer in the income distribution of his or her reference group (e.g., neighbours or colleagues). He argued that consumption expenditures are strongly influenced by comparisons with other people's consumption and that the utility index is therefore a function of relative, rather than absolute, consumption expenditure. The predictions of the model are that a person who is placed in the lower end of the income distribution of his reference group will save little because he will have to spend to keep pace with the groups' consumption level. Conversely, a person who has a relatively high income will save. Duesenberry also argued that past income would play a role because past income has shaped present consumption habits, which may be difficult to change in the short term.

Friedman (1957) and Modigliani and Brumberg (1954) proposed that future income or lifetime income would be the most important determinant for saving and consumption when formulating *the permanent income theory* and *the life-cycle hypothesis* (LCH), respectively. Modigliani and Brumberg based the LCH on the view that individuals are forward-looking and that saving is a function of future expected income and the individual's rate of time preference. A consumer's budget constraint over his or her lifetime, assuming that he or she does not want to leave a bequest, is his or her wealth plus current and future income. If we also assume that the marginal utility of consumption is decreasing and that the time preference rate is equal to the market interest rate, then it is reasonable to assume that people prefer to have a smooth consumption level over their entire lifetime. Due to the typical rising income profile that most workers have until they retire, the main predictions of the model are that people will borrow when young, repay their loans and start paying for retirement as they age, and then not save in retirement. In this model, there is no direct relationship between income and saving when saving behaviour is studied over a short period of time. Instead, saving is linked to the consumer's stage in his or her life-cycle. According to this model, the main reason for saving is consumption smoothing. The first versions of the model were based on numerous restrictive assumptions about preferences and the financial market. However, over time, the model has been elaborated so that new variables have been added and some assumptions have been relaxed (see Browning & Lusardi, 1996). For example, uncertainty about length of life, uncertainty about future income or inflation, the presence of liquidity constraints and a bequest motive are factors that have been incorporated into the model. Although empirical investigations show that households do not smooth consumption over the life-cycle as much as predicted by the model (Deaton, 1992), the LCH remains the most commonly used framework in economics for studies of saving behaviour.

Based on observations of people's actual saving behaviour, Shefrin and Thaler (1988) developed what they called the 'behavioural life-cycle hypothesis' (BLCH), which is based on an assumption of two sets of preferences that may conflict: short-term and long-term preferences. They introduced a dual personality model that included the far-sighted 'Planner' and the myopic 'Doer'. In the standard LCH, it is assumed that the trade-off between consuming now or later is made in a rational and consistent manner. The BLCH acknowledges that acting in this manner may not be so easy to do because of a lack of self-control. Saving occurs when the 'Planner' foresees the risk of over-spending and takes measures to prevent the 'Doer' from behaving short-sightedly. The model also incorporates the notion of mental accounting (see Chapter 8), and the BLCH states that the propensity to spend income is higher for a regular income compared to a lump-sum income. Sherfin and Thaler showed that this model could explain many observations of saving behaviour better than the LCH.

13.3   PSYCHOLOGICAL APPROACHES

The review above shows that many psychological constructs in the economic literature on saving can be found. Compared to the efforts of economists, there is less psychological research on saving. Nevertheless, psychological studies of saving also provide us with useful insights about the factors that foster saving. Below, we discuss some of these studies and examine concepts that are typically used in psychological research.

13.3.1   *Expectations*

Katona (1975) suggests that people's expectations would influence their decisions about saving and spending. He argues that, because most consumers receive the same news about economic development through the mass media, many will form the same expectations. Hence, in a population, there may be a majority of optimistic or pessimistic consumers, which may in turn influence aggregate demand (Huth, Eppright, & Taube, 1994). Through numerous surveys, Katona and his colleagues have found support for the notion that, when people are optimistic and confident about their future economic situation, they are more willing to spend money and to borrow compared to when they are pessimistic. These researchers have developed the 'Index of Consumer Sentiment' (ICS) to assess expectations in a population. The ICS consists of five questions: two that concern personal financial situation, two that concern the national economy, and one that concerns whether it is a good or bad time to buy durable goods. The ICS was introduced in the 1940s and is still used around the world. The index has been found to provide advance warnings regarding changes in demand of certain products, particularly automobiles and durable goods (e.g., Huth et al., 1994). Studies of the link between the index and actual saving behaviour suggest that the ICS can be used to predict spending and saving at the household level and that higher confidence is associated with lower saving (Souleles, 2003). Van Raaij and Gianotten (1990) find that the index questions concerning expectations of one's personal economic situation correlate with the consumption of durables and are the most useful when predicting behaviour at the micro level.

Using UK data, Brown and Taylor (2006) found that optimism is related to lower saving and that current financial expectations can predict future consumption. Similarly, Guariglia, (2001), also using UK panel data, found that households save more when they expect their financial situation to deteriorate. Hence, the results support the relationship between expectations of the future financial situation and the willingness to save.

Another aspect of expectations that influences saving is uncertainty. A person who is uncertain about how his or her future income will develop tends to save more and borrow less. Dardanoni (1991) studied the variability of earnings in different occupations and found that people who work in occupations with high earnings variability save more than others. Guariglia (2001) found that households saved more when they are uncertain about their future finances. This relationship may be linked to the precautionary saving motive (see below). If people have a financial buffer, then they reduce the risk of not being able to pay for unexpected expenses.

13.3.2   Time Orientation

Many variables used in saving models are related to variations in how people address the future: how far into the future people think (time horizon), how they value consumption in the present versus in the future (time preference), and whether they think about the future consequences of their actions (consideration of future consequences).

The time horizon refers to the length of the time period that one uses when a person plans his or her future spending and saving. Both Nyhus (2002) and Wärneryd (1999) found that the time horizon (the next couple of months, next year, the next couple of years, the next 5–10 years, or more than 10 years from now) have strong associations with saving. People with short time horizons typically save less than people who are planning further into the future. Similarly, Lusardi (1999) found that thinking about retirement is a strong predictor of retirement saving. She finds that one-third of people in the United States aged 52–61 have not begun to think about retirement, which is why their retirement saving was so low.

Rabinovich and Webley (2007) found that people who have longer time horizons have the highest probability of reaching their saving goals. Those who have planned and managed to save have longer time horizons than those who have planned saving but have failed to do so. People with short time horizons are less likely to save and are less likely to reach their saving goals.

As discussed above, the time preference expresses the preference for immediate utility over delayed utility (Frederick et al., 2002). A person who has a strong preference for immediate consumption is expected to spend in the present period at the cost of future periods and may even borrow to do so. Hershfield et al. (2013) showed that it is possible to influence people's concern for the future. In their study, people were shown age-processed pictures of themselves to make them think more about their future well-being, and this manipulation increased their willingness to wait for greater future awards. Hence, when people are encouraged to think about their future selves, they care more about their future.

Strathman, Gleicher, Boninger and Edwards (1994) have developed a scale to measure a related psychological construct that is promising with respect to predicting saving behaviour. The scale is called 'Consideration of Future Consequences' (CFC) and is defined as the extent to which people consider the potential distant outcomes of their current behaviours and are influenced by those potential outcomes. The CFC is assumed to be a stable individual trait; however, Toepoel (2010) found that it is stable over a period of one year but that it is a changeable construct over longer periods of time. At one end of the continuum of the CFC scale, we find individuals who consider future outcomes when making decisions about the present and are willing to sacrifice present well-being to achieve long-term goals. On the other end of the continuum, we find individuals who are uninterested in considering the future consequences of present actions and are concerned with maximizing immediate utility. In a recent review, Joireman and King (2016) summarize the findings concerning CFC and financial behaviour: Higher CFC is associated with lower levels of temporal discounting, problematic gambling, credit card debt, higher levels of saving and intentions to enrol in a 401(k) retirement plan in the United States. More research is necessary to conclude that CFC is an important determinant of saving behaviour, but to date, the findings are encouraging.

13.3.3   Attitude towards Saving

Both Keynes (1936) and Katona (1975) argued that most people have positive attitudes towards saving. An attitude is an expression of favour or disfavour towards something, and it is likely that people who hold a favourable attitude towards saving will save more than people who find saving unfavourable.

Julander (1975) conducted an experiment with 215 women in Sweden. He found that attitudes towards saving positively correlated with several measures of saving behaviour. In another Swedish study, Lindqvist; Julander and Fjæstad (1978) reported that attitudes towards saving were positive among all respondents, particularly among elderly people. They did not find any robust relationships between saving and attitudes except for two of the attitude factors that positively correlated with total bank saving and some other asset components. Lindqvist (1981) tested the effects of attitudes towards saving and four different estimates of saving: bank saving, repayments of debts, total savings and the amount that the household could withdraw from the bank at the time of the interview. Using a 14-item scale for attitudes and controlling for many socio-economic variables, he reported that the scale had little predictive power.

Furnham (1985) collected data on beliefs, saving habits and saving attitudes in Britain. He identified five saving attitude factors and found that they were positively related to age and educational level. Furnham also found that people could simultaneously think that saving is pointless but beneficial and concluded that people can hold different attitudes towards their own saving as opposed to attitudes towards saving in general. This contradiction may be one of the reasons for the difference in results across studies concerning the role of attitudes. Another reason for the variation in findings was provided by Rabinovich, Morton and Postmes (2010). They tested the relationship between saving attitudes and saving intentions and found that attitudes and intentions were related only for people with a distant-future time perspective and not for people with a short-term time perspective.

13.3.4   Saving Motives

One approach to studying individual saving behaviour is to focus on the reasons for saving. If we understand people's motivations for saving, then it may be easier to predict and understand saving. We may also find methods of stimulating saving.

Katona (1975) conducted two surveys (in 1960 and 1966) in which people were asked about their reasons for saving. He grouped them into the following categories, ordered by how frequently they were noted: (1) for emergencies, corresponding to the 'precautionary saving motive'; (2) for retirement; (3) for children and family needs; and (4) for other purposes (including a house or vacation). Few of the respondents in his surveys noted the other motives discussed in the savings literature (e.g., Keynes, 1936; Browning & Lusardi, 1996), which include bequests, earning interest or improvement. Subsequent studies showed that the four motives may considered as the most important, although people may use different names for them and focus on different underlying dimensions. For example, Lee and Hanna (2015) used data from the Surveys of Consumer Finance to study responses to open-ended questions on the reason for saving. They categorized the answers into six saving goals. The retirement and security goals were the most frequently noted (40%), whereas the self-actualization goal was noted by only 1–2% of the respondents. The other saving goals identified were saving for basic needs, saving for emergency/safety, saving for love/societal needs and saving for esteem/luxuries. These can easily be defined into Katona's categories.

The high importance of the precautionary motive has been supported in Dutch (Alessie, Lusardi, & Aldershof, 1997), Swedish (Lindqvist et al., 1978) and British (Canova, Rattazzi, & Webley, 2005) studies. The precautionary motive has been analysed in numerous studies (Browning & Lusardi, 1996), but the results regarding its impact are inconclusive, ranging from very important to unimportant. Kennickell and Lusardi (2004) show how the discrepancies in estimates may be explained by differences in the measurement of important variables and failures to consider alternative methods of satisfying the need for precaution. Another explanation for the varying results may be that there is insufficient variation in the precautionary motive. If everybody says precautionary saving is important, then it is not a good predictor of actual saving. Carroll (1997) proposes that the precautionary motive will only influence those with little money – or with less saving than their preferred buffer. He assumes that people typically have a small wealth/income ratio target for their saving. If wealth is below the target, then the precautionary motive dominates saving behaviour because people are afraid of being poor in future periods. However, if wealth is above this target, then impatience (high time preference) dominates and available resources beyond the target will be consumed. Hence, according to this 'buffer stock' model, the precautionary motive only motivates people who have not saved enough to meet their need for a financial buffer.

Mastrogiacomo and Alessie (2015) studied the empirical relevance of the retirement savings motive. Using Dutch data, they tested whether wage receivers and the self-employed consider the importance of the saving motives differently. They found that the self-employed think that, except for the precautionary saving motive, all saving motives are more important than do wage earners. However, they did not find large effects of saving motives on saving rates. They found a savings rate of approximately 15% of permanent income in their sample and concluded that only one-third of this value may be attributed to saving motives, with only 2 percentage points being due to the retirement saving motive. Using the US Survey of Consumer Finances, Fisher and Anong (2012) found that 46% of the sample of non-retired households saved regularly, 32% saved irregularly and 22% did not save. The precautionary and retirement motives increase the likelihood of saving regularly or irregularly, but only the retirement motive can distinguish regular from irregular savers.

Another line of research is concerned with co-existing saving motives and changes in motives at different stages of the life-cycle (Schunk, 2007). The idea behind this research is that households may save for many reasons simultaneously. Canova et al. (2005) find support for a hierarchical structure of motives. Through interviews with 97 British adults who all planned to save the next year, they identify 15 salient saving goals, which they rank according to how frequently they were noted. At the bottom of the hierarchy are concrete goals, such as purchases, holidays and having money available, whereas at the top of the hierarchy are abstract goals, such as self-esteem and self-gratification. The intermediate goals are speculation, security, and debt avoidance. When testing the predictive power of the six goals on actual saving behaviour, retirement/security and self-actualization have the strongest association with saving.

One interesting aspect of multiple saving goals has been documented by Soman and Zhao (2011). They find that having many simultaneous saving goals may have a negative impact on saving. Using data from India, Hong Kong and Canada, they find that having one saving goal leads to higher saving than not having a saving goal but having one goal leads to higher saving rates than multiple goals. Having only one goal seems to make the implementation of saving plans easier.

Knowing why people save may be a key to understanding saving behaviour, but more research should be conducted in this area. We know that people have saving goals: precaution, retirement, specific goals such as a house or a holiday. However, how strongly these motives influence actual behaviour remains unclear. In particular, it is interesting to explore whether the same asset can satisfy several saving motives simultaneously (the value of a house may satisfy both the precautionary, retirement saving and bequest motive). It may also be the case that some motives are only important for segments of the population and that we would find stronger links between saving and motives if segments were analysed separately.

13.3.5   Personality

Some studies have focused on the links between personality and saving behaviour. In this line of research, the so-called Big Five taxonomy (Digman, 1990) is often used. This model advocates that a person's personality can be described by five broad dimensions, i.e., emotional stability, extraversion, conscientiousness, agreeableness, and openness, and that these dimensions are relatively stable over time.

Brandstätter (1996) finds that emotional stability, introversion and conscientiousness are associated with the respondents' saving the previous year. He proposes a model where personality traits indirectly influence saving through attitudes towards saving. Wärneryd (1996) elaborates on this work and links the concept of thrift to the personality dimension of 'conscientiousness'. Conscientiousness includes the degree of self-discipline, planning, and competence. In a study of Dutch households, he finds that conscientiousness is related to financial self-control. He also finds that conscientiousness and agreeableness are significantly related to saving behaviour and intention to save. The strength of these relationships is mediated by saving attitudes.

Nyhus and Webley (2001) used Dutch household data and found that emotional stability and introversion are positively linked with saving whereas autonomy and agreeableness are negatively related to saving. Emotional stability is found to be related to saving intentions. They do not find significant effects of conscientiousness on any of the saving measures. Using UK data, Brown and Taylor (2014) found that extraversion is negatively associated with the value of assets held, whereas openness to experience is positively related to financial wealth holding. They concluded that conscientiousness and emotional stability have little importance for wealth. Finally, Mosca and McCrory (2016) found that extraversion and emotional stability are associated with wealth among older Irish couples. They found a positive effect of conscientiousness but only at the lower end of the wealth distribution.

Emotional stability and introversion have been found to be positively linked to saving across studies, although the opposite result concerning extraversion is found by Mosca and McCrory. Conscientiousness and agreeableness also seem to have an impact on saving, but the effects may be indirect through attitudes, intentions and self-control. Additionally, more research in this area is necessary before we can draw conclusions about the role of personality for saving behaviour.

13.3.6 *Financial Literacy and Financial Education*

The traditional neo-classical economic models of saving behaviour assume that people are rational decision-makers and understand financial information and the decisions that they make. However, saving behaviour involves numerous complex decisions about the timing of spending and the choice of financial instruments. One must perform calculations when planning ahead and to be able to navigate an increasingly complex financial market. We have already discussed how psychological variables are associated with saving. Other factors to consider are understanding and knowledge. Research on financial literacy shows that many individuals are unable to perform simple economic calculations and do not understand basic economic concepts. Hence, they cannot perform the calculations and make the judgements that the economic models assume. International surveys of financial understanding in the general population show that low financial knowledge is a problem in many countries (Atkinson & Messy, 2012; Lusardi & Mitchell, 2011).

The degree of financial literacy is related to several types of financial behaviour that may have direct or indirect effects on saving. Van Rooij, Lusardi, and Alessie (2012) found a positive relationship between financial literacy and the net worth of wealth that may be explained by the positive link between financial literacy and planning and saving for retirement (Lusardi & Mitchell, 2011). Financial literacy is also linked to other types of behaviour that will have an indirect effect on saving. People who are financially literate are more likely to invest in the stock market (Van Rooij, Lusardi, & Alessie, 2011), less likely to use expensive credit and mortgage options (Campbell, 2006), and less likely to have payment problems (Lusardi & Tufano, 2009). Hence, it seems reasonable to conclude that there is a robust link between financial literacy and saving and that the link may be both direct and indirect.

Therefore, one long-term recommendation for politicians is to include financial education in the school curriculum. Children and adolescents should learn enough about finance so that they are capable of making sound decisions on behalf of themselves and their families in their adult lives. Better financial understanding is likely to increase saving at both the individual and aggregate levels (Batty, Collins, & Odders-White, 2015). In addition, through proper financial education, it may be possible to foster long-term thinking and positive attitudes towards saving. These factors will be easier to change through the school system than through campaigns aimed at adults who have already established habits and opinions. Hence, using the school system to foster knowledge and attitudes may be the most influential measure for politicians who want to stimulate saving, and this method is now a major strategy in many OECD countries (OECD, 2015).

Although more financial knowledge may have positive effects on saving behaviour, Thaler (2015) warns that financial education will have a limited effect on behaviour unless saving decisions are made easy. He advocates carefully designed saving arrangements, where people are automatically enrolled in saving schemes (but with the option to opt out) and where they pre-commit to increasing their savings rate in the future. Hence, he advocates contractual saving rather than discretionary saving. Even with more knowledge about personal finance, it may still be difficult to resist temptations to spend more than planned.

13.4 SUMMARY

The research on saving behaviour is voluminous, and the review above has only covered a small part of it. The literature review is challenging because the definition of saving behaviour may vary from study to study. To date, we can conclude that a great deal is known about the factors that influence saving, but further research remains necessary. People's income level determines their ability to save, and therefore, it is an important predictor of saving. However, there is large variation in the saving behaviour between people in the same age and income groups, and psychological concepts may help explain this heterogeneity. The differences may be due to variation in the willingness to save (Katona, 1975). Although economists have often assumed that the variables that cause the willingness to save would cancel out at the aggregate level, psychologists have shown that this is not the case.

In this chapter, we have observed that variables related to time are important for saving behaviour. People have expectations about their future situations, which may be uncertain, and these expectations influence their decisions in the present. However, people also differ in how long into the future they think and in the extent to which they consider the future consequences of their decisions.

People vary in their attitudes towards saving and their saving motives, and they have different personalities. All of these factors have been found to be related to saving behaviour; however, we need more research to establish the portion of saving that can be attributed to such variables. Surveys have also revealed large differences in financial knowledge, which, in turn, influence how sensibly people handle their money.

To date, we know little about the relationships between the different psychological concepts and for which segments of the population they are important. Hence, future studies should focus on how motives, the time horizon, attitudes, personality, financial literacy and other psychological concepts work together and how they may have different impacts on low- and high-income households, for example.

REVIEW QUESTIONS

1. Imagine you were to ask people about their savings. What type of assets would you include in your measure to produce a measure that can be meaningfully compared across households?
2. Try to find the latest measures of the Consumer Sentiment Index in your country (or in another country). How would you explain the development in the index over the past few years? How do you think consumer sentiment will influence saving behaviour the next year?
3. Review the individual factors that have been found to be related to saving behaviour. Assuming that you were to propose a model of how these factors would influence your own saving behaviour, how would you propose that they are related?

REFERENCES

Alessie, R., Lusardi, A., & Aldershof, T. (1997). Income and wealth over the life cycle. Evidence from panel data. *Review of Income and Wealth, 43*, 1–32.

Antonides, G. (1988). Scrapping a durable consumption good. *(Unpublished doctoral dissertation).* Erasmus University, Rotterdam, The Netherlands.

Atkinson, A., & Messy, F. (2012). *Measuring financial literacy: Results of the OECD/International network on Financial Education (INFE) pilot study.* OECD Working Papers on Finances, Insurance and Private Pensions. No. 15. Paris: OECD.

Batty, M., Collins, J. M., & Odders-White, E. (2015). Experimental evidence on the effects of financial education on elementary school students' knowledge, behavior, and attitudes. *Journal of Consumer Affairs, 49*, 69–96.

Böhm-Bawerk, E. v. (1959 [1889]). *Capital and interest.* South Holland: Libertarian Press.

Brandstätter, H. (1996). *Saving, income, and emotional climate of households related to personality structure.* Progress Report No. 38. CentER, Tilburg University, The Netherlands.

Brown, S., & Taylor, K. (2006). Financial expectations, consumption and saving: A microeconomic analysis. *Fiscal Studies, 27*, 313–338.

Brown, S., & Taylor, K. (2014). Household finances and the 'Big Five' personality traits. *Journal of Economic Psychology, 45*, 197–212.

Browning, M., & Lusardi, A. (1996). Household saving: Micro theories and micro facts. *Journal of Economic Literature, 34*, 1797–1855.

Campbell, J. Y. (2006). Household finance. *The Journal of Finance, 61*, 1553–1604.

Canova, L., Rattazzi, A. M. M., & Webley, P. (2005). The hierarchical structure of saving motives. *Journal of Economic Psychology, 26*, 21–34.

Carroll, C. D. (1997). Buffer-stock saving and the life cycle/permanent income hypothesis. *Quarterly Journal of Economics, 112*, 1–56.

Chabris, C. F., Laibson, D., Morris, C. L., Schuldt, J. P., & Taubinsky, D. (2008). Individual laboratory-measured discount rates predict field behaviour. *Journal of Risk and Uncertainty, 37*, 237–269.

Dardanoni, V. (1991). Precautionary savings under income uncertainty: A cross-sectional analysis. *Applied Economics, 23*, 153–160.

Deaton, A. (1992). *Understanding consumption*. Oxford: Oxford University Press.

Digman, J. M. (1990). Personality structure: Emergence of the five-factor model. *Annual Review of Psychology, 41*, 417–440.

Donkers B., & van Soest, A. (1999). Subjective measures of household preferences and financial decisions. *Journal of Economic Psychology, 20*, 613–642.

Duesenberry, J. S. (1949). *Income, saving and the theory of consumer behavior*. Cambridge, MA: Harvard University Press.

Fisher, I. (1930) *The theory of interest*. London: Macmillan.

Fisher, P. J., & Anong, S. T. (2012). Relationship of saving motives to saving habits. *Journal of Financial Counselling and Planning, 23*, 63–79.

Frederick, S., Loewenstein, G., & O'Donoghue, T.(2002). Time discounting and time preference: A critical review. *Journal of Economic Literature, XL*, 351–401.

Friedman, M. (1957). *A theory of the consumption function*. Princeton, NJ: Princeton University Press.

Furnham, A. (1985). Why do people save? Attitudes to, and habits of saving money in Britain. *Journal of Applied Social Psychology, 15*, 354–373.

Furnham, A. (1999). The saving and spending habits of young people. *Journal of Economic Psychology, 20, 6*, 677–697.

Guariglia, A. (2001). Saving behaviour and earnings uncertainty: Evidence from the British Household Panel Survey. *Journal of Population Economics, 14*, 619–634.

Hershfield, H. E., Goldstein, D. G., Sharpe, W. F., Fox, J., Yeykeliset, L., Carstensen, L. L., & Bailenson, J. N. (2013). Increasing saving behaviour through age-progressed renderings of the future self. *Journal of Marketing Research, 48*, s23–s37.

Huth, W. L., Eppright, D. R., & Taube, P. M. (1994). The Indexes of Consumer Sentiment and confidence: Leading or misleading guides to future buyer behavior. *Journal of Business Research, 29*, 199–206.

Joireman, J., & King, S. (2016). Individual differences in the consideration of future and (more) immediate consequences: A review and directions for future research. *Social and Personality Psychology Compass, 10/5*, 313–326.

Julander, C. -R. (1975). Sparande och effecter av okad kunskap om inkomstens använding [Saving behaviour and the effects of increased knowledge of the use of income]. Unpublished doctoral dissertation. Stockholm, Sweden, Stockholm School of Economics.

Katona, G. (1975). *Psychological economics*. New York: Elsevier Scientific Publishing Company.

Kennickell, A., & Lusardi, A. (2004). Disentangling the importance of the precautionary saving motive. (NBER Working Paper No. 10888). Retrieved from https://www.federalreserve.gov/econresdata/scf/files/precautionarynov052.pdf

Keynes, J. M. (1936). *The general theory of employment, interest, and money*. London: Macmillan.

Kuznets, S. (1946). *National product since 1869*. New York: National Bureau of Economic Research.

Lee, J. M., & Hanna, S. D. (2015). Saving goals and saving behavior from a perspective of Maslow's hierarchy of needs. *Journal of Financial Counseling and Planning, 26*, 129–147.

Lindqvist, A. (1981). Hushållens sparande: Beteendevetenskapliga måtninger av hushållens sparbeteende [The saving behaviour of households: Behavioural measures of households' saving behaviour]. Unpublished doctoral dissertation. Stockholm, Sweden, Stockholm School of Economics.

Lindqvist, A., Julander, C. -R., & Fjæstad, B. (1978). *Utveckling av beteendevetenskapliga indikatorer på sparande*. [Development of behavioral science indicators on saving]. Rapport 2, 'Sparande och sparbeteende'. Stockholm, Sweden: EFI.

Lowe, S., & Meers, J. (2015). Responsibilisation of everyday life: Housing and welfare state change. In Z. Irving, M. Fenger, & J. Hudson (Eds.), *Social policy review 27. Analysis and debate in social policy* (pp. 53–72). Bristol: Policy Press.

Lusardi, A. (1999). Information, expectations and savings for retirement. In H. Aaron (Ed.), *Behavioral dimensions of retirement economics* (pp. 81–115). Washington, DC: Brookings Institution and Russsell Sage Foundation.

Lusardi, A., & Mitchell, O. S. (2011). Financial literacy around the world: An overview. *Journal of Pension Economics and Finance, 10*, 497–508.

Lusardi, A., & Tufano, P. (2009). Debt literacy, financial experience, and over-indebtedness. NBER Working Paper No. 14808. Cambridge, MA: NBER.

Mastrogiacomo, M., & Alessie, R. (2015). Where are the retirement savings of self-employed? An analysis of 'unconventional' retirement accounts. De Nederlandsche Bank Working Paper, No. 454.

Modigliani, F. (1949). Fluctuations in the saving-income ratio: A problem in economic forecasting. *Studies in Income and Wealth, 11*, 371–438.

Modigliani, F., & Brumberg, R. (1954). Utility analysis and the consumption function: An interpretation of cross-section data. In K. K. Kurihara (Ed.), *Post-Keynesian economics* (pp. 388–436). New Brunswick, NJ: Rutgers University Press.

Mosca, I., & McCrory, C. (2016). Personality and wealth accumulation among older couples: Do dispositional characteristics pay dividends? *Journal of Economic Psychology, 56*, 1–19.

Nyhus, E. K. (2002). Psychological determinants of household saving behaviour. Doctoral dissertation. Retrieved from http://hdl.handle.net/11250/164358

Nyhus, E. K., & Webley, P. (2001). The role of personality for saving and borrowing behaviour. *European Journal of Personality, 15*, S85–S103.

OECD (2015). *National strategies for financial education: OECD/INFE policy handbook*. Paris: OECD.

Rabinovich, A., Morton, T., & Postmes, T. (2010). Time perspective and attitude-behaviour consistency in future-oriented behaviours. *British Journal of Social Psychology, 49*, 69–89.

Rabinovich, A., & Webley, P. (2007). Filling the gap between planning and doing: Psychological factors involved in the successful implementation of saving intention. *Journal of Economic Psychology, 28*, 444–461.

Ritzema, J. (1992). An extended behavioural life-cycle model. *Unpublished manuscript. Erasmus University*, Rotterdam, The Netherlands.

Schunk, D. (2007). What determines the saving behaviour of German households? An examination of saving motives and saving decisions. MEA Discussion Paper 124-2007. Mannheim: MEA, University of Mannheim.

Shefrin, H., & Thaler, R. H. (1988). The behavioral life-cycle hypothesis. *Economic Inquiry, 26*, 609–643.

Soman, D., & Zhao, M. (2011). The fewer the better: Number of goals and savings behaviour. *Journal of Marketing Research, 48*, 944–957.

Souleles, N. S. (2003). Expectations, heterogeneous forecast errors, and consumption: Micro evidence from the Michigan Consumer Sentiment Surveys. *Journal of Money, Credit and Banking, 26*, 39–72.

Strathman, A., Gleicher, F., Boninger, D. S., & Edwards, C. S. (1994). The consideration of future consequences: Weighing immediate and distant outcomes of behavior. *Journal of Personality and Social Psychology, 66*, 742–752.

Thaler, R. H. (2015). *The making of behavioral economics: Misbehaving*. New York: W. W. Norton & Company.

Toepoel, V. (2010). Is consideration of future consequences a changeable construct? *Personality and Individual Differences, 48*, 951–956.

Van Raaij, W. F., & Gianotten, H. J. (1990). Consumer confidence, expenditure, saving and credit. *Journal of Economic Psychology, 11*, 269–290.

Van Rooij, M., Lusardi, A., & Alessie, R. (2011). Financial literacy and stock market participation. *Journal of Financial Economics, 101*, 449–472.

Van Rooij, M., Lusardi, A., & Alessie, R. (2012). Financial literacy, retirement planning, and household wealth. *The Economic Journal, 122,* 449–478.

Wämeryd, K. E. (1996). Personality and saving (VSB-CentER savings project progress report No. 39). Tilburg, The Netherlands: Tilburg University.

Wärneryd, K. E. (1999). *The psychology of saving: A study on economic psychology.* Cheltenham: Edward Elgar Publishing.

Webley, P., & Nyhus, E. (2006). Parents' influence on children's future orientation and saving. *Journal of Economic Psychology, 27,* 140–164.

FURTHER READING

Kotlikoff, L. L. (1989). *What determines savings?* Cambridge, MA: The MIT Press.

Wärneryd, K. E. (1999). *The psychology of saving: A study on economic psychology.* Cheltenham: Edward Elgar Publishing.

14 The Psychology of Borrowing and Over-Indebtedness

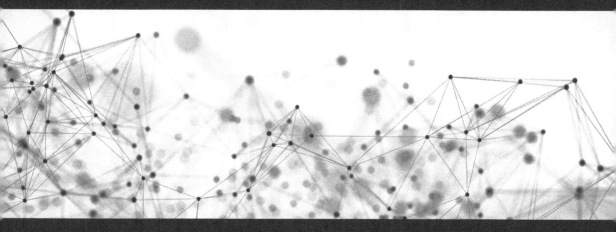

ROB RANYARD, SANDIE MCHUGH AND SIMON MCNAIR

CHAPTER OUTLINE

LEARNING OUTCOMES

BY THE END OF THIS CHAPTER YOU SHOULD BE ABLE TO:

1. Identify psychological and other determinants of borrowing and discuss the processes of credit information search, evaluation and choice.
2. Understand the nature of borrowers' repayment strategies and give examples of how borrowers might default.
3. Describe the psychological consequences of over-indebtedness and suggest how such problems might be prevented or supported.

14.1   INTRODUCTION

Personal and household borrowing, like saving, is a quintessential intertemporal decision; the borrower agrees to take out a loan now and to repay it some time in the future – often in instalments, and usually with interest. When the loan is taken out, it is referred to as a 'credit agreement', and this remains the case as long as the borrower can comfortably afford the repayments. If, however, repayments become burdensome, or the borrower defaults, the loan is described as a debt; somewhat dramatically, the borrower is said to be in a state of indebtedness. Over-indebtedness means that the sum-total of payment demands, for example utility bills as well as loan repayments, are causing unsustainable financial stress.

According to economic life-cycle theory (Modigliani & Brumberg, 1954), people should borrow in order to maximize their overall life-cycle utility. Consistent with this, there is evidence that borrowing is broadly related to the life-cycle. First, it increases with age to a peak at the mid-forties and then begins to decline (e.g. SCHUFA, 2010). Second, being married is related to increased use of credit (Chien & Devaney, 2001), presumably as such arrangements typically entail major purchases, and/or the arrival of children.

Consider, though, that total personal debt in the United Kingdom reached some of the highest rates on record in the post-2008 period, £1.46 billion at its height in 2010 (The Money Charity, 2010). Moreover, recent figures estimated that around one in eight households are over-indebted, around 12% of the population (Gibbons & Vaid, 2015). These are international phenomena; for example, in the United States, credit card debt increased 214% from 1990 to 2004 (Hodges, 2009), with affairs being similar in the EU (Department of Trade and Industry, 2005). Worryingly, in the United Kingdom, the Competition and Markets Authority (2014) predicted a return to pre-crisis debt levels from 2020 onwards. Clearly, understanding the psychology of borrowing and over-indebtedness has never been more necessary, and this chapter reviews existing research to that end.

Credit has existed in all societies since money was invented. For example, Tebbutt (1983) documented how pawnbrokers, who lend money secured on property such as clothes and jewellery, were a key source of credit for British working-class people as early as the nineteenth century. The trade thrived from about 1850 to 1910 but had substantially declined by 1930. Borrowers were protected from exploitation by laws including the Pawnbrokers' Acts of 1872, which set out maximum interest charges, a maximum 'ticket fee' and the consequences of not redeeming the item (usually its loss).

In the United States from the 1940s, fixed instalment loans from banks and retailers were major sources of consumer credit. Important survey findings by George Katona and colleagues showed that the Consumer Sentiment Index, which assesses people's confidence regarding their own and the country's current and future economic positions, could predict the overall rate of US consumer credit borrowing. They also found that instalment credit was taken more by younger, middle- and upper-income people, and those with rising income expectations (see Katona, 1975).

From the 1970s, the personal credit market has expanded exponentially and continues to be an important driver of economic growth (ECRI, 2015). At the same time, the *acceptability* of credit use has undergone an immense change. Credit is now much more widely-viewed as an acceptable vehicle to facilitate consumption (Watkins, 2000) with younger generations tending to have more positive views of credit (e.g. Livingstone & Lunt, 1992). In today's credit market, the use of revolving credit such as store and credit cards, and payday loans, now rivals fixed instalment loans.

In Section 14.2, drawing on Kamleitner and Kirchler's (2007) three-stage model of the borrowing process, we present theory and research on the determinants of personal borrowing (stage 1), credit choice processes (stage 2), and subsequent repayment strategies (stage 3). Following this we examine the causes and psychological consequences of over-indebtedness. Finally, we consider the policy implications of the research reviewed.

14.2   DETERMINANTS OF BORROWING

The first stage of credit use reviewed by Kamleitner and Kirchler (2007) involves deciding whether to borrow at all, as opposed to, for example, postponing a purchase or using existing savings. Here we consider basic motivations for, and barriers to, borrowing and some psychological characteristics associated with it.

14.2.1   *Maintenance Versus Improvement*

Norton (1993) made a useful distinction between credit use for 'maintenance' or for 'improvement' of one's circumstances. Berthoud and Kempson's research (1992) identified similar distinctions according to people's economic lifestyles and goals. First, those experiencing financial hardship tended to borrow to make ends meet, whereas those who were rather better off, and of a materialistic disposition, were more likely to borrow to fund a consumerist lifestyle, for example, changing cars and household consumer durables relatively frequently. Both hardship (maintenance) and improvement-oriented borrowing seem to be durable characteristics of borrowing behaviour. The former echoes Tebbutt's (1983) analysis of pawnbroker borrowing in Victorian Britain and is particularly associated with lower incomes. The latter echoes Katona's (1975) findings of borrowing as a means of improvement associated more with higher-income earners.

Using credit to improve one's lifestyle seems likely to be motivated in part by social comparisons that create a desire to elevate one's consumption in order to buffer self-worth. In essence, people benchmark themselves against their peers and increase consumption to bridge perceived gaps (Karlsson, Dellgran, Klingander, & Gärling, 2004). Studies have reported that engaging in social comparisons increases willingness to borrow (Roland-Lévy & Walker, 1994) and that those who feel they are evenly matched with their peers report being less amenable to borrowing (Groenland & Nyhus, 1994).

14.2.2   *Financial Exclusion and Access to Credit*

Clearly, the decision to use credit will be affected by its availability and accessibility. An extensive literature exists concerning the 'financially excluded': those who typically cannot access mainstream financial services (estimated at 1.5 million households in the United Kingdom; Blake & de Jong, 2008). This is a continuing problem associated with factors such as race, gender, income, education and where people live (Dymski, 2005). Lower-income earners and the less well-educated are more likely to have their credit applications rejected (Zhu & Meeks, 1994). Furthermore, non-white applicants are more likely to be rejected than white applicants to whom they otherwise compare (Dymski, 2005). Such financial barriers can translate into a higher prevalence of 'alternative credit', such as payday loans and pawnbroking, among the excluded (Croden, 2000). Gallmeyer and Roberts (2009) noted that high-cost payday loan providers are typically found in higher volumes in areas where lower-earners, minorities, or younger people live. More generally, those on lower income and those with higher pre-existing debts are typically subjected to higher interest rates when borrowing (Berthoud & Kempson, 1992), which may dissuade people from accessing credit and further perpetuate exclusion.

14.2.3   *Psychological Factors*

Economic psychologists have often considered the influence that psychological factors may have *relative* to more immutable ones, such as socio-demographic considerations (Lea, Webley & Walker, 1995; McNair, Summers, Bruine de Bruin, & Ranyard, 2016; Webley & Nyhus, 2001). Various individual-level behavioural and dispositional characteristics associated with borrowing behaviour have been identified. At a behavioural level, for example, those with more credit cards typically hold more debt (Norvilitis et al., 2006). This might be because people who pay by credit typically focus more on a product's benefits than its cost (Chatterjee & Rose, 2012). Also, engaging in more active money management behaviours, such as keeping track of one's bank balance, has been found to be inversely related to amount of debt (Garðarsdóttir & Dittmar, 2012; Lea et al., 1995).

At a more dispositional level, several aspects of time perspective and self-control have been found to relate to debt levels, such as impulsivity (associated with unsecured but not secured debt; Ottaviani & Vandone, 2011), and present orientation (Meier & Sprenger, 2010). Also, low self-control has been associated with making greater use of higher-cost credit (Gathergood, 2012). Finally, heavy users of credit also tend to view money as a means of displaying power or prestige (Yamauchi & Templer, 1982) and tend to score higher on measures of materialism (Garðarsdóttir & Dittmar, 2012; Watson, 2003).

14.3   CREDIT CHOICE PROCESSES

The second stage of the borrowing process involves evaluating and deciding on several key things, especially the amount to borrow, the lender, the cost, whether to use secured or unsecured credit, or revolving or fixed instalment credit – and in the case of the latter, the repayment level and loan duration.

14.3.1   Information Search

Chang and Hanna (1992) noted that information search in the credit market is worth the cost in time and effort, since there is substantial variation in cost across providers. However, they reported that only 20% of borrowers had tried to get any information about multiple lenders or credit terms. Those that had done so tended to be younger and have higher levels of education. In addition, Berthoud and Kempson (1992) found that nearly half of their respondents borrowed from a credit source they had previously used, with others reporting they made more spontaneous choices.

In a process-tracing study, Ranyard, Hinkley, Williamson and McHugh (2006) presented borrowers with realistic car and washing machine purchase scenarios, allowing participants to seek information about three credit options before choosing. Relevant information was readily available from the interviewer. As well as loan duration, many sought information across options about monthly repayment, total cost, and annual percentage rate of interest (APR). This suggests that when information search costs are low, consumers will seek more information on credit attributes important for good decision-making. A recent survey of consumers' use of credit cards found evidence of substantial active information search and switching of lenders in the UK market (Financial Conduct Authority, 2016). This may be due to the proliferation of financial comparison websites that reduce search costs.

14.3.2   Evaluation

How should borrowers evaluate credit options? Since borrowing involves outcomes at different points in time, i.e., receiving a loan now and repaying it later, discounted utility theories are relevant (Estalami, 2001; Frederick, Loewenstein, & O'Donoghue, 2002). However, these theories have only been investigated in the context of relatively simple intertemporal choices (see Chapter 3) rather than more complex ones such as instalment credit, which involves a series of future outcomes. Based on in-depth interviews with borrowers, Ranyard and Craig (1995) proposed an alternative, dual mental accounting model in which credit options are represented in a simplified manner as mental accounts (Thaler, 1999). In this model an instalment credit option is represented in terms of two alternative mental accounts: a *total account*, in which all future repayments are treated as equivalent to a total current cost; and a *recurrent budget period* account, whereby each future monthly budget period is seen as equivalent, or similar to, the current budget period. In the latter case, each future repayment is integrated into its associated budget period, so that the weekly or monthly repayment amount is the most important aspect of cost. The loan duration, or number of budget periods in which the repayment is required, is also important from this perspective. Evaluating instalment credit in terms of these alternative mental accounts is often an important element in the credit choice process (see Box 14.1).

14.3.3   Choice

Bettman, Luce and Payne (1998) reviewed research on how people choose between multi-attribute options and found that people use alternative decision strategies

Box 14.1 Fixed instalment credit as a multi-attribute decision

Imagine that you have decided to take out a bank loan for £7,500 and that you have been given information from two banks (Table 14.1).

- The total cost is the financial charge for the whole transaction, plus the amount borrowed.
- The APR, or annual percentage rate, is the average amount charged by the lender per unit of time (one year) as a percentage of the amount borrowed, taking into account that the amount borrowed increases when interest is added and decreases as repayments are made.
- The FCM is the financial charge per month.

Which Credit Offer Should You Choose?
The offer from bank A is for a longer duration but with a much lower monthly repayment. The other measures of cost are also in conflict, with the total cost of A being a little higher but the APR and FCM being rather lower. From a rational economic perspective, the best credit offer is that offering the lowest 'true' interest rate, the APR. From this perspective, then, A is preferable because of the lower APR (and FCM). However, from a total account perspective, B is better as the total cost is less. Finally, from a recurrent budget period account, A is better because of the lower monthly repayments, but B is better because the cost runs for fewer budget periods. This conflict must be resolved by weighing the short-term budget pressures of higher repayments against the long-term benefits of fewer repayments.

Table 14.1 *Comparison of loan offers*

Bank	Duration of loan	Monthly repayment (£)	Total cost (£)	APR (%)	FCM (£)
A	48 months	180	8640	7.3	23.75
B	24 months	353	8472	12.6	40.50

that range from those based on all available information to decision heuristics using information selectively. Box 14.1 shows how choices between two fixed instalment credit options can be represented in terms of loan duration and the cost attributes: annual percentage rate of interest (APR), financial charge per month (FCM), total cost and monthly repayment.

Ranyard et al. (2006) classified the choice strategies of a subset of their participants in a think-aloud condition (N = 32) into two basic categories: comparative and non-comparative. Many of the former type, which was the most frequent, involved the simple decision heuristic, 'take the best APR'. Some participants said that they did this to reduce total cost. Other strategies compared total cost, monthly repayments and loan duration. These are consistent with the alternative mental account representations described earlier. Follow-up experiments systematically varying total cost and APR information confirmed that APR was a major determinant of credit choice, but also found that its effect was moderated by total cost information (McHugh, Ranyard, & Lewis, 2011).

The role of interest rates in consumer credit choice has been investigated since Katona's (1975) surveys found that most borrowers were unaware of the interest rate charged on their loans. This was one of the considerations that led to the US 'truth in lending' legislation of the 1960s that required lenders to disclose the APR. This requirement was introduced into the UK in the Consumer Credit Act of 1975; subsequently its disclosure has become a requirement internationally. On the positive side, it is a widely accepted standard of comparison based on a standard time period that is, as we saw, easy to use with a simple 'take the best APR' rule. On the negative side, however, APR is a complex statistic that can be misunderstood (Office of Fair Trading, 2004). Some borrowers believe that an APR of 10%, for example, means that the interest charged would be 10% of amount borrowed regardless of loan duration, while others believe it is a rate measure based on the initial, not the average amount borrowed (McHugh et al., 2011; Ranyard & Craig, 1995). Finally, it has been found that with flexible credit, estimates of the loan duration or total cost are less accurate when the APR is given (McHugh et al., 2011; Ranyard & Craig, 1993).

The role of two other important aspects of the cost of borrowing, the financial charge and the total cost, has also been investigated. These aspects of cost are limited because they are absolute measures that do not take into account the duration of the loan. Nevertheless, they are easy to understand and consistent with one of the ways that people naturally think about instalment credit, in terms of the total account. In addition, we have found that: (1) with revolving credit, estimates of loan duration are more accurate when the total cost is given (Ranyard & Craig, 1993); and (2) together with loan duration information, it leads to higher credit card repayments (McHugh et al., 2011). These findings have important implications for credit cost information disclosure (see Section 14.7).

14.4   REPAYMENT STRATEGIES

With revolving credit such as store and credit cards, the choice of repayment level is made periodically during the third stage of the borrowing process. A common repayment strategy that borrowers adopt is to choose the highest repayment level that is affordable within recurrent budget period constraints in order to reduce total cost and loan duration (Ranyard et al., 2006). Consistent with this, there is evidence that credit card repayment levels rise with disposable income (McHugh & Ranyard, 2012). There is other evidence, however, that debtors tend to pay off smaller debts first, thus reducing the overall number of outstanding debts, rather than prioritize debt accruing the highest rate of interest (Amar, Ariely, Ayal, Cryder, & Rick, 2011). In addition, repayment decisions depend on psychological dispositions and states, as well as contextual variables. With respect to the former, for example, concern for future consequences has been found to correlate with credit card repayment levels (Navarro-Martinez et al., 2011).

With respect to contextual factors, the mere presence of minimum repayment information on credit card statements has been found to influence repayment decisions. For example, Stewart (2009) manipulated the inclusion of minimum repayment information on hypothetical credit card statements. He found that the mean partial repayment was significantly lower for a group presented with this information, 23% of the outstanding balance compared to 40% for the group not presented with it (see also Navarro-Martinez et al., 2011). Recent studies have investigated ways to mitigate this anchoring effect. Salisbury (2014) found that informing people of the repayment necessary to repay in three years, as required by the US CARD Act of 2010, had a significant effect, increasing the proportion of credit card users repaying at that level, and sometimes raised the proportion repaying more than that amount. A large-scale US survey analysed by Jones, Loibl and Tennyson (2015) found that this effect was stronger among those who were aware of the added three-year information. However, it has also been reported that a significant number of users may pay *less* when the three-year payment amount is less than they would have paid otherwise (Hershfield & Roese, 2015). Nevertheless, we have found that anchors higher than three-year repayment amounts increase the proportion of users repaying at or above such higher levels (McHugh & Ranyard, 2016).

14.5   ROUTES TO OVER-INDEBTEDNESS

Borrowers have competing demands on their financial resources, and this can lead to missed credit repayments or missed payments on household bills. Several such occasions indicate a situation developing towards over-indebtedness. A review by Ford (1988) identified three broad groups of factors associated with defaulting: (1) the macroeconomic and social environment; (2) changes in personal circumstances that can disrupt the household's income or expenditure (e.g. redundancy); and (3) psychological factors including those discussed earlier. In 40 interviews with over-indebted people, Ford found that disruptions to already tight budgets were major causes of arrears in almost every case, often in combination; specifically 'labour market change, matrimonial breakdown and the maintenance requirements of poor quality property ...' (Ford, 1988, p. 115).

Similarly, Berthoud and Kempson (1992) found that their respondents explained problem debts as being mainly due to reduced income or other changes in circumstances (34% of respondents); insufficient income (25%); unexpected bills (10%); or overlooked payments (8%). Around 10% of those in the lowest income range had multiple problem debts, compared to 1% or less for those in above-average income ranges. Having multiple debt occurrences was also related to having children, having more credit commitments and a less unfavourable attitude to arrears. As Ford (1988) foresaw, recent surveys have recorded how over-indebtedness has persisted. A 2011 UK survey reported that 13% of respondents were spending more than 30% of their income on unsecured credit repayments; furthermore, 7% were more than three months in arrears on bills or credit repayments (Department of Business, Information and Skills, 2012). In France, the number of over-indebtedness cases filed with the authorities in recent years has been almost a quarter of a million a year (Banque de France, 2014). These recent surveys continue to identify low income and shocks to household budgets as major contributors to over-indebtedness. In addition, the French survey found that critical factors in over-indebtedness included being generally less committed to budget management and building up precautionary savings, and using revolving credit as a substitute for income. Related to this, in Gathergood's (2012) UK survey, lower levels of financial literacy were associated with over-indebtedness. Finally, another important finding from the French survey was that more than half of the over-indebted sample waited between three months and a year before seeking support.

The relative role of psychological factors was investigated in a longitudinal study by Webley and Nyhus (2001) that tracked debtors and non-debtors over three surveys. Antecedent variables contributing significantly to the prediction of debt-status, thereby indicating causation, included having a lower income and a time preference for spending immediately. On the other hand, a cross-lagged analysis indicated that several psychological variables were a consequence of over-indebtedness, including having a less unfavourable attitude towards debt; a time preference for spending immediately; shorter planning horizons; and using certain 'low-tech' money management techniques (e.g. carrying less cash). Future longitudinal studies could further clarify the complex relationships between psychological factors and debt status over time.

14.6   PSYCHOLOGICAL CONSEQUENCES OF DEBT

The psychological consequences of debt can be profound, with Fitch, Hamilton, Bassett, and Davey (2011) having concluded that 'plausible data exist which indicate that indebtedness may contribute to the development of mental health problems' (p. 153). A 2012 survey found that 74% of those with serious debt problems reported feeling unhappy about their situation, with 70% of these having indicated that they felt anxious; and 56% said that their debt impinged on their family relationships (Money Advice Service, 2013). In this section we detail some of the most widely reported psychological consequences of debt, focusing on depression, and stress and anxiety.

14.6.1   *Depression*

Using data from the British Household Panel Survey (BHPS), Wildman (2003) observed higher levels of depressive symptoms (such as loss of sleep, feelings of inadequacy) among those who felt financially strained. Similar findings were reported by Bridges and Disney (2010) in their analysis of the UK's Families and Children's Survey. Over a six-year period, they observed a 17% incidence of depression among those who were currently experiencing financial difficulty, compared to 6% among those who were not currently experiencing but had previously experienced financial difficulty, and just 2% among respondents who neither currently nor previously had financial difficulties. Skapinakis, Weich, Lewis, Singleton, and Araya (2006) found that financial difficulty also significantly exacerbated existing mental well-being issues: depressed individuals with financial difficulties were four times as likely to report depression 18 months later, compared to twice as likely for depressed individuals not experiencing financial issues. Interestingly, BHSP research by Brown, Taylor, and Wheatley Price (2005) only found an association between debt and depressive symptoms for *unsecured* (i.e. non-mortgage) debt. Furthermore, Bridges and Disney noted that the association between debt and depression is mainly accounted for by *subjective* factors rather than *objective* financial indicators. Finally, feelings of hopelessness, worthlessness, and demoralization (e.g. at not being able to make repayments, or at receiving income support) appeared to mediate the link between debt and depression (Butterworth, Fairweather, Anstey, & Windsor, 2006).

14.6.2   Stress and Anxiety

Nettleton and Burrows (1998) used BHPS data to study the negative impact of mortgage debt. They observed that such debt led to larger increases in stress for women than men over a 12-month period, with some suggestion that significant increases in stress may be limited to women. Taylor, Pevalin, and Todd (2007) offered some conflicting findings, however, having observed significant increases in stress for men who entered into mortgage arrears in the past year, while women showed increases in stress only over a longer period of time. Taylor et al. noted that stress due to housing repayment difficulties was associated with larger increases in stress than unemployment, or divorce. The association between debt and anxiety also appears to differ by age. Drentea (2000) found that younger adults (less than 30 years) reported higher financial anxiety levels concerning credit card debt. Notably, the amount of debt did not predict age differences in anxiety (adults in their forties had the highest debt levels), but younger adults were more likely to be in default, and had higher debt-to-income ratios. Similar confirmation that higher credit card debt-to-income ratios are related to higher financial stress came from Drentea and Lavrakas (2000). There are some conflicting results, however, with Norvilitis, Szablicki, and Wilson (2003) having found no link between credit card debt and stress among a student sample.

Other research has isolated financial anxiety as a special case of anxiety that can account for stress levels separately from more generalized stress and anxiety. For example, Marjanovic, Greenglass, Fiksenbaum, and Bell (2013) proposed their construct of 'financial threat' which comprises worries, preoccupations, and feelings of risk pertaining specifically to financial matters. They proposed that this construct is dispositional in nature, and that individuals more predisposed to experiencing financial threat will in turn experience higher stress due to financial instability. Shapiro and Burchell (2012) similarly observed a form of financial anxiety that is discernible from general anxiety; interestingly, they found that higher financial anxiety had behavioural consequences, such as being more avoidant of financial information, and having taken longer to cognitively process it.

14.7   POLICY IMPLICATIONS

14.7.1   Credit Information Disclosure

The research reviewed in Section 14.3 first of all suggests that an accurate value of the APR of all credit offers should be disclosed clearly at an appropriate point in the sales process. Disturbingly, a recent survey by the European Commission found that APRs were often not disclosed and furthermore, those advertised by some lenders across the EU were often inaccurate (ECRI, 2015). Second, for all fixed repayment credit, a clear presentation of the monthly repayment, the loan duration and either the financial charge (or total cost) is important. Third, as illustrated in Box 14.1, an alternative measure of relative cost, the financial charge per month (FCM), could be routinely provided. This is a user-friendly measure on a familiar scale that can help borrowers to compare the relative costs of different credit options more transparently. Finally, total cost and loan duration information for a range of monthly repayments should be presented on credit card statements to alleviate the minimum repayment anchoring effect (McHugh & Ranyard, 2016).

14.7.2 Financial Education

A controlled evaluation of mandatory high school financial education programmes in three US states found that after three years of implementation the average credit score of students was substantially higher than those of comparable students in states not implementing such programmes (Brown, Collins, Schmeiser, & Urban, 2014). Nevertheless, a recent meta-analysis by Fernandes, Lynch, and Netemeyer (2014) found that financial education initiatives account for only 0.1% of a change in people's financial behaviour. The authors note that a failure to consider the role of psychological characteristics in financial behaviour likely explains this limited effectiveness. For example, the psychological consequences of debt discussed in Section 14.6 may interfere with people's capacity to apply practical skills, and addressing this could help students to benefit from such programmes.

The research reviewed in Section 14.4 suggests that helping students to understand credit cost measures such as APR may be particularly important. One way to do this would be via the teaching and learning of an approximate APR formula (Yard, 2004), essentially drawing attention to APR's relation to the average, rather than the initial loan. Coaching in how to effectively use price-comparison websites, which can often return a lot of comparative data about products, may be a further practical element of financial education that could help reduce the cognitive costs typically associated with the information search stage of the credit decision process.

It is becoming clearer that financial education should comprise a more holistic approach than mere calculative skills. Psychological resilience to adaptively cope with financial difficulty would seem to encompass a candidate category of skills that should be incorporated into financial education. For example, learning coping skills to counteract avoidance or denial of financial difficulty may overcome debtors' tendencies to delay seeking help. Such a shift in perspective towards elevating the importance of resiliency skills for financial capability is now occurring (Consumer Financial Protection Bureau, 2015; Money Advice Service, 2015).

14.7.3 Supporting Those in Financial Distress

In the United Kingdom, only 8%–13% of severely indebted individuals seek help (Money Advice Service, 2013); many over-indebted people either delay, or do not seek advice at all. Perhaps crucially, the onus remains on debtors *themselves* to seek help with their financial difficulties. The stress and anxiety that one might experience concerning financial difficulty may trigger avoidant behaviour, for example, as the prospects of addressing issues of debt may prove too emotionally challenging. As such, there exists a counter-intuitive situation whereby we know debtors can experience tremendous psychological pressures that may make it difficult for them to address their financial issues directly, yet support structures rely on self-presentation. While incorporating coping skills into financial education, as noted, may prove beneficial, there is also an argument to be made for more top-down, proactive approaches to assisting those in financial difficulty.

In Amsterdam, for example, the 'Vroeg eropaf' system launched in 2008 sees major creditors such as utility companies, and social housing organizations and land-lords contacting local authorities to alert them to individuals in arrears. The author-ities then arrange for a debt advisor to directly contact the debtor in order to offer support, and put in place an action plan to overcome the financial issues. The CEO of the initiative recently reported that evictions in the city decreased by 15% between the launch of the service and 2013, and that for every €1 invested by the City into the scheme, there has been a return of €2.22 (Siebols, 2016).

14.8 SUMMARY

In this chapter we first reviewed research on the psychology of borrowing, begin-ning with an outline of changes in borrowing over the years. We noted that finan-cial exclusion limits access to mainstream credit, resulting in higher costs for those least able to afford it. The psychological factors associated with borrowing include attitudes to debt, materialism and social comparisons, less active money manage-ment behaviours, present orientation and financial literacy. At the point of credit choice, information search has been found to be limited in some vulnerable groups, although recent technological developments have lowered the psychological costs of search. We argued that discounted utility is less useful for understanding how peo-ple evaluate credit alternatives than a mental accounting perspective and presented evidence on how people choose instalment credit options using important attributes such as loan duration, monthly repayment, the annual percentage rate and total cost. Although the APR is useful for borrowers, it is a complex statistic that can be misun-derstood; monthly repayment and total cost are also important and consistent with people's mental account representations. A common repayment strategy is to choose the highest level that is affordable to reduce the total cost and the length of the loan. However, minimum repayment information lowers repayment levels; this can be counteracted with information on the consequences of much higher repayments. Routes to over-indebtedness are varied but are often linked to low income and a com-bination of life events leading to income shocks. Research indicates that those expe-riencing such circumstances are more likely to avoid over-indebtedness if they have maintained precautionary savings, engage in active money management, and refrain from using credit as a source of income. Some of the psychological factors associated with over-indebtedness, such as present orientation and attitudes to repayment, may be consequences rather than causes. A growing body of research has shown that being in debt can lead to significant psychological detriment, including depression, stress and anxiety. The research reviewed has policy implications for credit informa-tion disclosure, financial education and how to best support those in financial distress.

REVIEW QUESTIONS

1. Why do people borrow, and what steps can they take to make good credit decisions?
2. What determines a borrower's level of repayment and why might borrowers default?
3. What are the psychological consequences of over-indebtedness and how might such problems be prevented or supported?

REFERENCES

Amar, M., Ariely, D., Ayal, S., Cryder, C. E., & Rick, S. I. (2011). Winning the battle but losing the war: The psychology of debt management. *Journal of Marketing Research*, 48(SPL), S38–S50. http://dx.doi:10.1509/jmkr.48.SPL.S38

Banque de France (2014). *Study of paths leading to over-indebtedness*. Retrieved from https://www.banque-france.fr/fileadmin/user_upload/banque_de_france/La_Banque_de_France/study-of-paths-leading-to-over-indebtedness.pdf

Berthoud, R., & Kempson, E. (1992). Credit and debt. *The PSI Report*. London: Policy Studies Institute.

Bettman, J. R., Luce, M. F., & Payne, J. W. (1998). Constructive consumer choice processes. *Journal of Consumer Research*, 25(3), 187–217. http://dx.doi.org/10.1086/209535

Blake, S., & de Jong, E. (2008). *Financial exclusion: A guide for donors and funders*. Retrieved from http://www.friendsprovidentfoundation.org/wp-content/uploads/2013/03/NPC_-_Full_Report.pdf

Bridges, S., & Disney, R. (2010). Debt and depression. *Journal of Health Economics*, 29(3), 388–403. http://dx.doi.org/10.1016/j.jhealeco.2010.02.003

Brown, A. M., Collins, J. M., Schmeiser, M. D., & Urban, C. (2014). *State mandated financial education and the credit behavior of young adults*. Divisions of Research & Statistics and Monetary Affairs, Finance and Economics Discussion Series, (2014-68). Washington, DC: Federal Reserve Board.

Brown, S., Taylor, K., & Wheatley Price, S. (2005). Debt and distress: Evaluating the psychological cost of credit. *Journal of Economic Psychology*, 26(5), 642–663. http://dx.doi.org/10.1016/j.joep.2005.01.002

Butterworth, P., Fairweather, A. K., Anstey, K. J., & Windsor, T. D. (2006). Hopelessness, demoralization and suicidal behaviour: The backdrop to welfare reform in Australia. *Australian and New Zealand Journal of Psychiatry*, 40(8), 648–656. http://dx.doi.org/10.1111/j.1440-1614.2006.01864.x

Chang, Y. C. R., & Hanna, S. (1992). Consumer credit search behaviour. *Journal of Consumer Studies & Home Economics*, 16(3), 207–227. http://dx.doi.org/10.1111/j.1470-6431.1992.tb00513.x

Chatterjee, P., & Rose, R .L. (2012). Do payment mechanisms change the way consumers perceived products? *Journal of Consumer Research*, 38(6), 1129–1139. http:/dx.doi.org/10.1086/661730

Chien, Y. W., & Devaney, S. A. (2001). The effects of credit attitude and socioeconomic factors on credit card and installment debt. *Journal of Consumer Affairs*, 35(1), 162–179. http://dx.doi.org/10.1111/j.1745-6606.2001.tb00107.x

Competition and Markets Authority. (2014). *Problem debt: A report commissioned by the Consumer Protection Partnership*. London: Her Majesty's Stationery Office.

Consumer Financial Protection Bureau. (2015). *Financial well-being: The goal of financial education*. Washington, DC: CFPB.

Croden, N. (2000). Credit use among low income groups. In A. Fleiss (Ed.), *Research Yearbook 1999/2000, Department of Social Security* (pp. 7–16). Leeds: Corporate Document Services.

Department of Business, Information and Skills (2012). *Credit, debt and financial difficulty in Britain* (2011). Retrieved from https://www.gov.uk/government/uploads/system/uploads/attachment_data/file/36991/12-948-credit-debt-financial-difficulty-in-britain-2011.pdf

Department of Trade and Industry. (2005). *Consumer Credit Law. A consultation on the proposed European Consumer Credit Directive.* Retrieved from http://www.berr.gov.uk/files/file14388.pdf (accessed 26 Jan. 2010).

Drentea, P. (2000). Age, debt and anxiety. *Journal of Health and Social Behavior, 41*(4), 437–450. http://dx.doi.org/10.2307/2676296

Drentea, P., & Lavrakas, P. J. (2000). Over the limit: The association among health, race and debt. *Social Science and Medicine, 50*(4), 517–529. http://dx.doi.org/10.1016/S0277-9536(99)00298-1

Dymski, G. A. (2005). Financial globalization, social exclusion and financial crisis. *International Review of Applied Economics, 19*(4), 439–457. http://dx.doi.org/10.1080/02692170500213319

ECRI (2015). *Towards a balanced contribution of household credit to the economy.* European Credit Research Institute: Brussels. Retrieved from: https://www.ceps.eu/system/files/CEPS-ECRI%20TFR%20Household%20Credit.pdf

Estalami, H. (2001). Determinants of discount rates in consumer credit decisions. *Journal of Marketing Theory and Practice, 9*(1), 63–73. http://dx.doi.org/10.1080/10696679.2001.11501886

Fernandes, D., Lynch Jr, J. G., & Netemeyer, R. G. (2014). Financial literacy, financial education, and downstream financial behaviors. *Management Science, 60*(8), 1861–1883. http://dx.doi.org/10.1287

Financial Conduct Authority. (2016) *Credit card market survey: Interim report.* Retrieved from http://www.fca.org.uk/your-fca/documents/market-studies/ms14-6-2-ccms-interim-report

Fitch, C., Hamilton, S., Bassett, P., & Davey, R. (2011). The relationship between personal debt and mental health: A systematic review. *Mental Health Review Journal, 16*(4), 153–166. http://dx.doi.org/10.1108/13619321111202313

Ford, J. (1988). *The indebted society: Credit and default in the 1980s.* London: Routledge.

Frederick, S., Loewenstein, G., & O'Donoghue, T. (2002). Time discounting and time preference: A critical review. *Journal of Economic Literature, 40*(2), 351–401. http://dx.doi.org/10.157/jel.40.2.351

Gallmeyer, A., & Roberts, W. T. (2009). Payday lenders and economically distressed communities: A spatial analysis of financial predation. *Social Science Journal, 46*(3), 521–538. http://dx.doi.org/10.1016/j.soscij.2009.02.008

Garðarsdóttir, R. B., & Dittmar, H. (2012). The relationship of materialism to debt and financial well-being: The case of Iceland's perceived prosperity. *Journal of Economic Psychology, 33*(3), 471–481. http://dx.doi.org/10.1016/j.joep.2011.12.008

Gathergood, J. (2012). Self-control, financial literacy and consumer over-indebtedness. *Journal of Economic Psychology, 33*(3), 590–602. http://dx.doi.org/10.1016/j.joep.2011.11.006

Gibbons, D., & Vaid, L. (2015). *Britain in the red: Provisional report.* Retrieved from https://www.tuc.org.uk/sites/default/files/Britain%20in%20%20the%20Red%20preliminary%20report.pdf

Groenland, E. A. G., & Nyhus, E. K. (1994, July). Determinants of time preference, saving, and economic behavior: A comparison between Norway and The Netherlands. Paper presented at the IAREP/SABE conference, Erasmus University, Rotterdam.

Hershfield, H. E., & Roese, N. J. (2015). Dual payoff scenario warnings on credit card statements elicit suboptimal payoff decisions. *Journal of Consumer Psychology, 25*(1), 15–27. http://dx.doi.org/10.1016/j.jcps.2014.06.005

Hodges, M. (2009) *America's total debt report.* Grandfather Economic Report Series. Retrieved from http://mwhodges.home.att.net/nat-debt/debt-nat.htm on 25/1/10.

Jones, L. E., Loibl, C., & Tennyson, S. (2015). Effects of informational nudges on consumer debt repayment behaviors. *Journal of Economic Psychology, 51*, 16–33. http://dx.doi.org/10.1016/j.joep.2015.06.009

Kamleitner, B., & Kirchler, E (2007). Consumer credit use: A process model and literature review. *European Review of Applied Psychology, 57*, 267–283. http://dx.doi.org/j.erap.2006.09.003

Karlsson, N., Dellgran, P., Klingander, B., & Gärling, T. (2004). Household consumption: Influences of aspiration level, social comparison, and money management. *Journal of Economic Psychology*, *25*(6), 753–769. http://dx.doi.org/10.1016/j.joep.2003.07.003

Katona, G. (1975). *Psychological economics*. Oxford: Elsevier.

Lea, S. E. G., Webley, P., & Walker, C. M. (1995). Psychological factors in consumer debt: Money management, economic socialization, and credit use. *Journal of Economic Psychology*, *16*, 681–701. http://dx.doi.org/10.1016/0167-4870(95)00013-4

Livingstone, S. M., & Lunt, P. K. (1992). Predicting personal debt and debt repayment: Psychological, social and economic determinants. *Journal of Economic Psychology*, *13*(1), 111–134. http://dx.doi.org/10.1016/0167-4870(92)90055-C

Marjanovic, Z., Greenglass, E. R., Fiksenbaum, L., & Bell, C. M. (2013). Psychometric evaluation of the Financial Threat Scale (FTS) in the context of the great recession. *Journal of Economic Psychology*, *36*, 1–10. http://dx.doi.org/10.1016/j.joep.2013.02.005

McHugh, S., & Ranyard, R. (2012). Credit repayment decisions: The role of long-term consequence information, economic and psychological factors. *Review of Behavioral Finance*, *4*(2), 98–112. http://dx.doi.org/10.1108/19405971211284880

McHugh, S., & Ranyard, R. (2016). Consumers' credit card repayment decisions: The role of higher anchors and future repayment concern. *Journal of Economic Psychology*, *52*, 102–114. http://dx.doi.org/10.1016/j.joep.2015.12.003

McHugh, S., Ranyard, R., & Lewis, A. (2011). Understanding and knowledge of credit cost and duration: Effects on credit judgements and decisions. *Journal of Economic Psychology*, *32*(4), 609–620. http://dx.doi.org/10.1016/j.joep.2011.02.005

McNair, S.J., Summers, B., Bruine de Bruin, W., & Ranyard, R. (2016). Individual-level factors predicting consumer financial behaviour at a time of high-pressure. *Personality and Individual Differences*, *99*, 211–216. http://dx.doi.org/10.1016/j.paid.2016.05.034

Meier, S., & Sprenger, C. (2010). Present-biased preferences and credit card borrowing. *American Economic Journal: Applied Economics*, *2*(1): 193–210. http://dx.doi.org/10.1257/app.2.1.193

Modigliani, F., & Brumberg, R.H. (1954). Utility analysis and the consumption function: an interpretation of cross-section data. In K. K. Kurihara (Ed.), *Post-Keynesian economics* (pp. 388–436). New Brunswick, N J. Rutgers University Press.

Money Advice Service. (2013). *The financial capability of the UK*. London: Money Advice Service.

Money Advice Service. (2015). *The financial capability strategy for the UK*. London: Money Advice Service.

Navarro-Martinez, D. J., Salisbury, L. C., Lemon, K. N., Matthews, W. J., & Harris, A. J. L. (2011). Minimum required payment and supplemental information disclosure effects on consumer debt repayment decisions. *Journal of Marketing Research*, *48*, 60–77. http://dx.doi.org/10.1509/jmkr.48.SPL.S60

Nettleton, S., & Burrows, R. (1998). Mortgage debt, insecure home ownership and health: An exploratory analysis. *Sociology of Health & Illness*, *20*(5), 731–753. http://dx.doi.org/10.1111/1467-9566.00127

Norton, C. M. (1993). The social psychology of credit. *Credit World*, *82*(1), 18–22.

Norvilitis, J., Merwin, M., Osberg, T., Roehling, P., Young, P., & Kamas, M. (2006). Personality factors, money attitudes, financial knowledge, and credit-card debt in college students. *Journal of Applied Social Psychology*, *36*(6), 1395–1413. http://dx.doi.org/10.1111/j.0021-9029.2006.00065.x/

Norvilitis, J. M., Szablicki, P. B., & Wilson, S. D. (2003). Factors influencing levels of credit-card debt in college students. *Journal of Applied Social Psychology*, *33*, 935–947. http://dx.doi.org/10.1111/j.1559-1816.2003.tb01932.x

Office of Fair Trading. (2004). *Credit card survey (OFT 709)*. London: HMSO.

Ottaviani, C., & Vandone, D. (2011). Impulsivity and household indebtedness: Evidence from real life. *Journal of Economic Psychology*, *32*(5), 754–761. http://dx.doi.org/10.1016/j.joep.2011.05.002

Ranyard, R., & Craig, G. (1993). Estimating the duration of a flexible loan: The effect of supplementary information. *Journal of Economic Psychology*, *14*(2), 317–335. http://dx.doi.org/10.1016/0167-4870(93)90005-6

Ranyard, R., & Craig, G. (1995). Evaluating and budgeting with instalment credit: An interview study. *Journal of Economic Psychology*, *16*(3), 449–467. http://dx.doi.org/10.1016/0167-4870(95)00020-0.

Ranyard, R., Hinkley, L., Williamson, J., & McHugh, S. (2006). The role of mental accounting in consumer credit decision processes. *Journal of Economic Psychology*, *27*(4), 571–588. http://dx.doi.org/10.1016/j.joep.2005.11.001

Roland-Lévy, C., & Walker, C. M. (1994, July). Savings and debts: The impact of the family structure on the processes of money management. Paper presented at the IAREP/SABE conference, Erasmus University, Rotterdam.

Salisbury, L. C. (2014). Minimum payment warnings and information disclosure effects on consumer debt repayment decisions. *Journal of Public Policy and Marketing*, *33*(1), 49–64. http://dx.doi.org/10.1509/jppm.11.116

SCHUFA. (2010). *SCHUFA Kredit Kompass 2010*. Wiesbaden, Germany: SCHUFA Holdings A. G.

Shapiro, G. K., & Burchell, B. J. (2012). Measuring financial anxiety. *Journal of Neuroscience, Psychology, and Economics*, *5*(2), 92–103. http://dx.doi.org/10.1037/a0027647

Siebols, J. (2016). Early detection of late payment problems in Amsterdam: Vroeg Eropaf. *ECRI News*, *50*, 4–5. Retrieved from http://www.ecri.eu/new/system/files/ECRI%20Newsletter%20no%2050(1)_0.pdf

Skapinakis, P., Weich, S., Lewis, G., Singleton, N., & Araya, R. (2006). Socio-economic position and common mental disorders: Longitudinal study in the general population in the UK. *British Journal of Psychiatry*, *189*(2), 109–17. http://dx.doi.org/10.1192/bjp.bp.105.014449

Stewart, N. (2009). The cost of anchoring on credit-card minimum repayments. *Psychological Science*, *20*(1), 39–41. http://dx.doi.org/10.1111/j.1467-9280.2008.02255.x

Taylor, M. P., Pevalin, D. J., & Todd, J. (2007). The psychological costs of unsustainable housing commitments. *Psychological Medicine*, *37*(7), 1027–1036. http://dx.doi.org/10.1017/S0033291706009767

Tebbutt, M. (1983). *Making ends meet: Pawnbroking and working-class credit*. London: Methuen.

Thaler, R. H. (1999). Mental accounting matters. *Journal of Behavioral Decision Making*, *12*, 183–206. http://dx.doi.org/10.1002/(SICI)1099-0771(199909)12:3<183::AID-BDM318>3.0.CO;2-F

The Money Charity. (2010). *The Money statistics – September 2010*. Retrieved from http://themoney-charity.org.uk/media/september-2010.pdf

Watkins, J. P. (2000). Corporate power and the evolution of consumer credit. *Journal of Economic Issues*, *34*(4), 909–932. http://dx.doi.org/10.1080/00213624.2000.11506321

Watson, J. J. (2003). The relationship of materialism to spending tendencies, saving, and debt. *Journal of Economic Psychology*, *24*(6), 723–739. http://dx.doi.org/10.1016/j.joep.2003.06.001

Webley, P., & Nyhus, E. K. (2001). Life-cycle and dispositional routes into problem debt. *British Journal of Psychology*, *92*, 423–446. http://dx.doi.org/10.1348/000712601162275

Wildman, J. (2003). Income related inequalities in mental health in Great Britain: Analysing the causes of health inequality over time. *Journal of Health Economics*, *22*(2), 295–312. http://dx.doi.org/10.1016/S0167-6296(02)00101-7

Yamauchi, K. T., & Templer, D. (1982). The development of a money attitude scale. *Journal of Personality Assessment*, *46*(5), 522–528. http://dx.doi.org/10.1207/s15327752jpa4605_14

Yard, S. (2004). Consumer loans with fixed monthly payments: Information problems and solutions based on some Swedish experiences. *International Journal of Bank Marketing*, *22*, 65–80. http://dx.doi.org/10.1108/02652320410514933

Zhu, L .Y., & Meeks, C. B. (1994). Effects of low income families' ability and willingness to use consumer credit on subsequent outstanding credit balances. *Journal of Consumer Affairs*, *28*(2), 403–422. http://dx.doi.org/10.1111/j.1745-6606.1994.tb00859.x

FURTHER READING

BPS. (2014). *Behaviour change: Personal debt.* Retrieved from http://www.bps.org.uk/system/files/Public%20files/debt.pdf

Furnham, A. (1984). Many sides of the coin: The psychology of money usage. Personality and Individual Differences. http://dx.doi.org/10.1016/0191-8869(84)90025-4

Gross, D. B., & Souleles, N. S. (2002). Do liquidity constraints and interest rates matter for consumer behavior? Evidence from credit card data. *Quarterly Journal of Economics, 117*(1), 149–185. http://dx.doi.org/10.3386/w8314

Hardaway, C. R., & Cornelius, M. D. (2014). Economic hardship and adolescent problem drinking: Family processes as mediating influences. *Journal of Youth and Adolescence, 43*(7), 1191–1202. http://dx.doi.org/10.1007/s10964-013-0063-x

Kamleitner, B., Hoelzl, E., & Kirchler, E. (2012). Credit use: Psychological perspectives on a multifaceted phenomenon. *International Journal of Psychology, 47*(1), 1–27.

Lovibond, P. F., & Lovibond, S. H. (1995). The structure of negative emotional states: Comparison of the Depression Anxiety Stress Scales (DASS) with the Beck Depression and Anxiety Inventories. *Behaviour Research and Therapy, 33*(3), 335–343. http://dx.doi.org/10.1016/0005-7967(94)00075-U

OECD (2016). *PISA 2015 Assessment and Analytical Framework: Science, Reading, Mathematic and Financial Literacy, PISA.* Paris: OECD. Retrieved from http://dx.doi.org/10.1787/9789264255425-en

Office for Budget Responsibility. (2015). *Economic and fiscal outlook (July 2015).* Retrieved from http://budgetresponsibility.org.uk/docs/dlm_uploads/July-2015-EFO-234224.pdf

Prelec, D., & Simester, D. (2001). Always leave home without it: A further investigation of the credit-card effect on willingness to pay. *Marketing Letters, 12*(1), 5–12. http://dx.doi.org/10.1023/A:1008196717017

Santiago, C. D., Wadsworth, M. E., & Stump, J. (2011). Socioeconomic status, neighborhood disadvantage, and poverty-related stress: Prospective effects on psychological syndromes among diverse low-income families. *Journal of Economic Psychology, 32*(2), 218–230. http://dx.doi.org/10.1016/j.joep.2009.10.008

Shefrin, H. M., & Thaler, R. H. (1988). The behavioral life-cycle hypothesis. *Economic Inquiry, 26,* 609–643. http://dx.doi.org/10.1111/j.1465-7295.1988.tb01520.x

Skinner, M. L., Elder, G. H., & Conger, R. D. (1992). Linking economic hardship to adolescent aggression. *Journal of Youth and Adolescence, 21*(3), 259–276. http://dx.doi.org/10.1007/BF01537018

Soman, D., & Cheema, A. (2002). The effect of credit on spending decisions: The role of the credit limit and credibility. *Marketing Science, 21*(1), 32–53. http://dx.doi.org/10.1287/mksc.21.1.32.155

The Money Charity. (2016). *The money statistics – February 2016.* Retrieved from: http://themoneycharity.org.uk/media/February-2016-Money-Statistics.pdf

Williams, D. T., Cheadle, J. E., & Goosby, B. J. (2013). Hard times and heartbreak: Linking economic hardship and relationship distress. *Journal of Family Issues,* 1–27. http://dx.doi.org/10.1177/0192513X13501666

15 Behaviour in Financial Markets

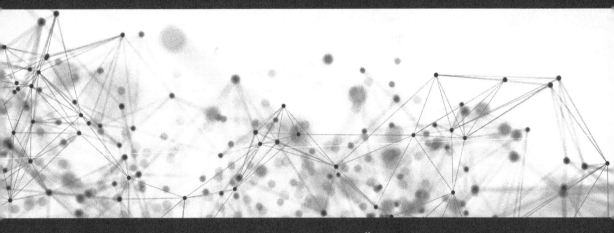

MARTIN HEDESSTRÖM

CHAPTER OUTLINE

LEARNING OUTCOMES

BY THE END OF THIS CHAPTER YOU SHOULD BE ABLE TO:

1. Describe common errors that stock market investors make, and how they are explained psychologically.
2. Explain how psychological factors might contribute to rising or falling stock prices.
3. Discuss how economic psychology can contribute towards developing a better understanding of behaviour in financial markets.

15.1   INTRODUCTION

Making stock market decisions has during the last few decades has changed from being an activity confined to only a few and mainly professional investors to becoming most people's concern, at least in the richer parts of the world. For example, citizens are increasingly expected to make their own decisions on how their retirement savings should be invested. While some may see this as an exciting opportunity, others are left bewildered. How to choose which funds to invest in? When is the right time to buy stocks and when is it advisable to sell? As there are no simple answers to such questions, investors often rely on their intuition. This chapter selectively reviews economic psychology research on behaviour in financial markets, mainly focusing on the stock market. Knowing how psychological factors affect financial behaviour is important in order to improve investors' ability to make good choices. It also helps us better understand, and perhaps be able to forecast or even prevent, negative events such as stock market crashes with wide-reaching implications for society as a whole.

15.2   DO STOCKS ALWAYS TRADE AT THE 'RIGHT' PRICE?

15.2.1   The Traditional Finance Perspective: Markets Are Efficient

Few would contest that stock market investors are affected by psychological factors. According to traditional finance, however, investor behaviour is best predicted by models that assume rationality. Mistakes, it is argued, cancel out at the aggregate level and have no or negligible effects on stock prices. In financial lingua, markets are efficient (Fama, 1991). This implies that a stock's price always reflects all publicly available information about 'fundamentals' – factors with a potential bearing on the future prospects of the stock company – and should not change unless new information emerges. Since it is not possible to forecast whether new fundamental information will exceed or fall short of expectancies, stock prices follow a 'random walk'. As a consequence, future stock prices are entirely unpredictable from past price movements or any public information. If a stock is temporarily under-priced, the efficient market hypothesis predicts that sophisticated investors, so-called 'arbitrageurs', will soon realize this and therefore buy the stock. If arbitrageurs instead identify a stock as over-priced, they sell it or, if they do not own it, use a procedure called 'short-selling', by which they borrow the over-priced stock from some other investor and sell it with the intention to later buy it back at a lower price before returning it to its owner. In this way, arbitrage brings stock prices back to levels justified by fundamentals. In efficient markets, a mispriced stock is like a $100 bill dropped on the sidewalk—it won't be long until someone picks it up.

15.2.2   *The Psychological Perspective*

Behavioural finance refers to economic psychology research on behaviour in financial markets. This line of research emerged in the 1970s in response to difficulties found in the traditional financial paradigm to encompass some observed patterns in market data. For example, extreme and long-lasting increases in stock prices followed by sudden sharp declines ('booms and busts') and other 'anomalies' suggest that stock mispricing can persist for longer than predicted by the efficient market hypothesis, and indicate that the ability of sophisticated investors to restore stocks' 'true' value is limited. While limits to arbitrage can partly be explained by structural factors, such as rules restricting fund managers' ability to 'short-sell' stocks, behavioural finance offers additional explanations based on psychological research on judgement and decision-making. Behavioural finance acknowledges that stock investors are boundedly rational (Simon, 1955) and form judgements influenced by cognitive biases, emotions, and other people's actions. Furthermore, investors hold preferences that are inconsistent with the standard economic expected utility framework by, for example, being loss averse (Kahneman & Tversky, 1984). Using such insights, behavioural finance seeks to increase understanding of why stock mispricings emerge and persist, by modelling investor behaviour in a descriptively more accurate way than standard economic models which assume that investors behave as if they were completely rational, preference-consistent, and unaffected by emotions. Furthermore, while traditional finance would be interested in psychological factors only to the extent that they were shown to predictably affect stock prices, behavioural finance explores the psychology of investor behaviour even in cases where stock prices are not necessarily affected but consequences for the investors themselves may be substantial. Figure 15.1 provides an overview of the behavioural stock market phenomena discussed in this chapter, their psychological explanations, and their consequences for stock prices and investments.

15.2.3   *Evidence of Investor Skill*

If markets were efficient, investors should not be able either to consistently outperform or underperform the stock market at large, since prices vary randomly over time. The only way to increase expected returns would be by investing in riskier stocks, as returns constitute compensation for carrying risk. A significant body of evidence suggests that the average actively managed fund does not achieve risk-adjusted returns superior to the stock market at large (e.g., Carhart, 1997). The difficulty in consistently 'beating the market' is often used as strong evidence for market efficiency.

A counter-argument is provided by studies that find that some stock fund managers consistently outperform their colleagues. For example, Kacperczyk, Nieuwerburgh, and Veldkamp (2014) identify a small segment of fund managers, who are both the best stock-pickers when prices are on the rise (in 'bull markets') as well as the best at timing when to move out of stocks and into safer investments in periods of general stock price declines ('bear markets'). Moreover, non-professional investors – also called individual investors – earn on average lower returns than professionals which indicates that knowledge and experience result in skill (Barber, Lee, Liu, & Odean,

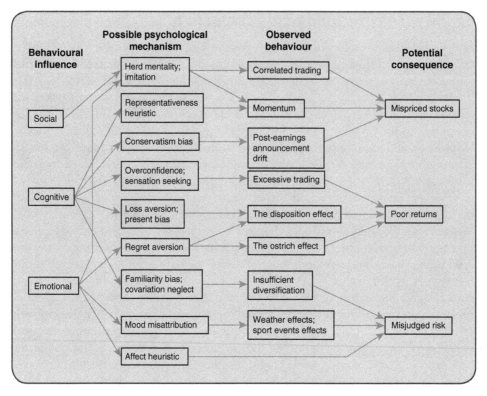

FIGURE 15.1 *Overview of stock market behaviours discussed in this chapter, their psychological explanations, and their potential consequences for stock prices and investments.*

2009). Several studies document consistent over-performance or under-performance among sections of investors, and investment skill has been empirically linked with individual factors such as genetics (Barnea, Cronqvist, & Siegel, 2010), cognitive ability (Korniotis & Kumar, 2013), and IQ (Grinblatt, Keloharju, & Linnainmaa, 2012).

15.3   COGNITIVE INFLUENCES ON INVESTOR BEHAVIOUR

15.3.1   Over-Confidence, Sensation Seeking, and Excessive Trading

Investors' poor investment performance is partly attributed to poor choices of which stocks to buy and which to sell and when (Hvidkjaer, 2008). Another suggested reason is excessive trading. Instead of holding onto stocks that they own, investors tend to sell and buy stocks too frequently, which incurs unnecessary costs in the form of commissions, fees, and taxes. Studies show that the more often investors change stocks in their portfolio, the poorer is their return, and that this applies to both professional and individual investors (Barber & Odean, 2000; Carhart, 1997).

The main explanation forwarded for excessive trading is that investors are, on average, overconfident with regards to their stock-picking ability. In order to buy stocks that they perceive as under-valued, they need to first free capital by selling stocks that they own, resulting in a high portfolio turnover. Barber and Odean (2001) made an initial empirical case for this argument by analysing the trading records of individual investors using gender as a proxy for overconfidence. Since psychological research demonstrates that within 'masculine' task domains, men are generally more overconfident than women (e.g., Beyer & Bowden, 1997), the researchers hypothesized and found that men trade more and earn poorer risk-adjusted returns than women.

Overconfidence models that seek to explain excessive trading assume that investors learn to be overconfident by taking credit for successes but attributing failures to external factors. As a consequence, the degree to which investors over-estimate the precision of their forecasts develops over time as a function of previous trading success. In studies of market data, it is this type of overconfidence – in psychology referred to as miscalibration – that is typically inferred. Yet, experimental studies in which miscalibration is measured through psychometric scales show little or no correlation with trading frequency (e.g., Glaser & Weber, 2007). It is instead the belief that one is better than the average (or median) investor that has been empirically linked with high trading frequency (e.g., Dorn & Huberman, 2005). However, since the 'better-than-average' type of overconfidence has been shown to be a relatively stable personality trait (Jonsson & Allwood, 2003), these findings do not buttress the 'learning-to-be-overconfident' explanation of excessive trading. While some suggest that failure to empirically link miscalibration with trading volume is due to measurement problems (Barber & Odean, 2011), others conclude that reasons for excessive trading should be looked for elsewhere.

An alternative explanation for why some stock investors trade too frequently is that they are prone to sensation seeking and thus enjoy the thrill of trading. Since driving behaviour is known to be strongly related to sensation seeking, Grinblatt and Keloharju (2009) hypothesized and found that trading rates among Finnish individual investors correlate with how many speeding tickets they have recently received. Further evidence stems from studies showing drops in trading volumes at times when there is a particularly large jackpot in regional or national lotteries, and that this drop is the largest for risky, lottery-like, stocks (Dorn, Dorn, & Sengmueller, 2014). In the Taiwanese stock market, which unlike most markets is heavily dominated by individual rather than institutional investors, trading dropped by about one fourth when a legal lottery was introduced on the island in 2002, which suggests that investing and gambling were treated by at least some as substitutes (Barber et al., 2009). Furthermore, Markiewicz and Weber (2013) showed that individual investors' trading volume was predicted by their score on a psychometric test of risk propensity in horse race betting and casino gambling, but not by their score for risk propensity in investment contexts. Some may thus simply enjoy trading and focus more on the thrill and less on the profit.

15.3.2   Under-Reaction, Over-Reaction, and Momentum

When a company announces its earnings for the preceding quarter, the stock price rises if the news exceeds expectations or, if falling short, drops. While this is in line with the efficient market hypothesis, the widely reported observation that prices in the former case tend to continue to rise and in the latter case continue to fall over subsequent weeks is not. This anomaly is labelled post-announcement price drift (Bernard & Thomas, 1989). Psychological accounts for this price pattern have been proposed. For example, Barberis, Shleifer and Vishny (1998) suggest that since investors, like most people, are conservatively biased (Slovic & Lichtenstein, 1971), they under-weigh new information relative to their prior beliefs and therefore initially under-react to earnings announcements. In the weeks following the announcement, implications of the news are gradually acknowledged among investors who therefore buy (or sell) the stock, which causes its price to slowly 'drift' towards its current fundamental value.

However, if an earnings announcement points in the same direction as consecutive preceding announcements, investors may overinterpret this as a trend and thus instead over-react to the news (De Bondt & Thaler, 1985). Over-reaction is furthermore often observed within the first 15 minutes following an earnings announcement, although the resulting sharp price change tends to partially revert within the next few hours (Patell & Wolfson, 1984).

A related robust finding is that in the short term (3–12 months), stock prices that have started rising tend to continue to rise while stock prices that fall often continue their decline. This is called 'momentum' (Jegadeesh & Titman, 1993). When stocks have shown a steady price increase or decrease over a longer period, however, prices generally revert. De Bondt and Thaler (1985) show that stocks that have been extreme losers over a three-year period do better in the following three-year period than previous extreme winners. Momentum, Barberis et al. (1998) argue, occurs as unsophisticated investors ('noise traders') use a representative heuristic (Kahneman & Tversky, 1984) which leads them to mistakenly interpret random price movements as representative of an underlying trend. Having identified the 'trend', they extrapolate it into the future and therefore buy the rising stock. This drives the stock's price upwards until, at a certain stage, an actual trend is formed. Even rational investors then buy the rising stock, further fuelling the momentum. Momentum has been suggested to contribute to the formation of 'bubbles' where stock prices are pushed far beyond their fundamental value before inevitably collapsing (Caginalp, Porter, & Smith, 2000).

15.3.3 The Disposition Effect: Selling Winners Too Early and Losers Too Late

Momentum and under-reaction and over-reaction to news exemplify anomalies argued to contribute to the mispricing of stocks (see Figure 15.1). Other psychologically influenced regularities in investor behaviour may not violate market efficiency but are nonetheless inconsistent with the notion of rational investors. One such regularity is the 'disposition effect', referring to the observation that investors seem disposed to sell winners early and hold on to losers (Shefrin & Statman, 1985). One reason why this behaviour is broadly categorized as an investment mistake is that it is tax inefficient. For tax purposes, investors should postpone taxable gains by continuing to hold their profitable investments, and capture tax losses by selling their losing investments. In addition, selling winners early is likely to leave investors missing out on some returns that might be earned due to momentum. The disposition effect is demonstrated in market data as well as in experiments (Odean,

1998; Weber & Camerer, 1998) but appears to diminish with financial knowledge and experience (Dhar & Zhu, 2006). Nonetheless, Frazzini (2006) shows that even investment professionals are susceptible to the disposition effect and that this adversely affects their returns.

The disposition effect has been explained through prospect theory (Kahneman & Tversky, 1979), which predicts that investors after a gain will be risk-averse and thus prefer to realize the gain rather than risk losing it. Conversely, after a loss, they will be risk-seeking and therefore choose to hold on to their risky stock. This explanation has been criticized on several grounds (Barberis & Xiong, 2009; Hens & Vlcek, 2011). Recent theoretical models suggest that while disposition behaviour in some cases is consistent with prospect theory, in other cases, it is not. When failing to account for the disposition effect, prospect theory is shown to predict either the opposite behaviour or that disposition-prone investors would not invest in stocks in the first place.

Barberis and Xiong (2012) propose an explanation for the disposition effect that does not presuppose the prospect theory value function. Investors may prefer to sell a winning stock early for a small gain rather than later for a possibly larger gain because they are present-biased – they value what happens today over what will happen tomorrow. For the same reason, they prefer to hold on to a losing stock instead of realizing the loss.

15.3.4 *Diversification*

In order to avoid unnecessary risks, investors are advised not to 'put all their eggs in one basket'. The reason why risk diversification is recommended has to do with co-variation of returns: it is more likely that firms within the same industry (or country) do poorly at the same time than firms in dissimilar industries (countries) (Markowitz, 1952). Yet, investors often diversify insufficiently. Analysing bank assets, stocks, and mutual funds owned by each Swedish household during a four-year period, Calvet, Campbell, and Sodini (2007) find that while better-educated, richer and financially literate households hold better-diversified investment portfolios, some households suffer large losses from under-diversification.

One manifestation of insufficient diversification is that stock portfolios are often heavily tilted towards companies from the investor's home country (French & Poterba, 1991). As economic reasons do not justify the magnitude of this 'home bias', it may partly be explained by the fact that people tend to feel more optimistic about matters with which they are familiar and that familiarity lessens perceptions of risk (Heath & Tversky, 1991). This could also explain why people often own (too much) stock in the company where they are employed (Huberman & Sengmueller, 2004) and in companies whose the headquarters are located close to their home and whose CEO shares their ethnicity (Grinblatt & Keloharju, 2001).

In order for diversification to effectively reduce portfolio risk, price movements of included stocks must not co-vary excessively. Some investors may incorrectly believe that any multi-asset portfolio will be well diversified (Goetzmann & Kumar, 2008) and hence use a naïve diversification heuristics that involves including many stocks (or stock funds) in their portfolio without sufficiently considering co-variation. This was illustrated in a study by Hedesström, Svedsäter, and Gärling (2009), where the majority of risk-averse experimental participants chose a portfolio of specialized funds instead of a single well-diversified fund that in fact constituted the least risky option.

Naïve diversification heuristics may furthermore make investors susceptible to how investment options are presented. For example, Benartzi and Thaler (2001) show that many participants in US employee pension plans simply divide their contributions evenly across all funds in the plan. In plans offering a majority of stock funds, most is therefore invested in stocks, while in plans offering a majority of interest funds, most is invested in interest-bearing securities.

15.4 EMOTIONAL INFLUENCES

Emotional factors can impact the quality of stock investors' choices and hence their returns. Emotions may also, on an aggregated level, contribute to how investor sentiment – a general feeling of optimism or pessimism among market participants – develops and sometimes results in 'booms and busts'. While there is ample evidence of emotions' central role in information processing and decision-making (Damasio, 1994), behavioural finance has only started to explore their influence on stock market decisions. As a first step, studies seek to establish whether such influence exists at all.

A common research method is to analyse market data using proxy variables believed or known to induce positive or negative mood. Good weather, for instance, is known to improve mood, and studies show that stock prices are more likely to rise during sunny days than during cloudy days (e.g., Saunders, 1993). This is taken as evidence that being in a good mood makes investors more optimistic and therefore more willing to take risks and buy stocks. Conversely, being in a bad mood is assumed to increase pessimism and risk aversion, and consequently make investors more prone to sell their stocks and move into safer investments.

Further support for the suggestion that mood affects investors' risk attitude is reported by Kamstra, Kramer, and Levi (2003) who document below-average stock returns during winter months and attribute this to shorter daylight hours ('winter blues'). Markets in the Southern Hemisphere exhibited the same pattern as markets in the Northern, that is, with a six-months delay. Other examples of mood proxies demonstrated to correlate with stock prices are geomagnetic storms (Krivelyova & Robotti, 2003) and the full moon phase of the lunar cycle (Yuan, Zheng, & Zhu, 2006), both associated with depressed mood, and, in Muslim countries, the fasting month of Ramadan, which is presumed to enhance social identity and life satisfaction and therefore mood (Białkowski, Etebari, & Wisniewski, 2012). In a similar vein, Edmans, Garcia, and Norli (2007) document significant stock market declines following losses by national soccer teams in international competitions.

Studies using mood proxies are, similar to proxy studies of overconfidence, questioned on the ground that mood is inferred rather than measured. Some studies seek to provide more direct evidence of how mood affects investor behaviour. For example, Kramer and Weber (2012) asked experimental participants to make hypothetical investment choices on three different occasions spread out across the year, as well as completing a seasonal affect disorder questionnaire. A high score on this scale was shown to predict more pronounced seasonal variation in risk-taking, thereby providing support to Kamstra et al.'s (2003) claim that seasonal variation in stock returns is caused by variation in sunlight and not by some other seasonal factor. In another attempt to provide an improved measure of mood, Bollen, Mao, and Zeng (2011) constructed an index based on daily Twitter feeds and found Twitter mood to be positively correlated with stock price movements.

Another approach is conducting experiments where mood is induced. Kuhnen and Knutson (2011) showed participants pictures inducing positive, negative or neutral mood before asking them to make repeated hypothetical choices between stocks and bonds. Participants exposed to pictures inducing positive and arousing emotions, such as excitement, took more risks and were more confident in their ability. Negative emotions, such as anxiety, had the opposite effect. In another study, experimental participants were mood-induced by music or by reading mood-laden statements before making hypothetical trading choices in a foreign exchange market (Au, Chan, Wang, & Vertinsky, 2003). Participants induced with a negative mood made less risky choices. They also made more accurate judgements and earned better returns than participants induced with a good mood. This result is consistent with psychological research showing that people in unpleasant affective states tend to engage in effortful and systematic information processing, whereas pleasant affective states foster use of less effortful heuristic strategies more likely to lead to biased judgements (Wyer, Clore, & Isbell, 1999).

While the above-reviewed studies target 'incidental' moods, that is, emotional states that are unrelated to the task at hand but misattributed as being relevant (Schwartz & Clore, 1983), emotional states can also be 'integral', that is, evoked by task-relevant stimuli. In an investment context, integral emotions could arise from, for example, experiencing gains or losses. Lo and Repin (2002) observed professional stock traders during live trading and found that even the most seasoned traders exhibited significant emotional response, evidenced by elevated levels of skin conductance and cardiovascular variables, when stock prices rose or fell more than usual or suddenly changed direction. While it is generally a good idea to keep a 'cool head' when making investment choices (Lo, Repin, & Steenbarger, 2005), psychological research shows that emotions in fact can contribute to better decision-making by drawing attention to relevant aspects of the choice (Ketelaar & Clore, 1997). In an experiment by Seo and Feldman Barret (2007), participants made hypothetical stock investment decisions and rated their current feelings each day for 20 consecutive business days, after which they received a cash prize matching their performance. Individuals who experienced the most intense feelings were found to achieve the highest returns. However, returns were also superior among those who reported their emotions in a more specific and differentiated fashion than others. These findings support Au et al.'s (2003) suggestion that a central challenge, especially for investment professionals working in a fast-paced environment, may be to effectively monitor and regulate emotional responses in order to avoid the biasing impact of incidental emotional states, while retaining the informational advantages conferred by integral emotions.

Emotions arising from assessing particular investment options may be used as decision cues. The 'affect heuristic' predicts that having a good (bad) feeling about something make people overly associate it with positive (or negative) attributes and therefore choose it (or not choose it). In an experimental study, MacGregor, Slovic, Dreman, and Berry (2000) showed that holding a positive affective attitude towards a certain industry made participants expect stocks of companies within that industry to both yield higher returns and be less risky than stocks from other industries, thereby ignoring the fact that risk and return are in general negatively correlated.

Moreover, merely anticipating emotions may influence investment behaviour. Summers and Duxbury (2012) argue that investors' reluctance to sell stocks that have diminished in value, as manifested in the disposition effect, is due to the fact that they want to avoid regret associated with realizing the loss. In a series of experiments the degree to which participants were responsible for their stock purchases was systematically varied, and their emotional responses to various outcomes measured. Selling losing stocks produced different emotions depending on degree of responsibility: high responsibility resulted in feelings of regret while low responsibility resulted in disappointment. Irrational retention of loser stocks was detected only among high-responsibility participants. Analysing market data, Lehenkari (2012) found supporting evidence in that stock investors showed a weaker tendency to hold on to losers received via inheritance or gift than to losers that they had purchased themselves. Furthermore, in Au et al.'s (2003) experiment, participants ignored new information that would make them regret their previous investment decisions. These findings are all consistent with the 'ostrich effect', referring to the observation that investors in times of poor stock market performances seem inclined to 'bury their heads in the sand'. For example, Swedish pension savers log on to their online accounts much less frequently in bear markets than in bull markets, presumably in order to shield themselves from feelings of regret (Karlsson, Loewenstein, & Seppi, 2009).

15.5   SOCIAL INFLUENCES

In many areas of social life, people conform to others when making decisions. Social influence is either normative or informational (Deutsch & Gerard, 1955). In the former case, people conform due to external social pressure or internalized social norms; in the latter case, the motive is to acquire and use information from others. When a group of investors follow each other into (or out of) the same stocks, this is referred to as herding. Informational herding, or an 'information cascade', arises when investors ignore their own 'private' information and instead imitate other investors' choices because they believe the others to be better informed. Shiller (2015) offers an everyday illustration (here slightly revised): Imagine that you choose between two unfamiliar, apparently similar restaurants situated on each side of a street. You have received mixed evaluations about one of the restaurants (A) and favourable evaluations about the other (B). When approaching the restaurants you note that restaurant A is more crowded than restaurant B. You infer that this must be for a good reason and therefore ignore your private information about the evaluations and instead choose the same restaurant as the majority.

Whether herding is rational or irrational is debated. Ignoring private information can be beneficial when a market possesses the 'wisdom of crowds' (Surowiecki, 2004), referring to the observation that the average judgement among a large group of individuals who all make independent judgements is generally more accurate than any one individual. In an information cascade, however, judgements are not made independently and markets therefore are not 'wise'. Yet, even when stock prices are pushed far beyond their fundamental levels, following the herd is not necessarily irrational since bubbles may inflate for years. In such cases, following a 'contrarian' investment strategy (selling when most others buy and vice versa) can prove costly. To illustrate, funds that opted not to 'ride the trend' during the price surge in technology stock around the turn of the millennium lost investors. Some were, as a consequence, forced out of business long before prices finally reverted. A further reason for fund managers to herd is that unprofitable investments are likely to hurt their reputation considerably less if others have made the same mistakes (Scharfstein & Stein, 1990). Reputational herding is an example of normative social influence.

While it may seem self-evident that investors influence each other, this turns out to be hard to prove. Lakonishok, Shleifer, and Vishny (1992) introduced a way to empirically measure correlated trading across groups of investors. The idea is to analyse the buying pressure on a given stock for a homogeneous subgroup (e.g., pension funds; mutual funds; individual investors). For the market as a whole each purchase is balanced by a sale, and the number of buyers thus equals the number of sellers. However, for a given subgroup and a given stock, there can be an excess of buyers or sellers, which suggests that the investors composing the subgroup herd.

Using this measure, Dorn, Huberman, and Sengmueller (2008) found that individual investors at a German discount broker traded more similarly than expected by chance, and interpret this as evidence of herd behaviour. In a typical stock and quarter, 57% of the investors were on the same side of the market, while the figure would be 50% in perfectly efficient markets. Early studies showed no, or only weak, evidence of correlated trading among professional investors. For example, Lakonishok et al. (1992) found 50.1% of US pension funds to be on the same side of the market in a typical stock and quarter. However, using a less conservative measure, Sias (2004) reports compelling evidence of herding also among fund managers.

It is important to note that herd-like behaviour, as evidenced by correlated trades, may not always result from imitation. Social influence can also be indirect. Investors may, for example, independently of each other use identical information sources or investment strategies, in which case, correlated trades indicate 'clustering' rather than herding. To distinguish herding from clustering in market data is difficult. Experimental approaches facilitate this distinction, but experimental evidence of herding is mixed and its generalizability to real markets has been questioned (see review in Andersson, Hedesström, & Gärling, 2014).

Success stories and advice from friends, colleagues, and neighbours can also influence investors. Kaustia and Knüpfer (2012) show that Finnish investors are particularly likely to buy stocks for the first time when people living within their own postal code area have recently made good returns on their stocks. Interestingly, the likelihood of entering the stock market does not diminish with a poor performance of neighbours, possibly indicating that people only talk about their investments when they are successful.

Additionally, investors are influenced by experts. Malmendier and Shanthikumar (2007) report that investors yield inferior returns by following buy recommendations from stock market analysts without taking into account that analysts often have financial incentives to tout particular stocks. Besides, analysts themselves herd; they often release forecasts similar to those previously announced by other analysts even when this is not justified by the information at hand (Trueman, 1994).

15.6 POLICY IMPLICATIONS

Through depicting investors' behaviour with enhanced accuracy, behavioural finance may gradually increase stock market predictability and thereby improve the odds of avoiding future bubbles and crashes. Yet, there is no consensus regarding whether contemporary behavioural finance models better predict investor behaviour than traditional economic models. Gärling, Kirchler, Lewis, and van Raaij (2009) provide an overview of how psychological factors may have contributed to the 2007–2008 financial crisis. In this case, it was the credit market and not the stock market in which the crisis originated but, as the authors point out, common for the financial system as a whole is an institutionalized focus on short-term profits. Gärling et al. (2009) suggest that in order to help prevent or mitigate future market collapses, behavioural finance research should focus less on disproving the efficient market hypothesis and more on questions relating to how market functionality might be improved. For example, bonuses to stock portfolio managers typically reward annual or even quarterly performance, which encourages short-term investment strategies such as momentum trading and herding. One way to counteract short-termism would be instead to incentivize longer-term performance.

What could be done to help citizens make the difficult stock market investment decisions required of them when, for example, saving for retirement? Thaler and Sunstein (2008) argue that educational efforts aimed at increasing financial knowledge alone are unlikely to suffice. Investors may also need sensible 'nudges', for example, by having investment alternatives presented to them in a psychologically informed way that increases the likelihood of making a good choice. Additionally, a well-diversified age-tailored default option should be provided for those who do not wish to make their own selection of funds.

15.7 SUMMARY

Some stock investors consistently earn better risk-adjusted returns than the stock market at large. Most, however, fail to do so, in part because they trade too frequently. This may in turn be due to overconfidence or thrill seeking. Furthermore, investors tend to initially under-react to news and sell winners too early and losers too late. Their decisions are affected by emotions and by other investors' behaviour, which may cause price bubbles bound to burst. A challenge for economic psychology is to explore ways of counteracting short-termism in financial markets.

REVIEW QUESTIONS

1. Describe at least three different research findings that appear to contradict the efficient market hypothesis.
2. What is the psychological explanation for why people invest heavily in stocks from their home country?
3. Why, according to behavioural finance, do stock prices rise more on sunny than on cloudy days?
4. For what reasons might investors make similar choices as other investors?

REFERENCES

Andersson, M., Hedesström, M., & Gärling, T. (2014). A social-psychological perspective on herding in stock markets. *Journal of Behavioral Finance, 15*(3), 226–234. DOI: 10.1080/15427560.2014.941062

Au, K., Chan, F., Wang, D., & Vertinsky, I. (2003). Mood in foreign exchange trading: Cognitive processes and performance. *Organizational Behavior and Human Decision Processes, 91*, 322–338. DOI: 10.1016/S0749-5978(02)00510-1

Barber, B. M., Lee, Y. T., Liu, Y. J., & Odean, T. (2009). Just how much do individual investors lose by trading? *Review of Financial Studies, 22*, 609–632. DOI: 10.1093/rfs/hhn046

Barber, B. M., & Odean, T. (2000). Trading is hazardous to your wealth: The common stock investment performance of individual investors. *Journal of Finance, 55*(2), 773–806. DOI: 10.1111/0022-1082.00226

Barber, B. M., & Odean, T. (2001). Boys will be boys: Gender, overconfidence, and common stock investment. *Quarterly Journal of Economics, 116*, 261–292. DOI: 10.1162/003355301556400

Barber, B. M., & Odean, T. (2011). The behavior of individual investors. In G. Constantinides, M. Harris, & R. Stulz (Eds.), *Handbook of the economics of finance*. Amsterdam: Elsevier.

Barberis, N., Shleifer, A., & Vishny, R. (1998). A model of investor sentiment. *Journal of Financial Economics, 49*(3), 307–343.

Barberis, N., & Xiong, W. (2009). What drives the disposition effect? An analysis of a long-standing preference-based explanation. *Journal of Finance, 64*, 751–784. DOI: 10.1111/j.1540-6261.2009.01448.x

Barberis, N., & Xiong, W. (2012). Realization utility. *Journal of Financial Economics, 104*, 251–271. DOI: 10.1016/j.jfineco.2011.10.005

Barnea, A., Cronqvist, H., & Siegel, S. (2010). Nature or nurture: What determines investor behavior? *Journal of Financial Economics, 98*(3), 583–604. DOI: 10.1016/j.jfineco.2010.08.001

Benartzi, S., & Thaler, R. H. (2001). Naïve diversification strategies in defined contribution plans. *American Economic Review, 91*, 79–99. DOI: 10.1257/aer.91.1.79

Bernard, V. L., & Thomas, J. K. (1989). Post-earnings-announcement drift: Delayed price response or risk premium? *Journal of Accounting Research, 27*, 1–36. DOI: 10.2307/2491062

Beyer, S., & Bowden, E. M. (1997). Gender differences in self-perceptions: Convergent evidence from three measures of accuracy and bias. *Personality and Social Psychology Bulletin, 23*(2), 157–172. DOI: 10.1177/0146167297232005

Białkowski, J., Etebari, A., & Wisniewski, T. P. (2012). Fast profits: Investor sentiment and stock returns during Ramadan. *Journal of Banking and Finance, 36*, 835–845. DOI: 10.1016/j.jbankfin.2011.09.014

Bollen, J., Mao, H., & Zeng, X. (2011). Twitter mood predicts the stock market. *Journal of Computational Science, 2*, 1–8. DOI: 10.1016/j.jocs.2010.12.007

Caginalp, G., Porter, D. P. & Smith, V. L. (2000). Overreactions, momentum, liquidity, and price bubbles in laboratory and field asset markets. *Journal of Psychology and Financial Markets, 1*(1), 24–48. DOI: 10.1207/S15327760JPFM0101_04

Calvet, L. E., Campbell, J. Y., & Sodini, P. (2007). Down or out: Assessing the welfare costs of household investment mistakes. *Journal of Political Economy, 115*, 707–747. DOI: 10.1086/524204

Carhart, M. M. (1997). On persistence in mutual fund performance. *Journal of Finance, 52*, 57–82. DOI: 10.1111/j.1540-6261.1997.tb03808.x

Damasio, A. R. (1994). *Descartes' error: Emotion, reason, and the human brain*. New York: Avon.

De Bondt, W. F., & Thaler, R. H. (1985). Does the stock market overreact? *Journal of Finance, 40*(3), 793–805. DOI: 10.1111/j.1540-6261.1985.tb05004.x

Deutsch, M., & Gerard, H. G. (1955). A study of normative and informational social influence upon individual judgment. *Journal of Abnormal and Social Psychology, 51*, 629–636. DOI: 10.1037/h0046408

Dhar, R., & Zhu, N. (2006). Up close and personal: Investor sophistication and the disposition effect. *Management Science, 52*(5), 726–740. DOI: 10.1287/mnsc.1040.0473

Dorn, A. J., Dorn, D., & Sengmueller, P. (2014). Trading as gambling. *Management Science.* DOI: 10.1287/mnsc.2014.1979

Dorn, D., & Huberman, G. (2005). Talk and action: What individual investors say and what they do. *Review of Finance, 9*(4), 437–481. DOI: 10.1007/s10679-005-4997-z

Dorn, D., Huberman, G., & Sengmueller, P. (2008). Correlated trading and returns. *Journal of Finance, 63*(2), 885–920. DOI: 10.1111/j.1540-6261.2008.01334.x

Edmans, A., Garcia, D., & Norli, Ø. (2007). Sports sentiment and stock returns. *Journal of Finance, 62*(4), 1967–1998. DOI: 10.1111/j.1540-6261.2007.01262.x

Fama, E. F. (1991). Efficient capital markets: II. *Journal of Finance, 46*(5), 1575–1617. DOI: 10.1111/j.1540-6261.1991.tb04636.x

Frazzini, A. (2006). The disposition effect and underreaction to news. *Journal of Finance, 61*(4), 2017–2046. DOI: 10.1111/j.1540-6261.2006.00896.x

French, K. R., & Poterba, J. M. (1991). Investor diversification and international equity markets. *American Economic Review, 81,* 222–226.

Gärling, T., Kirchler, E., Lewis, A., & van Raaij, F. (2009). Psychology, financial decision making, and financial crises. *Psychological Science in the Public Interest, 10*(1), 1–47. DOI: 10.1177/1529100610378437

Glaser, M., & Weber, M. (2007). Overconfidence and trading volume. *The Geneva Risk and Insurance Review, 32*(1), 1–36. DOI: 10.1007/s10713-007-0003-3

Goetzmann, W. N., & Kumar, A. (2008). Equity portfolio diversification. *Review of Finance, 12,* 433–463. DOI: 10.1093/rof/rfn005

Grinblatt, M., & Keloharju, M. (2001). Distance, language, and cultural bias: The role of investor sophistication. *Journal of Finance, 46,* 1053–1073.

Grinblatt, M., & Keloharju, M. (2009). Sensation seeking, overconfidence, and trading activity. *Journal of Finance, 64*(2), 549–578. DOI: 10.2139/ssrn.890985

Grinblatt, M., Keloharju, M., & Linnainmaa, J. T. (2012). IQ, trading behavior, and performance. *Journal of Financial Economics, 104*(2), 339–362. DOI: 10.1016/j.jfineco.2011.05.016

Heath, C., & Tversky, A. (1991). Preference and belief: Ambiguity and competence in choice under uncertainty. *Journal of Risk and Uncertainty, 4*(1), 5–28. DOI: 10.1007/BF00057884

Hedesström, M., Svedsäter, H., & Gärling, T. (2009). Naïve diversification in the Swedish premium pension scheme: Experimental evidence. *Applied Psychology, 58*(3), 403–417. DOI: 10.1111/j.1464-0597.2009.00399.x

Hens, T., & Vlcek, M. (2011). Does prospect theory explain the disposition effect? *Journal of Behavioral Finance, 12*(3), 141–157. DOI: 10.2139/ssrn.970450

Huberman, G., & Sengmueller, P. (2004). Performance and employer stock in 401(k) plans. *Review of Finance, 8*(3), 403–443. DOI: 10.1007/s10679-004-2544-y

Hvidkjaer, S. (2008). Small trades and the cross-section of stock returns. *Review of Financial Studies, 21,* 1123–1151. DOI: 10.1093/rfs/hhn049

Jegadeesh, N., & Titman, S. (1993). Returns to buying winners and selling losers: Implications for stock market efficiency. *Journal of Finance, 48*(1), 65–91. DOI: 10.1111/j.1540-6261.1993.tb04702.x

Jonsson, A. C., & Allwood, C. M. (2003). Stability and variability in the realism of confidence judgments over time, content domain, and gender. *Personality and Individual Differences, 34*(4), 559–574. DOI: 10.1016/S0191-8869(02)00028-4

Kacperczyk, M., Nieuwerburgh, S. V., & Veldkamp, L. (2014). Time-varying fund manager skill. *ournal of Finance, 69*(4), 1455–1484. DOI: 10.1111/jofi.12084

Kahneman, D., & Tversky, A. (1979). Prospect theory: An analysis of decision under risk. *Econometrica, 47*(2), 263–291. DOI: 10.2307/1914185

Kahneman, D., & Tversky, A. (1984). Choices, values and frames. *American Psychologist, 39,* 341–350. DOI: 10.1037/0003-066X.39.4.341

Kamstra, M. J., Kramer, L. A., & Levi, M. D. (2003). Winter blues: A SAD stock market cycle. *American Economic Review, 93*, 324–343. DOI: 10.1257/000282803321455322

Karlsson, N., Loewenstein, G. F., & Seppi, D. J. (2009). The ostrich effect: Selective attention to information. *Journal of Risk and Uncertainty, 38*(2), 95–115. DOI: 10.1007/s11166-009-9060-6

Kaustia, M., & Knüpfer, S. (2012). Peer performance and stock market entry. *Journal of Financial Economics, 104*(2), 321–338. DOI: 10.1016/j.jfineco.2011.01.010

Ketelaar, T., & Clore, G. L. (1997). Emotion and reason: The proximate effects and ultimate functions of emotion. In G.Matthews (Ed.), *Cognitive science perspectives on personality and emotion* (pp. 355–395). New York: Elsevier.

Korniotis, G. M., & Kumar, A. (2013). Do portfolio distortions reflect superior information or psychological biases? *Journal of Financial and Quantitative Analysis, 48*(1), 1–45. DOI: 10.1017/S0022109012000610

Kramer, L. A., & Weber, J. M. (2012). This is your portfolio on winter seasonal affective disorder and risk aversion in financial decision making. *Social Psychological and Personality Science, 3*(2), 193–199. DOI: 10.1177/1948550611415694

Krivelyova, A., & Robotti, C. (2003). Playing the field. Geomagnetic storms and international stock markets. Working Paper, Federal Reserve Bank of Atlanta.

Kuhnen, C. M., & Knutson, B. (2011). The impact of affect on beliefs, preferences and financial decisions. *Journal of Financial and Quantitative Analysis, 46*, 605–626.

Lakonishok, J., Shleifer, A., & Vishny, R. W. (1992). The impact of institutional trading on stock prices. *Journal of Financial Economics, 32*(1), 23–43. DOI: 10.1016/0304-405X(92)90023-Q

Lehenkari, M. (2012). In search of the underlying mechanism of the disposition effect. *Journal of Behavioral Decision Making, 25*(2), 196–209. DOI: 10.1002/bdm.727

Lo, A., & Repin, D. V. (2002). The psychophysiology of real-time financial risk processing. *Journal of Cognitive Neuroscience, 14*(3), 323–339. DOI: 10.1162/089892902317361877

Lo, A., Repin, D. V., & Steenbarger, B. N. (2005). Fear and greed in financial markets: A clinical study of day-traders. *American Economic Review, 95*, 352–359. DOI: 10.1257/000282805774670095

MacGregor, D. G., Slovic, P., Dreman, D., & Berry, M. (2000). Imagery, affect, and financial judgment. *Journal of Psychology and Financial Markets, 1*, 104–110. DOI: 10.1207/S15327760JPFM0102_2

Malmendier, U., & Shanthikumar, D. (2007). Are small investors naïve about incentives? *Journal of Financial Economics, 85*, 457–489. DOI: 10.1016/j.jfineco.2007.02.001

Markiewicz, Ł., & Weber, E. U. (2013). Dospert's gambling risk-taking propensity scale predicts excessive stock trading. *Journal of Behavioral Finance, 14*(1), 65–78. DOI: 10.1080/15427560.2013.762000

Markowitz, H. (1952). Portfolio selection. *Journal of Finance, 7*, 77–91. DOI: 10.2307/2975974

Odean, T. (1998). Are investors reluctant to realize their losses? *Journal of Finance, 53*, 1775–1798. DOI: 10.1111/0022-1082.00072

Patell, J. M., & Wolfson, M. A. (1984). The intraday speed of adjustment of stock prices to earnings and dividend announcements. *Journal of Financial Economics, 13*(2), 223–252.

Saunders, E. M. (1993). Stock prices and Wall Street weather. *American Economic Review, 83*, 1337–1345.

Scharfstein, D. S. & Stein, J. C. (1990). Herd behavior and investment. *American Economic Review, 80*, 465–479.

Schwartz, N., & Clore, G. L. (1983). Mood, misattribution, and judgments of well-being: Informative and directive functions of affective states. *Journal of Personality and Social Psychology, 45*(3), 513–523. DOI: 10.1037/0022-3514.45.3.513

Seo, M.-G., & Feldman Barret, L. (2007). Being emotional during decision making: good or bad? An empirical investigation. *Academy of Management Journal, 50*, 923–940.

Shefrin, H., & Statman, M. (1985). The disposition to sell winners too early and ride losers too long: Theory and evidence. *Journal of Finance, 40*(3), 77–790. DOI: 10.1111/j.1540-6261.1985.tb05002.x

Shiller, R. J. (2015). *Irrational exuberance*. Princeton, NJ: Princeton University Press.

Sias, R. W. (2004). Institutional herding. *Review of Financial Studies, 17*, 165–206. DOI: 10.1093/rfs/hhg035

Simon, H. A. (1955). A behavioral model of rational choice. *Quarterly Journal of Economics, 69*, 99–118. DOI: 10.2307/1884852

Slovic, P., & Lichtenstein, S. (1971). Comparison of Bayesian and regression approaches to the study of information processing in judgment. *Organizational Behavior & Human Processes, 6*, 649–744. DOI: 10.1016/0030-5073(71)90033-X

Summers, B., & Duxbury, D. (2012). Decision-dependent emotions and behavioral anomalies. *Organizational Behavior and Human Decision Processes, 118*(2), 226–238. DOI: 10.1016/j.obhdp.2012.03.004

Surowiecki, J. (2004). *The wisdom of crowds: Why the many are smarter than the few and how collective wisdom shapes business, economies, societies, and nations.* London: Little Brown.

Thaler, R. H., & Sunstein, C. R. (2008). *Nudge: Improving decisions about health, wealth and happiness.* New Haven, CT: Yale University Press.

Trueman, B. (1994). Analyst forecasts and herding behavior. *Review of Financial Studies, 7*(1), 97–124. DOI: 10.1093/rfs/7.1.97

Weber, M., & Camerer, C. F. (1998). The disposition effect in securities trading: An experimental analysis. *Journal of Economic Behavior & Organization, 33*, 167–184. DOI: 10.1016/S0167-2681(97)00089-9

Wyer, R. S., Clore, G. L., & Isbell, L. (1999). Affect and information processing. In M. Zanna (Ed.), *Advances in experimental social psychology* (pp. 1–77). New York: Academic Press.

Yuan, K., Zheng, L., & Zhu, Q. (2006). Are investors moonstruck? Lunar phases and stock returns. *Journal of Empirical Finance, 13*(1), 1–23. DOI: 10.1016/j.jempfin.2005.06.001

FURTHER READING

Shiller, R. J. (2015). *Irrational exuberance.* Princeton, NJ: Princeton University Press.

Shleifer, A. (2000). *Inefficient markets: An introduction to behavioral finance.* New York: Oxford University Press.

16 Tax Behaviour

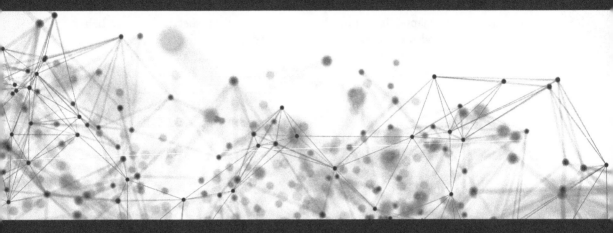

ERICH KIRCHLER AND ERIK HOELZL

CHAPTER OUTLINE

LEARNING OUTCOMES

BY THE END OF THIS CHAPTER YOU SHOULD BE ABLE TO:

1. Describe psychological explanations of the behaviour of individual taxpayers and companies.
2. Discuss the relationship between taxpayers and tax authorities with respect to interaction climates, trust, and power.
3. Give examples of regulation strategies and practical implications.

16.1 INTRODUCTION

The aim of this chapter is to introduce psychological perspectives on tax behaviour. Taxpaying and tax evasion are important economic behaviours that concern citizens, companies and governments. Because taxpaying can be viewed as a social dilemma, individual attempts to evade taxes have negative effects on the community and in consequence again on the individual. On the one hand, it is important to understand what influences tax behaviour. Factors range from audits and fines to attitudes towards taxes and tax evasion, social norms and justice. On the other hand, it is important to understand how tax behaviour can be regulated. Approaches range from command-and-control strategies to responsive strategies. This chapter proposes that the interaction climate between taxpayers and tax authorities matters, and that the coordination of power and trust into a comprehensive approach to understanding and regulating tax behaviour is key.

16.2 TAXES AND TAX COMPLIANCE

From the perspective of governments, taxes are used to fund public goods, to influence markets, and to regulate the behaviour of citizens and companies. Taxes can be an instrument to shape behaviour by providing incentives (e.g., to consume healthy food and engage in environmentally-friendly activities) or by increasing costs to control undesirable behaviour (e.g., smoking and excessive consumption of energy; Freiberg, 2010). Moreover, taxes are a policy instrument applied to redistribute wealth across society. A progressive tax system can reduce the unequal distribution of wealth and has been found to be positively related to social well-being at the aggregate national level (Oishi, Schimmack, & Diener, 2012). Governments pass tax laws, and tax compliance refers to the degree to which citizens and companies follow these laws.

From the perspective of taxpayers, taxes are often seen as a burden which citizens and companies try to avoid (Kirchler, 2007). Consequently, the classical economic approach to regulate tax behaviour was auditing and imposing sanctions on illegal actions (Allingham & Sandmo, 1972; Srinivasan, 1973) to ensure tax compliance. Tax evasion, i.e., illegal methods to reduce the tax burden, can to some extent be influenced by such command-and-control approaches (Slemrod, Blumenthal, & Christian, 2001). However, many studies have shown that the effect is rather weak (e.g., Andreoni, Erard, & Feinstein, 1998). These studies suggest that audits and fines explain only part of tax behaviour and are without effect on tax avoidance, i.e., legal methods to reduce the tax burden such as exploiting loopholes in the tax law.

Economic psychology acknowledges that tax behaviour depends partly on audits and fines. However, to understand the motives for tax compliance it is necessary to understand taxpayers' attitudes towards taxes, their knowledge and understanding of tax laws, their personal and social norms, and fairness concerns related to distributive and procedural justice. Alm, Kirchler and Muehlbacher (2012) summarized the determinants of compliance as studied by economists and psychologists. Besides socio-demographic characteristics, the effects of audits and fines, marginal tax rate, income level, opportunities to evade by various occupational groups, complexity of the tax law, attitudes and tax morale, personal, social and societal norms, and the complex facets of distributive, procedural and retributive justice were investigated (see also Kirchler, 2007; Pickhardt & Prinz, 2014). Table 16.1 provides an overview of determinants of tax compliance in the form of broad generalizations.

The following sections will focus on selected topics on the levels of individual tax-payers, companies, and tax authorities. An integrative view on the interaction climate between taxpayers and tax authorities is introduced. The chapter ends with practical implications to increase tax compliance.

Table 16.1 *Economic and psychological determinants of tax compliance*

Determinants	Effect
Economic determinants	
Audits	Higher probability of audits increases compliance, but subjective probability appears to have a larger impact than objective probability
Fines	High fines increase compliance, but need to be in line with retributive justice
Marginal tax rate	Tax rate effects on compliance are mixed
Income size	Income effects on compliance are mixed
Opportunity to avoid or to evade taxes	Higher opportunities to avoid or to evade taxes reduce compliance
Psychological determinants	
Complexity of tax law	High complexity and subjective incompetence reduce compliance
Attitudes	Viewing tax evasion as only a minor crime and negative attitudes towards taxes and tax authorities reduce compliance
Personal norms	Internalized ethical values and the personal tendency to obey laws increase compliance
Social and societal norms	Ethical values of the social group and of a society as a whole increase compliance
Distributive justice	High fairness in terms of horizontal fairness (an individual's tax burden in comparison to others), vertical fairness (individual tax burden in comparison to those capable of contributing more or less) and exchange fairness (tax burden relative to the provision of public goods financed by tax revenues) increases compliance
Procedural justice	High fairness of tax-related decision-making procedures (e.g., having a voice in policy making, transparency) increases compliance
Retributive justice	High fairness of the form and severity of the punishment imposed on tax offenders increases compliance

Source: Adapted from Alm, Kirchler and Muehlbacher (2012, p. 138), with permission from Elsevier B.V.

16.3   TAX ATTITUDES BY INDIVIDUAL TAXPAYERS

16.3.1   Tax Laws and Tax Evasion

Tax law is extraordinarily complex. Not surprisingly, then, the majority of taxpaying citizens have difficulties in understanding what is right and what is wrong. Even tax authorities and tax advisors express difficulties in drawing a clear borderline between what is legally right and what is wrong. This is a long-standing problem. More than half a century ago, Schmölders (1959) found that politicians in the German parliament and members of its finance committee had a poor understanding of fiscal policy. In the meantime, the tax code of many countries has become even more complex. Owens and Hamilton (2004) reported that the entire tax code of the Internal Revenue Service in the United States quadrupled in number of words from 1955 to 2000. People blame the complexity of tax law for their feelings of tax incompetence and lack of interest in the system (McKerchar, 2001) and feel it is necessary to consult tax practitioners (Sakurai & Braithwaite, 2003). Niemirowski and Wearing (2003) found a high level of agreement among taxpayers with the statement: 'Because I do not want to make any mistakes, I use a tax professional to prepare my tax return.' The demand for tax practitioners does not seem primarily driven by the desire to avoid paying taxes, but by a dual motivation to report correctly but at the same time pay no more than is required (Frecknall-Hughes & Kirchler, 2015).

Tax evasion is often not seen as a serious crime, despite the majority of taxpayers' willingness to abide by the law. In German surveys conducted by Schmölders (1959), approximately half of the respondents compared a person deliberately evading taxes with a cunning business man, while only one quarter judged such a person as a thief or deceiver. Similar results were reported by Song and Yarbrough (1978) and Vogel (1974). In Kirchler's (1998) study on social representations of taxes, respondents were asked to describe and evaluate a typical taxpayer, an honest taxpayer, and a tax evader. The description and evaluation of tax evaders were quite positive. Whereas typical taxpayers were rated most negatively and honest taxpayers most positively, tax evaders were evaluated neutrally. Moreover, tax evaders were described as being the most intelligent and as being rather hard-working, whereas the typical taxpayer was perceived as being rather lazy and not very intelligent. Honest people were perceived as hard working, but as less intelligent than tax evaders. While these findings suggest that attitudes towards tax evasion are positive, there may have been changes in the recent past. The OECD (2013) initiative of enhanced relationships and cooperative compliance has led to changes of paradigms and to investment in trust. The recent success of tax authorities in the fight against tax evasion on a large scale, especially in Germany, as well as the public shaming of tax avoidance by globally operating companies and their sophisticated, tax-efficient profit shifting strategies, have led to a greater awareness in the population of the necessity of taxes. It can be assumed that large-scale tax evasion is seen as serious crime, whereas small-scale evasion might still be seen as minor crime. Indeed, a representative survey study on tax morale in Germany found that the population believes it is important to comply with the tax laws. Tax morale – which Torgler (2007) defines as an intrinsic motivation arising from the moral obligation to pay taxes correctly – is high. At the same time, citizens expect more fairness: 95% believe that the state is too wasteful with their money and 85% think their personal tax burden is too high. In addition, many think that the tax code is too complicated and unfair (Bund der Steuerzahler Deutschland e.V., 2014).

16.3.2   Taxes as Burden and Restrictions

Taxes are often seen as a burden. Despite citizens' appreciation of public goods and policy regulations of consumer behaviour, organizations and markets, citizens dislike paying taxes and sometimes are even willing to take on additional costs in order to avoid taxes. They have a stronger preference for avoiding tax-related costs than for avoiding equal-sized or even larger monetary costs unrelated to taxes. For example, Sussman and Olivola (2011) showed that consumers considered goods advertised as 'tax-free', i.e., with a price reduction in the magnitude of the sales tax, to be more attractive than goods with a larger price reduction not linked to tax. Representations of taxes and reactions to tax burden differ between groups of taxpayers, e.g., employees and self-employed. The self-employed and entrepreneurs who take the gross income and collect value added tax often perceive taxes as too high, do not perceive a balanced return of benefits, claim taxes to be unfairly distributed and as limiting their freedom. In a study by Kirchler (1998), blue-collar workers, white-collar workers, civil servants, self-employed and entrepreneurs wrote down what came to their minds when thinking about taxes. Analyses of these free associations showed clear differences between the groups. Blue-collar workers, white-collar workers, and civil servants mentioned public goods, welfare, social security, and justice. Thus, they had an exchange between paying taxes and receiving benefits in mind. The self-employed and entrepreneurs mentioned audits and fines and taxes as a disincentive to work, as public constraint, the complexity of tax law, bureaucracy and the non-transparent public use of tax revenues. Thus, these groups thought of taxes in terms of high compliance costs, and as a limitation on their freedom to run their businesses.

Taxes can be seen as restrictions. People often resist attempts to limit their freedom of choice. According to reactance theory (Brehm, 1966), restricted freedom is often responded to by doing the opposite of what is requested. If the self-employed and entrepreneurs perceive taxes as a restriction on their freedom, they are likely to develop reactance motives which manifest in a decreased tax morale and a search for opportunities to avoid or evade taxes. Especially in their early business years, the self-employed and entrepreneurs may experience taxes as an unbearable loss when they focus on their gross income (including the value added tax collected and to be passed on to tax authorities) and feel as if they are paying taxes 'out of pocket'. The longer they run their business, the more they will shift their focus: they are likely to develop strategies to separate direct and indirect taxes from their income and keep (mental) accounts for income tax, social security payments, or valued added tax (Muehlbacher & Kirchler, 2013). When tax revenues are (mentally) kept aside, taxes are not seen as being paid out of pocket, and are seen more as a forgone gain rather than a painful loss. Kirchler (1999) investigated whether self-employed' and entrepreneurs' resistance to taxes was dependent on the length of time they had run their business: a shorter business history was correlated with increased perceived restrictions of freedom and consequently higher intentions to evade taxes.

16.4   PROFIT SHIFTING AND AGGRESSIVE TAX PLANNING BY COMPANIES

16.4.1   Legal and Psychological Perspectives

In the globalized economic world, companies have formed multinational corporations. Tax planning schemes allow them to legally reduce tax liability to a minimum by so-called *profit shifting*, i.e., moving the taxable profit to a country with lower tax rates. Tax planning schemes have become a major competitive factor contributing to steadily declining corporate tax rates in the European Union. Tax policy and discussions about efficient reactions to tax avoidance schemes are dominated by the OECD initiative against aggressive profit reductions and transfers of profits (OECD, 2013). While the initiative aims at regulating the transfer of profits by international corporations, its success depends on new regulations in different countries and on the attitudes of taxpayers towards tax avoidance and tax evasion.

The struggle of individuals and businesses to improve their financial situation is widely accepted in society and perceived as a prerequisite of wealth. From a legal perspective, tax evasion is illegal, whereas tax avoidance and tax flight are usually considered legal behaviours which – though not following the spirit of the law – do follow the letter of the law (Frecknall-Hughes, 2013). From a macro-economic perspective, and apart from legal considerations, tax avoidance, tax evasion, and tax flight have similar negative effects on the national budget. From a psychological perspective, taxpayers perceive tax avoidance, tax evasion, and tax flight differently along legal and moral dimensions (Kirchler, Maciejovsky, & Schneider, 2003). In Kirchler et al.'s study, fiscal officers, students of economics and business administration specializing in auditing and accounting, business lawyers and entrepreneurs were asked to produce free associations to the terms tax avoidance, tax flight and tax evasion. All three activities were perceived as possibilities to save taxes. However, evasion was judged as illegal and immoral behaviour, whereas avoidance was perceived as legal and not immoral; tax flight was considered legal but immoral behaviour. Since the time of that study, citizens' views may have changed through recent media reports and public discussion of aggressive tax planning and profit shifting by multinational firms.

16.4.2   Policy Perspectives

Some recent contributions highlight the necessity of responding to multinational corporations' activities by developing rules and instruments to effectively control their tax behaviour. The OECD released recommendations on how to combat aggressive tax planning in 2013. Fuest, Spengel, Finke, Heckemeyer, and Nusser (2013) discussed policy options for tackling profit shifting and tax avoidance by multinational firms, such as extension of source taxation, residence taxation, fundamental reforms of corporate income taxation, and stricter reporting and transparency requirements. Hey, Schreiber, Pönnighaus, and Bierbrauer (2013) underline the need for an international consensus on how to jointly regulate the taxpaying behaviour of citizens and businesses in order to effectively combat aggressive tax avoidance and to increase tax justice.

The problem, however, is that the tax planning strategies of multinational firms are not illegal. By exploiting the possibilities offered by complex and ambivalent laws, their activities may be at the border of the law but hardly over the border. They follow the letter of the law. In order to enhance willingness to comply with the spirit of the law, it seems necessary to establish a sense of right-doing and wrong-doing in corporate business and in society. If aggressive tax planning and tax avoidance strategies are made public, and if the public understands that egoistic profit-maximizing strategies are directed against the community, citizens' reactions (e.g., consumer boycotts) may have more impact on tax planning than complex laws that are adjusted by lawyers who chase the 'robbers' who continue exploiting ambivalences and loopholes in the law.

Citizens' judgements of unfairness of tax avoidance and evasion probably result from an everyday understanding of moral and immoral conduct, and probably not from an informed judgement against the background of the complex tax law. In Section 16.5, we consider how governments can design regulation strategies to strengthen the sense of right-doing for the community, to condemn what is against the community's welfare, and to enhance cooperation by individuals and companies.

16.5   REGULATION STRATEGIES BY TAX AUTHORITIES

16.5.1   *Regulation and Power*

Governments regulate the behaviour of citizens and companies through laws and institutions, specifically through tax laws and tax authorities. 'Regulation is essentially about the use of power and the debates about the nature of regulation are similar to those about the nature of "power" in political science discourse, "social control" in sociological discourse and "sanctions" in criminological discourse' (Freiberg, 2010, p. 84).

Power is defined as the potential and perceived ability of one party to influence the behaviour of another party (e.g., Freiberg, 2010; French & Raven, 1959; see also Gangl, Hofmann, & Kirchler, 2015). French and Raven (1959) and Raven (1965) developed the concept of bases of social power which distinguishes between coercive power, reward power, legitimate power, expert power, referent power, and information power. These different bases of power can be integrated into a two-dimensional structure of harsh (i.e., coercive and reward power) and soft (i.e., legitimate, expert, referent and information power) forms of power (Raven, Schwarzwald, & Koslowsky, 1998), which we will discuss under the generalized terms *coercive power* versus *legitimate power*.

Coercive power is related to the tax authorities' potential to punish. In a taxpaying context, coercive power aims at strictly monitoring taxpayers' behaviour and punishing misbehaviour. Until recently, the tools most often used to regulate tax behaviour were founded in the concept of coercive power and manifested as command-and-control approaches through audits and fines. The concept of coercive power is based on legal compulsion as those who do not obey the rules of the authority will face criminal sanctions.

Legitimate power is related to citizens' perceptions of tax authorities' rightfulness and expertise. In a taxpaying context, the concept of legitimate power is founded on other bases than compulsion and pressure, instead trying to convince taxpayers that voluntarily cooperating is the right course of action (Raven, 1965, 1992, 1993; and also Pierro, Raven, Amato, & Bélanger, 2013; Tyler, 2006).

16.5.2 Forms of Regulation

With regard to forms of regulation, coercive power is related to prescriptive regulation. According to Freiberg (2010), prescriptive regulation relies on rules or statements that specify precisely what is required to be done. Such regulation enforces adherence to rules and statements, focuses on deterrence-based compliance, and is quite rigid. In contrast to this rigid, authoritarian paradigm, performance-based regulation and principle-based regulation are more flexible and are related to legitimate power. While performance-based regulation specifies desired outcomes, it is flexible with regard to the means applied to reach these outcomes. Principle-based regulation relies on agreements on conduct that are accepted in a group and expressed by objectives and duties at a high level of generality (Freiberg, 2010). While rigid forms of regulation, i.e., authorities approaching taxpayers in undifferentiated ways, are likely to be perceived as a manifestation of coercive power, more flexible forms of regulation are likely to be perceived in terms of power based on expertise and legitimization. Moreover, flexible forms of regulation stimulate the development of trust in authorities.

Flexibility means that tax authorities treat taxpayers in differentiated, partly individualized ways. V. Braithwaite (2003) has identified five motivational postures of taxpayers: Commitment and capitulation reflect an overall positive orientation towards tax authorities, whereas resistance, disengagement and game playing reflect a negative orientation. Commitment and capitulation are positively related to tax compliance, whereas the other three postures are related to tax avoidance and evasion. While commitment and capitulation are the most prevalent motivational postures, resistance, game playing, and disengagement are found less frequently.

Motivational postures describe the stance of taxpayers that tax authorities have to manage when seeking to change taxpaying behaviour. The Australian Taxation Office has developed a model which links motivating factors in taxpayers' compliance behaviour to the appropriate response by the tax office. Figure 16.1 shows the model, adapted from V. Braithwaite (2003) and James, Hasseldine, Hite and Toumi (2003): depending on the motivational posture of taxpayers, regulatory strategies should vary, encompassing self-regulation, enforced self-regulation, discretionary command regulation, and non-discretionary command regulation. When taxpayers admit wrongdoing, correct their mistakes and begin meeting the law's expectations, the tax officials' task is to educate, keep records, and deliver services and advice. Indeed, provision of services has been found to be significantly related to compliance (Gangl et al., 2013). When taxpayers behave in an adversarial fashion, show resistance and

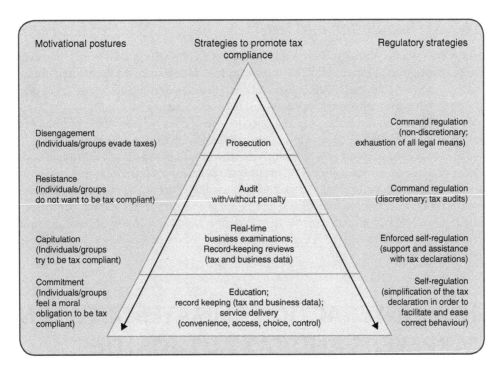

FIGURE 16.1 *Australian Taxation Office compliance model.*

Source: Adapted from Braithwaite, 2003, p. 3, and from James et al., 2003, with permission from Ashgate.

disengagement, tax officials should respond with much harder measures such as command regulation, and finally respond with prosecution.

It can be hypothesized that rigid, authoritarian regulation based on prescriptive rules and enforcement by coercive power manifestation leads to the impression that tax authorities are approaching compliant and less compliant taxpayers in a uniform way. The applied command-and-control tools are directed to all taxpayers independent of their motivation, their willingness and ability to comply, or their intent to free-ride. This undifferentiated approach may cause negative feelings such as uncertainty, anger, and anxiety. It may lead to perceptions of arbitrariness, and it may undermine trust.

On the other hand, more flexible regulation, especially responsive regulation, should lead to the perception of professionalism and expertise on the part of authorities. Distinctive measures – applied to react to commitment or resistance appropriately – are assumed to be perceived as necessary and just. Regulators need to have a variety of regulatory measures available, to apply them in response to taxpayers' behaviour, and to be realistic enough to use 'the iron fist' in case of repeated evasion. Ayres and Braithwaite (1992) in their model of responsive regulation assume that compliance is most likely when tax authorities follow an explicit enforcement pyramid: they propose a 'tit for tat' approach, by which increasing non-compliance is dealt with increasing seriousness of sanctions (Freiberg, 2010). Severe sanctions, serving as well-targeted threats, are assumed to increase honest taxpayers' feelings of security and protection against free-riders, and as protection of collective responsibility.

16.5.3 *Regulation and Trust*

Flexible regulation through both legitimate power and well-directed coercive power should strengthen the perception of the authorities as legitimized experts, and consequently increase trust in the authorities and cooperation with the authorities. It can also be argued that trust among citizens and trust between citizens and authorities are necessary preconditions for the accepted and effective use of coercive power and punishment by the authorities (Bailliet & van Lange, 2013; Parks, Joireman, & van Lange, 2013).

In the tax context, trust was differentiated into reason-based trust and implicit trust in the socio-cognitive trust theory (Castelfranchi & Falcone, 2010). Reason-based trust means that the tax authorities are trusted because they pursue relevant goals, because taxpayers depend on the authorities, and because the authorities appear competent and benevolent. In contrast, implicit trust is defined as an automatic and unconscious trust reaction to the perception that the tax authorities are part of one's own community, sharing one's own values.

16.6 INTERACTION CLIMATES BETWEEN TAXPAYERS AND TAX AUTHORITIES

16.6.1 *Antagonistic and Synergistic Interaction Climates*

In their synopsis of economic and psychological determinants of tax compliance, Kirchler, Hoelzl, and Wahl (2008) distinguish – on the one extreme – between an antagonistic interaction climate, i.e., taxpayers and authorities working against each other, and a synergistic interaction climate, i.e., taxpayers and authorities working together, on the other extreme. While the use of power, especially coercive power in a distrustful relationship between citizens and authorities, is assumed to foster an antagonistic climate, mutual trust and protective power are assumed to strengthen cooperation and foster a synergistic climate.

In an antagonistic interaction climate, mutual trust between taxpayers and authorities is eroded and compliance needs to be enforced. Tax authorities approach taxpayers as potential criminals who only comply with the law if forced to. Taxpayers feel prosecuted, repulse the tight net of rules limiting their freedom, and hide from the enforcing authorities by trying to take rational, utility-maximizing decisions whether to comply or to evade, on the basis of perceived audit probability and severity of fines in case of detected evasion. There is no binding psychological contract between the authorities and taxpayers prescribing cooperation, and no intrinsic motivation to follow the rules (V. Braithwaite, 2003; Feld & Frey, 2007; 2010; Rousseau, 1995). In an antagonistic climate, taxpayers neither trust in the benevolence of authorities nor in the cooperativeness of other taxpayers. If the authorities are not perceived as cooperative and other taxpayers are assumed not to pay their taxes properly, the intent to avoid and evade one's one tax duty is likely to be strong (Rothstein, 2000).

In a synergistic interaction climate, taxpayers and authorities trust in each other's willingness to cooperate voluntarily. A powerful legal system, a strong economy and especially an efficient government that provides essential services and guarantees public goods can establish binding rules of fair play. Tax authorities are not seen as dominant agencies that enforce tax compliance, but as agents acting in the service of citizens towards the well-being of the community. Both legitimate power and reason-based trust in authorities are the prerequisites of a synergistic climate.

Authorities using fair procedures and engaging in assisting taxpayers rather than exclusively focusing on audits and fines are perceived as trustworthy. A strong psychological contract ensures voluntary cooperation. This resembles the trust paradigm identified by Alm and Torgler (2011) as one of the three paradigms of tax administration. In the traditional enforcement paradigm, taxpayers are treated as potential criminals. In the service paradigm, tax authorities acknowledge the necessity to make tax compliance easier by way of offering service. In the trust paradigm, the importance of building trust between interacting parties is emphasized, and trust is based on the expectation of both taxpayers and tax authorities that the other party will act beneficially (Gambetta, 1988).

16.6.2   Slippery Slope Framework

In the slippery slope framework, Kirchler, Hoelzl, and Wahl (2008) and Kirchler, Kogler, and Muehlbacher (2014) propose that in an antagonistic interaction climate, the strong power of the authorities leads to enforced compliance. In a synergistic climate, strong mutual trust leads to voluntary cooperation (Figure 16.2). Voluntary

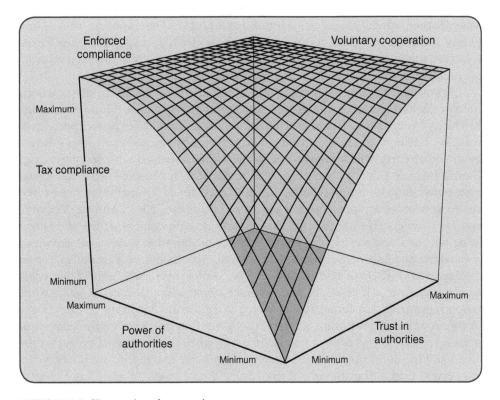

FIGURE 16.2 *Slippery slope framework.*

Source: Adapted from Kirchler, Hoelzl, & Wahl, 2008, p. 212, with permission by Elsevier.

cooperation depends primarily on trust in the state and its authorities; however, if cooperation does not occur voluntarily, tax compliance needs to be secured by force. Power includes all the measures that serve the purpose of deterrence, e.g., efficient tax audits and high fines for evasion. On the other hand, trust in the authorities requires tax laws which are understood by the taxpayers, services helping to comply, positive attitudes towards taxation and high tax morale by taxpayers, distributional and procedural fairness, and the belief that compliance is the norm rather than the exception, i.e., social norms demanding cooperation. Moreover, trust also originates from proper use of power, in the sense that the authorities protect the cooperative majority from free-riders.

The assumptions of the slippery slope framework were tested empirically by Wahl, Kastlunger, and Kirchler (2010). Specifically, it was examined whether tax compliance is high in cases of trustworthy authorities as well as in cases of deterrence. Moreover, the quality of compliance was examined. In a laboratory experiment, participants imagined living in a fictitious country and paying their taxes to authorities that were either trusted or not, and powerful or not. In 20 experimental periods, participants earned income and filed tax returns. It was found that participants were most compliant if authorities were described as trustworthy rather than untrustworthy and powerful rather than weak. Voluntary cooperation was high when authorities were described as trustworthy, and enforced compliance was high when the country was described as being ruled by powerful authorities. Similar results were reported by Kastlunger, Lozza, Kirchler, and Schabmann (2013), Kogler, Batrancea, Nichita, Pantya, Belianin and Kirchler (2013), and by Muehlbacher, Kirchler, and Schwarzenberger (2011). They confirm the assumptions of the slippery slope framework and show also that taxpayers feeling forced to contribute by the authorities attempt to think strategically about how to avoid tax pressure, rather than cooperating spontaneously.

The power-enhancing and trust-building measures proposed in the slippery slope framework have complex interactions and dynamics over time (Hofmann, Gangl, Kirchler, & Stark, 2014). Power exerted by authorities may evoke suspicion and mistrust by citizens, resulting in a vicious circle: mistrust by one party provokes mistrust by the other party, which justifies and deepens the mistrust by the first party (e.g., Castelfranchi & Falcone, 2010, Farrell & Knight, 2003; Nooteboom, 2002). However, power can also positively affect trust. The power of an institution can be perceived as a necessary precondition for trust (Bachmann, 2001). Mulder, Verboon, and De Cremer (2009) argue that the law and its enforcement define the norms to be followed, and sanctioning systems can be perceived as a means of enforcing societal norms. As a consequence, trust would increase due to authorities' power (Mulder, van Dijk, De Cremer, & Wilke, 2006). Korczynski (2000) argued that while trust is undermined if power is used to coerce cooperation, trust can increase when power is exerted by an authority that is seen as legitimate. According to Choudhury (2008), power and monitoring decrease trust when they are based on surveillance or unclear regulations, whereas the opposite is true when the exertion of power is rule-based and the authorities monitor behaviour in a fair manner. In summary, when the power of tax authorities is perceived as legitimate power, it likely has a positive effect on citizens' trust.

16.7   PRACTICAL IMPLICATIONS

Institutions and authorities are beginning to recognize that trust-building measures promote cooperation. New forms of interaction between authorities and taxpayers, termed cooperative relationships or horizontal monitoring, are being tested out in several countries. Beginning in 2005 in the Netherlands, tax authorities are switching from traditional vertical monitoring to horizontal monitoring (Stevens, Pheijffer, van den Broek, Keijzer, & van der Hel-van Dijk, 2012). Vertical monitoring is based on checking tax files retroactively, whereas horizontal monitoring focuses on fair play, understanding and transparency between taxpayers and the authorities, and the planning of future activities of businesses and their tax consequences. Horizontal monitoring is based on a trust relationship between taxpayers and the authorities which is recorded in a compliance agreement, and on an effective tax control framework.

If taxpayers are perceived to be selfish, profit-maximizing individuals, unavoidably it must be concluded that contributions will not made voluntarily but only be paid when enforced. The strategies to secure tax compliance in this situation are audits and fines (Allingham & Sandmo, 1972; Srinivasan, 1973). However, evidence grows that these strategies are less successful than predicted by theory. Therefore, it is necessary to adopt strategies building on both economic and psychological arguments to promote cooperation (Alm & Torgler, 2011; J. Braithwaite, 2005; 2008; V. Braithwaite, 2009; James, Hasseldine, Hite, & Toumi, 2003). Reviews of empirical studies in economics and psychology provide ample evidence of the manifold determinants of tax compliance which have practical implications (Kirchler 2007). The following list contains some suggested measures (Alm & Torgler, 2011; Alm, Kirchler, & Muehlbacher, 2012):

1. Monitoring and audits are important to protect honest taxpayers from free-riders. Audits need to be focused on at-risk groups and effectively implemented. Audits need to be perceived as a manifestation of power with the aim of protecting cooperative citizens from free-riders. Negative sanctions need to be adequate in level and form, in line with retributive justice.

2. Tax authorities need to be well trained, and they need to cooperate intensively with legislators, judges, and international authorities in order to fight tax evasion and excessive tax avoidance. There is also need to strengthen the dialogue between commissioners, businesses and researchers. Tax authorities, and above all tax auditors, need to be efficiently trained so that they are both experts in tax law and experts in applying different regulation strategies effectively.

3. Tax law needs to be simplified so that taxpayers understand it and can abide by the law. Instead of a plethora of rules with exceptions, principles of behaviour need to be fixed in law to minimize the space for interpretation and negotiation. Services for taxpayers need to be improved. Taxpayers need to be segmented according to their needs, so that appropriate services can be offered to facilitate tax honesty.

4. Distributive justice and procedural justice need to be taken seriously. The use of tax money needs to be transparent; advertising campaigns should be used to inform the public of the services available, so that the fair exchange of tax contributions, on the one hand, for state services on the other is clear. Procedures for determining tax contributions need to be transparent and fair, and tax authorities need to ensure adherence to these procedures.

5. Establishment and communication of social norms of correct behaviour are necessary. Measures need to be taken that strengthen the identification of citizens and companies with the community.

16.8   SUMMARY

To summarize, this chapter highlighted that tax behaviour can only partly be understood by a simple reaction to audits and fines. It showed that it is necessary to understand how citizens see taxes in general, and tax laws and tax authorities in particular. It also showed that at the company level, it is necessary to move towards a system that can reduce tax avoidance, not only tax evasion. For tax authorities, one potential way is to rethink regulation strategies. Several recent approaches highlight the interaction between the power of tax authorities and the trust of citizens and companies in the tax authorities. These approaches incorporate important psychological concepts into tax policy and regulation.

REVIEW QUESTIONS

1. What is responsive regulation?
2. Give four examples of economic and psychological determinants of tax compliance.
3. Describe the concepts antagonistic and synergistic interaction climate.
4. Is tax evasion perceived as a serious crime? Describe the empirical findings on this matter.
5. What are the differences between tax evasion and tax avoidance from a legal perspective and from a psychological perspective?

REFERENCES

Allingham, M. G., & Sandmo, A. (1972). Income tax evasion: A theoretical analysis. *Journal of Public Economics, 1*(3–4), 323–338. DOI:10.1016/0047-2727(72)90010-2

Alm, J., Kirchler, E., & Muehlbacher, S. (2012). Combining psychology and economics in the analysis of compliance: From enforcement to cooperation. *Economic Analysis and Policy, 42*(2), 133–151. DOI:10.1016/S0313-5926(12)50016-0

Alm, J., & Torgler, B. (2011). Do ethics matter? Tax compliance and morality. *Journal of Business Ethics, 101*(4), 635–651. DOI:10.1007/s10551-011-0761-9

Andreoni, J., Erard, B., & Feinstein, J. S. (1998). Tax compliance. *Journal of Economic Literature, 36*(2), 818–860. Retrieved from http://www.jstor.org/stable/2565123

Ayres, I., & Braithwaite, J. (1992). *Responsive regulation: Transcending the deregulation debate.* New York: Oxford University Press.

Bachmann, R. (2001). Trust, power and control in trans-organizational relations. *Organization Studies, 22*(2), 337–365. DOI:10.1177/0170840601222007

Bailliet, D., & van Lange, P. A. M. (2013). Trust, punishment, and cooperation across 18 societies: A meta analysis. *Perspectives on Psychological Science, 8*(4), 363–379. DOI:10.1177/1745691613488533

Braithwaite, J. (2005). *Markets in vice, markets in virtue.* Leichhardt, Australia: The Federation Press.

Braithwaite, J. (2008). *Regulatory capitalism. How it works, ideas for making it work better.* Cheltenham: Elsevier.

Braithwaite, V. (2003). A new approach to tax compliance. In V. Braithwaite (Ed.), *Taxing democracy: Understanding tax avoidance and tax evasion* (pp. 1–11). Aldershot: Ashgate.

Braithwaite, V. (2009). *Defiance in taxation and governance. Resisting and dismissing authority in a democracy.* Cheltenham: Edward Elgar.

Brehm, J. W. (1966). *Theory of psychological reactance.* New York: Academic Press.

Bund der Steuerzahler Deutschland e.V. (2014, July 24). *Die Steuermoral ist top.* Retrieved from http://www.steuerzahler.de/Die-Steuermoral-ist-top/62049c71880i1p637/index.html

Castelfranchi, C., & Falcone, R. (2010). *Trust theory. A socio-cognitive and computational model.* Chichester: Wiley.

Choudhury, E. (2008). Trust in administration: An integrative approach to optimal trust. *Administration & Society, 40*(6), 586–620. DOI:10.1177/0095399708321681

Farrell, H., & Knight, J. (2003). Trust, institutions, and institutional change: Industrial districts and the social capital hypothesis. *Politics and Society, 31*(4), 537–566. DOI:10.1177/0032329203256954

Feld, L. P., & Frey, B. S. (2007). Tax compliance as the result of a psychological tax contract: The role of incentives and responsive regulation. *Law & Policy, 29*(1), 102–120. DOI:10.1111/j.1467-9930.2007.00248.x

Feld, L. P., & Frey, B. S. (2010). Tax evasion and the psychological tax contract. In J. Alm, J. Martinez-Vazquez, & B. Torgler (Eds.), *Developing alternative frameworks for explaining tax compliance* (pp. 74–94). London: Routledge.

Frecknall-Hughes, J. (2013, May). What is tax avoidance? A consideration of different viewpoints. Presentation at the DIBT Research Seminar, Vienna University of Economics and Business.

Frecknall-Hughes, J., & Kirchler, E. (2015). Towards a general theory of tax practice. *Social & Legal Studies, 24*, 289–312. DOI:10.1177/0964663915571787

Freiberg, A. (2010). *The tools of regulation.* Leichhardt, Australia: The Federation Press.

French, J. R., & Raven, B. (1959). The bases of social power. In D. Cartwright (Ed.), *Studies in social power* (pp. 150–167). Ann Arbor: University of Michigan Press.

Fuest, C., Spengel, C., Finke, K., Heckemeyer, J. H., & Nusser, H. (2013). Profit shifting and 'aggressive' tax planning by multinational firms: Issues and options for reform. *World Tax Journal, October*, 307–324.

Gambetta, D. (Ed.). (1988). *Trust: Making and breaking co-operative relations.* Oxford: Basil Blackwell.

Gangl, K., Hofmann, E., & Kirchler, E. (2015). Tax authorities' interaction with taxpayers: A conception of compliance in social dilemmas by power and trust. *New Ideas in Psychology, 37*, 13–23. DOI:10.1016/j.newideapsych.2014.12.001

Gangl, K., Muehlbacher, S., de Groot, M., Goslinga, S., Hofmann, E., ... & Kirchler, E. (2013). 'How can I help you?' Perceived service orientation of tax authorities and tax compliance. *FinanzArchiv, 69*(4), 487–510. DOI:10.1628/001522113X675683

Hey, J., Schreiber, U., Pönnighaus, F., & Bierbrauer, F. (2013). Steueroasen und „legale Steuervermeidung": Wie kann größere Steuergerechtigkeit erreicht werden? *ifo Schnelldienst, 66*(11), 3–6.

Hofmann, E., Gangl, K., Kirchler, E., & Stark, J. (2014). Enhancing tax compliance through coercive and legitimate power of tax authorities by concurrently diminishing or facilitating trust in tax authorities. *Law & Policy, 36*(3), 290–313. DOI:10.1111/lapo.12021

James, S., Hasseldine, J. D., Hite, P. A., & Toumi, M. (2003, December). Tax compliance policy: An international comparison and new evidence on normative appeals and auditing. Paper presented at the ESRC Future Governance Workshop, Institute for Advanced Studies, Vienna, Austria.

Kastlunger, B., Lozza, E., Kirchler, E., & Schabmann, A. (2013). Powerful authorities and trusting citizens: The slippery slope framework and tax compliance in Italy. *Journal of Economic Psychology, 34*(1), 36–54. DOI:10.1016/j.joep.2012.11.007

Kirchler, E. (1998). Differential representations of taxes: Analysis of free associations and judgments of five employment groups. *Journal of Socio Economics, 27*(1), 117–131. DOI:10.1016/S1053-5357(99)80080-8

Kirchler, E. (1999). Reactance to taxation: Employers' attitudes towards taxes. *Journal of Socio Economics, 28*(2), 131–138. DOI:10.1016/S1053-5357(99)00003-7

Kirchler, E. (2007). *The economic psychology of tax behaviour.* Cambridge: Cambridge University Press.

Kirchler, E., Hoelzl, E., & Wahl, I. (2008). Enforced versus voluntary tax compliance: The 'slippery slope' framework. *Journal of Economic Psychology, 29*(2), 210–225. DOI:10.1016/j.joep.2007.05.004

Kirchler, E., Kogler, C., & Muehlbacher, S. (2014). Cooperative tax compliance: From deterrence to deference. *Current Directions in Psychological Science, 23*(2), 87–92. DOI:10.1177/0963721413516975

Kirchler, E., Maciejovsky, B., & Schneider, F. (2003). Everyday representations of tax avoidance, tax evasion, and tax flight: Do legal differences matter? *Journal of Economic Psychology, 24*(4), 535–553. DOI:10.1016/S0167-4870(02)00164-2

Kogler, C., Batrancea, L., Nichita, A., Pantya, J., Belianin, A., & Kirchler, E. (2013). Trust and power as determinants of tax compliance: Testing the assumptions of the slippery slope framework in Austria, Hungary, Romania and Russia. *Journal of Economic Psychology, 34*(1), 169–180. DOI:10.1016/j.joep.2012.09.010

Korczynski, M. (2000). The political economy of trust. *Journal of Management Studies, 37*(1), 1–21. DOI:10.1111/1467-6486.00170

McKerchar, M. (2001). The study of income tax complexity and unintentional noncompliance: Research method and preliminary findings. Atax Discussion Paper No. 6. Available at SSRN: http://ssrn.com/abstract=623627 or http://dx.doi.org/10.2139/ssrn.623627.

Muehlbacher, S., & Kirchler, E. (2013). Mental accounting of self-employed taxpayers: On the mental segregation of the net income and the tax due. *FinanzArchiv, 69*(4), 412–438. DOI:10.1628/001522113X675656

Muehlbacher, S., Kirchler, E., & Schwarzenberger, H. (2011). Voluntary vs. enforced tax compliance: Empirical evidence for the 'slippery slope' framework. *European Journal of Law & Economics, 32*(1), 89–97. DOI:10.1007/s10657-011-9236-9

Mulder, L. B., van Dijk, E., De Cremer, D., & Wilke, H. A. M. (2006). Undermining trust and cooperation: The paradox of sanctioning systems in social dilemmas. *Journal of Experimental Social Psychology, 42*(2), 147–162. DOI:10.1016/j.jesp.2005.03.002

Mulder, L. B., Verboon, P., & De Cremer, D. (2009). Sanctions and moral judgments: The moderating effect of sanction severity and trust in authorities. *European Journal of Social Psychology, 39*(2), 255–269. DOI:10.1002/ejsp.506

Niemirowski, P., & Wearing, A. (2003). Taxation agents and taxpayer compliance. *Journal of Australian Taxation, 6*(2), 166–200.

Nooteboom, B. (2002). *Trust: Forms, foundations, functions, failures and figures.* Cheltenham: Edward Elgar.

OECD (2013). *Co-operative compliance: A framework: from enhanced relationship to co-operative compliance.* Paris: OECD. DOI:10.1787/9789264200852-en

Oishi, S., Schimmack, U., & Diener, E. (2012). Progressive taxation and the subjective well-being of nations. *Psychological Science, 23*(1), 86–92. DOI:10.1177/0956797611420882

Owens, J., & Hamilton, S. (2004). Experience and innovations in other countries. In H. J. Aaron, & J. Slemrod (Eds.), *The crisis in tax administration* (pp. 347–388). Washington, DC: Brookings Institution Press.

Parks, C. D., Joireman, J., & van Lange, P. A. M. (2013). Cooperation, trust, and antagonism: How public goods are promoted. *Psychological Science in the Public Interest, 14*(3), 119–165. DOI:10.1177/1529100612474436

Pierro, A., Raven, B. H., Amato, C., & Bélanger, J. J. (2013). Bases of social power, leadership styles, and organizational commitment. *International Journal of Psychology, 48*(6), 1122–1134. DOI:10.1080/00207594.2012.733398

Pickhardt, M., & Prinz, A. (2014). Behavioral dynamics of tax evasion. A survey. *Journal of Economic Psychology, 40*, 1–19. DOI:10.1016/j.joep.2013.08.006

Raven, B. H. (1965). Social influence and power. In I. D. Steiner, & M. Fishbein (Eds.), *Current studies in social psychology* (pp. 371–382). New York: Holt, Rinehart and Winston.

Raven, B. H. (1992). A power/interaction model of interpersonal influence: French and Raven thirty years later. *Journal of Social Behavior and Personality, 7*(2), 217–244.

Raven, B. H. (1993). The bases of power: Origins and recent developments. *Journal of Social Issues, 49*(4), 227–251. DOI:10.1111/j.1540-4560.1993.tb01191.x

Raven, B. H., Schwarzwald, J., & Koslowsky, M. (1998). Conceptualizing and measuring a power/interaction model of interpersonal influence. *Journal of Applied Social Psychology, 28*(4), 307–332. DOI:10.1111/j.1559-1816.1998.tb01708.x

Rothstein, B. (2000). Trust, social dilemmas, and collective memories: On the rise and decline of the Swedish model. *Journal of Theoretical Politics, 12*(4), 477–499. DOI:10.1177/0951692800012004007

Rousseau, D. (1995). *Psychological contracts in organization: Understanding written and unwritten agreements*. Thousand Oaks, CA: Sage.

Sakurai, Y., & Braithwaite, V. (2003). Taxpayers' perceptions of practitioners: Finding one who is effective and does the right thing? *Journal of Business Ethics, 46*(4), 375–387. DOI:10.1023/A:1025641518700

Schmölders, G. (1959). Fiscal psychology: A new branch of public finance. *National Tax Journal, 12*(4), 340–345. Retrieved from http://www.jstor.org/stable/41790780

Slemrod, J., Blumenthal, M., & Christian, C. (2001). Taxpayer response to an increased probability of audit: Evidence from a controlled experiment in Minnesota. *Journal of Public Economics, 79*(3), 455–483. DOI:10.1016/S0047-2727(99)00107-3

Song, Y., & Yarbrough, T. E. (1978). Tax ethics and taxpayer attitudes: A survey. *Public Administration Review, 38*(5), 442–452. DOI:10.2307/975503

Srinivasan, T. N. (1973). Tax evasion: A model. *Journal of Public Economics, 2*(4), 339–346. DOI:10.1016/0047-2727(73)90024-8

Stevens, L. G. M., Pheijffer, M., van den Broek, J. G. A., Keijzer, T. J. & van der Hel-van Dijk, E. C. J. M. (2012). *Tax supervision – Made to measure*. Committee Horizontal Monitoring and Customs Administration. Available at http://download.belastingdienst.nl/belastingdienst/docs/tax_supervision_made_to_measure_tz0151z1fdeng.pdf.

Sussman, A. B., & Olivola, C. Y. (2011). Axe the tax: Taxes are disliked more than equivalent costs. *Journal of Marketing Research, 48*(SPL), S91–S101. DOI:10.1509/jmkr.48.SPL.S91.

Torgler, B. (2007). *Tax compliance and tax morale: A theoretical and empirical analysis*. Cheltenham: Edward Elgar.

Tyler, T. R. (2006). Psychological perspectives on legitimacy and legitimation. *Annual Review of Psychology, 57*, 375–400. DOI:10.1146/annurev.psych.57.102904.190038

Vogel, J. (1974). Taxation and public opinion in Sweden: An interpretation of recent survey data. *National Tax Journal, 27*(4), 499–513. Retrieved from http://www.jstor.org/stable/41861983

Wahl, I., Kastlunger, B., & Kirchler, E. (2010). Trust in authorities and power to enforce tax compliance: An empirical analysis of the 'slippery slope framework'. *Law & Policy, 32*(4), 383–406. DOI:10.1111/j.1467-9930.2010.00327.x

FURTHER READING

Braithwaite, V. (2009). *Defiance in taxation and governance. Resisting and dismissing authority in a democracy*. Cheltenham: Edward Elgar.

Freiberg, A. (2010). *The tools of regulation*. Leichhardt, Australia: The Federation Press.

Kirchler, E. (2007). *The economic psychology of tax behaviour*. Cambridge: Cambridge University Press.

PART 5

Economic Activity

17 Volunteer Organizations: Motivating with Awards

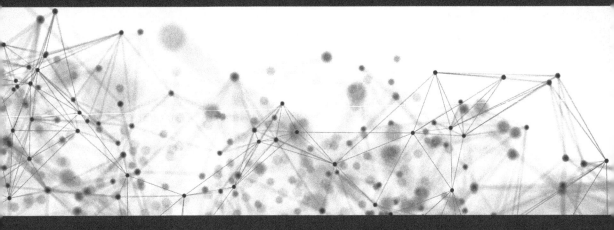

BRUNO S. FREY AND JANA GALLUS

CHAPTER OUTLINE

LEARNING OUTCOMES

BY THE END OF THIS CHAPTER YOU SHOULD BE ABLE TO:

1. Comprehend the nature, origins, and scope of awards.
2. Understand in what way and to what extent award recipients are motivated.
3. Identify why awards are of particular importance in volunteer organizations.

17.1   INTRODUCTION

This chapter deals with a largely neglected issue in the social sciences. While awards exist in all forms of society, in all sectors and in all ages, economists and other social scientists have largely neglected to study them. Our contribution seeks to establish awards as a valuable additional incentive instrument for volunteers. Awards have distinctive features setting them apart from monetary or material rewards, on the one hand, and pure praise, on the other.

After distinguishing between motivational issues in for-profits compared to non-profits, we show that both forms of organization face similar challenges with respect to incentivizing workers (Section 17.2). We discuss the various areas in which awards have been used and consider their distinctive characteristics (Section 17.3). Section 17.4 analyses conditions for successfully bestowing awards. Section 17.5 discusses the empirical evidence available so far on the effects of awards on performance, and Section 17.6 presents the conclusion.

17.2   ORGANIZATIONAL FORMS

17.2.1   For-Profit Firms

Voluntary organizations and for-profit firms are commonly conceived of as polar opposites along a continuum of organizational forms. Corporations hire and bind employees with a formal contract in which the tasks to be performed are exactly specified, and the compensation is precisely determined so that the value of the firm is maximized. Principal-Agent Theory (Holmström, 1979; Jensen & Meckling, 1976; Ross, 1973) acknowledges that it is rarely possible to fully specify the tasks expected from employees because it is in most cases impossible to fully anticipate the performance needed in the future. Moreover, it is often impossible to monitor to what extent employees fulfil the requirements. Based on these restrictions with respect to the formulation of employment contracts, it has been concluded that mechanisms have to be introduced that align the interests of the owners of the firm (the shareholders, as principals) with those of the employees (the agents).

Pay-for-performance has been suggested as an effective means for bringing the divergent interests of the two groups together. This idea rests on the fundamental micro-economic assumption that people are solely motivated by extrinsic incentives. Their behaviour is taken to be entirely determined by monetary considerations, i.e., the incentive provided by the wages to be received. If the contract is not well fulfilled, negative sanctions including dismissal or legal sanctions may be enforced.

Pay-for-performance has, however, led to severe negative consequences in the economy. It has been overlooked that some employees, in particular, managers, have to some extent been able to determine the criteria relevant to receive a bonus. They have also been able to manipulate the performance measurement so that they meet the criteria. As a result, the income of managers has virtually exploded, and the distribution of income has been strongly tilted in favour of high-income recipients (Bebchuk & Fried, 2009). The fact that in most Western countries the rich have become much richer, while the incomes of the middle and lower classes have stagnated, has been the subject of much political and social concern (e.g. Piketty, 2014).

17.2.2   Voluntary Organizations

Individuals working voluntarily and without payment in an organization with a humanitarian or other social goal are usually not subject to formal enforcement mechanisms. Though it might be legally possible to hold volunteers accountable if they have signed a contract, volunteer organizations are most reluctant to apply negative sanctions as this is inconsistent with their goals. They are rightly concerned that if they use force, they will lose many, if not most of their volunteers. People's intent to engage in a social activity is predominantly based on intrinsic motivations. They are willing to work for free because they want to do something useful for society, in accordance with the values they hold dear. Volunteering also raises their self-esteem. Compared to these intrinsic motivations, extrinsic ones such as learning new tasks, gaining social esteem, or furthering a specific career orientation play a small role (see e.g., Oostlander et al., 2012, p. 26).

A major challenge for organizations working with volunteers is to uphold the retention rate over an extended period of time. Many volunteers commit themselves only for a rather short time. A survey among Swiss institutions reveals that 60% have been active between 0 and 5 years, and only 7% have been active for 15 years and longer. Moreover, they have spent relatively few hours as volunteers. 83% work between 0 and 5 hours per week, and only 3% work more than 10 hours (Oostlander et al., 2012, p. 9). In many organizations depending on voluntary work, it has become increasingly difficult to motivate volunteers to stay. Thus, for example, Wikipedia faces increasing difficulties in retaining editors. A study in 2009 found that 60% of registered editors never completed another edit after their first 24 hours (Panciera, Halfaker, & Terveen, 2009). The community of editors behind Wikipedia has been steadily shrinking after having reached a peak in 2007 (Halfaker, Geiger, Morgan, & Riedl, 2013).

17.2.3   Similarities

The previous sections have argued that there are fundamental differences between for-profit-firms and voluntary organizations. However, on closer inspection, the differences are quite small, and in some respects even disappear. Organizations in both sectors have to motivate individuals to go beyond the call of duty.

It has increasingly been realized that corporations cannot easily motivate their employees by applying extrinsic incentives only. Intrinsic motivation – which is at the heart of voluntary organizations – plays a significant role also in firms working in a strict market environment. A firm's management has to rely on intrinsic motivation in areas where formal contracts and monitoring are difficult, impossible, or too costly to apply. There is extensive empirical evidence that one of the most important resources of firms, creativity, crucially depends on employees having an intrinsic interest in the work they do (Amabile, 1997). The literature on crowding-out effects has firmly established that monetary incentives as well as the threat of negative sanctions under relevant conditions undermine intrinsic motivation (for psychological evidence, see Deci, Koestner, & Ryan, 1999); the concept was introduced into economics and management theory by Bénabou and Tirole (2003), Frey (1997), and Frey and Jegen (2001).

The fact that intrinsic motivation is relevant both for voluntary organizations and for-profit-firms moves them closer together. The psychological determinants of intrinsic motivation, in particular, self-determination and autonomy, become more important compared to extrinsic incentives such as performance pay, other types of bonuses, and negative sanctions in the form of threat of dismissal.

Both types of institutions have to take into consideration the following aspects related to the instruments used to reach their goals:

- *Monetary incentives play a limited role.* Neither of the two types of institution can reach their goals relying solely on such extrinsic incentives. This insight deviates fundamentally from standard economics claiming that it is always possible to induce people by money, the only condition being that the monetary incentive is high enough.

- *An attempt to substitute pay for intrinsic motivation backfires.* Indeed, the higher the monetary compensation is, the lower is intrinsic motivation, which is required for a creative organization and economy.

- *Intrinsic motivation can be maintained and raised by acknowledging that one of the most important, if not the most important, motivator for people is social recognition.* Income is, of course, also relevant; but it is subject to decreasing marginal returns. Once a reasonable income level has been reached, income loses its attraction compared to the need for appreciation. What is considered a 'reasonable' real disposable income depends on circumstances, such as family size. Even more important is the social environment, i.e., the personal comparisons undertaken with referent peers. People tend to compare themselves to individuals and families with a higher income level, which continually pushes up the income level taken to be acceptable. Extensive research on happiness suggests that increases in income have a rather short-lived effect on subjective well-being (see e.g., Easterlin, 2001; Frey, 2008; Frey & Stutzer, 2002a, 2002b; Layard, 2011).

- *Praise addresses people's desire for recognition*, provided it is honest. It has the disadvantage that its effect evaporates rather quickly and also praise may not be given too often.

- *Giving awards is an effective way to cater for people's desire to be appreciated.* Awards are always given in a public ceremony, which makes the act known to peers and family whose judgement is particularly valuable. Orders, crosses, medals, decorations, trophies, prizes, and other honours are designed to raise the intrinsic motivation of the recipients.

At first sight, for-profit institutions seem to basically differ from volunteer institutions with respect to the incentive systems they use. We have shown that there are more similarities between them than one would expect. In particular, the central role of intrinsic motivation for performance and how it can be crowded out by external interventions makes it important to carefully search for alternatives to monetary incentives. The next sections deal more fully with awards as motivators and supporters of intrinsic motivation.

17.3   AWARDS AS MOTIVATION

17.3.1   Ubiquity of Awards

Historically, the use of awards is intimately related to monarchic systems. However, even staunch republics have from early on relied on orders to reward merit. Up to this day awards have remained ubiquitous both in monarchies and in republics.

17.3.2   State Orders

The French Republic hands out the highly valued Légion d'honneur, which ranges from the Chevalier up to the Grand Croix. Napoléon Bonaparte founded it when he was First Consul, and later extended it when he became Emperor. The Légion d'honneur served as the model for many other modern orders of merit, which are often subdivided into similar classes.

Today, the best-known order probably is the Order of the Garter. It was founded in 1348 and is given as the British sovereign's personal gift. The United Kingdom has many other orders ceremonially bequeathed by the Queen. In most cases, however, it is the British government who decides who is honoured.

Not only monarchs and governments bestow awards. Non-profit organizations hand out a large number of honours, too. In the arts and media, sports, religion, the voluntary sector, and academia, awards are most prominent. More surprisingly, even the for-profit sector, which is supposedly only geared to increasing financial gain, sports an astonishing number and diversity of honours.

17.3.3   Arts and Media

The Academy Awards (the Oscars) and the prizes given at the film festivals in Cannes, Venice, Locarno, or Berlin, feature many different categories to recognize persons involved in the movie industry. The Emmy Awards honour outstanding achievement in television, and the Grammy Awards are given for artistic significance in the field of recording in the United States. There are several major literary prizes handed out in various countries around the globe, such as the Pulitzer Prize, the British Man Booker Prize or France's Prix Goncourt, and, of course, the Nobel Prize in Literature.

17.3.4   Sports

At regular intervals, the titles Olympic or World Champion, as well as national, regional, and city champions, are awarded. In chess, there are International Masters (IM) and Grand Masters (GM). Athletes get the honour of being elected Sports Personality of the Year and are admitted into one of the many halls of fame. In soccer, the FIFA accords Orders of Merit to honour particularly successful players. At world championships, not only is the winning team awarded a golden trophy; specific players are also singled out for their special performance, being made Man of the Match or given the Golden Ball, Golden Boot, or Golden Glove (all of which are sponsored by private firms).

17.3.5 Academia

Universities hand out the titles of honorary doctor or senator, and professional scientific associations award an enormous number of medals and prizes. The best known are certainly the Nobel Prizes and the Fields Medal in mathematics, the pinnacle of the academic honour system. Moreover, there is a complicated system of titles (not always connected to functions), such as that of lecturer, reader, assistant professor, associate professor (with and without tenure), full professor, named professor, university professor, distinguished professor, and senior professor.

Many prestigious fellowships exist in academies of science, some of which also allow for the use of post-nominal letters as they are known from state orders. Examples are Fellow of the Royal Society (FRS), founded in 1660, and Fellow of the American Academy of Arts and Sciences, founded in 1780. Finally, there is a flood of best paper awards handed out at conferences and by journals. Academia is, next to the military and the arts, one of the domains with most awards.

17.3.6 Business

Titles are very important, even if they are at times little related to functions, such as vice-president, senior vice-president, or first senior vice-president. The number of titles of Chief Officers has virtually exploded. There is a CEO (Chief Executive Officer), a COO (Chief Operating Officer), a CFO (Chief Financial Officer), and many other variants. Firms also commend their own employees for being Salesman of the Week or Employee of the Month. The media actively engage in this activity, for instance, by regularly choosing the Manager of the Month, of the Year, or even of the Century. In a somewhat similar manner, non-profit organizations devoted to business issues equally make an effort to yield influence by bestowing awards. The World Economic Forum, for example, appoints young people it considers to be representative of contemporary leadership to its club of Young Global Leaders.

17.3.7 The Voluntary and Humanitarian Sector

Non-profit organizations bequeath many different awards; indeed it is often their main way of expressing recognition and gratitude to their workers. The International Committee of the Red Cross, for instance, bestows the Florence Nightingale Medal on nurses for 'exceptional courage and devotion'. At a more local level, voluntary organizations such as the fire fighters recognize their members' courage and engagement with many different forms of honours, which are mostly based on tenure or courageous deeds in the face of danger. Volunteer fire departments are the prevalent organizational form in which awards play a major role. These awards are given by non-state entities such as the Austrian Federal Fire Service Association, which has eight different awards, including a Grand Cross of Merit and a Ring of Honour. Finally, award schemes are also used in service clubs such as the Rotary or the Lions, which constitute yet another form of organization active in the humanitarian sector.

This section has illustrated the ubiquity of awards in history as well as in today's world, including in domains that at a first glance seem to be solely governed by money.

17.3.8 Characteristics of Awards

Awards create social value with regard to two different aspects:

- Awards provide *hedonic benefits* to the winners who feel recognized and honoured. Awards raise a person's subjective well-being. This positive effect extends not only to individual winners but also to members of organizations and inhabitants of cities receiving awards. But awards may also produce negative external effects on the people who had hoped to win an award but failed to do so. In this case, awards can reduce satisfaction.

- Awards can be used for instrumental purposes. The givers are able to raise the *performance of their organization* by inducing the necessary changes in the behaviour of employees trying to win the award. Persons not winning an expected award may hope to get the award in the future and therefore put in the effort desired by the giver. Moreover, the award may reinforce important norms, such as helpfulness, and signal what kind of behaviour is deemed honourable. Thus, even persons who do not win an award may be positively influenced in their behaviour and follow the role models created with the award. However, awards may also backfire when disgruntled non-recipients reduce their work effort, or even resort to sabotage.

17.3.9 Differences between Awards and Monetary Incentives

Prizes, or awards, have distinctive advantages over monetary compensation in several respects:

- *Awards are always given in public and often attract media attention.* They have greater visibility than bonuses and other monetary rewards. In most corporations employees are prohibited from revealing their incomes and the bonuses they have received. Recognizing a person is better accomplished by handing out awards than by transferring money to a bank account.

- *Awards can be bequeathed for broad achievements and the performance they honour need only be vaguely specified.* In contrast, pay-for-performance requires that performance can be defined ex ante and measured ex post.

- *Awards strengthen employees' commitment to the organization honouring* them. The intrinsic motivation to perform well and in the interest of the employer is strengthened. In contrast, when an attempt is made to measure performance by pay, this intrinsic work motivation may well be crowded out. All that matters is to reach the criteria in order to get the bonus promised, while the content of work becomes secondary.

- *Awards establish a bond of loyalty between the givers and recipients.* This element of trust refers to both sides. In market settings, there is no such requirement of loyalty.

- *Awards can be used to structure and shape a field.* In the reasons given for bequeathing an award, as well as in the ceremony accompanying the award's conferral, the givers communicate what is important to them, what should be achieved, and how this should be done.

- *Awards are a low cost way to honour persons as well as organizations.* The costs most often consist only of a piece of ribbon given at an award ceremony.

- *Awards are not subject to taxation.* In contrast, monetary bonuses and other material rewards, including fringe benefits (e.g., expensive company cars or luxurious apartments), are taxed.

- *Bequeathing awards provides private benefits to the decision-makers in the award giving institutions.* The media and the social attention gained raise their status in society, making them important people. In the case of famous recipients, award givers may share in their glory.

The reasons given indicate that awards have indeed quite different characteristics from monetary incentives. If wisely used, awards can motivate persons to perform well in tasks which are difficult, or even impossible, to address by offering money. This applies in particular to organizations based on voluntary work for which awards in many respects are almost ideal. However, as is the case with all instruments designed to motivate, it is crucial to apply them in an appropriate way.

17.4 CONDITIONS FOR SUCCESSFULLY GIVING AWARDS TO VOLUNTEERS

Awards need to be applied in a careful way to raise the motivation of volunteers. Wrongly and carelessly applied, they may even backfire, undermining the intrinsic motivation of the persons engaging in voluntary work.

There are six important considerations to be observed.

1. Awards are a suitable motivator when the tasks to be fulfilled cannot be exactly defined and much must be left to the volunteers themselves. A pertinent example is care for the elderly and sick, whose needs greatly differ from each other, not least due to idiosyncratic personality traits. The volunteer in charge must be given sufficient discretion to help in an appropriate way. Bureaucratic rules are inimical to the task. Awards are also suitable when the goals of an organization are inconsistent with the use of money. Most people would, for instance, consider it as immoral if priests were paid a bonus for each person becoming a member of their church. Similarly, most patients would find it inadmissible if their

physician performed an operation on them solely because of the income increase achieved.

2. The award giver must make a great effort to recognize the specific motivation and contribution of an awardee. This requires a good knowledge of the persons singled out to receive an award; it does not suffice to speak about the work performed in general terms.

3. Awards are usually given to individual persons; in rare cases also to teams and organizations as a whole (Frey & Gallus, 2015). Other persons in the same work group, or performing similar tasks elsewhere, may get angry if they do not also receive an award. One might expect that the non-winners would create an atmosphere of dissatisfaction in a work group or even the organization as a whole, reducing the quality of performance, and in the extreme case, leading to sabotage. In order to minimize such results, the award giver can make it clear that the person awarded stands for a whole team, and that he or she represents the other members. Such procedures may even lead others to be proud about the award conferral. Our research suggests that such feelings of jealousy do not usually occur, and that handing out awards to particular people rarely leads to negative reactions (Neckermann, Cueni, & Frey, 2014; Neckermann & Frey, 2013).

4. Awards must be kept scarce. If they are handed out in great numbers, they are no longer taken seriously by both recipients and the public. This is easier said than done. The leaders of an organization have an incentive to hand out awards because it is a low cost way to motivate people. The constitution of many orders therefore limits the number of recipients, but in actual fact these limitations are rarely observed. The Legion d'honneur provides an example. There are not supposed to be more than 1,250 Commandeurs and 250 Grands officiers. In actual fact, however, in 2010, there were 3,009 Commandeurs and 314 Grands officiers.

5. Awards are most effective if they come as a surprise. This is at least partly the case when the award giver has discretionary power over whom to honour. In contrast, other awards come as a normal addition to the monetary compensation (for the distinction between discretionary and confirmatory awards, see Gallus & Frey, 2017). British diplomats in important positions can safely expect to receive an order, normally the Order of St. Michael and St. George, going with the attribute Sir or Dame. Purely confirmatory awards have a weaker effect on motivation than discretionary awards.

6. The award givers must make an effort not to give awards to persons undeserving of this honour. Two cases can be distinguished. Either the persons awarded behaved badly in the past, or they may do so in the future. Other award recipients may be ashamed of being associated with such people and might send back their own award. To honour such undeserving people strongly reduces the reputation of the award and of the award giver.

The conditions for awards to be successful are quite stringent. The requirements present a challenge to the managers of all organizations, and in particular to the leaders of voluntary organizations.

17.5   EFFECTS OF AWARDS ON PERFORMANCE

Many observers, most prominently academic economists committed to standard neo-classical economics (Mankiw, 2015; Mas-Colell, Whinston, & Green, 1995), would doubt whether awards have any effect on subsequent performance. They are at best ready to accept that the recipients of awards experience joy, but would affirm that the effect on performance is negligible and transient. Recent research on the effects of awards in a few cases supports this notion, but in many other cases it has been shown that awards do indeed raise performance over an extended period of time.

A study by Malmendier and Tate (2009), for instance, reaches the unexpected result that CEOs who are made 'Best Managers' or receive other coveted titles by the business press thereafter exert less effort for their firm. They start spending their time on image boosting activities such as writing books, while still demanding higher compensation. The awards apparently interfere with the principal–agent relationship and are shown to harm the respective firms' performance (see also Wade, Porac, Pollock, & Graffin, 2006).

In our own research on awards in academia, however, we find positive effects on the desired performance dimensions. The American Economic Association regularly honours 'that American economist under the age of forty who is judged to have made the most significant contribution to economic thought and knowledge' with the pres-tigious John Bates Clark Medal. The medal was awarded biannually from 1947 to 2009 and annually ever since. A considerable number of its winners have subsequently been awarded the Nobel Prize (12 out of 37). Using the synthetic control method to construct a control group, we find that five years after award receipt, medallists have published 13% more quality weighted publications compared to the counterfactual scenario of no award receipt. By then, the number of citations to papers they had pub-lished before the award has increased by 50% compared to the counterfactual (Chan, Frey, Gallus, & Torgler, 2014). Our analysis of the much-appreciated Fellowship of the Econometric Society yields similar results. We see considerably higher productivity (proxied by weighted publications) and attention (citations) for the award recipients' work (for a contrasting result focusing on a special case, see Borjas & Doran, 2013).

Other studies of ours more directly consider the motivational effects of awards on performance, ruling out the possibility that award recipients' performance is simply increased by external factors (e.g., more and better co-authors; in line with Merton's (1968) Matthew Effect). Neckermann, Cueni, and Frey (2014) studied an award given to employees in a call centre for their social activities, such as helping a colleague. This award, accompanied by a sum of $150, is found to increase performance also on core duties, which is not included in the award conditions.

One of the few studies analysing the causal effects of awards on motivation in the voluntary sector looks at purely symbolic awards given to Wikipedia editors (Gallus, 2016). The study focuses on the declining newcomer retention rates and asks whether awards can be usefully applied to help ease this problem. The author implemented an award scheme with reputable Wikipedia editors. Each month, 150 newcomers were given the symbolic award (i.e., it was posted on their talk page) and their names were included on the monthly list of award winners displayed on the official award page. The field experiment shows that such awards, with no material or career-related benefit, have a substantive and statistically highly significant effect on performance. The award increased the volunteer retention rate by no less than 25% in the following month. It also raised its recipients' willingness to engage in behind-the-scenes community work, such as discussing content. Overall, these results show that awards can play an important role in settings where material incentives are of no avail.

17.6   SUMMARY

Voluntary organizations either cannot or do not want to force workers to continue working for them. Under these conditions other instruments beyond money or binding contracts must be sought to bind volunteers to an organization and keep their motivation high. We have argued that awards have many features that help in reaching that goal. Awards are quite distinct from praise and from monetary incentives and are particularly suited to organizations relying on volunteers. We have emphasized that there are stringent requirements to meet so that awards motivate volunteers to perform. Raising volunteers' intrinsic motivation by honouring them with awards is no easy task. The six conditions for awards to be successful present a challenge to the leaders of voluntary organizations; but it should be a welcome challenge in view of the great opportunities that award conferrals offer.

REVIEW QUESTIONS

1. What are the major differences between monetary incentives and awards?
2. In what way can awards be used in the for-profit sector?
3. What are the major advantages of using awards in the voluntary sector?
4. What is the overall outcome of the existing empirical literature on the effects of awards on performance?

REFERENCES

Amabile, T. (1997). Motivating creativity in organizations: On doing what you love and loving what you do. *California Management Review, 40*, 39–58.

Bebchuk, L. A., & Fried, J. M. (2009). *Pay without performance: The unfulfilled promise of executive compensation.* Cambridge, MA: Harvard University Press.

Bénabou, R., & Tirole, J. (2003). Intrinsic and extrinsic motivation. *Review of Economic Studies, 70*, 489–520.

Borjas, G. J., & Doran, K. B. (2013). Prizes and productivity: how winning the Fields Medal affects scientific output. NBER Working Paper No. 19445. DOI: 10.3386/w19445

Chan, H. F., Frey, B. S., Gallus, J., & Torgler, B. (2014). Academic honors and performance. *Labour Economics, 31*, 188–204.

Deci, E. L., Koestner, R., & Ryan, R. M. (1999). A meta-analytic review of experiments examining the effects of extrinsic rewards on intrinsic motivation. *Psychological Bulletin, 125*, 627–668.

Easterlin, R. A. (2001). Income and happiness: Towards a unified theory. *Economic Journal, 111*, 465–484.

Frey, B. S. (1997). *Not just for the money: An economic theory of personal motivation.* Cheltenham: Edward Elgar Publishing.

Frey, B. S. (2008). *Happiness: A revolution in economics.* Cambridge, MA: MIT Press.

Frey, B. S., & Gallus, J. (2015). Awards as non-monetary incentives. *Evidence-based HRM, 4*(1), 81–90.

Frey, B. S., & Jegen, R. (2001). Motivation crowding theory. *Journal of Economic Surveys, 15*, 589–611.

Frey, B. S. & Stutzer, A. (2002a). *Happiness and economics: How the economy and institutions affect human well-being.* Princeton, NJ: Princeton University Press.

Frey, B. S. & Stutzer, A. (2002b). What can economists learn from happiness research? *Journal of Economic Literature, 40*, 402–435.

Gallus, J. (2016). Fostering public good contributions with symbolic awards: A large-scale natural field experiment at Wikipedia. *Management Science,* Article in Advance. http://dx.doi.org/10.1287/mnsc.2016.2540

Gallus, J. & Frey, B. S. (2017). Awards as Strategic Signals. *Journal of Management Inquiry, 26*(1), 76–85.

Halfaker, A., Geiger, R. S., Morgan, J. T., & Riedl, J. (2013). The rise and decline of an open collaboration system: How Wikipedia's reaction to popularity is causing its decline. *American Behavioral Scientist, 20*, 1–25.

Holmström, B. (1979). Moral hazard and observability. *Bell Journal of Economics, 10*, 74–91.

Jensen, M. C., & Meckling, W. H. (1976). Theory of the firm: Managerial behavior, agency costs and ownership structure. *Journal of Financial Economics, 3*, 305–360.

Layard, R. (2011). *Happiness: Lessons from a new science* (2nd ed.). New York: Penguin.

Malmendier, U., & Tate, G. (2009). Superstar CEOs. *Quarterly Journal of Economics, 124*, 1593–1638.

Mankiw, G. N. (2015). *Principles of microeconomics* (7th ed.). Stamford, CT: Cengage Learning.

Mas-Colell, A., Whinston, M. D. & Green, J. R. (1985). *Microeconomic theory.* Oxford: Oxford University Press.

Merton, R. K. (1968). The Matthew effect in science. *Science, 159*, 56–63.

Neckermann, S., Cueni, R., & Frey, B. S. (2014). Awards at work. *Labour Economics, 31*, 205–217.

Neckermann, S., & Frey, B. S. (2013). And the winner is…? The motivating power of employee awards. *Journal of Socio-Economics, 46*, 66–77.

Oostlander, J, van Schie, S., Ott, N., Güntert, S. T., & Wehner, T. (2012). Bericht zur Studie „Freiwillig 2011". Mimeo, Zentrum für Organisations- und Arbeitswissenschaften, ETH-Zurich, 3 December.

Panciera, K., Halfaker, A., & Terveen, L. (2009). Wikipedians are born, not made: A study of power editors on Wikipedia. *Proceedings of GROUP 2009*, 51–60. DOI: 10.1145/1531674.1531682

Piketty, T. (2014). *Capital in the twenty-first century.* Cambridge, MA: Harvard University Press.

Ross, S. A. (1973). The economic theory of agency: The principal's problem. *American Economic Review, 63*, 134–139.

Wade, J. B., Porac, J. F., Pollock, T., & Graffin, S. D. (2006). The burden of celebrity: The impact of CEO certification contests on CEO pay and performance. *Academy of Management Journal, 49*, 643–660.

FURTHER READING

Anheier, H. K. (2000). *Managing non-profit organisations: Towards a new approach.* London: Centre for Civil Society, London School of Economics and Political Science.

Brennan, G., & Pettit, P. (2004). *The economy of esteem: An essay on civil and political society.* Oxford: Oxford University Press.

Frey, B. S. (2005). Knight fever: towards an economics of awards. CESifo Working Paper No. 1468. http://www.iew.uzh.ch/wp/iewwp239.pdf.

Frey, B. S., & Gallus, J. (2017). *Honours versus Money: The Economics of Awards.* Oxford: Oxford University Press.

Powell, W. W., & Steinberg, R. (Eds.). (2006). *The nonprofit sector: A research handbook.* New Haven, CT: Yale University Press.

18 Entrepreneurial Activity

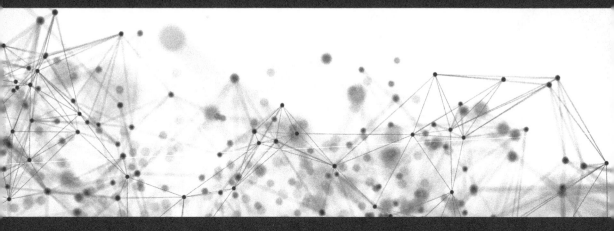

ARTUR DOMURAT AND TADEUSZ TYSZKA

CHAPTER OUTLINE

LEARNING OUTCOMES

BY THE END OF THIS CHAPTER YOU SHOULD BE ABLE TO:

1. Explain how psychological and environmental factors support or restrain people from entrepreneurial activity.
2. Identify some of the psychological traps in entrepreneurial activity.
3. Discuss the problem of whether entrepreneurship can be taught or whether becoming an entrepreneur requires specific innate entrepreneurial predispositions.

18.1   INTRODUCTION

There were 21.6 million small and medium enterprises in European Union (EU) in 2013, which constituted 99.8% of all active enterprises in non-financial business sectors. They generated 28% of the 2013 EU GDP (gross domestic product) and provided jobs to 88.8 million people, constituting 66.8% of total employment in the 28 EU countries (Muller et al., 2014). In particular, opportunity-seeking, innovative, and fast-growing new enterprises account for economic growth (Wong, Ho, & Autio, 2005). Undoubtedly entrepreneurship is important for market economies.

The field of entrepreneurship research is wide-ranging and interdisciplinary (Simpeh, 2011). There are numerous interesting issues related to entrepreneurial activities, such as business ethics, leadership, business administration and human resource management. Naturally, we do not cover all of them within this chapter; rather, we have chosen issues that are most important from a psychological perspective.

First, we describe environmental factors and motivations that promote or discourage people from entrepreneurial activities. Then we describe personal characteristics regarded as potentially distinguishing entrepreneurs from other people: achievement motivation, locus of control of reinforcement, risk attitudes and self-efficacy. Next, we consider some psychological traps that might influence entrepreneurial decisions and actions. Finally, we address the question of whether entrepreneurs are born or whether one can learn to be a successful entrepreneur.

18.1.1   Who Are the Entrepreneurs?

Perhaps the first person to define entrepreneurship and entrepreneurs was the eighteenth-century French economist Richard Cantillon (1959 [1730]). He described an entrepreneur as a person who buys commodities for a specific price and intends to sell them at a higher price which is still unknown. In this view, an entrepreneur is mainly a merchant who deals with risk or uncertainty. John Stuart Mill (1902 [1848]) popularized the term 'entrepreneur'. He proposed a broader view of an entrepreneur as a person who takes risks and manages a business. A still broader view was proposed by Alfred Marshall (1920 [1890]) who saw an entrepreneur as a person playing different roles, from providing capital for a company to carrying out administrative and managerial tasks. Although the specific term 'entrepreneur' cannot be found in his texts, the notion of an entrepreneur is present in them, insofar as various entrepreneurial roles such as coordinator, innovator, arbitrager, manager and investor are mentioned. In this view, the entrepreneur is a manager with the highest position in a company, a supervisor of both capital and the labour force, and a person who is responsible for the rationalization of production.

In line with the tradition started by Cantillon, Frank Knight (1921) also linked entrepreneurial activity with risk and uncertainty. Knight made a sharp distinction between these two concepts, emphasizing that risks may be evaluated with known probabilities, whereas uncertainty involves unknown probabilities. A person may insure against risks, while uncertainty involves issues which are difficult to estimate because one lacks the appropriate knowledge to make computations. It is therefore impossible to insure against factors involving uncertainty, and these factors define the uniqueness of entrepreneurial activity:

> The essential and outstanding fact is that the 'instance' in question is so entirely unique that there are no others or not a sufficient number to make it possible to tabulate enough like it to form a basis for any inference of value about any real probability in the case we are interested in.
>
> (Knight, 1921, p. 39)

The tradition of connecting entrepreneurship with risk-taking and uncertainty was decried by Joseph-Alois Schumpeter (1934 [1911]). He claimed that risk-taking was not a distinctive feature of entrepreneurs, as it is more characteristic of the capitalist, who expects to make future profits from capital (Schumpeter, 1947). The key aspect of entrepreneurship is 'creative destruction', i.e. innovative activity that goes beyond everyday routine and changes markets, causing their disequilibrium. Being an innovator is a necessary condition for being an entrepreneur, and someone whose activity is not 'creative destruction' is not an entrepreneur. Entrepreneurial innovativeness is not the same as inventiveness. The inventor designs things that were previously unavailable or unknown. The innovator understands the importance of inventions and transforms inventions into market offers (Schumpeter, 1947). Schumpeter also drew a likely psychological portrait of innovative entrepreneurs, seeing them as unique, open-minded and optimistic people, who realize their passion and are able to convince others of their innovative vision (Schumpeter, 1934 [1911]).

A pragmatic, practice-oriented definition was developed by Ahmad and Seymour (2008) to compare entrepreneurship across different countries in the OECD's worldwide research. Entrepreneurial activity characterizes business owners who seek to generate value and create or expand economic activities, and who identify and exploit new products, processes and markets. This working definition embraces the thoughts of Cantillon, Schumpeter and other scholars, and emphasizes measurable aspects of entrepreneurial activity (e.g., enterprise birth rates, temporal changes in company size, proportion of high-growth firms, etc.).

Researchers have distinguished between different types of entrepreneur. Some have studied people who have launched new companies. Such entrepreneurs may differ from non-founders (Begley & Boyd, 1987). Also, researchers studying innovative activity distinguish growth-oriented vs. current income-oriented entrepreneurs (Kolvereid, 1992). Still others distinguish between opportunity-driven and necessity-driven entrepreneurs. The first group is enticed into entrepreneurship more out of choice, while the latter group has no other option, needing to provide jobs for themselves (Reynolds et al., 2002).

18.2   ENVIRONMENTAL FACTORS AND ENTREPRENEURSHIP

In common with many other economists, Campbell (1992) emphasizes that the choice to start up one's own business or to become a wage-earner is dependent on comparing the expected future income streams of these choices while also considering the fixed costs of operating a business. A person becomes an entrepreneur when they expect higher future profits from entrepreneurial activity than from wages. However, in addition to financial rewards, non-economic personal benefits, such as feelings of independence or achievement, satisfaction from vision realization, etc., can also be rewards of entrepreneurship. Thus, economists use the notion of utility; a more general concept than profit. Oswald and Blanchflower (1998) claim that people decide to start a business when the utility of self-employment is higher than the utility of working for others.

A society's level of entrepreneurship also depends upon economic growth, the possibility of employing other people and other external factors: technological, demographic and socio-cultural (Bosma, de Wit, & Carree, 2005). For instance, people aspiring to self-employment must possess enough capital to overcome any financial constraints, and possibly have access to credit. Shane (1996) investigated how such environmental factors influenced fluctuations in the number of US entrepreneurs between 1899 and 1988. Entrepreneurial activity rose when interest rates were low, prior rates of entrepreneurship were high and economic growth was high. Furthermore, entrepreneurship rates (the number of extant businesses divided by the US population in a given year) were positively correlated with technological changes (measured as the number of patents relative to the population).

However, not only economic conditions matter. People reveal interest in starting their own firms particularly in communities where entrepreneurship is prestigious and already popular (Giannetti & Simonov, 2009). Max Weber emphasized this cultural aspect of entrepreneurship, highlighting its religious, cultural and normative roots. He posited that the Protestant ethic – valuing work, time, the accumulation of assets and money and their reasonable use, an ascetic life and frugality – shaped people's entrepreneurial motivations. These beliefs were said to create a specific climate in a society, called the 'spirit of capitalism', causing people to be interested in economic activities and driving them to accumulate wealth. Weber suggested that factory owners, merchants, managers and key decision-makers in companies formed a new social class which was motivated by Protestant work ethic principles (Weber, 1958).

18.3   REASONS FOR ENGAGING IN ENTREPRENEURIAL ACTIVITY

Several studies have tried to identify the reasons driving individuals to become entrepreneurs. Scheinberg and MacMillan (1988) surveyed over 1,400 business owners in 11 countries, asking them about the reasons for starting their business. Factor analysis of 38 items presented to the subjects yielded six factors: need for approval, perceived instrumentality of wealth, communitarianism, need for personal development, need for independence, and need for escape from previous job. Follow-up studies with fewer items produced similar factors driving business creation. For example, Shane, Kolvereid and Westhead (1991) found four broad factors: recognition, independence, learning and following role models. Birley and Westhead's (1994) survey of 405 UK business owners identified seven factors: need for approval, need for personal development, need for independence, welfare considerations, perceived instrumentality of wealth, tax reduction, and following role models. Carter et al. (2003), summarizing these and similar research efforts, concluded that entrepreneurs tend to mention six categories of reasons for going into business:

1. *Innovation.* This refers to doing something new, e.g., developing an idea for a new product or service, bringing a new technology to fruition or innovating at work. Here, people who have accumulated experience in their job may be dissatisfied with being unable to express their own initiative and may decide to leave and start up their own business to implement their own ideas (Naffziger, Hornsby, & Kuratko, 1994).

2. *Pursuing self-directed goals.* This motive refers to the need for personal development and was emphasized by McClelland (1961), who argued that people in entrepreneurial societies are inclined to compete with their own subjective standards of excellence and are eager to continually do things better.

3. *Independence.* Much research into why people opt for self-employment mentions autonomy and independence in making decisions as important motivators. This involves the drive to make one's own choices, to control one's own time, with the flexibility of allocating it to work or leisure, and to be one's own boss (e.g., Feldman & Bolino, 2000).

4. *Recognition.* This motive describes the need for others' approval: gaining social status and being recognized in one's family or society for one's success or business achievements.

5. *Roles.* This involves the following of family traditions or following the example of an admired person. Bosma et al. (2012) found that this reason is particularly relevant to young entrepreneurs with a high level of general formal education but who lack entrepreneurial experience. The tendency to follow other entrepreneurs declines as previous entrepreneurial experience growths.

6. *Financial success.* Studies show that entrepreneurial activity is often motivated by profit: people often become entrepreneurs to earn more money, increase their wealth and achieve financial security. However, the average entrepreneur does not earn more than the average wage earner (Evans & Leighton, 1989). A comparison of the employed and self-employed in the United States showed that median initial earnings of self-employed people were lower and grew slower, reaching a median income 35% lower after 10 years (Hamilton, 2000). Some authors conclude that, although financial reward is important for most entrepreneurs, they see it as a measure of their success and performance rather than it being their primary reason for developing an enterprise.

A significant weakness in the above studies is that they involved entrepreneurs' retrospective explanations for going into business (Carter et al., 2003). When Carter et al. compared reasons for career choice given by nascent entrepreneurs and non-entrepreneurs, they found that the above-mentioned motives were not specific to nascent entrepreneurs: both groups reported the same reasons for their choices. The authors suggested that the retrospective stories of entrepreneurs could easily be distorted in line with their previous experience or stereotypes. Thus, it is unclear whether motives such as independence, financial success, self-actualization, etc. are specific to entrepreneurs or whether they are equally characteristic of non-entrepreneurs. Moreover, the motives driving an individual to develop their own business may change across different phases of a business's development. Some entrepreneurs aver that financial success was the most critical for them during the start-up phase, but that later, when their business was expanding, other motives became more crucial.

18.4   PERSONALITY CHARACTERISTICS OF ENTREPRENEURS

Numerous studies of entrepreneurship have attempted to identify the psychological reasons why some people become entrepreneurs while others do not. Some have tried to pinpoint personality traits differentiating entrepreneurs from other people, focusing both on general traits – particularly the Big Five model of personality – and characteristics which may be specific to entrepreneurs.

Zhao and Seibert (2006) performed meta-analysis on the results of 23 studies comparing entrepreneurs with managers on the Big Five dimensions. They concluded that entrepreneurs were higher in Conscientiousness and Openness and lower in Neuroticism and Agreeableness. However, these effects were generally rather weak.

Slightly stronger effects were found for relationships between entrepreneurship and specific traits: achievement motivation, locus of control, risk attitudes and self-efficacy. All these characteristics are commonly considered essential for entrepreneurship.

18.4.1   *Achievement Motivation*

Achievement motivation is defined as a desire to do well in order to attain feelings of accomplishment, and may explain the commitment and perseverance necessary for entrepreneurial endeavor (Stewart & Roth, 2007). Indeed, entrepreneurial activities seem to produce more achievement satisfaction than other occupational activities. Therefore, unsurprisingly, many studies have considered achievement motivation's relationship with entrepreneurship.

Meta-analyses generally indicate that achievement motivation is significantly related to both the choice of an entrepreneurial career and performance (Collins, Hanges, & Locke, 2004). Similarly, Stewart and Roth (2007), who conducted a meta-analysis of studies on the achievement motivation of entrepreneurs and managers, also found that entrepreneurs generally exhibit moderately higher achievement motivation than managers. Nevertheless, some studies have reported no difference in the achievement motivation of entrepreneurs and managers (e.g., Cromie & Johns, 1983).

Differences in studies' outcomes may arise from several sources: variations in measurement, samples, etc. For example, some studies used the Thematic Apperception Test (TAT) or other projective tests, while others used personality questionnaires such as the Personality Research Form (PRF) or Edwards Personal Preference Schedule (EPPS). Measuring achievement motivation as an unconscious drive in a projective test might lead to different results than when measuring it as a conscious need in a personality questionnaire. A major sampling issue is that different studies have focused on different types of entrepreneur: small business owners, founders of firms, growth-oriented entrepreneurs, current income-oriented entrepreneurs, etc. For example, it might be expected that growth-oriented entrepreneurs would display greater achievement motivation than owners of firms focusing on maintaining current income, and there is empirical support for this (Stewart et al., 1999). Summing up, in general, people opting for entrepreneurial careers tend to be higher in achievement motivation and this is particularly true of growth-oriented entrepreneurs.

18.4.2   Locus of Control

After the need for achievement, the second most frequently studied specific motivational trait associated with entrepreneurship is locus of control (Pandey & Tewary, 1979). In essence, locus of control describes the extent to which individuals believe they can control outcomes affecting them. People with a more internal locus of control believe that their personal actions allow them to directly affect outcomes and have an impact upon the world. In contrast, people with a more external locus of control are more likely to believe that outcomes and their destiny are beyond their influence, and they are dependent on external circumstances such as chance, powerful others or fate (Rotter, 1966). To measure the construct, Rotter developed the Introversion-Extraversion (I-E) scale.

Greater internality would be expected to result in greater interest in entrepreneurial activities because these permit one to have a direct impact on events and observe the results of one's own decisions. Consistent with this, some studies show business owners to be more internal compared to general populations (e.g., Durand, 1975). On the other hand, other studies show that they do not differ from managers (Brockhaus, 1982). A meta-analysis on the results of 20 studies using Rotter's I-E scale performed by Rauch and Frese (2007) revealed that entrepreneurs demonstrate greater internality than general populations, but that differences are not as strong as they are for need for achievement.

18.4.3   Risk Attitudes

As noted by Wärneryd (1988), the very definition of entrepreneurship suggests entrepreneurs should be more risk-seeking than other people. Furthermore, everyday observations of entrepreneurs' activities, the annual failure rate of new ventures, etc., might lead one to assume that entrepreneurs are more risk-tolerant than other people. Is this assumption justified, or is it simply a stereotype concerning entrepreneurship?

Countless empirical studies have addressed the above question. Many have indicated that entrepreneurs do indeed have a higher risk propensity than conventionally employed people, including managers. For example, research by Stewart et al. (1999) using the Jackson Personality Inventory, consisting of 10 true/false statements concerning risk in social, ethical and financial areas, revealed entrepreneurs to have a more positive attitude towards risk than non-entrepreneurs. Similar results were found by Begley and Boyd (1987) and Carland et al. (1995) among others. Stewart and Roth's (2001) meta-analysis of 12 studies published between 1980 and 1999 also found that in many instances entrepreneurs' risk propensity was greater than that of managers. Moreover, growth-oriented entrepreneurs had higher risk propensities than current income-oriented entrepreneurs.

However, several studies have shown entrepreneurs to be no more risk-tolerant than managers. Brockhaus (1980) compared entrepreneurs' risk-taking propensity with that of two groups of managers using the Kogan-Wallach Choice Dilemmas Questionnaire (CDQ) which faces individuals with 12 decision scenarios involving risky activities. For example, a decision might concern accepting a job offer from a newly established company with an uncertain future. Individuals have to choose the level of probability which would justify taking the risky action. The scenarios relate to different life domains such as careers, health, stock exchange investments, marriage, etc. Brockhaus found no statistically significant differences in risk-taking propensity between company owners and managers. Furthermore, Xu and Ruef (2004) found that nascent entrepreneurs were actually more risk-averse than non-entrepreneurs. Meta-analysing 14 studies not included in Stewart and Roth's (2001) analysis, Miner and Raju (2004) observed a similar tendency. Given such contradictory findings, results of studies on entrepreneurs' risk-taking propensity appear to be inconclusive.

The above contradictory conclusions may stem from various sources. Again, one issue is variation in samples. Different types of entrepreneurs have been studied and these are likely to differ with respect to risk attitudes. For instance, owners of inherited businesses may tolerate less investment risk than those who have launched a new firm (Puri & Robinson, 2013). Nascent entrepreneurs may be more risk-averse than those who have already achieved success, and, almost by definition, growth-oriented entrepreneurs should be more risk-prone than current income-oriented entrepreneurs. Similarly, differences in risk attitudes would be expected between opportunity-driven and necessity-driven entrepreneurs.

Differences in theoretical concepts focused upon and in measures of risk attitudes used may be even more important in explaining the contradictory conclusions concerning risk attitudes among entrepreneurs. Indeed, the most commonly accepted way of measuring risk attitudes in decision theory is to present an individual with a lottery and ask them to determine its so-called certainty equivalent. For example, an individual is offered a lottery where they may receive either 100 units or nothing with equal probabilities of 0.5, and is asked to indicate a certain amount for which they would be indifferent between receiving the certain payoff and playing the lottery. These are static measures. Some have argued that such measures have limited success in predicting individual differences in naturalistic risk-taking. Perhaps observing risk-taking behaviour in naturally occurring risky situations would provide more reliable measures. Wärneryd (1996) found that these two types of risk attitude measure were very poorly correlated. Finally, risk taking is domain-specific (Weber, Blais, & Betz, 2002), individuals not necessarily displaying similar risk-propensity across various domains (finance, health, etc.). This implies that risk attitudes do not reflect a stable trait. Thus, the issue of whether entrepreneurs are more risk-seeking than other people is complex and still lacks a definitive answer.

18.4.4   Self-Efficacy

As mentioned earlier, according to Knight (1921), it is the belief in one's own competences and skills in managing uncertain situations which distinguishes entrepreneurs
from other people. This personality characteristic causes some people to become
entrepreneurs, others to become managers and others to become wage earners
(Knight, 1921, p. 27).

Many years after Knight, Albert Bandura (1994) developed the concept of self-
efficacy, understood as one's belief in one's ability to succeed in a task. According to
Bandura, self-efficacy may be built on differing foundations. Perhaps the most effective is personal experience. When one experiences success, one starts to believe in
one's ability to succeed in tasks. When a series of failures is experienced, self-efficacy
is undermined. Bandura argues that even vicarious experience – seeing others similar
to oneself succeeding in something – may help build self-efficacy.

Knight's claim that self-efficacy is a distinctive characteristic of entrepreneurs
enjoys much support (Rauch & Frese, 2007). Studies using various self-efficacy
measurement methods consistently characterize entrepreneurs as having higher
levels of this trait than wage earners. Also, self-efficacy significantly correlates with
business creation, business success, etc. (Rauch & Frese, 2007). However, these
relationships are generally modest. For example, Chen, Greene, and Crick (1998)
asked entrepreneurs and managers to rate their confidence in dealing with different
types of business tasks. For some, but not all, of these tasks entrepreneurs had higher
self-efficacy than managers. Using Schwarzer and Jerusalem's (1995) 10-item Generalized Self-Efficacy Scale, Tyszka et al. (2011) compared a sample of business owners,
divided into opportunity-driven vs. necessity-driven entrepreneurs, with a group of
non-entrepreneurial employees. Opportunity-driven, but not necessity-driven, entrepreneurs revealed higher levels of self-efficacy than the employees.

18.4.5   Commentary on Personality Characteristics

Summarizing, findings on relationships between personality traits and entrepreneurship are often in conflict. From this, some conclude that, in general, personality is
not a valuable predictor of entrepreneurial behaviour (e.g., Brockhaus & Horwitz,
1986), and that personality traits are secondary to situational factors in impacting
entrepreneurial activity. Others claim that the connection between personality and
entrepreneurship may be more complex than studies acknowledge. Characteristics
relevant to starting a venture may be irrelevant to more experienced entrepreneurs'
activities. For instance, while openness to experience may integrate with a creative
mindset for new business funders, it may be less important when sustaining a venture
(Hisrich, Langan-Fox, & Grant, 2007).

Moreover, Hisrich et al. (2007) note that while personality characteristics may or
may not predispose one to entrepreneurial activity, entrepreneurial activity may also
shape an individual's characteristics. People learn how to become and act as an entrepreneur, and this may affect their personality. For instance, Littunen's (2000) longitudinal study of 123 Finnish entrepreneurs demonstrated that achievement motivation
and locus of control evolve in time: the pursuit of mastery increases and attributions
of outcomes to other people decrease with growing entrepreneurial experience.

However, other researchers (e.g., Collins et al., 2004; Stewart & Roth, 2001) claim that examining the entrepreneurial personality is valuable, suggesting that contradictory conclusions arise from variations in concepts studied and measurements and samples used. Thus, when referring to risk propensity, achievement motivation and so on, we should be more specific about these concepts. For example, studies of the role of achievement motivation should differentiate between conscious and unconscious achievement motivation, and studies of the role of risk attitudes should be specific as to whether we mean static or dynamic risk attitude. Naturally, we should also be specific as to the type of entrepreneur studied: business founders versus non-founders, growth-oriented versus current income-oriented entrepreneurs, opportunity-driven versus necessity-driven entrepreneurs, etc.

The mixed results concerning the influence of individual predispositions, attitudes and personality on entrepreneurial activities may also be attributable to the distinction between soft vs. hard situations (Rauch & Frese, 2007). An example of a soft situation occurs when establishing a new firm or project, where an entrepreneur decides on organizational structure, employment and the scope of an activity. In such situations people have freedom to decide on their behaviour and choices, so personality can be more influential. In contrast, in hard situations, people must act with regard to external rules or expectations. Such situations occur once a company is established and a person's actions are driven by standardized expectations or objective procedures (the rules and laws of accounting, employment law, etc.). Traits and attitudes are less likely to manifest themselves here.

18.5 PSYCHOLOGICAL TRAPS IN ENTREPRENEURSHIP

The literature on cognitive biases in human judgement and decision-making is extensive. Numerous studies show that both lay people and experts engage in heuristic reasoning and are affected by biases (Kahneman, Slovic, & Tversky, 1982). Entrepreneurs act in situations that facilitate susceptibility to cognitive biases. They must often adapt to novel and changing situations. In such circumstances they can be overwhelmed by the amount of information involving different sources and domains: employees, contractors, competitors, accountants, etc. Operating under the time pressure or the pressure of other people's demands, the possibilities of analyzing incoming information precisely and cautiously are limited; but entrepreneurs need to evaluate which information is critical and which issues should be prioritized. Unsurprisingly, under such circumstances they are prone to cognitive biases and other pitfalls.

One bias of particular relevance to entrepreneurial behaviour is overconfidence. This consists of a person believing that their judgements are reliable to a greater extent than their objective accuracy justifies. For example, when people rate their answer as 100% certain, they may be wrong in 20% of cases rather than 0% of cases. Using Fischhoff and Lichtenstein's questionnaire to measure overconfidence, Busenitz and Barney (1997) found that entrepreneurs were more prone to this bias than managers in large organizations.

When making judgements about the probability of an event under uncertainty, people tend to rely on several heuristics. One such heuristic is the law of small numbers. Here, people tend to believe that small samples represent a population equally as well as large samples (Tversky & Kahneman, 1971). For example, when five consecutive tosses of a coin result in 'heads', people tend to believe that the coin is biased towards 'heads'.

Busenitz and Barney (1997) tested whether entrepreneurs are more susceptible to bias concerning the law of small numbers than other people. They constructed scenarios portraying real-life situations, e.g.:

> Mr Johnson is about to invest in a new machine and has narrowed his options to Machine A, which is made in the United States or Machine B, which is made overseas. Both machines are equally capable of performing the same function. In considering this decision, Mr Johnson says to his friend, 'You know, it seems that every time I buy a piece of equipment made by a foreign manufacturer, it breaks down in the first month of use.'
>
> After further discussion, Mr Johnson's friend remembers a recent industrial report that gives a significantly higher ranking to Machine B (the one made overseas) than to Machine A. This report bases its recommendation on extensive testing as well as on feedback from dozens of users. If you were in Mr Johnson's position, which machine would you purchase? Why?

In the above scenario, when opting to purchase Machine A, the decision-maker bases their decision on a representativeness heuristic, generalizing from a small non-random sample. When opting to purchase Machine B, the decision-maker bases their decision on reliable statistical data. Relative to managers in large organizations, Busenitz and Barney found that entrepreneurs tended to prefer Machine A, to rely more on their choices, and make more justifications based on the law of small numbers. The authors speculated that entrepreneurs may need to base their decisions on simple heuristics because they often have to adapt to novel and changing situations under the pressure of time or other people's demands, with limited possibilities of precisely and cautiously analyzing all the available information.

There are also biases where entrepreneurs seem less vulnerable than others, e.g., the status quo bias: the tendency to prefer a current state to a change. Burmeister and Schade (2007) analysed susceptibility to this bias across groups of students, bankers and entrepreneurs. Entrepreneurs were as susceptible as students but less susceptible than bankers. Entrepreneurs also seem less vulnerable than others to counterfactual thinking, i.e. thinking what would have happened had one acted or chosen differently. Such thoughts often produce negative emotions such as regret or guilt. They can hinder concentration on the present and future, and instead result in over-contemplation of past decisions or events. Baron's (2000) study demonstrated that nascent entrepreneurs were less susceptible to counterfactual thinking than potential entrepreneurs (people interested in launching a business) and non-entrepreneurs (people having no interest in starting a new venture).

18.6   TEACHING ENTREPRENEURSHIP

Entrepreneurial activity characterizes business owners who seek to generate value and create or expand economic activities, and who identify and exploit new products, processes and markets. When ordinary people think of entrepreneurship they find it easy to think of business people who have made big fortunes, e.g. Bill Gates (Microsoft) or Larry Page and Sergey Brin (Google). Biographies of such entrepreneurs encourage the idea that 'real' entrepreneurs are born and that entrepreneurial success requires a specific 'entrepreneurial profile'. Popular books and web sites present checklists and offer evaluations of how well people fit this profile (see, e.g., Isenberg, 2010). Their superficial credibility probably arises from the disproportionate attention paid to the extraordinary creativity, drive, initiative and social skills attributed to famous entrepreneurs. Such beliefs are simplified myths (Kuratko, 2009). Although entrepreneurs do differ from other people in some psychological characteristics (e.g., achievement motivation or self-confidence), such differences are not great. Moreover, entrepreneurs perform many different business activities and they may compensate for some personal deficiencies by employing others, e.g., hiring managers and employees with higher stress resistance or better communication skills, specialists with specific knowledge (such as technicians, accountants and R&D specialists), etc.

A management science guru, Peter Drucker (1985) claims that entrepreneurship is not magic or a mystery and everyone can learn it. Indeed, Gorman, Hanlon and King (1997) reviewed 63 empirical articles addressing the efficiency of entrepreneurial education. The studies used different methodologies, for example, surveying opinions of school graduates, programme attendees and entrepreneurs in the post-start-up phase. Investigations involved graduates' or attendees' awareness of entrepreneurship as a possible career choice, or evaluations of the influence of entrepreneurial education in shaping entrepreneurial attitudes and intentions. The authors concluded that most studies indicate that entrepreneurship can be taught, or at least encouraged, by entrepreneurial education.

However, it should be borne in mind that people undertaking entrepreneurial education may have had a strong prior intention to start a business. Meta-analysing 73 studies, Bae et al. (2014) found that engaging in entrepreneurially-oriented education was more strongly related to entrepreneurial intentions than engaging in general business education. Nevertheless, post-education entrepreneurial intentions correlated highly with intentions prior to enrolling in entrepreneurial education. This indicated that those undertaking entrepreneurial education already had stronger prior intentions to start their own businesses.

Basic entrepreneurial education is provided by programmes in business schools and universities. The general purpose of these programmes is to develop students' abilities to discover and exploit business opportunities. Naturally, such programmes also offer other specific business-related knowledge, such as how to write convincing business plans, how to launch a new venture, how to finance an enterprise and how to design organizational structures and define job positions (Baron & Shane, 2008).

In addition to formal academic education, academic institutions also offer programmes supporting student entrepreneurial activity. One form of programme provides spaces on campus where student entrepreneurs can develop their own ventures. Three major types of programme are business hatcheries, business incubators and business accelerators. Business hatcheries provide a 24/7 available work space to facilitate business start-ups while student entrepreneurs pursue their education. Thus, they offer support for ventures in their earliest-stage. Hatcheries do not need specially designed spaces: they can use any vacant campus space. As well as a convenient space, hatcheries provide monitoring and counselling by faculty. Business incubators are organizations that help early-stage ventures overcome introductory barriers and survive the launch phase. They provide a work place, infrastructure and services for free or at subsidized rates to a cohort of young firms. Typically, the firms co-work in a shared office space, have common access to administrative, accounting and legal advisory services, facilitate training in business skills and foster new business relationship networks. Incubators focus mainly on innovation and discovering opportunities. Business accelerators are more structured programmes accelerating the growth of ventures (companies) already in existence. They adopt start-ups with high potential and support their corporate growth, helping them to build organizational structures and implement business processes in a substantially shorter time. Comprehensive description of these three programmes can be found in *Entrepreneurship Programs and the Modern University*, by Morris, Kuratko and Cornwall (2013).

Entrepreneurship education and support programmes offer not only 'hard' economic and business knowledge, but also develop or train advantageous 'entrepreneurial' psychological skills and attitudes. For example, for entrepreneurial success it is useful to know how to deal with one's own characteristics (e.g., manage stress and one's emotions, develop creativity and alertness to opportunities, be aware of cognitive traps and one's own risk attitude), and how to foster good interactions with other people (e.g., when negotiating, managing organizational conflicts, and building cooperative working relationships: Baron & Shane, 2008). Such soft psychological characteristics may also evolve. Hansemark's (1998) longitudinal study demonstrated significant increases in the need for achievement and internal locus of control among attendees of a one-year entrepreneurship programme when compared to control groups, which showed no significant change. Also, DeTienne and Chandler (2004) investigated whether training in skills that enhanced creativity influenced opportunity recognition among business students, and found that recipients of the training discovered more business opportunities when compared to both their performance before the training and a control group of untrained students.

18.7 SUMMARY

Entrepreneurial activity characterizes those business owners who seek to generate value and create or expand economic activities, and who identify and exploit new products, processes and markets. Entrepreneurial activity is inspired by environmental factors, including economic conditions, as well as cultural and normative factors. The main reasons that entrepreneurs tend to give for going into business are: doing something new, pursuing self-directed goals, being independent in making decisions, a need for other people's approval, following an example and achieving financial success. Some relationships are found between entrepreneurship and specific psychological characteristics: achievement motivation, locus of control, risk attitudes and self-efficacy. However, these relationships are generally rather weak. Like other people, entrepreneurs often engage in heuristic reasoning and are affected by biases. Entrepreneurship can be taught. There are entrepreneurial programmes aiming at the development of students' abilities to discover and to exploit business opportunities.

REVIEW QUESTIONS

1. In which respects do entrepreneurs differ from other people?
2. Do entrepreneurs like to take risks?
3. What drives people to become entrepreneurs?
4. Why are entrepreneurs susceptible to specific psychological traps?
5. Are entrepreneurs born or made?

REFERENCES

Ahmad, N., & Seymour, R. G. (2008). Defining entrepreneurial activity: Definitions supporting frameworks for data collection. OECD Statistics Working Paper, Paris, OECD.

Bae, T. J., Qian, S., Miao, C., & Fiet, J. O. (2014). The relationship between entrepreneurship education and entrepreneurial intentions: A meta-analytic review. *Entrepreneurship Theory and Practice*, 38(2), 217–254.

Bandura, A. (1994). Self-efficacy, in V. S.Ramachandran (Ed.), *Encyclopedia of human behavior* (vol. 4; pp. 71–81). New York: Academic Press.

Baron, R. A. (2000). Counterfactual thinking and venture formation: The potential effects of thinking about 'what might have been'. *Journal of Business Venturing*, 15(1) 79–91.

Baron, R. A., & Shane, S. (2008). *Entrepreneurship: A process perspective* (2nd ed.). Mason, OH: Thompson South-Western.

Begley, T. M., & Boyd, D. P. (1987). Psychological characteristics associated with performance in entrepreneurial firms and smaller businesses. *Journal of Business Venturing*, 2(1), 79–93.

Birley, S., & Westhead, P. (1994). A taxonomy of business start-up reasons and their impact on firm growth and size. *Journal of Business Venturing*, 9(1), 7–31.

Bosma, N., de Wit, G., & Carree, M. (2005). Modelling entrepreneurship: Unifying the equilibrium and entry/exit approach. *Small Business Economics*, 25(1), 35–48.

Bosma, N., Hessels, J., Schutjens, V., Van Praag, M., & Verheul, I. (2012). Entrepreneurship and role models. *Journal of Economic Psychology*, 33(2), 410–424.

Brockhaus, R. H. (1980). Risk taking propensity of entrepreneurs. *Academy of Management Journal*, 23(3), 509–520.

Brockhaus, R. H. (1982). The psychology of the entrepreneur. In C. A. Kent, D. L. Sexton, & K. H. Vesper (Eds.), *Encyclopedia of entrepreneurship* (pp. 39–57). Englewood Cliffs, NJ: Prentice-Hall.

Brockhaus, R. H., & Horwitz, P. S. (1986). The psychology of the entrepreneur. In D. L. Sexton, & R.W. Smilor (Eds.), *The art and the science of entrepreneurship* (pp. 25–48). Cambridge, MA: Ballinger Publishing Company.

Burmeister, K., & Schade, C. (2007). Are entrepreneurs' decisions more biased? An experimental investigation of the susceptibility to status quo bias. *Journal of Business Venturing*, 22(3), 340–362.

Busenitz, L. W., & Barney, J. B. (1997). Differences between entrepreneurs and managers in large organizations: Biases and heuristics in strategic decision-making. *Journal of Business Venturing*, 12(1), 9–30.

Campbell, C. (1992). A decision theory model for entrepreneurial acts. *Entrepreneurship Theory and Practice*, 17(1), 21–27.

Cantillon, R. (1959 [1730]). *Essai sur la nature du commerce en général* [Essay on the nature of trade in general]. London: Frank Cass and Company. Tłum ang. Henry Higgs. Library of Economics and Liberty. Available at: http://www.econlib.org/library/NPDBooks/Cantillon/cntNT0.html.

Carland, J. W. III, Carland, J. W., Carland, J. C., & Pearce, J. W. (1995). Risk taking propensity among entrepreneurs, small business owners, and managers. *Journal of Business and Entrepreneurship*, 7(1), 15–23.

Carter, N. M., Gartner, W. B., Shaver, K. G., & Gatewood, E. J. (2003). The career reasons of nascent entrepreneurs. *Journal of Business Venturing, 18*(1), 13–39.

Chen, C. C., Greene, P. G., & Crick, A. (1998). Does entrepreneurial self-efficacy distinguish entrepreneurs from managers? *Journal of Business Venturing, 13*(4), 295–316.

Collins, C. J., Hanges, P. J., & Locke, E. A. (2004). The relationship of achievement motivation to entrepreneurial behavior: A meta-analysis. *Human Performance, 17*(1), 95–117.

Cromie, S., & Johns, S. (1983). Irish entrepreneurs: Some personal characteristics. *Journal of Occupational Behavior, 4*(4), 317–324.

DeTienne, D. R., & Chandler, G. N. (2004). Opportunity identification and its role in the entrepreneurial classroom: A pedagogical approach and empirical test. *Academy of Management Learning & Education, 3*(3), 242–257.

Drucker, P. F. (1985). *Innovation and entrepreneurship. Practice and principles.* New York: Harper and Row.

Durand, D. E. (1975). Effects of achievement motivation and skill training on the entrepreneurial behavior of black businessmen. *Organizational Behavior and Human Performance, 14*(1), 76–90.

Evans, D. S., & Leighton, L. S. (1989). Some empirical aspects of entrepreneurship. *The American Economic Review, 79*(3), 519–535.

Feldman, D. C., & Bolino, M. C. (2000). Career patterns of the self-employed: Career motivations and career outcomes. *Journal of Small Business Management, 38*(3), 53–67.

Giannetti, M., & Simonov, A. (2009). Social interactions and entrepreneurial activity. *Journal of Economics & Management Strategy, 18*(3), 665–709.

Gorman, G., Hanlon, D., & King, W. (1997). Some research perspectives on entrepreneurship education, enterprise education and education for small business management: A ten-year literature review. *International Small Business Journal, 15*(3), 56–77.

Hamilton, B. H. (2000). Does entrepreneurship pay? An empirical analysis of returns to self-employment. *Journal of Political Economy 108*(3), 604–631.

Hansemark, O. C. (1998). The effects of an entrepreneurship programme on need for achievement and locus of control of reinforcement. *International Journal of Entrepreneurial Behavior & Research, 4*(1), 28–50.

Hisrich, R., Langan-Fox, J., & Grant, S. (2007). Entrepreneurship research and practice: A call to action for psychology. *American Psychologist, 62*(6), 575–589.

Isenberg, D. (2010). Should you be an entrepreneur? Take this test. *Harvard Business Review 12* Feb. Retrieved from https://hbr.org/2010/02/should-you-be-an-entrepreneur

Kahneman D., Slovic P., & Tversky, A. (Eds.). (1982). *Judgment under uncertainty: Heuristics and biases.* New York: Cambridge University Press.

Knight, F. H. (1921). *Risk, uncertainty, and profit.* Boston: Hart, Schaffner and Marx; Houghton Mifflin Company. http://www.econlib.org/LIBRARY/Knight/knRUP1.html

Kolvereid, L. (1992). Growth aspirations among Norwegian entrepreneurs. *Journal of Business Venturing, 7*(3), 209–222.

Kuratko, D. F. (2009). *Entrepreneurship: Theory, process, practice* (8th ed.). Mason, OH: Southwestern/Cengage Publishers.

Littunen, H. (2000). Entrepreneurship and the characteristics of the entrepreneurial personality. *International Journal of Entrepreneurial Behavior & Research, 6*(6), 295–310.

Marshall, A. (1920 [1890]). *Principles of economics.* Library of Economics and Liberty. Available at: http://www.econlib.org/library/Marshall/marP.html.

McClelland, D. C. (1961). *The achieving society.* Princeton, NJ: Van Nostrand.

Mill, J. S. (1902 [1848]). *Principles of political economy with some of their applications to social philosophy.* London: Longmans, Green, and Company.

Miner, J. B., & Raju, N. S. (2004). Risk propensity differences between managers and entrepreneurs and between low- and high-growth entrepreneurs: A reply in a more conservative vein. *Journal of Applied Psychology, 89*(1), 3–13.

Morris, M. H., Kuratko, D. F., & Cornwall, J. R. (2013). *Entrepreneurship programs and the modern university*. Cheltenham: Edward Elgar Publishing.

Muller, P., Gagliardi, C., Caliandro, C., Bohn. N. U., & Klitou, D. (2014). *Annual report on European SMEs 2013/2014: A partial and fragile recovery*. Brussels: European Commission.

Naffziger, D., Hornsby, J., & Kuratko, D. (1994). A proposed research model of entrepreneurial motivation. *Entrepreneurship Theory and Practice*, *18*(3), 29–42.

Oswald, A., & Blanchflower, D. (1998). What makes an entrepreneur? *Journal of Labor Economics*, *16*(1), 26–60.

Pandey, J., & Tewary, N. B. (1979). Locus of control and achievement values of entrepreneurs. *Journal of Occupational Psychology*, *52*(2), 107–111.

Puri, M., & Robinson, D. T. (2013). The economic psychology of entrepreneurship and family business. *Journal of Economics & Management Strategy 22*(2), 423–444.

Rauch, A., & Frese, M. (2007). Let's put the person back into entrepreneurship research: A meta-analysis on the relationship between business owners' personality traits, business creation, and success. *European Journal of Work and Organizational Psychology*, *16*(4), 353–385.

Reynolds, P. D., Camp, S. M., Bygrave, W. D., Autio, E., & Hay, M. (2002). *Global Entrepreneurship Monitor 2001 executive report*. London: Babson College, London Business School.

Rotter, J. B. (1966). Generalized expectancies of internal versus external control of reinforcements. *Psychological Monographs*, *80*, 1–20.

Scheinberg, S., & MacMillan, I. C. (1988). An 11 country study of motivations to start a business. In B. Kirchoff, W. Long, W. McMullan, K. H. Vesper, & W. Wetzel (Eds.), *Frontiers of entrepreneurship research* (pp. 669–687). Wellesley, MA: Babson College.

Schumpeter, J. A. (1934 [1911]). *The theory of economic development*. New York: Oxford University Press.

Schumpeter, J. A. (1947). The creative response in economic history. *Journal of Economic History*, *7*(2), 149–159.

Schwarzer, R., & Jerusalem, M. (1995). Generalized self-efficacy scale. In J. Weinman, S. Wright, & M.Johnston (Eds.), *Measures in health psychology: A user's portfolio. Causal and control beliefs* (pp. 35–37). Windsor: NFER-Nelson.

Shane, S. (1996). Explaining variation in rates of entrepreneurship in the United States: 1899–1988. *Journal of Management*, *22*(5), 747–781.

Shane, S., Kolvereid, L., & Westhead, P. (1991). An exploratory examination of reasons leading to new firm formation across country and gender. *Journal of Business Venturing 6*(6), 431–446.

Simpeh, K. N. (2011). Entrepreneurship theories and empirical research: A summary review of the literature. *European Journal of Business and Management*, *3*(6), 1–8.

Stewart, Jr., R. H., & Roth, P. L. (2001) Risk propensity differences between entrepreneurs and managers: A meta-analytic review. *Journal of Applied Psychology*, *86*(1), 145–153.

Stewart Jr, W. H., & Roth, P. L. (2007). A meta-analysis of achievement motivation differences between entrepreneurs and managers. *Journal of Small Business Management*, *45*(4), 401–421.

Stewart Jr., W. H., Watson, W. E., Carland, J. C., & Carland, J.W . (1999). A proclivity for entrepreneurship: A comparison of entrepreneurs, small business owners, and corporate managers. *Journal of Business Venturing*, *14*(2), 189–214.

Tversky, A., & Kahneman, D. (1971). Belief in law of small numbers. *Psychological Bulletin*, *76*(2), 105–110.

Tyszka, T., Cieślik, J., Domurat, A., & Macko, A. (2011). Motivation, self-efficacy, and risk attitudes among entrepreneurs during transition to a market economy. *Journal of Socio-Economics*, *40*(2), 124–131.

Wärneryd, K. -E. (1988). The psychology of innovative entrepreneurship. In W. F. van Raaij, G. M. Veldhoven, & K. E.Wärneryd (Eds.), *Handbook of economic psychology* (pp. 404–447). Dordrecht: Kluwer.

Wärneryd, K. -E. (1996). Risk attitudes and risky behavior. *Journal of Economic Psychology*, *17*(6), 749–770.

Weber, E. U., Blais, A. -R., & Betz, N. E. (2002). A domain-specific risk-attitude scale: Measuring risk perceptions and risk behaviors. *Journal of Behavioral Decision Making, 15*(4), 263–290.

Weber, M. (1958). *The Protestant ethic and the spirit of capitalism.* New York: Scribner.

Wong, P. K., Ho, Y. P., & Autio, E. (2005). Entrepreneurship, innovation and economic growth: Evidence from GEM data. *Small Business Economics, 24*(3), 335–350.

Xu, H., & Ruef, M. (2004). The myth of the risk-tolerant entrepreneur. *Strategic Organization, 2*(4), 331–355.

Zhao, H., & Seibert, S.E. (2006). The Big Five personality dimensions and entrepreneurial status: A meta-analytical review. *Journal of Applied Psychology, 91*(2), 259–271.

FURTHER READING

Baum, J. R., Frese, M., & Baron, R. A. (Eds.). (2007). *The psychology of entrepreneurship.* Mahwah, NJ: Lawrence Erlbaum.

Kuratko, D. F. (2009). *Entrepreneurship: Theory, process, practice* (8th ed.). Mason, OH: Southwestern/ Cengage Publishers.

19 The Economic Psychology of Gambling

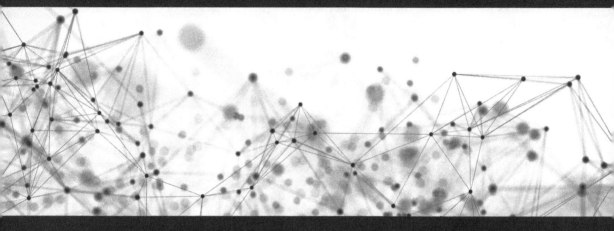

JUEMIN XU AND NIGEL HARVEY

CHAPTER OUTLINE

LEARNING OUTCOMES

BY THE END OF THIS CHAPTER YOU SHOULD BE ABLE TO:

1. Describe cognitive biases, fallacies and real expertise related to gambling.
2. Give examples of the manifestation of these biases, fallacies and real expertise in common forms of gambling.
3. Understand potential reasons behind problem gambling.

19.1   INTRODUCTION

Gambling, being a game of money, allows us a peep into the psychology of money. It has a long history (Schwartz, 2006): indeed, it is one of the earliest types of decision-making to have been systematically studied (Bernoulli, 1954 [1738]). Typically, it involves winning or losing money with uncertainties. To gamblers, uncertainty is intertwined with luck. Their belief in luck manifests itself in cognitive biases, fallacies, and real skills. In the United Kingdom, 72% of adults gambled in 2010 and 56% of them gambled in games other than the National Lottery (Wardle et al., 2011). Gambling is a popular activity worthy of economic and psychological analysis. In what follows, we discuss six popular forms of gambling and indicate how they illustrate the way that people reason about money and probability (Table 19.1). Then, we discuss the economic, psychological and neurological roots of problem gambling.

19.2   LOTTERIES

Lotteries are a common form of gambling. There are at least 180 lotteries worldwide and the total size of lottery industry is estimated to be $284 billion (Markel, La Fleur, & La Fleur, 2015). In the United Kingdom, 59% of adults purchased the National

Table 19.1 *Common forms of gambling*

Games	Characteristics	Prevalence as a percentage all UK adults (Wardle et al., 2011)	Biases, fallacies, and other reasons to gamble
Lottery	Low frequency, fixed odds, pure chance	National Lottery 59 Other lotteries 25	Overestimation of low odds
Scratch cards	High frequency, fixed odds, pure chance	24	The availability heuristic Entrapment
Roulette	High frequency, fixed odds, pure chance	In a casino 5 Online games that include roulette 13	The representativeness heuristic Illusions of control
Fruit machines	High frequency, fixed odds, pure chance	18	The gambler's fallacy The hot hand effect Superstitious behaviour
Sports betting	High frequency, flexible odds, may involve real skills	Horse racing 16 Football 4 Dog racing 4 Other sports events 9	The near-miss effect Mental accounting Loss chasing
Card games	High frequency, flexible odds, may involve real skills	Poker (pub or club) 2 Casino card games 5 Online games that include card games 13	High testosterone levels Abnormal levels of neurotransmitters Abnormal brain activity Card counting (a real skill)

Lottery tickets in 2009 (Wardle et al., 2011). The chance of winning the jackpot (first prize) is typically extremely low. As an example, consider Lotto, one of the games offered by the UK National Lottery. With a £2 lottery ticket, the buyer chooses six numbers from a range between one and 59 or, alternatively, they take the Lucky Dip option and a machine picks the six numbers for them. There are two draws every week, one on Wednesday and one on Saturday. To win the jackpot, all six numbers on the lottery ticket must match the six winning numbers. There are 45,057,474 combinations of six winning numbers. In 2015, the jackpot size fluctuated from £886,754 to £43 million (Camelot, 2015). Apart from the jackpot, there are smaller prizes for people with tickets that have fewer than six numbers that match those selected. For those with five matching numbers, the prize is estimated to be £1000. There is also £100 for those with four matching numbers, £25 for those with tickets with three, and a free Lotto ticket for those with two.

Every time a person buys a £2 lottery ticket, they are expected to lose half of the money. The chance of winning any prize is 1 out of 9.3. Clearly, buying a lottery ticket is not an efficient way to make money. Other lotteries in the world are also fairly similar to the lottery games organized by the UK National Lottery and have similar returns. For example, the expected return from participating in Powerball in the United States is about $0.90 for a $2 ticket and 1 in 24.87 buyers wins a prize. It is clear from these odds that buying lottery tickets does not earn money. So why do people do it?

Lottery buyers may miscalculate and believe they can make money. According to prospect theory, people tend to overestimate low odds of winning (Kahneman & Tversky, 1979). Because the extremely low odds of winning the jackpot are far lower than what people experience in everyday life, they may not be able to estimate just how tiny they actually are.

Our understanding of the environment comes from experience. According to decision-by-sampling theory (Stewart, Chater, & Brown, 2006), people are likely to use a small chance that they have retained in memory as a substitute for a minuscule chance that they have never encountered before: this would result in an overestimation of winning. Another way that this could happen is by use of the availability heuristic (Tversky & Kahneman, 1973): people's attention may have been drawn to news coverage of a number of highly impressive jackpot wins and, as a result, they would overestimate their chances of winning (Bordalo, Gennaioli, & Shleifer, 2012). The bigger the jackpot, the more jackpot winners are reported and the more people buy lottery tickets (Cook & Clotfelter, 1991; Matheson & Grote, 2004).

There are other motivations for playing: people may play lottery together with friends as a social activity; they may also buy lottery tickets to experience excitement; they may be 'entrapped' by the thought that, if they stop buying tickets, they will miss the jackpot (Beckert & Lutter, 2013; Binde, 2013; Forrest, Simmons, & Chesters, 2002).

People invent methods to increase their chances of winning. The randomness of the lottery is closely monitored by its organizers, the regulation bodies, lottery machine engineers, independent researchers, and millions of buyers (Camelot, 2016a; Gambling Commission, 2012; Konstantinou, Liagkou, Spirakis, Stamatiou, & Yung, 2005). However, this does not stop people trying to increase their chances of winning. Searching online using keywords such as 'predict lottery' and 'lottery tips' produces numerous suggestions for doing so. These tips for increasing the chances of winning can often be traced back to well-known cognitive biases. For example, people using the representativeness heuristic are likely to expect that the winning numbers should look random. As a result, they avoid numbers that do not look random enough, such as those with regular intervals or those that do not distribute sparsely across the whole range of possible numbers (Holtgraves & Skeel, 1992; Hardoon, Baboushkin, Derevensky, & Gupta, 2001). Also, given their susceptibility to the illusion of control (Langer, 1975), people overestimate their ability to choose winning numbers. This is likely to be why they prefer numbers that they have chosen themselves (Wohl & Enzle, 2002). In addition, there is evidence that people are affected by the gambler's fallacy. If certain numbers have recently appeared among the winning ones, people tend not to bet on them whereas, if particular numbers have not appeared for a long time, they are more likely to bet on them (Clotfelter & Cook, 1991; Terrell, 1994). People may attempt to find out which their lucky numbers are by visiting temples, observing candle tears, examining incense ashes, and so on (Ariyabuddhiphongs & Chanchalermporn, 2007).

19.3 SCRATCH CARDS

Twenty-four per cent of all UK adults played scratch cards in 2010 (Wardle et al., 2011). A scratch card is typically a paper card coated with a layer of black silver ink. The ink can be scratched off to reveal numbers or symbols underneath. The UK National Lottery sells them for prices ranging between £1 and £10. For example, one scratch card that is sold for £10 and called the £4 Million Blue claims to have four top prizes of £4 million each. It contains a number of games on one card. The first one involves finding the UK National Lottery logo: if, after the ink has been scratched off, the Lotto symbol appears, the purchaser wins £4 million. Other games are similar, though some prizes are smaller than £4 million. The odds of winning after purchasing a scratch card range from a 1-in-4,347,890 chance of winning £4 million to a 1-in-6 chance of winning £10 (Camelot, 2016b). The buyer is expected to lose £3 for every £10 purchase.

The main difference between scratch cards and the lottery is that results from scratch cards are instant. Because the result of the gamble is revealed within seconds after buying the scratch card, people can quickly buy another card, if they wish. This makes it easier for people to become addicted to purchasing scratch cards: if they win, they may feel lucky and buy another scratch card; if they lose, they may display the gambler's fallacy and decide to have another try (Griffiths, 2000). Another difference is that after the initial print run of the scratch cards, the winning chance changes after winning cards have been claimed. People display 'near-miss' effects with scratch cards, which we will discuss in detail in Section 19.5 in the context of fruit machines.

19.4 ROULETTE

In 2010, 9% of the adult population in the United Kingdom played casino games, including roulette, whereas 13% gambled online, again including roulette (Wardle et al., 2011). Roulette requires no skill. It is a game of pure chance. The odds are completely clear and transparent. The rules are simple. There are 37 slots on the European roulette wheel (38 on the American one). Numbers range from 0 to 36 (with an extra 00 slot on the American roulette wheel). Half are red, half are black, and 0 and 00 are green. Gamblers can choose to bet on a single slot or a selection of slots. The pay-out for a single number is 35 to 1, the pay-out for even or odd, red or black is 1 to 1, and the pay-out for any selection of 12 numbers is 2 to 1. The expected return in European roulette is 36/37 for any choice. (For American roulette the expected return is 36/38.) The result of the roulette game is available immediately and gamblers can play again immediately.

Roulette is a good game to discuss loss chasing (Cohen, 1972). Loss chasing is characteristic of problem gamblers, according to the *Diagnostic and Statistical Manual of Mental Disorders*, 5th edition (DSM-5) (American Psychiatric Association, 2014). To normal people, if something brings pleasure, they do more of it; if something brings pain, they do less of it. Losing money is certainly painful, or at least unpleasant. However, it is quite common for gamblers to gamble more after losing. They chase their loss in an attempt to get their money back. Gamblers may have a mental account for one session of gambling (Shefrin & Statman, 1985; Thaler & Johnson, 1990). When they are losing, they would face a sure loss if they stop. When they are still gambling, the book is not yet closed. They have not 'lost'. In other words, they would be facing an uncertain loss with some possibility of winning back their money. According to prospect theory, people tend to be risk-seeking when choosing between a large uncertain loss and a smaller sure loss (Kahneman & Tversky, 1979). For example, the vast majority of people prefer an 80% chance of losing 4000 Israeli shekels to a sure loss of 3000 shekels (the median family monthly net income). Furthermore, once they have lost, they somehow believe that their luck will turn; they cannot always lose, God must be fair. This is the gambler's fallacy (Croson & Sundali, 2005). In order to catch the anticipated forthcoming good luck, they must continue gambling.

There is even a betting strategy based on the gambler's fallacy. It is called the martingale (Snell, 1982; Wagenaar, 1988). It claims to guarantee winning in a gambling session. The original model of the martingale strategy is based on coin flip but it 'works' in roulette as well. Here is an example: Your first stake is £1 on red. If you win, you stop. If you lose £1, you double your stake to £2. If you win, you stop. If you lose again, you double your stake again to £4. If you win, you stop. If you lose again, you double the stake again to £8. And so on. Now suppose that you have lost three times but, finally, won. You will get £8 − £4 − £2 − £1 = £1, if you bet on the 1:1 pay-out choice. This sounds like a brilliant strategy because, no matter how many times you lose, you can always win in the end.

Unfortunately, there is a catch: it is quite possible that a gambler will run out of funds after a losing streak. The roulette ball does not remember its history. Thus, that gambler is no more likely to win after a losing streak than in any other round. Of course, for gamblers who have an infinite amount of money, the martingale is a reasonable strategy. But nobody has an infinite amount of money. In a limited number of rounds, the return could deviate far away from the expected value. With erroneous beliefs, people can be trapped in loss chasing and become problem gamblers. Though it difficult to ascertain how many people use the martingale strategy, there are written records of it covering hundreds of years at least (Scarne, 1961). One vivid story is by Casanova (1966 [1797]): 'Playing the martingale, continually doubling my stake, I won every day during the rest of the carnival. I was fortunate enough never to lose the sixth card … I still played the martingale, but with such bad luck that I was soon left without a sequin.'

19.5 FRUIT MACHINES

In 2010, 18% of all UK adults played fruit machines (Wardle et al., 2011). Fruit machines are said to be most addictive form of gambling because of their highly stimulating sounds and colours. According to Turner and Horbay (2004), it takes just over a year to become addicted to them, whereas it takes over three years with traditional table games, such as roulette.

Fruit machines look like vending machines and work like them. Typically, they have three to five reels on which pictures are depicted. The player inserts a coin and then pulls down a handle or presses a button. The reels spin. When they stop, the combination of pictures forms a certain pattern. If the combination comprises three pictures that are the same (or some other designated pattern), a reward is given. The most common winning combination is 777. The odds of fruit machines are unknown. The fact that it is a game of pure chance and that the owners of the machines make money indicates that luck is unlikely to be on the gamblers' side.

One of the main phenomena identified in studies of fruit machine gambling is the effects of a near miss. This is a losing pattern that is very similar to a winning one. For example, the three reels may stop at 776, a combination very similar to the winning 777. A near miss makes the gamblers feel that luck is with them and that success is on its way. As a result, near-miss experiences tend to encourage more gambling (Griffiths, 1991; Reid, 1986).

In natural environments to which we are adapted by evolution, a near miss may indeed be close to a win. For example, almost catching prey clearly indicates that prey is nearby and your skill levels are probably adequate to make a kill. In these circumstances, it makes sense to continue to hunt. However, in artificial environments, this link may no longer hold. A 776 in a fruit machine does not indicate that the result of the next spin is likely to be 777. A piece of valid natural reasoning has been hijacked. In fact, by using functional magnetic resonance imaging, it has been found that the part of brain that responds to real winning also responds to a near miss (Clark, Lawrence, Astley-Jones, & Gray, 2009). This supports the notion that a near miss is a loss that is mistaken for a gain. Confusion between losses and gains could lead to problem gambling. This is because near misses that are registered in the brain as gains will result in gamblers' receiving positive reinforcement even when they are losing money. As a result, they would encourage people to gamble more.

19.6 SPORTS BETTING

In 2010, 16% of UK adults gambled on horse races, 4% on football matches, 4% on dog races, and 9% played on other types of sports betting (Wardle et al., 2011). In sports betting, people bet money on the outcome of sports events. Here we include non-human sports events, such as horse racing and dog racing, as well as human sports events like football, tennis, and so on. This is because the format of the gambling is similar and gambling houses include betting on non-human sports as sports betting. Gamblers can bet against the bookmaker or against each other in a betting exchange. Traditionally, the bookmaker sets the odds, the gamblers bet that a certain event will occur (back) and the bookmaker bets that it will not (lay). This traditional form of gambling can be done in gambling outlets or on the bookmakers' websites.

Betting exchange typically takes place on bookmakers' websites. Gamblers bet against each other. They can offer to 'back' a certain event, or to 'lay' a certain event. Their counterparts can see the offers and choose the best odds. Bookmakers in this scenario work as risk-free exchange houses and do not get involved in the price setting of the odds. They display matches and settle the bets for a small percentage of commission. Different bets can be made on one event. For example, for a single football match, there can be bets on the total score, the first half score, the second half score, the first team or player to score a goal, the number of goals over or under a certain number, and so on. The range of odds can be wide. For example, they can range from 4:3 for 'both teams to score' to 150:1 for 'over 9.5 goals'. Hence, gamblers can select from a wide range of different risk levels.

Gamblers who back a certain event can choose to hedge their position by laying that event in the exchange. This could reduce or eliminate the risk they are exposed to. For example, a gambler who has placed £10 on odds of 150:1 for 'over 9.5 goals' may find that the prevailing odds for the same event become 50:1 after four goals in the first half. He may decide to lay 50:1 'over 9.5 goals' for £20 backer's stake. In other words, he now believes the final result will not exceed 9.5 goals and so he accepts a £20 stake from another gambler who believes the final result will exceed 9.5 goals. If the final score is over 9.5, he will win £1490 from his first bet, lose £980 from his second bet, and so win £510 overall (minus commission). If the final score is under 9.5, he will lose the £10 stake in the first bet, win the £20 stake in the second bet, and so win £10 overall (minus commission). At half time, this gambler can guarantee making a profit, no matter what the final score is. Such hedging can be regarded as a gambling strategy that allows control of risk exposure in mid-game.

Many gamblers believe that there is useful knowledge to be learned about different sports. There are books, columns and websites that provide tips for betting. Betting companies also sell past records to people who want to carry out analyses. However, researchers have not found much evidence of expertise. Ladouceur, Giroux and Jacques (1998) found that experts won more times than randomly selected betters but did not win any more money. Experts were just being cautious and chose safe bets. If this is to be called an expert strategy, then so should not gambling at all as this would have a non-negative return of zero. Gamblers feel empowered by knowing the past records of sports teams and the latest updates. Their confidence level is increased, but their performance level is not (Cantinotti, Ladouceur, & Jacques, 2004).

Superstition is common in sports gambling. Windross (2003) found that the majority of people betting on horse racing believed in luck and practised superstitious ceremonies to create good luck. The superstitious behaviours include choosing a lucky number or lucky colour, finding a lucky letter combination in horse names, combining the numbers of the two previous winning horses, and so on. Gamblers believe luck can be observed and manipulated. Superstitious rituals are the methods to obtain good luck. Some rituals can appear bizarre and dangerous. For example, in

South-east Asia, some people run in front of trucks on highways to read their number plates. The number plate gives clues to the lucky number. The closer the gambler runs to the truck, the luckier the number.

Ayton and Fischer (2004) discovered that people who were told that a run of the same outcome was the result of random process predicted the trend would reverse whereas those who were told that the same sequence was the result of skilled performance predicted that it would continue. This begs an obvious question: do gamblers believe that sports betting is skill-based or not? If they believe that it is their skills that give them an edge, they should predict they are more likely to win after winning and therefore become more risk-seeking. Xu and Harvey (2014) discovered the opposite: in sports gambling, gamblers predicted the trend in their betting performance would reverse. They chose safer odds after winning and riskier odds after losing. Interestingly, this actually produced a hot hand effect because safer odds are more likely to produce a win and risky odds are more likely to produce a loss. However, safer odds do not have high payoffs. Hence, gamblers who have experienced a winning streak may feel that their gambling performance has improved, even though they have not actually made more profits. This echoes the observation by Ladouceur et al. (1998) that experts did not make more money in spite of the higher probability of winning. They might become experts simply by winning more times rather than winning more money. They can be experts and problem gamblers at the same time.

19.7 CARD GAMES

Wardle et al. (2011) report that, in 2010, 2% of adults in the United Kingdom played poker in a pub or club, 5% went to a casino to gamble on games (including poker and blackjack), and 13% played online games (including poker and blackjack). There are many different kinds of card games. Some of them, such as blackjack and poker, have elements both of luck and of real expertise. In blackjack, the players take cards in rounds and the winner is the person who reaches 21 points or who is the closest to 21 without exceeding 21. It is played between the dealer of the house and one or more gamblers. If players can remember the cards that have already appeared in the game, they will have a better chance of guessing the cards that are going to appear.

In a lottery and roulette, anomalies are rare and when they happen, it is difficult to profit from them; in card games, there are real cases of sustainable successes. One of the legends is the MIT blackjack team (Mezrich, 2002). They used a card counting technique. Cards A, 2, 3, 4, 5, 6, are marked as +1, cards 7, 8, 9 are marked as 0, cards 10, J, Q, K are marked −1. The gambler keeps adding the value of the cards as they appear. If the sum is negative, it means there are more small cards in the undistributed deck. This is advantageous to the house and so gamblers should decrease their stake. Though the profit level of the MIT blackjack team has not been verified, statistically it is possible to profit from blackjack, poker and other card games (DeDonno & Detterman, 2008; Javarone, 2015; Turner, 2008).

It is not easy to make money by playing card games because success is largely influenced by holding good cards and gamblers may not have enough funds to survive potential losses. Hurley and Pavlov (2011) carried out a simulation based on the card counting technique. They found that, although the expected return was positive with the card counting technique, with minimum stake of $100, the 95% confidence interval of return ranged between –$59,570 and $76,044. It is a risky business. The gamblers must be prepared for difficult periods during their search for positive returns. There are also exogenous risks that are not related to card games *per se*. For example, casinos do not welcome card counters and they may restrict entry for such players. If this happens when the players are losing, it may be difficult to play enough games to reach the expected value. It is possible that people become problem gamblers in the belief that they will win their losses back.

Poker games often involve a combination of the suit and the points of the cards. There are many different kinds of poker games. The rank of the card combinations from low to high normally are: single, pair, three of a kind, straight (consecutive cards), flush (cards of the same suit). There are small variations in ranking orders in different games. Texas Hold'em is a popular card game. It has three to five community cards visible to all players. Players can use the community cards with their own two secret cards to form combinations. They can decide to increase the stake or to fold as the games goes along. Players win either by having the highest rank of the combination or by being the only person remaining.

In Texas Hold'em, players guess each other's cards by observing their stake change and other emotional signals. Card games are available online or in a casino. There is evidence of real expertise in this game (Fiedler & Rock, 2009; Hannum & Cabot, 2009). It is also possible to teach neural networks to play Texas Hold'em to a professional level using evolutionary methods (Nicolai & Hilderman, 2009). The argument that it is a skill-based game may give it a status of a sport rather than gambling.

19.8   PROBLEM GAMBLING

Problem gambling (gambling addiction, pathological gambling) is a mental disorder defined by DSM-5 as 'persistent and recurrent problematic gambling behavior leading to clinically significant impairment or distress' (American Psychiatric Association, 2014). According to the British Gambling Prevalence Survey in 2010, 1.5% of men, 0.3% of women and 0.9% of the entire adult population are problem gamblers (Wardle et al., 2011).

Problem gambling is a major psychological disorder: in terms of the size of the patient population, it is in the same league as depression or panic disorder (Bebbington et al., 2009). It is positively correlated to being male, young, having a low level of education, and having a low socio-economic status (Wardle et al., 2011). Internet gambling, because of its constant availability and convenience, may exacerbate problem gambling: Gainsbury et al. (2015) found that half of problem gamblers reported that convenient online payment increased their monetary losses. Internet gamblers also gamble in more games because they are offered a wider choice than that offered by traditional casino or gambling shops (Gainsbury et al., 2015).

Most forms of gambling in most situations have negative expected returns. Why would people become addicted to negative returns? Neurological research has cast some light on this. Problem gamblers viewing gambling scenarios show decreased brain activity in regions that control impulse, emotion, and decision-making and that respond to loss but increased activity in those regions associated with pleasure and risk taking (Potenza, 2014; Potenza et al. 2003; van Holst, van Den Brink, Veltman, &

Goudriaan, 2010). Some medical treatments used for substance abuse are used to treat problem gambling and have been found to be effective (Bullock & Potenza, 2013). There is also some evidence that problem gambling is associated with abnormal levels of various neurotransmitters, such as serotonin, dopamine, endogenous opioids and hormones (Grant, Brewer, & Potenza, 2006). It is not yet clear whether these anomalies in neurological function are inherited (Eisen et al., 1998).

People with high testosterone levels are more risk-seeking than their counterparts with low testosterone levels (Stanton, Liening, & Schultheiss, 2011). Men naturally have higher testosterone levels than women and they are more risk-seeking. Adolescent males and females in different stage of puberty have different levels of testosterone and their testosterone levels are positively related to their risk-seeking behaviours (Op de Macks et al., 2011). Injecting women with testosterone results in reduced sensitivity to loss and increased risk-seeking (Eisenegger & Naef, 2011; Van Honk et al., 2004). Furthermore, a low ratio of the length of the index finger to the ring finger (an indicator of pre-birth testosterone levels inside the mother's uterus) is associated with high levels of risk-seeking (Neave, Laing, Fink, & Manning, 2003; Stenstrom, Saad, Nepomuceno, & Mendenhall, 2011). All these findings imply that risk preference has a biological basis and can be influenced by long-term and short-term testosterone levels.

Blaszczynski and Nower (2002) suggested that there are three kinds of problem gamblers: (1) gamblers with poor judgement and decision-making skills; (2) those who gamble in order to satisfy emotional needs; and (3) gamblers with neurological or neurochemical dysfunctions.

The first of these do not have any psychopathology before they start gambling. They embark upon their gambling habit because it represents an easily accessible or social activity. They may experience excitement from their gambling, they may experience illusions of control or other kinds of irrational belief, and, for the reasons we have discussed, they may believe that they can win. After losing, they may start to chase their losses and, as a result, they may lose even more. Evidence suggests that this type of gambler can gain control over their habit with minimal intervention provided by sound economic reasoning (Hodgins, 2005).

The second type of gambler often has a family history of problem gambling, together with emotional and biological vulnerabilities (e.g., depression, anxiety). Gambling provides an escape from these problems (Gambino, Fitzgerald, Shaffer, Renner, & Courtage, 1993 Jacobs, 1988; Lesieur & Rothschild, 1989).

The third type of problem gambler typically exhibits impulsive or antisocial behaviours that are independent of their gambling. Such behaviours include substance abuse, suicidality, irritability, low tolerance for boredom, and criminal behaviour not related to gambling. In other words, they have weak control over their behaviours that is manifested not only in gambling but also in other ways (Carlton et al., 1987; Goldstein, Manowitz, Nora, Swartzburg & Carlton, 1985).

For less severe problem gamblers, brief interventions such as warning messages have been used to reduce the gambling behaviour. This approach appears to be useful to some of them (Hodgins, 2005) but not for others (Steenbergh, Whelan, Meyers, May & Floyd, 2004). Courses of cognitive-behavioural therapy (CBT) typically last longer than brief interventions: in Gooding and Tarrier's (2009) study, the minimum CBT session length was four hours. There are different variants of CBT. These range from correction of perceptions about gambling, desensitization to images of gambling, and reduction in motivations to gamble. Some studies have shown that CBT is effective in reducing gambling behaviours (Gooding & Tarrier, 2009; Sylvain, Ladouceur,

& Boisvert, 1997). Psychopharmacological treatments have also been used, with or without behavioural therapies, to reduce problem gambling and some have been found to be effective (Bullock & Potenza, 2013; Leung & Cottler, 2009).

19.9 SUMMARY

Gambling is a mix of biases, fallacies, and real expertise. It provides terrific opportunities to study monetary decision-making. In this chapter, we have described a variety of phenomena associated with the economic psychology of gambling and have shown how they may be explained in different gambling contexts.

People tend to overestimate low odds of winning (Tversky & Kahneman, 1992). This overestimation may arise from use of the availability heuristic, from illusions of control, or from over-inflated confidence associated with the acquisition of knowledge specific to the gambling domain. Gamblers also have techniques that they believe enhance their chances of winning: these include superstitious practices and choosing random-looking lottery numbers. Some of these techniques are effective: real skills in some card games can bring profit. However, the vast majority of gamblers are likely to lose money in the long run. Once they have lost, many of them become susceptible to loss chasing. They believe their luck is going to turn and they must bet again to win the money back. As long as they continue to gamble, the book is still open and losses are not yet realized. They have to keep gambling to prevent that happening. As a result, they often end up losing more money. The brain may fail to discriminate adequately between wins and losses: there is evidence that indicates that near misses activate the same brain regions as wins. Confusion arising from this could also encourage the continuation of gambling.

People may become problem gamblers because they overestimate their chances of winning, because they suffer emotional vulnerabilities that are temporarily offset by gambling, or because they have neurological abnormalities manifest in various antisocial behaviours that include gambling. Problem gamblers may have abnormal brain activities or neurotransmitter levels. High testosterone level predicts high risk preference.

REVIEW QUESTIONS

1. Is it possible to make a profit from buying lottery tickets? If so, please describe a method for doing so.
2. What is the function of experts' advice in sports gambling? What will happen if experts no longer give out advice?

REFERENCES

American Psychiatric Association. (2014). *Diagnostic and statistical manual of mental disorders (DSM-5)*. Washington, DC: APA. www.psychiatry.org/psychiatrists/practice/dsm/dsm-5

Ariyabuddhiphongs, V., & Chanchalermporn, N. (2007). A test of social cognitive theory. Reciprocal and sequential effects: Hope, superstitious belief and environmental factors among lottery gamblers in Thailand. *Journal of Gambling Studies, 23*, 201–214. DOI: 10.1007/s10899-006-9035-3

Ayton, P., & Fischer, I. (2004). The hot hand fallacy and the gambler's fallacy: Two faces of subjective randomness? *Memory & Cognition, 32*(8), 1369–1378. DOI: 10.3758/BF03206327

Bebbington, P., Brugha, T., Coid, J., Crawford, M., Deverill, C., D'Souza, J., ... & Jotangia, D. (2009). *Adult psychiatric morbidity in England, 2007.* Edited by S. McManus et al. London: Information Centre for Health and Social Care.

Beckert, J., & Lutter, M. (2013). Why the poor play the Lottery: Sociological approaches to explaining class-based Lottery play. *Sociology, 47*(6), 1152–1170. DOI: 10.1177/0038038512457854

Bernoulli, D. (1954 [1738]). Exposition of a new theory on the measurement of risk. (Ed. & Trans.). *Econometrica, 22*(1), 23–36. DOI:10.2307/1909829

Binde, P. (2013). Why people gamble: A model with five motivational dimensions. *International Gambling Studies, 13*(1), 81–97. DOI :10.1080/14459795.2012.712150

Blaszczynski, A., & Nower, L. (2002). A pathways model of problem and pathological gambling. *Addiction, 97,* 487–499. DOI: 10.1046/j.1360-0443.2002.00015.x

Bordalo, P., Gennaioli, N., & Shleifer, A. (2012). Salience theory of choice under risk. *Quarterly Journal of Economics, 127,* 1243–1285. DOI: 10.1093/qje/qjs018

Bullock, S., & Potenza, M. (2013). Update on the pharmacological treatment of pathological gambling. *Current Psychopharmacology, 2,* 204–211. DOI: 10.2174/22115560113029990008

Camelot. (2015). Lotto draw history. Retrieved from https://www.national-lottery.co.uk/results/lotto/draw-history (accessed 31 Dec. 2015).

Camelot. (2016a). Lotto: Players' guide. Retrieved from https://www.national-lottery.co.uk/games/in-store/players-guide/lotto (accessed 7 March 2016).

Camelot. (2016b). £4 Million Blue Game procedures. Retrieved from https://www.national-lottery.co.uk/c/files/scratchcards/4millionblue.pdf~2 (accessed 7 March 2016).

Cantinotti, M., Ladouceur, R., & Jacques, C. (2004). Sports betting: Can gamblers beat randomness? *Psychology of Addictive Behaviors, 18*(2), 143–147. DOI: 10.1037/0893-164X.18.2.143

Carlton, P. L., Manowitz, P., McBride, H., Nora, R., Swartzburg, M., & Goldstein, L. (1987). Attention deficit disorder and pathological gambling. *Journal of Clinical Psychiatry, 48,* 487–488.

Casanova, G. (1966 [1797]). *History of my life,* trans. W. R. Trask, 12 vols. New York: Harcourt, Brace & World.

Clark, L., Lawrence, A. J., Astley-Jones, F., & Gray, N. (2009). Gambling near-misses enhance motivation to gamble and recruit win-related brain circuitry. *Neuron, 61*(3), 481–490. DOI: 10.1037/a0032389

Clotfelter, C. T., & Cook, P. J. (1991). Lotteries in the real world. *Journal of Risk and Uncertainty, 4*(3), 227–232. DOI: 10.1007/BF00114154

Cohen, J. (1972). *Psychological probability.* London: Allen & Unwin.

Cook, P. J., & Clotfelter, C. T. (1991). The peculiar scale economies of Lotto. Retrieved from www.nber.org/papers/w3766

Croson, R., & Sundali, J. (2005). The gambler's fallacy and the hot hand: Empirical data from casinos. *Journal of Risk and Uncertainty, 30*(3), 195–209. DOI: 10.1007/s11166-005-1153-2

DeDonno, M. A., & Detterman, D. K. (2008). Poker is a skill. *Gaming Law Review, 12*(1), 31–36. DOI: 10.1089/glr.2008.12105

Eisen, S. A., Lin, N., Lyons, M. I. J., Errer, J. F. S. C. H., Riffith, K. G., Illiam, W. R., & Tsuang, M. I. N. G. T. (1998). Familial influences on gambling behavior: An analysis of 3359 twin pairs, *Addiction, 93*(9), 1375–1384. DOI: 10.1046/j.1360-0443.1998.93913758.x

Eisenegger, C., & Naef, M. (2011). Combining behavioral endocrinology and experimental economics: Testosterone and social decision making. *Journal of Visualized Experiments, 49.* DOI: 10.3791/2065

Fiedler, I. C., & Rock, J. (2009). Quantifying skill in games: Theory and empirical evidence for poker. *Gaming Law Review and Economics, 13*(1), 50–57. DOI:10.1089/glre.2008.13106

Forrest, D., Simmons, R., & Chesters, N. (2002). Buying a dream: Alternative models of demand for Lotto. *Economic Inquiry, 40*(3), 485–496. DOI: 10.1093/ei/40.3.485

Gainsbury, S. M., Russell, A., Wood, R., Hing, N., & Blaszczynski, A. (2015). How risky is Internet gambling? A comparison of subgroups of Internet gamblers based on problem gambling status. *New Media & Society, 17*(6), 861–879. DOI: 10.1177/1461444813518185

Gambino, B., Fitzgerald, R., Shaffer, H., Renner, J., & Courtage, P. (1993). Perceived family history of problem gamblers and scores on SOGS. *Journal of Gambling Studies*, 9, 169–184. DOI: 10.1007/BF01014866

Gambling Commission. (2012). *Machine standards category B3 & B4*. www.gamblingcommission. gov.uk/pdf/machine%20standards%20category%20b3%20and%20b4%20june%202012%20revision%202.pdf

Goldstein, L., Manowitz, P., Nora, R., Swartzburg, M., & Carlton, P. L. (1985). Differential EEG activation and pathological gambling. *Biological Psychiatry*, 20, 1232–1234. DOI:10.1016/0006-3223(85)90180-5

Gooding, P., & Tarrier, N. (2009). A systematic review and meta-analysis of cognitive-behavioural interventions to reduce problem gambling: Hedging our bets? *Behaviour Research and Therapy*, 47(7), 592–607. DOI:10.1016/j.brat.2009.04.002

Grant, J., Brewer, J., & Potenza, M. (2006). The neurobiology of substance and behavioral addictions. *CNS Spectrums*, 11(12), 924–930. dx.doi.org/10.1017/s109285290001511x

Griffiths, M. (1991). Psychobiology of the near-miss in fruit machine gambling. *The Journal of Psychology*, 125(3), 347–357. DOI:10.1080/00223980.1991.10543298

Griffiths, M. (2000). Scratchcard gambling among adolescent males. *Journal of Gambling Studies*, 16(1), 79–91. DOI: 10.1023/A:1009483401308

Hannum, R., & Cabot, A. (2009). Toward legalization of poker: The skill vs. chance debate. *UNLV Gaming Research & Review Journal*. Retrieved from digitalscholarship.unlv.edu/grrj/vol13/iss1/1

Hardoon, K. K., Baboushkin, H. R., Derevensky, J. L., & Gupta, R. (2001). Underlying cognitions in the selection of lottery tickets. *Journal of Clinical Psychology*, 57(6), 749–763. DOI: 10.1002/jclp.1047

Hodgins, D. C. (2005). Implications of a brief intervention trial for problem gambling for future outcome research. *Journal of Gambling Studies*, 21, 13–19. DOI: 10.1007/s10899-004-1917-7

Holtgraves, T., & Skeel, J. (1992). Cognitive biases in playing the Lottery: Estimating the odds and choosing the numbers' representativeness. *Journal of Applied Social Psychology*, 22(12), 934–952. DOI: 10.1111/j.1559-1816.1992.tb00935.x

Hurley, W. J., & Pavlov, A. (2011). There will be blood: On the risk-return characteristics of a blackjack counting system. *Chance*, 24(2), 47–52. DOI: 10.1007/s00144-011-0019-4

Jacobs, D. F. (1988). Evidence for a common dissociative like reaction among addicts. *Journal of Gambling Behavior*, 4, 27–37. DOI: 10.1007/BF01043526

Javarone, M. A. (2015). Is poker a skill game? New insights from statistical physics, 5. *Physics and Society*. DOI: 10.1209/0295-5075/110/58003

Kahneman, D., & Tversky, A. (1979). Prospect theory: An analysis of decision under risk, *Econometrica*, 47(2), 263–292. DOI: 10.1111/j.1536-7150.2011.00774.x

Konstantinou, E., Liagkou, V., Spirakis, P., Stamatiou, Y., Yung, M. (2005). 'Trust engineering': From requirements to system design and maintenance: A working national lottery system experience. *Information Security, Lecture Notes in Computer Science*, 3650, 44–58. DOI: 10.1007/11556992_4

Ladouceur, R., Giroux, I., & Jacques, C. (1998). Winning on the horses: How much strategy and knowledge are needed? *The Journal of Psychology*, 132(2), 133–142. DOI: 10.1080/00223989809599154

Langer, E. (1975). The illusion of control. *Journal of Personality and Social Psychology*, 32(2), 311–328. DOI: 10.1037/0022-3514.32.2.311

Lesieur, H. R., & Rothschild, J. (1989). Children of Gamblers Anonymous members. *Journal of Gambling Behavior*, 5, 269–282. DOI: 10.1007/BF01672428

Leung, K. S., & Cottler, L. B. (2009). Treatment of pathological gambling. *Current Opinion in Psychiatry*, 22, 69–74. DOI: 10.1097/YCO.0b013e32831575d9

Markel, T., La Fleur, B., & La Fleur, B. (2015). *La Fleur's 2015 world lottery almanac*. Rockville, MD.

Matheson, V. A., & Grote, K. R. (2004). Lotto fever: Do lottery players act rationally around large jackpots? *Economics Letters*, 83(2), 233–237. DOI: 10.1016/j.econlet.2003.11.010

Mezrich, B. (2002). *Bringing down the house: The inside story of six MIT students who took Vegas for millions*. New York: Free Press.

Neave, N., Laing, S., Fink, B., & Manning, J. T. (2003). Second to fourth digit ratio, testosterone and perceived male dominance. *Proceedings of the Royal Society of London, B, 270*(1529), 2167–2172. DOI: 10.1098/rspb.2003.2502

Nicolai, G., & Hilderman, R. J. (2009). No-limit Texas Hold'em Poker agents created with evolutionary neural networks. In CIG2009 - 2009 IEEE Symposium on Computational Intelligence and Games (pp. 125–131). DOI: 10.1109/CIG.2009.5286485

Op de Macks, Z. A., Gunther Moor, B., Overgaauw, S., Güroğlu, B., Dahl, R. E., & Crone, E. A. (2011). Testosterone levels correspond with increased ventral striatum activation in response to monetary rewards in adolescents. *Developmental Cognitive Neuroscience, 1*(4), 506–516. DOI: 10.1016/j.dcn.2011.06.003

Potenza, M. N. (2014). The neural bases of cognitive processes in gambling disorder. *Trends in Cognitive Sciences, 18*(8), 429–438. DOI: 10.1016/j.tics.2014.03.007

Potenza, M. N., Steinberg, M. A., Skudlarski, P., Fulbright, R.K., Lacadie, C.M., Wilber, M.K., ... & Wexler, B. E. (2003). Gambling urges in pathological gambling: A functional magnetic resonance imaging study. *Archives of General Psychiatry, 60*(8), 828–836. DOI: 10.1001/archpsyc.60.8.828

Reid, R. L. (1986). The psychology of the near miss. *Journal of Gambling Behavior, 2*(1), 32–39. DOI: 10.1007/BF01019932

Scarne, J., 1961. *Scarne's complete guide to gambling*. New York : Simon & Schuster.

Schwartz, D. G. (2006). *Roll the bones: The history of gambling*, New York: Gotham.

Shefrin, H., & Statman, M. (1985). The disposition to sell winners too early and ride losers too long: Theory and evidence. *Journal of Finance, 40*, 777–790. DOI: 10.1111/j.1540-6261.1985.tb05002.x

Snell, J. L. (1982). Gambling, probability and martingales. *The Mathematical Intelligencer, 4*(3), 118–124. DOI: 10.1007/BF03024242

Stanton, S. J., Liening, S. H., & Schultheiss, O. C. (2011). Testosterone is positively associated with risk taking in the Iowa Gambling Task. *Hormones and Behavior, 59*(2), 252–6. DOI: 10.1016/j.yhbeh.2010.12.003

Steenbergh, T. A., Whelan, J. P., Meyers, A. W., May, R. K., & Floyd, K. (2004). Impact of warning and brief intervention messages on knowledge of gambling risk, irrational beliefs and behaviour. *International Gambling Studies, 4*(1), 3–16. DOI: 10.1080/1445979042000224377

Stenstrom, E., Saad, G., Nepomuceno, M. V., & Mendenhall, Z. (2011). Testosterone and domain-specific risk: Digit ratios (2D:4D and rel2) as predictors of recreational, financial, and social risk-taking behaviors. *Personality and Individual Differences, 51*(4), 412–416. DOI: 10.1016/j.paid.2010.07.003

Stewart, N., Chater, N., & Brown, G. D. a. (2006). Decision by sampling. *Cognitive Psychology, 53*(1), 1–26. DOI: 10.1016/j.cogpsych.2005.10.003

Sylvain, C., Ladouceur, R., & Boisvert, J. (1997). Cognitive and behavioral treatment of pathological gambling: A controlled study. *Journal of Consulting and Clinical Psychology, 65*, (5), 727–732. DOI: 10.1037//0022-006X.65.5.727

Terrell, D. (1994). A test of the gambler's fallacy: Evidence from pari-mutuel games. *Journal of Risk and Uncertainty, 8*(3), 309–317. DOI: 10.1007/BF01064047

Thaler, R., & Johnson, E. J. (1990). Gambling with the house money and trying to break even: The effects of prior outcomes on risky choice. *Management Science. 36*, 643–660. DOI: 10.1287/mnsc.36.6.643

Turner, N. E. (2008). Viewpoint: Poker is an acquired skill. *Gaming Law Review and Economics, 12*(3), 229–230. DOI: 10.1089/glre.2008.12305

Turner, N., & Horbay, R. (2004). How do slot machines and other electronic gambling machines actually work? *Journal of Gambling Issues, 11*. Retrieved from http://jgi.camh.net/doi/abs/10.4309/jgi.2004.11.21 (accessed 31 March 2016).

Tversky, A., & Kahneman, D. (1973). Availability: A heuristic for judging frequency and probability. *Cognitive Psychology, 5*(2), 207–232. DOI: 10.1016/0010-0285(73)90033-9

Tversky, A., & Kahneman, D. (1992). Advances in prospect theory: Cumulative representation of uncertainty. *Journal of Risk and Uncertainty, 5*(4), 297–323. DOI:10.1007/BF00122574

Van Holst, R. J., Van Den Brink, W., Veltman, D. J., & Goudriaan, A. E. (2010). Brain imaging studies in pathological gambling. *Current Psychiatry Reports*, *12*(5), 418–425. DOI: 10.1007/ s11920-010-0141-7

Van Honk, J., Schutter, D. J. L. G., Hermans, E. J., Putman, P., Tuiten, A., & Koppeschaar, H. (2004). Testosterone shifts the balance between sensitivity for punishment and reward in healthy young women. *Psychoneuroendocrinology*, *29*(7), 937–43. DOI: 10.1016/j.psyneuen.2003.08.007

Wagenaar, W. A. (1988). *Paradoxes of gambling behaviour.* Mahwah, NJ: Lawrence Erlbaum Associates.

Wardle, H., Moody, A., Spence, S., Orford, J., Volberg, R., Jotangia, D., ... et al. (2011). *British Gambling Prevalence Survey 2010.* London: Stationery Office.

Windross, A. J. (2003). The luck of the draw: Superstition in gambling. *Gambling Research*, *15*(1), 63–77.

Wohl, M. J. A., & Enzle, M. E. (2002). The deployment of personal luck: Sympathetic magic and illusory control in games of pure chance. *Personality and Social Psychology Bulletin*, *28*(10), 1388–1397. DOI: 10.1177/014616702236870

Xu, J., & Harvey, N. (2014). Carry on winning: The gamblers' fallacy creates hot hand effects in online gambling. *Cognition*, *131*(2), 173–180. DOI: 10.1016/j.cognition.2014.01.002

FURTHER READING

Gobet, F., & Schiller, M. (Eds.). (2014). *Problem gambling: Cognition, prevention and treatment.* Basingstoke: Palgrave Macmillan.

Walker, M. B. (1992). *The psychology of gambling.* New York: Pergamon Press.

PART 6

Life-Span Perspectives

20 Economic Socialization: Childhood, Adolescence, and Early Adulthood

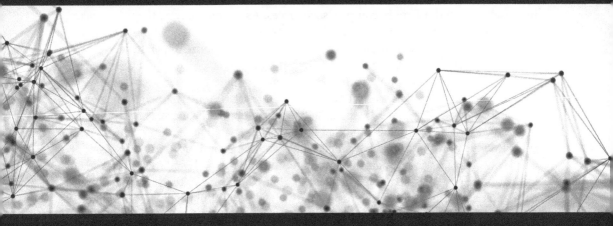

ANNETTE OTTO AND JOYCE SERIDO

CHAPTER OUTLINE

LEARNING OUTCOMES

BY THE END OF THIS CHAPTER YOU SHOULD BE ABLE TO:

1. Name antecedent skills and developmental tasks that signal the acquisition of knowledge and skills associated with economic behaviour and maturation during childhood, adolescence, and early adulthood.

2. Explain the socializing role of parents with regard to the development of economic behaviour.

3. Demonstrate how Bronfenbrenner's bioecological model can help us understand individual development towards financial autonomy.

20.1   INTRODUCTION

Autonomy is a key indicator of adult status in many cultures, that is, individual ability to make – and assume personal responsibility for – everyday life choices and the increasing demands of more complex social roles. As people mature, they also make more complex economic choices. A child may choose to save money for a toy, rather than spend it on sweets or magazines; an adolescent may choose to play video games with friends rather than spend the allowance at the cinema; a young adult may cycle to work rather than take public transport or pay the high cost of petrol to drive a car. Whether cycling to work is motivated out of concern for the environment or personal health, for pleasure or to save driving time, the behaviour has economic consequences (e.g., the cost of bicycle maintenance and repair is less than that of a car or the annual cost of public transport). These examples illustrate that economic behaviours, opportunities, and responsibilities change with age. Indeed, the early choices of everyday life can be regarded as economic behaviours that contribute to the financial knowledge and behaviours needed to independently manage adult financial responsibilities (Serido, Shim, & Tang, 2013). We refer to this ability as *financial* autonomy.

In a 24/7 global economy, today's financial options and economic choices demand a high level of financial knowledge and skills. Thus, to function in a complex world, children, adolescents, and early adults need to develop and integrate skills and knowledge across many settings – settings that are important to them at each stage of their life (Larson, 2002). There is evidence that feeling financially competent is related to early adults' financial, psychological, and subjective well-being (Gutter & Copur, 2011; Serido, Shim, Mishra, & Tang, 2010). This probably best explains why it is important to understand the development of economic skills and contributing factors.

Many of the competencies needed to achieve financial autonomy in adulthood – such as future orientation (Webley & Nyhus, 2006), self-regulation (Kochanska, Coy, & Murray, 2001), self-efficacy (Bandura, 1994), and executive function (Drever et al., 2015) – develop early in life. Throughout this chapter, we will explain the ways in which children, adolescents, and early adults develop the economic knowledge and skills needed at respective stages in their lives as a framework for understanding economic socialization as a developmental progression of financial autonomy.

This chapter begins by providing a contextual framework for understanding economic socialization as a developmental process (i.e., leading to financial autonomy, a developmental task of late adolescence). Then, we present a review of the socializing role of parents before empirical support for the economic socialization process during childhood, adolescence, and early adulthood is provided. The chapter ends with a summary and suggestions for further reading.

20.2   A CONTEXTUAL FRAMEWORK FOR ECONOMIC BEHAVIOUR DEVELOPMENT

Successful maturation is an unfolding process of navigating age-graded challenges. But individuals do not develop independent of their environment; both are changing. A lifespan model that captures the dynamic and complex interactions of internal (individual) and external (environmental) factors in human ontology has been presented by Bronfenbrenner (1986; 2005). Bronfenbrenner's bioecological model (2005) is based on the notion that development involves relations between individuals and multi-layered ecologies occurring across the lifespan. This lifespan developmental perspective incorporates the interacting and interrelated factors of the ever-changing social and cultural environment to which people adapt. In this model, development emerges from the interaction of the individual and the social environmental context (see Box 20.1).

Advances in technology over the past 30 years, including online access to consumer goods and financial services over the World Wide Web, are examples of a chronosystem change. The change introduces new levels of economic complexity and abstraction, demanding a higher level of economic awareness worldwide. The impact at each level, however, is not uniform. Financial inclusion policies provide a

Box 20.1 Bronfenbrenner's bioecological model

Bronfenbrenner (2005) distinguishes four different ecological environments: (1) the *microsystem*, which includes the immediate environment, the home or the family, the playground, the school, and the peer group (a person can be part of more than one microsystem); (2) the *mesosystem*, which contains the interacting microsystems, such as the school and the family, the family and the friends, the family and the neighbourhood, etc.; (3) the *exosystem* as the structure of the larger community in which people live, that indirectly influence the developing person; and (4) the *macrosystem*, which includes general cultural, political, social, legal, religious, educational and economic values. There is also the *chronosystem* as the final parameter, which refers to historical change over time that affects the four levels of the ecological environment (Figure 20.1).

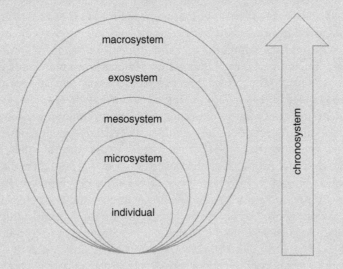

FIGURE 20.1 *Bronfenbrenner's bioecological model.*

Source: Bronfenbrenner 2005. Reproduced with permission of SAGE Publishing.

good illustration. At a macrosystem level, policies regarding bank accounts for children, the type of account, the age at which they can open an account, who has access to the account, and tax treatment of these accounts differ by country (see Loke & Sherraden, 2009, for a global comparison of Child Development Account policies). Even within the same country, the impact differs at each level. To mention a specific case, Ghana introduced a mobile banking policy to improve access to financial services for individuals living in remote areas. Despite this macrosystem level change, less than one-third of young people between 15 and 24 years of age in Ghana reported having no physical access to banks but more than two-thirds reported not having used any financial services in the past year (Montez, 2010). The combination of macrosystem and exosystem influences is illustrated by the variation in the level of understanding about the banking services from children of different countries (Jahoda, 1981; Ng, 1983, 1985). Irrespective of age differences, children in Hong Kong showed advanced levels of understanding of the sources of income of banks and banking activities (Ng, 1983), compared to children from New Zealand (Ng, 1985) and Scotland (Jahoda, 1981). Ng (1983) explained the economic maturity of the Hong Kong children in terms of macrosystem influences: the high levels of consumer activity and the business ethos of the Hong Kong society. Ng posited that, 'Socially, life would be difficult for them if they did not grasp socio-economic concepts at an early age' (p. 221). Financial interactions within the mesosystem encompass parents and schools or schools and financial institutions working together to assist children and young people in making deposits to accumulate larger sums of money (Sherraden, Johnson, Elliott, Porterfield, & Rainford, 2007). Finally, parental strategies to teach their children to save (Bucciol & Veronesi, 2014) exemplify the influence of the microsystem.

Individual development lies at the centre of Bronfenbrenner's model. He stresses that individuals shape their environment through their own behaviour (Bronfenbrenner, 1994). Although individuals play an active part in shaping their environment (*human agency*, see Bandura, 2006), they do this within the constraints of the overall economic, social, and cultural conditions. They actively choose from possible alternatives that are available to them and they do this in different ways (*bounded agency*, Schoon, 2007). By way of example, Leiser and colleagues (Leiser, Sevón, & Levy, 1990) found that attitudes towards wealth, poverty, and unemployment differed between the ten countries they compared and sometimes also within different segments of the same population (in Israel). Suggested explanations involve differences in locus of control and uncertainty avoidance, as well as in individualistic versus collectivistic values (see Hofstede, 1980). Comparing six countries, Bowes, Flanagan, and Taylor (2001) illustrated that what adolescents think about children's involvement in (and payment for) different types of household work reflected general differences in social and political characteristics. For a summary of cross-cultural differences regarding the economic socialization of children, see Leiser et al. (1990). The findings of these studies are in line with Vygotsky's view of cognitive development (1978). Vygotsky considers culture and assumes that children's intellectual ability develops gradually through assistance provided by peers who are more capable and adults (scaffolding). According to Vygotsky, scaffolding helps children develop their overall cognitive abilities. When exposed to new information that is intriguing and at the same time not too difficult to grasp, children's cognitive development advances. Often, these helpful adults are parents, other family members (grandparents), or siblings. They may provide assistance or function as role model (see Section 20.3).

20.3   THE ROLE OF PARENTS IN ECONOMIC SOCIALIZATION

Economic behaviour develops as individuals exchange goods and services within social groups. It is thus reasonable to consider the development of economic behaviour as a social learning process. From a social learning theory perspective (Bandura & Walters, 1963), children learn about money and financial behaviour by observing and imitating the most relevant models (observational learning; Bandura, 1977), including parents. The social learning theory can help us understand the process by which an individual learns attitudes, knowledge, and skills to become a competent economic agent. Note, as active agents, children often create the very reinforcements that strengthen new patterns of behaviour.

According to LeVine (1974), parents have three basic goals for their children. First, a survival goal, such that parents promote the physical survival and health of the child. Second, an economic goal, in which parents foster the skills and behaviours the child will need for independent economic functioning as an adult. When these goals are met, parents will encourage the child to seek status and self-fulfilment. Thus, parents can be expected to promote financial autonomy. In the literature, we find support for this assumption, not only from the perspective of parents but also from children, adolescents, and young adults.

For a long time, the role of parents as economic socialization agents has mainly been investigated in connection with their attitudes towards the management of their child's pocket money use (Feather, 1991; Furnham & Thomas, 1984; Lewis & Scott, 2003; Marshall & Magruder, 1960; Prevey, 1945). According to a study conducted in France, pocket money and allowances may play a more educative role during adolescence than during childhood (Lassarre, 1996). A study in Australia (Feather, 1991) established that the behaviour of parents is likely influenced by their value system: Giving pocket money or setting up an allowance system was either justified by group thinking (children as part of the family whose needs should be met) or individualistic values (pocket money and allowances are thought to provide for opportunities to learn to become more independent).

Early on, parents were broadly characterized as 'educators' and 'regulators' of their children's behaviour, based on their socializing practices and their socialization goals within the economic domain (Furnham, 1993). As educators, parents expose the child to all aspects of the economic world; as regulators, parents try to protect the child where possible. Leiser and Ganin (1996) introduced a similar distinction between parents who engage their children in discussions about financial matters in order to teach their children the skills they need to reach economic independence in the future, and parents who avoid such discussions to protect their children from economic worries and responsibilities.

Another approach to parents as socialization agents in the economic domain is the consideration of parenting style. Based on the dimensions of demandingness and responsiveness, Baumrind (1991) described parents who are demanding and responsive as authoritative, parents who are demanding without being responsive as authoritarian, and parents who are responsive and not demanding as permissive. Parents who are neither responsive nor demanding have been described as neglectful

(Maccoby & Martin, 1983). Drawing on this approach, Carlson and Grossbart (1988) investigated mothers' attitudes towards advertising and child consumption in relation to parenting style. Authoritative mothers were more active in consumer communication, reported more media mediation efforts, and in general, were less positive about advertising, compared to authoritarian and neglectful mothers. More recently, associations were found between parenting style and economic behaviours such as saving and spending (i.e., careful, deliberate, well-informed, prudent or impulsive shopping) in adolescents and young adults (Ashby, Schoon, & Webley, 2011; Kim, Yang, & Lee, 2015; Otto, 2009).

Parents influence the development of their children's knowledge and skills concerning the use of money both indirectly (by observation and participation) and intentionally (through lessons) (Bucciol & Veronesi, 2014; Webley & Nyhus, 2006). A common form of indirect parental economic socialization is role-modelling. Children internalize the attitudes and behaviours modelled by parents. Whether or not parents are aware of it, they transmit the financial values, norms, and behaviours that contribute to their children's economic well-being (Danes, 1994). Imitation without understanding of the purpose or implications of those behaviours, however, may be problematic. For instance, early adults may pay by credit card, as their parents did, but not pay off the monthly balance because they did not observe that behaviour. Intentional and direct parental teaching of specific financial knowledge and application of that knowledge may engender feelings of self-confidence and competence about managing finances independently (Serido et al., 2013). Studies of college students have evidenced that the influence of parents continues into early adulthood (Jorgensen & Savla, 2010; Serido et al., 2010; Shim Barber, Card, Xiao, & Serido, 2010; Shim, Xiao, Barber, & Lyons, 2009). In a study by Shim and colleagues (Shim et al., 2010), college students whose parents taught them how to use a credit card, how to be a smart shopper, and how to finance college were more likely to act on those behaviours while at school. Similarly, adolescents who received more financial information from their parents were more likely to set financial goals and save money compared to adolescents who did not (Koonce, Mimura, Mauldin, Rupured, & Jordan, 2008). On the face of it, the quality of the parent–child communication regarding financial topics is an important predictor of the financial, psychological, and personal well-being of early adults. In the previously cited study (Shim et al., 2010), the researchers found support that positive parental economic socialization, including role-modelling and explicit teaching, promoted healthy financial attitudes and perceived control, and these factors in turn promoted responsible financial behaviour.

Although the extant literature provides support for parents as primary economic socializing agents, the influence of other socialization agents is likely to play a role. For children and adolescents, siblings, peers, teachers, or grandparents may influence their economic knowledge and skills. For early adults, romantic partners may become an important source of economic socialization, as they separate from their parents and begin to form committed romantic relationships. The role of alternative economic socializing influences, however, is less studied (Gudmunson & Danes, 2011). The growing body of research on financial literacy and the role of formal education is an exception, which we do not consider here due to space limitations (for a review, see OECD, 2014).

20.4   THE STUDY OF ECONOMIC BEHAVIOUR DEVELOPMENT FROM CHILDHOOD THROUGH EARLY ADULTHOOD

In the following sections, we present the types of studies and the insights from those studies that describe developmental tasks that signal the acquisition of knowledge and skills associated with economic maturation during childhood, adolescence, and early adulthood.

20.4.1   Childhood

Experiments and qualitative studies (e.g., role-play, group discussions, and interviews) provide insight into the economic behaviour and understanding of children. Experiments allow children to demonstrate their understanding of abstract concepts with tangible objects. Experimental studies on children's saving (Otto, Schots, Westerman, & Webley, 2006; Sonuga-Barke & Webley, 1993; Webley et al., 1991) revealed age differences in the use of saving strategies: Whereas 12-year-old children used the deposit function of the bank to avoid temptation, children aged 6 and 9 years old did not. Although a lot can be learned from the behaviour of children through experimental studies, it could be short-sighted to infer from their behaviour a certain level of understanding without further probing to understand what they did (or why) in their own words. Qualitative studies allow children to express their views and perspectives. For instance, one interview study with children aged 8–11 years old (Webley, 1996) revealed that the children's ideas about fair swaps and the value they ascribe to a marble is more likely related to its size, popularity, and scarcity, than to the price paid for it in a shop. It may be helpful to use additional material such as stories and pictures to gain insight into children's views of a certain topic (see Leiser and Halachmi's (2006) investigation of children's understanding of market forces). One way to balance the two is to ask the parents about their child's typical behaviour.

Children as young as 5 or 6 have been found to think of a bank as a source of money (Berti & Bombi, 1988), or to think of money in the bank as money that is lost (Sonuga-Barke & Webley, 1993; Webley, Levine, & Lewis, 1991). How can this be explained? In the early years of research on economic socialization, Stacey (1982) identified a number of stages related to the economic understanding of children and adolescents. This approach is characterized by an assumption of deficiency because it examines when and how children are becoming more adult-like, mature, and rational and it implies that in their early years, children lack the cognitive understanding that adults possess. According to Stacey, children make economic inferences about work as a source of money around the age of 6–8, while 7–9-year-olds would be able to understand socio-economic differences such as rich and poor. The findings are based on rather small samples that cannot be considered representative, but have shed some light on children's ideas about money, possessions, social differentiation, and inequality (see Bonn, Earle, Lea, & Webley, 1999, for an investigation of children in South Africa, and Emler & Dickinson, 1985, for Scottish children's representations of economic inequalities).

During childhood, a number of skills develop that can be considered antecedent skills needed for solving economic problems that are important to children, such as swapping, bargaining, and making choices about small amounts of (pocket) money. A relevant component of maturity regarding the use of money would be the pre-schooler's understanding of numbers. On average, 5-year-olds are able to carry out simple additions and subtractions through counting (Gilmore & Spelke, 2008). Next to basic numeracy skills (Lusardi, 2008; Friedline, 2015), saving to reach a specific amount of (pocket) money requires problem-solving and mathematical ability (Webley, 1996). To understand monetary transactions at a market or in a shop, children need to know the value of the coins required and make correct calculations to understand and check the change they receive (Berti & Bombi, 1988; Scheinholtz, Holden, & Kalish, 2012; Strauss, 1952). Another helpful skill for saving is the ability to delay gratification (Ainslie, 1975; Wood, 1998) and there is empirical support that individual differences in regulatory strength can be observed early in life (Mischel & Ayduk, 2011). Studies set up to investigate choices (see Chapter 3 in this volume) of pre-schoolers between a small reward now (e.g., a marshmallow or a sticker) and a larger reward later (e.g., two marshmallows or more stickers) discovered that children need to understand the difference in quantity of a reward as well as the temporality of the reward to develop and exhibit future-oriented self-control (Garon, Longard, Bryson, & Moore, 2012). Related to this is the development of children's sense of time (around age 8 or 9, children are able to accurately distinguish the time order of events, Friedman & Lyon, 2005) and gain the ability to anticipate future events (Atance & Meltzoff, 2005). This is important since a number of economic behaviours, such as saving and borrowing, are time-related. Involved in children's temporal understanding is the development of memory (Suddendorf & Moore, 2011) and, recently, relationships were found between languages, which grammatically separate the future and the present and intertemporal financial decision making in children (Chen, 2013) as well as time preferences in adults (Sutter, Angerer, Glätzle-Rützler, & Lergetporer, 2014).

Taken together, numeracy, self-control, an understanding of the present and the future, and the ability to delay gratification can be considered developmental antecedents acquired during childhood that contribute to economic maturity and autonomy. The everyday experiences of children affect their understanding of economic concepts, and these experiences depend on age and participation in economic life (Leiser & Ganin, 1996; Marshall & Magruder, 1960), the context (Bonn et al., 1999), and the social environment of the children (Berti & Bombi, 1988). Yet, it is unclear, which concepts and competencies should be taught by whom and when. More research is needed to further our understanding of how children develop positive financial habits, and what role values, attitudes, and emotions play in the acquisition of appropriate economic skills and knowledge during childhood and thereafter.

20.4.2 Adolescence

With adolescent samples, interviews have been used to elicit how adolescents think and feel about economic choices while experiments demonstrate levels of understanding through choice of strategy or success. Based on in-depth interviews with 30 adolescent girls (15 from an urban area in northern France and 15 from an urban area in the Midwestern United States), Palan, Gentina, and Muratore (2010) revealed that consumption autonomy can be broken down into four dimensions: attitudinal, emotional, functional, and financial autonomy. The establishment of autonomy is a main theme of adolescence as a transitional period. Adolescents increasingly seek independence and control over their lives. Compared to children, they have more opportunities to make autonomous choices, particularly with regard to personal issues, such as hairstyle, choice of clothing, time spent away from home, and how to spend allowance money or earnings (Daddis & Smetana, 2005; Wray-Lake, Crouter, & McHale, 2010). The degree to which adolescents seek autonomy may be influenced by cultural factors (Fuligni, Tseng, & Lam, 1999) and the degree with which parents grant autonomy.

Leiser and Ganin (1996) emphasize the importance of adolescence 'as the age at which economic knowledge and attitudes become more systematic and better coordinated' (p. 105). Compared to children, adolescents can be expected to start dealing with money from sources other than parents (e.g., income from small jobs during out-of-school-hours) and this may, at least in part, free them from adult economic control (Alhabeeb, 1996). At the same time, adolescents have more spending opportunities and spending autonomy than children (Palan et al., 2010).

During adolescence, regulatory skills mature (Collins & Steinberg, 2008) and cognitive control improves (Luna, 2009). This development is important, since intentional self-regulation is key when it comes to the individual's contribution to his or her positive development (Lerner, Dowling, & Anderson, 2003). Adolescents are able to think about possibilities beyond the immediate present, think ahead, plan, and work towards future goals (Keating, 1980; Larson, 2014). These skills in combination with cognitive self-regulation are relevant for making decisions about money (spending versus not spending) as 'the conflict between "having now" versus "having later" requires the person to engage in self-regulation' (Faber & Vohs, 2004, p. 509).

From a lifespan perspective, adolescence is the period with the greatest engagement in sensation-seeking behaviours; that is, across cultures, adolescents are keenest to seek novelties. Engaging in sensation-seeking behaviours may be necessary to develop social skills (Steinberg, 2004) that promote independence in adulthood (cf. Luna, 2009). However, in an economic context, urgency and sensation-seeking (dimensions of impulsivity) were found to be correlated with adolescent gambling (Romo et al. 2014). Adolescents, who are more impulsive than adults (Pechmann, Levine, Loughlin, & Leslie, 2005) and who have yet to master self-controlling techniques, are likely to find postponing consumption more difficult than adults. It is during this time, however, that adolescents make decisions (e.g., educational decisions), that will ultimately affect their financial future (Webley, Burgoyne, Lea, & Young, 2001). Leaving the parental home to acquire higher or further education after compulsory education may contribute to the student group feeling more capable about managing a budget and paying bills. In contrast, choosing to work full-time and continuing to live at home may contribute to a feeling of greater independence from parents among the working group because they are earning money. In the short term, the student defers earnings and incurs fees and debt while in school (Cho, Xu,

& Kiss, 2015; Davies & Lea, 1995), whereas the worker may be able to save money for the future. Yet over a lifetime, the student may earn much more from a higher-paying career than the less-educated counterpart (Baum, Ma, & Payea, 2013).

20.4.3 Early Adulthood

Much of what is known about early adults and money comes from survey studies conducted with college students primarily in Western industrialized countries. This research has focused on the level of financial knowledge (e.g., OECD, 2014; Peng, Bartholomae, Fox, & Cravener, 2007), economic socialization (Jorgensen & Savla, 2010; Kim & Chatterjee, 2013; Shim et al., 2010), beliefs, attitudes, and values (Allen, Edwards, Hayhoe, & Leach, 2007; Harrison, Agnew, & Serido, 2015; Serido et al., 2013; Webley & Nyhus, 2006), as well as financial behaviours (Robb & Woodyard, 2011; Shim et al., 2010), and well-being (Gutter & Copur, 2011; Serido et al., 2013; Shim, Serido, & Barber, 2011). These studies suggest that young adults have limited financial knowledge; parental economic socialization continues into the early adult years; attitudes strongly influence actual behaviours; and responsible financial behaviours are associated with better outcomes, both concurrently and over time.

In post-industrialized societies, economic autonomy during the transition to adulthood is an indication of positive development (Eccles, Templeton, Barber, & Stone, 2003). Although the research on early adults outside Western industrialized countries is sparse, most societies expect youth to transition to adult roles, including the transition from school to work (National Research Council and Institute of Medicine, 2005). Consequently, making day-to-day economic choices becomes an increasingly complex task, requiring the development of more advanced skills.

As youth mature (18–24 years), they adopt a more relativistic view of the world and their place in it (e.g., Perry, 1970; 1981). Whereas childhood and adolescent development emphasize progressively rational thinking (e.g., objective, scientific processing) as the antecedent to cognitive maturity (Piaget, 1972), adult development places increasing importance on subjective experience and contextual interactions as catalysts for growth (Cartwright, 2001). This developmental shift to more relativistic decision-making coincides with the need to assume greater personal and financial responsibility (Arnett, 2000).

Decision-making increasingly refers to a process of selecting the most adaptive action – the one most applicable to the current situation that aligns with the current working model, based on previous knowledge and experience – rather than a right or wrong choice (Sinnott, 1998). In this sense, adult economic choices must be based on relevant information available in real-life situations that take into account objective knowledge as well as personal values and responsibility (Gudmunson & Danes, 2011). Early socialization experiences may be reinterpreted in the context of uncertainty and economic constraint. In balancing the need to become economically self-sufficient with the desire to consume, early adults develop a deeper understanding of the tasks they must master.

We would like to point out that research on early adults outside Western industrialized countries is sparse, and that generalizations to countries with different levels of economic and political development should be treated with caution. In the main, there is much more to learn about economic socialization during this developmental period and the dynamic interaction among economic conditions, economic behaviours, and economic socialization.

20.5   SUMMARY

We began the chapter noting the fundamental need for individuals to develop economic knowledge and skills to achieve financial autonomy. We also provided a developmental framework for understanding how economic socialization shapes individual knowledge and skills within contextual settings – and emphasized that both the individual and the contextual settings change over time. We described the role of parents in the development of economic behaviour and highlighted skills and tasks necessary for achieving financial autonomy that develop in childhood, adolescence, and early adulthood. We argue that economic behaviour, particularly the knowledge and skills learned in childhood through early adulthood, is an important aspect of individual development and a rich area for future study.

REVIEW QUESTIONS

1. How do developmental theories help us understand economic socialization as a behavioural process?
2. Why do economic psychologists use different research methods?
3. How might the theoretical framework be used to study cultural sub-groups of industrialized societies (e.g., immigrant populations, non-minority populations)?

REFERENCES

Ainslie, G. (1975). Specious reward: A behavioural theory of impulsiveness and impulse control. *Psychological Bulletin, 82,* 463–496.

Alhabeeb, M. J. (1996). Teenagers' money, discretionary spending and saving. *Financial Counseling and Planning, 7,* 123–132.

Allen, M. W., Edwards, R., Hayhoe, C. R., & Leach, L. (2007). Imagined interactions, family money management patterns and coalitions, and attitudes toward money and credit. *Journal of Family and Economic Issues, 28,* 3–22.

Arnett, J. J. (2000). Emerging adulthood: A theory of development from the late teens through the twenties. *American Psychologist, 55,* 469.

Ashby, J. S., Schoon, I., & Webley, P. (2011). Save now, save later? Linkages between saving behavior in adolescence and adulthood. *European Psychologist, 16,* 227–237.

Atance, C. M., & Meltzoff, A. N. (2005). My future self: Young children's ability to anticipate and explain future states. *Cognitive Development, 20,* 341–361.

Bandura, A. (1977). *Social learning theory.* Englewood Cliffs, NJ: Prentice-Hall.

Bandura, A. (1994). Self-efficacy. In V. S. Ramachaudran (Ed.), *Encyclopedia of human behavior* (vol. 4; pp. 71–81). New York: Academic Press.

Bandura, A. (2006). Toward a psychology of human agency. *Perspectives on Psychological Science, 1,* 164–180.

Bandura, A., & Walters, R. H. (1963). *Social learning and personality development*. New York: Holt, Rinehart, and Winston.

Baum, S., Ma, J., & Payea, K. (2013). *Education pays 2013: The benefits of higher education for individuals and society*. New York: The College Board. http://trends.collegeboard.org/sites/default/files/education-pays-2013-full-report.pdf

Baumrind, D. (1991). Effective parenting during the early adolescent transition. In P. A. E. Cowan, & M. Hetherington (Eds.), *Family transitions* (pp. 111–163). Hillsdale, NJ: Lawrence Erlbaum Associates.

Berti, A. E., & Bombi, A. S. (1988). *The child's construction of economics*. Cambridge: Cambridge University Press.

Bonn, M., Earle, D., Lea, S. E. G., & Webley, P. (1999). South African children's views of wealth, poverty, inequality and unemployment. *Journal of Economic Psychology, 20*, 593–612.

Bowes, J. M., Flanagan, C., & Taylor, A. J. (2001). Adolescents' ideas about individual and social responsibility in relation to children's household work: Some international comparisons. *International Journal of Behavioral Development, 25*, 60–68.

Bronfenbrenner, U. (1986). Ecology of the family as a context for human development: Research perspectives. *Developmental Psychology, 22*, 723–742.

Bronfenbrenner, U. (1994). Ecological models of human development: Research models and fugitive findings. In R. H. Wozinak, & K. W. Fischer (Eds.), *Scientific environments*. Hillsdale, NJ: Erlbaum.

Bronfenbrenner, U. (2005). *Making human beings human: Bioecological perspectives on human development*. Thousand Oaks, CA: Sage Publications.

Bucciol, A., & Veronesi, M. (2014). Teaching children to save: What is the best strategy for lifetime savings? *Journal of Economic Psychology, 45*, 1–17.

Carlson, L., & Grossbart, S. (1988). Parental style and consumer socialization of children. *Journal of Consumer Research, 15*, 77–94.

Cartwright, K. B. (2001). Cognitive developmental theory and spiritual development. *Journal of Adult Development, 8*(4), 213–220.

Chen, M. K. (2013). The effect of language on economic behavior: Evidence from savings rates, health behaviors, and retirement assets. *American Economic Review, 103*, 690–731.

Cho, S. H., Xu, Y., & Kiss, D. E. (2015). Understanding student loan decisions: A literature review. *Family and Consumer Sciences Research Journal, 43*(3): 229–243.

Collins, W. A., & Steinberg, L. (2008). Adolescent development in interpersonal context. In W. Damon, & R. M. Lerner (Eds.), *Child and adolescent development: An advanced course* (pp. 551–590). Hoboken, NJ: John Wiley & Sons, Inc.

Daddis, C., & Smetana, J. (2005). Middle-class African American families' expectations for adolescents' behavioural autonomy. *International Journal of Behavioral Development, 29*, 371–381.

Danes, S. M. (1994). Parental perceptions of children's financial socialization. *Journal of Financial Counseling and Planning, 5*, 127–149.

Davies, E., & Lea, S. E. G. (1995). Student attitudes to student debt. *Journal of Economic Psychology, 16* (4): 663–679.

Drever, A. I., Odders-White, E., Kalish, C. W., Else-Quest, N. M., Hoagland, E. M., & Nelms, E. N. (2015). Foundations of financial well-being: Insights into the role of executive function, financial socialization, and experience-based learning in childhood and youth. *Journal of Consumer Affairs, 49*, 13–38.

Eccles, J., Templeton, J., Barber, B., & Stone, M. (2003). Adolescence and emerging adulthood: The critical passage ways to adulthood. In M. H. Bornstein, L. Davidson, C. L. M. Keyes, & K. A. Moore (Eds.), *Well-being: Positive development across the life course* (pp. 383–406). Mahwah, NJ: Lawrence Erlbaum Associates.

Emler, N., & Dickinson, J. (1985). Children's representation of economic inequalities: The effects of social class. *British Journal of Developmental Psychology, 3*(2), 191–198.

Faber, R. J., & Vohs, K. D. (2004). To buy or not to buy? Self-control and self-regulatory failure in purchase behavior. In R. R. Baumeister, & K. D. Vohs (Eds.), *Handbook of self-regulation: Research, theory, and application* (pp. 509–524). New York: Guilford Press.

Feather, N. T. (1991). Variables relating to the allocation of pocket money to children: Parental reasons and values. *British Journal of Social Psychology, 30*, 221–234.

Friedline, T. (2015). A developmental perspective on children's economic agency. *Journal of Consumer Affairs, 49*, 39–68.

Friedman, W. J., & Lyon, T. D. (2005). Development of temporal-reconstructive abilities. *Child Development, 76*(6), 1202–1216.

Fuligni, A. J., Tseng, V., & Lam, M. (1999). Attitudes toward family obligations among American adolescents with Asian, Latin American, and European backgrounds. *Child Development, 70*, 1030–1044.

Furnham, A. (1993). *Reaching for the counter. The new child consumers: Regulation or education*. London: Social Affairs Unit.

Furnham, A., & Thomas, P. (1984). Adults' perceptions of the economic socialization of children. *Journal of Adolescence, 7*, 217–231.

Garon, N. M., Longard, J., Bryson, S. E., & Moore, C. (2012). Making decisions about now and later: Development of future-oriented self-control. *Cognitive Development, 27*, 314–322.

Gilmore, C. K., & Spelke, E. S. (2008). Children's understanding of the relationship between addition and subtraction. *Cognition, 107*, 932–945.

Gudmunson, C. G., & Danes, S. M. (2011). Family financial socialization: Theory and critical review. *Journal of Family and Economic Issues, 32*(4), 644–667.

Gutter, M., & Copur, Z. (2011). Financial behaviors and financial well-being of college students: Evidence from a national survey. *Journal of Family and Economic Issues, 32* (4): 699–714.

Harrison, N., Agnew, S., & Serido, J. (2015). Attitudes to debt among indebted undergraduates: A cross-national exploratory factor analysis. *Journal of Economic Psychology, 46*, 62–73.

Hofstede, G. (1980). Motivation, leadership, and organization: Do American theories apply abroad? *Organizational dynamics, 9*, 42–63.

Jahoda, G. (1981). The development of thinking about economic institutions: The bank. *Cahiers de Psychologie Cognitive, 1*, 55–78.

Jorgensen, B. L., & Savla, J. (2010). Financial literacy of young adults: The importance of parental socialization. *Family Relations, 59*, 465–478.

Keating, D. P. (1980). Thinking processes in adolescence. In J. Adelson (Ed.), *Handbook of adolescent psychology* (pp. 211–246). New York: Wiley.

Kim, J., & Chatterjee, S. (2013). Childhood financial socialization and young adults' financial management. *Journal of Financial Counseling and Planning, 24*, 61–79.

Kim, C., Yang, Z., & Lee, H. (2015). Parental style, parental practices, and socialization outcomes: An investigation of their linkages in the consumer socialization context. *Journal of Economic Psychology, 49*, 15–33.

Kochanska, G., Coy, K. C., & Murray, K. T. (2001). The development of self-regulation in the first four years of life. *Child Development, 72*, 1091–1111.

Koonce, J. C., Mimura, Y., Mauldin, T. A., Rupured, A. M., & Jordan, J. (2008). Financial information: Is it related to savings and investing knowledge and financial behavior of teenagers? *Journal of Financial Counseling and Planning, 19*, 19–28.

Larson, R. (2002). Globalization, societal change, and new technologies: What they mean for the future of adolescence. *Journal of Research on Adolescence, 12*(1), 1–30.

Larson, R. W. (2014). Studying experience: Pursuing the 'something more'. In R. M. Lerner, A. C. Petersen, R. K. Silbereisen, & J. Brooks-Gunn (Eds.), *The developmental science of adolescence: History through autobiography* (pp. 267–276). London: Psychology Press.

Lassarre, D. (1996). Consumer education in French families and schools. In P. Lunt, & A. Furnham (Eds.), *Economic socialization: The economic beliefs and behaviours of young people* (pp. 130–148). Cheltenham: Edward Elgar.

Leiser, D., & Ganin, M. (1996). Economic participation and economic socialization. In P. Lunt & A. Furnham (Eds.), *Economic Socialization: The Economic Beliefs and Behaviours of Young People* (pp. 93–109). Cheltenham: Edward Elgar.

Leiser, D., & Halachmi, R. B. (2006). Children's understanding of market forces. *Journal of Economic Psychology, 27*, 6–19.

Leiser, D., Sevón, G., & Levy, D. (1990). Children's economic socialization: Summarizing the cross-cultural comparison of ten countries. *Journal of Economic Psychology, 11*, 591–614.

Lerner, R. M., Dowling, E. M., & Anderson, P. M. (2003). Positive youth development: Thriving as the basis of personhood and civil society. *Applied Developmental Science, 7*, 172–180.

LeVine, R. (1974). Parental goals: A cross-cultural view. *The Teachers College Record, 76*(2), 226–239.

Lewis, A., & Scott, A. (2003). A study of economic socialization: Financial practices in the home and the preferred role of schools among parents with children under 16. *Citizenship, Social and Economics Education, 5*, 138–147.

Loke, V., & Sherraden, M. (2009). Building assets from birth: A global comparison of child development account policies. *International Journal of Social Welfare, 18*(2), 119–129.

Luna, B. (2009). Developmental changes in cognitive control through adolescence. *Advances in Child Development and Behaviour, 37*, 233–278.

Lusardi, A. (2008). *Financial literacy: An essential tool for informed consumer choice?* No. w14084. Cambridge, MA: National Bureau of Economic Research.

Maccoby, E. E., & Martin, J. A. (1983). Socialization in the context of the family: Parent-child interaction. In P. H. Mussen (Series Ed.) & E. M. Hetherington (Vol. Ed.), *Handbook of child psychology: Vol. 4. Socialization, personality, and social development* (4th ed., pp. 1–101). New York: Wiley.

Marshall, H., & Magruder, L. (1960). Relations between parent money education practices and children's knowledge and use of money. *Child Development, 31*, 253–284.

Mischel, W., & Ayduk, O. (2011). Willpower in a cognitive affective processing system: The dynamics of delay of gratification. In K. Vohs, & R. Baumeister (Eds.), *Handbook of self-regulation: research, theory, and applications* (pp. 83–105). New York: The Guilford Press.

Montez, D. (2010). Young Africans' access to financial information and services: lessons from surveys in Kenya and Ghana. Retrieved from http://www.youtheconomicopportunities.org/taxonomy/term/93 (accessed 18 November 2015).

National Research Council and Institute of Medicine (2005). *Growing up global: The changing transitions to adulthood in developing countries.* Panel on Transitions to Adulthood in Developing Countries. C. B. Lloyd (Ed.), Committee on Population and Board on Children, Youth, and Families. Division of Behavioral and Social Sciences and Education. Washington, DC: The National Academies Press.

Ng, S. H. (1983). Children's ideas about the bank and shop profit: Developmental stages and the influence of cognitive contrasts and conflict. *Journal of Economic Psychology, 4*, 209–221.

Ng, S. H. (1985). Children's ideas about the bank: A New Zealand replication. *European Journal of Social Psychology, 15*, 121–123.

OECD (2014), *PISA 2012 results: Students and money: financial literacy skills for the 21st century* (vol. VI), PISA, OECD Publishing. http://dx.doi.org/10.1787/9789264208094-en

Otto, A. M. C. (2009). The economic psychology of adolescent saving. Unpublished thesis. University of Exeter, UK.

Otto, A. M. C., Schots, P. A., Westerman, J. A., & Webley, P. (2006). Children's use of saving strategies: An experimental approach. *Journal of Economic Psychology, 27*, 57–72.

Palan, K. M., Gentina, E., & Muratore, I. (2010). Adolescent consumption autonomy: A cross-cultural examination. *Journal of Business Research, 63*, 1342–1348.

Pechmann, C., Levine, L., Loughlin, S., & Leslie, F. (2005). Impulsive and self-conscious: Adolescents' vulnerability to advertising and promotion. *Journal of Public Policy & Marketing, 24*, 202–221.

Peng, T. C. M., Bartholomae, S., Fox, J. J., & Cravener, G. (2007). The impact of personal finance education delivered in high school and college courses. *Journal of Family and Economic Issues, 28*, 265–284.

Perry, W. G., Jr. (1970). *Forms of intellectual and ethical development in the college years: A scheme.* New York: Holt, Rinehart, and Winston.

Perry, W. G., Jr. (1981). Cognitive and ethical growth: The making of meaning. In A. W. Chickering and Associates, *The modern American college: Responding to the new realities of diverse students and a changing society* (pp. 76–116). San Francisco: Jossey-Bass.

Piaget, J. (1972). Intellectual evolution from adolescence to adulthood. *Human Development, 15,* 1–12.

Prevey, E. E. (1945). A quantitative study of family practices in training children in the use of money. *Journal of Educational Psychology, 36,* 411–428.

Robb, C. A., & Woodyard, A. (2011). Financial knowledge and best practice behavior. *Journal of Financial Counseling and Planning, 22,* 60–70.

Romo, L., Kotbagi, G., Platey, S., Coeffec, A., Boz, F., & Kern, L. (2014). Gambling and impulsivity: An exploratory study in a French adolescent population. *Open Journal of Medical Psychology, 3,* 306–313.

Scheinholtz, L., Holden, K., & Kalish, C. (2012). Cognitive development and children's understanding of personal finance. In D. J. Lamdin (Ed.), *Consumer knowledge and financial decisions* (pp. 29–47). New York: Springer.

Schoon, I. (2007). Adaptations to changing times: Agency in context. *International Journal of Psychology, 42,* 94–101.

Serido, J., Shim, S., Mishra, A., & Tang, C. (2010). Financial parenting, financial coping behaviours, and well-being of emerging adults. *Family Relations, 59,* 453–464.

Serido, J., Shim, S., & Tang, C. (2013). A developmental model of financial capability: A framework for promoting a successful transition to adulthood. *International Journal of Behavioral Development, 37,* 287–297.

Sherraden, M. S., Johnson, L., Elliott, W., Porterfield, S., & Rainford, W. (2007). School-based children's saving accounts for college: The I Can Save program. *Children and Youth Services Review, 29,* 294–312.

Shim, S., Barber, B. L., Card, N. A., Xiao, J. J., & Serido, J. (2010). Financial socialization of first-year college students: The roles of parents, work, and education. *Journal of Youth and Adolescence, 39,* 1457–1470.

Shim, S., Serido, J., & Barber, B. L., (2011). A consumer way of thinking: Linking consumer socialization and consumption motivation perspectives to adolescent development. *Journal of Research on Adolescence: Decade in Review, 21,* 290–299.

Shim, S., Xiao, J. J., Barber, B. L., & Lyons, A. C. (2009). Pathways to life success: A conceptual model of financial well-being for young adults. *Journal of Applied Developmental Psychology, 30,* 708–723.

Sinnott, J. (1998). *The development of logic in adulthood: Postformal thought and its applications.* New York: Plenum Press.

Sonuga-Barke, E. J. S., & Webley, P. (1993). *Children's saving: A study in the development of economic behaviour.* Hillsdale, NJ: Lawrence Erlbaum.

Stacey, B. G. (1982). Economic socialization in the pre-adult years. *British Journal of Social Psychology, 21,* 159–173.

Steinberg, L. (2004). Risk taking in adolescence: What changes, and why? *Annals of the New York Academy of Sciences, 1021,* 51–58.

Strauss, A. L. (1952). The development and transformation of monetary meanings in the child. *American Sociological Review, 17*(3), 275–286.

Suddendorf, T., & Moore, C. (2011). Introduction to the special issue: The development of episodic foresight. *Cognitive Development, 26,* 295–298.

Sutter, M., Angerer, S., Glätzle-Rützler, D., & Lergetporer, P. (2014). The effects of language on children's intertemporal choices. Working Paper.

Vygotsky, L. (1978). *Mind in society: The development of higher mental processes.* Cambridge, MA: Harvard University Press.

Webley, P. (1996). Playing the market: The autonomous economic world of children. In P. Lunt & A. Furnham (Eds.), *Economic socialization: The economic beliefs and behaviours of young children* (pp. 149–161). Cheltenham: Edward Elgar.

Webley, P., Burgoyne, C., Lea, S. E. G., & Young, B. (2001). *The economic psychology of everyday life.* Hove, East Sussex: Psychology Press.

Webley, P., Levine, M., & Lewis, A. (1991). A study in economic psychology: Children's saving in a play economy. *Human Relations, 44,* 127–146.

Webley, P., & Nyhus, E. K. (2006). Parents' influence on children's future orientation and saving. *Journal of Economic Psychology, 27,* 140–164.

Wood, M. (1998). Socio-economic status, delay of gratification, and impulse buying. *Journal of Economic Psychology, 19,* 295–320.

Wray-Lake, L., Crouter, A. C., & McHale, S. M. (2010). Developmental patterns in decision-making autonomy across middle childhood and adolescence: European American parents' perspectives. *Child Development, 81,* 636–651.

FURTHER READING

Batty, M., Collins, M., & Odders-White, E. (2015). Experimental evidence on the effects of financial education on elementary school students' knowledge, behavior, and attitudes. *Journal of Consumer Affairs, 49,* 69–96.

OECD (2014), *PISA 2012 results: Students and money: financial literacy skills for the 21st century* (vol. VI), PISA, OECD Publishing. http://dx.doi.org/10.1787/9789264208094-en

Webley, P. (2005). Children's understanding of economics. In M. Barrett, & E. Buchanan-Barrow (Eds.), *Children's understanding of society* (pp. 43–67). Hove, East Sussex: Psychology Press.

21 Childhood Psychological Predictors of Lifelong Economic Outcomes

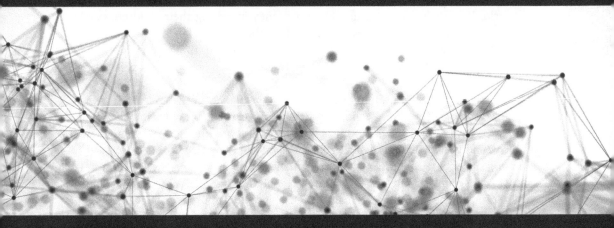

MARK EGAN, MICHAEL DALY, AND LIAM DELANEY

CHAPTER OUTLINE

LEARNING OUTCOMES

BY THE END OF THIS CHAPTER YOU SHOULD BE ABLE TO:

1. Explain how cognitive and noncognitive skills differ from each other and give examples of each type of skill.

2. Give examples of studies showing how cognitive and noncognitive skills predict future economic outcomes.

3. Review the main methodological challenges in the field and discuss how these could be overcome.

21.1 INTRODUCTION

Which psychological characteristics help children become economically successful adults? This is a question of interest to parents, governments and academics all over the world. Parents invest time, energy and money in raising their children, partly with the goal of fostering qualities which will help them succeed in life. Governments structure health and education policies to help children maximize their potential, and academics study the characteristics in childhood which lead to success in school and the labour market.

In this chapter we summarize the results of a large body of research from economics and psychology examining childhood psychological predictors of adult economic outcomes. We follow recent economics literature by classifying these predictors into cognitive and noncognitive skills[1] and we focus on the two broad domains of school and work since these encompass the principal individual-level indicators of economic success (e.g., employment, earnings, educational attainment). Where possible, we cite literature reviews and meta-analyses which provide the strongest available evidence by aggregating the results of many studies.

Economists have long recognized the importance of cognitive ability as a determinant of economic success. Since the turn of the millennium, however, researchers in economics and psychology have become increasingly interested in the role of noncognitive skills in shaping economic outcomes. Noncognitive skills, also called soft skills, socio-emotional skills and character, refer to relatively stable individual differences in psychological characteristics, which are not captured by conventional tests of cognitive ability but which may contribute to economic success. They include personality traits, attitudes and abilities, such as self-control, interpersonal skills, motivation, conscientiousness, agreeableness, locus of control, and many others. Growing evidence linking these psychological differences to educational and labour market success has led some economists to consider noncognitive skills to be as important as cognitive skills in predicting economic outcomes, if not more so (e.g., Heckman, Stixrud, & Urzua, 2006).

This chapter is structured as follows. Using the framework of cognitive and noncognitive skills, we summarize the empirical evidence on some of the main childhood psychological differences which predict success in school and work. We examine how this evidence has been incorporated into an economic model of lifespan development and review the main methodological challenges of the field. Finally, we discuss the policy implications of this stream of research and make concluding remarks.

21.2 LITERATURE REVIEW

21.2.1 Overview

Two major methodological developments in the twentieth century laid the foundations for the scientific study of childhood psychological differences and adult outcomes. The first was the development of reliable psychometric tools to quantify individual psychological differences, beginning with the creation of the modern IQ test in 1905 (Boake, 2002). Hundreds of more sophisticated intelligence tests were later developed, notably the Stanford-Binet scale, the Wechsler Adult Intelligence Scale and Raven's Progressive Matrices. As theories of personality and psychometric measurement developed throughout the century, psychologists produced a diverse array of scales to measure psychological differences not captured by intelligence tests, including the NEO Five-Factor Inventory, the Brief Self-Control Scale, the Rotter Locus of Control Scale and the General Health Questionnaire. The second methodological development was the establishment, principally in Britain and the United States, of prospective longitudinal studies following hundreds or thousands of participants over the course of their lives.[2] Many of these studies have followed their participants from birth and include information on their background and childhood psychological characteristics as well as later educational and labour market outcomes.

Because of these methodological advances, modern researchers can draw on a rich set of measurement tools across many different studies to examine how individual psychological differences in childhood predict economic outcomes occurring years or even decades later. Using the framework of cognitive and noncognitive skills, we now examine the predictive power of some of these differences in forecasting future economic success.

21.2.2 Cognitive Skills

Cognitive skills refer to the subcomponents of intelligence, which has been broadly defined as

> a very general capability that, among other things, involves the ability to reason, plan, solve problems, think abstractly, comprehend complex ideas, learn quickly and learn from experience. It is not merely book learning, a narrow academic skill, or test-taking smarts. Rather, it reflects a broader and deeper capability for comprehending our surroundings—'catching on', 'making sense' of things, or 'figuring out' what to do.
>
> (Gottfredson, 1997, p. 13)

One influential model of intelligence, based on an analysis of over 400 data-sets of cognitive ability test scores, conceives of a three-stratum hierarchy that includes general intelligence (also known as 'g') at the top, broad domains at the second level such as processing speed, fluid and crystallized intelligence, general memory and learning, and narrow specific abilities at the bottom level such as mathematical and lexical knowledge, reading speed and comprehension, listening and communication ability, working memory capacity and many others (Carroll, 1993).

Intelligence has been a lauded trait in human society since antiquity and has obvious implications for economic success. Individuals with better reasoning skills, memory and decision-making capabilities are more likely to perform well in school, gain entry into more competitive universities, and enter cognitively demanding professions which typically provide higher remuneration. Furthermore, a robust finding from many studies is that intelligence is relatively stable over time. Children who score highly on intelligence tests tend to score highly as adults; an illustrative example is a study of 106 Scottish adults which found that their intelligence scores at age

11 correlated moderately high (r = 0.67 when correcting for range restriction) with their scores on the same test at age 90 (Deary, Pattie, & Starr, 2013). Highly intelligent children are therefore likely to become intelligent adults and continue to benefit from their greater mental faculties over time.

Although history contains many examples of child prodigies whose remarkable cognitive abilities attracted much attention, the effects of high childhood intelligence on later life outcomes were not systematically studied until the 1920s, when the American psychologist Lewis Terman began to track the life outcomes of 1,528 high-IQ children in California (Terman, 1925). Terman found that by mid-life the study participants were earning twice as much as the average white-collar worker, were substantially more educated than the average American and, contrary to contemporary expectations that high intelligence would be compensated for by a deficiency in other areas (e.g., by having poor health or limited social skills), were on average as healthy and well adjusted as the general population (Terman, 1959).

More recent studies have examined the predictive power of childhood intelligence using larger and more representative samples. A study of 70,000 English children found that higher intelligence at age 11 predicted better performance at age 16 on national examination tests in all 25 subjects examined. For those scoring a standard deviation above (below) the mean intelligence score, 91% (16%) achieved the criterion of five or more General Certificates of Secondary Education (GSCEs) at grades A–C (Deary, Strand, Smith, & Fernandes, 2007). Upon leaving education and entering the labour market, high-IQ children have also been found to be more likely to avoid unemployment (Caspi, Wright, Moffitt, & Silva, 1998), become managers as opposed to employees (Daly, Egan, & O'Reilly, 2015), and experience more positive social mobility (Deary et al., 2005). Lastly, a meta-analysis of studies comparing intelligence scores elicited before age 19 with socioeconomic success after age 29 found that, on average, higher cognitive ability correlated positively with better educational attainment (r = 0.56, N = 20 studies), occupational status (r = 0.45, N = 21) and income (r = 0.21, N = 15) (Strenze, 2007).

In summary, there is strong evidence that higher cognitive ability in childhood contributes substantially to later educational attainment and success in the labour force. However, while intelligence is advantageous in these areas, it is not a guarantee of success. As noted by Heckman and Rubinstein (2001), 'numerous instances can be cited of people with high IQs who fail to achieve success in life because they lacked self-discipline and of people with low IQs who succeeded by virtue of persistence, reliability and self-discipline' (p. 145). Kuhn and Weinberger (2005) cite practical evidence of the demand for skills other than cognitive ability in the labour market; a nationwide survey of American employers found that their five most valued qualities in employees were, in descending order of importance, communication skills, motivation/initiative, teamwork skills, leadership and academic achievement. The first four of these are noncognitive skills, suggesting these abilities play an important role in determining labour market success. Finally, empirical evidence suggesting a relative parity of importance of noncognitive and cognitive skills comes from two analyses of Swedish data which used skill measures elicited during mandatory military enlistment at age 18–19 to predict future earnings. Lindqvist and Vestman's (2011) analysis of almost 15,000 men found that a 1 standard deviation increase in cognitive and noncognitive skills predicted 8.9% and 6.9% higher earnings respectively; Lundborg, Nilsson, and Rooth's (2014) analysis of over 275,000 male siblings found respective increases of 11% and 7.7%.

21.2.3 Noncognitive Skills

While there is disagreement on the definition of noncognitive skills, the term is generally used 'to contrast a variety of behaviours, personality characteristics, and attitudes with academic skills, aptitudes, and attainment' (Gutman & Schoon, 2013, p. 7). Noncognitive skills encompass a much broader spectrum of psychological differences than cognitive skills. They include relatively stable personality traits (i.e., one's characteristic patterns of thoughts, feelings, and behaviours) such as conscientiousness and self-control, more flexible constructs such as motivation and expectations, metacognitive strategies such as setting goals and being aware of one's strengths and weaknesses, and socio-emotional skills such as social awareness and empathy. The importance of these abilities may seem unsurprising: a person who is thorough, hard-working, goal-oriented, motivated and has high expectations of what they can achieve should perform better in school and work than someone of equal cognitive ability who lacks these traits. However, the empirical evidence on their predictive power for socioeconomic outcomes has been neglected in the economics literature until relatively recently.

The economist James Heckman has produced an influential set of studies analysing the long-run effects of the Michigan-based Perry Preschool Program which demonstrate the importance of noncognitive skills in childhood for future labour market success. Heckman et al. (2010) found that amongst disadvantaged young children who were randomly assigned to receive daily preschool, girls achieved higher rates of high school graduation and boys went on to experience higher earnings and employment in adulthood than a comparable group of children who did not attend the preschool programme. These effects operated, at least in part, through a reduction in externalizing behaviour (Heckman, Pinto, & Savelyev, 2013). An important caveat of this study is that it used a small sample and had an unusually large effect size, making its scalability unclear. Moreover, the short-run impact of such interventions is more mixed; a meta-analysis of 84 American pre-school programmes spanning five decades found that their average effect on cognitive and achievement scores, as measured at the end of the intervention period, varied substantially and that larger studies tended to have smaller effect sizes (Duncan & Magnuson, 2013).

We now describe the childhood noncognitive skills which are most predictive of educational and labour market outcomes.[3] Adapting the classification schemes of recent literature reviews on the predictive power of childhood noncognitive skills by Gutman and Schoon (2013) and Goodman, Joshi, Nasim, and Tyler (2015), we focus on six areas, some of which overlap with each other: 1. Self-control; 2. Self-perception; 3. Socio-emotional skills; 4. Motivation; 5. Mental health; and 6. Metacognitive strategies.

Self-Control

Self-control, also known as willpower, self-discipline and self-regulation, refers to the 'capacity for altering one's own responses, especially to bring them into line with standards such as ideals, values, morals, and social expectations, and to support the pursuit of long-term goals' (Baumeister, Vohs, & Tice, 2007, p. 351).

The value of self-control in children was demonstrated by Walter Mischel and colleagues in the early 1970s in a series of seminal delay-of-gratification experiments collectively known as the 'Marshmallow Tests'. Four-year-old children were offered a single treat such as a marshmallow immediately or two marshmallows if they could wait 15 minutes. Children who were able to wait longer had higher Scholastic Aptitude Test (SAT) scores a decade later (Shoda, Mischel, & Peake, 1990). Larger studies from New Zealand and Great Britain using parent- and teacher-rated self-control measures have also found striking long-run benefits of good self-control in childhood, including higher income (Moffitt et al., 2011) and lower unemployment (Daly, Delaney, Egan, & Baumeister, 2015). Notably, the predictive strength of self-control was comparable to cognitive ability in both these studies. Lastly, self-control is thought to be a key antecedent of the personality trait conscientiousness (Eisenberg, Duckworth, Spinrad, & Valiente, 2014), which is the tendency to be organized, responsible and hard-working. Of the 'Big Five' personality traits (openness, conscientiousness, extraversion, agreeableness, neuroticism), a recent overview of the personality literature concluded that conscientiousness is the trait most predictive of positive outcomes in a wide variety of domains, including educational attainment, job performance and earnings (Almlund, Duckworth, Heckman, & Kautz, 2011).

A related concept to low self-control in economics is 'impatience', used to denote individuals who smaller-sooner rewards over larger-later rewards when asked to choose between alternatives (e.g., preferring £100 now rather than £300 in one year). While only a small number of studies have examined childhood impatience and later economic outcomes, their results accord with the self-control literature in psychology. For example, a Swedish longitudinal study of almost 12,000 individuals found that more impatient choices on a time preference measure at age 13 predicted worse school performance, lower labour supply and reduced lifetime income (Golsteyn, Grönqvist, & Lindahl, 2014). Taken together, these results suggest that children who are self-controlled, conscientious and future oriented are much more likely to perform well in school and the labour market.

Self-Perception

A child's beliefs about the effect of their actions, operationalized in this section by locus of control and self-efficacy, are potentially very important in that they may become self-fulfilling. For example, a student who believes there are no returns to studying is unlikely to study very hard.

Locus of control is the extent to which individuals believe that they can control events around them. A person who believes in their own ability to effect change is characterized as having an 'internal' locus of control, as opposed to someone with an 'external' locus of control, who believes that luck or fate play a larger role in determining their life outcomes. An example is a child with an external locus of control who attributes their poor test scores to the difficulty of the test rather than their own efforts. Self-efficacy measures the strength of an individual's belief in their own ability to complete tasks and meet their goals. Research examining self-efficacy in children has typically focused on academic achievement as an outcome. Self-efficacy in this context can include both a student's belief in their innate ability to perform well in a given subject, as well as their ability to organize their own learning activities and goals in order to maximize their academic performance.

A meta-analysis of 98 studies involving students from primary to university level found that, on average, greater internal locus of control correlated modestly with better academic performance ($r = 0.18$), and this effect was stronger for adolescents than children (Findley & Cooper, 1983). Similarly, there is strong evidence linking high self-efficacy to better academic outcomes: a meta-analysis of studies published between 1977 and 1988 found that higher self-efficacy correlated with greater persistence on academic tasks ($r = 0.34$, $N = 18$ studies) and better academic performance ($r = 0.38$, $N = 38$) (Multon, Brown, & Lent, 1991).

Socio-Emotional Skills

Although the term socio-emotional skills is sometimes used interchangeably with noncognitive skills, it specifically refers to the ability to understand and manage emotions, set and achieve goals, feel and show empathy for others, hold positive relationships and make responsible decisions (CASEL, 2015). Aside from promoting greater well-being for the child, these skills should provide a better foundation for academic engagement by improving classroom behaviour, reducing conduct problems, and increasing the motivation to learn.

Durlak, Weissberg, Dymnicki, Taylor, and Schellinger (2011) conducted a meta-analysis of 213 school-based socio-emotional learning (SEL) programmes covering 270,034 students ranging from ages 5 to 18. Compared to children in control groups who did not receive such training, SEL programme participants had significantly more positive attitudes, fewer conduct problems and better emotional well-being, effects which persisted even among the 33 studies with follow-up periods longer than 6 months. These improvements in psychological functioning also translated into an 11 percentile-point improvement in academic performance among the 35 studies which measured this outcome. While these effects represent impressive evidence of the value of SEL training, to date there remains much less evidence on whether such programmes also improve children's future labour market performance.

Motivation

Different levels of motivation are a plausible explanation for differences in performance, since motivation may act as a spur to increased focus and effort. Although there are many theories of motivation (Eccles & Wigfield, 2002), we focus here on intrinsic motivation. A person who is intrinsically motivated performs an activity because they enjoy it for its own sake rather than for instrumental reasons, such as the prospect of a reward. Intrinsic motivation in students is typically measured by asking them to rate to what extent they agree with statements such as 'I experience pleasure and satisfaction while learning new things'. A meta-analysis of 10 studies including over 4,000 students by Taylor et al. (2014) found that children who were more intrinsically motivated performed better in school. The authors also conducted a longitudinal study of 319 Canadian high school students which found that higher intrinsic motivation predicted better grades one year later even after taking into account baseline grades.

One gap in this literature identified by Goodman et al. (2015) is that there are no studies examining whether childhood intrinsic motivation predicts long-term economic outcomes in adulthood.

Mental Health

Although mental health does not fit neatly under the heading of noncognitive 'skills', it is an important psychological characteristic which varies across individuals and has a large impact on socioeconomic prospects. Children and adolescents who experience severe anxiety and depression and other psychological problems have been found to be substantially more likely to perform worse in school, experience higher rates of youth unemployment and in one study to have family incomes 28% lower than others at age 50. Additionally, Smith and Smith (2010) used data from the American Panel Study of Income Dynamics (PSID) to show that siblings who recalled as adults having had childhood psychological problems had worse educational attainment and 20% lower family incomes than their siblings who did not recall such problems. Based on those data, the authors estimated the lifetime economic costs of childhood distress to be over $2 trillion in the United States alone.

Perhaps surprisingly, given the relatively greater attention given to physical health compared to mental health in most Western societies, a recent literature review concluded that poor mental health in early life has a far larger negative impact than poor physical health on long-run economic outcomes (Delaney & Smith, 2012). These large but hitherto relatively neglected effects have led the noted labour economist Richard Layard to dub mental health a 'new frontier for labour economics', one requiring greater study and attention from policy-makers (Layard, 2013). One area requiring further study is the need to identify the relative economic penalties of the range of possible mental health conditions, such as depression and anxiety, ADHD, conduct and personality disorders, alcoholism and drug dependence (Currie & Stabile, 2009; Lundborg, Nilsson, & Rooth, 2014).

Metacognitive Strategies

Metacognitive strategies are goal-oriented efforts to influence one's own learning behaviours and processes by focusing awareness on thinking and selecting, monitoring, and planning strategies that are most conducive to learning. In other words, these strategies encourage 'thinking about thinking'. Teaching these skills to children encourages them to proactively understand the processes that help them learn, rather than being passive agents waiting to receive information. The tools used to teach these strategies in the classroom can include checklists which encourage self-monitoring on tasks, reserving class time for thinking aloud approaches to problems, and after completing a task, evaluating the learning experience and identifying ways to improve.

Gutman and Schoon (2013) cite four meta-analyses covering 148 studies examining the efficacy of school-based interventions which teach metacognitive strategies. Those meta-analyses unanimously conclude that teaching children these strategies improves academic performance in a meaningful way across a wide variety of subjects, from elementary school to university level. However, it is still unclear to what extent these improvements persist in the long term, and whether they transfer to non-academic domains, such as the labour market.

21.3 LIFECOURSE PERSPECTIVE

The previous section summarizes research showing that childhood cognitive and noncognitive skills matter for educational and labour market success. One challenge for researchers is the need to synthesize this body of research in order to address the deeper questions arising from this literature. Why do children have different levels of cognitive and noncognitive abilities in the first place? Which factors encourage or inhibit the development of these skills over time? How malleable are these skills during childhood and adolescence?

The main framework in economics to examine the development of economically relevant psychological differences has been developed by Heckman and colleagues over the last decade. Cunha and Heckman (2007) describe a lifecourse model of skill development which presents a framework for understanding how cognitive and noncognitive skills develop in children. The model posits that children are born with a set of traits determined by their inherited genes and the prenatal environment. Throughout childhood and into adolescence, their development is influenced by their parents, schools, the broader environment, their health and their own efforts. Parents who are more nurturing, attentive and effective supervisors of their children will causally affect their child's skills in a positive way, as will schools which provide a safe and enriching learning environment. Children with good physical and mental health will miss fewer school days, and children with good self-control and who are academically motivated will learn more in school. Thus the model predicts that important life outcomes will be shaped by the combined influence of a child's cognitive and noncognitive skills as well as their broader environment.

Two important characteristics of this model are self-productivity and dynamic complementarity. Self-productivity means that the process of skill formation at one stage (e.g., adolescence) depends on the skills acquired at a previous stage (e.g., childhood). For example, a child with high levels of concentration, motivation and well-developed socio-emotional skills will be more likely to engage productively with their school environment, and this engagement will contribute to the extent to which they grow into an adolescent with good cognitive and noncognitive ability. Cognitive and noncognitive skills may therefore dynamically interact to shape subsequent skill development; a concept summarized with the phrase 'skills beget skills'. Dynamic complementarity means that skills produced at one stage raise the productivity of future investments. Imagine an intervention which successfully improves the academic motivation and socio-emotional skills of a group of 5-year-olds. Suppose these gains compound over time by improving the children's engagement with their schooling and increasing their ambition to attend university. By age 18, the children have developed a larger stock of cognitive and noncognitive skills. Subsequent interventions which encourage school-leavers to proceed to tertiary education (e.g., via grants or access programmes) may now be more effective than if they had targeted less able and motivated young people who did not benefit from the original intervention. As is suggested by this example, an implied feature of dynamic complementarity is that early investments should be followed up with later investments in order for the initial investment to be maximally productive.

The dynamic nature of skill development is constrained by the existence of sensitive and critical periods for investment. Investments are relatively more productive during sensitive periods. Critical periods refer to timeframes within which investments must be made if they are to be successful; during any other period, they will not be effective. Heckman (2008) cites the examples that 'if a second language is learned before age 12, the child speaks it without an accent (sensitive period) ... a child born with a cataract on the eye will be blind for life if the cataract is not removed within the first year of life (critical period)' (p. 17). The existence of sensitive and critical periods for skill development is borne out by extensive research demonstrating greater plasticity in early life for the development of social skills in humans and animals, followed by decreasing plasticity with age (see Knudsen, Heckman, Cameron, & Shonkoff, 2006).

There is some evidence suggesting that a critical period for the development of cognitive skills is before the age of 3. One notable study by O'Connor, Rutter, Beckett, Keaveney & Kreppner (2000) examined Romanian infants raised in extremely deprived orphanage environments who were adopted by families in the United Kingdom. Children raised in these environments had severely impaired social and cognitive development and high sensitivity to stress. Because many of the 165 children examined were adopted at different ages, they experienced different amounts of exposure to the orphanage environment. On average, children who spent more time in the orphanage before being adopted had worse cognitive performance than children who were adopted before the age of 6 months. However, this finding must be interpreted with the proviso that this study used a small sample, and the evidence base supporting the malleability of early-life IQ is still relatively limited.

Noncognitive skills appear to be much more malleable than cognitive skills. This is suggested by comparisons of test-retest rank-order stability estimates, which show that while IQ reaches terminal stability at age 6–8, personality does not reach comparable stability until at least age 50 (Almlund, Duckworth, Heckman, & Kautz, 2011). Further, Heckman and Kautz's (2013) review of 25 interventions targeted from pre-school age to young adulthood found evidence to suggest that interventions improve longrun outcomes chiefly by improving noncognitive skills, whereas only very early (before age 3) interventions improve IQ in a lasting way. As children grow into adolescents and become more entrenched in their habits and preferences, it becomes relatively more difficult to improve noncognitive skills and there is less potential for self-productivity (e.g., improving academic motivation at age 18 does not have the same potential for positive knock-on effects as intervening at age 5). This pattern of evidence suggests a decreasing gradient of sensitivity for investment as children grow older, implying that interventions to improve noncognitive skills should begin very early in life in order to be maximally effective.

21.4   METHODOLOGICAL CHALLENGES

The main strength of this field has been its use of randomized trials and observational longitudinal studies to link childhood psychological differences with socioeconomic outcomes occurring years or decades later. Using variables elicited in childhood to predict future outcomes also allows researchers to avoid issues of reverse causality, which may occur when examining psychological measures and economic outcomes elicited simultaneously in adulthood (e.g., does unemployment cause poor mental health, vice versa, or do they mutually influence each other?). However, there remain significant methodological challenges for future researchers to address, some of which are inseparable from the use of these longitudinal studies.

First, the research cited in this chapter overwhelmingly relies on data from Great Britain and the United States. This reflects the reality that very few countries invest in and make high-quality longitudinal data-sets available to researchers. Nonetheless it exacerbates a problem common across the social sciences of relying on samples from 'Western, educated, industrialized, rich, democratic countries' (called the 'WEIRD' problem by Henrich, Heine, & Norenzayan, 2010). Given that identifying the skills which help children grow into economically successful adults is a research topic with global relevance, it is essential to develop a wider evidence base in order to expand the relevance of these findings to different countries and cultures.

The second issue is measurement error. Because noncognitive skills are usually elicited via self-report or observer report, they are typically considered to be more prone to measurement error than IQ tests. Consider a question designed to measure the personality trait conscientiousness which asks a person to rate how hard-working they are on a scale of 1 (not at all) to 7 (extremely). Respondents may prefer not to describe themselves negatively and thus overstate how hard-working they are. Alternatively, respondents may have different benchmarks of what constitutes hard work and thus provide scores which are not comparable. This problem of subjective interpretation of response scales can make it difficult to make meaningful comparisons across different groups. In extreme cases, subjective ratings seem to directly contradict objective evidence: for example, among OECD countries South Korea ranks first in annual hours worked but second last in self-reported conscientiousness scores (Heckman & Kautz, 2013). Measurement error in the assessment of noncognitive skills may also arise from the fact that researchers are often obliged to work with pre-existing older secondary data. This may mean using psychological measures which seem out-of-date or not designed for purpose. For example, many childhood psychological measures in the National Child Development Study were elicited in the 1960s. Modern researchers using these measures to answer contemporary research questions therefore rely on questionnaires which are over 50 years old (for an example of how researchers may address this issue by validating such measures against modern scales, see Daly, Delaney, Egan, & Baumeister, 2015).

Although the problems involved with measuring noncognitive skills are well known, even cognitive skills may be inaccurately measured if IQ tests capture factors other than intelligence. A recent meta-analysis of 2,008 individuals found that providing incentives such as candy or money increased IQ scores by an average of 0.64 standard deviations, suggesting that motivation plays an important role in determining scores in low-stakes IQ tests (Duckworth et al., 2011). Relatedly, highly neurotic individuals may perform poorly on IQ tests due to test anxiety (Moutafi, Furnham, & Tsaousis, 2006). Personality can therefore have a direct effect on IQ scores (for a full discussion of measurement error in this area, see Borghans, Golsteyn, Heckman, & Humphries, 2011), suggesting that the predictive power of cognitive ability for economic outcomes may be overstated if personality is not taken into account.

The third issue, arguably the most important of the three highlighted here, is causal inference. While many studies show that a certain childhood noncognitive skill predicts a later socioeconomic outcome, considerably fewer use research designs which can demonstrate a causal relationship (as might be obtained by randomizing participants into treatment and control groups). Instead researchers typically rely on observational data and attempt to isolate the contributing role of a skill on an outcome by including an array of statistical control variables (e.g., examining whether academic motivation predicts future employment while taking into account gender and socioeconomic status). A limitation of this method is that there may be background variables not present in the data which influence both the skill and outcome being examined (e.g., perhaps cognitive ability in early life causes later motivation and employment levels). Failing to control for these confounding variables can produce misleading results and potentially lead to misguided interventions. The issue is exacerbated by the fact that different researchers in different disciplines do not consistently examine the same noncognitive skills or outcomes, or control for the same background factors. This problem is likely to persist until the field adopts a cohesive theoretical framework which provides guidance on which noncognitive skills and outcomes researchers should prioritize.

21.5   POLICY IMPLICATIONS

Given that early life cognitive and noncognitive skills are strong predictors of future economic success, governments may wish to implement policies which promote these skills, thereby creating more economically productive populations and bringing greater well-being and prosperity to society. The theoretical case for prioritizing investment in children rather than adults is that the economic return is likely to be higher due to the mechanisms of self-productivity and dynamic complementarity (Cunha & Heckman, 2007). The results of interventions, such as the Perry Preschool Program, and a meta-analysis of 30 interventions from 21 countries across Europe, Asia, Africa, Central and South America (Nores & Barnett, 2010) suggest that early childhood interventions can improve cognitive and noncognitive skills in a lasting way. However, two important distinctions between these skill types emerge from the literature. First, early intervention programmes lead more consistently to improvements in noncognitive skills than cognitive skills. Second, while better cognitive skills are a robust predictor of better performance in school and work, there is no comparable single noncognitive skill with the same predictive power. Instead, as noted by Gutman and Schoon (2013), 'there are many [noncognitive] skills that are inter-linked and the enhancement of one of these skills without improvement of the others is unlikely to lead to lasting changes' (p. 43).

Investing in cognitive and noncognitive skills in early life may be an effective way to address social inequality. Gaps in test scores open up early in life across socioeconomic groups and are stable by age 8–9, suggesting the education children receive after this age is not effective at closing these gaps (Heckman, 2006). For this reason, Heckman and Kautz (2013) argue that 'waiting until kindergarten to address these gaps is too late. It creates achievement gaps for disadvantaged children that are costly to close' (p. 7). Interventions might therefore be designed to address the portion of these gaps which is attributable to variation in the quality of family life in the child's early years. Such interventions might include pre- and post-natal nutritional supplementation programmes (e.g., iron, iodine), home visitations which teach parenting skills, early preschool programmes which promote cognitive and socio-emotional development, and school-based programmes extending into adolescence in order to take advantage of dynamic complementarities.

The practical implementation of such interventions would ideally adhere to certain best practices in order to identify the cognitive and noncognitive pathways to economic success while addressing the limitations of prior literature. Broadly speaking, the ideal intervention would: (1) target a large, representative sample to ensure that the findings were relevant to the broader population and provide sufficient power for statistical analyses; (2) implement a randomized design with low rates of attrition over time to demonstrate causality; (3) use established strategies (where available) to improve cognitive and noncognitive skills which take into account their changing malleability over the lifespan; (4) assess cognitive and noncognitive skills via a multi-method approach to minimize measurement error (e.g., combining scores on individual tests and behavioural tasks with self-, informant and observer ratings); and (5) examine a wide set of outcome variables in order to evaluate the full range of effects of the programme.

21.6   CONCLUSION

We began this chapter by asking which psychological characteristics help children become economically successful adults. A large body of research in economics and psychology confirms that early-life cognitive and noncognitive skills play a substantial role in shaping outcomes in education and the labour market. Indeed, by focusing only on the domains of school and work in this chapter, we have omitted considerable evidence showing that greater childhood cognitive and noncognitive skills also predict better outcomes in areas such as health, criminality and well-being.

Future research in this area should move towards identifying the noncognitive skills which are causal determinants of later socioeconomic success, rather than merely predictors of it. It would also be useful to broaden the outcomes examined beyond academic achievement and extend the follow-up periods of interventions; knowing whether, for example, improvements in early-life socio-emotional skills also lead to consistently better labour market outcomes could substantially change the cost-benefit evaluations of early interventions. Lastly, while there is consensus on the importance of early childhood interventions, there is no gold standard intervention template which delineates which specific skills and outcomes should be targeted and the optimum duration and intensity for programmes to produce the greatest economic return.

21.7   SUMMARY

This chapter reviewed the evidence on childhood psychological predictors of adult economic outcomes. Our central finding is that better childhood cognitive skills and noncognitive skills (i.e. self-control, self-perception, socio-emotional skills, motivation, mental health and metacognitive strategies) consistently predict better outcomes in areas such as employment, education, income and socioeconomic status. Interventions which improve these skills in early life appear to be effective ways to improve children's long-term prospects.

NOTES

1. We use the term 'noncognitive skills' to maintain consistency with prior literature. However, there is considerable debate about whether this term is appropriate for categorizing such a diverse collection of psychological differences, or even whether these differences reflect deeper underlying preferences rather than skills per se.
2. The UK Data Service website (http://ukdataservice.ac.uk/) contains examples of such studies. It hosts, among others, the National Child Development Study (cohort members born 1958), the British Cohort Study (1970), the Longitudinal Study of Young People in England (1989/90) and the Millennium Cohort Study (2000).
3. Due to space limitations, our review is not exhaustive; for example we omit evidence on achievement striving, grit, and creativity. See Table 1 of Heckman and Kautz (2013) for a complete list of noncognitive skills, categorized using the taxonomy of the Big Five personality traits.

REVIEW QUESTIONS

1. Distinguish between cognitive and noncognitive skills and the ways in which they are measured.
2. What is the evidence on the malleability of cognitive vs. noncognitive skills? How does this malleability change over the lifespan?
3. How might the implications of this stream of research be practically addressed in the real world?

REFERENCES

Almlund, M., Duckworth, A., Heckman, J., & Kautz, T. (2011). Personality psychology and economics. NBER Working Paper No. 16822.

Baumeister, R., Vohs, K., & Tice, D. (2007). The strength model of self-control. *Current Directions in Psychological Science, 16,* 351–355. DOI:10.1111/j.1467-8721.2007.00534.x

Boake, C. (2002). From the Binet-Simon to the Weschler-Bellevue: Tracing the history of intelligence testing. *Journal of Clinical and Experimental Psychology, 2*(3), 383–405. DOI:10.1076/jcen.24.3.383.981

Borghans, L., Golsteyn, B., Heckman, J., & Humphries, J. (2011). Identification problems in personality psychology. *Personality and Individual Differences, 51,* 315–320. DOI:10.1016/j.paid.2011.03.029

Carroll, J. (1993). *Human cognitive abilities.* Cambridge: Cambridge University Press.

CASEL. (2015). *SEL Defined.* Retrieved from http://www.casel.org/social-and-emotional-learning/ (accessed 7 May 2015).

Caspi, A., Wright, B., Moffitt, T., & Silva, P. (1998). Early failure in the labor market: Childhood and adolescent predictors of unemployment in the transition to adulthood. *American Sociological Review, 63,* 424–451. DOI:10.2107/2657557

Cunha, F., & Heckman, J. (2007). The technology of skill formation. *American Economic Review, 97,* 31–47. DOI:10.1257/aer.97.2.31

Currie, J., & Stabile, M. (2009). Mental health in childhood and human capital. In J. Gruber (Ed.), *An economic perspective on the problems of disadvantaged youth.* Chicago: University of Chicago Press for NBER.

Daly, M., Delaney, L., Egan, M., & Baumeister, R. (2015). Childhood self-control and unemployment throughout the life span: Evidence from two British cohort studies. *Psychological Science, 26,* 709–721. DOI:10.1177/0956797615569001

Daly, M., Egan, M., & O'Reilly, F. (2015). Childhood general cognitive ability predicts leadership role occupancy across life: Evidence from 17,000 cohort study participants. *The Leadership Quarterly*, *26*, 321–341. DOI:10.1016/j.leaqua.2015.03.006

Deary, I., Pattie, A., & Starr, J. (2013). The stability of intelligence from age 11 to age 90 years: The Lothian Birth Cohort of 1921. *Psychological Science*, *24*, 2161–2168. DOI:10.1177/0956797613486487

Deary, I., Strand, S., Smith, P., & Fernandes, C. (2007). Intelligence and educational achievement. *Intelligence*, *35*, 13–21. DOI:10.1016/j.intell.2006.02.001

Deary, I., Taylor, M., Hart, C., Wilson, V., Smith, G., Blane, D., & Starr, J. (2005). Intergenerational social mobility and mid-life status attainment: Influences of childhood intelligence, childhood social factors, and education. *Intelligence*, *33*, 455–472. DOI:10.1016/j.intell.2005.06.003

Delaney, L., & Smith, J. (2012). Childhood health: Trends and consequences over the life course. *The Future of Children*, *22*, 43–63. DOI:10.1353/foc.2012.0003

Duckworth, A., Quinn, P., Lynam, D., Loeber, R., & Stouthamer-Loeber, M. (2011). Role of test motivation in intelligence testing. *Proceedings of the National Academy of Sciences*, *108*(19), 7716–7720. DOI:10.1073/pnas.1018601108

Duncan, G., & Magnuson, K. (2013). Investing in preschool programs. *Journal of Economic Perspectives*, *27*, 109–132. DOI:10.1257/jep.27.2.109

Durlak, J., Weissberg, R., Dymnicki, A., Taylor, R., & Schellinger, K. (2011). The impact of enhancing students' social and emotional learning: A meta-analysis of school-based universal interventions. *Child Development*, *82*, 405–432. DOI:10.1111/j.1467-8624.2010.01564.x

Eccles, J., & Wigfield, A. (2002). Motivational beliefs, values, and goals. *Annual Review of Psychology*, *53*, 109–132. DOI:10.1146/annurev.psych.53.100901.135153

Egan, M., Daly, M., & Delaney, L. (2015). Childhood psychological distress and youth unemployment: Evidence from two British cohort studies. *Social Science & Medicine*, *124*, 11–17. DOI:10.1016/j.socscimed.2014.11.021

Eisenberg, N., Duckworth, A., Spinrad, T., & Valiente, C. (2014). Conscientiousness: Origins in childhood? *Developmental Psychology*, *50*, 1331–1349. DOI:10.1037/a0030977

Findley, M., & Cooper, H. (1983). Locus of control and academic achievement: A literature review. *Journal of Personality and Social Psychology*, *44*, 419–427. DOI:10.1037/0022-3514.44.2.419

Fletcher, J. (2009). Adolescent depression and educational attainment: Results using sibling fixed effects. *Health Economics*, *19*, 855–871. DOI:10.1002/hec.1526

Golsteyn, B., Grönqvist, H., & Lindahl, L. (2014). Adolescent time preferences predict lifetime outcomes. *Economic Journal*, *124*, 739–761. DOI:10.1111/ecoj.12095

Goodman, A., Joshi, H., Nasim, B., & Tyler, C. (2015). *Social and emotional skills in childhood and their long-term effects on adult life*. London: Institute of Education.

Goodman, A., Joyce, R., & Smith, J. (2011). The long shadow cast by childhood physical and mental problems on adult life. *Proceedings of the National Academy of Sciences*, *108*, 6032–6037. DOI:10.1073/pnas.1016970108

Gottfredson, L. (1997). Mainstream science on intelligence: An editorial with 52 signatories, history, and bibliography. *Intelligence*, *24*, 13–21. DOI:10.1016/s0160-2896(97)90011-8

Gutman, L. M., & Schoon, I. (2013). *The impact of non-cognitive skills on outcomes for young people: Literature review*. London: Institute of Education.

Heckman, J. (2006). Skill formation and the economics of investing in disadvantaged children. *Science*, *312*, 1900–1902. DOI:10.1126/science.1128898

Heckman, J. (2008). Schools, skills and synapses. *Economic Inquiry*, *46*, 289–324. DOI:10.1111/j.1465-7295.2008.00163.x

Heckman, J., & Kautz, T. (2013). Fostering and measuring skills: Interventions that improve character and cognition. NBER Working Paper No. 19656.

Heckman, J. J., Moon, S. H., Pinto, R., Savelyev, P. A., & Yavitz, A. Q. (2010). Analyzing social experiments as implemented: A reexamination of the evidence from the HighScope Perry Preschool Program. *Quantitative Economics*, *1*, 1–46. DOI:10.3982/qe8

Heckman, J., Pinto, R., & Savelyev, P. (2013). Understanding the mechanisms through which an influential early childhood program boosted adult outcomes. *American Economic Review, 103,* 2052–2086. DOI:10.1257/aer.103.6.2052

Heckman, J., & Rubinstein, Y. (2001). The importance of noncognitive skills: Lessons from the GED testing program. *American Economic Review, 91,* 145–149. DOI:10.1257/aer.91.2.145

Heckman, J., Stixrud, J., & Urzua, S. (2006). The effects of cognitive and noncognitive abilities on labor market outcomes and social behavior. *Journal of Labor Economics, 24,* 411–482. DOI:10.1086/504455

Henrich, J., Heine, S., & Norenzayan, A. (2010). The weirdest people in the world?. *Behavioral and Brain Sciences, 33,* 61–83. DOI:10.1017/s0140525x0999152x

Knudsen, E., Heckman, J., Cameron, J., & Shonkoff, J. (2006). Economic, neurobiological, and behavioral perspectives on building America's future workforce. *Proceedings of the National Academy of Sciences, 103,* 10155–10162. DOI:10.1073/pnas.0600888103

Kuhn, P., & Weinberger, C. (2005). Leadership skills and wages. *Journal of Labor Economics, 21,* 395–436. DOI:10.1086/430282

Layard, R. (2013). Mental health: The new frontier for labour economics. *IZA Journal of Labor Policy, 2,* 1–16. DOI: 10.1186/2193-9004-2-2

Lindqvist, E., & Vestman, R. (2011). The labor market returns to cognitive and noncognitive ability: Evidence from the Swedish enlistment. *American Economic Journal: Applied Economics, 3,* 101–128. DOI:10.1257/app.3.1.101

Lundborg, P., Nilsson, A., & Rooth, D. (2014). Adolescent health and adult labor market outcomes. *Journal of Health Economics, 37,* 25–40. DOI:10.1016/j.jhealeco.2014.05.003

Moffitt, T., Arseneault, L., Belsky, D., Dickson, N., Hancox, R., & Harrington, H. et al. (2011). A gradient of childhood self-control predicts health, wealth, and public safety. *Proceedings of the National Academy of Sciences, 108,* 2693–2698. DOI:10.1073/pnas.1010076108

Moutafi, J., Furnham, A., & Tsaousis, I. (2006). Is the relationship between intelligence and trait neuroticism mediated by test anxiety?. *Personality and Individual Differences, 40,* 587–597. DOI:10.1016/j.paid.2005.08.004

Multon, K., Brown, S., & Lent, R. (1991). Relation of self-efficacy beliefs to academic outcomes: A meta-analytic investigation. *Journal of Counseling Psychology, 38,* 30–38. DOI:10.1037/0022-0167.38.1.30

Nores, M., & Barnett, W. (2010). Benefits of early childhood interventions across the world: (Under) investing in the very young. *Economics of Education Review, 29,* 271–282. DOI:10.1016/j.econedurev.2009.09.001

O'Connor, T., Rutter, M., Beckett, C., Keaveney, L., & Kreppner, J. (2000). The effects of global severe privation on cognitive competence: Extension and longitudinal follow-up. *Child Development, 7 1,* 376–390. DOI:10.1111/1467-8624.00151

Shoda, Y., Mischel, W., & Peake, P. (1990). Predicting adolescent cognitive and self-regulatory competencies from preschool delay of gratification: Identifying diagnostic conditions. *Developmental Psychology, 26,* 978–986. DOI:10.1037//0012-1649.26.6.978

Smith, J., & Smith, G. (2010). Long-term economic costs of psychological problems during childhood. *Social Science & Medicine, 71,* 110–115. DOI:10.1016/j.socscimed.2010.02.046

Strenze, T. (2007). Intelligence and socioeconomic success: A meta-analytic review of longitudinal research. *Intelligence, 35,* 401–426. DOI:10.1016/j.intell.2006.09.004

Taylor, G., Jungert, T., Mageau, G., Schattke, K., Dedic, H., Rosenfield, S., & Koestner, R. (2014). A self-determination theory approach to predicting school achievement over time: the unique role of intrinsic motivation. *Contemporary Educational Psychology, 39,* 342–358. DOI:10.1016/j.cedpsych.2014.08.002

Terman, L. M. (Ed.). (1925). *Genetic studies of genius, vol. I: Mental and physical traits of a thousand gifted children.* Stanford, CA: Stanford University Press.

Terman, L. M. (Ed.). (1959). *Genetic studies of genius, vol. V: The gifted group at mid-life, thirty-five years' follow-up of the superior child.* Stanford, CA: Stanford University Press.

FURTHER READING

Goodman, A., Joshi, H., Nasim, B., & Tyler, C. (2015). *Social and emotional skills in childhood and their long-term effects on adult life.* London: Institute of Education.

Gutman, L. M., & Schoon, I. (2013). *The impact of non-cognitive skills on outcomes for young people: Literature review.* London: Institute of Education.

Heckman, J., & Kautz, T. (2013). Fostering and measuring skills: Interventions that improve character and cognition. NBER Working Paper No. 19656.

22 The Economic Psychology of Financial Decision-Making and Money Management in the Household

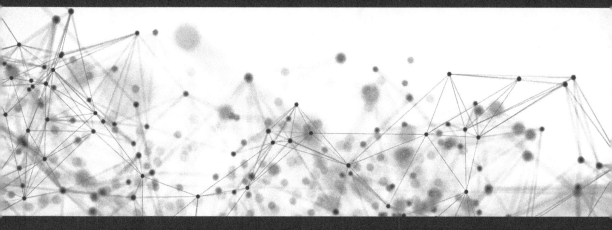

STEFANIE J. SONNENBERG

CHAPTER OUTLINE

LEARNING OUTCOMES

BY THE END OF THIS CHAPTER YOU SHOULD BE ABLE TO:

1. Discuss the relevance of an economic psychological approach to understanding the household or the family.

2. Provide examples of the range of factors that shape financial decisions and money management in the household.

3. Examine the role that gender and gender norms might play in explaining the findings in this field.

22.1 INTRODUCTION

Many decisions in our life have economic repercussions – albeit to varying degrees, and often despite our conscious intentions. The decisions we make in our private lives are no exception. Imagine this common scenario: You meet someone you like and become a couple. You start talking about living together – after some deliberation, you decide to set up home. Once you have found a home, what will you buy for your new place and how much money will you spend on new items? How are you going decide on any future joint purchases (e.g., furniture, holidays)? How will you deal with household bills (e.g., who/whose money will pay these)? Are you going to pool all your money, or will you keep your incomes separate? Will you get married, buy a property, have any children?

These seemingly mundane, private questions touch upon broader 'public' issues – this is why private households are considered important sites for studying wider economic processes. In this chapter, we will therefore turn our focus on intimate relationships and families. In doing so, we are going to explore the private household from the economic psychologist's perspective, concentrating on two specific domains of research, namely, (1) *financial decision-making* and (2) *money management*. First, though, we need to consider some key terms used throughout this chapter.

22.1.1 The Household and Family in Economics and Psychology

The use of terms such as 'household' or 'family' might seem straightforward – and many studies take their meaning for granted. Kirchler's work (e.g., 1988a) is an exception: it makes an explicit effort to distinguish between 'family' and 'household'. Kirchler (1988a) conceptualizes the family as a group of two or more people who dwell together and who are linked by kinship, marriage or adoption. In contrast, a 'household' is defined as the number of people residing in the same housing unit. From a psychological perspective, the key difference between the two lies in the greater physical/emotional intimacy which exists between members of the same family.

In the context of everyday life, 'family' and 'household' frequently overlap as the majority of households comprise some form of family. In line with previous work, we will therefore use these terms interchangeably. Yet, the nature of what constitutes a family is not fixed but changes in accordance with socio-cultural, political, legal and economic forces. For example, the rise of non-married, long-term cohabitation, the growth of extended step-families and the recent legal institution of civil partnerships and marriage for same-sex couples indicate that households are becoming increasingly diverse. We therefore should not take the meaning of 'household' or 'family' for granted.

The household is an important analytic unit for economists because the decisions made in private households often have financial repercussions on a public (i.e., aggregate) level. As such, the household has attracted much attention in economics where it is assumed to be a fairly straightforward, single decision-making entity (Kirchler, 1995). However, sociologists have long been challenging this assumption, demonstrating that households often do not resemble the economist's stylized version of an unproblematic decision-making unit (e.g., Pahl, 1983; Vogler & Pahl, 1994). From a psychological perspective, too, the economist's version appears suspect: as already noted, households often comprise families whose composition might vary considerably. While the treatment of households as single and *equivalent* decision-making units might be analytically necessary for economic modelling, in psychological terms, families seem considerably more complex.

Our personal experience often confirms the psychological complexity of family life. Contrary to the economist's abstract notion of the household, families are typically characterized by diverse interpersonal relationships and the existence of emotional bonds between family members (Kirchler, 1988a; 1998b). Therefore, a person's experience of belonging to a family is likely to be profoundly different to their membership in any other social group (Kirchler, 1988a). Moreover, interactions between family members tend to span relatively long periods of time. While this has led to the supposition that families are characterized by internal cohesion and the pursuit of common goals, as Burgoyne and Kirchler (2008) have pointed out, they also entail conflicting interests that have to be negotiated. These considerations have given rise to psychological approaches which start from the premise of the household-as-family (i.e., acknowledging its interpersonal complexities). With this in mind, we will now examine the economic psychology of household (1) financial decision-making and (2) money management.

22.2 FINANCIAL DECISION-MAKING IN THE HOUSEHOLD

In exploring the economic psychology of household decision-making, our focus will be on purchase decisions that have direct, tangible financial consequences. In the late 1980s, Erich Kirchler began a programme of research looking at such decisions within the family, arguing for a contextualized and process-oriented understanding of households and household financial decision-making. Kirchler and colleagues' work sets out from the following social-psychological observations:

1. Economic decisions in the household cannot be considered as one-off, linear or clearly defined events. Instead, such decisions should be theorized and studied as inseparable from the ongoing flow of everyday family life (Kirchler 1988a; 1995; 1999b).

2. Household economic decisions, especially purchase decisions, are not necessarily straightforward. Instead, decisions of this kind can represent an important cause of conflict within intimate relationships and ongoing negotiations might be required.

These social psychological observations differ markedly from normative economic models of decision-making where decisions are regarded as linear, rationally leading to the choice of the best alternative. From a psychological perspective, decision-making appears decidedly less well-defined, more 'messy', and moulded by its specific interactional context. On the basis of this premise, Kirchler's work has drawn attention to the importance of understanding not only a household's decision history but also the social influence processes that shape economic decision-making in family contexts (see also Simpson, Griskevicius, & Rothman, 2012; Su, Zhou, Zhou, & Li, 2008).

22.2.1 Relationship Quality, Perceived Expertise and Decision History

What, then, determines how household money is spent? In a methodologically innovative series of studies, Kirchler (1988b) and colleagues (Kirchler, Rodler, Hölzl, & Meier, 2001) asked couples to keep a detailed diary of their specific commodity purchases, including careful descriptions of the circumstances in which their decision-making processes took place (e.g., 'where were you when talking about the commodity?, who else was present?'). Each partner completed the diary separately, thus allowing the degree of overlap between partners' individual responses to be examined.

Relationship quality (i.e., the extent to which couples reported to be happy with their relationship) was found to have a bearing on couple's economic decisions: happier couples were more frequently in agreement over household purchases, and their economic decisions involved fewer conflicts (Kirchler, 1988b). Husbands' responses also suggested that, in comparison to less happy spouses, happier partners discussed purchase options more frequently prior to spending; unhappy couples, conversely, seemed more likely to be involved in post-purchase discussions (i.e., once an item had already been bought). Overall, the results suggested that happy couples are more frequently involved in making joint purchase decision than their less happy counterparts. In particular, Kirchler concluded that happier couples appear to resolve potential conflicts before any purchase takes place, whereas less happy couples tend to seek agreement after a purchase has already been made – which, in turn, may contribute to conflict. Subsequent work also revealed that happy and unhappy couples tend to differ in their social influence patterns which, as we shall see below, likewise link to how purchase decisions are made (Kirchler, 1993).

Kirchler (1988b) also found that perceived expertise played a role in couples' economic decision-making. In line with previous marketing evidence, findings indicated that the partner who is seen to possess relatively greater expertise concerning a specific product, or product category, tends to dominate decisions about its acquisition. Perceived expertise, in turn, seemed to be associated with gender. Kirchler found some evidence of the existence of gender role segmentation – that is, differences between women and men – in household purchase decision-making. For instance, women seemed to have greater say in purchases involving clothing and food, whereas men had greater control over decisions concerning cars and car-related items. These gender differences are in line with previous marketing research and have been replicated in later work (Penz & Kirchler, 2012). Meier, Kirchler and Hubert (1999) also found gender differences in saving decisions and perceived expertise in high-risk investments.

Kirchler's (1988b) diary study was the first to provide empirical evidence in support of the claim that a couple's prior decision history is crucial for understanding specific spending decisions. The diary findings demonstrated that 'utility debts' play a role in the household economic decision-making process, suggesting that partners who have dominated a previous decision are usually required to yield in a subsequent purchase decision. In other words, the potential 'utility gains' made by dominating a spending decision (i.e., 'getting one's way') become debts that need to be 'repaid' at a later stage (i.e., by letting one's partner have 'their way' in a subsequent choice).

22.2.2 The Importance of Social Influence

Partners or family members may not always be in agreement when it comes to the usefulness or value of purchasing a specific commodity or service. In this case, they need to find ways of aligning their preferences, that is, they may resort to social influence strategies in trying to sway one another's preferences for/against the service or commodity in question. As Kirchler (1988a) states: 'To reach an agreement, at least one of the involved parties must be willing to modify his/her subjective utility function or to be able to persuade the other(s) to yield ... The attempts to persuade the other to acquiesce are termed bargaining strategies and tactics' (p. 264).

In order to examine the role of social influence in household decision-making, Kirchler (1990) developed a taxonomy of 18 influence strategies which describe different tactics that partners may use to persuade one another when making purchase decisions. This taxonomy is summarized in Table 22.1. Kirchler and colleagues then examined the role these social influence tactics play in household purchase decisions, particularly when taking into account different types of purchase conflict (Kirchler, 1990; 1993; 1999a; Penz & Kirchler, 2012). They also explored which specific features of a couple's relationship (e.g., relationship satisfaction, marital power, egalitarian versus patriarchal attitudes) impact on partners' use of these influence tactics.

For example, Kirchler (1990; 1993) presented partners with different vignettes that described a specific purchase decision. The vignettes varied regarding the particular type of purchase conflict they depicted, namely, (1) a *probability conflict* (partners agree on the value/need for a particular product, e.g., a car, but not on the specific item representing that category, i.e., the type of car); (2) *value conflict* (partners disagree on the value of a particular product/service, e.g., a holiday); or (3) *distribution conflict* (partners disagree on what resources should be spent on). Following presentation of the vignettes, to examine how couples would influence their partner if similar situations arose within their own household, Kirchler (1990; 1993) interviewed or surveyed each spouse separately to examine partners' respective endorsement of the 18 influence tactics outlined above (see Table 22.1). He found that influence tactics such as integrative bargaining, reason, overt display of desires/wishes and indirect coalition appeared to be used more frequently than persuasive tactics, acting helpless and negative emotions (Kirchler, 1993; 1999a). There was also substantial evidence to suggest that people's use of particular influence tactics was significantly shaped by situational characteristics. In particular, the type of purchase conflict, features of the relationship and gender were found to have an impact on the reported social influence tactics.

Table 22.1 *Taxonomy of 18 social influence strategies used in household purchase decision-making (adapted from Kirchler, 1990)*

Strategy content (i.e., focus of tactic)	Strategy label	Example of strategy (i.e., behavioural expression of tactic)
Emotion	(1) Positive Emotion	Manipulation, humour, flattery, seductive behaviour
	(2) Negative Emotion	Threats, cynicism, ridicule, shouting
Physical force	(3) Helplessness	Crying, showing weakness, acting helpless/ill
	(4) Aggression	Using force, violence, aggression
Resources	(5) Rewards	Offering services/resources, being attentive
	(6) Punishments	Withdrawing (financial) resources, punishing
Presence	(7) Insisting	'Nagging', returning to the subject until the other yields, exhausting the other
	(8) Withdrawal	Leaving the scene, changing the subject, refusing to share responsibility
Information	(9) Overt Information	Talking openly about importance/interest to self, asking for cooperation, presenting one's own needs
	(10) Distorted Information	Lying, withholding or distorting relevant information
Persons	(11) Indirect Coalition	Referring to other people (e.g., children, neighbours), emphasizing utility of purchase to children
	(12) Direct Coalition	Discussing/talking about the issue in the presence of others
Fact	(13) Buying Autonomously ('Fait accompli')	Deciding without consulting partner, buying product/service without partner's consent
Roles/Role segmentation	(14) Yielding to Roles	Autonomous decision by partner according to established role; yielding as partner is regarded as responsible for the product
	(15) Role-Based Decision	Deciding in line with established role segmentation or family norms
Bargaining	(16) Trade-Offs	Offers of trade-offs, bookkeeping, reminding of past favours
	(17) Integrative Bargaining	Searching for the best solution that satisfies both partners
Reason	(18) Reasoned Argument	Logical argumentation, presenting factual arguments, talking in an emotionally neutral way about product alternatives

22.2.3 Situational and Interpersonal Characteristics: Purchase Conflicts, Relationship Features and Gender

The economic psychology of the household reveals that the nature of a particular financial decision and of a couple's relationship can have a significant impact on the decision-making process and its outcome. With respect to the former, Kirchler (1993) found that in distributional conflicts, trade-offs and integrative bargaining were the most frequent social influence tactics, whereas in value conflicts, persuasive tactics were predominant. Regarding the nature of couples' relationships, Kirchler (1990) found differences between couples categorized as egalitarian and those characterized as patriarchal. In comparison to patriarchal couples, partners within an egalitarian relationship were more likely to use persuasive tactics or coalition-making. Partners' use of influence tactics was also found to vary as a function of relationship quality (Kirchler, 1993). For instance, in comparison to partners who were less satisfied with their marriage, happy spouses more frequently endorsed finding integrative solutions and were less likely to endorse autonomous decision-making. Happy couples reported using positive emotions and overt acknowledgement of their wishes and reason more frequently and, correspondingly, resorted less to negative tactics (e.g., providing distorted information, displaying negative emotions, aggression).

Partners' use of influence strategies was also found to vary over time as a function of relationship length (Kirchler, 1993). For example, influence strategies such as autonomous purchases, deciding according to roles and yielding according to roles were found more frequently in more established couples. In other words, there seemed to be greater 'spontaneous' (i.e., automatic) consensus in older couples than younger ones who were more likely to engage in negotiations over purchases. Moreover, positive emotions, overt information and bargaining tactics were reported less frequently in older couples than in their younger counterparts.

Interestingly, contrary to economic assumptions, psychological evidence also indicates that when it comes to individual preferences or social influence tactics in joint economic decisions, spouses seem to know little about one another (Kirchler, 1988a; 1999a). For instance, Kirchler (1999a) examined the reliability of partners' self-reports and found that spouses were not particularly accurate in their judgement of their partner's influence tactics, nor in their assessment of the overlap between their own and their partner's use of social influence strategies.[1] Kirchler concludes that 'spouses are probably not explicitly aware of what is going on in detail and perhaps do not always know how they *muddle through* the process of making joint economic decisions' (1999, p. 15, emphasis added).

Finally, gender appears to play a role in the social influences processes underlying household economic decision-making. For instance, Kirchler (1993) found that women reported 'acting helpless' and 'leaving the scene', offering trade-offs and searching for integrative solutions more frequently than their male counterparts. Conversely, men seemed more likely to decide on purchases autonomously, without consulting a partner. The gendered nature of these social influence strategies echoes the finding of gender role segmentation/specialization in household purchases. Moreover, there is some evidence that these gender differences persist across different cultures and despite an increasing emphasis on gender equality. For example, Penz and Kirchler (2012) found that Vietnamese middle-class families appeared to preserve their traditional social influence patterns with regard to purchase decisions; women were still found to be responsible for the purchase of items traditionally regarded as falling within a woman's domain (e.g., cooking items, kitchen ware), whereas men seemed to dominate purchase decisions involving computer equipment and cars.

Overall, however, we should perhaps regard these gender differences with a degree of caution – especially since the reported differences often reflect commonly held gender stereotypes. It is conceivable that couples report influence tactics that they deem to be in line with pre-existing stereotypes or normative expectations but which may not, in fact, reflect their actual decision-making processes.

So far, we have focused on the psychological determinants of economic decision-making in the household. In particular, we have examined joint purchases made with household money. But what counts as joint household money? Who contributes what to household funds and how are these managed on a day-to-day basis? We will now turn to the economic psychological literature that deals with precisely these questions.

22.3 HOUSEHOLD MONEY MANAGEMENT

Economic psychology research on household money management (e.g., Burgoyne, 1990; Burgoyne & Lewis, 1994; Burgoyne & Routh, 2001) was originally inspired by sociological findings. Sociologists have long recognized the need to examine the 'inner workings' of the household – specifically the ways in which household members organize, control and manage their monetary resources. During the 1980s, the sociological pioneer in this field, Jan Pahl (1980; 1983), began to examine the ways in which monetary resources are allocated, organized and managed within individual households. She developed a typology of household money management systems (see Box 22.1) to reflect how the couples in her studies dealt with money (Pahl, 1989).

Box 22.1 Typology of household money management systems

1. *Female Whole Wage* – the husband passes his wage packet (minus money for his personal spending) to his wife who, in turn, has sole responsibility for managing the household's expenses.

2. *Male Whole Wage* – the husband keeps his own income and is responsible for managing all household money (potentially leaving a non-employed wife without any personal spending money).

3. *Housekeeping Allowance* – the breadwinner (traditionally the husband) hands over a sum of money for housekeeping expenses to the other partner, while keeping control over the remainder.

4. *Pooling* – both partners have access to all, or nearly all, household income and both are regarded as equally responsible for managing the common pool (that is, money in a joint account).

5. *Independent Management* – both partners have independent incomes which are kept separate (i.e., in separate accounts) and partners may be responsible for paying different household bills or for the purchase of different household items.

Source: Adapted from Pahl (1989).

Subsequent work has drawn heavily on Pahl's original typology, which has allowed researchers not only to describe patterns of money management *within* households but also to distinguish *between* different kinds of household on the basis of their financial organization (e.g., Burgoyne, 1990; Vogler, 1994; Vogler & Pahl, 1994). Moreover, Pahl's typology has provided scholars with a tool for tracking changes in money management patterns over time. While 'pooling' tends to be the most widely reported system of household money management (Lauer & Yodanis, 2011; Laurie & Gershuny, 2000), there have been considerable changes over time in people's use of the other systems. For example, the use of the 'housekeeping allowance' has undergone a rapid decline (Pahl, 2005; Vogler & Pahl, 1994). Conversely, there has been a marked rise in the popularity of the 'independent management' system (i.e., partners managing their finances independently). While early findings in this area were predominantly based on surveys and interview studies with married couples, more recent evidence including other types of household suggests that independent household money management occurs relatively more frequently in re-married couples and non-married cohabitants (Ashby & Burgoyne, 2008; 2009; Burgoyne & Morison, 1997; Vogler, 2005; Vogler, Lyonette, & Wiggins, 2008) and within same-sex relationships (Burgoyne & Clarke, 2011; Burns, Burgoyne, & Clarke, 2008).

Why, though, should psychologists be concerned with categorizing or systematizing couples' household money management in this way? Money management in the household turns out to have psychological significance since the specific money management system a household adopts can have significant consequences for individual family members and their well-being. This is because each of the systems of money management outlined in Box 22.1 has implications regarding the extent to which individual family members can access and control household money. These systems of money management also have repercussion for individual spending – that is, the extent to which family members can use household resources as personal spending money (PSM). For instance, imagine a couple in which both partner are employed full-time: partners may decide to adopt an 'independent management' system – that is, the couple may decide to keep their respective incomes separate and split the cost of bills and general household expenditure 50/50. The adoption of this particular system of managing money could leave the partner on lower pay – usually the woman – with significantly less disposable income after their portion of the essential household expenses has been paid (Burgoyne & Sonnenberg, 2009). We will examine shortly the specific implications that different money management systems have for men's and women's access to financial resources.

Over the last decade, Pahl's original typology of household money management systems has been undergoing several adaptations. This has partly been in recognition of the fact that systems of money management are likely to evolve over time. For example, changes in employment patterns (i.e., increase in the number of families with more than one income earner) as well as technological developments (e.g., online banking and the possibility of paying online for goods and services) are likely to have repercussions for how households manage their financial resources. Recent modifications to the original taxonomy have also been due to growing concerns among economic psychologists about the accuracy with which these systems capture what couples really *do* with their money. For example,

Burgoyne's research recognized that income pooling often entails sharing financial resources to varying degrees. Spouses or partners may combine some but not all of their individual incomes in a common pool (e.g., a joint bank account) to which they may either contribute equal amounts or, alternatively, individual contributions may vary (e.g., the partner on a higher income may contribute more). In acknowledgement of these subtleties, Burgoyne and colleagues further subdivided Pahl's original 'pooling' system into different forms of 'part-pooling' (Ashby & Burgoyne, 2008; Burgoyne, Clarke, Reibstein, & Edmunds, 2006; Burgoyne, Reibstein, Edmunds, & Dolman, 2007; see also Pahl, 2005). What, then, are the key findings from studying household money management systems? Here, again, gender seems to play a pivotal role.

22.3.1 *Money Management and Gender*

As already mentioned, the ways in which household income is allocated and managed can have significant repercussions for the well-being of individual family members (Burgoyne, 1990; Pahl, 1995; 2005; Vogler, 2005; Vogler, Lyonette, & Wiggins, 2008). Early sociological findings indicated that, even in households where overall income is perfectly adequate, women and children may be living in relative poverty – that is, there is often a higher incidence of financial deprivation among women (Vogler, 1994; Vogler & Pahl, 1994).

To date, the gender differences in partners' access to household money and patterns of consumption remain a frequent and persistent theme in this field (see Bennett, 2013). Often marked differences between men and women have emerged in several domains, and especially in relation to the important distinction between financial *management* and financial *control* (see Vogler, 1994; Vogler & Pahl, 1993; 1994). According to this distinction, the management of financial resources describes the more mundane aspects of dealing with the day-to-day money matters (e.g., routine payment for goods, services, bills) whereas financial control refers to having the 'final say' in the household's economic decisions. Women tend to be in charge of financial management in households where overall income is low, when making ends meet is often difficult and can be rather hard work (Antonides, 2011; Pahl, 1989; Vogler & Pahl, 1994). As family income increases, both financial control and management are more likely to become bestowed on the male partner. The specific pattern by which financial control and management are conferred can lead to significant gender differences in access to money: for example, in those lower-income households where men have a high degree of financial control, women might not only find themselves at an economic disadvantage but also be more likely to experience greater financial deprivation (e.g., Vogler & Pahl, 1994).

Another domain in which gender differences have emerged concerns access to personal spending money (PSM). For example, even in households where all income appears to be pooled in one bank account and is seemingly viewed as 'joint' money, wives seem to feel more constrained when it comes to accessing money for their own personal use, especially if their contribution to overall household income is less than their husband's (Burgoyne, 1990; Burgoyne et al., 2006; 2007).

Research has also pointed to the existence of gender difference in the domain of spending. For example, women who are in paid employment frequently appear to be more family-focused than their male partners when it comes to spending household money: women tend to dedicate a relatively larger proportion of their earnings to children and child-related expenses (Nyman, 1999; Pahl, 1995; 2000). Different expectations regarding men and women's contribution to family-related expenditure have also been demonstrated experimentally (Burgoyne & Routh, 2001; Sonnenberg, Burgoyne, & Routh, 2011). It appears, then, that there are differences in the social norms or expectations that govern how men and women's financial contributions should be allocated, controlled and spent.

22.3.2 Explaining Gender Differences

Several explanations of gender differences in household money management have been proposed. Some regard the discrepancies between men and women in access to/control over money primarily as a function of the particular money management system adopted by the household (e.g., Nyman, 1999). However, this tends to ignore the ways in which adoption of a specific system of money management (e.g., the use of the whole wage or housekeeping allowance system) might relate to the actual source(s) of household income or partners' relative financial contributions. Some theorists have therefore argued that gender differences in access to/control over household money are a function of the traditional division of labour and partners' respective employment status. Blood and Wolfe (1960) initially captured this idea in their relative resource contribution theory which proposes that the greater a spouse's or partner's financial contribution (traditionally the man's), the greater the control that is afforded over the common budget. Also, this theory suggests that the partner who contributes most in financial terms has greater power in purchase decision-making (see Kirchler, 1988a; 1988b). This explanation is supported by some findings that the greater the perceived contribution to the household's finances, the greater the share in and access to the household's resources (Nyman & Dema, 2007).

However, other findings challenge this explanation. For example, relative resource contribution theory implies that we should see fewer (or no) gender differences in control over household money in families where both partners contribute the same amount to the common budget. Yet, despite demographic changes in women's labour market participation and increases in women's contribution to overall family income, the observed inequalities between men and women persist and seem relatively resistant to these broader developments. For instance, findings suggest that women, even when they are the family's main income earner, tend to curb their potential for greater financial control: that is, employed women not only tend to allocate resources differently to their husbands (e.g., devoting a higher proportion of their income to children; Pahl, 1995; 2000; Nyman, 1999; Yodanis & Lauer, 2007), but they also seem to downplay their role as 'good providers' (Commuri & Gentry, 2005). It has been argued that this might be an attempt to uphold the normative status of the male partner as the 'head of the household' (Vogler, 1998; Vogler & Pahl, 1993). The importance of upholding the notion of the 'male breadwinner' – regardless of the male partner's actual financial input – for the continuance of gender inequalities has also been emphasized in more recent work (Dema-Moreno & Diaz-Martinez, 2010; Vogler et al., 2006).

22.3.3 *The Psychology of Perceived Ownership and Entitlement*

The existence of gender differences in control over/access to household money not only seems puzzling from a socio-structural perspective (i.e., given the increase in women's labour market participation) but also from a social-psychological standpoint. This is because the gender disparities observed in research on household money management appear to contradict another key theme that has emerged from the same literature – namely, that the majority of people describe marriage as a partnership of equals in which all resources should be shared (Burgoyne, 1990; Burgoyne & Lewis, 1994; Nyman, 1999). For instance, when asked, in theory, how to organize household finances most people appear to endorse an ideal of equality (Burgoyne & Routh, 2001). Yet this apparent commitment to equal financial sharing is not always borne out by people's actual monetary arrangements; that is, there appears to be a paradox with regard to people's commitment to sharing, on the one hand, and their monetary practices, on the other (see Sonnenberg, 2008).[2]

To understand this paradox, Burgoyne has argued that, despite people's endorsement of marriage as a partnership of equals, there exists an unspoken rule according to which the partner who contributes the greater share to the household fund should be entitled to greater financial control as well as to more PSM. While this argument is reminiscent of the relative resource contribution approach mentioned above, unlike sociologists' focus on structural ('objective') explanations, economic psychologists emphasize the role psychological ('subjective') factors play in this regard. For instance, Burgoyne and Sonnenberg's (2009) research with non-married cohabiting couples demonstrates that one of the key determinants of a couple's money management practices is the psychological – or perceived – ownership of money. Findings from interview studies with different types of couples (including heterosexual and gay/lesbian cohabiting or married couples) suggest that it is difficult to comprehend household money management without taking into account subjective factors, such as the perceived ownership of money, notions of entitlement and sense of financial responsibility (Ashby & Burgoyne, 2008; 2009; Burgoyne et al., 2006; 2007).

In particular, Burgoyne and colleagues' work indicates that perceived ownership of money underpins the extent to which household income is treated as a collective or individual resource (Burgoyne et al., 2006) – that is, 'perceived ownership captures the degree to which partners are seen as, and feel themselves to be, psychologically entitled to access and control money, regardless of its source' (Burgoyne & Sonnenberg, 2009, p. 101). For example, one partner might inherit a sum of money: while some couples might psychologically regard this as belonging to the inheritor, other couples might consider this sum as jointly owned (i.e., regardless of its source) and for collective use. Conversely, while one partner may not contribute any income or assets to the relationship, a couple might nevertheless psychologically regard the other partner's money as belonging to them both, with both partners having equal control and access to it (Burgoyne & Sonnenberg, 2009).

Burgoyne et al. (2006) identify three broad categories of perceived ownership of household money, namely, (1) distinct or separate ownership; (2) blurred or transitional ownership; and (3) shared ownership. However, these categories are seen as subject to change and to re-definition/re-negotiation over time. Burgoyne and Sonnenberg (2009) observe that there can be a subtle interaction between the perceived ownership of household money and the expectations or meanings a couple might attach to their relationships at a particular stage. In other words, perceived ownership of household money is likely to respond to changes in the nature of a couple's relationship as well as in the couple's economic circumstances. From an economic psychological perspective, then, it is this notion of perceived ownership that determines and shapes partners' respective sense of entitlement to the family's resources.

22.3.4   The Importance of Social Norms

Sonnenberg, Burgoyne and Routh (2011) explored the role of social norms in the context of couples' transitions to marriage and parenthood. They presented respondents with vignettes that depicted a couple about to get married and another approaching the birth of a first child. The relative income of the hypothetical partners was varied experimentally across vignettes. Respondents were asked to indicate the type of financial organization they considered 'best' for each couple and to signal which partner (if either) should have access to more PSM. In line with previous research (Burgoyne & Routh, 2001), Sonnenberg et al. found that the 'joint pool' (i.e., pooling of all income with both partners contributing equally to decisions about how to use it) was most commonly regarded as the 'best' way to organize household finances overall – which provides further evidence in support of the normative view of marriage as a partnership of equals in which all resources should be shared.

However, Sonnenberg et al.'s (2011) findings also showed a clear causal link between the degree of income disparity between partners (as depicted in the vignettes) and the perceived suitability of different systems of financial allocation and views on PSM. For example, more traditional ways of managing household money – such as the housekeeping allowance system – were more likely to be considered 'best' in cases where one partner was depicted as the main breadwinner and when a woman, in a couple's transition to parenthood, was depicted as earning considerably more than her male partner. Conversely, independent management and part-pooling with different contributions from each partner were more likely to be chosen as the most suitable systems in situations where the man was portrayed as earning considerably more than his female counterpart. Differences in partners' respective incomes were also related to views on PSM: in the transition to marriage, higher-income earners and breadwinners were seen as entitled to more PSM than their partners – which links to the notion of perceived ownership discussed above. These findings suggest that women's higher income is normatively viewed differently to men's higher earnings, with women's extra income being treated as 'family money' while a man's extra earnings are more likely to be regarded as his own to manage and spend. In other words, the perceived ownership of (extra) income seems to vary as a function of gender.

22.4   CONCLUSION

Taken together, the findings discussed in this chapter point to an inextricable link between the private sphere and the economic domain. However, despite the important strides economic psychologists have made in advancing our understanding of economic decision making and money management in families (i.e., lifting the 'lid' on the household), there has been a relative paucity of both research and theory development in this domain. This may partly be due to the methodological challenges posed in this area. For instance, to what extent do our methods allow us to capture the *actual* dynamics of financial decision-making or money management? The psychologist's data tend to derive from various forms of self-report (e.g., surveys, interviews, diaries) and measurement is therefore relatively static. Moreover, asking household members about economic matters is rarely a neutral or 'objective' information-gathering exercise – instead, it can tap into what it *means* to be a family – which may distort our insights into actual financial practices (see Sonnenberg, 2008). Finally, the potential 'fuzziness' and changing nature of families may also have consequences for empirical and theoretical development.

22.5   SUMMARY

Standard economic models regard the household as a relatively unproblematic rational decision-making unit. These normative models rest on the assumption that, for analytic purposes, all households (i.e., family relationships) can be considered equivalent and that a common standard of living exists among members of the same household. Economic psychologists challenge these assumptions and, in recognition of the fact that households generally consist of families, focus on the ways in which contextual and interpersonal dynamics impinge on financial decisions and control over/access to monetary resources. This chapter reviews two distinct strands of research in economic psychology. Research on household financial decision-making demonstrates that couples' purchase decisions are frequently shaped by social psychological factors, such as relationship quality, perceived expertise as well as couples' previous decision histories. Studies in this field also show that purchase decisions are contingent not only on partners' use of social influence strategies but also on gender and broader situational characteristics (e.g., type of purchase conflict). These findings suggest that decision-making in families does not correspond to normative models – instead, people appear to 'muddle through' (Kirchler, 1999a) the joint decision-making process.

We also review research on household money management which suggests that there is considerable variation between households with regard to how financial resources are controlled and managed. Findings in this field suggest that the type of money management system a household adopts can have significant implications for individual family members' ability to access monetary resources. Moreover, evidence suggests that household money management practices are gendered, reflecting subjective notions of ownership of and entitlement to the family's resources. Both strands of economic psychological work point to the importance of social norms and stereotypical expectations – particularly concerning gender – when studying economic processes in the household. We conclude that although progress has been made in 'unpacking' the household, there is still much scope for theoretical and methodological development – especially as the nature of the household or family continues to evolve.

NOTES

1. Again, relationship quality was found to have some bearing here: happier spouses provided more accurate reports of their partner's behaviour (i.e., there was greater descriptive accuracy and overlap between self-reports) than people in less satisfactory relationships.
2. This contradiction reflects the lack of consistency observed more generally in relation to the ideology and practice of marital equality (e.g., Knudson-Martin & Mahoney, 1998).

REVIEW QUESTIONS

1. How would you define a *household* or a *family*? To what extent can these be considered similar? What distinguishes families from households in psychological terms?
2. Define and describe the key psychological factors associated with making household purchase decisions. Explain these factors by drawing on empirical evidence.
3. In what ways is gender linked to household money management? Describe three key findings in this area by distinguishing between management and control of money.

REFERENCES

Antonides, G. (2011). The division of household tasks and household financial management. *Journal of Psychology, 219*, 198–208.

Ashby, K. J., & Burgoyne, C. B. (2008). Separate financial entities? Beyond categories of money management. *Journal of Socio-Economics, 37*, 458–480.

Ashby, K. J., & Burgoyne, C. B. (2009). The financial practices and perceptions behind separate systems of household financial management. *Journal of Socio-Economics, 38*, 519–529.

Bennett, F. (2013). Researching within-household distribution: Overview, developments, debates, and methodological challenges. *Journal of Marriage and Family, 75*, 582–597.

Blood, R. O., & Wolfe, D. M. (1960). *Husbands and wives*. Glencoe, IL: The Free Press.

Burgoyne, C. B. (1990). Money in marriage: How patterns of allocation both reflect and conceal power. *The Sociological Review, 38*, 634–665.

Burgoyne, C. B., & Clarke, V. (2011). Money management and views of civil partnership in same-sex couples: Results from a UK survey of non-heterosexuals. *The Sociological Review, 59*, 685–706.

Burgoyne, C. B., Clarke, V., Reibstein, J. R., & Edmunds, A. E. (2006). 'All my worldly goods I share with you'? Managing money at the transition to heterosexual marriage. *The Sociological Review, 54*, 619–637.

Burgoyne, C. B., & Kirchler, E. (2008). Financial decisions in the household. In A. Lewis (Ed.), *Psychology and economic behaviour* (pp. 132–154). Cambridge: Cambridge University Press.

Burgoyne, C. B., & Lewis, A. (1994). Distributive justice in marriage: Equality or equity? *Journal of Community & Applied Social Psychology, 4*, 101–114.

Burgoyne, C. B., & Morison, V. (1997). Money in remarriage: Keeping things simple and separate. *The Sociological Review, 45*, 363–395.

Burgoyne, C. B., Reibstein, J., Edmunds, A., & Dolman, V. (2007). Money management systems in early marriage: Factors influencing change and stability. *Journal of Economic Psychology, 28*, 214–228.

Burgoyne, C. B., & Routh, D. A. (2001). Beliefs about financial organization in marriage: The 'Equality Rules OK' norm? *Zeitschrift für Sozialpsychologie, 32*, 162–170.

Burgoyne, C. B., & Sonnenberg, S. J. (2009). Financial practices in cohabiting heterosexual couples: A perspective from economic psychology. In J.Miles, & R.Probert (Eds.), *Sharing lives, dividing assets: An interdisciplinary study* (pp. 89–108). Oxford: Hart Publishing.

Burns, M. L., Burgoyne, C. B., & Clarke, V. (2008). Financial affairs? Money management in same-sex relationships. *Journal of Socio-Economics, 37*, 481–501.

Commuri, S., & Gentry, J. W. (2005). Resource allocation in households with women as chief wage earners. *Journal of Consumer Research, 32*, 185–195.

Dema-Moreno, S., & Diaz-Martinez, C. (2010). Gender inequalities and the role of money in Spanish dual-income couples. *European Societies, 12*, 65–84.

Kirchler, E. (1988a). Household economic decision making. In W. F. van Raaij, G. M. van Veld-hoven, & K.-E. Wärneryd (Eds.), *Handbook of economic psychology*. Dordrecht: Kluwer Academic Publishers.

Kirchler, E. (1988b). Diary reports on daily economic decisions of happy versus unhappy couples. *Journal of Economic Psychology, 9*, 327–357.

Kirchler, E. (1990). Spouses' influence strategies in purchase decisions as dependent on conflict type and relationship characteristics. *Journal of Economic Psychology, 11*, 101–118.

Kirchler, E. (1993). Spouses' joint purchase decisions: Determinants of influence tactics for mud-dling through the process. *Journal of Economic Psychology, 14*, 405–438.

Kirchler, E. (1995). Studying economic decisions within private households: A critical review and design for a 'couple experience diary'. *Journal of Economic Psychology, 11*, 101–118.

Kirchler, E. (1999a). Unbelievable similarity: Accuracy in spouses' reports on their partners' tactics to influence joint economic decisions. *Journal of Applied Psychology, 48*, 329–348.

Kirchler, E. (1999b). Household decision making. In P. E. Earl, & S. Kemp (Eds.), *The Elgar companion to consumer research and economic psychology*. Cheltenham: Edward Elgar.

Kirchler, E., Rodler, C., Hölzl, E., & Meier, K. (2001). *Conflict and decision making in close relationships: Love, money and daily routines*. Hove: Psychology Press.

Knudson-Martin, C., & Mahoney, A. (1998). Language and processes in the construction of equality in new marriages. *Family Relations, 47*, 81–91.

Lauer, S. R., & Yodanis, C. (2011). Individualized marriage and the integration of resources. *Journal of Marriage and Family, 73*, 669–683.

Laurie, H., & Gershuny, J. (2000). Couples, work and money. In R. Berthoud, & J. Gershuny (Eds.), *Seven years in the lives of British families: Evidence on the dynamics of social change from the British Household Panel Survey* (pp. 45–72). Bristol: The Policy Press.

Meier, K., Kirchler, E., & Hubert, A.-H. (1999). Savings and investment decisions within private households: Spouses' dominance in decisions on various forms of investment. *Journal of Economic Psychology, 20*, 499–519.

Nyman, C. (1999). Gender equality in the 'most equal country in the world'? Money and marriage in Sweden. *The Sociological Review, 47*, 766–793.

Nyman, C., & Dema, S. (2007). An overview: Research on couples and money. In J. Stocks, C. Diaz, & B. Hallerod (Eds.), *Modern couples sharing money, sharing life* (pp. 7–29). Basingstoke: Palgrave Macmillan.

Pahl, J. (1980). Patterns of money management within marriage. *Journal of Social Policy, 9*, 313–335.

Pahl, J. (1983). The allocation of money and the structuring of inequality within marriage. *The Sociological Review, 31*, 227–262.

Pahl, J. (1989). *Money and marriage*. London: Macmillan.

Pahl, J. (1995). His money, her money: Recent research on financial organisation in marriage. *Journal of Economic Psychology, 16*, 361–376.

Pahl, J. (2000). The gendering of spending within households. *Radical Statistics, 75*, 38–48.

Pahl, J. (2005). Individualisation in couple finances: Who pays for the children? *Social Policy and Society, 4*, 381–391.

Penz, E., & Kirchler, E. (2012). Sex-role specialization in a transforming market: Empirical evidence from Vietnamese middle-class households. *Journal of Makromarketing, 32*, 61–73.

Simpson, J. A., Griskevicius, V., & Rothman, A. J. (2012). Consumer decisions in relationships. *Journal of Consumer Psychology, 22*, 304–314.

Sonnenberg, S. J. (2008). Household financial organisation and discursive practice: Managing money and identity. *Journal of Socio-Economics, 37*, 533–551.

Sonnenberg, S. J., Burgoyne, C. B., & Routh, D. A. (2011). Income disparity and norms relating to intra-household financial organisation in the UK: A dimensional analysis. *Journal of Socio-Economics, 40*, 573–582.

Su, C., Zhou, K. Z., Zhou, N., & Li, J. J. (2008). Harmonizing conflict in husband–wife purchase decision making: Perceived fairness and spousal influence dynamics. *Journal of the Academy of Marketing Science, 36*, 378–394.

Vogler, C. (1994). Money in the household. In M. Anderson, F. Bechhofer, & J. Gershuny (Eds.), *The social and political economy of the household* (pp. 225–266). Oxford: Oxford University Press.

Vogler, C. (1998). Money in the household: some underlying issues of power. *The Sociological Review, 46*, 687–713.

Vogler, C. (2005). Cohabiting couples: Rethinking money in the household at the beginning of the twenty-first century. *The Sociological Review, 53*, 1–29.

Vogler, C., Brockmann, M., & Wiggins, R. D. (2006). Intimate relationships and changing patterns of money management at the beginning of the twenty-first century. *British Journal of Sociology, 3*, 455–482.

Vogler, C., Lyonette, C., & Wiggins, R. D. (2008). Money, power and spending decisions in intimate relationships. *Sociological Review, 56*, 117–143.

Vogler, C., & Pahl, J. (1993). Social and economic change and the organisation of money within marriage. *Work, Employment & Society, 7*, 71–95.

Vogler, C., & Pahl, J. (1994). Money, power and inequality within marriage. *The Sociological Review, 42*, 263–288.

Yodanis, C., & Lauer, S. (2007). Managing money in marriage: Multilevel and cross-national effects of the breadwinner role. *Journal of Marriage and Family, 69*, 1307–1325.

FURTHER READING

Kirchler, E., Rodler, C., Hölzl, E., & Meier, K. (2001). *Conflict and decision making in close relationships: Love, money and daily routines*. Hove: Psychology Press.

23 Ageing and Economic Decision-Making

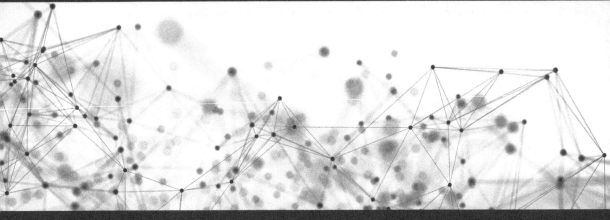

WÄNDI BRUINE DE BRUIN

CHAPTER OUTLINE

LEARNING OUTCOMES

BY THE END OF THIS CHAPTER YOU SHOULD BE ABLE TO:

1. Identify skills relevant to making good decisions and understand how these skills change with age.
2. Suggest interventions to address age-related changes in decision-relevant skill sets.
3. Suggest research developments required to better understand and inform older adults' economic decisions.

23.1   INTRODUCTION

Population age is increasing worldwide (Kinsella & Phillips, 2005). Adults of all ages face economic decisions, including about spending, borrowing, saving and investment. Over recent decades, the number of options has been expanding for many financial products, thus making consumer choices more difficult (Schwartz, 2004). Although financial decisions occur across the adult life span, complex financial decisions about home mortgages and long-term investments are more common in older age (Hershey, Austin, & Guitierrez, 2015).

Saving for retirement has become more complicated, with employers in many countries shifting from defined benefit to defined contribution plans. Employees are increasingly being made responsible for their own retirement planning. Even decisions about when to retire are becoming more complex, including options to keep working part-time, to change job status, or even to switch careers while transitioning into retirement (Shultz & Wang, 2011; Weierich et al., 2011). Once retired, older adults may be less likely to recover from financial problems, due to being on a fixed income and unable to find work to supplement income (Jin, Joyce, Phillips, & Sibieta 2011).

As adults get older, they may also face the challenge of financially supporting their elderly parents as well as their young-adult children (Grundy & Henretta, 2006). Other age-related life changes can have financial consequences. Increased longevity and higher divorce rates may spur decisions about re-marriage and step-families (Coleman, Ganong, & Fine, 2000). Age-related illnesses may lead to difficult decisions for both patients and caregivers, regarding possible treatments and end of life (Fischhoff, 1999; Parker et al., 2007).

Better economic decision outcomes are observed among individuals with better decision-making competence (Bruine de Bruin, Parker, & Fischhoff, 2007; Parker, Bruine de Bruin, & Fischhoff, 2015). However, the relationship between age and decision performance depends on the specific decision task at hand (Bruine de Bruin, Parker, & Fischhoff, 2012). Some decision tasks may require skills that decline with age, and others may require skills that improve with age. Below, we review skills that have been deemed relevant to making good economic decisions, and how they change with age.

23.2   THE ROLE OF COGNITIVE DELIBERATION IN DECISION-MAKING

Traditionally, normative theories viewed decision-making as an exercise in cognitive deliberation. Good decisions were seen as involving systematic comparisons of available options, so as to select the one with the best expected future outcomes (Edwards, 1954; Keren & Bruine de Bruin, 2003). Fluid cognitive abilities form the 'mechanics' underlying cognitive deliberation, including processing speed, working memory and executive functions (Salthouse, 2004). Fluid cognitive abilities have been associated with better performance on hypothetical decision tasks, including those involving financial discount rates, and applying decision rules to consumer choices (Bruine de Bruin et al., 2007; Del Missier, Mäntylä, & Bruine de Bruin, 2012; Li, Baldassi, Johnson, & Weber, 2013; Stanovich & West, 2008). Fluid cognitive abilities have also been associated with better real-world financial outcomes such as fewer credit-related financial mistakes and better credit scores, even after taking into account demographic variables (Agarwal, Driscoll, Gabaix, & Laibson, 2009; Li, Gao, Enkavi, Zaval, Weber, & Johnson, 2015). In part, these findings may reflect that individuals with better fluid cognitive abilities also have better decision-making competence and numeracy (Bruine de Bruin et al., 2007; Parker & Fischhoff, 2005; Peters, Västfjäll, Slovic, Mertz, Mazzocco, & Dickert, 2006).

23.2.1   Age-Related Changes in Cognitive Deliberation

It has been well documented that abilities relevant to cognitive deliberation, such as processing speed and working memory, decrease with age from the mid-twenties (for reviews, see Peters & Bruine de Bruin, 2012; Salthouse, 2004; Strough, Parker, & Bruine de Bruin, 2015; Zaval, Li, Johnson, & Weber, 2015). Due to such cognitive ageing, older adults perform worse on cognitively demanding decision tasks (Bruine de Bruin et al., 2012; Del Missier, Mäntylä, Hansson, Bruine de Bruin, Parker, & Nilson, 2013; Finucane, Mertz, Slovic, & Schmidt, 2005; Li et al., 2013). For example, older adults are more likely than younger adults to show errors in applying decision rules to select options from a choice set (Bruine de Bruin et al., 2012; Del Missier et al., 2013).

Cognitively demanding tasks are more effortful for older adults than for younger adults, as seen in increased systolic blood pressure as compared to baseline (Ennis, Hess, & Smith, 2013; Hess & Ennis, 2012). To reduce cognitive deliberation, older adults may therefore consider less information when comparing choice options (Johnson, 1990). One possible consequence is that older adults perform worse on consumer decisions that require comparisons across many alternatives (Besedeš, Deck, Sarangi, & Shor, 2012). Older adults' reduced cognitive deliberation may also explain why their choices between gambles are less in line with expected value calculations (Weller, Levin, & Denburg, 2011). In conclusion, age-related cognitive decline may lead older adults to be challenged by the complexities of economic decisions.

23.3   THE ROLE OF EXPERIENCE-BASED KNOWLEDGE IN DECISION-MAKING

Experts rely less on cognitive deliberation, because they have learned how to tackle decisions in their domain (Ericsson, Prietula, & Cokely, 2007). Such experience-based knowledge is a form of 'crystallized intelligence', which accumulates with life experience and deliberate training in their domain. Experience-based financial knowledge is also referred to as financial literacy, which has been associated with better financial decisions in the psychological laboratory (Li et al., 2013), as well as better credit scores, debt reduction, and retirement planning in the real world (Li et al., 2015; Lusardi & Mitchell, 2014; Lusardi & Tufano, 2009). Financial experts have learned to complete financial decision tasks in fewer steps and less time, while also searching more quickly for higher-level information (Hershey, Walsh, Read, & Chulef, 1990). People who have learned the economic cost-benefit rule in economics courses are less likely to violate it in their financial decisions (Larrick, Nisbett, & Morgan, 1993). Yet, experience-based knowledge can also undermine performance when financial 'experts' become overconfident about what they think they have learned (Törngren & Montgomery, 2004).

23.3.1 Age-Related Changes in Experience-Based Knowledge

Experience-based knowledge improves with age (Park, Lautenschlager, Hedden, Davidson, Smith, & Smith, 2002; Salthouse, 2004). Older adults' greater practical experience in specific financial domains may allow them to rely more on learned economic principles and less on cognitive deliberation, therefore performing at least as well as younger adults (Li et al., 2013; 2015). Due to experience-based knowledge, performance on credit-related decision tasks tends to peak when people are in their fifties despite cognitive ageing (Agarwal et al., 2009). Older adults' ability to avoid the 'sunk cost' bias is related to age-related changes in semantic memory (or learned world knowledge), perhaps about the importance of ignoring irrecoverable losses (Del Missier et al., 2013). Possibly because older adults have more consumer experience, their preferences for shopping discount cards may be more consistent than younger adults' preferences (Tentori, Osherson, Hasher, & May, 2001).

Unfortunately, experience is no guarantee for improved decision-making. Older adults have developed automated 'scripts', which facilitate decisions (Park, 1999) but can prevent them from rethinking their habitual purchases (Lambert-Pandrout & Laurent, 2010; Lambert-Pandrout, Laurent, & Lapersonne, 2005). Older adults may also be misled by experience, such as when repeated exposure to misleading health claims increases the likelihood of misremembering them as true (Skurnik, Yoon, Park, & Schwarz, 2005). Thus, it appears that older adults' experience-based knowledge can have positive and negative effects on decision quality.

23.4 THE ROLE OF EMOTIONS IN DECISION-MAKING

Emotional processes are fast, automatic, and tend to guide cognitions (Zajonc, 1980; Slovic, Finucane, Peters, & MacGregor, 2002). In judgement and decision research, emotions were traditionally seen as posing a threat to the quality of cognitive deliberation (Peters, Västfjäll, Gärling, & Slovic, 2006). More recent views have identified a wider role for emotions in decision-making, such as giving meaning to information, allowing comparisons between options in affective terms, putting a 'spotlight' on information that is important, and motivating decision-makers (Peters, 2006). Each of these roles can be served by emotions that are integral to the decision, such as when risky technologies evoke negative emotions (Slovic et al., 2002). Individuals may also be influenced by incidental emotions that are not relevant to the decision such as when weather-induced mood affects their purchasing of risky assets (Hirsh-leifer & Schumway, 2003).

23.4.1   Age-Related Changes in Emotions

Older adults tend to report less negative affect than younger adults (Carstensen, Pasu-pathi, Mayr, & Nesselroade, 2000; Charles, Reynolds, & Gatz, 2001). Older adults ruminate less about adverse life events (Sütterlin, Paap, Babic, Kübler, & Vögele, 2012; Torges, Stewart, & Nolen-Hoeksema, 2008), which may explain why they are better than younger adults at discontinuing prior investments that are no longer beneficial (Bruine de Bruin, Strough, & Parker, 2014). However, older adults' aversion to neg-ative affect could contribute to rash decisions to retire after a frustrating day at work (Weierich et al., 2011). In conclusion, older adults' reliance on emotions can have detrimental or beneficial effects on decisions, depending on the role of emotions in the task at hand (see Finucane, 2008; Peters & Bruine de Bruin, 2012).

23.5   THE ROLE OF MOTIVATION AND STRATEGIES IN DECISION-MAKING

Engaging with cognitively demanding problems can be frustrating (Fagerlin, Zikmund-Fisher, Ubel, Jankovic, Derry, & Smith, 2007). To reduce cognitive effort, deci-sion-makers may choose to 'satisfice' or select the first option they deem good enough, rather than 'maximize' or compare all options in order to find the best one (Simon, 1956). Although such short cuts reduce effort, they introduce the risk of not selecting the best option (Payne, Bettman, & Johnson, 1993). However, the tendency to keep searching for the best option even after completing decisions has been associated with regret and depression (Iyengar, Wells, & Schwartz, 2006; Schwartz, Ward, Monterosso, Lyubomirsky, White, & Lehman, 2002; Sparks, Ehrlinger, & Eibach, 2012).

23.5.1   Age-Related Changes in Motivation and Strategies

Because cognitive deliberation is especially effortful for older adults, they may be less motivated to engage in it (Ennis et al., 2013; Hess & Ennis, 2012). Older adults are more likely than younger adults to self-identify as satisficers rather than maximiz-ers (Bruine de Bruin, Parker, & Strough, 2016). They prefer decision strategies that require less information processing (Chen & Sun, 2003; Johnson, 1990), especially when decisions lack personal relevance (Hess, Queen, & Ennis, 2013). Older adults do switch to more deliberative processing when they are explicitly instructed to give reasons for their choices, thus highlighting the role of motivation (Kim, Goldstein, Hasher, & Zacks, 2005).

Adult ageing brings a shift from deliberation-focused to emotion-focused goals, with older adults aiming to optimize positive-affective experiences in the limited time they have left (Carstensen & Mikels, 2005; Mather & Carstensen, 2005). Perhaps as a result, older adults are more likely to seek and remember positive than negative information (Carstensen & Mikels, 2005; Mather & Carstensen, 2005). Despite age-related declines in working memory, there are no age differences in memory for positive-affective information (Mikels, Larkin, Reuter-Lorenz, & Carstensen, 2005). Older adults also list more positive than negative attributes of decision options, which contributes to their greater choice satisfaction (Kim, Healey, Goldstein, Hasher, & Wiprzycka, 2008). Older adults rate health brochures as more informative if they contain more positive than negative information (Shamaskin, Mikels, & Reed, 2010). This so-called 'positivity effect' affects older adults across a wide range of tasks, with varying effects on performance quality (Carstensen & Mikels, 2005; Mather & Carstensen, 2005).

23.6 INTERVENTIONS

If people face problems in making specific decisions, policy-makers and practitioners may decide to design interventions. Possible interventions include decision aids, training, delegation, and 'nudge' interventions. Sections 23.6.1–23.6.3 suggest how these interventions may be designed to support older adults' decisions. Overall, when targeting older adults, interventions may be more effective if they take into account age-related changes in cognitive deliberation, experience-based knowledge, emotions, and motivation.

23.6.1 *Decision Aids*

Decision aids may be designed to support a specific decision, such as which loan to choose or how to save for retirement. Older people may spontaneously write down information when making consumer decisions, thus reducing demands on working memory with their own decision aids (Cole & Balasubramanian, 1993; Morrow, 2003). When presenting information, focusing on the main points and removing less relevant details may improve understanding, especially for low-numerate individuals (Peters, Dieckmann, Dixon, Hibbard, & Mertz, 2007). Older adults may perform better when being presented with a smaller choice set, which is less cognitively demanding to consider (Tanius, Wood, Hanoch, & Rice, 2009). A 'tournament' strategy that introduces smaller sub-sets of options may improve older adults' decisions (Besedeš, Deck, Sarangi, & Schor, in press). Because older adults are increasingly searching the Internet for information, web-based retirement calculators and search engines may also be useful, as long as the technology is easy to use and builds on their experience-based knowledge (Morrow, 2003). Visual displays may also make risk information easier to process, with initial evidence suggesting benefits to older adults (Galesic, Garcia-Retamero, & Gigerenzer, 2009). For example, icon arrays show icons in one colour to represent individuals with negative outcomes and icons in another colour to show the rest of the at-risk population.

One potential limitation of decision aids is that people may not be motivated to engage with the presented information. To motivate older adults to make better decisions, it is important to present information that older adults actually want and need, and that improves their self-efficacy in implementing recommended behaviours (Strough, Bruine de Bruin, & Peters, 2015). Care should be taken to describe decision-relevant information in emotionally meaningful terms and to build on experience-based knowledge (Finucane, 2008).

Adding narratives of other people's personal experiences may compel people of all ages to engage with presented information, at the risk of distracting from statistical facts (Bekker et al., 2013; Winterbottom et al., 2008). Especially low-numerate individuals pay more attention to narratives than to statistics (Dieckmann, Slovic, & Peters, 2009). Although age differences in responses to decision aids have not been systematically studied, older adults may like narratives because they prefer information that is emotion-focused rather than fact-based (Williams & Drolet, 2005).

To further motivate older adults' engagement with decision aids, accompanying instructions should encourage a focus on emotional reactions rather than on specific informational details (Mikels et al., 2010). Older adults may also perform better when they are asked to give reasons for their choices (Kim et al., 2005), which could be incorporated into decision aids.

23.6.2 Training

Experience-based knowledge and associated scripts support older adults' economic decisions despite age-related cognitive decline (Agarwal et al., 2009; Li et al., 2013; 2015; Park, 1999). To build experience-based knowledge, individuals should probably be trained in economic decision-making from an early age because developing expertise takes many years of deliberate practice (Ericsson et al., 2007). If successful, training in economic decision-making should benefit adults of all ages, as economic decisions are made across the life span (Hershey et al., 2015). Youth development accounts and other practical interventions can potentially promote good financial habits and responsibility (Shobe & Sturm, 2007). Teaching simple rules may be more effective than teaching complex rules, which can create cognitive overload and choice avoidance (Schwartz, 2004). People who apply simple rules to retirement planning tend to save as much as those who engage in complex planning, and more than those who have no plan (Binswanger & Carman, 2012). Yet, evidence is mixed about the effectiveness of training in financial decision-making, especially in the long run (Fernandes, Lynch, & Netemeyer, 2014).

23.6.3 Delegation

Older adults value their independence when making decisions (Delaney, Strough, Bruine de Bruin, & Parker, 2015). Yet, it has been argued that older adults prefer to delegate some complex decisions to others so as to reduce their cognitive effort (Finucane et al., 2005; Mather, 2006; Yates & Patalano, 1999). Perhaps such preferences depend on the degree to which older adults perceive age-related decline in deliberative skills relevant to decision-making (Bruine de Bruin et al., 2012). Nevertheless, older adults are more likely than younger adults to have financial advisors (Milner & Rosenstreich, 2013). They also experience more complex financial decisions than younger adults (Hershey et al., 2015).

People may feel anxious about going to financial advisors (Gerrans & Hershey, in press. Their financial decisions may instead be influenced by family members, friends, and colleagues (Loibl & Hira, 2006). Older adults prefer to spend time with meaningful social partners (Fung, Carstensen, & Lutz, 1999), potentially informing their choice of financial advisors. In married couples, the spouse with the relatively higher level of educational attainment tends to take more responsibility for the household financial decisions (Fonseca, Mullen, Zamarro, & Zissimopoulous, 2012). Married women may therefore leave financial decisions to their husbands, and miss opportunities to develop the financial literacy they may need if they outlive their husbands (Hsu, 2011). Moreover, older adults who delegate help to others may put themselves at risk of financial abuse (Acierno et al., 2010).

23.6.4   Nudges

'Nudge' interventions are those that design a choice environment to promote choices that will be beneficial to most decision-makers. One 'nudge' strategy involves setting the 'default' to a recommended option. Because people of all ages often defer difficult decisions, setting the default to a beneficial option makes it more likely that people will end up choosing it (Johnson & Goldstein, 2003). One often-cited example of default setting pertains to improving employees' retirement savings by introducing default enrolment and automatic increases in contributions from the first pay cheque after a raise (Thaler & Bernartzi, 2004.

Like any intervention strategy, nudging also has its limitations. Most notably, nudging will only be ethical for situations in which there is one recommended course of action. Another limitation is that people may dislike the paternalism inherent in nudging (cf. Thaler & Sunstein, 2003). However, if older adults are more willing to leave some difficult decisions to others, then they may show reduced resistance to nudge interventions.

23.7   DIRECTIONS FOR FUTURE RESEARCH

Research on ageing and decision-making competence has made great strides in recent years (see Hess, Strough, & Löckenhoff, 2015). Below are suggestions for future research focussed on improved measurement, samples, and intervention development.

23.7.1   Better Measures

Measures of decision-making competence have mostly involved hypothetical decision tasks. Because those hypothetical tasks are often unrealistic and lack real-world consequences, their external validity can be questioned. Concerns about external validity may be somewhat reduced by the finding that better performance on hypothetical decision-making tasks is associated with better real-world decision outcomes

(Bruine de Bruin et al., 2007; Weller, Moholy, Bossard, & Levin, 2015). However, older adults may be less motivated to perform well on complex numerical tasks (Bruine de Bruin, McNair, Taylor, Summers, & Strough, 2015), especially if tasks lack personal relevance due to their hypothetical nature (Hess et al., 2013). More tests are needed of real-world decision-making performance and how it changes across the life-span.

Additionally, a better understanding is needed of the skills that support decision-making competence in older age. Age-related cognitive declines are well documented, through a battery of validated measures of fluid cognitive ability, working memory, and executive functioning (Salthouse, 2004). By comparison, less is known about the skills and strategies that improve with age to support older adults' decisions. One reason for this paucity may be the lack of validated measures of domain-specific experience, emotional processing, and motivation. Existing measures are often based on self-reports rather than actual performance (Appelt, Milch, Handgraaf, & Weber, 2011), which raises concerns due to older adults being less confident than younger adults about their performance on complex decision tasks (Bruine de Bruin et al., 2012).

Moreover, validated measures of domain-specific experience-based economic knowledge have not yet been developed, leading researchers to use other measures of crystallized intelligence (e.g., vocabulary knowledge) as a proxy (Li et al., 2013, 2015). Although there is a growing literature on the importance of financial literacy for economic decisions (Lusardi & Mitchell, 2014), large variation exists in how financial literacy has been defined and operationalized (Hung, Parker, & Yoong, 2009; Huston, 2010). Reliable and valid measures are needed to examine how such skills develop across the life-span and improve as a result of interventions.

23.7.2   Better Samples

Many studies on ageing and decision-making have recruited community-dwelling older adults and university-attending younger adults. As a result, any observed differences between older adults and younger adults may be explained by factors associated with socio-economic status and education. A better strategy would be to recruit older and younger adults in the same way, by seeking diverse convenience samples of community-dwellers (e.g., Bruine de Bruin et al., 2007). Even better but more costly recruitment strategies would involve selecting representative samples from a specific city (e.g., Del Missier et al., 2013; Mikels et al., 2010), or country (Bruine de Bruin et al., 2014; 2016).

Furthermore, longitudinal research is needed to examine how decision-making competence develops with age. Most studies that have been conducted to date have used cross-sectional designs, leaving it unclear whether reported age differences may be the result of cohort effects rather than ageing (e.g., Schaie, 1965). Longitudinal studies are also needed to examine decision performance across the entire life span, including childhood and adolescence in addition to older adulthood (e.g., Weller, Levin, Rose, & Bossard, 2012).

23.7.3   Better Intervention Development and Evaluation

To develop effective interventions, it is important to have a solid understanding of the wants and needs of the target audience, the problems they face in making recommended decisions, and how those problems are best resolved (Bruine de Bruin

& Bostrom, 2013). The literature reviewed in this chapter informed the above-mentioned suggestions that interventions targeting older adults should take into account age-related declines in cognitive ability, experience-based knowledge, emotions, and motivation. However, most of these suggestions have not yet been applied to the development or evaluation of interventions targeting older adults' economic decisions.

In many domains, interventions are developed solely by domain experts, who no longer think or talk like non-experts (Bruine de Bruin & Bostrom, 2013). Yet, effective intervention development requires interdisciplinary teams, including experts who understand the specific domain as well as social scientists who understand how to assess and address an audience's wants and needs (Fischhoff, Brewer, & Downs, 2011; Morgan, Fischhoff, Bostrom, & Atman, 2002). Forming interdisciplinary teams can be a challenge, because experts from different fields have developed their own specialist terminologies, theories of behaviour change, and research methodologies. Effective team work can be facilitated by defining clear intervention design goals, and sharing the best evidence of how those goals have been met in the past (Wong-Parodi & Strauss, 2014). Perhaps most of all, it is important that the effectiveness of intervention strategies is systematically tested before proceeding with their widespread implementation (Bruine de Bruin & Bostrom, 2013). Ultimately, the goal is to help older adults to obtain better financial outcomes and associated well-being.

23.8 SUMMARY

People of all ages face important economic decisions, which may increase in complexity as they age. Older adults' ability to engage in cognitively demanding economic decisions may be undermined by age-related changes in fluid cognitive ability, such as processing speed, working memory and executive functions. However, older age also brings changes in experience-based knowledge, emotions and motivation. Older adults' increased experience and associated knowledge reduce the need to think hard while making familiar economic decisions. Older adults' better emotion regulation can help them to walk away from decisions involving 'sunk costs' or irrecoverable losses. Older adults' selective motivation affects how much effort they put into their decision-making. Interventions to help older adults with their economic decisions should take into account these age-related changes, by building on their strengths while addressing any weaknesses. This chapter discusses the promise of decision aids, training, delegation and 'nudge' interventions. Better measures, samples and intervention tests are needed so as to promote our ability to understand and improve older adults' economic decisions.

ACKNOWLEDGEMENTS

Funding was received from the European Union Seventh Framework Programme (FP7-People-2013-CIG-618522; PI: Bruine de Bruin). This chapter has greatly benefited from comments by Cäzilia Loibl, Ellen Peters, JoNell Strough, and Joshua Weller.

REVIEW QUESTIONS

1. What skills are relevant to making good decisions?
2. How do these skills change with age?
3. What interventions can be developed to address age-related changes in decision-relevant skill sets?
4. What is needed to better understand and inform older adults' economic decisions?

REFERENCES

Acierno, R., Hernandez, M. A., Amstadter, A. B., Resnick, H. S., Steve, K., Muzzy, W., & Kilpatrick, D. (2010). Prevalence and correlates of emotional, physical, sexual, and financial abuse and potential neglect in the United States: The national elder mistreatment study. *American Journal of Public Health*, 100, 292–297.

Agarwal, S., Driscoll, J. C., Gabaix, X., & Laibson, D. (2009). The age of reason: Financial decisions over the life-cycle with implications for regulation. *SSRN-973790*.

Appelt, K. C., Milch, K. F., Handgraaf, M. J., & Weber, E. U. (2011). The Decision Making Individual Differences Inventory and guidelines for the study of individual differences in judgment and decision-making research. *Judgment and Decision Making*, 6, 252–262.

Bekker, H. L., Winterbottom, A. E., Butow, P., Dillard, A. J., Feldman-Stewart, D., Fowler, F. J. ... & Volk, R. J. (2013). Do personal stories make patient decision aids more effective? *BMC Medical Informatics & Decision Making*, 13, 1–9.

Besedeš, T., Deck, C., Sarangi, S., & Shor, M. (2012). Age effects and heuristics in decision making. *The Review of Economics and Statistics*, 94, 580–595.

Besedeš, T., Deck, C., Sarangi, S., & Shor, M. (in press). Reducing choice overload without reducing choices. *The Review of Economics and Statistics*.

Binswanger, J., & Carman, K. G. (2012). How real people make long-term decisions: The case of retirement preparation. *Journal of Economic Behavior and Organization*, 81, 39–60.

Bruine de Bruin, W., & Bostrom, A. (2013). Assessing what to address in science communication. *Proceedings of the National Academy of Sciences*, 110, 14062–14068.

Bruine de Bruin, W., McNair, S., Taylor, A. L., Summers, B., & Strough, J. (2015). 'Thinking about numbers is not my idea of fun': Need for cognition mediates age differences in numeracy performance. *Medical Decision Making*, 35, 22–26.

Bruine de Bruin, W., Parker, A. M., & Fischhoff, B. (2007). Individual differences in adult decision-making competence. *Journal of Personality and Social Psychology*, 92, 938–956.

Bruine de Bruin, W., Parker, A. M.. & Fischhoff, B. (2012). Explaining adult age differences in decision-making competence. *Journal of Behavioral Decision Making*, 25, 352–360.

Bruine de Bruin, W., Parker, A. M., & Strough, J. (2016). Choosing to be happy? Age differences in 'maximizing' decision strategies and experienced emotional well-being. *Psychology and Aging*, 31, 295–300.

Bruine de Bruin, W., Strough, J., & Parker, A. M. (2014). Getting older isn't all that bad: Better decisions and coping when facing 'sunk costs'. *Psychology and Aging*, 29, 642–647.

Carstensen, L. L., & Mikels, J. A. (2005). At the intersection of emotion and cognition. *Current Directions in Psychological Science*, 14, 117–121.

Carstensen, L. L., Pasupathi, M., Mayr, U., & Nesselroade, J. R. (2000). Emotional experience in everyday life across the adult life span. *Journal of Personality and Social Psychology*, 79, 644–655.

Charles, S. T., Reynolds, C. A., & Gatz, M. (2001). Age-related differences and change in positive and negative affect over 23 years. *Journal of Personality and Social Psychology*, 80, 136–151.

Chen, Y., & Sun, Y. (2003). Age differences in financial decision-making: Using simple heuristics. *Educational Gerontology*, 29, 627–635.

Cole, C.A., & Balasubramanian, S. K. (1993). Age differences in consumers' search for information: Public policy implications. *Journal of Consumer Research, 20,* 157–169.

Coleman, M., Ganong, L., & Fine, M. (2000). Reinvestigating remarriage: Another decade of progress. *Journal of Marriage and the Family, 62,* 1288–1307.

Delaney, R., Strough, J., Bruine de Bruin, W., & Parker, A. (2015). Variations in decision-making profiles by age and gender: A cluster-analytic approach. *Personality and Individual Differences, 85,* 19–24.

Del Missier, F., Mäntylä, T., & Bruine de Bruin, W. (2012). Decision-making competence, executive functioning, and general cognitive abilities. *Journal of Behavioral Decision Making, 25,* 331–351.

Del Missier, F., Mäntylä, T., Hansson, P., Bruine de Bruin, W., Parker, A. M., & Nilsson, K. (2013). The multifold relationship between memory and decision making: An individual differences study. *Journal of Experimental Psychology: Learning, Memory, and Cognition, 39,* 1344–1364.

Dieckmann, N. F., Slovic, P., & Peters, E. (2009). The use of narrative evidence and explicit likelihood by decision makers varying in numeracy. *Risk Analysis, 29,* 1473–1488.

Edwards, W. (1954). The theory of decision making. *Psychological Bulletin, 51,* 380–417.

Ennis, G. E., Hess, T. M., & Smith, B. T. (2013). The impact of age and motivation on cognitive effort: Implications for cognitive engagement in older adulthood. *Psychology and Aging, 28,* 495–504.

Ericsson, K. A., Prietula, M. J., & Cokely, E. T. (2007). The making of an expert. *Harvard Business Review, 85,* 114–122.

Fagerlin, A., Zikmund-Fisher, B. J., Ubel, P. A., Jankovic, A., Derry, H. A., & Smith, D. M. (2007). Measuring numeracy without a math test: Development of the subjective numeracy scale. *Medical Decision Making, 27,* 672–680.

Fernandes, D., Lynch, J. G., & Netemeyer, R. G. (2014). Financial literacy, financial education and downstream financial behaviors. *Management Science, 60,* 1861–1883.

Finucane, M. L. (2008). Emotion, affect, and risk communication with older adults: Challenges and opportunities. *Journal of Risk Research, 11,* 983–997.

Finucane, M. L., Mertz, C. K., Slovic, P., & Schmidt, E. S. (2005). Task complexity and older adults' decision-making competence. *Psychology and Aging, 20,* 71–84.

Finucane, M. L., Slovic, P., Hibbard, J. H., Peters, E., Mertz, C. K., & MacGregor, D. G. (2002). Aging and decision-making competence: An analysis of comprehension and consistency skills in older versus younger adults considering health-plan options. *Journal of Behavioral Decision Making, 15,* 141–164.

Fischhoff, B. (1999). What do patients want? Help in making effective choices. *Effective Clinical Practice, 2,* 198–200.

Fischhoff, B., Brewer, N. T., & Downs, J. S. (2011). *Communicating risks and benefits: An evidence-based user guide.* Silver Spring, MD: US Department of Health and Human Services, Food and Drug Administration.

Fonseca, R., Mullen, K. J., Zamarro, G., & Zissimopoulous, J. (2012). What explains the gender gap in financial literacy? The role of household decision making. *Journal of Consumer Affairs, 46,* 90–106.

Fung, H. H., Carstensen, L. L., & Lutz, A. M. (1999). Influence of time on social preferences: Implications for life-span development. *Psychology and Aging, 14,* 595–604.

Galesic, M., Garcia-Retamero, R., & Gigerenzer, G. (2009). Using icon arrays to communicate medical risks: Overcoming low numeracy. *Health Psychology, 28,* 210–216.

Gerrans, P., & Hershey, D. A. (in press). Financial advisor anxiety, financial literacy, and financial advice seeking. *Journal of Consumer Affairs.*

Grundy, E., & Henretta, J. C. (2006). Between elderly parents and adult children: A new look at the intergenerational care provided by the 'sandwich generation'. *Aging and Society, 26,* 707–722.

Hershey, D. A., Austin, J. T., & Guitierrez, H. C. (2015). Financial decision making across the adult life span: Dynamic cognitive capacities and real-world competence. In: Hess, T. M., Strough, C. J., & C. Lockenhoff (Eds.), *Aging and decision making: Empirical and applied perspectives* (pp. 329–349). New York: Elsevier.

Hershey, D. A., Walsh, D. A., Read, S. J., & Chulef, A. S. (1990). The effects of expertise on financial problem solving: Evidence for goal directed problem-solving scripts. *Organizational Behavior and Human Decision Processes, 46*, 77–101.

Hess, T. M., & Ennis, G. E. (2012). Age differences in the effort and costs associated with cognitive activity. *The Journals of Gerontology, Series B: Psychological Sciences and Social Sciences, 67*, 447–455.

Hess, T. M., Queen, T. L., & Ennis, G. E. (2013). Age and self-relevance effects on information search during decision making. *Journals of Gerontology Series B: Psychological Sciences & Social Sciences, 68*, 703–711.

Hess, T. M., Strough, C. J., & Löckenhoff, C. (2015). *Aging and decision making: Empirical and applied perspectives.* New York: Elsevier.

Hira, T. K. (1997). Financial attitudes, beliefs, and behaviours: Differences by age. *Journal of Consumer Studies and Home Economics, 21*, 271–290.

Hirshleifer, D., & Schumway, T. (2003). Good day sunshine: Stock returns and the weather. *Journal of Finance, 58*, 1009–1032.

Hsu, J. W. (2011). Aging and strategic learning: The impact of spousal incentives of financial literacy. *Networks Financial Institute at Indiana State University, 2011-WP-06.*

Hung, A., Parker, A. M., & Yoong, J. (2009). Defining and measuring financial literacy. RAND Working Paper Series WR-706.

Huston, S. J. (2010). Measuring financial literacy. *Journal of Consumer Affairs, 44*, 296–316.

Iyengar, S. S., Wells, R. E., & Schwartz, B. (2006). Doing better but feeling worse. Looking for the 'best' job undermines satisfaction. *Psychological Science, 17*, 143–150.

Jin, W., Joyce, R., Phillips, D., & Sibieta, L. (2011). *Poverty and inequality in the UK: 2011.* London: The Institute for Fiscal Studies.

Johnson, E. J., & Goldstein, D. (2003). Do defaults save lives? *Science, 302*, 1338–1339.

Johnson, M. M. S. (1990). Age differences in decision making: A process methodology for examining strategic information processing. *Journal of Gerontology: Psychological Sciences, 45*, P75–P78.

Keren, G., & Bruine de Bruin, W. (2003). On the assessment of decision quality: Considerations regarding utility, conflict, and accountability. In D. Hardman, & L. Macchi (Eds.), *Thinking: Psychological perspectives on reasoning, judgment and decision making* (pp. 347–363). New York: Wiley.

Kim, S., Goldstein, D., Hasher, L., & Zacks, R. T. (2005). Framing effects in younger and older adults. *The Journals of Gerontology Series B: Psychological Science and Social Science, 60*, 215–218.

Kim, S., Healey, M. K., Goldstein, D., Hasher, L., & Wiprzycka, U. J. (2008). Age differences in choice satisfaction: A positivity effect in decision making. *Psychology and Aging, 23*, 33–38.

Kinsella, K. G., & Phillips, D. R. (2005). Global aging: The challenges of success. *Population Bulletin, 60*, 3–42.

Lambert-Pandrout, R., & Laurent, G. (2010). Why do older consumers buy older brands? The role of attachment and declining innovativeness. *Journal of Marketing, 74*, 104–121.

Lambert-Pandrout, R., Laurent, G., & Lapersonne, E. (2005). Repeat purchasing of new automobiles by older consumers: Empirical evidence and interpretations. *Journal of Marketing, 69*, 97–113.

Larrick, R. P., Nisbett, R. E., & Morgan, J. N. (1993). Who uses the cost-benefit rules of choice? Implications for the normative status of microeconomic theory. *Organizational Behavior and Human Decision Processes, 56*, 331–347.

Li, Y., Baldassi, M., Johnson, E. J., & Weber, E. U. (2013). Complementary cognitive abilities: Economic decision making and aging. *Psychology and Aging, 28*, 595–613.

Li, Y., Gao, J., Enkavi, A. Z., Zaval, L., Weber, E. U., & Johnson, E. J. (2015). Sound credit scores and financial decisions despite cognitive aging. *Proceedings of the National Academy of Sciences*, *112*, 65–69.

Loibl, C., & Hira, T. (2006). A workplace and gender-related perspective on financial planning information sources and knowledge outcomes. *Financial Services Review*, *15*, 21–42.

Lusardi, A., & Mitchell, O. S. (2014). The economic importance of financial literacy: Theory and evidence. *Journal of Economic Literature*, *52*, 5–44.

Lusardi, A., & Tufano, P. (2009). Teach workers about the perils of debt. *Harvard Business Review*, *87*, 22–24.

Mather, M. (2006). A review of decision-making processes: Weighing the risks and benefits of aging. In L. L. Carstensen, & R. Hartel (Eds.), *When I'm 64* (pp. 145–173). Washington, DC: National Academies Press.

Mather, M., & Carstensen, L. L. (2005). Aging and motivated cognition: The positivity effect in attention and memory. *Trends in Cognitive Science*, *9*, 496–502.

Mikels, J. A., Larkin, G. R., Reuter-Lorenz, P. A., & Carstensen, L. L. (2005). Divergent trajectories in the aging mind: Changes in working memory for affective versus visual information with age. *Psychology and Aging*, *20*, 542–553.

Mikels, J. A., Löckenhoff, C. E., Maglio, S. A., Carstensen, L. A., Goldstein, M. K., & Garber, A. (2010). Following your heart or your head: Focusing on emotions versus information differentially influences. *Journal of Experimental Psychology: Applied*, *16*, 87–95.

Milner, T., & Rosenstreich, D. (2013). Insights into mature consumers of financial services. *Journal of Consumer Marketing*, *30*, 248–257.

Morgan, M. G., Fischhoff, B., Bostrom, A., & Atman, C. J. (2002) *Risk communication: A mental models approach*. Cambridge: Cambridge University Press.

Morrow, D. G. (2003). Technology as environmental support for older adults' daily lives. I: N. Charness, & K. W. Schaie (Eds.), *The impact of technology on successful aging* (pp. 290–305). New York: Springer.

Oswald, F., & Wahl, H. W. (2004). Housing and health in later life. *Reviews on Environmental Health*, *19*, 223–252.

Park, D. C. (1999). Aging and the controlled and automatic processing of medical information and medical intentions (pp. 3–24). In D. C. Park, R.W. Morell, & K. Shifren (Eds.), *Processing of medical information in aging patients: Cognitive and human factors perspectives*. Mahwah, NJ: Lawrence Erlbaum.

Park, D. C., Lautenschlager, G., Hedden, T., Davidson, N. S., Smith, A. D., & Smith, P. K. (2002). Models of visuospatial and verbal memory across the adult life span. *Psychology and Aging*, *17*, 299–320.

Parker, A. M., Bruine de Bruin, W., & Fischhoff, B. (2015). Negative decision outcomes are more common among people with lower decision-making competence: An item-level analysis of the Decision Outcome Inventory (DOI). *Frontiers in Psychology*, *363*, 1–7.

Parker, A. M., & Fischhoff, B. (2005). Decision-making competence: External validation through an individual-differences approach. *Journal of Behavioral Decision Making*, *18*, 1–27.

Parker, S. M., Clayton, J. M., Hancock, K., Walder, S., Butow, P. N., Carrick, S., Currow, D., ... & Tattersall, M. H. N. (2007). A review of prognostic/end-of-life communication with adults in the advanced stages of life-limiting illness: patient/caregiver preferences for the content, style, and timing of information. *Journal of Pain and Symptom Management*, *34*, 81–93.

Payne, J. W., Bettman, J. R., & Johnson, E. J. (1993). *The adaptive decision maker*. New York: Cambridge University Press.

Peters, E. (2006). The functions of affect in the construction of preferences. In S. Lichtenstein & P. Slovic (Eds.), *The construction of preference*. New York: Cambridge University Press.

Peters, E., & Bruine de Bruin, W. (2012). Aging and decision skills. In M. K. Dhami, A. Schlottmann, & M. Waldmann (Eds.), *Judgment and decision making as a skill: Learning, development, and evolution*. New York: Cambridge University Press.

Peters, E., Dieckmann, N., Dixon, A., Hibbard, J. H., & Mertz, C. K. (2007). Less is more in presenting quality information to consumers. *Medical Care Research and Review, 64*, 169–190.

Peters, E., Västfjäll, D., Gärling, T., & Slovic, P. (2006). Affect and decision making: A 'hot' topic. *Journal of Behavioral Decision Making, 19*, 79–85.

Peters, E., Västfjäll, D., Slovic, P., Mertz, C. K., Mazzocco, K., & Dickert, S. (2006). Numeracy and decision making. *Psychological Science, 17*, 407–413.

Salthouse, T. A. (2004). What and when of cognitive aging. *Current Directions in Cognitive Science, 13*, 140–144.

Schaie, K. W. (1965). A general model for the study of developmental problems. *Psychological Bulletin, 64*, 92–107.

Shamaskin A. M., Mikels, J. A., & Reed, A. E. (2010). Getting the message across: Age differences in the positive and negative framing of health care messages. *Psychology and Aging, 25*, 746–751.

Schwartz, B. (2004). *The paradox of choice: Why more is less.* New York: HarperCollins.

Schwartz, B., Ward, A., Monterosso, J., Lyubomirsky, S., White, K., & Lehman, D. R. (2002). Maximizing versus satisficing: Happiness is a matter of choice. *Journal of Personality and Social Psychology, 83*, 1178–1197.

Shobe, M. A., & Sturm, S. L. (2007). Youth individual development accounts: Retirement planning initiatives. *Children & Schools, 29*, 172–181.

Shultz, K. S., & Wang, M. (2011). Psychological perspectives on the changing nature of retirement. *American Psychologist, 66*, 170–179.

Simon, H. A. (1956). Rational choice and the structure of the environment. *Psychological Review, 63*, 129–138.

Skurnik, I., Yoon, C., Park, D. C., & Schwarz, N. (2005). How warnings about false claims become recommendations. *Journal of Consumer Research, 31*, 713–724.

Slovic, P., Finucane, M., Peters, E., & MacGregor, D. G. (2002). Rational actors or rational fools: Implications of the affect heuristic for behavioral economics. *Journal of Socio-Economics, 31*, 329–342.

Sparks, E. A., Ehrlinger, J., & Eibach, R. P. (2012). Failing to commit: Maximizers avoid commitment in a way that contributes to reduced satisfaction. *Personality and Individual Differences, 52*, 72–77.

Stanovich, K. E., & West, R. F. (2008). On the relative independence of thinking biases and cognitive ability. *Journal of Personality and Social Psychology, 94*, 672–695.

Strough, J., Bruine de Bruin, W., & Peters, E. (2015). New perspectives for motivating older adults to make better decisions. *Frontiers in Psychology, 6*, 1–10.

Strough, J., Parker, A. M., & Bruine de Bruin, W. (2015). Understanding life-span developmental changes in decision-making competence. In T. Hess, J. Strough, & C. Löckenhoff (Eds.), *Aging and decision making: Empirical and applied perspectives* (pp. 235–257). London: Elsevier Academic Press.

Sütterlin, S., Paap, M. C. S., Babic, S., Kübler, A., & Vögele, C. (2012). Rumination and age: Some things get better. *Journal of Aging Research, 267327*, 1–10.

Tanius, B. E., Wood, S., Hanoch, Y., & Rice, T. (2009). Aging and choice: Applications to Medicare Part D. *Judgment and Decision Making, 4*, 92–101.

Tentori, K., Osherson, D., Hasher, L., & May, C. (2001). Wisdom and aging: Irrational preferences in college students but not older adults. *Cognition, 81*, B87–B96.

Thaler, R. H., & Bernartzi, S. (2004). Save More Tomorrow ™: Using behavioral economics to increase employee saving. *Journal of Political Economy, 112*, S164–S187.

Thaler, R. H., & Sunstein, C. R. (2003). Libertarian paternalism. *American Economic Review, 93*, 175–179.

Torges, T. M., Stewart, A. J., & Nolen-Hoeksema, S. (2008). Regret resolution, aging, and adapting to loss. *Psychology and Aging, 23*, 169–180.

Törngren, G., & Montgomery, H. (2004). Worse than chance? Performance and confidence among professionals and laypeople in the stock market. *The Journal of Behavioral Finance, 5*, 148–153.

Weierich, M. R., Kensinger, E. A., Munnell, A. H., Sass, S. A., Dickerson, B. C., Wright, C. I., & Barrett, L. F. (2011). Older and wiser? An affective science perspective on age-related challenges in financial decision making. *Scan, 6,* 195–206.

Weller, J. A., Levin, I. P., & Denburg, N. L. (2011). Trajectory of risky decision making for potential gains and losses from ages 5 to 85. *Journal of Behavioral Decision Making, 24,* 331–344.

Weller, J. A., Levin, I. P., Rose, J. P., & Bossard, E. (2012). Assessment of decision-making competence in preadolescence. *Journal of Behavioral Decision Making, 25,* 414–426.

Weller, J. A., Moholy, M., Bossard, E., & Levin, I. (2015). Pre-teen decision-making competence predicts later interpersonal strengths and difficulties: A two-year prospective study. *Journal of Behavioral Decision Making, 28,* 76–88.

Williams, P., & Drolet, A. (2005). Age-related differences in responses to advertisements. *Journal of Consumer Research, 32,* 343–354.

Winterbottom, A., Bekker, H. L., Conner, M., & Mooney, A. (2008). Does narrative information bias individuals' decision making? *Social Science & Medicine, 67,* 2079–2088.

Wong-Parodi, G., & Strauss, B. H. (2014). Team science for science communication. *Proceedings of the National Academy of Sciences, 111,* 13658–13663.

Yates, J. F., & Patalano, A. L. (1999). Decision making and aging. In D. C. Park, R. W. Morrell, & K.Shifren (Eds.), *Processing of medical information in aging patients: Cognitive and human factors perspectives* (pp. 31–54). Mahwah, NJ: Lawrence Erlbaum.

Zajonc, R. B. (1980). Feeling and thinking: Preferences need no inferences. *American Psychologist, 35,* 151–175.

Zaval, L., Li, Y., Johnson, E. J., & Weber, E. U. (2015). Complementary contribution of fluid and crystallized intelligence to decision making across the life span. In T. M. Hess, C. J. Strough, & C. Lockenhoff (Eds.). *Aging and decision making: Empirical and applied perspectives* (pp. 329–349). New York: Elsevier.

FURTHER READING

Hess, T. M., Strough, C. J., & Löckenhoff, C. (2015). *Aging and decision making: Empirical and applied perspectives.* New York: Elsevier.

PART 7

Economic Psychology and Society

24 Psychological Determinants of Charitable Giving

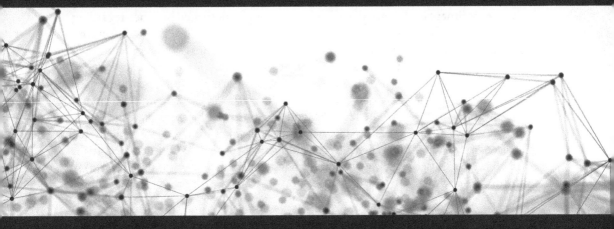

TEHILA KOGUT AND ILANA RITOV

CHAPTER OUTLINE

LEARNING OUTCOMES

BY THE END OF THIS CHAPTER YOU SHOULD BE ABLE TO:

1. Identify causes that elicit more help in donation decisions.
2. Give examples of individual differences in donation decisions.
3. Explain common biases in donation decisions.

24.1   INTRODUCTION

Behavioural economists and economic psychologists have paid much attention to altruism and pro-social behaviours in the past few decades, in part due to the growing body of experimental evidence that people are strongly motivated by other-regarding preferences – such as fairness and social norms – in their decisions concerning resource allocation (e.g., Fehr & Schmidt, 1999). These findings contradict traditional models that portray human behaviour as being purely self-interested. Cooperation, the provision of public goods, charitable giving, and informal helping behaviours are all difficult to explain purely on grounds of self-interest. In this chapter, we discuss the motivations behind such behaviours, and demonstrate the main biases in donation decisions. We present causes and victims that are likely to encourage donations, and discuss individual differences in the motivation to help. We present the main research methods used to study charitable giving, and conclude with some directions for future research.

24.2   DONATION DECISIONS: COSTS AND REWARDS

In the wake of prospect theory (Kahneman & Tversky, 1979), behavioural economic and decision-making research highlights heuristics and biases that stem from *loss aversion*, namely, the pronounced preference to avoid losses to acquiring gains. People's giving to charity appears to contradict this tendency, since people often give without expecting anything in return. Altruistic approaches suggest that people's charitable giving may be selfless and based mainly on the concern for the welfare of others. In particular, Batson's research suggests that giving may be genuinely selfless when it is based on empathic concern for the intended recipient (e.g., Batson, Ahmad, & Stocks, 2011). In contrast, social exchange theory posits that altruism only exists when benefits outweigh costs (Maner et al., 2002). Such approaches view donation decisions as being similar to purchasing decisions, i.e., that the decision to help others involves a balance between expenses and rewards, even when no external rewards ensue (such as tax breaks, honour, appreciation, or a sign of wealth and status). According to these approaches, the joy of giving is its own reward. In other words, people achieve an internal reward – such as pleasure, happiness or moral satisfaction – from the act of giving (Batson & Shaw, 1991).

24.2.1   Warm Glow

Andreoni's *warm glow giving* theory (e.g., Andreoni, 1990) is based on the notion that people receive utility from the act of giving, thanks to the positive emotional feelings that they experience from helping others. This idea had already been mooted by Adam Smith in his seminal work *The Theory of Moral Sentiments* (1759), which states that *Homo economicus* – who seeks happiness for him/herself – will not find it, but the person who helps others will. Recent findings that donors get more satisfaction from giving a dollar directly to charity than from witnessing a dollar of their tax money go directly to that same charity suggest that people derive an internal satisfaction from the very act of giving, rather than from just achieving the donation goal per se (Andreoni & Payne, 2003). Giving can enhance people's self-image, and reduce feelings of guilt (Konečki, 1972; Regan et al., 1972). People often feel better about themselves after helping (Dunn et al., 2008), and happier people give more (Konow & Earley, 2008). Specifically, Dunn et al. (2014) suggest that giving increases happiness, particularly when it satisfies one or more core human needs of relatedness, competence, and autonomy. Thus, giving and happiness can enforce each other in a virtuous cycle (Dunn, Aknin, & Norton, 2014).

24.2.2 Moral Satisfaction

Kahneman and Knetch (1992) suggest that a donor's reward from the act of giving stems from the sense of moral satisfaction that they derive from the donation. They found a significant correlation between willingness to donate, and ratings of the perceived morality of different causes, such that people are more willing to donate to a cause that they perceive as being more moral. Comparing purchasing decisions with charitable giving, Ritov and Kahneman (1997) suggest that while the former is sensitive to scope (i.e., people are willing to pay more when they get a greater amount of the resource that they are buying), people are less sensitive to scope when it comes to charitable giving, since the experience of moral satisfaction that they gain as a result is likely to be similar whether the donation helps a hundred people, or just one.

24.3 CAUSES THAT ELICIT MORE HELP

Although people may vary in their perception of the respective morality and importance of various causes, some causes tend to attract more help than others. Generally, expressions such as 'medical research', 'hospitals and hospices', 'children and young people' attract the highest proportion of donors (Charities Aid Foundation, 2012). In addition, research has identified a number of other principles and features that trigger a greater positive response.

24.3.1 Features of Causes that Trigger a Greater Positive Response

Epstein (2006) suggests that people respond more readily to sudden crises, which evoke stronger emotions, than to ongoing or chronic conditions, even when the latter concerns a greater tragedy involving more victims. Moreover, people exhibit an *immediacy bias*, namely, they donate disproportionately more to humanitarian crises that spark immediate emotions (Huber, Van Boven, McGraw, & Johnson-Graham, 2011). People are also more willing to help victims of disasters of natural causes than victims of man-made disasters, who are more likely to be blamed for their plight

(Zagefka et al., 2011). On the other hand, when it comes to compensation for misfortune, victims of human-caused accidents are awarded higher compensation than victims of natural accidents, even when all other circumstances are identical (Ritov & Baron, 1994).

Social and geographic closeness of the potential donor to the recipient, as well as perceptions of shared group membership, also tend to increase giving (Chen & Li, 2009). When people recognize aspects of themselves in the other, the other's welfare becomes more self-relevant (Sturmer, Snyder, Kropp, & Siem, 2006). The *similarity-breeds-liking* principle (Byrne, 1997) suggests that people are more willing to help others when they feel that they share similar characteristics or beliefs (for a review, see Bar-Tal, 2000, pp. 1–14). Research suggests that people tend to help in-group victims more than out-group victims (Dovidio et al., 1997). For example, people tend to help people of their own nationality (Levine & Thompson, 2004) or fellow supporters of the same sports team (Levine, Prosser, Evans, & Reicher, 2005). Recent research suggests that this preference for helping in-group victims is related to *perceived responsibility*, in that in-group victims elicit a greater sense of responsibility, which in turn increases helping (Erlandsson, Björklund, & Bäckström, 2015).

24.3.2   Why Do Different People Give to Different Causes?

Apart from the general tendency to help certain types of causes, people may differ in the degree to which they are affected by, or willing to donate to, different causes. For example, being personally acquainted with a victim of a given misfortune increases a person's donations to other victims of the same misfortune, due to their greater perceived closeness and responsibility to them (Small & Simonsohn, 2008).

Furthermore, causes that evoke fears or anxieties in the observer are more likely to elicit their attention and help. In our own recent research, we found that people's donations are positively correlated with their perceived likelihood of falling victim themselves to the misfortune in question. In addition, refusing to donate to victims of an intimidating misfortune is often perceived as 'tempting fate', and increasing the sense of one's own vulnerability (Kogut & Ritov, 2011a). For example, people tend to donate more to an association that helps people with cancer when they feel personally more susceptible to cancer themselves. Interestingly, this sense of vulnerability intensifies when the respondent is reminded that they had recently forgone an opportunity to donate.

24.3.3   The Magnitude of the Problem

One of the objectively most important aspects of a public problem or cause is its scope. Some problems may affect several individuals, while others may involve thousands of people, or an entire region. One might expect people's reactions to mass disasters to be stronger, thereby increasing donations to such causes. However, research in the past few decades consistently shows that people's willingness to support public causes is insensitive to the magnitude of quantitative outcomes (e.g., Baron, 1997; Desvousges et al. 1993; Frederick & Fischhoff, 1998; Kahneman & Ritov, 1994). In particular, Hsee and Rottenstreich's study (2004) found that, while subjective values are highly sensitive to the presence or absence of a stimulus (i.e., a change from nil to any number), they are largely insensitive to any further variations in scope, especially when affect-rich stimuli are considered.

Epstein (2006) describes the discrepancy between donation amounts given to different causes, and the number of people affected in each case. For example, she shows that private donors in the United States spent on average approximately $1,839 for each individual affected by Hurricane Katrina (2005), but only $10 for each person diagnosed with AIDS, and only $3 or so for each victim of malaria – a disease that claims a million lives every year. Normatively, the scope or magnitude of a disaster and the number of people at risk should be the main factor increasing motivation to act. However, descriptively, our actions are often insensitive to, or even demotivated by, larger numbers of people at risk (Slovic, 2007). Such insensitivity to scope is typical of people's evaluation of human lives, especially when the recipients of help are identified (Kogut & Ritov, 2005a; 2005b; Slovic, 2007).

24.4   SPECIFIC INDIVIDUALS IN NEED

The *identifiable victim effect* refers to the tendency of individuals to offer greater aid to a specific individual in need about whom they have some identifying information, than to unidentifiable or statistical victims. This occurs even when said identification does not actually convey any truly individuating information (Jenni & Loewenstein, 1997; Small, Loewenstein, & Slovic, 2007). For example, Small and Loewenstein (2003) found that participants playing the part of Allocator in a dictator game gave more money to recipients who were identified only by a number, than to those who remained entirely anonymous.

24.4.1   The Singularity Effect

One feature that often distinguishes identified victims from unidentified ones is the fact that the former are typically encountered as single individuals, e.g., John, who needs a costly treatment to get cured of a rare disease; Miriam, the little girl who had just lost her parents, and so on. The very fact that identified victims are usually single individuals, rather than groups, can affect people's inclination to contribute to helping them. In our own research (Kogut & Ritov, 2005a; 2005b), we have found that the identifiable victim effect is largely limited to single victims. In a series of studies, we show that willingness to extend help is greatly affected by the victims' identifiability when a single victim is involved, but not when there are more than one. Specifically, we found that a single identified victim elicited higher contributions than an unidentified individual, but a group of eight identified individuals did not attract significantly higher contributions than a group of unidentified individuals. Indeed, we found that a single identified victim received higher donations than an entire *group* of victims (whether identified or not) – even when the amount of money needed to save the individual child or the group of children was the same ($300,000) – thus controlling for the 'drop in the bucket effect'. This phenomenon, known as the singularity effect, appears to be largely explained by the emotions evoked when considering the victims' plight. In particular, the reported level of the prospective donor's distress (i.e., feelings of concern, agitation, or sadness) significantly predicted their willingness to contribute, suggesting that the intensified emotional response to the single identified victim is a key factor in the effect. Thus, due to their spontaneous emotional response to the single victim, respondents' contributions to that victim were higher, overall, than contributions to the group.

Recently, Västfjäll, Slovic, Mayorga and Peters (2015) showed that the effect of identification diminishes even with two victims. Their findings support Slovic's *collapse model* of people's response to numerous victims (Slovic, 2007), demonstrating a sharp drop in emotions and donations even with two victims. According to Slovic's model, as the group grows ever larger and becomes represented by numbers rather than images, large numbers of victims become merely dry statistics that fail to spark any emotions or motivate actions.

Cameron and Payne (2011) provide an alternative account to the 'collapse model' of compassion, suggesting that people anticipate the needs of large groups to be potentially overwhelming. As a result, they engage in a form of emotion regulation, to avoid experiencing overwhelming levels of emotion. Because groups are more likely than individuals to trigger emotion regulation, people feel less for groups than for individuals, and are thus less likely to attend to their needs.

24.4.2 *Boundary Conditions*

Although a single identifiable victim in need sparks a spontaneous emotional reaction in the observer, this reaction can also bolster negative emotions and willingness to punish in situations when the victim is perceived in a negative light (Kogut, 2011a; Small & Loewenstein, 2006). Indeed, the same victim might evoke sympathy and caring if perceived to be innocent, but anger and blame if they are seen as responsible for their plight. For example, a young man with AIDS may evoke sympathy and caring if introduced as someone who contracted the disease because of his haemophilia, but anger and blame if presented as an intravenous drug user (Irwin, Jones, & Mundo, 1996). Thus, identifying a person in need can increase or decrease the help that they receive, depending on their perceived responsibility for their plight. When the victim is seen as being responsible for their situation, their identification can strengthen negative perceptions (such as blame), and decrease helping and donations (Kogut, 2011b).

The role of identifiability in increasing donations may also be limited to in-group victims, that is to say, identifying a victim leads to an increase in helping behaviour, particularly when they are a single individual who appears to belong to the respondent's own in-group. For example, contributions for rescuing tsunami victims were most generous when the targeted victim was depicted as a single individual compatriot, identified by name. Similarly, the expressed willingness to contribute to saving a sick child was amplified when a picture of the child was included, but only if he or she were thought to be of the same nationality as the respondent. Finally, the emotions prompted when considering the plight of victims were particularly intense when the victim in question was a single child – especially a compatriot (Kogut & Ritov, 2007).

Interestingly, recent findings suggest that certain circumstances involving groups or affiliations, such as the existence of intergroup conflict, may modify or even reverse the effect. Under such circumstances identifiability increases generosity towards a member of *the adversary* group, but it decreases generosity towards a member of one's own group (Ritov & Kogut, 2011). Thus, the role played by identifiability in intergroup contexts is complex, and further research is needed to understand it fully.

24.4.3   *Debiasing the Singularity Effect*

Small, Lowenstein and Slovic (2007) attempted to counteract the spontaneous reaction towards identifiable victims by teaching people about the effect, and encouraging them to think analytically about the greater value involved when more lives are at risk. They found that, while engaging in a deliberative mode of thought decreases contributions to single victims, it does not increase contributions to entire groups of victims. However, Hsee et al. (2013) found that asking donors to specify the amount needed to help one individual in a group or crowd of people in need, just before asking them to decide how much to donate to help the entire group, did increase donations to the group as a whole. The authors explain that this method is effective, because while initially people are scope-insensitive due to the singularity effect, when asked to donate to a group of people only in the second stage, they are scope-consistent, and anchored to their initial decision.

Increasing the unity of a group, that is, by making it look more like a single entity than a group of many individuals, can boost the role played by emotions in decisions about the group (Bartels & Burnett, 2011). For example, donations to help children in need increase when the children are of the same family, compared to when they have no shared affiliation (Smith, Faro, & Burson, 2013).

Arguing from a normative perspective, Singer (2009) has proposed the *effective altruism* approach, namely, that if people are truly motivated to help as many people as possible, they should direct their donation to the cause most likely to make the biggest 'bang for their buck', regardless of whether the need is chronic or sudden, natural or human-caused or its geographical location. Moreover, according to this approach, being aware of our tendency to follow our emotions in donation decisions, people should deliberately adopt the so-called *System 2* mode of thinking when making donation decisions, namely, to consider all causes and actions, and then act in the manner that brings about the greatest positive impact to others (whoever they may be). It should be noted that Singer's normative prescription is starkly at odds with empirical findings – such as the singularity effect and scope insensitivity in donation decisions – which must cast some doubt as to its likely effectiveness in practice.

24.5   EFFECTIVENESS AND IMPACT

Research suggests that people care about the impact or effectiveness of their donation, and tend to support projects that they believe will have a greater impact (i.e., provide more help with the same amount of donations, e.g., Duncan 2004). For example, people are less motivated to help when overhead costs are thought to be high (Sargeant & Woodliffe, 2007). People derive satisfaction from feeling that they have a personal say in solving a social problem, so campaigns that are close to reaching fundraising goals receive more donations than those that are far from attaining their targets (Cryder, Loewenstein, & Seltman, 2013). Similarly, providing tangible details about a charity's interventions significantly increases donations to that charity, by increasing perceptions of their impact (Cryder, Loewenstein, & Scheines, 2013).

Rubaltelli and Agnoli (2012) highlight the conflict between respondents' moral intuitions (e.g., fulfilling moral obligations and helping as many individuals in need as possible), and the cost entailed by following one's moral intuitions (e.g., spending money). They suggest that people might choose to help fewer people, since they suspect that this will require a smaller expense. Indeed, studies suggest that when the costs of the donation are lower, the level of giving increases (e.g., Karlan & List, 2007; Perrine & Heatheer, 2000). In addition, when people are faced with a massive crisis affecting large numbers of people, they are sometimes overwhelmed, and refrain from offering help altogether. This may be due to two reasons: they may perceive their help as being merely 'a drop in the bucket', i.e. insignificant in relation to the huge amount needed, or – as suggested by Västfjäll, Slovic and Mayorga (2015) – when many victims in need are involved, respondents may suspect that not all of them will be saved. They found that the negative emotions induced by the thought that some of the victims may not be helped decreases the 'warm glow' associated with helping those who are, and this in turn diminishes people's motivation to help. The authors suggest that this 'pseudo inefficacy' perception is irrational, since people should not be deterred from helping whoever can be helped, simply because some people might not be.

24.6   WHO HELPS – AND WHEN?

So far, we have described the general conditions that encourage or inhibit willingness to help. However, there are also personal factors that may account for individual differences in people's willingness to help others. Some of these may be temporary or incidental factors such as mood, fatigue, or an ongoing visceral need; other factors may be more consistent personality traits and tendencies such as values, beliefs, empathic propensity or well-being. In this section, we briefly discuss how some of these factors play a dominant role in the context of charitable giving.

24.6.1   Temporary Conditions

To help others, people must first recognize the needs of other people, and pay real attention to it. Research has shown that distractions by temporary external factors, such as noise, haste, or competing stimuli (e.g., Darley & Batson, 1973; Dickert & Slovic, 2009), or internal factors (such as having to deal with one's own concerns, losses and needs), constrain the amount of attention and energy one can allocate to the needs of others, thereby decreasing the amount of help that one provides (e.g., Thompson, Cowan, & Rosenhan, 1980). Attention and focus on others in need are preconditions for the triggering of empathic concern, which in turn is found to be a key factor in respondents' decision to help (Dickert & Slovic, 2009). For example, experiencing an ongoing visceral need such as hunger makes people less responsive to the needs of others – even when those needs match their own visceral state (Harel & Kogut, 2015).

Incidental moods can similarly affect the degree of help being proffered. Research suggests that both good and bad moods can increase the impetus to help, in contrast to neutral moods, which do not. Although happier people give more to charity (Konow & Earley, 2008), and a positive mood increases the incidence of helping (Forgas, Dunn, & Granland, 2008), victims with sad expressions – as Small and Verrochi (2009) have demonstrated – receive more donations, because their expressions also affected the potential donors' mood. In an attempt to reconcile this apparent contradiction, Anik et al. (2009) suggested that a positive mood tends to boost readiness to help others when it is induced by factors unrelated to the cause or need in question, while a negative mood tends to enhance such readiness when it is induced by reasons directly related to the person or people in need.

24.6.2   *Personality Traits, Beliefs and Tendencies*

Over and above transient influences, such as mood, individuals differ in more fundamental, stable characteristics related to their willingness to help others. Some of these – such as belief in a just world (BJW) – reflect a greater focus on the self, others reflect a greater concern for others (empathy), while some reflect the balance between the two. Specifically, the social value orientation approach (SVO) suggests that people fall into four categories when assessed by the extent to which they care about the outcome for others relative to themselves when allocating resources between themselves and others: (1) *individualistic orientation*; (2) *competitive orientation*; (3) *cooperative orientation*; and (4) *altruistic orientation* (Van Lange et al., 2007). Van Lange et al. also found that *prosocials* (i.e., cooperative and altruistic people) reportedly donating more, particularly to organizations aimed at helping the poor and the ill. Other values, like personal degrees of individualism and collectivist orientations may influence motivation for helping. For example, Kemmelmeier, Jambor and Letner (2006) have found higher levels of charitable giving in individualistic states (as compared with more collectivist states) in the United States, especially when the causes were compatible with individualistic causes; whereas collectivist values are related to greater donations to groups of needy people (rather than to single individuals in need) (Kogut, Slovic, & Västfjäll, 2015).

Belief in a just world (BJW) also reflects an inherent attitude and conviction that may increase the amount that one gives. People with strong BJW are more likely to help others, due to their belief that good deeds are ultimately rewarded. Such *BJW-for-the-self* (rather than for other people) was found to be positively correlated with willingness to help (Bègue et al. 2008; Bègue & Bastounis, 2003) and actual giving to charity (Bègue, 2014; Kogut, 2011b).

Since helping is related to the emotional reaction to the needs of others, both individual differences in empathic abilities and emotion regulation strategies may predict individual differences in the tendency to help others. Dickert, Sagara and Slovic (2011) suggest a two-stage model that incorporates affective influences on the decision to donate. In their studies, mood management – an inherently self-oriented process – plays a major role in a person's initial choice of whether or not to donate at all, while other-oriented emotions (such as empathy and compassion), play a greater role in their subsequent decision as to how much to donate. Such affective reactions can be induced by the donation cause in question, with stronger responses being induced by certain causes, or by the identity of the prospective recipient(s).

24.7 MAIN RESEARCH METHODS IN THE STUDY OF CHARITABLE GIVING

The main research methods used in studying charitable research include surveys, field studies, lab experiments with real donations or hypothetical scenarios, and experimental economics games (e.g., public good games, the dictator game, and the ultimatum game).

24.7.1 Surveys and Correlational Data

Survey research, including questionnaires and interviews, is one of the most common means of measurement in charitable donation research. Insights from such studies typically yield knowledge about which individuals give donations, and the causes that they tend to give to. They further reveal how populations differ in their donations to different causes, and help in understanding trends and predicting future changes in the size and nature of donations within specific populations. For example, survey studies examine the associations between a person's charitable giving and their financial situation (e.g., Belfield, & Beney, 2000; Carman, 2006), age and gender (e.g., Andreoni & Vesterlund, 2001; Wu, Huang, & Kao, 2004), or religious beliefs (e.g., Bekkers, 2003). Wilhelm (2007) describes the main limitations of such studies on charitable giving, such as their declarative character; the absence of significant data about donation amounts (which makes it difficult to draw reliable conclusions); the difficulty in estimating donations at the top of the distribution, without a high-income oversample; and the difficulty of comparing between different studies and populations, given the different questions and methods used in different surveys. Moreover, surveys typically provide only correlational relations that do not allow the causal roles of different factors to be explored.

24.7.2 Lab Experiments and Economic Games

Laboratory experiments are an important methodology in the study of charitable donations because they have the advantage of isolating the variables examined from other factors like individual differences, or situational factors. These studies include priming manipulations such as rational versus emotional priming (e.g., Small, Loewenstein, & Slovic, 2007); objective versus empathic priming (e.g., Batson et al., 1999); in-group versus out-group affiliation (e.g., Kogut & Ritov, 2007); ego depletion and self-control manipulations (e.g., Halali, Bereby-Meyer, & Meiran, 2014); or highlighting the awareness of being observed by others (Haley & Fessler, 2005). These methods allow an understanding of behavioural tendencies as well as their underlying mechanisms. Many studies use economic games, such as the dictator game and the ultimatum game, to study generosity. These studies consistently show that people are motivated by social concerns and fairness when faced with resource allocation dilemmas, and that they tend to share some of their endowment with an anonymous partner, even when no future reciprocity is likely, or even possible. Since lab experiments raise questions of external validity – i.e., whether people's actions in experiments are a true reflection of their behaviour in real-life situations (e.g., Levitt & List, 2007) – some researchers have opted to use natural field experiments, instead, when studying donation-related decision-making.

24.7.3   Field Studies

Field studies are studies that examine charitable giving in real-life situations, by comparing different treatments and observing people's behaviour in response to a real donation request. For example, such studies may compare people's levels of giving in response to door-to-door solicitations, versus solicitations by mail (Landry et al., 2008); in response to matching grants in different ratios (Karlan, List, & Shafir, 2011); or when the solicitor is a member of the majority, or a minority group (List & Price, 2009).

24.8   FUTURE RESEARCH DIRECTIONS

Although prosocial behaviour and charitable giving have been the focus of research for several decades, in various disciplines, many questions and challenges remain for future research. While existing research has examined personal, situational and societal factors (such as norms) that might increase or decrease charitable giving, the interactions between these factors have yet to be examined. For example, different motivations to help may result in help to different causes, or to different individuals in need.

Longitudinal studies on charitable giving are rare, but may help in understanding people's reactions to repeated requests for donations. In addition, longitudinal studies may help in monitoring and observing changes in trends in people's donation-related decision-making over a lifetime and in changing circumstances, in particular, their motivations for various pro-social behaviours, such as donating money, time, or indeed blood.

One of the limitations of the research that we have reviewed is its cultural context. Most of this research was carried out in the context of individualistic, Western cultures. Research into the broad conceptualizations of individualism versus collectivism has identified a host of differences between those two concepts in terms of focus of attention, self-definitions, motivations, emotional connections to in-groups, as well as belief systems and behavioural patterns (e.g., Oyserman & Lee, 2008). In the specific context of helping behaviour, research suggests that cultural values or norms can result in differences in willingness to help across different cultures (e.g., Kemmelmeier, Jambor, & Letner, 2006; Levine, Norenzayan, & Philbrick, 2001). Such research may contribute to our understanding of the role of cultural and educational factors in shaping people's reactions to the needs of others (beyond genetic factors), and may help in explaining the different psychological mechanisms underlying donation-related decisions.

24.9 SUMMARY

We reviewed a range of findings showing that humans are strongly motivated by other-regarding preferences in donation decisions. The question of what motivates people to help others and specifically to donate money to others, without expectation of reward has been of great interest to researchers in many fields for several decades. Research addressing the question examines personal factors, situational factors and societal factors that may increase or decrease pro-social behaviours. In this chapter we discussed situations and causes that are likely to affect willingness to help and increase donations. These include the effect of a disaster cause (natural vs. man-made disasters), group belonging of the victims (in-group vs. outgroup), and other features of the target of help (children vs. adults, single vs. groups, and identifiable vs. abstract). Our discussion highlighted biases in donation decisions, such as scope neglect and the identifiability effect. Finally, we presented some underlying mechanisms behind charitable giving decisions, such as affective mechanisms (like empathy and distress) attentional mechanisms and the consideration for effectiveness.

REVIEW QUESTIONS

1. How might recent findings contradict traditional models that portray human behavior as being purely self-interested?
2. Which causes elicit more charitable giving?
3. Define the 'singularity effect' and describe ways to reduce its influence on donation decisions.
4. Describe four individual differences in charitable giving and helping decisions.
5. What are the main research methods used in the study of charitable giving?

REFERENCES

Andreoni, J. (1990). Impure altruism and donations to public goods: A theory of warm-glow giving. *The Economic Journal, 100*(401), 464–477.

Andreoni, J., & Payne, A. (2003). Do government grants to private charities crowd out giving or fund-raising? *American Economic Review, 93,* 792–812.

Andreoni, J., & Vesterlund, L. (2001). Which is the fair sex? Gender differences in altruism. *The Quarterly Journal of Economics, 116*(1), 293–312.

Anik, L., Aknin, L. B., Norton, M. I., & Dunn, E. W. (2009). Feeling good about giving: The benefits (and costs) of self-interested charitable behavior. Harvard Business School Marketing Unit Working Paper, (10–012)

Baron, J. (1997). Biases in the quantitative measurement of values for public decisions. *Psychological Bulletin, 122,* 72–88.

Bar-Tal, D. (2000). *Shared beliefs in a society: Social psychological analysis.* London: Sage.

Bartels, D. M., & Burnett, R. C (2011). A group construal account of 'drop in the bucket' thinking in policy preference and moral judgment. *Journal of Experimental and Social Psychology, 47,* 50–57.

Batson, C., Ahmad, N., & Stocks, E. L. (2011). Four forms of prosocial motivation: Egoism, altruism, collectivism, and principlism. In D. Dunning (Ed.), *Social motivation* (pp. 103–126). New York: Psychology Press.

Batson, C. D., Ahmad, N., Yin, J., Bedell, S. J., Johnson, J. W., & Templin, C. M. (1999). Two threats to the common good: Self-interested egoism and empathy-induced altruism. *Personality and Social Psychology Bulletin, 25*, 3–16.

Batson, C. D., & Shaw, L. L. (1991). Evidence for altruism: Toward a pluralism of prosocial motives. *Psychological Inquiry, 2*, 107–122.

Bekkers, R. (2003). Trust, accreditation, and philanthropy in the Netherlands. *Nonprofit & Voluntary Sector Quarterly, 32*, 596–615.

Bègue, L. (2014). Do just-world believers practice private charity? *Journal of Applied Social Psychology, 44*, 71–76.

Bègue, L., & Bastounis, M. (2003). Two spheres of belief in justice: Extensive support for the bidimensional model of belief in a just world. *Journal of Personality, 71*, 435–463.

Bègue, L., Charmoillaux, M., Cochet, J., Cury, C., & De Suremain, F. (2008). Altruistic behavior and the bidimensional just world belief. *The American Journal of Psychology, 121*, 47–56.

Belfield, C. R., & Beney, A. P. (2000). What determines alumni generosity? Evidence for the UK. *Education Economics, 8*, 65–80.

Byrne, D. (1997). An overview (and underview) of research and theory within the attraction paradigm. *Journal of Social & Personal Relationships, 14*, 417–431.

Camerer, C., & Fehr, E. (2005). Measuring social norms and preferences using experimental games: A guide for social scientists. In J. Henrich, R. Boyd, S. Bowles, H. Gintis, E. Fehr, & R. McElreath (Eds.), *Foundations of human sociality: Experimental and ethnographic evidence from 15 small-scale societies* (pp. 55–95). Oxford: Oxford University Press.

Cameron, C. D., & Payne, B. K. (2011). Escaping affect: How motivated emotion regulation creates insensitivity to mass suffering. *Journal of Personality and Social Psychology, 100*(1), 1.

Carman, K. G. (2006). Social influences and the private provision of public goods: evidence from charitable contributions in the workplace. Discussion Paper, Stanford Institute for Economic Policy Research, Stanford University.

Charities Aid Foundation. (2012). *UK giving 2012*, November 2012.

Chen, Y., & Li, S. X. (2009): Group identity and social preferences, *The American Economic Review, 99*, 431–457.

Cryder, C. E., Loewenstein, G., & Scheines, R. (2013). The donor is in the details. *Organizational Behavior and Human Decision Processes, 120*(1), 15–23.

Cryder, C. E., Loewenstein, G., & Seltman, H. (2013). Goal gradient in helping behavior. *Journal of Experimental Social Psychology, 49*(6), 1078–1083.

Darley, J. M., & Batson, C.D. (1973). From Jerusalem to Jericho: A study of situational and dispositional variables in helping behavior. *Journal of Personality and Social Psychology, 27*, 100–108.

Desvousges, W. H., Johnson, F. R., Dunford, R. W., Boyle, K. J., Hudson, S. P., & Wilson, K. N. (1993). Measuring natural resource damages with contingent valuation: Tests of validity and reliability. In J. A. Hausman (Ed.), *Contingent valuation: A critical assessment* (pp. 91–164). Amsterdam: North-Holland.

Dickert S., Sagara N., Slovic P. (2011). Affective motivations to help others: a two-stage model of donation decisions. *Journal of Behavioral Decision Making, 4*, 297–306.

Dickert, S., & Slovic, P. (2009). Attentional mechanisms in the generation of sympathy. *Judgment and Decision Making, 4*, 297–306.

Dovidio, J. F., Gaertner, S. L., Validzic, A., Matoka, K., Johnson, B., & Frazier, S. (1997). Extending the benefits of recategorization: Evaluations, self-disclosure, and helping. *Journal of Experimental Social Psychology, 33*(4), 401–420.

Duncan, B. (2004). A theory of impact philanthropy. *Journal of Public Economics, 88*, 2159–2180.

Dunn, E. W., Aknin, L. B., & Norton, M. I. (2008). Spending money on others promotes happiness. *Science, 319*, 1687–1688.

Dunn, E. W., Aknin, L. B., & Norton, M. I. (2014). Prosocial spending and happiness: Using money to benefit others pays off. *Current Directions in Psychological Science, 23*, 41–47.

Epstein, K. (2006). Crisis mentality: Why sudden emergencies attract more funds than do chronic conditions, and how nonprofits can change that. *Stanford Social Innovation Review, Spring,* 48–57.

Epstein, S. (1994). Integration of the cognitive and the psychodynamic unconscious. *American Psychologist, 49,* 709–724.

Erlandsson, A., Björklund, F., & Bäckström, M. (2015). Emotional reactions, perceived impact and perceived responsibility mediate the identifiable victim effect, proportion dominance effect and in-group effect, respectively. *Organizational Behavior and Human Decision Processes, 127,* 1–14.

Fehr, E., & Schmidt, K., (1999). A theory of fairness, competition, and cooperation. *Quarterly Journal of Economics, 114,* 817–868.

Forgas, J. P., Dunn, E., & Granland, S. (2008). Are you being served…? An unobtrusive experiment of affective influences on helping in a department store. *European Journal of Social Psychology, 38,* 333–342.

Frederick, S., & Fischhoff, B. (1998). Scope (in)sensitivity in elicited valuations. *Risk, Decision and Policy, 3,* 109–123.

Halali, E., Bereby-Meyer, Y., & Meiran, N. (2014). Between self-interest and reciprocity: The social bright side of self-control failure. *Journal of Experimental Psychology: General, 143,* 745–754.

Haley, K. J. & Fessler, D. M. T. (2005). Nobody's watching? Subtle cues affect generosity in an anonymous economic game. *Evolution of Human Behavior, 26,* 245–256.

Harel, I., & Kogut, T. (2015). Visceral needs and donation decisions: Do people identify with suffering or with relief? *Journal of Experimental Social Psychology, 56,* 24–29.

Hsee, C., & Rottenstreich, Y. (2004). Music, pandas, and muggers: On the affective psychology of value. *Journal of Experimental Psychology General, 133,* 23–30.

Hsee, C. K., Zhang, J., Lu, Z. Y., & Xu, F. (2013). Unit asking: A method to boost donations and beyond. *Psychological Science.* Online 1 August.

Huber, M., Van Boven, L., McGraw, A. P., & Johnson-Graham, L. (2011). Whom to help? Immediacy bias in judgments and decisions about humanitarian aid. *Organizational Behavior and Human Decision Processes, 115*(2), 283–293.

Irwin, J. R., Jones, L. E., & Mundo, D. (1996). Risk perception and victim perception: The judgment of HIV cases. *Journal of Behavioral Decision Making, 9,* 1–22.

Jenni, K., & Loewenstein, G. (1997). Explaining the identifiable victim effect. *Journal of Risk and Uncertainty, 14*(3), 235–257.

Kahneman, D., & Frederick, S. (2002). Representativeness revisited: Attribute substitution in intuitive judgment. In T. Gilovich, D. Griffin, & D. Kahneman (Eds.), *Heuristics and biases* (pp. 49–81). New York: Cambridge University Press.

Kahneman, D., & Knetsch, J. (1992). Valuing public goods: The purchase of moral satisfaction. *Journal of Environmental Economics and Management, 22,* 57–70.

Kahneman, D., & Ritov, I. (1994). Determinants of stated willingness to pay for public goods: A study in the headline method. *Journal of Risk and Uncertainty, 9,* 5–38.

Kahneman, D., & Tversky, A. (1979). Prospect theory: An analysis of decision under risk. *Econometrica: Journal of the Econometric Society, 47*(2), 263–291.

Karlan, D., & List, J. A. (2007). Does price matter in charitable giving? Evidence from a large-scale natural field experiment. *The American Economic Review, 97*(5), 1774–1793.

Karlan, D., List, J. A., & Shafir, E. (2011). Small matches and charitable giving: Evidence from a natural field experiment. *Journal of Public Economics, 95,* 344–350.

Kemmelmeier, M., Jambor, E., & Letner, J. (2006). Individualism and good works: Cultural variation in giving and volunteering across the United States. *Journal of Cross-Cultural Psychology, 37,* 327–344.

Konow, J., & Earley, J. (2008). The hedonistic paradox: Is *Homo economicus* happier? *Journal of Public Economics, 92,* 1–33.

Kogut, T. (2011a). The role of perspective-taking and emotions in punishing identified and unidentified wrongdoers. *Cognition and Emotion, 25,* 1491–1499.

Kogut, T. (2011b). Someone to blame: When identifying a victim decreases helping. *Journal of Experimental Social Psychology, 47*, 748–755.

Kogut, T., & Ritov, I. (2005a). The 'identified victim' effect: An identified group, or just a single individual? *Journal of Behavioral Decision Making, 18*, 157–167.

Kogut, T., & Ritov, I. (2005b). The singularity of identified victims in separate and joint evaluations. *Organizational Behavior and Human Decision Processes, 97*, 106–116.

Kogut, T., & Ritov, I. (2007). Saving one of us: Outstanding willingness to help rescue a single identified compatriot. *Organizational Behavior and Human Decision Processes, 104*, 150–157.

Kogut, T., & Ritov, I. (2011). 'Protective donation': When donating to a cause decreases the sense of vulnerability. *Journal of Experimental Social Psychology, 47*, 1059–1069.

Kogut, T., Slovic, P., & Västfjäll, D. (2015). Scope insensitivity in helping decisions: Is it a matter of culture and values? *Journal of Experimental Psychology: General.* DOI: 10.1037 / 10039708

Konečki, V. J. (1972). Some effects of guilt on compliance. *Journal of Personality and Social Psychology, 23*, 30–32.

Landry, C. E., Lange, A., List, J. A., Price, M. K., & Rupp, N. G. (2008). *Is a donor in hand better than two in the bush? Evidence from a natural field experiment* (No. w14319). Cambridge, MA: National Bureau of Economic Research.

Levine, M., Prosser, A., Evans, D., & Reicher, S. (2005). Identity and emergency intervention: How social group membership and inclusiveness of group boundaries shape helping behavior. *Personality and Social Psychology Bulletin, 31*, 443–453.

Levine, M., & Thompson, K. (2004). Identity, place, and bystander intervention: Social categories and helping after natural disasters. *The Journal of Social Psychology, 144*, 229–245.

Levine, R. V., Norenzayan, A., & Philbrick, K. (2001). Cross-cultural differences in helping strangers. *Journal of Cross-Cultural Psychology, 32*, 543–560.

Levitt, S. D., & List, J. A. (2007). What do laboratory experiments measuring social preferences reveal about the real world? *The Journal of Economic Perspectives*, 153–174.

List, J. A., & Price, M. K. (2009). The role of social connections in charitable fundraising: Evidence from a natural field experiment. *Journal of Economic Behavior & Organization, 69*, 160–169.

Maner, J. K., Luce, C. L., Neuberg, S. L., Cialdini, R. B., Brown, S., & Sagarin, B. J. (2002). The effects of perspective taking on motivations for helping: Still no evidence for altruism. *Personality and Social Psychology Bulletin, 28*, 1601–1610.

Oyserman, D., & Lee, S. W. S. (2008). Does culture influence what and how we think? Effects of priming individualism and collectivism. *Psychological Bulletin, 134*, 311–342.

Perrine, R. M., & Heather, S. (2000). Effect of picture and even-a-penny-will-help appeals on anonymous donations to charity. *Psychological Reports, 86*(2), 551–559.

Regan, D. T., Williams, M., & Sparling, S. (1972). Voluntary expiation of guilt: A field experiment. *Journal of Personality and Social Psychology, 24*, 42–45.

Ritov, I., & Baron, J. (1994). Biases in decisions about compensation for misfortune: The role of expectation. *European Journal of Social Psychology, 24*, 525–539.

Ritov, I., & Kahneman, D. (1997). How people value the environment: Attitudes versus economic values. In M.Bazerman, D.Messick, A.Tenbrunsel, & K.Wade-Benzoni (Eds.), *Psychological perspectives to environmental and ethical issues.* Lexington, MA: The New Lexington Press.

Ritov, I., & Kogut, T. (2011). Ally or adversary: The effect of identifiability in inter-group conflict situations. *Organizational Behavior and Human Decision Process, 116*, 96–103.

Rubaltelli, E., & Agnoli, S. (2012). The emotional cost of charitable donations. *Cognition & Emotion, 26*, 769–785.

Sargeant, A., & Woodliffe, L. (2007). Gift giving: An interdisciplinary review. *International Journal of Nonprofit and Voluntary Sector Marketing, 12*(4), 275–307.

Singer, P. (2009). *The life you can save.* New York: Random House.

Sloman, S. A. (1996). The empirical case for two systems of reasoning. *Psychological Bulletin, 119*, 3–22.

Slovic, P. (2007). 'If I look at the mass I will never act': Psychic numbing and genocide. *Judgment and Decision Making, 2,* 79–95.

Small, D. A., & Loewenstein, G. (2003). Helping a victim or helping the victim: Altruism and identifiability. *Journal of Risk and Uncertainty, 26,* 5–16.

Small, D. A., & Loewenstein, G. (2006). The devil you know: The effects of identifiability on punitiveness. *Journal of Behavioral Decision Making, 18,* 311–318.

Small, D. A., Loewenstein, G., & Slovic, P. (2007). Sympathy and callousness: The impact of deliberative thought on donations to identifiable and statistical victims. *Organizational Behavior and Human Decision Processes, 102,* 143–153.

Small, D., & Simonsohn U. (2008). Friends of victims: Personal experience and prosocial behavior. *Journal of Consumer Research, 35,* 532–542.

Small, D. A., & Verrochi, N. M. (2009). The face of need: Facial emotion expression on charity advertisements. *Journal of Marketing Research, 46,* 777–787.

Smith, A. (1759). *The theory of moral sentiments,* Glasgow: R. Chapman. p. 357.

Smith, R. W., Faro, D., & Burson, K. A. (2013). More for the many: The influence of entitativity on charitable giving. *Journal of Consumer Research, 39.* 961–976.

Sturmer, S., Snyder, M., Kropp, A., & Siem, B. (2006). Empathy-motivated helping: The moderating role of group membership. *Personality and Social Psychology Bulletin, 32*(7), 943–956.

Thompson, W. C., Cowan, C. L., & Rosenhan, D. L. (1980). Focus of attention mediates the impact of negative affect on altruism. *Journal of Personality and Social Psychology, 38,* 291–300.

Van Lange, P.A.M., Bekkers, R., Schuyt, T., & Van Vugt, M. (2007). From games to giving: Social value orientation predicts donations to noble causes. *Basic and Applied Social Psychology, 29,* 375–384.

Västfjäll, D., Slovic, P., & Mayorga, M. (2015). Whoever saves one life saves the world: Confronting the challenge of pseudoinefficacy. Working Paper.

Västfjäll, D., Slovic, P., Mayorga, M., & Peters, E. (2015). Compassion fade: Affect and charity are greatest for a single child in need. *PLoS ONE.*

Wilhelm, M. O. (2007). The quality and comparability of survey data on charitable giving. *Nonprofit and Voluntary Sector Quarterly, 36,* 65–84.

Wu, S. Y., Huang, J. T., & Kao, A. P. (2004). An analysis of the peer effects in charitable giving: The case of Taiwan. *Journal of Family and Economic Issues, 25*(4), 483–505.

Zagefka, H., Noor, M., Randsley de Moura, G., Hopthrow, T., & Brown, R. (2011), Donating to disaster victims: responses to natural and humanly caused events. *European Journal of Social Psychology, 41,* 353–363.

FURTHER READING

Andreoni, J., & Payne, A. A. (2013). Charitable giving. *Handbook of Public Economics, 5,* 1–50.

Batson, C. D. (2014). *The altruism question: Toward a social-psychological answer.* New York: Psychology Press.

Oppenheimer, D. M., & Olivola, C. Y. (Eds.). (2011). *The science of giving: Experimental approaches to the study of charity.* New York: Psychology Press.

25 Life satisfaction and Emotional Well-Being: Psychological, Economic and Social Factors

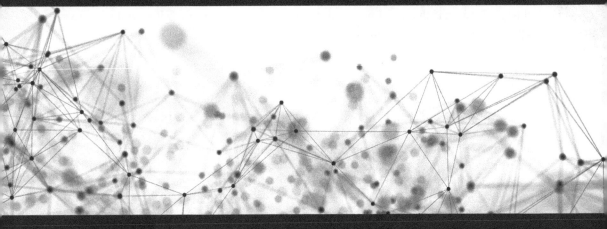

TOMMY GÄRLING AND AMELIE GAMBLE

CHAPTER OUTLINE

LEARNING OUTCOMES

BY THE END OF THIS CHAPTER YOU SHOULD BE ABLE TO:

1. Distinguish subjective well-being from material wealth and national social indicators.
2. Explain the advantages and disadvantages of different methods of measuring subjective well-being.
3. Understand how subjective well-being interacts with individual factors (personality, goal pursuit), economic factors (income, consumption), and social factors (relationships with family, friends, and romantic partners).

25.1 INTRODUCTION

An impression conveyed by the mass media is that people in affluent societies are not as happy and satisfied with their lives as one would expect them to be. Scientific research both supports and does not support this impression. It also disentangles many of the factors explaining why people are satisfied or dissatisfied. But why is it important to do this? An answer is that most people desire to be satisfied with their lives and want to know what makes them satisfied. Being satisfied with one's life has also important consequences for health, longevity, and success in life. Public health policies should therefore also be informed by scientific knowledge about life satisfaction.

In public health disciplines and politics, the broad term *well-being* is used. In Section 25.2. this chapter first contrasts the conventional well-being construct in economics to the chapter's main topic: the constructs of life satisfaction and emotional well-being developed in psychology. An umbrella term used in psychology is *subjective well-being*. In economics, the term *happiness* is currently used to refer to essentially the same construct.

All scientific research needs to develop methods for measuring the phenomena it aims to study. Measuring life satisfaction and the complementary construct of emotional well-being may appear insurmountable, however, the scientific evidence is that it is feasible. In Section 25.3, the different methods for measuring subjective well-being are described. The chapter ends with one section reviewing factors that influence subjective well-being and another reviewing what is known about its different consequences.

25.2 VIEWS OF WELL-BEING IN ECONOMICS AND PSYCHOLOGY

In economics, material wealth is the dominant objective indicator of well-being (Perlman & Marietta, 2005). It is assumed to be positively related to utility which is the term traditionally used for well-being. Happiness has later become a more commonly used term (Frey, 2008). A positive relationship between material wealth and utility or well-being depends on markets offering goods and services that citizens are able to consume so that they maximize their utility (or happiness).

If material wealth has the important role that it is supposed to have at the citizen level, this justifies use of economic national indicators for assessing the state of well-being of a country. The Gross Domestic Product (GDP) per capita is one such indicator but many others have been developed (e.g., income, spending, assets), are standardized and used in many countries. A general criticism of GDP as summarized in Van den Berg (2009) is that it provides limited information about citizens' well-being. A similar reason noted by others (Diener & Seligman, 2004) is that economic indicators exclude many potentially important factors, for instance, social capital, environmental pollution, and fair and effective government. Another criticism is methodological (Angner, 2009). Obtaining the indicators requires data collected by means of surveys known to be susceptible to various errors.

Social national indicators are used to complement economic indicators. The rationale is that such indicators assess life circumstances that are important for citizens' well-being (Dolan & White, 2007). The selection of indicators would optimally be based on theory. One proposed theoretical framework implies that capabilities (e.g., education, health) need to be provided for people to achieve a good life (Nussbaum, 2011). Related to this framework the *Human Development Index* was developed by United Nations to be used in international comparisons. In many countries around the world, different systems of social national indicators have been proposed to make possible the monitoring of citizens' well-being. Based on the 'capabilities approach' Diener et al. (2009, p. 25) give examples of proposed social indicators in seven different domains: (1) food, housing, income; (2) longevity; (3) work; (4) safety; (5) friends and family, education, neighborhood; (6) ability to help others; and (7) well-being from religion, spirituality or philosophy. Subjective well-being (life satisfaction, happiness, domain satisfaction) can be added to these domains.

Economic and social indicators were developed to meet the need for objective measures. The argument (substantiated in Section 25.3) is that an objective measure of subjective well-being is feasible. What are the advantages of such a measure? Subjective well-being as measured in populations of citizens tends to correlate with economic and social indicators, but also captures something beyond these indicators (Diener, Lucas, Schimmack, & Helliwell, 2009). Subjective well-being measures may thus provide information about what the objective indicators miss. They may also inform improvements of public goods and services. For instance, if such improvements involve tradeoffs, subjective well-being measures would help to determine the relative importance of different indicators. Finally, subjective well-being is in itself a goal both at the societal and citizen level.

25.3   MEASUREMENT OF SUBJECTIVE WELL-BEING

It seems simplistic to directly ask people themselves to report how satisfied they are with their lives. Yet, with minor modifications, self-report measures have in research proved to be of value. A distinction was made early on between a cognitive judgement of life satisfaction and recall from memory of positive and negative affect experienced in the past (Busseri & Sadava, 2011). The former is referred to as *life satisfaction* and the latter as *emotional well-being* or *affect balance*. Box 25.1 describes how life satisfaction is measured in questionnaires.

A measure of the affect balance is similarly obtained by means of self-report questionnaires (see the example in Pavot, 2008) in which people are asked to think of what they have been doing and experienced during the past four weeks (or any other specified past period or simply 'recently') and then to rate on a graded scale how frequently they have felt positive and negative evaluations or emotion states described by, for instance, the adjectives good, bad, glad, sad, agitated or relaxed. Duration may be rated instead of frequency. Sometimes ratings of intensity are combined with the ratings of frequency or duration but are usually omitted because the variation in intensity tends to be low (Diener, Larsen, Levine, & Emmons, 1985). The affect balance is

Box 25.1 Are you happy? Measurement of life satisfaction

Several methods of measurement that have been developed all converge on defining life satisfaction as a cognitive evaluation or judgement of how satisfying one's life is. They differ in whether participants answer a single question or several questions. They also differ in how participants are requested to answer the question(s). Frequently used methods include the *Ladder of Life Scale* used in the Gallup World Poll (www.gallup.com/services/170945/world-poll.aspx). In this method, participants are requested to say where they currently stand on 11 steps of an imaginary ladder with the lowest step representing the worst possible life for oneself and the highest step representing the best possible life for oneself.

In the *World Values Survey* (www.worldvaluessurvey.org) repeatedly conducted in over 100 countries, two separate questions are asked:'All things considered, how satisfied

are you with your life as a whole these days?' requesting a rating on a 10-point scale ranging from 1 (feeling completely dissatisfied) to 10 (feeling completely satisfied) and 'Taking all things together, would you say you are. . .' requesting that participants answer 'Very unhappy', 'Somewhat unhappy', 'Somewhat happy' or 'Very happy'.

Diener, Emmons, Larsen and Griffin (1985) developed the five-item *Satisfaction with Life Scale (SWLS)* which subsequently has been used in a large number of research studies. Participants are asked to rate on seven-point scales the degree to which they agree with the five statements, 'In most ways my life is close to my ideal', 'So far I have achieved the important things I want in life', 'The conditions of my life are excellent', 'I am satisfied with my life', and 'If I could live my life over again, I would change almost nothing'. A life satisfaction score is obtained by summation.

obtained after summation of the positive evaluations or emotion states with a positive sign and the negative evaluations or emotion states with a negative sign.

An alternative way of measuring emotional well-being during a past time interval is to aggregate recurrent reports of how positive or negative one feels at the moment (Kahneman, 1999). This method minimizes forgetting to which life-satisfaction judgements and recall of affect are susceptible. It is as yet a method that has been used infrequently. This may change since currently large-scale studies are under way (e.g., Killingworth & Gilbert, 2010) that use smartphones to ask people questions about how they feel at the moment and what may be causing this feeling.

A criticism of the affect balance is that it only taps hedonic aspects of emotional well-being, whereas aspects such as purpose of and meaning in life should also be important. These latter aspects are referred to as *psychological flourishing*. The point of departure for Diener et al. (2010b) in developing a new self-report scale that assesses psychological flourishing (see Table 25.1) was that universal psychological needs for self-determination, competence, and relatedness must be fulfilled for people to be satisfied with their lives (Ryan & Deci, 2000).

It is assumed that life-satisfaction judgements are primarily related to stable life circumstances (see Section 25.4). As one should expect, life-satisfaction judgements have therefore been found to be relatively stable over time (Eid & Diener, 2004). It has also been found that life-satisfaction judgements are related to satisfaction with different

Table 25.1 *Statements in the Flourishing Scale*

I lead a purposeful and meaningful life
My social relationships are supportive and rewarding
I am engaged and interested in my daily activities
I actively contribute to the happiness and well-being of others
I am competent and capable in the activities that are important to me
I am a good person and live a good life
People respect me
I am optimistic about my future

Note: Each statement is rated on a scale from 'strongly disagree' (1) to 'strongly agree' (7) and then summed to a total score.

Source: Adapted from Diener et al., 2010b, pp. 154–155.

domains of life such as family life, social life, work, and recreation (Schimmack, 2008). An additional issue that has been raised is how life-satisfaction judgements are related to the affect balance (Kim-Prieto, Diener, Tamir, Scollon, & Diener, 2005). A modest positive correlation is usually found in empirical studies. Situational factors such as the current weather are expected to influence and have been shown to influence positive or negative affect, and also life-satisfaction judgements but not to the same extent (Eid & Diener, 2004). A way of accounting for the positive correlation between life-satisfaction judgements and the affect balance is that the possession of material resources, which is a primary basis of life-satisfaction judgements, buffers the frequency of negative affect (e.g., worries) in everyday life (Kahneman & Deaton, 2010). Alternatively, thinking of material (as well as less tangible) possessions may increase positive affect (Gärling & Gamble, 2012).

Both the measures of life satisfaction and affect balance have been found to have acceptable reliability (Diener et al., 2009). Reliability of a measurement method is, however, a necessary but not a sufficient prerequisite. It also needs to be shown that the method validly measure what it should measure and nothing else. Comparing different methods is one way to determine this, and different self-report measures have thus been shown to correlate as expected. This is not due to the influence of a specific method since self-reports have also been shown to correlate as expected with other methods such as informant ratings and psychophysiological measures (Diener et al., 2009).

25.4 FACTORS INFLUENCING SUBJECTIVE WELL-BEING

What makes people happy and satisfied with their lives? One common belief is that some lucky people are disposed to be happy and satisfied with their lives literally from birth to death. Another belief is that some fortunate people are happy and satisfied with their lives because they have a high income and money saved in the bank. Still another belief is that people are happy and satisfied with their lives because they have a loving family and close friends.

Diener (1984) distinguished between top-down and bottom-up theoretical explanations of subjective well-being. As we shall see in this section, both personality (a top-down explanation), available material resources (a bottom-up explanation), and social relationships (another bottom-up explanation) contribute to an explanation of why people differ in how satisfied or dissatisfied they are with their lives. No single top-down or bottom-up explanation is sufficient.

25.4.1 *Individual Factors*

At the individual level, stable personality traits such as extraversion and emotional stability account for a large proportion of individual differences in subjective well-being (Lucas, 2008). A smaller proportion is accounted for by stable life circumstances including wealth, health, life-cycle stage, marital status, employment, and education (Diener, Suh, Lucas, & Smith, 1999). Yet, changes in life circumstances such as getting or losing a job, birth or death of a child, marriage, death of or divorce from a spouse, and injuries, illness or recovery from such conditions have large impacts. Although the time course is not known with certainty, changes in life circumstances (e.g., marriage) that increase subjective well-being tend to revert back to a set point which is roughly invariant for an individual but different for different individuals (Diener, Lucas, & Scollon, 2006). Full reversion from decreases in subjective well-being (e.g., divorce) may, however, never occur or will take a longer time.

If stable (and possibly genetically determined) personality traits are important determinants of subjective well-being, is it futile to implement public health policies to increase people's life satisfaction and emotional well-being? Even if it were true that, as approximately estimated, 50% of individual differences in subjective well-being are accounted for by personality traits, there is still a large part of the variation that can be influenced. It also needs to be taken into account that personality traits have both direct (temperamental) effects and indirect (behavioural) effects on subjective well-being.

A temperamental explanation of the influence of personality traits on subjective well-being is that emotionally unstable people respond with both stronger positive and negative affect than emotionally stable people. Extraverts compared to introverts similarly respond with stronger positive but weaker negative affect. A complementary behavioural explanation is that personality traits influence choice of and effort invested in activities that lead to positive subjective well-being outcomes.

Engagement in intentional goal-directed activities has positive influences on subjective well-being (Lyubomirsky, Sheldon, & Schkade, 2005). Such activities include exercising regularly, devoting effort to meaningful causes, eschewing social comparisons and contingent self-evaluations, and practising certain virtues, for instance, kindness, gratitude, forgiveness, and thoughtful self-reflection. In a similar vein, it may be argued that daily hassles and uplifts are important for how satisfied people are with their lives. In a survey, Jakobsson Bergstad et al. (2012)

showed that affect associated with frequent routine out-of-home activities (e.g., chauffeuring children to school or day-care centre; participating in sports, exercise or outdoor activities; purchasing non-durables; visiting relatives and friends) had a substantial impact on the weekly affect balance and a smaller but still measurable impact on life-satisfaction judgements. The results highlight that it is important for subjective well-being that communities provide services that facilitate routine out-of-home activities.

Activities in everyday life are instrumental in achieving goals such as raising one's salary by performing well at work, leading a happy family life, and having a relaxing leisure time. If goal progress is as expected, people are in a positive mood. The affect balance would thus be positively influenced by goal progress (Klug & Maier, 2014). Only scant research has, however, documented the negative effects of impediments to goal progress.

Time pressure is something many people in affluent societies encounter (Strazdins et al., 2011). A common complaint is having too many things to do in too short a time. Another common complaint is having too little free time. How does time pressure affect satisfaction with life and emotional well-being? Figure 25.1 presents the conceptual model proposed by Gärling, Krause, Gamble and Hartig (2014) to explain how time pressure reduces emotional well-being by interfering with goal progress in the life domains of work, family life, and leisure, as well as spilling over from one domain to another domain. An example of the latter is that, when a satisfactory work-leisure balance is threatened, this jeopardizes recovery from work stress that otherwise would have a positive effect on emotional well-being (Hartig, Johansson, & Kylin, 2003). Material wealth may increase time pressure since it makes available many competing free-time opportunities, thus paradoxically reducing emotional well-being. Less wealthy people who are denied these opportunities may also experience negative effects of time pressure when they have fewer resources to buy time, for instance, by hiring domestic services.

A market has emerged for courses in time management as well as technical time-management devices enhancing the functionality of the traditional calendar and clock, presumably in response to people's negative experience of time pressure in their everyday lives. Evaluations of time management courses in which participants

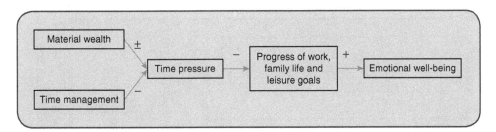

FIGURE 25.1 *Hypothesized conceptual model positing that progress of work, family life, and leisure goals increases emotional well-being, that time pressure negatively influencing performance of instrumental activities decreases goal progress and emotional well-being, that practising time management has indirect positive effects on emotional well-being by decreasing time pressure and its negative effects on goal progress, and that material wealth has indirect negative effects on emotional well-being by increasing and indirect positive effects by decreasing time pressure and its negative effects on goal progress.*

practise goal setting and planning appear to show that the courses boost overall life satisfaction, positive feelings such as enthusiasm and engagement, and a strong belief in being able to attain set goals (MacLeod, Coates, & Hetherton, 2008).

If people face many tasks or activities in everyday life such that they experience time pressure, deadlines motivate people to make progress in achieving set goals (Locke & Latham, 2002). Yet, deadlines set too strictly may result in detrimental effects on performance, exactly as having too much time may do. Unsuccessful coping with time pressure causing time stress would have even larger negative performance effects. Time stress would also change the affect balance in a negative direction (Gärling, Gamble, Fors, & Hjerm, 2015; Ng, Diener, Arora, & Harter, 2009). In Figure 25.2, time stress that negatively influences emotional well-being is added to the conceptual model as a parallel mediator to goal progress. Figure 25.2 also illustrates that the personality trait emotional stability may reduce time stress (Vollrath, 2000). Thus, people who are emotionally stable are perhaps more apt to cope with time pressure than those who are emotionally less stable.

25.4.2 Economic Factors

Subjective well-being has been assessed at national levels in studies conducted worldwide (www.worlddatabaseofhappiness.eur.nl) (Veenhoven, 2011). Analyses of such results (e.g., Ahuvia, 2008; Dolan, Peasgood, & White, 2008) demonstrate a substantial effect of material wealth (usually proxied by income) on differences in average life satisfaction between affluent and poor countries, whereas within already affluent countries, material wealth has a diminishing influence on citizens' life satisfaction. A paradoxical but controversial finding, first noted by Easterlin (1974), is that in some affluent countries average life satisfaction has over time increased less than GPD. One explanation is the relative income effect, implying that citizens compare themselves to others in evaluating their subjective well-being. Another is that people adapt to wealth increases by raised aspirations. A possible caveat in some studies is that the causal direction is not from material wealth to subjective well-being but the reverse (see Section 25.5).

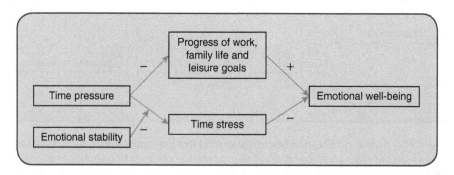

FIGURE 25.2 *How the hypothesized conceptual model in Figure 25.1 is augmented by positing that individuals with a less emotional stable personality frequently may fail to cope with time pressure leading to time stress which exaggerates the negative effects of time pressure on emotional well-being.*

Why should material wealth be important for subjective well-being? An obvious answer is that people have basic needs (e.g., food, housing, security) that must be met to make their lives enjoyable. Psychosocial prosperity becomes more important when material wealth increases (Diener, Ng, Harter, & Arora, 2010a). Presumably for this reason, increases in material wealth are more strongly reflected in changes in the affect balance than in life-satisfaction judgements. Yet, in affluent societies, the affect balance appears to be less influenced by income than life satisfaction (Kahneman & Deaton, 2010). The increase with income is still not linear but diminishing.

Important ingredients of affluent societies are large markets for luxury goods and services. Yet, the diminishing increase that life satisfaction has with income appears to be consistent with luxury consumption having less than expected positive effects. It may even appear as if people in these societies are entering endless loops of consumption where nothing is sufficient and others always have something better. It is generally assumed that a positive relation between material wealth and utility or well-being depends on markets offering goods and services allowing citizens to maximize their well-being. Do markets then fail in doing this, and if so why? Some things that make people happy (see Section 25.4.3) are not for sale. Yet, Dunn, Gilbert, and Wilson (2011) question whether this is a sufficient explanation, arguing instead that people do not spend their money in the right way. The reason is that they do not know what makes them happy. An example is that, contrary to what people believe, purchases of experiences in which they engage tend to lead to more happiness than purchases of goods in which they quickly lose interest (Killingsworth & Gilbert, 2010).

The paradox that luxury consumption fails to increase subjective well-being appears to be that preferences change due to hedonic adaptation (Frederick & Loewenstein, 1999). Hedonic adaptation is a component of the 'hedonic treadmill' effect (Diener et al., 2006). Significant improvements are after some time perceived as normal (adaptation), thus a desire for further improvements is aroused, and so forth (the treadmill). Consumption loops may possibly be understood in this way. Wilson and Gilbert (2008) suggest that the degree of attention to change influences adaptation. As an example, the experience of driving a new car evokes emotions (e.g., fun to drive) by attention to certain attributes (e.g., better acceleration). However, over time, attention to these attributes is reduced. The emotional impact is then reduced. On the other hand, attention to negative events may be sustained longer. For instance, having more space in your apartment is not noticed after some time, whereas a lack of space is experienced every day as being annoying.

Inequality of income distributions in affluent consumer societies negatively affects subjective well-being, in particular, among low-income citizens perceiving inequality. Oshio and Urakawa (2014) thus showed that answers to the question 'Do you think the disparity between the rich and the poor in Japan has grown in the past 5 years?' correlated negatively with ratings of overall happiness. One possible determinant is that inequality has resulted in substantial increases in credit purchases (Kamleitner, Hoelzl, & Kirchler, 2012) causing indebtedness that negatively influences subjective well-being. At the same time as people are susceptible to the 'treadmill' effect boosting their desires for luxury consumption, many are economically denied the possibility of consuming luxury products unless taking up credit. A possible source of the negative effects on subjective well-being is that the pleasure of consumption does not buffer the burden of repayments (Kamleitner, Hoelz, & Kirchler, 2010).

25.4.3 Social Factors

Human beings are, as Aristotle remarked, social animals. It is understandable then that so much pleasure in life is derived from various social interactions, with family members, friends, colleagues, and even strangers. A well-documented finding from an abundance of cross-sectional and longitudinal surveys is that marrying is accompanied by an uplift of subjective well-being, although later declining to the level before marrying (Myers, 1999). In asking directed questions in subjective well-being surveys, high ranks are generally given to close relationships with family, friends, and romantic partners. People who report having intimate friends are more satisfied with their lives than those who report having no intimate friends. Breaking up a close relationship is an extremely negative experience (Lucas, 2005), and much effort is invested in maintaining the relationship. Promises to keep in touch, sending postcards, making occasional telephone calls, and organizing reunions exemplify that effort is also made to maintain less close relationships.

Why do interpersonal relationships improve subjective well-being? Reversing the causality, a reason may be that happy people are attracted to each other. An emotional dividend from attachment and belongingness is another reason. A third reason is *social support* ranging from obtaining practical advice and assistance to sharing joys and sorrows, experiencing a partner's empathy, and being mentally supported and rewarded by the partner.

Subjective well-being is also increased if people contribute to an interpersonal relationship, that is, if they themselves provide social support. In experiments described in Lyubomirsky et al. (2005), participants were requested to practise kindness. They chose themselves to do five things beneficial to other people, either on a single day or spread out over a week. Examples of what participants did included helping a friend to solve a problem or to overcome some bad experience, buying something for a friend, lending out the car to a family member or visiting a hospice. Only if the kindness practice was concentrated in one day was an increase in subjective well-being observed. In another experiment, participants were requested to do different things or the same thing several times. After 10 weeks, a positive effect on subjective well-being was again observed but only for those who did different things. Several explanations are conceivable of why helping others increases subjective well-being. Probably the most important one is *reciprocation*. In any society, people are excluded if they do not help needy others and they also therefore expect that others would help them if they themselves were needy. Positive affect associated with helping others may have a long evolutionary history that accounts for the building of human societies. Small cohesive groups may be essential for this.

Charitable giving is an example at the societal level that may increase citizens' subjective well-being – both as givers and receivers. Box 25.2 describes a study showing how companies may contribute to this at the same time as they make a profit from selling demanded products. Other examples in societies are non-profit organizations that receive charitable donations from people to help those in need. That people donating may increase their emotional well-being should also be recognized.

Box 25.2 Charitable giving increases happiness

A. Gneezy, U. Gneezy, Nelson and Brown (2010) reported a study to investigate whether the happiness enhanced by charitable giving would increase if people were asked to 'pay what they want' (PWYW). In a US amusement park, photos were taken of people (N = 113,047) after the end of a ride on a roller-coaster-like attraction. People asked to purchase the photos were randomized to a 2 (either a regular US$12.95 price or PWYW) by 2 (no charitable giving or 50% charitable giving) experimental design. The results showed that 4.49% more purchases were made in the PWYW condition than in the regular-price condition when charitable giving was asked to be made. Significantly more was paid per photo (Mean = US$5.33) in the PWYW condition with charitable giving compared to US$0.92 with no charitable giving. Additional data did not show that spending more on purchasing the pictures crowded out additional spending in the amusement park. If the photo was considered of low value, few purchased it despite that they could decide on the price themselves. Neither was the company profit reduced by asking for charitable giving. The implication is that company profits ethics may not be in conflict with a society's well-being goals. It may thus be possible for companies to both increase selling desired goods and do good for society by increasing charitable giving to the benefits of both themselves and receivers.

25.5   CONSEQUENCES OF SUBJECTIVE WELL-BEING

It is undisputed that healthy people are more satisfied with their lives. But do people become healthier if they are satisfied with their lives? Do they live longer? Recent longitudinal evidence suggests qualified affirmative answers to both questions (Diener & Chan, 2011). In healthy populations, both morbidity and mortality are negatively related to life satisfaction. The most solid evidence is that the prevalence of cardiovascular diseases increases with prolonged negative affect states. In diseased populations, the evidence is, however, non-conclusive. Positive affective states do not seem to overcome illnesses despite being known to strengthen the immune system. It may also be questioned whether extreme degrees of positive affect foster over-optimism that disposes people to unhealthy life-styles. There is furthermore a risk of not seeking medical care when required.

High compared to low subjective well-being may add from four to 10 years to one's life. The additional years are also more enjoyable due to better health and a more active life. It is still too premature to specify which degree of subjective well-being is beneficial. This does not speak against public health policies to increase subjective well-being for people in whom it is low.

Living longer, being healthy, being satisfied with one's life, and experiencing predominantly positive affect (a positive affect balance) is for the majority of people a desirable goal. But if facing the choice between a shorter more satisfying life and a longer less satisfying life, which would people prefer? In real life, few people make this choice, but participants in an experiment described in Box 25.3 were asked to do. The results have a bearing on policy decisions that are based on Quality-Adjusted Life Years (QALY), for instance, decisions about allocating resources to a new medical treatment. If a treatment only prolongs an unhappy life, should the cost of the treatment be allocated differently? QALY is calculated by adding 1 for each additional year in perfect health but less than 1 depending on how much worse than perfect health is.

From a societal and individual perspective, it is germane to ask if life satisfaction and emotional well-being lead to success in life. In comparing longitudinal to cross-sectional surveys to support their causal interpretation, Lyubomirski, King, and Diener (2005) reach the conclusion that people who are satisfied with their lives and report a positive affect balance become more successful in the life domains of work (e.g., income, job performance and satisfaction), social relationships (e.g., marital happiness, number of and satisfaction with friends, positive perceptions of self and others), and health (e.g., absence of pain, little need of medical care, few work absences). Some experimental studies point in the same direction, although their results should only with caution be generalized to real life.

Box 25.3   A longer unhappy life may not be desirable: the James Dean effect

Diener, Wirtz and Oishi (2001) conducted a study of what lay people believe is a good life. They recruited as participants 115 undergraduates in their twenties and 55 parents and older friends aged from 34–63 years old with a mean of 46 years. Different vignettes presented in a questionnaire described the life of a fictitious character who was a never-married woman without children. All vignettes ended with the character's sudden and painless death in an automobile accident at the age of 30 or 60 years (50 years for the older participants). In a positive condition, the character's first part of life was extremely happy with enjoyable work, vacations, close friends, and pleasant leisure time. An extended positive condition added a slightly less positive extra five years before death. In a contrasting negative condition the character's first part of life was very depressed and angry with a monotonous job, no close friends, and leisure filled with solitary television viewing. In an extended negative condition a slightly less negative five years before death were added. The participants answered two questions: (1) 'Taking the character's life as a whole, how desirable do you think it was?' and (2) 'How much total happiness or unhappiness would you say the character experienced in her life?' Ratings were made on scales from 1 (most undesirable or unhappy) to 9 (most desirable or happy). The results showed that a longer life (death at age 50 or 60 years rather than at age 25 years) and a happy life compared to an unhappy life were rated more positively. However, for both the younger and the older participants, adding five less happy years to a happy life or five less unhappy years to an unhappy life did not increase the ratings of desirability or happiness. The main point is thus that death at a younger age is preferred to death at an older age if the last years are less happy. Yet, looking ahead people would likely prefer a longer to a shorter life.

25.6 SUMMARY

In this chapter we have addressed three questions that are important in any society: Are citizens satisfied or dissatisfied with their lives?, what makes them satisfied or dissatisfied?, and what are the consequences of being satisfied or dissatisfied? How should such questions be answered to influence policies? First, several types of national indicators (economic, social, subjective well-being) were described that are or may be relevant. Next our main focus was subjective well-being, consisting of a cognitive judgement of life satisfaction and emotional well-being defined as the balance of experienced positive and negative affect. We reviewed how life satisfaction and emotional well-being are reliably and validly measured by means of self-report ratings in questionnaires. In such measurements, the cognitive judgements of life satisfaction mainly reflect stable possessions of material and other resources and are therefore only modestly correlated with the less stable balance of positive and negative affect experienced in everyday life. We reviewed research showing that individual factors (personality, life-cycle stage, engagement in goal-directed activities), economic factors (material wealth, income), and social factors (receiving and giving social support, kindness) influence subjective well-being. We also noted that these influences are frequently complex, such that causality is difficult to infer. Finally, we reviewed other strands of research showing that subjective well-being has positive consequences for health, longevity, and life success.

REVIEW QUESTIONS

1. What is subjective well-being and how is it measured?
2. In which ways does economic wealth increase emotional well-being?
3. In which ways does economic wealth not increase emotional well-being?
4. What implications for public policy do measures of subjective well-being have?

REFERENCES

Ahuvia, A. (2008). Wealth, consumption and happiness. In A. Lewis (Ed.), *The Cambridge handbook of psychology and economic behavior* (pp. 199–226). Cambridge: Cambridge University Press.

Angner, E. (2009). The politics of happiness: Subjective vs. economic measures as measures of social well-being. In L. Bortolotti (Ed.), *Philosophy and happiness* (pp. 149–166). New York: Palgrave.

Busseri, M. A., & Sadava, S. W. (2011) A review of the tripartite structure of subjective well-being: Implications for conceptualization, operationalization, analysis, and synthesis. *Personality and Social Psychology Review*, *15*, 290–314. DOI:10.1177/1088868310391271

Diener, E. (1984). Subjective well-being. *Psychological Bulletin*, *95*, 542–575. DOI:10.1037/0033-2909.125.2.276

Diener, E., & Chan, M. Y. (2011). Happy people live longer: Subjective well-being contributes to health and longevity. *Applied Psychology: Health and Well-Being*, *3*, 1–43. DOI:10.1111/j.1758-0854.2010.01045.x

Diener, E., Emmons, R. A., Larsen, R. J., & Griffen, S. (1985). The satisfaction with life scale. *Journal of Personality Assessment, 49*, 71–75. DOI:10.1207/s15327752jpa4901_13

Diener, E., Larsen, R. J., Levine, S., & Emmons, R. A. (1985). Intensity and frequency: Dimensions underlying positive and negative affect. *Journal of Personality and Social Psychology, 48*, 1253–1265. DOI: 10.1037/0022-3514.48.5.1253

Diener, E., Lucas, R. E., Schimmack, U., & Helliwell, J. F. (2009). *Well-being for public policy.* New York: Oxford University Press.

Diener, E., Lucas, R. E., & Scollon, C. (2006). Beyond the hedonic treadmill: Revising the adaptation theory of well-being. *American Psychologist, 65*(4), 305–314. DOI: 10.1037/0003-066X.61.4.305

Diener, E., Ng, W., Harter, J., & Arora, R. (2010a). Wealth and happiness across the world: Material prosperity predicts life evaluation, whereas psychosocial prosperity predicts positive feelings. *Journal of Personality and Social Psychology, 99*, 52–61. DOI:10.1037/a0018066

Diener, E., & Seligman, M. E. P. (2004). Beyond money: Toward an economy of well-being. *Psychological Science in the Public Interest, 5*(1), 1–31. DOI:10.1111/j.0963-7214.2004.00501001.x.

Diener, E., Suh, E. M., Lucas, R. E., & Smith, H. L. (1999). Subjective well-being: Three decades of progress. *Psychological Bulletin, 125*, 276–302. DOI: 10.1037/0033-2909.125.2.276

Diener, E., Wirtz, D., & Oishi, S. (2001). End effects of rated life quality: The James Dean effect. *Psychological Science, 12*, 124–128. DOI: 10.1111/1467-9280.00321

Diener, E., Wirtz, D., Tov, W., Kim-Prieto, C., Choi, D., Oishi, S., & Biswas-Diener, R. (2010b). New well-being measures: Short scales to assess flourishing and positive and negative feelings. *Social Indicators Research, 97*, 143–156. DOI:10.1007/s11205-009-9493-y

Dolan, P., Peasgood, T., & White, M. P. (2008). Do we really know what makes us happy? A review of the economic literature on the factors associated with subjective well-being. *Journal of Economic Psychology, 29*, 94–122. DOI:10.1016/j.joep.2007.09.001

Dolan, P., & White, M. P. (2007). How can measures of subjective well-being be used to inform public policy? *Perspective on Psychological Science, 2*, 71–85. DOI:10.1111/j.1745-6916.2007.00030.x

Dunn, E. W., Gilbert, D. T., & Wilson, T. D. (2011). If money doesn't make you happy, then you probably aren't spending it right. *Journal of Consumer Psychology, 21*, 115–125. DOI: 10.1016/j.jcps.2011.02.002

Easterlin, R. A. (1974). Does economic growth improve the human lot? Some empirical evidence. In P. A. David, & M. W. Reder (Eds.), *Nations and households in economic growth* (pp. 89–125). New York: Academic Press.

Eid, M., & Diener, E. (2004). Global judgements of subjective well-being: Situational variability and long-term stability. *Social Indicators Research, 65*, 245–272.

Frederick, S., & Loewenstein, G. (1999). Hedonic adaptation. In D. Kahneman, E. Diener, & N. Schwartz (Eds.), *Well-being: The foundations of hedonic psychology* (pp. 302–329). New York: Russell Sage Foundation.

Frey, B. (2008). *Happiness: A revolution in economics.* Cambridge, MA: MIT Press.

Gärling, T., & Gamble, A. (2012). Influences on current mood of eliciting life-satisfaction judgments. *Journal of Positive Psychology, 7*, 219–229. DOI:10.1080/17439760.2012.674547

Gärling, T., Gamble, A., Fors, F., & Hjerm, M. (2015). Emotional well-being related to time pressure, impediment to goal progress, and stress-related symptoms. *Journal of Happiness Studies, 17*(5), 1789–1799. DOI: 10.1007/s10902-015-9670-4

Gärling, T., Krause, K., Gamble, A., & Hartig, T. (2014). Time pressure and emotional well-being. *PsyCH Journal, 3*, 132–143. DOI: 10.1002/pchj.52

Gneezy, A., Gneezy, U., Nelson, L. D., & Brown, A. (2010). Shared social responsibility: A field experiment in Pay-What-You-Want pricing and charitable giving. *Science, 329*, 325–327. DOI: 10.1126/science.1186744.

Hartig, T., Johansson, G., & Kylin, C. (2003). Residence in the social ecology of stress and restoration. *Journal of Social Issues, 59*, 611–636. DOI: 10.1111/1540-4560.00080

Jakobsson Bergstad, C., Gamble, A., Hagman, O., Polk, M., Gärling, T. ... & Olsson, L. E. (2012). Influences on subjective well-being of affect associated with routine out-of-home activities. *Applied Research in Quality of Life, 7*, 49–62. DOI:10.1007/s11482-011-9143-9.

Kahneman, D. (1999) Objective happiness. In D. Kahneman, E. Diener, & N. Schwarz (Eds.), *Well-being: The foundations of hedonic psychology* (pp. 3–25). New York: Russell Sage Foundation.

Kahneman, D., & Deaton, A. (2010). High income improves evaluation of life but not emotional well-being. *PNAS, 107*, 16489–16493. DOI:10.1073/pnas.1011492107.

Kamleitner, B., Hoelz, E., & Kirchler, E. (2010). Experiencing costs and benefits of a loan transaction: The role of cost-benefit associations. *Journal of Economic Psychology, 31*, 1047–1056. DOI: 10.1016/j. joep.2010.09.005

Kamleitner, B., Hoelzl, E., & Kirchler, E. (2012). Credit use: Psychological perspectives on a multifaceted phenomenon. *International Journal of Psychology, 47*(1), 1–27. DOI: 10.1080/00207594.2011.628674

Killingworth, M. A., & Gilbert, D. T. (2010). A wandering mind is an unhappy mind. *Science, 330*, 932. DOI: 10.1126/science.1192439

Kim-Prieto, C., Diener, E., Tamir, M., Scollon, C., & Diener, M. (2005). Integrating the diverse definitions of happiness: A time-sequential framework of subjective well-being. *Journal of Happiness Studies, 6*, 261–300. DOI: 10.1007/s10902-005-7226-8

Klug, H. J. P., & Maier, G. W. (2014). Linking goal progress and subjective well-being: A meta-analysis. *Journal of Happiness Studies, 16*, 37–65. DOI:10.1007/s10902-013-9493-0.

Locke, E. A., & Latham, G. P. (2002). Building a practically useful theory of goal setting and task motivation: A 35-year odyssey. *American Psychologist, 57*, 705–717. DOI:10.1037/0003-066X.57.9.705

Lucas, R. E. (2005). Time does not heal all wounds: A longitudinal study of reaction and adaptation to divorce. *Psychological Science, 16*, 945–950. DOI: 10.1111/j.0963-7214.2004.01501002.x

Lucas, R. E. (2008). Personality and subjective well-being. In M. Eid, & R. J. Larsen (Eds.), *The science of subjective well-being* (pp. 171–194). New York: Guilford Press.

Lyubomirsky, S., King, L., & Diener, E. (2005). The benefits of frequent positive affect: Does happiness lead to success? *Psychological Bulletin, 131*, 803–855. DOI:10.1037/0033-909.131.6.803.

Lyubomirsky, S., Sheldon, K. M., & Schkade, D. (2005). Pursuing happiness: The architecture of sustainable change. *Review of General Psychology, 9*, 111–131. DOI: 10.1037/1089-2680.9.2.111

MacLeod, A. K., Coates, E., & Hetherton, J. (2008). Increasing well-being through teaching goal-setting and planning skills: Results of a brief intervention. *Journal of Happiness Studies, 9*, 185–196. DOI:10.1007/s10902-007-9057-2

Myers, D. G. (1999). Close relationships and quality of life. In D. Kahneman, E. Diener, & N. Schwartz (Eds.), *Well-being: The foundations of hedonic psychology* (pp. 374–391). New York: Russell Sage Foundation.

Ng, W., Diener, E., Arora, R., & Harter, J. (2009). Affluence, feelings of stress, and well-being. *Social Indicators Research, 94*, 257–271. DOI:10.1007/s11205-008-9422-5

Nussbaum, M. C. (2011). *Creating capabilities.* Cambridge, MA: Harvard University Press.

Oshio, T., & Urakawa, K. (2014). The association between perceived income inequality and subjective well-being: Evidence from a social survey in Japan. *Social Indicators Research, 116*, 755–770. DOI: 10.1007/s11205-013-0323-x

Pavot, W. (2008). The assessment of subjective well-being. In M. Eid, & R. J. Larsen (Eds.), *The science of subjective well-being* (pp. 124–140). New York: Guilford Press.

Perlman, M., & Marietta, M. (2005). The politics of social accounting: Public goals and the evolution of the national accounts in Germany, the United Kingdom and the United States. *Review of Political Economy, 17*(2), 211–230. DOI:10.1080/09538250500067262

Ryan, R. M., & Deci, E. L. (2000). Self-determination theory and facilitation of intrinsic motivation, social development, and well-being. *American Psychologist, 55*, 68–78. DOI:10.1037/0003-066X.55.1.68

Schimmack, U. (2008). The structure of subjective well-being. In M. Eid, & R. J. Larsen (Eds.), *The science of subjective well-being* (pp. 97–123). New York: Guilford Press.

Strazdins, L., Griffin, A. L., Broom, D. H., Banwell, C., Korda, R., Dixon, J., Paolucci, F., & Glover, J. (2011). Time scarcity: Another health inequality? *Environment and Planning A, 43*, 545–559. DOI:10.1068/a4360

Van den Bergh, J. C. J. M. (2009). The GDP paradox. *Journal of Economic Psychology*, *30*, 117–135. DOI:10.1016/j.joep.2008.12.001

Veenhoven, R. (2011). *World database of happiness*. Rotterdam, The Netherlands: Erasmus University, Faculty of Social Sciences.

Vollrath, M. (2000). Personality and hassles among university students: A three-year longitudinal study. *European Journal of Personality*, *14*, 199–215. DOI: 10.1002/1099-0984(200005/06)

Wilson, T. D., & Gilbert, D. T. (2008). Explaining away: A model of affective adaptation. *Perspectives on Psychological Science*, *3*, 370–386. DOI:10.1111/j.1745-6924.2008.00085.x

FURTHER READING

Diener, E., Lucas, R. E., Schimmack, U., & Helliwell, J. F. (2009). *Well-being for public policy*. New York: Oxford University Press.

Eid, M., & Larsen, R. J. (Eds.). (2008). *The science of subjective well-being*. New York: Guilford Press.

Frey, B. (2008). *Happiness: A revolution in economics*. Cambridge, MA: MIT Press.

Kahneman, D., Diener, E., & Schwarz, N. (Eds.). (1999). *Well-being: The foundations of hedonic psychology*. New York: Russell Sage Foundation.

26 Living in Poverty: Understanding the Financial Behaviour of Vulnerable Groups

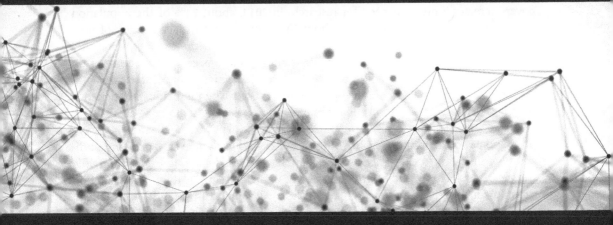

CÄZILIA LOIBL

CHAPTER OUTLINE

LEARNING OUTCOMES

BY THE END OF THIS CHAPTER YOU SHOULD BE ABLE TO:

1. Understand and describe behavioural perspectives on poverty.
2. Discuss the factors that influence how individuals and families of limited financial means make financial decisions.
3. Give examples of population groups that are vulnerable to financial hardship.

26.1 INTRODUCTION

This chapter provides an overview of financial decision-making by people living in poverty. Poverty is characterized as a lack of the resources required to meet an individual's or a family's needs. Poverty receives increased interest in economic psychology, for several reasons. First, the large number of individuals and families living in poverty creates a pressing need for research. In 2014, about 24% of the population in the European Union (EU-28) and about 14.5% of Americans face the risk of poverty (Eurostat, 2016; U.S. Census Bureau, 2015). This percentage can be significantly higher in less wealthy countries. Second, scarcity situations create unique decision environments that affect cognitive, behavioural and affective levels of decision competences. An example is the notion of a 'tunnel' vision when individuals experience shortfalls of money, time, food and other real-world poverty situations (Mullainathan & Shafir, 2013). Third, as a result of the lack of successful poverty alleviating interventions and policies and the growing interest in behavioural sciences, a growing number of ground-breaking research studies have been funded and published in only the past few years. These studies provide a better understanding of the unique decision situations in scarcity situations (e.g., Haushofer & Fehr, 2014; Mani, Mullainathan, Shafir, & Zhao, 2013; Shah, Mullainathan, & Shafir, 2012). These studies also point to the great need for research and provide guidance for particularly important policy areas that would benefit from a better understanding. An example are the mechanisms that improve the welfare of children who were born to families in poverty (e.g., Chetty, Hendren, & Katz, 2016; Gundersen & Ziliak, 2014). Finally, investigations on the causes and consequences of poverty invite a particularly wide range of research methods and interdisciplinary collaborations. Poverty is not only related to personal finances. Rather, it is associated with almost every aspect of life. Poverty solutions require innovative thinking, which is evident in the strategic goals of federal and private research-grant programmes.

This chapter first presents different definitions of poverty. Next, it explains the characteristics of financial decisions made by low-income individuals. This discussion is followed by descriptions of financial decision-making among three particularly vulnerable population groups: older people, children, and single mothers. The chapter ends with a final discussion of policy implications and a summary.

26.2 DEFINITION OF POVERTY

Poverty can be defined in a number of ways. Material definitions of poverty are based on household cash flow, the assets and liabilities. The goal is to identify insufficient income and limited assets (Haushofer & Fehr, 2014). Typically, material definitions of poverty are based on household income ('income poverty') because income data are best available. A widely used threshold is one based either on a percentage of the median household income of a population, e.g., 60% in the European Union (Eurostat, 2012a), or on a set amount, e.g., $11,770 for a single-person household in the United States, according to the federal poverty guidelines (U.S. Department of Health and Human Services, 2015).

If data are available, analysis of household income can be compared with expenditure data ('consumption poverty'). For example, poverty is indicated if household expenditures are below 60% of the median, after adjusting for different household types (Noll & Weick, 2012). Similarly, if asset data are available, asset-poor households can be defined as having less than 60% of the median value of the assets of a population. Households with both low incomes and limited assets are particularly vulnerable to poverty (Goebel & Grabka, 2011).

In contrast to these material definitions, subjective poverty describes the perception of poverty, for instance, with regard to a sense of material deprivation or feelings of financial distress. The European Union's Statistics on Income and Living Conditions, which collects data annually, uses nine questions to assess subjective poverty. Examples include whether a person can afford a one-week annual holiday away from home, catch up with late payments for mortgage/rent or utility bills, and keep the home adequately warm. Respondents are classified as deprived if they report to lack at least three of the nine items (Atkinson & Marlier, 2010).

Ideally, measures of both objective and subjective poverty are available to examine poverty fully. This broader view is typically taken in economic psychological literature. For instance, Mani et al. (2013) define poverty as a 'gap between one's needs and the resources available to fulfil them'. It is a definition that works whether an individual lives in a rich country or a poor one, and it includes individuals who experience temporary poverty, as well as those living in chronic poverty. To illustrate this definition, Mani et al. (2013) present findings from both Indian sugarcane farmers as well as shoppers at a New Jersey mall in the United States.

26.3 CHARACTERISTICS OF FINANCIAL BEHAVIOURS

Financial behaviours of individuals and families in poverty can appear at odds with their financial interests. For instance, low-income individuals are more likely to play the lottery (Haisley, Mostafa, & Loewenstein, 2008), overlook available social services (Bertrand, Mullainathan, & Shafir, 2004), neglect home maintenance (Van Zandt & Rohe, 2006), fail to save for emergencies or retirement (Thaler & Benartzi, 2004), borrow from high-interest, alternative financial services (Barr, 2012), and forego profitable small investments, such as those available through matched savings accounts (Loibl, Grinstein-Weiss, Zhan, & Red Bird, 2010).

Several explanations have been offered for the economic choices of low-income individuals. First, the financial environment can facilitate certain financial behaviours. Second, the characteristics of low-income individuals have been shown to negatively affect financial decision-making. Third, living in poverty with its limited access to credit and its higher risk of income and health shocks restricts low-income households' flexibility to cope with financial mistakes. Fourth, analysis of mental processes shows that resource scarcity limits self-control, reduces cognitive resources, and causes stress, fear and anxiety, which leads to short-sighted, risk-averse decisions while neglecting ongoing or longer-term problems. This section gives an overview of current theories and research on each of these topics.

26.3.1 Financial Environment

The financial environment in which low-income individuals and families live provides a host of obstacles and inconveniences that influence financial decisions and behaviours (Haushofer & Fehr, 2014). Rather than being served by local branches of mainstream banks and credit unions, low-income neighbourhoods have a larger number of alternative financial services (Mani et al., 2013). This informal credit market includes payday lenders, pawnshops, rent-to-own establishments, and merchants' lay-away plans. It means borrowing at higher interest rates and encountering greater limits on the amount of money that can be borrowed. For these reasons, the liquidity of low-income households tends to be more highly constrained than that of households above the poverty threshold (Haushofer & Fehr, 2014). This becomes evident, for instance, when people miss work or are late to arrive because they are unable to afford car repairs, when they are slow to afford computers and other new technology, or when they are less able to invest in health care and education, which provide returns mostly in the longer term (Mani et al., 2013).

Living in low-income neighbourhoods is also stressful in itself. Low-income areas are characterized by higher violence and crime rates, poorer access to health care, and fewer and less comprehensive social support services. These disadvantages for the financial well-being of low-income families are particularly evident in the 'Moving to Opportunity' experiment. In a real-world experiment conducted by the United States Department of Housing and Urban Development from 1994 to 1998, a random selection of families living in high-poverty urban neighbourhoods in five large cities received housing vouchers that allowed them to move to a better neighbourhood. Following up with the families shows that children who were small when the families moved benefited the most from the move with regard to their financial prospects. As adults they have higher incomes, live in better neighbourhoods, and in more stable families. In addition, the improved environment benefited the families' subjective well-being, mental and physical health (Chetty et al., 2016). These findings point to the possibilities of social-sector programmes, such as voucher or matched savings programmes, for helping low-income families build assets and afford to live in less poverty-stricken neighbourhoods.

26.3.2 Financial Literacy

Low-income households are not only characterized by limited financial resources. Lower earnings have been associated with lower levels of formal education and lower levels of financial literacy. Among low-income households, financial literacy is high with regard to daily financial management, such as budgeting, finding additional sources of income, and managing credit constraints. There is a good understanding of relevant social-sector programmes and banking services that these households use regularly, yet low-income individuals and families have been found to lack financial literacy with regard to financial planning and knowledge of the larger scope of policies and procedures of financial services (Buckland, 2010).

These problems are frequently observed among low-income women, particularly with regard to a lack of retirement planning (Lusardi & Mitchell, 2008). In data from German households, this link has been evident in the low take-up of government subsidies for private retirement savings, even though this option is targeted to lower-income individuals and families (Bucher-Koenen & Lusardi, 2011). Lower financial literacy is also associated with lower access to online financial information and less skill in using online financial services, such as electronic banking. Field data show that, while developing these skills requires intensive interventions that combine technological and financial literacy training to be effective, there is much interest from individuals with limited online skill in such training (Servon & Kaestner, 2008). In a review and meta-analysis of the effectiveness of financial literacy interventions, Fernandes, Lynch Jr., and Netemeyer (2014) provide a summary of current studies and document that low-income households show weaker responses in their financial behaviours, compared to general population samples, even after financial literacy interventions.

These findings have resulted, at the government level, in the creation of the Consumer Financial Protection Bureau in the United States and of the Financial Conduct Authority in the United Kingdom. These agencies are charged with defending consumer rights in the financial market place (Smith & Zywicki, 2015). Their particular focus is on safeguarding vulnerable population groups and their influence is visible in the design of an increasing number of financial products, such as credit card statements and mortgage contracts. With regard to credit card statements, for instance, the newly added information about how to pay off their balance in 36 months has helped consumers with reducing their credit card debt (Jones, Loibl, & Tennyson, forthcoming). In addition to their regulatory powers, the success of these agencies coincides with their interest in implementing 'nudges' from the behavioural economics literature.

26.3.3 Margins of Error

A number of studies suggest that behavioural biases in financial decision-making do not differ for people in low-income compared to higher-income households. Based on environmental as well as personal characteristics, however, financial behaviours among low-income individuals and families can be characterized as having 'narrow margins of error' (Bertrand et al., 2004; Bertrand, Mullainathan, & Shafir, 2006). This means that people with low earnings have less room for financial mistakes, and, if financial mistakes do occur, they tend to result in more serious outcomes, compared to those of wealthier households (Mani et al., 2013). For instance, adjustable rate mortgages with ballooning monthly mortgage payments can quickly become unmanageable for lower-income households, resulting in mortgage default and loss of the home (Moulton, Collins, Loibl, & Samek, 2015).

If biases and behaviours are no different from those of average people, simple interventions that focus on 'small situational barriers' can be effective. For instance, complicated fee schedules, inconvenient opening hours, and unfriendly loan officers are psychological barriers that prevent low-income individuals from using the banking services of mainstream financial institutions (Bertrand et al., 2006). Successful interventions may also engage mainstream financial institutions in social-sector programmes, such as matched savings account programmes, to help build trust between the low-income individual and the banking institution. Low-income individuals are also more likely to engage with the formal banking sector if welfare payments are deposited in bank accounts. This assumption will be tested in the 'Universal Credit' scheme that is to be rolled out in the United Kingdom over the next few years. Instead of housing benefits being paid to the landlord, they will be deposited monthly in the consumer's account.

26.3.4   *Resource Scarcity*

Scarcity describes how pressing demands make low-income individuals and families limit their focus on solving the most urgent problems while neglecting others. This behaviour has been described in a ground-breaking study by Shah et al. (2012). For instance, low-income homeowners may neglect regular, smaller home repairs because they are trying to make the monthly mortgage payment. They may wait until a small problem becomes a costly home maintenance item. Termed 'attentional neglect', this behaviour can also explain the use of high-cost short-term loans from payday lenders or loan sharks. The loan makes it easier to meet today's needs, which seem more pressing, and lessens the likelihood of weighing costs and benefits (Shah et al., 2012).

Laboratory experiments support this observation by showing that scarcity creates a focus on immediate and pressing expenses and, in turn, encourages the tendency to borrow. The proposed mechanism producing this outcome is that low-income individuals engage more strongly with financial problems, consequently using attentional resources and tiring the individual. Less energy is left for other problems, which then receive less attention (Shah et al., 2012). This is evident in a number of financial decisions, including saving too little, exposing children to food insecurity, and overlooking choices that would lead to improved health and higher education. Shah and colleagues argue that the scarcity-induced focus is not necessarily myopic decision-making or present-biased time preferences. It is rather the most 'convenient response to pressing demands'.

Digging deeper into the consequences of scarcity, reduced cognitive capacity has been found to influence financial decisions among low-income individuals and families. Mani et al. (2013) describe how financial problems capture attention and consume mental strength by triggering intrusive thoughts. This process reduces cognitive resources, leaving less energy for other tasks.

For instance, limited income requires difficult trade-offs on how to use disposable income. In addition, low-income households face larger credit constraints and a larger number of the kinds of risks that cannot easily be mitigated or eliminated, such as the risk of job loss, ill health, or eviction from housing. As a result, low-income households are less able to control their financial circumstances (Haushofer & Fehr, 2014).

In this context, cognitive capacity refers to the cognitive load caused by constant and distracting financial concerns. These concerns use up strength and leave fewer mental resources to allow for full consideration of other, less pressing problems (Mani et al., 2013). This understanding of the depletion of mental functioning of people in low-income circumstances aligns with the limited-resource model of self-control (Vohs, 2013) as well as with the notion that it harms the ability to exercise self-control (Bernheim, Ray, & Yeltekin, 2013).

In laboratory studies, Mani et al. (2013) show that financial challenges can have a different impact on the energy-levels of low-income and higher-income persons. These findings are confirmed in a field study comparing cognitive resources among farmers before and after they received the money for their annual harvest. Challenging financial conditions pre-harvest can result in lower mental resources. Mani et al. conclude that low-income households not only deal with financial, but also with cognitive, shortfalls. Policy interventions should take this into account. Interventions that simplify tasks and are carefully timed are most important: default settings, reminders, nudges for planning, low-literacy forms and texts, and simple rules in welfare pro-grammes. Ideally, interventions are aligned with less stressful times in the lives of low-income individuals and families.

26.3.5   Interrelation with Decision-Making

Another attempt to understand the mental processes of low-income individuals focuses on the question of whether low-income status reinforces itself through stress, unhappiness, fear, and anxiety. Haushofer and Fehr (2014) show that the demands faced by low-income households lead to short-sighted, risk-averse decisions, limited attention, and a preference for habitual behaviours. It is a circular process, which can worsen an individual's financial situation.

The cycle starts with individuals and families in poverty tending to be less tol-erant of risk and less able to take advantage of larger, future financial rewards than are households above the poverty level. It is well documented that subjective dis-count rates, which are a measure of a person's time horizon, increase with increasing liquidity constraints. Liquidity constraints also lead households to avoid risk. A safely received payment today helps meet pressing financial demands and offset other, less manageable financial risks. Therefore, it may be preferred over a larger, less costly payment in the future. Haushofer and Fehr (2014) emphasize that time and risk tol-erance does not reflect personality characteristics, but is rather a result of the life circumstances of low-income individuals and families.

This cycle continues in that poverty, with its limited access to credit and its larger number of financial risks, not only increases the household's material vulnerability, but also affects the family's mental well-being. Higher levels of stress and feelings of unhappiness, fear, or anxiety change low-income individuals: these factors cause higher levels of risk aversion and an increase in time discounting.

This understanding leads to the suggestion that, for interventions to be effective, they have to target the 'psychological costs of poverty' (Haushofer & Fehr, 2014). Commitment savings accounts and reminders to save are suggested as examples of small nudges. A successful example is a community-based, matched savings pro-gramme for individuals at the poverty level. Widely offered in the United States (Office of Community Services, 2012), savers typically save $1,000 over two years and receive a $2 match for each $1 saved. Such programs tend to include mandatory finan-cial education workshops and credit counselling. This type of savings programme supports the efforts of low-income individuals and families to find better housing in safer neighbourhoods, to get more education, and to start small businesses.

26.4   VULNERABLE POPULATION GROUPS

This section provides examples of the theories presented in the previous section. Three population groups, older adults, children, and single mothers, are particu-larly vulnerable to financial hardship. Their financial decisions and behaviours are described in this section.

26.4.1 Older Adults

Despite a growing body of research on poverty, little attention has been devoted to examining resource scarcity in older age. Difficulties adjusting to the lower pension income in early retirement, higher health care expenses, increasing demands to pay a contribution towards the cost of care (e.g., for long-term care), and the need to modify the home to meet changing health needs are reasons for tight financial situations in older age (Bucher-Koenen & Lusardi, 2011; van Rooij, Lusardi, & Alessie, 2011). In addition, an increasing number of older adults carry mortgage debt into retirement and have to service consumer debt that they had accumulated earlier in life. The reduction or slower adjustment of state pensions to general increases in cost of living has led in recent years to declines in purchase power, and the volatility of financial markets hampers financial planning. Many older adults are hesitant to seek professional help early, resulting in higher average debt burdens (Liersch, 2013). All of these factors add to the financial challenges confronted by older adults today more so than in the past. As a result, financial difficulties and indebtedness in older age are expected to intensify. In Germany, for example, no other age group shows faster growing poverty rates than the group of older adults (Krause, Schneider, Stilling, & Woltering, 2015). In 2016 only, the number of personal insolvencies among adults over 60 grew by 14%, to 10,683 cases. It is the second year with growing insolvencies among older adults, while the number of insolvencies among all other age groups is decreasing, according to industry groups. In the Netherlands older-aged debtors grew from 3% of clients at debt advisory services in 2008 to 8% in 2012 (Madern, 2014).

The consequences of financial distress can be severe in older age. An example of how financial distress can lead to decisions in older age that are focused on relieving short-term financial pressures while neglecting to take into account longer-term financial needs, are equity release schemes, such as lifetime mortgages and home reversion mortgages. Equity release schemes allow older homeowners over the age of 55 to borrow against the equity in their homes. There are at least two concerns with this increasingly popular financial product for 'house rich, cash poor' older adults. One concern relates to the fact that equity release schemes tend to be more expensive compared to other home loans, or compared to the costs of selling and moving to a smaller home. Lenders may only release 60–80% of a home's market value, depending on the age and financial standing of a borrower. Upfront fees are relatively high, including lender fees, upfront mortgage insurance, and closing costs. Older adults in financial distress may opt to use the equity-release loan to pay for these expenses. During the term of the equity release scheme, interest and mortgage insurance premiums accumulate, which further reduce the payout (The Money Advice Service, 2015).

A second concern with this financial product is the fact that the majority of borrowers decide, where possible, to take a lump sum payout rather than a line of credit or a guaranteed monthly payment (Fox O'Mahony & Overton, 2014). A fair amount of financial skill and planning is required to make the lump sum payout last as long as possible and to have funds available when later-life expenses like long-term care become necessary. In addition, older adults tend to have few options for responding to liquidity constraints once the lump sum is spent; for instance, they may not be healthy enough to accept a job for additional income (Lusardi, 2012). Because of these characteristics, the number of older adults who experience financial distress despite having released equity in their homes has been increasing along with the popularity of the product. Often, it is the only asset left in an aging, financially-distressed household (Fox O'Mahony & Overton, 2015).

In addition to affecting financial decision-making, financial distress in older adults has been associated with loneliness and isolation from family and social networks (Hawkley & Cacioppo, 2007). It is also linked with older adults' mental health, including self-esteem, morale, depression, and anxiety. Physical health is also affected when financial problems cause food insecurity, fuel poverty, avoidance of medical procedures, and failure to take medicine as prescribed. As a result, poverty can reduce a person's life expectancy (Kulkarni, Levin-Rector, Ezzati, & Murray, 2011).

26.4.2 Children

This section inquires whether economic socialization differs for children of low-income families (Webley & Nyhus, 2013). Two different views provide insight into this question: an economic socialization view and an institutional view (Elliott, Webley, & Friedline, 2011). The economic socialization position posits that families are the main means for children to learn about money and practise financial behaviours. Parents explain financial concepts to children and children learn by observing how their parents make financial decisions (Friedline, 2012).

The institutional position, however, argues that this may not be enough. According to this view, children of low-income families are 'doubly disadvantaged' (Webley & Nyhus, 2013, p. 21). In general, parents vary in the attention they devote to their children, in their level of financial literacy, and in their ideas about when and how children should begin using financial services. In addition, due to resource scarcity and differing decision-making processes, adults in low-income families tend to use fewer of the services of mainstream financial institutions than families with high incomes. As a result, children of low-income families are likely to be exposed to limited varieties of financial resources and have fewer opportunities to practise financial behaviours. These differences can 'produce gaps in children's capabilities that translate into financial disadvantage' and are evident, for instance, in their having less familiarity with banking services, such as using a savings account from an early age (Friedline, 2012).

Structured children's savings accounts have been suggested as a solution to help children save at an early age and independently from their parents. Children's accounts, which children manage and control, can have a long-term impact. Low-income children who have savings in their own name have been shown to have significantly higher rates of university enrolment and degree attainment. For example, data from the United States show that low-income children with designated savings for higher education of up to $500 before they enter university, are over three times more likely to enrol in university and four times more likely to gradate with a degree than a child without a school savings account (Elliott, Song, & Nam, 2013). In wealthier households, by contrast, the parents' net worth, rather than children's savings, predict enrolment and degree attainment at university (Elliott, Destin, & Friedline, 2011).

26.4.3 Single Mothers

Single motherhood has been steadily increasing in western societies. The rise in divorce rates and births outside marriage, the latter currently being at 40% in the European Union (Eurostat, 2012b), leads to single-parent families that are most often headed by a mother (Rousou, Kouta, Middleton, & Karanikola, 2013).

The focus on single mothers is also warranted because they experience particularly high levels of financial hardship. In addition, financial stress is the strongest and most consistent predictor of elevated levels of anxiety, depression, and health problems among single mothers (Bull & Mittelmark, 2009; Olson & Banyard, 1993). There are several facets to the link between financial distress and the well-being of single mothers.

First, the association between financial distress and well-being is stronger for single mothers living in poverty. Single mothers tend to constitute a large portion of the poorest population groups across countries. Across Europe, nearly half of single-parent families are at risk of poverty, compared to only about 20% of families with two adults (Eurostat, 2011). Diary studies show that meeting basic needs, such as food security and payment of utility bills, are among their main financial concerns (Olson & Banyard, 1993).

Second, single mothers are less likely than married mothers to be employed full-time and, if they have employment, they tend to work in lower-paid professions. Earned income and the supportive nature of a work environment are missed among single mothers. In addition, the dual responsibility of caring for and providing for children causes work-family conflicts for many single mothers (Bull & Mittelmark, 2009; Whitehead, Burström, & Diderichsen, 2000).

Third, single mothers have smaller social networks compared to mothers living with a spouse or partner. This increases single mothers' vulnerability to financial shocks and decreases the margin for financial errors. Fourth, single mothers are the sole caretakers for their families. Child-related stress is greater with young children and increases with the number of children. Stress directly influences single mothers' decision-making ability when coping with financial hardship (Hope, Power, & Rodgers, 1999). Day-to-day financial pressures lead to short-sighted, risk-averse decisions and limited attention to longer-term financial goals.

Financial stressors have both short- and long-term consequences on the well-being of single mothers. In the short term, financial hardship influences mental and physical health, for instance, when the mother does not see a physician as often as needed. Long-term health effects have been documented for single mothers after a divorce. These mothers tend to be more likely to develop chronic illnesses after several years, especially in financial hardship situations (Rousou et al., 2013). By contrast, diary studies document the hands-on, self-reliant strategies of single mothers. They respond to financial hardship by taking action, such as budgeting carefully, negotiating with creditors, and stretching resources as much as possible (Olson & Banyard, 1993).

Taking a broader view, Edin and her team document the important role of financial stability when low-income mothers consider marriage (Edin, Kefalas, & Reed, 2004). Besides the quality of the relationship, financial stability is considered necessary for a stable marriage. Ownership of a home, a car, and furniture, and having some savings and the means to afford a nice wedding are financial goals for low-income mothers and their partners before they decide to actually get married.

26.5   POLICY IMPLICATIONS

Individuals and families who experience deprivation and financial distress have been at the focus of regulatory interventions (Willis, 2008). The creation of consumer financial protection agencies at the government level document the public desire to regulate the financial marketplace, in addition to providing financial information and education in an accessible manner to vulnerable population groups. Both regulatory and educational efforts are furthered by the growing number of insights from behavioural economics research (Halpern, 2014). For instance, the labelling of cash transfers to older adults in the UK as 'Winter Fuel Payment' resulted in about half of the cash transfer actually being used on fuel; what was expected was 3%. As the use of the cash transfer was not restricted to fuel, the policy documents the effectiveness of labelling for directing behaviour (Beatty, Blow, Crossley, & O'Dea, 2014). Another example for interventions at the intersection of economics and psychology is children savings accounts held in the children's own names. Mental accounting has been shown to strengthen children's feeling of ownership and can prevent parents from using the funds for other purposes in financial-distress situations (Friedline, 2014).

26.6   SUMMARY

This chapter provides an overview of how low-income individuals and families make financial decisions. These decisions are influenced by the financial environment, the level of financial literacy, and a range of linked and circular mental processes. Limited room for financial mistakes, resource scarcity, and a tendency towards present-biased, risk-averse decisions are typical of individuals and families living in poverty. Three population groups are particularly vulnerable to financial hardship. Older adults are vulnerable to financial distress because of a combination of lower financial literacy and unique psychological characteristics. These include the consequences of cognitive decline, a stronger reliance on emotions, and the guidance of past experiences. Another group vulnerable to financial hardship is children. Their financial learning is equally dependent on their parents' status as role models and their access to and familiarity with institutional resources. In this view, children of low-income families are 'doubly disadvantaged' because they may only be exposed to limited varieties of financial resources and have fewer opportunities to practise financial behaviours. A third group is single mothers, whose well-being is strongly and consistently dependent on their financial situation. Their lower-income, smaller support networks, and sole responsibility for caring for their children directly affect their financial decision-making.

REVIEW QUESTIONS

1. Describe how environmental factors affect the financial decision-making of people living in poverty.
2. Give three examples of mental processes that affect financial decisions made by low-income individuals.

3. Explain why low-income children are 'doubly disadvantaged' with regard to financial learning.
4. Why are single mothers more likely than others to experience financial hardship and a lower level of well-being?

REFERENCES

Atkinson, A. B., & Marlier, E. (2010). *Income and living conditions in Europe.* Luxembourg: Publications Office of the European Union.

Barr, M. S. (2012). *No slack: The financial lives of low-income Americans.* Washington, DC: Brookings Institution Press.

Beatty, T. K. M., Blow, L., Crossley, T. F., & O'Dea, C. (2014). Cash by any other name? Evidence on labeling from the UK Winter Fuel Payment. *Journal of Public Economics, 118*(October), 86–96.

Bernheim, B. D., Ray, D., & Yeltekin, S. (2013). *Poverty and self-control* (Vol. January). Cambridge, MA: National Bureau of Economic Research.

Bertrand, M., Mullainathan, S., & Shafir, E. (2004). A behavioral-economics view of poverty. *American Economic Review, 94*(2), 419–423.

Bertrand, M., Mullainathan, S., & Shafir, E. (2006). Behavioral economics and marketing in aid of decision making among the poor. *Journal of Public Policy & Marketing, 25*(1), 8–23.

Bucher-Koenen, T., & Lusardi, A. (2011). Financial literacy and retirement planning in Germany. *Journal of Pension Economics and Finance, 10*(4), 565–584.

Buckland, J. (2010). Are low-income Canadians financially literate? Placing financial literacy in the context of personal and structural constraints. *Adult Education Quarterly, 60*(4), 357–376.

Bull, T., & Mittelmark, M. B. (2009). Work life and mental wellbeing of single and non-single working mothers in Scandinavia. *Scandinavian Journal of Public Health, 37*, 562–568.

Chetty, R., Hendren, N., & Katz, L. F. (2016). The effects of exposure to better neighborhoods on children: New evidence from the Moving to Opportunity experiment. *American Economic Review, 106*(4), 855–902.

Edin, K., Kefalas, M. J., & Reed, J. M. (2004). Peek inside the black box: What marriage means for poor unmarried parents. *Journal of Marriage and Family, 66*(4), 1007–1014.

Elliott, W., Destin, M., & Friedline, T. (2011). Taking stock of ten years of research on the relationship between assets and children's educational outcomes: Implications for theory, policy and intervention. *Children and Youth Services Review, 33*(11), 2312–2328.

Elliott, W., Song, H.-A., & Nam, I. (2013). Small-dollar children's savings accounts and children's college outcomes by income level. *Children and Youth Services Review, 35*(3), 560–571.

Elliott, W., Webley, P., & Friedline, T. (2011). *Two accounts for why adolescent savings is predictive of young adult savings: An economic socialization perspective and an institutional perspective.* St. Louis: Center for Social Development, Washington University of St. Louis.

Eurostat. (2011). *Population at risk of poverty or social exclusion by household type (%), EU-27, 2011.* http://ec.europa.eu/eurostat/statistics-explained/index.php/File:Population_at_risk_of_poverty_or_social_exclusion_by_household_type_(%25),_EU-27,_2011.png.

Eurostat. (2012a). *Measuring material deprivation in the EU: Indicators for the whole population and child-specific indicators.* http://ec.europa.eu/eurostat/documents/3888793/5853037/KS-RA-12-018-EN.PDF.

Eurostat. (2012b). *Share of live births outside marriage.* http://ec.europa.eu/eurostat/tgm/table.do?tab=table&plugin=1&language=en&pcode=tps00018.

Eurostat. (2016). *People at risk of poverty or social exclusion.* http://ec.europa.eu/eurostat/statistics-explained/index.php/People_at_risk_of_poverty_or_social_exclusion.

Fernandes, D., Lynch Jr. J. G., & Netemeyer, R. G. (2014). Financial literacy, financial education, and downstream financial behaviors. *Management Science, 60*(8), 1861–1883.

Fox O'Mahony, L., & Overton, L. (2014). Financial advice, differentiated consumers, and the regulation of equity-release transactions. *Journal of Law and Society, 41*(3), 446–469.

Fox O'Mahony, L., & Overton, L. (2015). Asset-based welfare, equity release and the meaning of the owened home. *Housing Studies, 30*(3), 392–412.

Friedline, T. (2012). Predicting children's savings: The role of parents' savings for transferring financial advantage and opportunities for financial inclusion. *Children and Youth Services Review, 34,* 144–154.

Friedline, T. (2014). The independent effects of savings accounts in children's names on their savings outcomes in young adulthood. *Journal of Financial Counseling and Planning, 25*(1), 69–89.

Goebel, J., & Grabka, M. M. (2011). Zur Entwicklung der Altersarmut in Deutschland. *DIW Wochenbericht, 25,* 3–16.

Gundersen, C. G., & Ziliak, J. P. (2014). *Childhood food insecurity in the U.S.: Trends, causes, and policy options* (Vol. Fall). Princeton, NJ: Princeton University Press.

Haisley, E., Mostafa, R., & Loewenstein, G. (2008). Myopic risk-seeking: The impact of narrow decision bracketing on lottery play. *Journal of Risk and Uncertainty, 37*(1), 57–75.

Halpern, D. (2014). *What works? Evidence for decision makers.* London: United Kingdom Cabinet Office.

Haushofer, J., & Fehr, E. (2014). On the psychology of poverty. *Science, 344*(6186), 862–867.

Hawkley, L. C., & Cacioppo, J. T. (2007). Aging and loneliness: Downhill quickly? *Current Directions in Psychological Science, 16*(4), 187–191.

Hope, S., Power, C., & Rodgers, B. (1999). Does financial hardship account for elevated psychological distress in lone mothers? *Social Science and Medicine, 49*(12), 1637–1649.

Jones, L. E., Loibl, C., & Tennyson, S. (forthcoming). Effects of informational nudges on consumer debt repayment behaviors. *Journal of Economic Psychology.*

Krause, N. R., Schneider, U., Stilling, G., & Woltering, C. (2015). *Die zerklüftete Republik. Bericht zur regionalen Armutsentwicklung in Deutschland 2014.* Berlin: Deutscher Paritätischer Wohlfahrtsverband Gesamtverband e.V.

Kulkarni, S. C., Levin-Rector, A., Ezzati, M., & Murray, C. J. L. (2011). Falling behind: Life expectancy in US counties from 2000 to 2007 in an international context. *Population Health Metrics, 9*(16), 1–12.

Liersch, A. (2013). Überschuldungsstatistik 2012: Die amtliche Statistik zur Situation überschuldeter Personen in Deutschland [Over-indebtedness statistics 2012: The federal statistical report on the situation of over-indebted individuals in Germany]. *Wirtschaft und Statistik, November,* 795–804.

Loibl, C., Grinstein-Weiss, M., Zhan, M., & Red Bird, B. (2010). More than a penny saved: Long-term changes in behavior among savings program participants. *Journal of Consumer Affairs, 44*(Spring), 98–126.

Lusardi, A. (2012). Financial literacy and financial decision-making in older adults. *Generations - Journal of the American Society on Aging, 36*(2), 25–32.

Lusardi, A., & Mitchell, O. S. (2008). Planning and financial literacy: How do women fare? *American Economic Review, 98*(2), 413–417.

Madern, T. (2014). *Overkoepelende blik op de omvang en preventie van schulden in Nederland.* Utrecht: Nationaal Instituut voor Budgetvoorlichting (Nibud).

Mani, A., Mullainathan, S., Shafir, E., & Zhao, J. (2013). Poverty impedes cognitive function. *Science, 341*(6149), 976–980.

Moulton, S., Collins, J. M., Loibl, C., & Samek, A. (2015). Effecty of monitoring on mortgage delinquency: Evidence from a randomized field study. *Journal of Policy Analysis and Management, 34*(1), 184–207.

Mullainathan, S., & Shafir, E. (2013). *Scarcity: Why having too little means so much.* New York: Times Books, Henry Holt and Company.

Noll, H.-H., & Weick, S. (2012). Altersarmut: Tendenz steigend. *Informationsdienst Soziale Indikatoren* (47), 1–7.

Office of Community Services. (2012). *Assets for Independence program: Status at the conclusion of the eleventh year; results through September 30, 2010.* Washington, DC: U.S. Department of Health and Human Services, Administration for Children and Families.

Olson, S. L., & Banyard, V. (1993). 'Stop the world so I can get off for a while:' Sources of daily stress in the lives of low-income single mothers of young children. *Family Relations, 42*(January), 50–56.

Rousou, E., Kouta, C., Middleton, N., & Karanikola, M. (2013). Single mothers' self-assessment of health: A systematic exploration of the literature. *International Nursing Review, 60,* 425–434.

Servon, L. J., & Kaestner, R. (2008). Consumer financial literacy and the impact of online banking on the financial behavior of lower-income bank customers. *Journal of Consumer Affairs, 42*(Summer), 271–305.

Shah, A. K., Mullainathan, S., & Shafir, E. (2012). Some consequences of having too little. *Science, 338*(November 02), 682–685.

Smith, A. C., & Zywicki, T. (2015). Behavior, paternalism, and policy: Evaluating consumer financial protection. *New York University Journal of Law and Liberty, 9,* 201.

Thaler, R. H., & Benartzi, S. (2004). Save More Tomorrow$^{(TM)}$: Using behavioral economics to increase employee saving. *Journal of Political Economy, 112*(1), S164–S187.

The Money Advice Service. (2015). *What is equity release?* London: The Money Advice Service.

U.S. Census Bureau. (2015). *Income, poverty and health insurance coverage in the United States: 2014.* Washington, DC: Government Printer.

U.S. Department of Health and Human Services. (2015). *2015 poverty guidelines.* Washington, DC: Government Printer.

van Rooij, M. C. J., Lusardi, A., & Alessie, R. J. M. (2011). Financial literacy and retirement planning in the Netherlands. *Journal of Economic Psychology, 32*(4), 593–608.

Van Zandt, S., & Rohe, W. M. (2006). Do first-time home buyers improve their neighborhood quality? *Journal of Urban Affairs, 28*(5), 491–510.

Vohs, K. D. (2013). The poor's poor mental power. *Science, 341*(30 August), 969–970.

Webley, P., & Nyhus, E. K. (2013). Economic socialization, saving and assets in European young adults. *Economics of Education Review, 33,* 19–30.

Whitehead, M., Burström, B., & Diderichsen, F. (2000). Social policies and the pathways to inequalities in health: A comparative analysis of lone mothers in Britain and Sweden. *Social Science & Medicine, 50*(2), 255–270.

Willis, L. (2008). Against financial-literacy education. *Iowa Law Review, 94*(1).

FURTHER READING

Elliott, W., Destin, M., & Friedline, T. (2011). Taking stock of ten years of research on the relationship between assets and children's educational outcomes: Implications for theory, policy and intervention. *Children and Youth Services Review, 33*(11), 2312–2328.

Fernandes, D., Lynch Jr. J. G., & Netemeyer, R. G. (2014). Financial literacy, financial education, and downstream financial behaviors. *Management Science, 60*(8), 1861–1883.

Lusardi, A., & Mitchell, O. S. (2008). Planning and financial literacy: How do women fare? *American Economic Review, 98*(2), 413–417.

Shah, A. K., Mullainathan, S., & Shafir, E. (2012). Some consequences of having too little. *Science, 338*(November 02), 682–685.

27 Economic Psychology and Pro-Environmental Behaviour

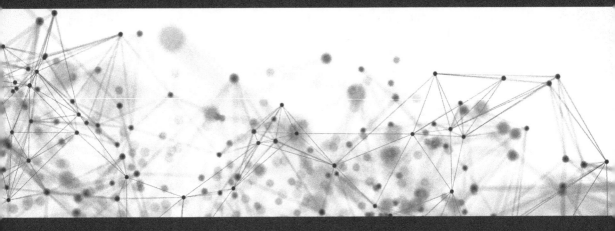

MICHEL HANDGRAAF, ANOUK GRIFFIOEN, JAN WILLEM BOLDERDIJK AND JOHN THØGERSEN

CHAPTER OUTLINE

LEARNING OUTCOMES

BY THE END OF THIS CHAPTER YOU SHOULD BE ABLE TO:

1. Review a range of studies and findings from recent economic psychology research in the environmental domain.
2. Consider environmental problems as large-scale social dilemmas, in which individuals have to trade off self-interest and collective interest, now and later.
3. Apply existing knowledge in the field of economic psychology to the domain of pro-environmental behaviour.

27.1 INTRODUCTION

In this chapter, we apply existing knowledge in the field of economic psychology to the domain of pro-environmental behaviour. In line with Stern (2000) and Lindenberg and Steg (2007, p. 118), we define environmental behaviour as 'all types of behaviour that changes the availability of materials or energy from the environment or alters the structure and dynamics of ecosystems or the biosphere'. Pro-environmental behaviour can be defined as behaviour that *improves* the quality of the environment or reduces a negative impact (Steg, Bolderdijk, Keizer, & Perlaviciute, 2014). The issue of climate change has recently become a primary focus of research in this domain, as it is generally seen as the most urgent and important problem related to the environment. Therefore, many of the examples given and research discussed here pertain to this specific problem. However, the economic psychology involved is equally relevant for other environmental problems, such as nature and resource conservation, the pollution of land, air, rivers and oceans, and the loss of species.

Evidence indicates that most people regard environmental issues as non-urgent and psychologically distant risks – spatially, temporally, and socially – which has led to deferred public decision-making about mitigation and adaptation responses (Leiserowitz, 2007). Moreover, even for people who do acknowledge the problem, this does not necessarily result in appropriate action, either because they view change as too costly in the short term, or because they are unaware of effective solutions or unable to implement them. Thus, any voluntary change in people's behaviour requires: (1) they believe there is a problem and, hence, experience a need for change; (2) they want to make changes; and (3) they are able to implement such changes. In each of these steps, psychological processes play a major role. Many of these processes manifest themselves as barriers to behaviour change (cf. Gifford's 'dragons of inaction', 2011), that may be difficult to overcome. Alternatively, some of these processes, notably problem awareness and goal intentions, may serve as positive motivators for change. The field of economic psychology, as discussed here, has generated a range of valuable concepts, theories and empirical insights useful when assessing the influence of such processes and translating them into effective policy.

We conceptualize environmental problems as large-scale social dilemmas, in which individuals have to trade off self-interest and collective interest, now and later. This requires them to deal with probabilities and complex information. In making those trade-offs, people do not rely solely on rational economic cost-benefit analyses. As has become clear throughout this book, rather (1) they use heuristics and are prone to biases that deviate from what theories based on the rationality assumption would predict (see e.g., Kahneman, 2003; Weber & Johnson, 2009), and (2) they consider other types of outcomes, such as social (how will my decisions influence the outcomes of others?) and normative (what will others think?) outcomes, in addition to possible financial and other private outcomes. Both reasons for not behaving like rational economic agents have been extensively studied by behavioural economists, economic and social psychologists, and decision scientists, and here we apply this knowledge to environmental behaviour.

27.2   BOUNDED RATIONALITY

There is extensive evidence that people are prone to systematic biases when they have to deal with probabilities and uncertainty, decisions over time, and complex information. In this section we link these biases to environmental behaviour.

27.2.1   *Perception and Evaluation of Environmental Issues*

Many environmental issues are shrouded in uncertainty: there is little exact knowledge about the effects of many types of pollution. Exact predictions about, for example, the local effects of climate change are currently impossible to make. People usually do not experience the negative effects of their behaviour on the environment, such as climate change, directly, as the changes occur too slowly for human perception. Moreover, large parts of the world are not yet strongly influenced by the indirect effects of climate change. As Weber (2006) notes, people can only learn about such risks through time-delayed, abstract, and often statistical information. This type of information is much less suitable to urge people into action than information that comes from direct experience. Thus, most people fail to be alarmed about the risk of environmental degradation and do not take precautions. Evolution has simply not prepared us to respond to such slow and distant risks. Indeed, people perceive climate change mainly as a threat to plants and animals and people elsewhere, but do not see it as a local issue affecting themselves, their family, and their community (Leiserowitz, 2007). This lack of perceived urgency is an important reason why the need to allocate resources to reduce these environmental impacts has a low priority for many people.

People also differ from person to person in how they deal with the same environmental risks. How people evaluate environmental problems can be captured in their environmental attitude. Eagly and Chaiken (1993, p. 1), define an attitude as 'a psychological tendency that is expressed by evaluating a particular entity with some degree of favor or disfavor'. With regard to environmental attitudes, the object of one's attitude is either the natural environment itself (or some aspects of it, e.g., air quality), or the attitude object is environmentally relevant behaviour (e.g., recycling or political activism). Environmental attitudes can be measured in many ways. Probably most used are environmental concern (Stern & Dietz, 1994) and the New Ecological Paradigm (NEP; Dunlap, Van Liere, Mertig, & Jones, 2000). One of the most influential theories in this field, which specifies an important role for attitudes on behaviour, is the Theory of Planned Behaviour (TPB; Ajzen, 1991). According to this theory, the most important predictors of behavioural intention are the attitude towards the behaviour, social norms and the perception of being able to carry out the behaviour. In a large meta-analysis, Bamberg and Moser (2007) found a mean correlation of $r = .42$ between pro-environmental attitude and pro-environmental behaviour, thus making pro-environmental attitude a very important factor in predicting the success of interventions.

27.2.2   *Resistance to Change*

Another important factor that influences people's behaviour is the general tendency to be change-averse – people dislike change. This is likely caused by a deeper and hard-wired dislike of uncertainty in general (Epstein, 1999): since change involves moving from a situation which is known to one that is less well known, change by definition introduces uncertainty. For investment decisions in the environmental domain, this uncertainty creates a threshold that needs to be crossed before people decide to change, which leads to a status quo bias (Kahneman, Knetsch, & Thaler, 1991). For example, although perhaps not energy-efficient, homeowners at least know how much money they are spending with their current heating system. To make investing in a more efficient system attractive enough, the new system has to do more than just improve their current outcomes, it must also compensate for this uncertainty threshold. The resulting status quo bias may manifest itself in the form of choice deferral, indecision, and procrastination, rather than in people making a definite choice against such a change (Anderson, 2003). Since sticking to the status quo usually means keeping all options open, this provides an extra reason for not investing: if a better alternative comes along, it remains an option to pick that alternative instead of accepting the current ones. The status quo bias has been established for climate change adaptation (Tam & McDaniels, 2013) and is likely an important reason why many people are reluctant to invest in fast-developing technologies like electric vehicles and solar panels.

The status quo bias also manifests itself through the 'default bias'. People tend to show a preference for an option that requires no action. Thus, whatever happens when no action is taken strongly predicts decision outcomes (Johnson & Goldstein, 2003). For example, in a study by Ebeling and Lotz (2015) on consumers' choice for renewable (green) versus conventional energy production, it turns out that setting the default choice to the more expensive 'green' energy (that is, where consumers have to actively opt out if they do not want it) increased the choice for the green option nearly tenfold. Defaults are effective for at least three reasons: (1) effort: the default requires no action and frees the consumer from laborious calculations; (2) implied endorsement: defaults are perceived as recommendations from experts or policy-makers; and (3) reference dependence: consumers adapt to the default, and see any negative departure from that as a loss. Since losses loom larger than gains (Kahneman et al., 1991), departing from the default means exposing oneself to a potential risk of losing. As can be inferred from these examples, policy-makers can make use of this bias to encourage pro-environmental behaviour by setting beneficial defaults, for example, requiring renewable energy to be the default option by energy suppliers (e.g., Toft, Schuitema & Thøgersen, 2014).

Environmental impacts often play out over long time scales. However, people tend to focus on their immediate concerns and discount future costs and benefits. Thus, even if future environmental outcomes are potentially catastrophic, they may not influence people's decisions about their energy use today (Hardisty & Weber, 2009). In general, this strong preference for now over later is problematic for pro-environmental decision-making: if people do not care enough for the future, investments in environmental measures are less likely to occur. One reason for this disproportionately large weight given to immediate outcomes is the fact that the future outcomes of decisions made today are never certain. Uncertainties exist both in the external world (new inventions, changing laws, future prices, effects of climate change) and within the decision-maker (changing preferences, the fact that one might not be there to enjoy future benefits). Thus, the fact that the immediate costs are often quite easy to estimate, whereas the future gains are uncertain, may negatively impact pro-environmental behaviour. Luckily, however, it seems that there are some individuals who are capable of factoring future consequences into their current considerations, and thus are less prone to discount delayed environmental consequences. One scale that measures such individual differences in preferences for now vs. the future, the Consideration of Future Consequences scale (CFC), has been linked to environmental decisions. Relative to people with low CFCs, people with high CFCs show stronger pro-environmental intentions and greater involvement in pro-environmental behaviour (Joireman, Lasane, Bennett, Richards, & Solaimani, 2001; Van Beek, Handgraaf, & Antonides, 2017). Similarly, people who have a strong affinity with future generations (Wade-Benzoni, 2008) also care more about future environmental outcomes.

Besides showcasing a somewhat reasonable tendency to discount the future in order to avoid uncertainty, people's patterns of preferences over time seem less logical. For instance, empirically observed discount rates are not constant over time, but seem to decline ('hyperbolic discounting'). For example, someone may prefer 10 euros today over 15 euros next week, yet prefer 15 euros in 5 weeks over 10 euros in 4 weeks. Thus, framing a decision as a trade-off between two future outcomes rather than between an immediate and a future outcome will diminish discounting (but see Sundblad, Biel, & Gärling (2011) who argue that environmental outcomes are not susceptible to this effect). Furthermore, intertemporal preferences vary across different types of choices: gains are discounted more than losses (the sign effect), and small amounts more than large amounts (the magnitude effect). When presented with sequences of multiple outcomes, people show a preference for increasing outcomes, which means that when able to choose several outcomes over a period of time they tend to 'save the best for last' (Frederick, Loewenstein, & O'Donoghue, 2002). The framing of a temporal decision in terms of acceleration vs. delay also matters: a delay frame ('How much extra would you want to receive to postpone a certain outcome?') produces higher discount rates than an accelerate frame ('How much would you want to pay to speed up a certain outcome?'; Weber et al., 2007).

These anomalies make it difficult to promote pro-environmental behaviour, since many pro-environmental decisions hardly fit what would seem the 'smart' and rational thing to do, and it is difficult to predict how people frame the decision themselves. On the other hand, however, knowledge about these anomalies can be of great benefit to policy-makers who want to try to minimize the negative effect of the general tendency to discount the future, for example, by pointing out that current investments in conservation measures lead to increasing patterns of outcomes over time, or by making informed decisions about how to frame an intervention in terms of gains or losses (e.g., Hardisty & Weber, 2009).

27.2.3   *Understanding, Knowledge and Feedback*

Even if people do experience a sense of urgency, have some understanding of environmental issues and intend to take action, they may not know *how* to do this (Ölander & Thøgersen, 1995). Gardner and Stern (2008) argue that people often misunderstand the effectiveness of their actions (see also Attari, DeKay, Davidson, & Bruine de Bruin, 2010). For example, turning off the lights when leaving a room is often considered an important way to save energy, but it actually saves relatively little. Such misunderstandings are not necessarily due to a lack of attention, intelligence or ability to find the information, but can also be caused by the fact that the information is presented in such a way that understanding is hindered. For example, Larrick and Soll (2008) show that people believe that gasoline consumption decreases linearly rather than nonlinearly as an automobile's gas mileage (in miles per gallon; mpg) increases. People do not sufficiently realize that switching from a 10 mpg car to a 15 mpg car yields much larger gas savings than switching from a 20 mpg car to a 25 mpg car. Consumers may thus erroneously assume that trading their already efficient car for an ultra-efficient car leads to more fuel savings than trading in their old SUV for a somewhat less inefficient SUV. Policy-makers can apply this insight: describing a vehicle's fuel efficiency in terms of fuel needed per unit of distance ('gallons per 100 miles) corrects this misperception and leads to more fuel-efficient choices (Schouten, Bolderdijk, & Steg, 2014). However, as Schultz (1999) suggests, knowledge on why and how to act is in itself not motivating, and for the information to actually translate into behaviour, motivation is necessary. Bolderdijk, Gorsira, Keizer and Steg (2013) find that only people with strong biospheric values (i.e., desirable goals, related to the interests of nonhuman species and the biosphere, which serve as a guiding principle for behaviour; Steg, De Groot, Dreijerink, Abrahamse, & Siero, 2011) respond to informational interventions. This suggests that these interventions are successful, not so much because they make people adjust their beliefs, but because they act as a reminder and make them more inclined to behave in accordance with values they already possess. A similar argument can be made for the pro-environmental attitudes, discussed earlier.

One way to motivate people to make pro-environmental decisions is by providing them with knowledge about the relationship between their actions and environmental impacts. This can be done through feedback (Dogan, Bolderdijk, & Steg, 2014; Grønhøj & Thøgersen, 2011). Feedback allows people to associate their behaviour with the environmental outcomes of this behaviour and allows them to make changes in the desired direction. As Abrahamse, Steg, Vlek and Rothengatter (2005) show in their extensive review, feedback is one of the more effective tools for reducing energy use. The way feedback is given is an important moderator of its effectiveness. In particular, the frequency of the feedback and the delay between behaviour and feedback are of paramount importance: the more frequent the feedback and the shorter the delay, the better the feedback works – frequent and immediate feedback enables people to associate cause (their behaviour) with a specific outcome (e.g., how much energy is used). Recent innovations in the field of smart metering allow for more precise and real-time feedback on energy use and costs. Many energy companies now offer much more sophisticated forms of feedback than the traditional monthly or yearly energy bill. Such feedback systems have been moderately successful, usually leading to savings of between 3 and 10%, and sometimes up to 15% (Abrahamse et al., 2005) or even 22% (Tiefenbeck et al., 2016).

27.3 THE ENVIRONMENT AS A SOCIAL DILEMMA

Most environmental problems can be characterized as large-scale social dilemmas (Dawes & Messick, 2000). These are situations in which there is a conflict between an individual's own interest and the interest of the larger group: Everyone is better off if more individuals would do the 'right thing', but for each individual a privately better outcome can always be gained by not cooperating ('defecting'). In the environmental domain, the structure of the social dilemma is as follows: If every individual reduces his or her environmental impact, this would be beneficial to the environment and thus for all individuals as well as future generations. However, if one individual decides not to reduce his or her environmental impact, this individual avoids the costs associated with doing so, and the individual's impact on the environment will be minimal. Hence, there is a personal incentive not to cooperate. Of course, if everyone defects, this does not bode well for the environment.

27.3.1 *Social Norms*

Despite the personal incentive not to cooperate, an average rate of cooperation of close to 50% is typical in social dilemma experiments (Sally, 1995). How come? Biel and Thøgersen (2007) suggest that social norms are an important reason for departure from rational choice in social dilemmas. In general, the opinions and behaviour of relevant others are an important factor in many situations. Thus, while defecting would be beneficial individually, the knowledge that others are also doing their fair share can motivate individuals to cooperate as well. There is an increasing volume of research demonstrating the usefulness of the social norms approach as a means to regulate environmental behaviour (Nolan, Schultz, Cialdini, Goldstein, & Griskevicius, 2008). In a field experiment (Schultz, Estrada, Schmitt, Sokoloski, & Silva-Send, 2015), feedback given with a descriptive social norm (i.e., whether or not the household was using more or less than a similar household) was effective, leading to a 7% reduction of energy use over 3 months, whereas simply giving feedback in terms of kW or costs was not effective. In many studies, social norms seem to act like a 'magnet': simply telling people what other people do (providing descriptive social norms) and what is commonly approved or disapproved of (providing injunctive social norms) has relatively strong and lasting positive effects on behaviour (Schultz, Nolan, Cialdini, Goldstein, & Griskevicius, 2007). It should be noted that in order to facilitate cooperation in social dilemmas (including pro-environmental behaviour) both descriptive norms *and* injunctive norms need to support cooperation (Thøgersen, 2006). According to Bicchieri (2006), a social norm is a behavioural rule for which a sufficiently large share of the population (1) knows the rule and knows that it applies to this particular situation, and (2) acknowledges the need for cooperation in social dilemmas and therefore prefers to cooperate. Whether such a preference for cooperation translates into actual behaviour depends on the belief of the individual that (1) a sufficient number of others will conform to the rule and (2) that a sufficient number of others expect them to conform to the rule in the situation. Thus, performance feedback may be even more effective if it is acknowledged by others, or if praise is given when positive goals are reached (Deci, Koestner, & Ryan, 1999; Handgraaf, Van Lidth de Jeude, & Appelt, 2013). Social recognition communicates an injunctive message; a reflection of what is approved or disapproved of in a given culture (Reno, Cialdini, & Kallgren, 1993). While social approval may be valued positively because it sometimes generates future benefits, it is believed that most people value social recognition positively (and disapproval negatively) for its own sake (Fehr & Falk, 2002).

Personal norms (Schwartz, 1977), are an individual's felt obligations toward a certain behaviour. Personal norms are important predictors of pro-environmental decisions and may differ between individuals (Bamberg & Moser, 2007). For example, people who have a highly pro-environmental personal norm may not be susceptible to any monetary incentive, since money is not the prime reason for their pro-environmental behaviour (Thøgersen, 1996). In fact, such people may respond negatively to financial incentives for behaviour they would display of their own accord anyway (crowding out; Bowles, 2008; Thøgersen, 1994). It is therefore important to know the personal norms of the target audience before starting an intervention.

Researchers who view pro-environmental behaviour primarily as caused by pro-social motivations, often base their research on the value–belief–norm theory of environmentalism (VBN theory; Stern, 2000) and the theory it is based on, the norm-activation model (NAM; Schwartz, 1977). VBN theory asserts that when individuals believe that something they value is threatened and that their actions can protect what they value, they will experience an obligation to take action. Accordingly, many studies provide evidence that positive moral norms contribute to pro-environmental behaviours like energy conservation (Black, Stern, & Elworth, 1985), recycling (Guagnano, Stern, & Dietz, 1995), travel mode choice (Hunecke, Blöbaum, Matthies, & Höger, 2001), and buying pro-environmental products (Thøgersen, 1999).

27.3.2   Self-Interest and Other-Oriented Motives in Social Dilemmas

However, of course, there are many environmentally relevant situations where the norm does not favour cooperation, or moral norms are lacking, where people collectively choose to defect rather than to cooperate. Self-interest is frequently assumed to be the main motivator for defecting in social dilemmas, both in economic theory and in the worldview of many individuals (Epley & Dunning, 2000). As Miller (1999) argues, self-interest is not per se the true underlying motive, but rather a social norm: Since people tend to think that it is normal to behave in a self-interested manner they therefore find it difficult to act for the greater good, even when such behaviour is in line with their private attitudes. Moreover, others may respond negatively to people who undertake actions that are against their own self-interest (Herrmann, Thöni, & Gächter, 2008). Violating this norm thus comes with psychological discomfort, which may weaken the link between pro-environmental attitudes and actual behaviour. Individuals may try to cope with this psychological discomfort by emphasizing selfish reasons and de-emphasizing unselfish reasons for this behaviour (Thøgersen, 2011).

Additionally, this norm of self-interest leads people to expect self-interested behaviour from others in social dilemmas, and can thus become a self-fulfilling prophecy – such expectations undermine trust in others to cooperate. People are unlikely to cooperate if they think that they are the only one cooperating (the 'Sucker Effect'; Kerr, 1983) or if they think that the effect of their cooperation is too small to matter (the 'Drop in the Bucket Effect'; Larrick & Soll, 2008). For example, consumers may erroneously assume that public endorsement of various environmental policies is low, leading them to 'defect' although they actually support the policy. By correcting these misperceptions, policy-makers may be able to restore trust and facilitate cooperation.

Despite this persistent self-fulfilling prophecy, research shows that in many situations in which self-interest could play a role, people's behaviour actually depends on other, more pro-social motivations. Circumstances may prime social or moral norms, as discussed earlier. For example, in cases where others' or the common interest are also at stake (like sharing a meal with friends, or the bill afterwards), people are definitely not expected to act in a self-interested manner. Thus, the norm of self-interest only guides behaviour when it is activated in the situation (Biel & Thøgersen, 2007). In a study by Nolan et al. (2008), the very same people that rated financial savings as a more important motivator for their own pro-environmental behaviour, were in reality more strongly influenced by social norms (information about their neighbour's energy conservation) than by financial cues. Correspondingly, in increasingly influential theories from Economic Psychology/Behavioural Economics, the assumption that people are self-interested, rational, maximizing agents has been relaxed (Fehr & Fischbacher, 2002). People also care for their outcomes relative to others and even about others' outcomes per se.

These motivations have been referred to by many different names, including: social preferences, social motives, other-regarding preferences, welfare trade-off ratios, and Social Value Orientation (SVO; Murphy, Ackermann, & Handgraaf, 2011). Within the SVO framework it is assumed that people vary in their motivations or goals when evaluating different resource allocations between themselves and others. For example, an individual may try to maximize her own payoff (individualistic), maximize the difference between her own and others' outcomes (competitive), minimize the difference between her own and others' payoff (inequality averse), or maximize joint pay-offs (pro-social). It has been shown that such SVOs influence the extent to which people are willing to cooperate in the social dilemma represented by the environment (Schultz, 2001). Gärling, Fujii, Gärling and Jakobsson (2003) find that pro-selfs are influenced more by environmental consequences for themselves, whereas pro-socials focus more on the joint outcomes.

27.3.3 Appealing to Self-Interest by Means of Financial Incentives

Interventions focused on changing behaviour and investment decisions in the environmental domain traditionally focus on monetary rewards, for example, to encourage energy conservation (Abrahamse et al., 2005). Indeed, monetary incentives are one way for policy-makers to resolve or reduce the social dilemma: they make cooperation individually (more) rewarding. Policy-makers seem to prefer this approach (Evans, McMeekin, & Southerton, 2012). There are also many examples of monetary incentives as successful drivers of pro-environmental behaviour (Stern, 1999), such as the successful government subsidy schemes on solar panels, hybrid and electric vehicles, fines on pollution and per-can fees for trash disposal.

However, in addition to the positive effects, monetary incentives may have negative side effects that diminish their effectiveness (Bowles, 2008; Fehr & Falk, 2002). As Bolderdijk and Steg (2015) argue, incentives not only have an instrumental function (they represent value), but they also have a psychological impact. Among others, they can crowd out intrinsic motivation, and lead to a cost/benefit mindset (Deci et al., 1999). This is especially problematic when a cost/benefit analysis favours the wrong behaviour, which is frequently the case when small amounts of money are at stake. To illustrate, a 50% reduction in household electricity use generally only leads to saving tens of euros per month (VaasaETT, 2012), and this may not be a sufficient driver for behaviour change. In fact, it has been shown that small energy savings are perceived as being more 'worthwhile' when they are expressed in grams CO_2 saved instead of equivalent monetary savings (Dogan, Bolderdijk, & Steg, 2014). Financial disincentives, on the other hand, can even be counterproductive as people may justify their norm-violating behaviour – 'a fine is a price' (Gneezy & Rustichini, 2000). Also, from a policy standpoint, disincentives restrict people's freedom, and thus may produce resistance (Schuitema, Steg, & Rothengatter, 2010).

Moreover, for many types of pro-environmental behaviour, financial incentives are not borne by the person responsible for the behaviour. For example, often people (renters, hotel guests, employees) do not pay directly for how much energy or water they use (Griffioen, Handgraaf, & Antonides, forthcoming; Randolph & Troy, 2008). Not coincidentally, the highest levels of energy or water use often occur in these situations (Kempton, Darley, & Stern, 1992). Of course adding (financial) incentives to these situations (e.g., by rewarding energy-conscious employees) could work, but this is frequently impractical and requires costly monitoring. Thus, incentives may be very effective in specific situations where it is easy to employ financial incentives, such as tax schemes, and focused on one-off purchases. When targeting more habitual behaviour, financial incentives may be prone to the discussed negative side effects and other methods may be more appropriate.

27.4   CONCLUSION

In this chapter we have discussed a large number of theories and findings from economic psychology that are relevant for behaviour in the environmental domain. It is clear that there is currently a large base of knowledge that can help policy-makers create more successful interventions. At the same time, however, solving this multi-faceted problem, with its social dilemma aspects, temporal trade-offs, the uncertainty and risk involved, and intricately linked multitude of relevant behaviours remains a huge challenge. As argued, changing voluntary environmental behaviour requires that people believe there is a problem, want to make changes and have the ability to implement those changes. The psychological factors described in this chapter play a major role in each of these steps, and we therefore believe that knowledge about these factors and their interplay is of paramount importance.

It is important to note that many questions have not been answered yet, in particular about the interaction of the different factors, their impact in the real world, and the relationships between different behaviours. For example, studies have shown that simply hoping for additive effects of combined interventions is overly simplistic and that combining two factors that in isolation have positive effects may actually lead to a cancelling out of both (e.g., Schwartz, Bruine de Bruin, Fischoff, & Lave, 2015). Hence, it is important to gain a better understanding of the way these factors work when simultaneously present. Another complication is that interventions targeting specific pro-environmental behaviour may influence related behaviours, which is commonly referred to as behavioural spillover. The literature on this topic is as yet quite mixed. Some studies show evidence for positive spillover: one pro-environmental behaviour leads to other pro-environmental behaviours (Lanzini & Thøgersen, 2014), where others show negative spillover, when one pro-environmental behaviour inhibits other pro-environmental behaviours (Thøgersen & Crompton, 2009). Attempts have been made to make sense of these seemingly contrasting results and variables that may influence the direction of spillover have been suggested (see e.g., Mullen & Monin, 2016; Truelove, Carrico, Weber, Raimi, & Vandenbergh, 2014).

Furthermore, although knowledge does exist that specifies the role of the discussed psychological factors for environmental behaviour, many of them have not been properly tested in the field. Implementation on a larger scale and assessing the effectiveness of (combinations of) interventions in practice in, for example, randomized controlled trials is rare (for exceptions, see Allcott, 2011). Promising in this respect is the recent increasing recognition of the importance of behavioural factors by policy-makers. Many governments have recently introduced Behavioural Intervention Teams (BITs) to test knowledge from the behavioural sciences as a way to improve and monitor the effect of interventions.

27.5 SUMMARY

In this chapter we present environmental problems as large-scale social dilemmas, in which individuals are bounded rational decision-makers who have to incur personal costs now in order to enjoy uncertain collective benefits later. We first discuss the systematic biases people have when dealing with uncertainties and probabilities and apply this specifically to environmental behaviour. We argue that the way people deal with uncertainty and probabilities results in a strong bias towards the status quo. Moreover, even when motivated, people frequently lack the knowledge to effectively improve their behaviour and decision-making. Change is therefore difficult to achieve. We also review the anomalous decision patterns that may arise in decision-making over time. The fact that people are very impatient and reluctant to make investments now that will only pay off later is particularly problematic for pro-environmental behaviour. In the second part of this chapter we discuss self-interested and other-oriented motives in pro-environmental behaviour. Self-interest is a strong motivator in social dilemmas, which can be problematic for environmental issues. We discuss how financial incentives can be successful (e.g., subsidies on solar panels), but can be problematic for a number of reasons as well (e.g., crowding out of intrinsic motivation). As an alternative to financial incentives we suggest social norms. Since dealing with environmental issues critically depends on human behaviour (be it in the form of behaviour change or decisions to invest in technological solutions), it is important to be aware of the psychology involved. We conclude that current findings from economic psychology can help policy-makers create more successful interventions, but also believe that the factors discussed should be tested on a larger scale in the field.

REVIEW QUESTIONS

1. Explain what the status quo bias entails.
2. Name five mechanisms that can result in a status quo bias and explain them.
3. Explain how defaults can be used to stimulate pro-environmental decisions.
4. Explain how the norm of self-interest can influence pro-environmental behaviour.
5. Explain why feedback helps to change behaviour
6. Name the key features of successful feedback.

REFERENCES

Abrahamse, W., Steg, L., Vlek, C., & Rothengatter, T. (2005). A review of intervention studies aimed at household energy conservation. *Journal of Environmental Psychology, 25*(3), 273–291.

Ajzen, I. (1991). The theory of planned behavior. *Organizational Behavior and Human Decision Processes, 50*(2), 179–211.

Allcott, H. (2011). Social norms and energy conservation. *Journal of Public Economics, 95*, 1082–1095.

Anderson, C. J. (2003). The psychology of doing nothing: Forms of decision avoidance result from reason and emotion. *Psychological Bulletin, 129*(1), 139–167.

Attari, S. Z., DeKay, M. L., Davidson, C. I., & Bruine de Bruin, W. (2010). Public perceptions of energy consumption and savings. *Proceedings of the National Academy of Sciences, 107*(37), 16054–16059.

Bamberg, S., & Möser, G. (2007). Twenty years after Hines, Hungerford, and Tomera: A new meta-analysis of psycho-social determinants of pro-environmental behaviour. *Journal of Environmental Psychology, 27*(1), 14–25.

Bicchieri, C. (2006). *The grammar of society. The nature and dynamics of social norms.* Cambridge: Cambridge University Press.

Biel, A., & Thøgersen, J. (2007). Activation of social norms in social dilemmas: A review of the evidence and reflections on the implications for environmental behaviour. *Journal of Economic Psychology, 28*, 93–112.

Black, J. S., Stern, P. C., & Elworth, J. T. (1985). Personal and contextual influences on household energy adaptations. *Journal of Applied Psychology, 70*(1), 3–21.

Bolderdijk, J. W., Gorsira, M., Keizer, K., & Steg, L. (2013). Values determine the (in)effectiveness of informational interventions in promoting pro-environmental behaviour. *PloS one, 8*(12), e83911.

Bolderdijk, J. W., & Steg, L. (2015). Promoting sustainable consumption: The risks of using financial incentives. In L. A. Reisch, & J. Thøgersen (Eds.), *Handbook of research on sustainable consumption.* Cheltenham: Edward Elgar.

Bowles, S. (2008). Policies designed for self-interested citizens may undermine 'the moral sentiments': Evidence from economic experiments. *Science, 320*(5883), 1605–1609.

Dawes, R. M., & Messick, D. M. (2000). Social dilemmas. *International Journal of Psychology, 35*(2), 111–116.

Deci, E. L., Koestner, R., & Ryan, R. M. (1999). A meta-analytic review of experiments examining the effects of extrinsic rewards on intrinsic motivation. *Psychological Bulletin, 125*(6), 627–668.

Dogan, E., Bolderdijk, J. W., & Steg, L. (2014). Making small numbers count: Environmental and financial feedback in promoting eco-driving behaviours. *Journal of Consumer Policy, 37*, 413–422.

Dunlap, R. E., Van Liere, K. D., Mertig, A. G., & Jones, R. E. (2000). New trends in measuring environmental attitudes: measuring endorsement of the new ecological paradigm: A revised NEP scale. *Journal of Social Issues, 56*(3), 425–442.

Eagly, A. H., & Chaiken, S. (1993). *The psychology of attitudes.* New York: Harcourt Brace Jovanovich College Publishers.

Ebeling, F., & Lotz, S. (2015). Domestic uptake of green energy promoted by opt-out tariffs. *Nature Climate Change, 5*, 868–871.

Epley, N., & Dunning, D. (2000). Feeling 'holier than thou': Are self-serving assessments produced by errors in self-or social prediction? *Journal of Personality and Social Psychology, 79*(6), 861.

Epstein, L. G. (1999). A definition of uncertainty aversion. *The Review of Economic Studies, 66*(3), 579–608.

Evans, D., McMeekin, A., & Southerton, D. (2012). Sustainable consumption, behaviour change policies and theories of practice. *Collegium, 12*, 113–129.

Fehr, E., & Falk, A. (2002). Psychological foundations of incentives. *European Economic Review, 46*(4), 687–724.

Fehr, E., & Fischbacher, U. (2002). Why social preferences matter: The impact of non-selfish motives on competition, cooperation and incentives. *The Economic Journal, 112*(478), C1–C33.

Frederick, S., Loewenstein, G., & O'Donoghue, T. (2002). Time discounting and time preference: A critical review. *Journal of Economic Literature, 40*(2), 351–401.

Gardner, G. T., & Stern, P. C. (2002). *Environmental problems and human behaviour* (2nd ed.). Boston, MA: Pearson Custom Publishing.

Gardner, G. T., & Stern, P. C. (2008). The short list: The most effective actions US households can take to curb climate change. *Environment: Science and Policy for Sustainable Development, 50*(5), 12–25.

Gärling, T., Fujii, S., Gärling, A., & Jakobsson, C. (2003). Moderating effects of social value orientation on determinants of proenvironmental behaviour intention. *Journal of Environmental Psychology, 23*(1), 1–9.

Gifford, R. (2011). The dragons of inaction: Psychological barriers that limit climate change mitigation and adaptation. *American Psychologist, 66*(4), 290–302.

Gneezy, U., & Rustichini, A. (2000). A fine is a price. *Journal of Legal Studies, 29*, 1–17.

Griffioen, A. M., Handgraaf, M. J. J., & Antonides, G. (forthcoming). Which construal level combinations are most effective? A field experiment on energy conservation. Manuscript in preparation.

Grønhøj, A., & Thøgersen, J. (2011). Feedback on household electricity consumption: Learning and social influence processes. *International Journal of Consumer Studies, 35*(2), 138–145.

Guagnano, G. A., Stern, P. C., & Dietz, T. (1995). Influences on attitude-behavior relationships: A natural experiment with curbside recycling. *Environment and Behavior, 27*(5), 699–718.

Handgraaf, M. J. J., Van Lidth de Jeude, M. A., & Appelt, K. C. (2013). Public praise vs. private pay: Effects of rewards on energy conservation in the workplace. *Ecological Economics, 86*, 86–92.

Hardisty, D. J., & Weber, E. U. (2009). Discounting future green: Money versus the environment. *Journal of Experimental Psychology: General, 138*(3), 329–340.

Herrmann, B., Thöni, C., & Gächter, S. (2008). Antisocial punishment across societies. *Science, 319*(5868), 1362–1367.

Hunecke, M., Blöbaum, A., Matthies, E., & Höger, R. (2001). Responsibility and environment ecological norm orientation and external factors in the domain of travel mode choice behaviour. *Environment and Behavior, 33*(6), 830–852.

Johnson, E. J., & Goldstein, D. (2003). Do defaults save lives? *Science, 302*(5649), 1338–1339.

Joireman, J. A., Lasane, T. P., Bennett, J., Richards, D., & Solaimani, S. (2001). Integrating social value orientation and the consideration of future consequences within the extended norm activation model of proenvironmental behaviour. *British Journal of Social Psychology, 40*(1), 133–155.

Kahneman, D. (2003). A perspective on judgment and choice: Mapping bounded rationality. *American Psychologist, 58*(9), 697–720.

Kahneman, D., Knetsch, J. L., & Thaler, R. H. (1991). Anomalies: The endowment effect, loss aversion, and status quo bias. *The Journal of Economic Perspectives, 5*(1), 193–206.

Kempton, W., Darley, J. M., & Stern, P. C. (1992). Psychological research for the new energy problems: Strategies and opportunities. *American Psychologist, 47*(10), 1213–1223.

Kerr, N. L. (1983). Motivation losses in small groups: A social dilemma analysis. *Journal of Personality and Social Psychology, 45*(4), 819–828.

Lanzini, P., & Thøgersen, J. (2014). Behavioural spillover in the environmental domain: An intervention study. *Journal of Environmental Psychology, 40*, 381–390.

Larrick, R. P., & Soll, J. B. (2008). The MPG illusion. *Science, 320*(5883), 1593–1594.

Leiserowitz, A. (2007). Communicating the risks of global warming: American risk perceptions, affective images, and interpretive communities. In S. C. Moser, & L. Dilling (Eds.), *Creating a climate for change: Communicating climate change and facilitating social change* (pp. 44–63). Cambridge: Cambridge University Press.

Lindenberg, S., & Steg, L. (2007). Normative, gain and hedonic goal frames guiding environmental behaviour. *Journal of Social Issues, 63*(1), 117–137.

Miller, D. T. (1999). The norm of self-interest. *American Psychologist, 54*(12), 1053–1060.

Mullen, E., & Monin, B. (2016). Consistency versus licensing effects of past moral behaviour. *Annual Review of Psychology, 67*, 363–385.

Murphy, R. O., Ackermann, K. A., & Handgraaf, M. J. J. (2011). Measuring social value orientation. *Judgment and Decision Making, 6*(8), 771–781.

Nolan, J. M., Schultz, P. W., Cialdini, R. B., Goldstein, N. J., & Griskevicius, V. (2008). Normative social influence is underdetected. *Personality and Social Psychology Bulletin, 34*(7), 913–923.

Ölander, F., & Thøgersen, J. (1995). Understanding of consumer behaviour as a prerequisite for environmental protection. *Journal of Consumer Policy, 18*, 317–357.

Randolph, B., & Troy, P. (2008). Attitudes to conservation and water consumption. *Environmental Science & Policy, 11*, 441–455.

Reno, R. R., Cialdini, R. B., & Kallgren, C. A. (1993). The transsituational influence of social norms. *Journal of Personality and Social Psychology, 64*(1), 104–112.

Sally, D. (1995). Conversation and cooperation in social dilemmas: A meta-analysis of experiments from 1958 to 1992. *Rationality and Society, 7*(1), 58–92.

Schouten, T. M., Bolderdijk, J. W., & Steg, L. (2014). Framing car fuel efficiency: Linearity heuristic for fuel consumption and fuel-efficiency ratings. *Energy Efficiency, 7*(5), 891–901.

Schuitema, G., Steg, L., & Rothengatter, J. A. (2010). The acceptability, personal outcome expectations, and expected effects of transport pricing policies. *Journal of Environmental Psychology, 30*(4), 587–593.

Schultz, P. W. (1999). Changing behaviour with normative feedback interventions: A field experiment on curbside recycling. *Basic and Applied Social Psychology, 21*(1), 25–36.

Schultz, P. W. (2001). The structure of environmental concern: Concern for self, other people, and the biosphere. *Journal of Environmental Psychology, 21*(4), 327–339.

Schultz, P. W., Estrada, M., Schmitt, J., Sokoloski, R., & Silva-Send, N. (2015). Using in-home displays to provide smart meter feedback about household electricity consumption: A randomized control trial comparing kilowatts, cost, and social norms. *Energy, 90*, 351–358.

Schultz, P. W., Nolan, J. M., Cialdini, R. B., Goldstein, N. J., & Griskevicius, V. (2007). The constructive, destructive, and reconstructive power of social norms. *Psychological Science, 18*(5), 429–434.

Schwartz, D., Bruine de Bruin, W., Fischhoff, B., & Lave, L. (2015). Advertising energy saving programs: The potential environmental cost of emphasizing monetary savings. *Journal of Experimental Psychology: Applied, 21*(2), 158–166.

Schwartz, S. H. (1977). Normative influences on altruism. *Advances in Experimental Social Psychology, 10*, 221–279.

Steg, L., Bolderdijk, J. W., Keizer, K., & Perlaviciute, G. (2014). An integrated framework for encouraging pro-environmental behaviour: The role of values, situational factors and goals. *Journal of Environmental Psychology, 38*, 104–115.

Steg, L., De Groot, J. I., Dreijerink, L., Abrahamse, W., & Siero, F. (2011). General antecedents of personal norms, policy acceptability, and intentions: The role of values, worldviews, and environmental concern. *Society and Natural Resources, 24*(4), 349–367.

Stern, P. C. (1999). Information, incentives, and proenvironmental consumer behaviour. *Journal of Consumer Policy, 22*(4), 461–478.

Stern, P. C. (2000). New environmental theories: Toward a coherent theory of environmentally significant behaviour. *Journal of Social Issues, 56*(3), 407–424.

Stern, P. C., & Dietz, T. (1994). The value basis of environmental concern. *Journal of Social Issues, 50*(3), 65–84.

Sundblad, E.-L., Biel, A., & Gärling, T. (2011). Timing of climate change consequences and intention to mitigate carbon dioxide emissions. *Umweltpsychologie, 15*(2), 123–134.

Tam, J., McDaniels, T. L. (2013). Understanding individual risk perceptions and preferences for climate change adaptations in biological conservation. *Environmental Science & Policy, 27*, 114–123.

Thøgersen, J. (1994). Monetary incentives and environmental concern. Effects of a differentiated garbage fee. *Journal of Consumer Policy, 17*, 407–442.

Thøgersen, J. (1996). Recycling and morality. A critical review of the literature. *Environment and Behavior, 28*, 536–558.

Thøgersen, J. (1999). Spillover processes in the development of a sustainable consumption pattern. *Journal of Economic Psychology, 20*(1), 53–81.

Thøgersen, J. (2006). Norms for environmentally responsible behaviour: An extended taxonomy. *Journal of Environmental Psychology, 26*, 247–336.

Thøgersen, J. (2011). Green shopping for selfish reasons or the common good? *American Behavioural Scientist, 55*(8), 1052–1076.

Thøgersen, J., & Crompton, T. (2009). Simple and painless? The limitations of spillover in environmental campaigning. *Journal of Consumer Policy, 32*(2), 141–163.

Tiefenbeck, V., Goette, L., Degen, K., & Tasic, V. (2016). Overcoming salience bias: How real-time feedback fosters resource conservation. *Management*, February 2017. http://doi.org/10.1287/mnsc.2016.2646

Toft, M. B., Schuitema, G., & Thøgersen, J. (2014). The importance of framing for consumer acceptance of the smart grid: A three country study. *Energy Research and Social Science, 3*, 113–123.

Truelove, H. B., Carrico, A. R., Weber, E. U., Raimi, K. T., & Vandenbergh, M. P. (2014). Positive and negative spillover of pro-environmental behaviour: An integrative review and theoretical framework. *Global Environmental Change, 29*, 127–138.

VaasaETT (2012). World energy retail market rankings. VaasaETT publication. www.vaasaett.com.

Van Beek, J., Handgraaf, M., & Antonides, G. (2017). Time orientation effects on health behavior. In M. Altman (Ed.), *Handbook of behavioral economics and smart decision-making: Rational decision-making within the bounds of reason.* Edward Elgar.

Wade-Benzoni, K. A. (2008). Maple trees and weeping willows: The role of time, uncertainty, and affinity in intergenerational decisions. *Negotiation and Conflict Management Research, 1*(3), 220–245.

Weber, E. U. (2006). Experience-based and description-based perceptions of long-term risk: Why global warming does not scare us (yet). *Climatic Change, 77*(1–2), 103–120.

Weber, E. U., & Johnson, E. J. (2009). Mindful judgment and decision making. *Annual Review of Psychology, 60*, 53–85.

Weber, E. U., Johnson, E. J., Milch, K. F., Chang, H., Brodscholl, J. C., & Goldstein, D. G. (2007). Asymmetric discounting in intertemporal choice: A query-theory account. *Psychological Science, 18*(6), 516–523.

FURTHER READING

Gardner, G. T., & Stern, P. C. (2002). *Environmental problems and human behaviour* (2nd ed.). Boston, MA: Pearson Custom Publishing.

Gifford, R. (2014). Environmental psychology matters. *Annual Review of Psychology, 65*(1), 541–579.

Swim, J. K., Stern, P. C., Doherty, T. J., Clayton, S., Reser, J. P., ... & Howard, G. S. (2011). Psychology's contributions to understanding and addressing global climate change. *American Psychologist, 66*(4), 241–250.

28 Insurance Behaviour and Society

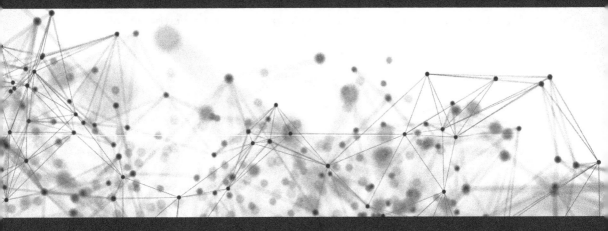

ROB RANYARD, JOHN K. ASHTON AND BILL HEBENTON

CHAPTER OUTLINE

LEARNING OUTCOMES

BY THE END OF THIS CHAPTER YOU SHOULD BE ABLE TO:

1. Compare and contrast the subjectively expected utility and bounded rationality accounts of insurance purchase decisions.

2. Discuss the causes of insurance mis-selling and approaches to insurance consumer protection.

3. Explain the economic concept of moral hazard in relation to insurance behaviour, in particular with reference to insurance fraud and deterrence.

28.1   INTRODUCTION

A personal or household insurance policy is a contract whereby an insurer, in exchange for a monetary premium, will pay agreed compensation if one of the specified, uncontrollable events covered by the policy occurs during the insured period, usually one year. Some insurance, such as motor insurance, is mandatory. Most insurance, however, is discretionary, meaning that its purchase is a personal or household decision. Internationally, such insurance is a major financial market, with products to insure against all manner of risks of financial loss, including those due to natural disasters, travel hazards, personal injury and ill-health, and crime.

To insure, or not to insure (and if so, which policy to choose) is a decision involving risk and uncertainty. The psychology of insurance decision making is a domain of utility-based theories such as subjectively expected utility (SEU; Savage, 1954) and prospect theory (Kahneman & Tversky, 1979), and of those based on bounded rationality and psychological processes, such as the positive theory of insurance demand (Kunreuther & Pauly, 2006) and the risk defusing operator model (Huber, 2012). In Section 28.2, we review research (including the above theories) on the psychology of insurance as a risk protection decision.

Turning to the wider societal issues surrounding personal and household insurance, its primary benefit is to protect people from risks of large, low probability financial losses, in exchange for certain, but small and manageable, costs. Some of its significant detriments, on the other hand, relate to the potential moral hazards of insurance. First, it has been argued that taking out insurance may result in a greater tendency for risky, perhaps reckless, behaviour (Parsons, 2003). Second, in part because of the complexity of insurance products, it is a market rich in opportunities for mis-selling and overpricing (Ericson & Doyle, 2006). Third, fraudulent claims are possible. In the UK, for example, insurers suspect that false claims for whiplash neck injury have steadily increased, since the claim rate trend is upwards and out of line with similar European countries, while at the same time vehicle safety has substantially improved (Levene, 2015). Finally, because of possible reputational damage to 'trust-relations' with consumers, together with the financial costs in detecting and prosecuting insurance fraud, insurers may find it expedient to turn a blind eye, and pass on the cost of such claims in higher premiums, to the detriment of the honest majority (Bacher, 1995; Vianene & Dedene, 2004).

Following our discussion of the psychology of insurance purchase decisions we consider the nature and causes of insurance mis-selling and review approaches to consumer protection. We then elucidate the nature and significance of moral hazard, and summarize what is known of the prevalence of fraud. Following this, we consider the role of evolving government regulatory activity, and the practices of insurance firms to prevent moral hazard and insurance fraud.

28.2   INSURANCE AS RISK PROTECTION

28.2.1   *Subjectively Expected Utility*

Consider a relatively simple insurance decision: whether to insure a cycle against theft, accidental damage or vandalism. A typical choice is represented in Figure 28.1

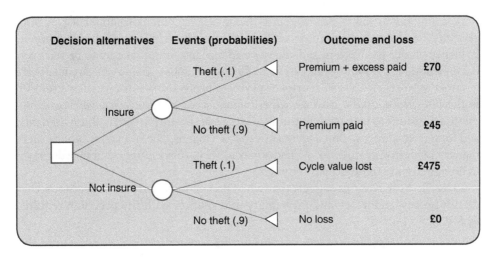

FIGURE 28.1 *A cycle insurance decision represented as a decision tree.*

as a decision tree in which the probability of the events covered is assumed to be one in ten (.01); the value of the cycle is £475 (new for old replacement cover); the insurance premium for one year is £45; and the excess (or deductible, to be paid in the event of a claim) is £25. In this example the long-run expected loss is the same whether insurance is taken or not.[1] On this expected value criterion, the purchaser should be indifferent between the two alternatives. However, as explained in Chapter 2 in this volume, the more widely accepted rational principle for decisions involving uncertainty is the subjectively expected utility (SEU) of the two options, which takes into account the decision-maker's personal beliefs about the probabilities of the insured events and the utility, or subjective value, of asset positions following the possible outcomes. Kunreuther, Onculer and Slovic (1998) further argue that future asset positions should be discounted relative to those experienced in the present. While discounted SEU may be an appropriate principle to guide rational insurance decisions, various strands of evidence, discussed below, show some of the ways in which insurance behaviour does not conform to it.

In order to follow the prescriptions of SEU theory for rational insurance choice, it is necessary to have precise information about the probabilities of the insured events and the costs and benefits of alternative policies. Hogarth and Kunreuther (1995) argued that people often lack such information and make insurance decisions under conditions of ignorance. Related to this, Williamson, Ranyard and Cuthbert (2000) carried out a simulation study which allowed participants to control their level of ignorance by seeking as much information as they wanted about an extended warranty policy. About 20% of their adult, non-student sample asked no questions at all before deciding whether to purchase it, therefore remaining ignorant in Hogarth and Kunreuther's sense; nearly all of these decided against buying insurance. Those who did seek information tended to focus on the monetary costs and benefits and the general terms and conditions, with less than 20% asking questions about risk-related factors such as the reliability of the insured product. In addition, verbal protocols revealed quantitative thinking comparing financial costs and benefits, but only qualitative thinking about probabilities of loss (see also Ranyard, Hinkley, & Williamson, 2001).

A second prediction of SEU theory is that insurance purchase should display price elasticity, i.e., as the premium decreases, the take-up of insurance should increase. Evidence on this has been mixed. Survey evidence has found take-up to be relatively price inelastic for Dutch health care (van Dijk et al., 2008), long-term care insurance (Cramer & Jensen, 2006) and mortgage payment protection insurance (hereafter PPI) in the UK (Pryce, 2001). Also, an experimental study reported that whereas hypothetical decisions to take health insurance were not sensitive to price, those for dental and long-term care insurance were (Royalty & Hagens, 2005). Finally, other experiments (Ganderton et al., 2000; Williamson et al., 2000) have found insurance decisions to be significantly influenced by cost.

Overall, these findings suggest that when people make insurance decisions, they do not process monetary and probability information with the precision required by SEU.

28.2.2 Bounded Rationality

A seminal critique of SEU theory was advanced by Simon (1957) in developing the bounded rationality perspective, which recognizes humans' limited capacity to process information in complex environments. Many insurance products are mind-bogglingly complex, and even relatively simple insurance decisions have a surprising degree of complexity. Loewenstein et al. (2013) identified extensive complexity in the US health insurance market with individual insurers offering many policies with minor or trivial differences. They argue that the difficulty of dealing with this is one of the reasons that people pay more than necessary for their health care.

Ranyard (2006) summarized some of the implications of bounded rationality for insurance decisions as follows:

- people construct *simplified representations* of insured events, neglecting to fully consider the details of cover specified in policy documents;
- their judgements of the probability of occurrence of insured events are based on *judgement heuristics* and subject to bias (Tversky & Kahneman, 1974); such judgements are not precise, they are rather coarse;
- their evaluations of the monetary costs and benefits of insurance policies are subject to *framing effects* (Johnson, Hershey, Meszaros & Kunreuther, 1993);
- they tend to use simple decision rules (*decision heuristics*) to make insurance decisions (Huber, 2007, 2012; Kunreuther & Pauly, 2006).
- *simplified representations*. Surveys have found that people's understanding of the breadth of their insurance cover can be rather limited. For example, a UK survey found that many credit users with PPI were unaware of the details of their cover (Office of Fair Trading, 2006). Related to this, Ranyard and McHugh (2012a; 2012b) found in experiments with realistic scenarios that decisions to purchase PPI with a credit option were not affected by the level of cover, i.e., basic versus premium, even though the latter covered a wider range of insured events. One interpretation of this is that insurance cover is intrinsically difficult to evaluate (Hsee, 1996).

- *judgement heuristics.* Weinstein and Klein (1996) observed that people underestimate the chances of bad things happening to them, compared to the chances that they will happen to other people. They call this phenomenon the *optimism bias*. For example, Weinstein (1987) found that people generally believe they are less likely to be made redundant than other people. The optimism bias could be one factor underlying decisions not to insure against natural disasters, even in groups for whom such insurance is heavily subsidized (Kunreuther et al., 1978). It has also been found that judgements of the probability of insured events can be influenced by how easy it is to recall or imagine the event, or its vividness (Johnson et al., 1993).

- *framing costs and benefits.* Two assumptions of prospect theory are consistent with the bounded rationality perspective. First, and perhaps most important, is the insight that people tend to evaluate decision outcomes in terms of gains and losses relative to a reference point (which can shift) rather than in terms of the final asset positions assumed by SEU theory. Second, Johnson et al. (1993) found that insurance decisions are influenced by how insurance costs are framed. To make it seem cheaper, they are often advertised in terms of daily cost, for example the slogan: 'Real peace of mind from 98p a day'. Conversely, when people consider the long-term costs of expenditure they make different consumer decisions, perhaps ones more consistent with their long-term goals (Read & Powell, 2002). Ranyard and McHugh (2005) found that for hypothetical choices between credit options with and without PPI, bank customers who were informed of the total cost as well as the monthly cost of the insurance were significantly more likely to reject it compared to a group only presented with the latter.

- *decision heuristics.* Kunreuther and Pauly (2006) argued that one decision heuristic people use is not considering taking insurance unless the probability of loss exceeds a threshold. They also suggest that a loss value threshold also needs to be exceeded. In support of this, some of Ranyard et al.'s (2001) participants would not purchase PPI for a lower loan amount but would do so for a higher amount, saying that they anticipated being able to bear the smaller financial loss. Kunreuther and Pauly's positive theory of insurance demand proposes that above these thresholds people engage in a prospect theory-like evaluation process (with certain provisos).

  In contrast, Huber's (2007, 2012) theory specifies only a probability detection threshold, above which further heuristics are used to make risk protection decisions. His model proposes that if people detect a risk in a preferred option, they then search for a suitable *risk-defusing operator* (RDO). If this search is successful, and if one of the RDOs is judged to be effective, then the choice of the preferred option is confirmed. Huber has identified several types of RDO, including: *planned, pre-outcome compensation*, doing something at the time of the decision which would compensate for the negative outcome if it occurred; and *worst-case plans*, mental activity at the point of decision anticipating the negative outcome by drawing up a plan to limit the effects of the loss if it occurs. Insurance belongs to the former category, incurring a prior cost to be weighed against the benefit of defusing the risk in this way. Instead, a worst-case plan could be devised as a means of managing the risk with no upfront costs. The choice for someone who detects a risk, then, is not between accepting insurance or not, but rather between insurance and an alternative RDO such as a worst-case plan. Support for this was found in the studies of extended warranty and consumer's PPI decisions discussed earlier (Ranyard et al., 2001; Williamson et al., 2000); concurrent and retrospective verbal reports contained several examples of RDOs, including taking insurance and worst case plans such as a plan to sell a product bought on credit if repayment difficulties emerge.

28.2.3   *Worry, Peace of Mind and Experience of Loss*

Zaleskiewicz, Piskorz and Borkowska (2002) investigated the role of emotion in decisions to purchase insurance against flood. They found that feelings of fear were evoked when thinking about this kind of catastrophic event. In less severe circumstances, the negative emotion of worry about risks of financial loss is perhaps more typical; in an experimental study, Schade, Kunreuther and Koellinger (2012) found that people's disposition to worry was strongly correlated with what they were willing to pay for insurance.

A related consideration is *anticipated* emotions, especially anticipated worry of financial loss. That is, the cognitive appraisal of how worried you would feel if you took a particular decision and a loss were to occur. This may drive the search for an effective RDO, for example, comparing insurance to worst-case plans. The reduction of anticipated worry is often referred to in insurance marketing as giving 'peace of mind'. Ranyard and McHugh (2012a) found that anticipated worry about repayment difficulties and the anticipated peace of mind offered by PPI were significant predictors of willingness to purchase such insurance.

Finally, Slovic, Finucane, Peters, and MacGregor (2004) and others, argue that the role of emotion is fundamentally linked to an experiential, in contrast to an analytic, mode of thought. Consequently, if risk management decisions are emotion-based, then they may be related to previous experience of the insured events. Various studies (e.g., Ranyard et al., 2001; Zaleskiewicz et al., 2002) have found that insurance take-up is greater for those who have experienced them.

28.3   MIS-SELLING

Financial mis-selling is a widely used term with many meanings; aggressive, ignorant or incompetent sales tactics, a failure to appropriately advise customers and deliberate strategies to sell financial services which customers do not need. These are all circumstances where a customer is unaware of being financially disadvantaged (Black & Nobels, 1998). Mis-selling episodes have occurred repeatedly in many nations, have been notable in the insurance as well as banking and investment sectors and have resulted in increasing corporate costs, consumer detriment and a substantial mis-allocation of resources. Financial firms internationally have faced fines and loss of reputation, have been required to provide substantial levels of customer redress and have suffered a substantial decline in public trust. For example in the United Kingdom, over £20 billion was paid to customers in redress for mis-sold PPI in the 2000s (see Ferran, 2012).

Clearly financial mis-selling causes substantial customer harm and displays failure of ethical behaviour. Mis-selling is also a matter of regulatory judgement and arises when regulatory demands and expectations differ from firms' identities and expectations (Gilad, 2011). However, the concept and incidence of mis-selling are controversial and disputed. Mis-selling could be exaggerated by customer complaints (McAllister & Erffmeyer, 2003) arising as the financial industry is mistrusted and the potential for customer fraud exists.

28.3.1 Causes

Despite the scope and importance of financial mis-selling, evidence as to its causes is relatively sparse. To date, much of the empirical literature from management, sociology and criminology (e.g., Aldridge, 1997; Ericson & Doyle, 2006; MacLean, 2008) has examined case studies of mis-selling in life insurance and pensions. This reports on the extent of financial mis-selling, the promotional ethos pervading finance and harmful corporate cultures within insurance firms. Alternatively contributions from economics and finance have often examined single practices associated with mis-selling, such as commission-based sales (e.g., Inderst & Ottaviani, 2009), the framing of financial information and product complexity (Carlin & Manso, 2010).

Central to most economic explanations of financial services mis-selling has been customers' limited comprehension of financial services (Altman, 2012) and the suboptimal way in which decisions are presented by firms (Hirshleifer, 2001) to exploit customers' decision-making anomalies (Frey & Eichenberger, 1994). As discussed earlier, in order to make appropriate financial decisions, individuals are expected to have a clear understanding of the financial services' characteristics, how their preferences relate to these characteristics and their future demands for this service. However, a substantial proportion of consumers have poor comprehension of financial services (e.g., Bucks & Pence, 2008) particularly the young, old, and less wealthy. Further, people with distinct lifestyles, levels of education and politics have very different abilities to make personal financial decisions (Aldridge, 1998).

A related concern is that insurance policies are often sold within a bundle of distinct financial services. Several studies have identified circumstances where customers make sub-optimal choices when jointly purchasing additional or add-on services (e.g., Ellison, 2005; Gabaix & Laibson, 2006). This cause of mis-selling is particularly associated with the sale of PPI, which provides varying combinations of accident, sickness and unemployment insurance and is used to protect the loan payments of policyholders in the event of loss of income. PPI is unusual in that it provides cover to both the borrower if they default on their debt after unexpected circumstances and also to the lender which is assured the loan will be repaid. This outcome is attractive to many lenders and lowers interest rates by reducing the probability of default. The mis-selling concern for PPI has been the form of distribution with credit and the resulting high cost and low quality of this service. As the insurance is an additional add-on service combined with a primary good desired by the customer, i.e. credit, the attention placed on the PPI purchase decision by the customer may be limited. This enabled PPI to be sold assumptively, by adding this to a credit agreement without the customers' knowledge, and it was over-priced to cross-subsidize the loan (Ashton & Hudson, 2014). All of this displays aspects of a situational monopoly (Baker & Siegelman, 2014).

Insurance is also often sold using the advice of a financial advisor or insurance broker; agents who are often remunerated on a commission basis. This creates incentives to inflate the perceived value of a financial service if it pays more commission (Inderst & Ottaviani, 2009). Such a critical interpretation arises as insurance policies associated with higher commission could be aggressively sold in preference to less profitable yet more suitable services. Commission-based sales can also lead to 'product churning' where a customer is encouraged to change policies frequently, thereby enhancing commission payments to the financial advisor, albeit at a cost to the customer.

Organizational theories can also explain mis-selling as an outcome of immoral yet rational actors operating in their own self-interest or as a circumstance arising from the culture observed across the firm. Insights from sociology (Aldridge, 1997), legal scholarship (e.g., Blair & Stout, 2001), economics (Guiso, Sapienza, & Zingales, 2007) and psychology (Gärling, Kirchler, Lewis, & van Raaij, 2009) all report that the social context of the marketplace can shape norms of customer and corporate behaviour. Financial mis-selling can therefore be a function of 'rogue advisors' existing in an otherwise faultless company. Alternatively, the entire firm or even industry could be 'dysfunctional', enabling the normalization of mis-selling practices.

'Rogue advisor' explanations have considered mis-selling through two principal approaches (Pinto, Leana, & Pol, 2008). Pressure or opportunity theory suggests that characteristics of the business environment create pressure to violate laws and norms, and the opportunity to do so without detection. Alternatively illegitimate actions are taken to gain resources and for pecuniary benefit, with organizational actors being 'amoral rational calculators' who weigh the costs of breaking rules for self-advantage (Daboub, Rasheed, Priem, & Gray, 1995).

Corporate culture also provides a process through which 'dysfunctional' firms can arise. Here misconduct is socially constructed within the firm, with financial advisors ill-trained or uninformed as to the insurance service they are selling. These concerns can be amplified by how advisors are recruited, or by the network of friends and family to which they may sell insurance (Ericson & Doyle, 2006). Under these circumstances wrongdoing becomes normalized (Balch & Armstrong, 2010) as individuals act in their dysfunctional, socially constructed view of the world in an uncalculating way (MacLean, 2008) viewing financial mis-selling as a normal commercial practice.

28.3.2   Consumer Protection

In light of the foregoing, the regulation and correction of mis-selling behaviours reflect anxieties with commission, customer literacy, firms' culture, and self-interested employee and firm behaviours. While the financial regulation of financial mis-selling has varied significantly internationally, different intellectual themes of neo-liberalism, consumer protection and 'culture'-driven regulatory solutions have emerged (Moloney, 2015). Neo-liberal policies have promoted less regulatory intervention and greater public engagement with financial markets. This form of regulation seeks to facilitate the unfettered disciplinary influence of market forces, to constrain bureaucratic regulation and encourage customers to accept responsibility for their own actions and personal well-being. The role of the state and the regulator is to facilitate these outcomes through enhancing consumer literacy and enable continuous, impersonal and non-bureaucratic market monitoring by citizens.

This process has its detractors. Questions arise as to whether efficient markets actually exist and whether market monitoring can lead to effective disciplining of financial firms. Against the backdrop of the increasing marketability of financial services (Boot, 2011), the major losses suffered by customers in financial crises and the malaise surrounding many financial mis-selling and fraud cases, consumer protection and conduct of business regulation have become a more significant influence on financial regulation. Within this policy tradition, key actions have included restrictions on commission, product level regulation and even banning or restricting certain business models and modes of distribution. Such actions have assumed that the customer is vulnerable and requires protection from unscrupulous market participants.

Lastly, in recent years, it has been advocated that business cultures and the social context of finance should become a focus of regulatory intervention (e.g., Financial Stability Board, 2014; Tennyson, 2010). Transforming mendacious corporate cultures, enhancing the accountability of corporate managers, the salvage and reconstruction of corporate reputations and rebuilding public trust are therefore a new focus of financial regulation in many nations. These approaches are nascent, need to develop and would benefit from more public discussion and academic discourse.

28.4   INSURANCE FRAUD

28.4.1   *Moral Hazard*

Some of the most interesting empirical and theoretical work on the phenomenon of insurance fraud has sought to focus on the dominant neo-classical economics concept of 'moral hazard', a term usually associated with the effect that insurance has on the incentive to avoid a loss.[2] Moral hazard is traditionally focused on the 'insured' party and the reward structure the insurance environment provides. Yet recent work would suggest, rather, that moral hazard comprises the ways in which an insurance relationship fosters behaviour by any party in the relationship that immorally increases risk to others. That is, how private insurance is socially organized also offers incentives to other parties in the insurance relationship to engage in risky behaviour with immoral consequences. Insurers themselves can be influenced in ways which encourage them to put others at risk, including their policyholders, employees, competitors, and government regulatory machinery (see, e.g., Baker & Simon, 2002; Ericson et al., 2000). From this broader perspective, both mis-selling and fraudulent claims can be seen as part of the intrinsic and embedded problem of moral hazard that infuses insurance behaviour and society.

Conventionally put, moral hazard is about insurers making judgements: insurance fraud is about the behaviour of policyholders (Powers, 2012). However, these are inescapably interlinked (see Okura, 2013). There are empirical studies, within and across varied cultural contexts, which illustrate how moral hazards embedded in the social organization of private insurance lead to various kinds of immoral risky behaviour by those insured, insurance companies, and their employees, and to intensified efforts to regulate this behaviour (Ericson & Doyle, 2006; Faber, 1997; Jou, 2013; Jou & Hebenton, 2007; Raphael, 1995). This recognition that moral risks are not limited to the insured person is key to understanding the insurance fraud/moral hazard overlap and how it plays out in the wider moral economy of insurance.

28.4.2 Prevalence

The Global Economic Crime Survey (2005) concluded, not unexpectedly, that fraud is 'a significant and growing threat worldwide' (Price Waterhouse Coopers/Martin Luther University, 2006). Yet, for individual countries it is obvious that the dynamic nature and prevalence of fraud (in which insurance comprises an important element) are largely unknown; accordingly efforts to combat such criminality are underdeveloped. In the United Kingdom, for instance, a 2006 official report has outlined the lack of knowledge of either the extent, costs or indeed comprehensive nature of types of fraud (Attorney-General's Office, 2006). Regarding the extent of fraud in the United Kingdom, the report notes an estimate of corporate fraud was £72 billion a year. The most recent industry wide figures suggest undetected insurance fraud at approximately £2.1 billion (see HM Treasury, 2016). Similarly, on types of fraud, while there is good information about such frauds where the victims are large organizations or government departments, where the victims are small businesses or individuals, much goes unreported (HM Treasury, 2016). Internationally, commentators within the insurance sector have also pointed to particular difficulties in estimating the prevalence and costs of insurance fraud (Coalition Against Insurance Fraud (CAIF), 2003; NICB, 2000). There are at least three problems. First, the covert nature of fraud (Dionne, 2000); second, sensitivity to change (CAIF, 2003); and, finally, lack of consensus on what actually constitutes insurance fraud and on which form of fraud to focus (Derrig, 2002).

At the practical level, insurance fraud has many aspects – given the phenomenon's creative dynamism. Fraudulent activities are commonly classified under three main categories: (1) exaggeration of an otherwise legitimate claim; (2) premeditated fabrication of a claim; and (3) fraudulent known disclosure or misrepresentation of material facts. All insurance frauds, however, 'share the distinctive common characteristic that, unlike bad debts, for example, or conventional property crime such as burglary, they are not self-disclosing. Their essence is to appear as normal and to be processed and paid in a routine manner' (Clarke, 1990, p. 1). It follows that insurers will normally only have an idea of the nature and extent of a fraud if they take specific detection measures. While the three-way classification is broadly accepted, it is also pointed out that any adequate typology of insurance fraud must include an understanding of internally versus externally perpetrated fraud, together with fraud committed at the underwriting stage as well as the claims stage (see Vianene & Dedene, 2004). Even the common assumption within the industry that around 10% of all claims are fraudulent is untested (HM Treasury, 2016). Given all the measurement difficulties, estimated figures, for instance, on insurance claims fraud, can only at best highlight the substantial size of the insurance fraud problem.

28.4.3   Detection and Deterrence

A contemporary regulatory framework for detection and deterrence has moved apace (HM Treasury, 2016). Fraud-deterrent activities have sought specifically to develop means for: improving claim screening facilities; providing special training for front-line office staff and claim handling personnel; investing in specialized 'big data' analytics; improving communication and cooperation within the industry and between the industry and police and prosecution; and improving internal audit.

At the international level, there is a trend to establish national centralized insurance fraud bureaux (in the United States, Canada, most EU states). These agencies normally have duties to help insurers and other stakeholders to investigate cases of suspected fraud so that they can be readily prosecuted. The other clear trend is towards an operational shared database, pooling intelligence across the sector and ensuring appropriate protocols for information sharing with the police. Contemporary anti-fraud regulation in the United States, for example, appears to have a number of interlocking components: a national agency, sponsored by insurers, with an associated database – the National Insurance Crime Bureau (NICB); most states have classified insurance fraud as a serious crime and provide immunity for those who report fraud.

In the United Kingdom, in 2006, the insurance industry itself established an Insurance Fraud Bureau to improve the capability of member insurers to prevent, detect and investigate organized insurance fraud. Another important initiative is the industry-funded Insurance Fraud Enforcement Division, a specialist police unit part of the City of London Police dedicated to tackling insurance fraud in England and Wales. It was established in 2012 and by the end of 2015 had secured 207 convictions at court (HM Treasury, 2016). The Sentencing Council in England and Wales has also issued specific guidelines on fraud in May 2014 recognizing the physical harm that insurance fraud can inflict, and recommending longer sentences.

In recent years, many insurers have turned to predictive analytics, reducing the need for tedious hands-on account management (Parente, 2012). Quantitative analysts use data mining tools to build programs that produce fraud propensity scores. Predictive modelling tends to be more accurate than other fraud detection methods. Information can be collected and cross-referenced from a variety of sources and in this context, social network analysis tools have proven effective in identifying organized fraud activities by modelling relationships in claims (Bologa, Bologa, & Florea., 2013). Social network tools allow for appropriate links and nodes to be analysed and evidenced conclusions drawn quickly. Text mining software accesses the unstructured text, parses it to distil meaningful data and analyses the newly created data to gain a deeper understanding of the claim. Facebook, YouTube and other social media websites are routinely mined for discriminating evidence of the claimant.

Yet, in spite of all of the emergent anti-fraud activities outlined above, the ultimate value of deterrence through higher detection probabilities and increased sanctions is largely unknown. As with deterrence on criminal sanctions in general, difficulties of accurately estimating effects are legion. Daniel Nagin succinctly summarized the current state of theory and empirical knowledge about deterrence. 'When deterrence effects are unpacked, it is clear that sanction threats are not universally efficacious: Magnitudes of deterrent effects range from none to seemingly very large' (Nagin, 2013, p. 199). Deterrent effects remain to be demonstrated in the insurance field.

Tennyson (2008) rightly points both to the high transaction costs in direct detection practices and use of enforcement, and that although deterrence may work for the 'hard', 'organized' end of fraud, 'soft' fraud by 'everyday' claimants may require a greater focus on the social normative and psychological dimensions of fraud behaviour. There is also relevant evidence from the European Social Survey and consumer fraud surveys (Accenture, 2010; Lopes, 2010). Effective prevention, as opposed to deterrent activities, requires a better understanding of moral hazard in the context of the links between fraud practices and consumer behaviour and attitudes towards institutional and contractual insurance practices. Interestingly, evidence is already emerging on fraud preventive 'nudge' approaches, drawing on behavioural science, and including use of 'moral cues' (see Cabinet Office, 2012; Shu et al., 2012). The layout and content of documentation or websites, and the way in which relations with customers are conducted can influence the way in which customers behave. In particular, customers can be persuaded to be more open and honest than they might otherwise have intended (HM Treasury, 2016).

Insurance fraud is therefore not just a regulatory or enforcement problem or an issue of increasing awareness of how insurance works among policyholders but is informed by a range of behavioural factors. Moreover, there is now a far greater appreciation of how the legal, organizational and commercial constraints under which the insurance industry operates often impact negatively upon the success of existing fraud prevention, detection and investigation practices (HM Treasury, 2016; Morley et al., 2006).

28.5 SUMMARY

Personal and household insurance can protect the population from risks of large, low probability financial losses in exchange for a manageable cost. Rational models prescribe that insurance purchase decisions should be made by weighing the utility of loss outcomes by the probabilities of their occurrence. In contrast, research from bounded rationality perspectives has revealed how people construct simplified representations of insured events, base probability judgements on heuristics, are susceptible to cost framing effects and use simple decision rules based on judgement thresholds. Furthermore, emotions such as worry, and anticipated peace of mind influence insurance choices.

While insurance brings societal benefits, it can also bring significant detriments related to its moral hazards. In recent years, for example, concerns have grown that much insurance held by individuals may be inappropriate for their needs or obtained due to misleading information provided by the seller. Such mis-selling of insurance has many sources, including the complexity of insurance products, the limited understanding of some consumers, the bundling of insurance with other products, pecuniary incentives, malevolent behaviour or the culture of the entire firm. Neo-liberal approaches to consumer protection encourage consumers to accept responsibility for their insurance decisions and to inform and educate themselves accordingly. Others argue that this is insufficient and in addition, consumer protection and the conduct of business regulation should be strengthened.

Insurance fraud, which exists on a continuum, is also detrimental to society. Although most estimates show it is widespread, its actual prevalence is unclear, in part because much insurance fraud goes undetected. Recent developments in combating fraud include high-level coordination of detection activity, the use of predictive analytics, revised guidelines on sentencing and the use of moral cues to discourage false claims. More generally, studies across varied cultural contexts illustrate how moral hazards embedded in the social organization of insurance lead to various kinds of immoral risky behaviour by those insured, insurance companies, and their employees. This recognition that moral risks are not limited to the insured person is key to understanding the insurance fraud-moral hazard overlap and how it plays out in the wider moral economy of insurance.

NOTES

1. Expected losses: insure, $(£70 \times .1) + (£45 \times .9) = £47.50$; not insure, $£475 \times .1 = £47.50$.
2. Rowell and Connelly (2012) provide an engaging account of the genesis of the term in theological and probability literatures.

REVIEW QUESTIONS

1. Describe and discuss some of the ways that bounded rationality and emotion can affect insurance purchase decisions.
2. What conditions enable the mis-selling of insurance?
3. In what ways is the concept of moral hazard important for an adequate understanding of insurance fraud?

REFERENCES

Accenture. (2010). *Insurance consumer fraud survey*. Retrieved from https://www.accenture.com/gb-en

Aldridge, A. (1997). Engaging with promotional culture: Organised consumerism and the personal financial services industry. *Sociology, 31*(3), 389–408.

Aldridge, A. (1998). Habitus and cultural capital in the field of personal finance. *The Sociological Review, 46*(1), 1–23.

Altman, M. (2012). Implications of behavioural economics for financial literacy and public policy. *Journal of Socio-Economics, 41*(5), 677–690.

Ashton, J. K., & Hudson, R. (2014). Do lenders cross subsidise loans by selling payment protection insurance? *International Journal of the Economics of Business, 21*(1), 121–138.

Attorney General's Office (2006). *Fraud Review Team: Interim report*. London: Attorney General's Office.

Bacher, J-L. (1995). Insurance, fraud and justice. *European Journal on Criminal Policy and Research, 3*, 84–92.

Baker, T., & Siegelman, P. (2014). 'You want insurance with that': Using behavioral economics to protect consumers from add-on insurance products. *Connecticut Insurance Law Journal, 29*(1), 1–60.

Baker, T., & Simon, J. (Eds.). (2002). *Embracing risk: The changing culture of insurance and responsibility*. Chicago: University of Chicago Press.

Balch, D. R., & Armstrong, R. W. (2010). Ethical marginality: The Icarus syndrome and banality of wrongdoing. *Journal of Business Ethics, 92*(2), 291–303.

Black, J., & Nobels, R. (1998). Personal pension mis-selling: The causes and lessons of regulatory failure. *The Modern Law Review, 61*(6), 789–820.

Blair, M. M., & Stout, L. A. (2001). Trust, trustworthiness and the behavioural foundations of corporate law. *University of Pennsylvania Law Review, 149*(June), 1735–1810.

Bologa, A., Bologa, R., & Florea, A. (2013). Big data and specific analysis methods for insurance fraud detection, *Database Systems Journal, 4*, 30–39.

Boot, A. W. A. (2011). Banking at the cross-roads, How to deal with marketability and complexity. *Review of Development Finance, 1*(3–4), 167–183.

Bucks, B., & Pence, K. (2008). Do borrowers know their mortgage terms? *Journal of Urban Economics, 64*(2), 218–233.

Cabinet Office. (2012). *Behavioural insights to reduce fraud, error and debt.* London: Behavioural Insights Team, Cabinet Office.

Carlin, B. I., & Manso, G. (2010). Obfuscation, learning and the evolution of investor sophistication. *Review of Financial Studies, 24*(3), 754–785.

Clarke, M. (1990). The control of insurance fraud: A comparative view. *British Journal of Criminology, 30*, 1–23.

Coalition Against Insurance Fraud (CAIF) (2003). *Insurance fraud: The crime you pay for.* Washington, DC: CAIF.

Cramer, A. T., & Jensen, G. A. (2006). Why don't people buy long-term-care insurance? *Journals of Gerontology: Series B: Psychological Sciences and Social Sciences, 61*, 185–193.

Daboub, A. J., Rasheed, A. M. A., Priem, R. L., & Gray, D. A. (1995). Top management ream characteristics and corporate illegal activity. *The Academy of Management Review, 20*(1), 138–170.

Derrig, R.A.(2002). Insurance fraud. *Journal of Risk and Insurance, 69*, 272–287.

Dionne, G. (2000). The empirical measure and information problems with emphasis on insurance fraud. In G. Dionne (Ed.), *Handbook of insurance* (pp. 395–414). Boston, MA: Kluwer Academic Publishers.

Ellison, G. (2005). A model of add on pricing. *Quarterly Journal of Economics, 120*(2), 585–637.

Ericson, R. V., Barry, D., & Doyle, A. (2000). The moral hazards of neoliberalism: Lessons from the private insurance industry. *Economy and Society, 29*, 532–558.

Ericson, R. V., & Doyle, A. (2006). The institutionalization of deceptive sales in life insurance. *British Journal of Criminology, 46*(6), 993–1010.

Faber, E. (1997). Shipping and scuttling: Criminogenesis in marine insurance. *Crime, Law and Social Change, 28*, 111–135.

Ferran, E. (2012). Regulatory lessons from the payment protection insurance mis-selling scandal in the UK. *European Business Organization Law Review, 13*(2), 247–270.

Financial Stability Board. (2014). *Guidance on supervisory interaction with financial institutions on risk culture. A framework for assessing risk culture,* Basel, Switzerland: Financial Stability Board.

Frey, B. S., & Eichenberger, R. (1994). Economic incentives transform psychological anomalies. *Journal of Economic Behaviour and Organization, 23*(2), 215–234.

Gabaix, X., & Laibson, D. (2006). Shrouded attributes, consumer myopia, and information suppression in competitive markets. *The Quarterly Journal of Economics, 121*(2), 505–540.

Ganderton, P. T., Brookshire, D. S., McKee, M., Stewart, S., & Thurston, H. (2000). Buying insurance for disaster-type risks: Experimental evidence. *Journal of Risk and Uncertainty, 20*, 271–289.

Gärling, T., Kirchler, E. Lewis, A., & van Raaij, F. (2009). Psychology, financial decision making, and financial crises. *Psychological Science in the Public Interest, 10*(1), 1–47.

Gilad, S. (2011). Institutionalising fairness in financial markets: Mission impossible? *Regulation and Governance, 5*(3), 309–332.

Guiso, L., Sapienza, P., & Zingales, L. (2007). Trusting the stock market. *ECGI Working Paper Series in Finance,* No. 170/2007, European University Institute, Florence.

Hirshleifer, D. (2001). Investor psychology and asset pricing. *Journal of Finance, 56*(4), 1533–1597.

HM Treasury (2016). *Insurance Fraud Task Force, Final report.* London: Her Majesty's Treasury and Ministry of Justice.

Hogarth, R. M., & Kunreuther, H. (1995). Decision making under ignorance: Arguing with yourself. *Journal of Risk and Uncertainty, 10*(1), 15–36.

Hsee, C. K. (1996). The evaluability hypothesis: An explanation of preference reversals between joint and separate evaluations of alternatives. *Organizational Behavior and Human Choice Processes, 46,* 247–257.

Huber, O. (2007). Behavior in risky decisions: Focus on risk defusing. In M. Abdellaoui, R. D. Luce, M. J. Machina, & B. Munier (Eds.), *Uncertainty and risk: Mental, formal, experimental representations* (pp. 291–306). Berlin: Springer.

Huber, O. (2012). Risky decisions: Active risk management. *Current Directions in Psychological Science, 21,* 26–30.

Inderst, R., & Ottaviani M. (2009). Misselling through agents, *American Economic Review, 99*(3), 883–908.

Johnson, E., Hershey, J., Meszaros, J., & Kunreuther, H. (1993). Framing, probability distortions, and insurance decisions. *Journal of Risk and Uncertainty, 7,* 35–51.

Jou, S. (2013). 'Opportunist' insurance fraud under different political economies. In J. Liu, S. Jou, & B. Hebenton (Eds.), *Asian handbook of criminology* (pp. 99–114). New York: Springer.

Jou, S., & Hebenton, B. (2007). Insurance fraud in Taiwan: Reflections on regulatory effort and criminological complexity. *International Journal of the Sociology of Law, 35,* 127–142.

Kahneman, D., & Tversky, A. (1979). Prospect theory: Analysis of decision under risk. *Econometrica, 47,* 263–291.

Kunreuther, H., Ginsberg, R., Miller, L., Sagi, P., Slovic, P., Borkan, B., & Katz, N. (1978). *Disaster insurance protection: Public policy lessons.* New York, Wiley.

Kunreuther, H., Onculer, A., & Slovic, P. (1998). Time insensitivity for protective investments. *Journal of Risk and Uncertainty, 16,* 279–299.

Kunreuther, H., & Pauly, M. V. (2006). *Insurance decision-making and market behavior.* New York: Now Publishers.

Levene, T. (2015, October 3). Whiplash epidemic returns to be a pain in insurers' neck. *The Guardian,* p. 46.

Loewenstein, G., Friedman, J. Y., McGill, B., Ahmad, S., Linck, S., Sinkula, S., & Madrian, B. C. (2013). Consumers' misunderstanding of health insurance. *Journal of Health Economics, 32*(5), 850–862.

Lopes, C. A. (2010). Consumer morality in times of economic hardship. *International Journal of Consumer Studies, 34,* 112–120.

MacLean, T. L. (2008). Framing and organizational misconduct: a symbolic interactionist study. *Journal of Business Ethics, 78*(1), 3–16.

McAllister, D. T. & Erffmeyer, R. C. (2003). A content analysis of outcomes and responsibilities for consumer complaints to their party organizations. *Journal of Business Research, 56,* 341–351.

Moloney, N. (2010). Regulating the retail markets: Law, policy and financial crisis. *Current Legal Problems, 63*(1), 375–447.

Morley, N., Ball, L. J., & Ormerod, T. C. (2006). How the detection of insurance fraud succeeds and fails. *Psychology, Crime & Law, 12,* 163–180.

Nagin, D. (2013). Deterrence in the twenty-first century. In M. Tonry (Ed.), *Crime and justice in America: 1975–2025* (pp. 80–102). Chicago: University of Chicago Press.

National Insurance Crime Bureau (NICB) (2000). *National Insurance Fraud Forum: Discussion papers on key issues.* Washington, DC: NICB.

Office of Fair Trading. (2006). *Payment protection insurance. Report on the market study and proposed decision to make a market investigation reference.* London: HMSO.

Okura, M. (2013). The relationship between moral hazard and insurance fraud. *Journal of Risk Finance, 14,* 120–128.

Parente, S. (2012). Assessment of predictive modeling for identifying fraud within the Medicare program, *Health Management, Policy and Innovation, 1,* 8–37.

Parsons, C. (2003). Moral hazard in liability insurance. *Geneva Papers, 28,* 448–471.

Pinto, J., Leana, C. R., & Pol, F. K. (2008). Corrupt organisations or organisations of corrupt individuals? Two types of organisation-level corruption. *Academy of Management Review, 33*(3), 685–709.

Powers, M. R. (2012). *Acts of God and man: Rumination on risk and insurance.* New York: Columbia University Press.

Price Waterhouse Coopers/Martin-Luther University (2006). *Global Economic Crime Survey 2005.* Halle, Germany: PWC/Martin Luther University, Economy and Crime Research Centre.

Pryce, G. (2002). Theory and estimation of the mortgage payment protection insurance decision. *Scottish Journal of Political Economy, 49*, 216–234.

Ranyard, R. (2006).*The psychology of consumer credit risk management: The case of payment protection insurance in the UK.* London: OFT. http://www.oft.gov.uk/shared_oft/reports/financial_products/oft869annexec.pdf

Ranyard, R., Hinkley, L., & Williamson, J. (2001). Risk management in consumers' credit decision making: A process tracing study of repayment insurance choices. *Zeitschrift für Sozialpsychologie, 32*, 152–161.

Ranyard, R., & McHugh, S. (2005). Consumer credit and payment protection insurance decisions. Research report prepared for the Co-operative Bank.

Ranyard, R., & McHugh, S. (2012a). Defusing the risk of borrowing: The psychology of payment protection insurance decisions. *Journal of Economic Psychology, 33*, 738–748.

Ranyard, R. & McHugh, S. (2012b). Bounded rationality in credit consumers' payment protection insurance decisions: The effect of relative cost and level of cover. *Journal of Risk Research, 15*, 937–950.

Raphael, A. (1995). *Ultimate risk.* London: Corgi Books.

Read, D., & Powell, M. (2002). Reasons for sequence preferences. *Journal of Behavioral Decision Making, 15*, 433–460.

Rowell, D., & Connelly, L. B. (2012). A history of the term 'moral hazard'. *Journal of Risk and Insurance, 79*(4), 1051–1075.

Royalty, A. B., & Hagens, J. (2005). The effect of premiums on the decision to participate in health insurance and other fringe benefits offered by the employer: Evidence from a real-world experiment. *Journal of Health Economics, 24*, 95–112.

Savage, L. J. (1954). *Foundations of statistics.* Oxford: Wiley.

Schade, C., Kunreuther, H. C., & Koellinger, P. (2012). Protecting against low-probability disasters: The role of worry. *Journal of Behavioral Decision Making, 25*, 534–543.

Shu, L., Mazar, N., Gino, F., Ariely, D., & Bazerman, M. (2012). Signing at the beginning makes ethics salient and decreases dishonest self-reports in comparison to signing at the end. *Proceedings of the National Academy of Sciences, 109*(38), 15197–15200.

Simon, H. A. (1957). *Models of man: Social and rational.* New York: Wiley.

Slovic, P., Finucane, M. L., Peters, E., & MacGregor, D. G. (2004). Risk as analysis and risk as feelings: Some thoughts about affect, reason, risk, and rationality. *Risk Analysis, 24*(2), 311–322.

Tennyson, S. (2008). Moral, social and economic dimensions of insurance fraud claims. *Social Research, 75*(4), 1181–1204.

Tennyson, S. (2010). Rethinking consumer protection regulation in insurance markets. Policy Brief, 2010-PB-07, Networks Financial Institute at Indiana State University.

Tversky, A., & Kahneman, D. (1974). Judgment under uncertainty: Heuristics and biases. *Science, 185*(4157), 1124–1131.

van Dijk, M., Pomp, M., Douven, R., Laske-Aldershof, T., Schut, E., de Boer, W., & de Boo, A. (2008). Consumer price sensitivity in Dutch health insurance. *International Journal of Health Care Finance and Economics, 8*(4), 225–244.

Vianene, S., & Dedene, G., (2004). Insurance fraud: Issues and challenges. *The Geneva Papers on Risk and Insurance, 29*(2), 313–333.

Weinstein, N. D. (1987). Unrealistic optimism about susceptibility to health problems: Conclusions from a community-wide sample. *Journal of Behavioral Medicine, 10*(5), 481–500.

Weinstein, N. D., & Klein, W. M. (1996). Unrealistic optimism: Present and future. *Journal of Social & Clinical Psychology. Special Issue: Unrealistic optimism about personal risks, 15*(1), 1–8.

Williamson, J., Ranyard, R., & Cuthbert, L. J. (2000). Risk management in naturalistic insurance decisions: Evidence from a process tracing study. *Decision, Risk & Policy, 5*, 19–38.

Zaleskiewicz, T., Piskorz, Z., & Borkowska, A. (2002). Fear or money? Decisions on insuring oneself against flood. *Risk, Decision and Policy, 7*(03), 221–233.

FURTHER READING

Ericson, R. V., & Doyle, A. (2006). The institutionalization of deceptive sales in life insurance. *British Journal of Criminology, 46*(6), 993–1010.

Kunreuther, H., & Pauly, M. V. (2006). *Insurance decision-making and market behavior*. New York: Now Publishers.

Tennyson, S. (2008). Moral, social and economic dimensions of insurance fraud claims. *Social Research, 75*(4), 1181–1204.

Index

Printed in the USA
CPSIA information can be obtained
at www.ICGtesting.com
LVHW082118061023
760262LV00008B/1083

9 781118 926345